PREFACE

In a fundamental sense, *The Critical Reader, Thinker, and Writer* is not radical; nothing in it is experimental or untried. On the other hand, no other book provides such breadth and depth of resources for critical reading, thinking, and writing. However, the table of contents makes the book appear more traditional than in fact it is. Though the organization seems to result from the conventional types of written discourse, the apparently sharp distinctions between modes quickly disappear as students become engaged with the book. For example, Chapter 2, "Thinking Critically about Narratives," resolves a fundamental misunderstanding about the traditional categories of writing (narration, exposition, argumentation, and persuasion): "stories" can be used to explain, to argue, and to persuade. And since stories are dramas — characters (whether fictional or factual) performing actions in scenes for some purpose — critical reading involves a dramatistic method of analysis and evaluation. Even more important: the concepts and methods that students learn in each chapter, although explained in relation to particular types of discourse, are applicable pretty much across the board to all kinds of texts.

In the first chapter, "Critical Reading, Thinking, and Writing," students learn that reading, like writing, is a constructive process and that readers must bring a great deal of information to the text if they expect to take anything out. Even when the reader is uncritical, reading is not the passive absorption of what is "in" the text.

As we have just pointed out, the second chapter, "Thinking Critically about Narratives," gives students a dramatistic method of analysis (adapted, obviously, from the work of Kenneth Burke).

Chapter 3, "Thinking Critically about Exposition," focuses on the unwritten "contract" that the writer establishes with the reader. The reader has certain expectations concerning a text and its author, and judging the text on the basis of these expectations is a powerful aspect of critical reading. (It will hardly surprise instructors who use this book that much of the substance of Chapter 3 derives from speech act theory.)

Chapter 4 teaches students how to evaluate argumentative and persuasive discourse by analyzing the claims an author makes, the backing for those claims, the evidence for the conclusions drawn, and necessary qualifications or hedges. (Here our debt to Stephen Toulmin is obvious.) The chapter also contains an exceptionally rich section on that tried-and-true, extremely useful checklist for critical thinking: the informal fallacies.

The final chapter, a guide to writing based on library research, should be invaluable to students. First, an overview outlines the resources available and explains how to use them. Second, students can follow, step by step, as a research paper comes into being, from the initial survey of bibliographic resources to the placement and function of footnotes. We want to state, however, that our last chapter presents library research and researched writing as important aspects of critical thinking, not as the mechanical skills of learning footnote and bibliographic forms.

We have spent many hours searching for and thinking about the reading selections that we have included with each chapter. In the first place, we think all of them are interesting and that they will engage students. Second, the readings are balanced in a number of ways: current interest (for example, "The Creation of Patriarchy," by Gerda Lerner) with timeless issues (Thoreau's "Civil Disobedience"); contemporary authors (for instance, Barbara Mellix, John McPhee) with old masters (Swift, Emerson); the literature of fact with that of fiction and poetry.

We admit it's not coincidence that we have the same last name. In fact, W. Ross is the father of Geoffrey R. This coauthorship has had great advantages for us, and it will have even more value for the students and teachers who use *The Critical Reader, Thinker, and Writer*. W. Ross has taught reading and writing for some thirty years now, first at the University of Montana and, since 1966, at the University of Southern California. Geoffrey R., an administrator at the University of Southern California, has never taught. Thus, in writing the chapters of this book, in choosing the selections to be anthologized, and in developing learning aids such as discussion questions, headnotes, and exercises, the perceptions and tastes of a young layperson served to balance (and even, at times, counteract) the wonts and usages of an aging academic whose conservatism on occasion checked the untoward ebullience of his coauthor. The result, we think, is a book that has contemporary verve yet meets the criteria of theoretical soundness and classroom practicality. It will engage its readers and will be an effective teaching instrument.

For their reviews of the project in its various stages, we thank especially Robert Keith Miller, Suzanne S. Webb, and Blake Smith. Their reactions and suggestions had appreciable salutary influence on the development of this book.

Our relationship with Mayfield has been the kind authors dream of but seldom are lucky enough to experience, especially nowadays. We could not possibly thank by name everyone who has made a contribution, but we must single out a few. Sharon Montooth and Sally Peyrefitte smoothed the rough spots in our manuscript, banged out and touched up some of the dents, filled in lacunae and, in general, contributed their meticulous care and unfailing good taste.

Though the names of two authors appear on the spine of this book, we admit that a third person deserves as much credit as either of us. That

The Critical Reader,
Thinker, and Writer

The Critical Reader, Thinker, and Writer

W. ROSS WINTEROWD
University of Southern California

GEOFFREY R. WINTEROWD
University of Southern California

Mayfield Publishing Company

Mountain View, California
London · Toronto

LIBRARY OF CONGRESS CATALOGING-IN-PUBLICATION DATA
Winterowd, W. Ross.
    The critical reader, thinker, and writer / W. Ross Winterowd, Geoffrey
R. Winterowd.
        p.   cm.
    Includes index.
    ISBN 0-87484-926-8
    1. College readers. 2. English language—Rhetoric. 3. Critical
thinking.   I. Winterowd, Geoffrey R.   II. Title.
PE1417.W557   1991   91-36784
428.6—dc20   CIP

Manufactured in the United States of America
10 9 8 7 6 5 4 3 2

Mayfield Publishing Company
1240 Villa Street
Mountain View, CA 94041

Sponsoring editor, Thomas V. Broadbent; managing editor, Linda Toy;
production editor, Sharon Montooth; text and cover designer, David
Bullen; art director, Jeanne M. Schreiber; manufacturing manager, Martha
Branch; cover illustration, Gabriel Molano. The text was set in 10.5/12
Bembo and printed on 50# Finch Opaque by the Maple-Vail Book
Manufacturing Group.

ACKNOWLEDGMENTS

Margaret Atwood, "The Loneliness of the Military Historian" from *Harper's*, December
    1990. Reprinted by permission of Margaret Atwood, © 1990.

A. Scott Berg, *Goldwyn* by A. Scott Berg. Copyright © 1989 by A. Scott Berg.
    Reprinted by permission of Alfred A. Knofp, Inc.

Jorge Luis Borges, "The Library of Babel" from *Ficciones* by Jorge Luis Borges,
    translated by Anthony Kerrigan. Copyright © 1962 by Grove Press, Inc. Translated
    from the Spanish © 1956 by Emece Editores, S.A., Buenos Aires. Used by
    permission of Grove Press, Inc.

Acknowledgments and copyrights continue at the back of the book on
pages 631–634, which constitute an extension of the copyright page.

is our editor and Mayfield's editorial director, Tom Broadbent. Tom is, simply, the best in the business, and either his spirit or his person hovered over us during the whole course of our planning, our search for readings, and our drafting and then redrafting of the chapters. Tom should be given a good deal of the credit for whatever virtues teachers and students attribute to *The Critical Reader, Thinker, and Writer.*

W. Ross Winterowd
Geoffrey R. Winterowd

CONTENTS

1

Critical Reading, Thinking, and Writing

This book is designed to help you sharpen your ability to under-stand and evaluate texts. By *texts* we mean not only books but also newspaper reports and editorials, magazine articles, government docu-ments, advertisements, political tracts, letters — in short, all the written materials that are the basis of your lifelong education and probably your career as well.

Developing the ability to read and think critically is the most im-portant objective of a college education. A critical reader is not a cynic or perpetual objector. Rather, a critical reader assumes that most writers are reliable but knows that some are not; such a reader enters into a "mental dialogue" with the text, asking questions such as these: Are the data reliable? What is their source? Is the author's argument sound, or does its logic break down? What is the author *really* trying to accomplish with this text? What do other experts say about the author's ideas? What arguments might one advance *against* the author's point? What arguments might one advance *in favor of* the author's point? Do I understand the text in its overall purpose as well as in its details? What can I do to gain a better understanding?

Some texts contain misinformation, included either intentionally (to delude readers) or unintentionally (because the writer was not ade-quately informed). You should always evaluate the information in texts, asking yourself whether it is credible or not, probable or improbable; whether the sources of that information are reliable or unreliable; whether the reporting is accurate or inaccurate. Even if information is reliable, however, arguments based upon it may be faulty. For instance, it is a fact that young male drivers have a higher accident rate than young female drivers, but an argument that males should therefore be licensed to drive at a later age than females would not necessarily be valid. Critical reading entails the ability to analyze arguments and to judge whether or not they hold up.

Sometimes, however, you may have to choose between opposing points of view that are advanced by equally qualified writers who are using reliable data and arguing flawlessly. In such situations, you must examine your own fundamental values and choose one position or another in light of these value systems; self-examination, too, is a part of critical reading and thinking.

Almost all of the principles relating to critical thinking and reading apply also to effective writing. For example, a critical reader asks, Is the author reliable, and does he know what he's talking about? A good writer asks, How can I convince my reader that I'm reliable and know what I'm talking about? A critical reader asks, Are these data reliable? What is their source? A writer asks exactly the same questions. This book, then, is about effective writing as well as critical reading. *Critical thinking* is the basis for both.

HOW WE READ

If you know something about the *what* and the *how* of reading — the nature of written text and the process of arriving at the meaning — the strategies for critical reading presented throughout this book will be easier to understand.

One way to think about reading is to compare it with mining. With pick and shovel, the miner digs to find the treasure buried in the earth; with eyes and brain, the reader digs to discover the meaning buried in the text. Another way to think about reading is to compare it with the work of a detective. The detective reconstructs what happened by gathering bits of evidence and putting together a coherent picture, filling in the gaps by using logic and intuition. The meaning does not exist until the detective constructs it. That is, it is not "buried" in the materials the detective gathers, but comes into being through the detective's decisions about how to use and connect those materials.

Does the reader, like the miner, dig meaning out or, like the detective, construct (or reconstruct) meaning? The following sections of this chapter help you answer that question.

Exercise: Miner or Detective?

In your opinion at this point, is the reader more like a miner, digging meaning out, or like a detective, constructing meaning? Explain your opinion. The following questions might help you.

1. *If you pronounce the words in a text but don't understand the information or ideas, can you say that you have read the text? (What if someone asks you to summarize what you have read?)*

2. *No machine — even the most sophisticated computer — can "read" a text and then summarize the meaning. Do you think that at some time in the future, machines will be able to read, in the full sense of that word? Why, or why not?*

3. *If someone asks you to summarize a text that you have read, do you simply repeat the words and sentences of the text, or do you express the meaning in your own words? What does your answer imply about your reading process?*

Filling Gaps in Text

No text supplies the reader with every detail; all contain gaps that the reader must fill. Take the following brief text, for example:

> Ellen brought the lunch. The sandwiches were delicious.

Nothing in the text explicitly states that sandwiches were a part of the lunch, but the reader fills that gap automatically, like this:

> Ellen brought the lunch. *[The lunch consisted of sandwiches (and probably other things as well).]* The sandwiches were delicious.

The reader has supplied information that relates the parts of the text to one another.

The gaps that we are talking about here are not the result of sloppy writing or bad thinking; they are part of any text (and any coherent spoken discourse), for the writer could not possibly give readers every single detail about the subject. A good writer would not even try; the result would be something like this:

> Ellen brought the lunch. Lunch is the meal that people usually eat at noon. The lunch that Ellen brought contained sandwiches. Sandwiches are two pieces of bread with some kind of filling between them. The sandwiches that Ellen brought were delicious. . . .

You can perform an experiment that demonstrates how readers fill gaps in texts. Ask a friend or family member to read the following text quickly, but give the person no other information or instructions.

> The company outing was held on the shores of Lake Crystal. George arrived late, after the festivities were in full swing. He got a hot dog and soda and wandered out on the dock, joining a group who were chatting there. Soon the members of the group were shouting, and several of the people, including George, were gesturing violently.
>
> Just thirty minutes after he arrived, George, soaking wet, stomped back to his car and roared away from the lake.

After five minutes or so, ask the person to summarize the story. Here is a typical response:

> George went to the company outing at Lake Crystal. He got into an argument with some people, *and they threw him into the lake,* so he left the party in anger.

The original story gives no explanation for George's being wet when he leaves the outing. Nevertheless, the implication that he was thrown into the lake is very strong, and most readers fill the gap with that assumption to make the text coherent.

Here are further examples of information readers must supply to make texts coherent:

> The little girl was just learning to roller-skate. *[While she was learning, she fell down and injured her knees.]* She had bandages on both knees.

> When I last visited my parents, I had trouble falling asleep, too big for the hills and valleys scooped in the mattress by child-bodies. *[The author was sleeping in the bed that had been used by the children in the family. Probably she had slept in that same bed when she was a child.]* I heard my mother come in *[to my bedroom].* What did she want?
> — *Maxine Hong Kingston*

> Between San Jose and the turnoff to Monterey, *[Highway]* 101 rolls gracefully through the rich farming foothills of the Santa Cruz Mountains. The Hell's Angels, riding two abreast in each lane *[of Highway 101],* seemed out of place in little towns like Coyote and Gilroy. *[Highway 101 passes through the little towns of Coyote and Gilroy.]*
> — *Hunter S. Thompson*

As you can see, *every* text requires the reader to supply some of the information necessary to make for coherence. We will return to this basic concept from time to time throughout this book.

Exercise: Filling Gaps in Texts

What are the most important gap fillers you supply when you read the following text? To get you started, some of the gaps at the beginning have been filled in.
> *I came to a ramshackle place called Smitty's Trading Post. Smitty* [who must have been the proprietor] *was a merchant of relics. He could sell you a Frankfort, Kentucky, city bus that made its last run down Shively Street, or an ice cream wagon made of a golf cart, or a used bulldozer, or a bent horseshoe* [which were the relics he could sell you]. *I stopped to look* [at the relics]. *Lying flat as the ground, a piebald mongrel too tired to lift its head gave a one-eyed stare. I pulled on the locked door, peered through the windows grimed like coalminers' goggles, but I couldn't find*

Smitty. A pickup rattled in. A man with a wen above his eye said, "Smitty ain't here."

"Where is he?" I was just making talk.

"You the feller wantin' the harness?"

"Already got one."

"What'd you come for then?"

"I don't know. Have to talk to Smitty to find out."

"That's one I ain't heard," he said.

— *William Least Heat Moon,* Blue Highways

Cues: The Text as a Set of Instructions

Exactly how does the reader fill gaps in text? To answer this question, think for a moment about what happens when you read the following texts:

Misanthropy is a philistinic cogency.

The tenor wouldn't yell through the screen door. He was afraid it would strain his voice.

You can view the text as a set of cues or instructions that guide you in filling the gaps; some of these cues prompt you to look outside the text for meaning, whereas others prompt you to look within the text. Consider the first example. Most of the words may be unfamiliar to you. To find the meaning of the whole sentence, therefore, you would first have to find the meanings of the individual words by consulting a dictionary. Now consider the second example. Some of the words are cues that prompt you to search your "mental dictionary" for meanings: *tenor* (a male singer), *yell* (to use the vocal cords strenuously to produce a loud sound), *screen door* (a frame covered with a mesh of wire or plastic), *afraid* (fearful or very apprehensive), *strain* (to use a part of the body so vigorously that it is injured; or, to sift a substance to remove the large particles), and *voice* (the human sound-making capability).

Other words are cues that prompt you to look *within* the text for meaning. For example, the *he* that begins the second sentence gains its meaning from *the tenor* in the first sentence, and *it* in the second sentence gains its meaning from *yell through the screen door* in the first sentence. You refer to other parts of the text to find the meaning of *he* and *it*. To take another instance, consider what the following sentences prompt you to do.

"What is the solution to the problem on page ninety–eight?" asked the professor.

"How should I know?" replied the student.

To understand the student's reply, you must "fill out" the answer with the information contained in the professor's question: "How should I know *[what the solution to the problem on page ninety-eight is]*?"

In short, you can view the text as a set of cues that prompt you to look outside of the text for some meanings and within it for others. With most texts, your responses to the cues are automatic, unconscious, and instantaneous. But as a critical reader, you can analyze this process whenever you need to in order to see what is occurring. When you have trouble understanding a text, you can ask the following questions about the cues in the text.

1. Do I understand the meanings of technical terms that the author uses? For example, a discussion about economics might contain the important term *laissez-faire;* to understand an explanation of the sound systems of languages, you would need to know the meaning of *phoneme.*
2. Does the author use any common terms in special ways? In discussions of composition and rhetoric, for example, *invention* means finding or generating subject matter. It does not mean creating new mechanical or electronic devices, as it does in the more traditional sense.
3. Does the author supply the cues I need to see how one part of the text relates to the others? For example, the following text would puzzle any reader: "The cost of housing has risen so dramatically that families with moderate incomes cannot afford to own a home and must rent inadequate apartments in increasingly undesirable areas of the city. It must be a first priority of the new mayor." The reader asks, Precisely what must be a first priority of the new mayor?

Reconstructing the Text

Let's begin with two axioms:

1. We read to gain meaning, not to pronounce the text. It is possible to learn to pronounce the words in a text without knowing their meanings — which is exactly what most opera singers do with librettos in languages they do not understand. Moreover, some readers cannot speak and therefore cannot "read" the text aloud at all, yet they can still gain meaning from the text.
2. We read with our minds, not our eyes. (Sightless people learn to read braille with their fingertips.) Merely being able to see the text is not enough to enable us to read it.

As we saw in our discussion of filling gaps, reading is a constructive process, the reader always attempting to see how the parts of the text fit together to make a whole and using his or her own knowledge of the world to fill in what is left unstated. Cues provided by the language system prompt and guide the reader.

The writer constructs the text, but the readers must *reconstruct* it to make the meaning for themselves. Readers try very hard to find ways of making the text coherent—of seeing the overall relationships among the elements in a text. As you read the following passage (quoted in Herbert H. Clark and Eve V. Clark's *Psychology and Language*), you will find that you are attempting to make sense of the whole thing, not just of each individual sentence.

> The two of them glanced nervously at one another as they approached the man standing there expectantly. He talked to them for about ten minutes, but spoke loudly enough that everyone else in the room could hear too. Eventually he handed over two objects he had been given, one to each of them. After he had said a few more words, the ordeal was over. With her veil lifted, the two of them kissed, turned around, and rushed from the room arm in arm, with everyone else falling in behind.

When you finally realize that the passage is about a wedding, the sentences seem almost magically to come together as a unified whole. If the passage had been titled "A Wedding," it would have been much easier to understand.

To reconstruct a text that a writer has constructed, the reader must bring to the text two kinds of knowledge: *knowledge of the language system* and what might be called *world knowledge*.

Knowledge of the Language System

If you have been able to understand this chapter so far, or if you are able to understand the daily newspaper, *you have what amounts to a complete knowledge of the language system*. Granted, the type of knowledge you have may not enable you to analyze or describe the system (that is a job for professional linguists), but it does enable you to use the system.

Here is a brief demonstration that you have an extremely sophisticated knowledge of the language system. Which of the following two phrases is "correct" English?

> the first thirty pretty brown cows
> the first brown pretty thirty cows

You undoubtedly chose the first one, because that is the way a native English speaker would arrange the words in the phrase. You probably could not state the linguistic principle that explains why the first is preferable, but being able to do so is obviously not important, since you are able to recognize and use the "natural" order. [In case you are interested, the rule goes something like this: the sequence of modifiers for a noun in English is (1) article (*the*), (2) ordinal number (*first*), (3) cardinal number (*thirty*), (4) general attribute (*pretty*), and (5) specific attribute (*brown*).]

Exercise: Your Knowledge of the Language System

One member of each of the following pairs is "correct," or idiomatic, English—that is, what a person whose native language is English would say or write. Which ones are idiomatic? Try to explain the "rule" or principle that governs the correct usage (but do not be discouraged if you cannot give an explanation, for in most cases only a trained linguist could do so).

1a. *Bertrand no have enough money to buy a Rolls Royce.*
1b. *Bertrand does not have enough money to buy a Rolls Royce.*
2a. *Alexander Pushkin is author of novel* Dead Souls.
2b. *Alexander Pushkin is the author of the novel* Dead Souls.
3a. *The document official gives custody of the estate to a trustee.*
3b. *The official document gives custody of the estate to a trustee.*
4a. *There is no doubt that Jacqueline must lose weight.*
4b. *There is no doubt that Jacqueline lose weight must.*
5a. *Dabney bringed his computer to class with him.*
5b. *Dabney brought his computer to class with him.*

World Knowledge

Knowledge of the language system is indispensable, but it will get you only so far. You must also bring to a text all your other relevant experience, everything pertinent that you know about the world. Consider the first two sentences of John McPhee's *Coming into the Country:*

> My bandanna is rolled on the diagonal and retains water fairly well. I keep it knotted around my head, and now and again dip it into the river.

The amount of knowledge you must contribute in order to understand this passage is quite astounding. You must know, for instance,

1. what a *bandanna* is;
2. what rolling it on the *diagonal* would result in;
3. that it is not unusual for people to wear rolled bandannas around their heads;
4. that the bandanna is probably made of cotton, not synthetic material, since it retains water fairly well.

In a best-selling book entitled *Cultural Literacy,* E. D. Hirsch, Jr., and his colleagues Joseph Kett and James Trefil, all of the University of Virginia, compiled a list of some five thousand items that people must know in order to comprehend such unspecialized texts as articles in the daily newspaper and in magazines. Here is a sampling from that list:

acid rain	Bangkok	cartel
Degas	Ellington, Duke	fascism
gamma rays	holding company	Irish Republican Army
Jazz Age	*King Lear*	malignancy
NATO	orbit	Paine, Thomas
quasars	realpolitik	Scopes trial
Tarzan	United Nations	Van Allen Belt
WASP	x-ray	Yom Kippur
Zapata		

Even everyday statements such as the following require the reader to contribute a wealth of knowledge:

> Because one of our guests was Saudi Arabian, we could not serve roast pork.

To make sense of the above sentence, the reader must know that Saudi Arabia is a Moslem nation and that Moslems are forbidden by their religion to eat pork. Again, the reader's world knowledge is essential.

Exercise: Your World Knowledge

For a computer to be able to read, it would need an enormous bank of "world knowledge." For example, to understand the following passage a computer would need to "know" that crane *has two meanings: (1) a device for hoisting and (2) a bird. If the machine were to read the following sentences, it would need to know, among other things, that devices for lifting do not stand on one leg in the swamp, but that some birds do, and that birds are incapable of lifting twenty tons.*

1. *The crane was standing on one leg in the swamp.*
2. *The crane could lift twenty tons.*

Here is your problem. What "knowledge" would the computer need in order to understand the meaning of the word it *in the following sentences?*

1. *The cat fell off the roof because it was slanted.*
2. *The cat fell off the roof because it was sick.*

THE REALMS OF KNOWLEDGE

We can think of knowledge as a universe divided into two kingdoms: "the public domain" and "the private reserve." All of us have estates in both realms; the public domain consists of the general world knowledge that we share with other writers and readers, and the private reserve is the specialized knowledge that we share with other members of our in-groups.

The differences between *general knowledge* and *specialized knowledge* are important, as the following example points out. In *A Brief History of Time,* Stephen W. Hawking (believed by many to be the most important thinker in theoretical physics since Einstein) has this to say about his book:

> Where did the universe come from? How and why did it begin? Will it come to an end, and if so, how? These are questions that are of interest to us all. But modern science has become so technical that only a very small number of specialists are able to master the mathematics used to describe them. Yet the basic ideas about the origin and fate of the universe can be stated without mathematics in a form that people without a scientific education can understand. This is what I have attempted to do in this book. (vi)

When Stephen Hawking writes scientific papers, he is in the private reserve common to the relatively few others who share his specialty, but when he wrote *A Brief History of Time,* he was in the public domain.

Everyone should be able to *read critically* in the public domain — those texts addressed to the general, educated public. The principles of critical reading apply also in the private reserve of specialized texts, but in that domain the reader must also have the appropriate specialized knowledge. This book will call on you to read, and think critically about, texts in the public domain.

REVIEW

In your own words, explain the following concepts (all of which are central to this chapter):

text
gaps in texts
cues
knowledge of the language system
world knowledge
specialized knowledge
read

SUGGESTIONS FOR WRITING

1. In a brief essay, answer the question posed at the beginning of this chapter: Does the reader, like the miner, dig meaning out or, like the detective, construct meaning? Drawing on what you have learned from this chapter and your own experience as a reader, give the reasons that support your opinion. You might conclude that neither comparison is appropriate: that readers neither dig meanings out nor construct. Can you think of a more appropriate comparison?

2. What do you read? Why do you read? In an essay, present a survey of your own reading. You might think of the following categories: required reading (such as textbooks), pleasure reading (novels, comic strips), and reading for information (newspapers and news magazines, sets of instructions). The following is an example of part of such an essay:

> When I read for pleasure, I almost invariably choose nonfiction: nature books, biography, or so-called New Journalism. Recently, for example, I have enjoyed *Arctic Dreams,* by Barry Lopez; *In All His Glory,* a biography of William S. Paley, by Sally Bedell Smith; and *Rising from the Plains,* by John McPhee.

Arctic Dreams is a wonderfully informative book, introducing the reader to the geography, history, flora, and fauna of the Arctic regions, but from the standpoint of an imaginative observer who has been caught up in the magic of his subject. As Lopez says in his preface:

> The mind, full of curiosity and analysis, disassembles a land-scape and then reassembles the pieces — the nod of a flower, the color of the night sky, the murmur of an animal — trying to fathom its geography. At the same time the mind is trying to find its place within the land, to discover a way to dispel its own sense of estrangement.

This mixture of fact about the Arctic and the author's imaginative experience of those facts creates, for me, a wonderful reading experience.

3. Do a survey of the reading done by a group to which you belong: your family, the members of your club, your friends. Ask them what they read and why they read what they do. Write a report about the results of your survey, commenting on what the survey tells you about the group you have studied.

THE ACHIEVEMENT OF DESIRE

Richard Rodriguez

In *Hunger of Memory,* the book from which this reading is excerpted, Richard Rodriguez tells the story of his educational odyssey from the closeness of a minority family to the impersonality of the world of learning, a journey that involved major losses as well as major gains. Rodriguez details the importance that language has had in defining his identity. As he says on page 7,

> This autobiography . . . is a book about language. I write about poetry; the new Roman Catholic liturgy; learning to read; writing; political terminology. Language has been the great subject of my life. In college and graduate school, I was registered as an "English major." But well before then, from my first day of school, I was a student of language. Obsessed by the way it determined my public identity. The way it permits me to describe myself. . . .

Rodriguez, the son of Mexican Americans, grew up in Sacramento, California, where he attended parochial schools. He was a student at both Stanford and Columbia universities and did graduate work at the Warburg Institute in London and the University of California, Berkeley.

As you read the following selection, be aware of the importance that reading has had for Rodriguez. Has reading played a similar role in your life?

I stand in the ghetto classroom — "the guest speaker" — attempting to lecture on the mystery of the sounds of our words to rows of diffident students. "Don't you hear it? Listen! The music of our words. '*Sumer is i-cumen in.* . . .' And songs on the car radio. We need Aretha Franklin's voice to fill plain words with music — her life." In the face of their empty stares, I try to create an enthusiasm. But the girls in the back row turn to watch some boy passing outside. There are flutters of smiles, waves. And someone's mouth elongates heavy, silent words through the barrier of glass. Silent words — the lips straining to shape each voiceless syllable: "*Meet meee late errr.*" By the door, the instructor smiles at me, apparently hoping that I will be able to spark some enthusiasm in the class. But only one student seems to be listening. A girl, maybe fourteen. In this gray room her eyes shine with ambition. She keeps nodding and nodding at all that I say; she even takes notes. And each time I ask a question, she jerks up and down in her desk like a marionette, while her hand waves over the bowed heads of her classmates. It is myself (as a boy) I see as she faces me now (a man in my thirties).

The boy who first entered a classroom barely able to speak English, twenty years later concluded his studies in the stately quiet of the reading room in the British Museum. Thus with one sentence I can summarize my academic career. It will be harder to summarize what sort of life connects the boy to the man.

With every award, each graduation from one level of education to the next, people I'd meet would congratulate me. Their refrain always the same: "Your parents must be very proud." Sometimes then they'd ask me how I managed it — my "success." (How?) After a while, I had several quick answers to give in reply. I'd admit, for one thing, that I went to an excellent grammar school. (My earliest teachers, the nuns, made my success their ambition.) And my brother and both my sisters were very good students. (They often brought home the shiny school trophies I came to want.) And my mother and father always encouraged me. (At every graduation they were behind the stunning flash of the camera when I turned to look at the crowd.)

As important as these factors were, however, they account inadequately for my academic advance. Nor do they suggest what an odd success I managed. For although I was a very good student, I was also a very bad student. I was a "scholarship boy," a certain kind of scholarship boy. Always successful, I was always unconfident. Exhilarated by my progress. Sad. I became the prized student — anxious and eager to learn. Too eager, too anxious — an imitative and unoriginal pupil. My brother and two sisters enjoyed the advantages I did, and they grew to be as successful as I, but none of them ever seemed so anxious about their schooling. A second-grade student, I was the one who came home and corrected the "simple" grammatical mistakes of our parents. ("Two negatives make a positive.") Proudly I announced — to my family's startled silence — that a teacher had said I was losing all trace of a Spanish accent. I was oddly annoyed when I was unable to get parental help with a homework assignment. The night my father tried to help me with an arithmetic exercise, he kept reading the instructions, each time more deliberately, until I pried the textbook out of his hands, saying, "I'll try to figure it out some more by myself."

When I reached the third grade, I outgrew such behavior. I became *5*
more tactful, careful to keep separate the two very different worlds of my day. But then, with ever-increasing intensity, I devoted myself to my studies. I became bookish, puzzling to all my family. Ambition set me apart. When my brother saw me struggling home with stacks of library books, he would laugh, shouting: "Hey, Four Eyes!" My father opened a closet one day and was startled to find me inside, reading a novel. My mother would find me reading when I was supposed to be asleep or helping around the house or playing outside. In a voice angry or worried or just curious, she'd ask: "What do you see in your books?" It became the family's joke. When I was called and wouldn't reply, someone would say I must be hiding under my bed with a book.

(How did I manage my success?)

What I am about to say to you has taken me more than twenty years to admit: *A primary reason for my success in the classroom was that I couldn't forget that schooling was changing me and separating me from the life I enjoyed before becoming a student.* That simple realization! For years I never spoke to anyone about it. Never mentioned a thing to my family or my teachers or classmates. From a very early age, I understood enough, just enough about my classroom experiences to keep what I knew repressed, hidden beneath layers of embarrassment. Not until my last months as a graduate student, nearly thirty years old, was it possible for me to think much about the reasons for my academic success. Only then. At the end of my schooling, I needed to determine how far I had moved from my past. The adult finally confronted, and now must publicly say, what the child shuddered from knowing and could never admit to himself or to those many faces that smiled at his every success. ("Your parents must be very proud. . . .")

1

At the end, in the British Museum (too distracted to finish my dissertation) for weeks I read, speed-read, books by modern educational theorists, only to find infrequent and slight mention of students like me. (Much more is written about the more typical case, the lower-class student who barely is helped by his schooling.) Then one day, leafing through Richard Hoggart's *The Uses of Literacy,* I found, in his description of the scholarship boy, myself. For the first time I realized that there were other students like me, and so I was able to frame the meaning of my academic success, its consequent price — the loss.

Hoggart's description is distinguished, at least initially, by deep understanding. What he grasps very well is that the scholarship boy must move between environments, his home and the classroom, which are at cultural extremes, opposed. With his family, the boy has the intense pleasure of intimacy, the family's consolation in feeling public alienation. Lavish emotions texture home life. *Then,* at school, the instruction bids him to trust lonely reason primarily. Immediate needs set the pace of his parents" lives. From his mother and father the boy learns to trust spontaneity and nonrational ways of knowing. *Then,* at school, there is mental calm. Teachers emphasize the value of a reflectiveness that opens a space between thinking and immediate action.

Years of schooling must pass before the boy will be able to sketch   10 the cultural differences in his day as abstractly as this. But he senses those differences early. Perhaps as early as the night he brings home an assignment from school and finds the house too noisy for study.

> He has to be more and more alone, if he is going to "get on". He will have, probably unconsciously, to oppose the ethos of the hearth, the intense gregariousness of the working-class family

group. Since everything centres upon the living-room, there is unlikely to be a room of his own; the bedrooms are cold and inhospi-
table, and to warm them or the front room, if there is one, would
not only be expensive, but would require an imaginative leap—out
of the tradition—which most families are not capable of making.
There is a corner of the living-room table. On the other side Mother
is ironing, the wireless is on, someone is singing a snatch of song or
Father says intermittently whatever comes into his head. The boy
has to cut himself off mentally, so as to do his homework, as well
as he can.*

The next day, the lesson is as apparent at school. There are even rows of
desks. Discussion is ordered. The boy must rehearse his thoughts and
raise his hand before speaking out in a loud voice to an audience of
classmates. And there is time enough, and silence, to think about ideas
(big ideas) never considered at home by his parents.

Not for the working-class child alone is adjustment to the classroom difficult. Good schooling requires that any student alter early
childhood habits. But the working-class child is usually least prepared
for the change. And, unlike many middle-class children, he goes home
and sees in his parents a way of life not only different but starkly opposed
to that of the classroom. (He enters the house and hears his parents
talking in ways his teachers discourage.)

Without extraordinary determination and the great assistance of
others—at home and at school—there is little chance for success. Typi-
cally most working-class children are barely changed by the classroom.
The exception succeeds. The relative few become scholarship students.
Of these, Richard Hoggart estimates, most manage a fairly graceful
transition. Somehow they learn to live in the two very different worlds
of their day. There are some others, however, those Hoggart pejoratively
terms "scholarship boys," for whom success comes with special anxiety.
Scholarship boy: good student, troubled son. The child is "moderately
endowed," intellectually mediocre, Hoggart supposes—though it may
be more pertinent to note the special qualities of temperament in the
child. High-strung child. Brooding. Sensitive. Haunted by the knowledge that one *chooses* to become a student. (Education is not an inevitable
or natural step in growing up.) Here is a child who cannot forget that his
academic success distances him from a life he loved, even from his own
memory of himself.

Initially, he wavers, balances allegiance. ("The boy is himself [until
he reaches, say, the upper forms] very much of *both* the worlds of home
and school. He is enormously obedient to the dictates of the world of
school, but emotionally still strongly wants to continue as part of the

*All quotations in this chapter are from Richard Hoggart, *The Uses of Literacy* (London: Chatto and Windus, 1957), chapter 10.

family circle.") Gradually, necessarily, the balance is lost. The boy needs to spend more and more time studying, each night enclosing himself in the silence permitted and required by intense concentration. He takes his first step toward academic success, away from his family.

From the very first days, through the years following, it will be with his parents — the figures of lost authority, the persons toward whom he feels deepest love — that the change will be most powerfully measured. A separation will unravel between them. Advancing in his studies, the boy notices that his mother and father have not changed as much as he. Rather, when he sees them, they often remind him of the person he once was and the life he earlier shared with them. He realizes what some Romantics also know when they praise the working class for the capacity for human closeness, qualities of passion and spontaneity, that the rest of us experience in like measure only in the earliest part of our youth. For the Romantic, this doesn't make working-class life childish. Working-class life challenges precisely because it is an *adult* way of life.

The scholarship boy reaches a different conclusion. He cannot afford to admire his parents. (How could he and still pursue such a contrary life?) He permits himself embarrassment at their lack of education. And to evade nostalgia for the life he has lost, he concentrates on the benefits education will bestow upon him. He becomes especially ambitious. Without the support of old certainties and consolations, almost mechanically, he assumes the procedures and doctrines of the classroom. The kind of allegiance the young student might have given his mother and father only days earlier, he transfers to the teacher, the new figure of authority. "[The scholarship boy] tends to make a father-figure of his form-master," Hoggart observes.

But Hoggart's calm prose only makes me recall the urgency with which I came to idolize my grammar school teachers. I began by imitating their accents, using their diction, trusting their every direction. The very first facts they dispensed, I grasped with awe. Any book they told me to read, I read — then waited for them to tell me which books I enjoyed. Their every casual opinion I came to adopt and to trumpet when I returned home. I stayed after school "to help" — to get my teacher's undivided attention. It was the nun's encouragement that mattered most to me. (She understood exactly what — my parents never seemed to appraise so well — all my achievements entailed.) Memory gently caressed each word of praise bestowed in the classroom so that compliments teachers paid me years ago come quickly to mind even today.

The enthusiasm I felt in second-grade classes I flaunted before both my parents. The docile, obedient student came home a shrill and precocious son who insisted on correcting and teaching his parents with the remark: "My teacher told us. . . ."

I intended to hurt my mother and father. I was still angry at them for having encouraged me toward classroom English. But gradually this

15

anger was exhausted, replaced by guilt as school grew more and more attractive to me. I grew increasingly successful, a talkative student. My hand was raised in the classroom; I yearned to answer any question. At home, life was less noisy than it had been. (I spoke to classmates and teachers more often each day than to family members.) Quiet at home, I sat with my papers for hours each night. I never forgot that schooling had irretrievably changed my family's life. That knowledge, however, did not weaken ambition. Instead, it strengthened resolve. Those times I remembered the loss of my past with regret, I quickly reminded myself of all the things my teachers could give me. (They could make me an educated man.) I tightened my grip on pencil and books. I evaded nostalgia. Tried hard to forget. But one does not forget by trying to forget. One only remembers. I remembered too well that education had changed my family's life. I would not have become a scholarship boy had I not so often remembered.

Once she was sure that her children knew English, my mother would tell us, "You should keep up your Spanish." Voices playfully groaned in response. "¡*Pochos*!" my mother would tease. I listened silently.

After a while, I grew more calm at home. I developed tact. A fourth-grade student, I was no longer the show-off in front of my parents. I became a conventionally dutiful son, politely affectionate, cheerful enough, even—for reasons beyond choosing—my father's favorite. And much about my family life was easy then, comfortable, happy in the rhythm of our living together: hearing my father getting ready for work; eating the breakfast my mother had made me; looking up from a novel to hear my brother or one of my sisters playing with friends in the backyard; in winter, coming upon the house all lighted up after dark. 20

But withheld from my mother and father was any mention of what most mattered to me: the extraordinary experience of first-learning. Late afternoon: In the midst of preparing dinner, my mother would come up behind me while I was trying to read. Her head just over mine, her breath warmly scented with food. "What are you reading?" Or, "Tell me all about your new courses." I would barely respond, "Just the usual things, nothing special." (A half smile, then silence. Her head moving back in the silence. Silence! Instead of the flood of intimate sounds that had once flowed smoothly between us, there was this silence.) After dinner, I would rush to a bedroom with papers and books. As often as possible, I resisted parental pleas to "save lights" by coming to the kitchen to work. I kept so much, so often, to myself. Sad. Enthusiastic. Troubled by the excitement of coming upon new ideas. Eager. Fascinated by the promising texture of a brand-new book. I hoarded the pleasures of learning. Alone for hours. Enthralled. Nervous. I rarely looked away from my books—or back on my memories. Nights when relatives visited and the front rooms were warmed by Spanish sounds, I slipped quietly out of the house.

It mattered that education was changing me. It never ceased to matter. My brother and sisters would giggle at our mother's mispronounced words. They'd correct her gently. My mother laughed girlishly one night, trying not to pronounce *sheep* as *ship*. From a distance I listened sullenly. From that distance, pretending not to notice on another occasion, I saw my father looking at the title pages of my library books. That was the scene on my mind when I walked home with a fourth-grade companion and heard him say that his parents read to him every night. (A strange-sounding book — *Winnie the Pooh*.) Immediately, I wanted to know, "What is it like?" My companion, however, thought I wanted to know about the plot of the book. Another day, my mother surprised me by asking for a "nice" book to read. "Something not too hard you think I might like." Carefully I chose one, Willa Cather's *My Ántonia*. But when, several weeks later, I happened to see it next to her bed unread except for the first few pages, I was furious and suddenly wanted to cry. I grabbed up the book and took it back to my room and placed it in its place, alphabetically on my shelf.

"Your parents must be very proud of you." People began to say that to me about the time I was in sixth grade. To answer affirmatively, I'd smile. Shyly I'd smile, never betraying my sense of the irony: I was not proud of my mother and father. I was embarrassed by their lack of education. It was not that I ever thought they were stupid, though stupidly I took for granted their enormous native intelligence. Simply, what mattered to me was that they were not like my teachers.

But, "Why didn't you tell us about the award?" my mother demanded, her frown weakened by pride. At the grammar school ceremony several weeks after, her eyes were brighter than the trophy I'd won. Pushing back the hair from my forehead, she whispered that I had "shown" the *gringos*. A few minutes later, I heard my father speak to my teacher and felt ashamed of his labored, accented words. Then guilty for the shame. I felt such contrary feelings. (There is no simple roadmap through the heart of the scholarship boy.) My teacher was so soft-spoken and her words were edged sharp and clean. I admired her until it seemed to me that she spoke too carefully. Sensing that she was condescending to them, I became nervous. Resentful. Protective. I tried to move my parents away. "You both must be very proud of Richard," the nun said. They responded quickly. (They were proud.) "We are proud of all our children." Then this afterthought: "They sure didn't get their brains from us." They all laughed. I smiled.

Tightening the irony into a knot was the knowledge that my parents were always behind me. They made success possible. They evened the path. They sent their children to parochial schools because the nuns "teach better." They paid a tuition they couldn't afford. They spoke English to us.

For their children my parents wanted chances they never had — an easier way. It saddened my mother to learn that some relatives forced their children to start working right after high school. To *her* children she would say, "Get all the education you can." In schooling she recognized the key to job advancement. And with the remark she remembered her past.

As a girl new to America my mother had been awarded a high school diploma by teachers too careless or busy to notice that she hardly spoke English. On her own, she determined to learn how to type. That skill got her jobs typing envelopes in letter shops, and it encouraged in her an optimism about the possibility of advancement. (Each morning when her sisters put on uniforms, she chose a bright-colored dress.) The years of young womanhood passed, and her typing speed increased. She also became an excellent speller of words she mispronounced. "And I've never been to college," she'd say, smiling, when her children asked her to spell words they were too lazy to look up in a dictionary.

Typing, however, was dead-end work. Finally frustrating. When her youngest child started high school, my mother got a full-time office job once again. (Her paycheck combined with my father's to make us — in fact — what we had already become in our imagination of ourselves — middle class.) She worked then for the (California) state government in numbered civil service positions secured by examinations. The old ambition of her youth was rekindled. During the lunch hour, she consulted bulletin boards for announcements of openings. One day she saw mention of something called an "anti-poverty agency." A typing job. A glamorous job, part of the governor's staff. "A knowledge of Spanish required." Without hesitation she applied and became nervous only when the job was suddenly hers.

"Everyone comes to work all dressed up," she reported at night. And didn't need to say more than that her co-workers wouldn't let her answer the phones. She was only a typist, after all, albeit a very fast typist. And an excellent speller. One morning there was a letter to be sent to a Washington cabinet officer. On the dictating tape, a voice referred to urban guerrillas. My mother typed (the wrong word, correctly): "gorillas." The mistake horrified the anti-poverty bureaucrats who shortly after arranged to have her returned to her previous position. She would go no further. So she willed her ambition to her children. "Get all the education you can; with an education you can do anything." (With a good education *she* could have done anything.)

When I was in high school, I admitted to my mother that I planned to become a teacher someday. That seemed to please her. But I never tried to explain that it was not the occupation of teaching I yearned for as much as it was something more elusive: I wanted to *be* like my teachers, to possess their knowledge, to assume their authority, their confidence, even to assume a teacher's persona.

30

In contrast to my mother, my father never verbally encouraged his children's academic success. Nor did he often praise us. My mother had to remind him to "say something" to one of his children who scored some academic success. But whereas my mother saw in education the opportunity for job advancement, my father recognized that education provided an even more startling possibility: It could enable a person to escape from a life of mere labor.

In Mexico, orphaned when he was eight, my father left school to work as an "apprentice" for an uncle. Twelve years later, he left Mexico in frustration and arrived in America. He had great expectations then of becoming an engineer. ("Work for my hands and my head.") He knew a Catholic priest who promised to get him money enough to study full time for a high school diploma. But the promises came to nothing. Instead there was a dark succession of warehouse, cannery, and factory jobs. After work he went to night school along with my mother. A year, two passed. Nothing much changed, except that fatigue worked its way into the bone; then everything changed. He didn't talk anymore of becoming an engineer. He stayed outside on the steps of the school while my mother went inside to learn typing and shorthand.

By the time I was born, my father worked at "clean" jobs. For a time he was a janitor at a fancy department store. ("Easy work; the machines do it all.") Later he became a dental technician. ("Simple.") But by then he was pessimistic about the ultimate meaning of work and the possibility of ever escaping its claims. In some of my earliest memories of him, my father already seems aged by fatigue. (He has never really grown old like my mother.) From boyhood to manhood, I have remembered him in a single image: seated, asleep on the sofa, his head thrown back in a hideous corpselike grin, the evening newspaper spread out before him. "But look at all you've accomplished," his best friend said to him once. My father said nothing. Only smiled.

It was my father who laughed when I claimed to be tired by reading and writing. It was he who teased me for having soft hands. (He seemed to sense that some great achievement of leisure was implied by my papers and books.) It was my father who became angry while watching on television some woman at the Miss America contest tell the announcer that she was going to college. ("Majoring in fine arts.") "College!" he snarled. He despised the trivialization of higher education, the inflated grades and cheapened diplomas, the half education that so often passed as mass education in my generation.

It was my father again who wondered why I didn't display my awards on the wall of my bedroom. He said he liked to go to doctors' offices and see their certificates and degrees on the wall. ("Nice.") My citations from school got left in closets at home. The gleaming figure astride one of my trophies was broken, wingless, after hitting the ground. My medals were placed in a jar of loose change. And when I   *35* lost my high school diploma, my father found it as it was about to be thrown out with the trash. Without telling me, he put it away with his own things for safekeeping.

These memories slammed together at the instant of hearing that refrain familiar to all scholarship students: "Your parents must be very proud. . . ." Yes, my parents were proud. I knew it. But my parents regarded my progress with more than mere pride. They endured my early precocious behavior — but with what private anger and humiliation? As their children got older and would come home to challenge ideas both of them held, they argued before submitting to the force of logic or superior factual evidence with the disclaimer, "It's what we were taught in our time to believe." These discussions ended abruptly, though my mother remembered them on other occasions when she complained that our "big ideas" were going to our heads. More acute was her complaint that the family wasn't close anymore, like some others she knew. Why weren't we close, "more in the Mexican style"? Everyone is so private, she added. And she mimicked the yes and no answers she got in reply to her questions. Why didn't we talk more? (My father never asked.) I never said.

I was the first in my family who asked to leave home when it came time to go to college. I had been admitted to Stanford, one hundred miles away. My departure would only make physically apparent the separation that had occurred long before. But it was going too far. In the months preceding my leaving, I heard the question my mother never asked except indirectly. In the hot kitchen, tired at the end of her workday, she demanded to know, "Why aren't the colleges here in Sacramento good enough for you? They are for your brother and sister." In the middle of a car ride, not turning to face me, she wondered, "Why do you need to go so far away?" Late at night, ironing, she said with disgust, "Why do you have to put us through this big expense? You know your scholarship will never cover it all." But when September came there was a rush to get everything ready. In a bedroom that last night I packed the big brown valise, and my mother sat nearby sewing initials onto the clothes I would take. And she said no more about my leaving.

Months later, two weeks of Christmas vacation: The first hours home were the hardest. ("What's new?") My parents and I sat in the kitchen for a conversation. (But, lacking the same words to develop our sentences and to shape our interests, what was there to say? What could I tell them of the term paper I had just finished on the "universality of Shakespeare's appeal"?) I mentioned only small, obvious things: my dormitory life; weekend trips I had taken; random events. They responded with news of their own. (One was almost grateful for a family crisis about which there was much to discuss.) We tried to make our conversation seem like more than an interview.

2

From an early age I knew that my mother and father could read and write both Spanish and English. I had observed my father making his way through what, I now suppose, must have been income tax forms. On other occasions I waited apprehensively while my mother read onion–paper letters airmailed from Mexico with news of a relative's illness or death. For both my parents, however, reading was something done out of necessity and as quickly as possible. Never did I see either of them read an entire book. Nor did I see them read for pleasure. Their reading consisted of work manuals, prayer books, newspapers, recipes.

Richard Hoggart imagines how, at home,   *40*

> . . . [The scholarship boy] sees strewn around, and reads regularly himself, magazines which are never mentioned at school, which seem not to belong to the world to which the school introduces him; at school he hears about and reads books never mentioned at home. When he brings those books into the house they do not take their place with other books which the family are reading, for often there are none or almost none; his books look, rather, like strange tools.

In our house each school year would begin with my mother's careful instruction: "Don't write in your books so we can sell them at the end of the year." The remark was echoed in public by my teachers, but only in part: "Boys and girls, don't write in your books. You must learn to treat them with great care and respect."

OPEN THE DOORS OF YOUR MIND WITH BOOKS, read the red and white poster over the nun's desk in early September. It soon was apparent to me that reading was the classroom's central activity. Each course had its own book. And the information gathered from a book was unquestioned. READ TO LEARN, the sign on the wall advised in December. I privately wondered: What was the connection between reading and learning? Did one learn something only by reading it? Was an idea only an idea if it could be written down? In June, CONSIDER BOOKS YOUR BEST FRIENDS. Friends? Reading was, at best, only a chore. I needed to look up whole paragraphs of words in a dictionary. Lines of type were dizzying, the eye having to move slowly across the page, then down, and across . . . The sentences of the first books I read were coolly impersonal. Toned hard. What most bothered me, however, was the isolation reading required. To console myself for the loneliness I'd feel when I read, I tried reading in a very soft voice. Until: "Who is doing all that talking to his neighbor?" Shortly after, remedial reading classes were arranged for me with a very old nun.

At the end of each school day, for nearly six months, I would meet with her in the tiny room that served as the school's library but was actually only a storeroom for used textbooks and a vast collection of

National Geographics. Everything about our sessions pleased me: the smallness of the room; the noise of the janitor's broom hitting the edge of the long hallway outside the door; the green of the sun, lighting the wall; and the old woman's face blurred white with a beard. Most of the time we took turns. I began with my elementary text. Sentences of astonishing simplicity seemed to me lifeless and drab: "The boys ran from the rain . . . She wanted to sing . . . The kite rose in the blue." Then the old nun would read from her favorite books, usually biographies of early American presidents. Playfully she ran through complex sentences, calling the words alive with her voice, making it seem that the author somehow was speaking directly to me. I smiled just to listen to her. I sat there and sensed for the very first time some possibility of fellowship between a reader and a writer, a communication, never *intimate* like that I heard spoken words at home convey, but one nonetheless *personal.*

One day the nun concluded a session by asking me why I was so reluctant to read by myself. I tried to explain; said something about the way written words made me feel all alone — almost, I wanted to add but didn't, as when I spoke to myself in a room just emptied of furniture. She studied my face as I spoke; she seemed to be watching more than listening. In an uneventful voice she replied that I had nothing to fear. Didn't I realize that reading would open up whole new worlds? A book could open doors for me. It could introduce me to people and show me places I never imagined existed. She gestured toward the bookshelves. (Bare-breasted African women danced, and the shiny hubcaps of automobiles on the back covers of the *Geographic* gleamed in my mind.) I listened with respect. But her words were not very influential. I was thinking then of another consequence of literacy, one I was too shy to admit but nonetheless trusted. Books were going to make me "educated." *That* confidence enabled me, several months later, to overcome my fear of the silence.

In fourth grade I embarked upon a grandiose reading program. "Give me the names of important books," I would say to startled teachers. They soon found out that I had in mind "adult books." I ignored their suggestion of anything I suspected was written for children. (Not until I was in college, as a result, did I read *Huckleberry Finn* or *Alice's Adventures in Wonderland.*) Instead, I read *The Scarlet Letter* and Franklin's *Autobiography.* And whatever I read I read for extra credit. Each time I finished a book, I reported the achievement to a teacher and basked in the praise my effort earned. Despite my best efforts, however, there seemed to be more and more books I needed to read. At the library I would literally tremble as I came upon whole shelves of books I hadn't read. So I read and I read and I read: *Great Expectations;* all the short stories of Kipling; *The Babe Ruth Story;* the entire first volume of the *Encyclopaedia Britannica* (A-ANSTEY); the *Iliad; Moby Dick; Gone with the Wind; The Good Earth; Ramona; Forever Amber; The Lives of the Saints; Crime and Punishment; The Pearl.* . . . Librarians who initially frowned when I checked out the maximum ten books at a time started saving books they thought I might like. Teachers would say to the rest of the class, "I only wish the rest of you took reading as seriously as Richard obviously does."

But at home I would hear my mother wondering, "What do you see in your books?" (Was reading a hobby like her knitting? Was so much reading even healthy for a boy? Was it the sign of "brains"? Or was it just a convenient excuse for not helping around the house on Saturday mornings?) Always, "What do you see . . . ?" [45]

What *did* I see in my books? I had the idea that they were crucial for my academic success, though I couldn't have said exactly how or why. In the sixth grade I simply concluded that what gave a book its value was some major idea or theme it contained. If that core essence could be mined and memorized, I would become learned like my teachers. I decided to record in a notebook the themes of the books that I read. After reading *Robinson Crusoe,* I wrote that its theme was "the value of learning to live by oneself." When I completed *Wuthering Heights,* I noted the danger of "letting emotions get out of control." Rereading these brief moralistic appraisals usually left me disheartened. I couldn't believe that they were really the source of reading's value. But for many more years, they constituted the only means I had of describing to myself the educational value of books.

In spite of my earnestness, I found reading a pleasurable activity. I came to enjoy the lonely good company of books. Early on weekday mornings, I'd read in my bed. I'd feel a mysterious comfort then, reading in the dawn quiet — the bluegray silence interrupted by the occasional churning of the refrigerator motor a few rooms away or the more distant sounds of a city bus beginning its run. On weekends I'd go to the public library to read, surrounded by old men and women. Or, if the weather was fine, I would take my books to the park and read in the shade of a tree. A warm summer evening was my favorite reading time. Neighbors would leave for vacation and I would water their lawns. I would sit through the twilight on the front porches or in backyards, reading to the cool, whirling sounds of the sprinklers.

I also had favorite writers. But often those writers I enjoyed most I was least able to value. When I read William Saroyan's *The Human Comedy,* I was immediately pleased by the narrator's warmth and the charm of his story. But as quickly I became suspicious. A book so enjoyable to read couldn't be very "important." Another summer I determined to read all the novels of Dickens. Reading his fat novels, I loved the feeling I got — after the first hundred pages — of being at home in a fictional world where I knew the names of the characters and cared about what was going to happen to them. And it bothered me that I was forced away at the conclusion, when the fiction closed tight, like a fortune-teller's fist — the futures of all the major characters neatly resolved. I never knew how to take such feelings seriously, however. Nor did I suspect that these experiences could be part of a novel's meaning. Still, there were pleasures to sustain me after I'd finish my books. Carrying a volume back to the library, I would be pleased by its weight. I'd run my fingers along the edge of the pages and marvel at the breadth of my achievement. Around my room, growing stacks of paperback books reenforced my assurance.

I entered high school having read hundreds of books. My habit of reading made me a confident speaker and writer of English. Reading also enabled me to sense something of the shape, the major concerns, of Western thought. (I was able to say something about Dante and Descartes and Engels and James Baldwin in my high school term papers.) In these various ways, books brought me academic success as I hoped that they would. But I was not a good reader. Merely bookish, I lacked a point of view when I read. Rather, I read in order to acquire a point of view. I vacuumed books for epigrams, scraps of information, ideas, themes — anything to fill the hollow within me and make me feel educated. When one of my teachers suggested to his drowsy tenth-grade English class that a person could not have a "complicated idea" until he had read at least two thousand books, I heard the remark without detecting either its irony or its very complicated truth. I merely determined to compile a list of all the books I had ever read. Harsh with myself, I included only once a title I might have read several times. (How, after all, could one read a book more than once?) And I included only those books over a hundred pages in length. (Could anything shorter be a book?)

There was yet another high school list I compiled. One day I came *50* across a newspaper article about the retirement of an English professor at a nearby state college. The article was accompanied by a list of the "hundred most important books of Western Civilization." "More than anything else in my life," the professor told the reporter with finality, "these books have made me all that I am." That was the kind of remark I couldn't ignore. I clipped out the list and kept it for the several months it took me to read all of the titles. Most books, of course, I barely understood. While reading Plato's *Republic,* for instance, I needed to keep looking at the book jacket comments to remind myself what the text was about. Nevertheless, with the special patience and superstition of a scholarship boy, I looked at every word of the text. And by the time I reached the last word, relieved, I convinced myself that I had read *The Republic.* In a ceremony of great pride, I solemnly crossed Plato off my list.

3

The scholarship boy pleases most when he is young — the working-class child struggling for academic success. To his teachers, he offers great satisfaction; his success is their proudest achievement. Many other persons offer to help him. A businessman learns the boy's story and promises to underwrite part of the cost of his college education. A woman leaves him her entire library of several hundred books when she moves. His progress is featured in a newspaper article. Many people seem happy for him. They marvel. "How did you manage so fast?" From all sides, there is lavish praise and encouragement.

In his grammar school classroom, however, the boy already makes students around him uneasy. They scorn his desire to succeed. They scorn him for constantly wanting the teacher's attention and praise. "Kiss Ass," they call him when his hand swings up in response to every question he hears. Later, when he makes it to college, no one will mock him aloud. But he detects annoyance on the faces of some students and even some teachers who watch him. It puzzles him often. In college, then in graduate school, he behaves much as he always has. If anything is different about him it is that he dares to anticipate the successful conclusion of his studies. At last he feels that he belongs in the classroom, and this is exactly the source of the dissatisfaction he causes. To many persons around him, he appears too much the academic. There may be some things about him that recall his beginnings—his shabby clothes; his persistent poverty; or his dark skin (in those cases when it symbolizes his parents" disadvantaged condition)—but they only make clear how far he has moved from his past. He has used education to remake himself.

It bothers his fellow academics to face this. They will not say why exactly. (They sneer.) But their expectations become obvious when they are disappointed. They expect—they want—a student less changed by his schooling. If the scholarship boy, from a past so distant from the classroom, could remain in some basic way unchanged, he would be able to prove that it is possible for anyone to become educated without basically changing from the person one was.

Here is no fabulous hero, no idealized scholar-worker. The scholarship boy does not straddle, cannot reconcile, the two great opposing cultures of his life. His success is unromantic and plain. He sits in the classroom and offers those sitting beside him no calming reassurance about their own lives. He sits in the seminar room—a man with brown skin, the son of working-class Mexican immigrant parents. (Addressing the professor at the head of the table, his voice catches with nervousness.) There is no trace of his parents" accent in his speech. Instead he approximates the accents of teachers and classmates. Coming from *him* those sounds seem suddenly odd. Odd too is the effect produced when *he* uses academic jargon—bubbles at the tip of his tongue: "*Topos* . . . negative capability . . . vegetation imagery in Shakespearean comedy." He lifts an opinion from Coleridge, takes something else from Frye or Empson or Leavis. He even repeats exactly his professor's earlier comment. All his ideas are clearly borrowed. He seems to have no thought of his own. He chatters while his listeners smile—their look one of disdain.

When he is older and thus when so little of the person he was survives, the scholarship boy makes only too apparent his profound lack   55 of *self*-confidence. This is the conventional assessment that even Richard Hoggart repeats:

> [The scholarship boy] tends to over-stress the importance of exam-
> inations, of the piling-up of knowledge and of received opinions.
> He discovers a technique of apparent learning, of the acquiring of
> facts rather than of the handling and use of facts. He learns how to
> receive a purely literate education, one using only a small part of
> the personality and challenging only a limited area of his being. He
> begins to see life as a ladder, as a permanent examination with some
> praise and some further exhortation at each stage. He becomes an
> expert imbiber and doler-out; his competence will vary, but will
> rarely be accompanied by genuine enthusiasms. He rarely feels the
> reality of knowledge, of other men's thoughts and imaginings, on
> his own pulses. . . . He has something of the blinkered pony about
> him. . . .

But this is criticism more accurate than fair. The scholarship boy is a very bad student. He is the great mimic; a collector of thoughts, not a thinker; the very last person in class who ever feels obliged to have an opinion of his own. In large part, however, the reason he is such a bad student is because he realizes more often and more acutely than most other students — than Hoggart himself — that education requires radical self-reformation. As a very young boy, regarding his parents, as he struggles with an early homework assignment, he knows this too well. That is why he lacks self-assurance. He does not forget that the class-room is responsible for remaking him. He relies on his teacher, depends on all that he hears in the classroom and reads in his books. He becomes in every obvious way the worst student, a dummy mouthing the opin-ions of others. But he would not be so bad — nor would he become so successful, a *scholarship* boy — if he did not accurately perceive that the best synonym for primary "education" is "imitation."

Those who would take seriously the boy's success — and his fail-ure — would be forced to realize how great is the change any academic undergoes, how far one must move from one's past. It is easiest to ignore such considerations. So little is said about the scholarship boy in pages and pages of educational literature. Nothing is said of the silence that comes to separate the boy from his parents. Instead, one hears proposals for increasing the self-esteem of students and encouraging early intellec-tual independence. Paragraphs glitter with a constellation of terms like *creativity* and *originality*. (Ignored altogether is the function of imitation in a student's life.) Radical educationists meanwhile complain that ghetto schools "oppress" students by trying to mold them, stifling native char-acteristics. The truer critique would be just the reverse: not that schools change ghetto students too much, but that while they might promote the occasional scholarship student, they change most students barely at all.

From the story of the scholarship boy there is no specific pedagogy to glean. There is, however, a much larger lesson. His story makes clear that education is a long, unglamorous, even demeaning process — *a nurturing never natural to the person one was before one entered a classroom.* At once different from most other students, the scholarship boy is also the archetypal "good student." He exaggerates the difficulty of being a student, but his exaggeration reveals a general predicament. Others are changed by their schooling as much as he. They too must re-form themselves. They must develop the skill of memory long before they become truly critical thinkers. And when they read Plato for the first several times, it will be with awe more than deep comprehension.

The impact of schooling on the scholarship boy is only more apparent to the boy himself and to others. Finally, although he may be laughable — a blinkered pony — the boy will not let his critics forget their own change. He ends up too much like them. When he speaks, they hear themselves echoed. In his pedantry, they trace their own. His ambitions are theirs. If his failure were singular, they might readily pity him. But he is more troubling than that. They would not scorn him if this were not so.

4

Like me, Hoggart's imagined scholarship boy spends most of his years in the classroom afraid to long for his past. Only at the very end of his schooling does the boy-man become nostalgic. In this sudden change of heart, Richard Hoggart notes:

> He longs for the membership he lost, "he pines for some Nameless Eden where he never was". The nostalgia is the stronger and the more ambiguous because he is really "in quest of his own absconded self yet scared to find it". He both wants to go back and yet thinks he has gone beyond his class, feels himself weighted with knowledge of his own and their situation, which hereafter forbids him the simpler pleasures of his father and mother. . . .

According to Hoggart, the scholarship boy grows nostalgic because he remains the uncertain scholar, bright enough to have moved from his past, yet unable to feel easy, a part of a community of academics.

This analysis, however, only partially suggests what happened to me in my last year as a graduate student. When I traveled to London to write a dissertation on English Renaissance literature, I was finally confident of membership in a "community of scholars." But the pleasure that confidence gave me faded rapidly. After only two or three months in the reading room of the British Museum, it became clear that I had joined a lonely community. Around me each day were dour faces eclipsed by large piles of books. There were the regulars, like the old couple who arrived every morning, each holding a loop of the shopping bag which

60

contained all their notes. And there was the historian who chattered madly to herself. ("Oh dear! Oh! Now, what's this? What? Oh, my!") There were also the faces of young men and women worn by long study. And everywhere eyes turned away the moment our glance accidentally met. Some persons I sat beside day after day, yet we passed silently at the end of the day, strangers. Still, we were united by a common respect for the written word and for scholarship. We did form a union, though one in which we remained distant from one another.

More profound and unsettling was the bond I recognized with those writers whose books I consulted. Whenever I opened a text that hadn't been used for years, I realized that my special interests and skills united me to a mere handful of academics. We formed an exclusive — eccentric! — society, separated from others who would never care or be able to share our concerns. (The pages I turned were stiff like layers of dead skin.) I began to wonder: Who, beside my dissertation director and a few faculty members, would ever read what I wrote? And: Was my dissertation much more than an act of social withdrawal? These questions went unanswered in the silence of the Museum reading room. They remained to trouble me after I'd leave the library each afternoon and feel myself shy — unsteady, speaking simple sentences at the grocer's or the butcher's on my way back to my bed-sitter.

Meanwhile my file cards accumulated. A professional, I knew exactly how to search a book for pertinent information. I could quickly assess and summarize the usability of the many books I consulted. But whenever I started to write, I knew too much (and not enough) to be able to write anything but sentences that were overly cautious, timid, strained brittle under the heavy weight of footnotes and qualifications. I seemed unable to dare a passionate statement. I felt drawn by professionalism to the edge of sterility, capable of no more than pedantic, lifeless, unassailable prose.

Then nostalgia began.

After years spent unwilling to admit its attractions, I gestured nostalgically toward the past. I yearned for that time when I had not been so alone. I became impatient with books. I wanted experience more immediate. I feared the library's silence. I silently scorned the gray, timid faces around me. I grew to hate the growing pages of my dissertation on genre and Renaissance literature. (In my mind I heard relatives laughing as they tried to make sense of its title.) I wanted something — I couldn't say exactly what. I told myself that I wanted a more passionate life. And a life less thoughtful. And above all, I wanted to be less alone. One day I heard some Spanish academics whispering back and forth to each other, and their sounds seemed ghostly voices recalling my life. Yearning became preoccupation then. Boyhood memories beckoned, flooded my mind. (Laughing intimate voices. Bounding up the front steps of the porch. A sudden embrace inside the door.)

For weeks after, I turned to books by educational experts. I needed   65
to learn how far I had moved from my past — to determine how fast I
would be able to recover something of it once again. But I found little.
Only a chapter in a book by Richard Hoggart . . . I left the reading
room and the circle of faces.

I came home. After the year in England, I spent three summer
months living with my mother and father, relieved by how easy it was
to be home. It no longer seemed very important to me that we had little
to say. I felt easy sitting and eating and walking with them. I watched
them, nevertheless, looking for evidence of those elastic, sturdy strands
that bind generations in a web of inheritance. I thought as I watched my
mother one night: Of course a friend had been right when she told me
that I gestured and laughed just like my mother. Another time I saw for
myself: My father's eyes were much like my own, constantly watchful.

But after the early relief, this return, came suspicion, nagging until
I realized that I had not neatly sidestepped the impact of schooling. My
desire to do so was precisely the measure of how much I remained an
academic. *Negatively* (for that is how this idea first occurred to me): My
need to think so much and so abstractly about my parents and our
relationship was in itself an indication of my long education. My father
and mother did not pass their time thinking about the cultural meanings
of their experience. It was I who described their daily lives with airy
ideas. And yet, *positively:* The ability to consider experience so abstractly
allowed me to shape into desire what would otherwise have remained
indefinite, meaningless longing in the British Museum. If, because of
my schooling, I had grown culturally separated from my parents, my
education finally had given me ways of speaking and caring about
that fact.

My best teachers in college and graduate school, years before, had
tried to prepare me for this conclusion, I think, when they discussed
texts of aristocratic pastoral literature. Faithfully, I wrote down all that
they said. I memorized it: "The praise of the unlettered by the highly
educated is one of the primary themes of 'elitist' literature." But, "the
importance of the praise given the unsolitary, richly passionate and spontaneous life is that it simultaneously reflects the value of a reflective life."
I heard it all. But there was no way for any of it to mean very much to
me. I was a scholarship boy at the time, busily laddering my way up the
rungs of education. To pass an examination, I copied down exactly what
my teachers told me. It would require many more years of schooling (an
inevitable miseducation) in which I came to trust the silence of reading
and the habit of abstracting from immediate experience — moving away
from a life of closeness and immediacy I remembered with my parents,
growing older — before I turned unafraid to desire the past, and thereby
achieved what had eluded me for so long — the end of education.

FOR DISCUSSION AND WRITING

1. What sorts of readers do you think Rodriguez has in mind? (For example, is he writing for specialists in some field? For Mexican Americans? For teenagers?) On what evidence *in the text* do you base your opinion?

2. Explain "scholarship boy" (pars. 8–9). What sort of person and student is a "scholarship boy"? Cite evidence from the text to back your opinion. Is the "scholarship boy" a critical thinker? Explain.

3. Rodriguez tells of the consequences his mother suffered when she misspelled a word (par. 29).

   > One morning there was a letter to be sent to a Washington cabinet officer. On the dictating tape, a voice referred to urban guerrillas. My mother typed (the wrong word, correctly): "gorillas." The mistake horrified the anti-poverty bureaucrats who shortly after arranged to have her returned to her previous position. She would go no further.

   Why would such an apparently unimportant mistake have such grave consequences? What does it say about the typist's world knowledge?

4. Explain why Rodriguez was upset by his parents' failure to read for pleasure. What did pleasure reading mean to him? Do you share the same idea of pleasure reading? Why or why not?

5. Rodriguez says, "In the sixth grade I simply concluded that what gave a book its value was some major idea or theme it contained. If that core essence could be mined and memorized, I would become learned like my teachers" (par. 46). Clearly, the value of a book comes from other factors as well as the major idea. In your opinion, what are some of those factors?

6. Explain why Rodriguez did not actually read *The Republic* (par. 50).

7. What other aspects of reading do you think Rodriguez overlooked when he read the important books of world literature? Explain what the author means when he says, "I was not a good reader. Merely bookish . . ." (par. 49).

8. "How, after all, could one read a book more than once?" asks Rodriguez (par. 49). In what ways can one reread a book and truly call it reading?

9. In your own words, state the main point of this selection.

10. When asked by the nun why he was so reluctant to read by himself, what reason does Rodriguez give? Compare this with his mother's complaint about how their family was changing. Do you believe that there is some correlation between the two? Explain.

11. According to Rodriguez, what is the goal of education? Do you agree? If not, what do you think it is?

12. Why do you think this chapter of *Hunger of Memory* was titled "The Achievement of Desire" rather than "The Desire for Achievement"?

I DEVELOPED THE ABILITY TO READ CLOSELY

Mike Rose

Mike Rose, the son of Italian immigrants, grew up in what was a rapidly deteriorating section of Los Angeles.

> Right to the north of us was a record shop, a barber shop presided over by old Mr. Graff, Walt's Malts, a shoe repair shop with a big Cat's Paw decal in the window. . . .
>
> Behind our house was an unpaved alley that passed, just to the north, a power plant the length of a city block. Massive coils atop the building hissed and cracked through the day, but the doors never opened. I used to think it was abandoned — feeding itself on its own wild arcs — until one sweltering afternoon a man was electrocuted on the roof. The air was thick and still as two firemen — the only men present — brought down a charred and limp body without saying a word.
>
> The north and south traffic on Vermont was separated by tracks for the old yellow trolley cars, long since defunct. Across the street was a huge garage, a tiny hot dog stand run by a myopic and reclusive man named Freddie, and my dreamland, the Vermont Bowl. (p. 14–15)

Spurred by caring teachers and his own intellectual curiosity, Rose ultimately earned a bachelor's degree at Loyola University in Los Angeles and a doctorate at the University of California, Los Angeles, where he is currently associate director of the writing programs.

In this selection from his intellectual and professional autobiography, Mike Rose portrays four college professors who made a profound impact on his life. How does the selection relate to your own experience? Have teachers, friends, or relatives influenced your reading? From this selection, you will probably gain insights about your own development as a reader and critical reader.

From the midpoint of their freshman year, Loyola students had to take one philosophy course per semester: Logic, Philosophy of Nature, Philosophy of Man, General Ethics, Natural Theology, and so on. Logic was the first in the series, and I had barely gotten a C. The rest of the courses looked like a book fair of medieval scholasticism with the mold scraped off the bindings, and I dreaded their advent. But I was beginning my sophomore year at a time when the best and brightest of the Jesuit community were calling for an intellectually panoramic, socially progressive Catholicism, and while this lasted, I reaped the benefits. Sections of the next three courses I had to take would be taught by a young man who was studying for the priesthood and who was, himself, attempting to develop a personal philosophy that incorporated the mind and the body as well as the spirit.

Mr. Johnson could have strolled off a Wheaties box. Still in his twenties and a casting director's vision of those good looks thought to be all-American, Don Johnson had committed his very considerable intelligence to the study and teaching of philosophy. Jack MacFarland had introduced me to the Greeks, to Christian scholasticism, eighteenth-century deism, and French existentialism, but it was truly an introduction, a curtsy to that realm of the heavens where the philosophers dwell. Mr. Johnson provided a fuller course. He was methodical and spoke with vibrance and made connections between ancients and moderns with care. He did for philosophy what Mr. MacFarland had done for literary history: He gave me a directory of key names and notions.

We started in a traditional way with the Greek philosophers who preceded Socrates — Thales, Heraclitus, Empedocles — and worked our way down to Kant and Hegel. We read a little Aquinas, but we also read E. A. Burtt's *The Metaphysical Foundations of Modern Science,* and that gave me entry to Kepler, Copernicus, Galileo (which I was then spelling *Galelao*), and Newton. As he laid out his history of ideas, Mr. Johnson would consider aloud the particular philosophical issue involved, so we didn't, for example, simply get an outline of what Hegel believed, but we watched and listened as Don Johnson reasoned like Hegel and then raised his own questions about the Hegelian scheme. He was a working philosopher, and he was thinking out loud in front of us.

The Metaphysical Foundations of Modern Science was very tough going. It assumed not only a familiarity with Western thought but, as well, a sophistication in reading a theoretically rich argument. It was, in other words, the kind of book you encounter with increased frequency as you move through college. It combined the history of mathematics and science with philosophical investigation, and when I tried to read it, I'd end up rescanning the same sentences over and over, not understanding them, and, finally, slamming the book down on the desk — swearing at this golden boy Johnson and angry with myself. Here's a typical passage, one of the many I marked as being hopeless:

> We begin now to glimpse the tremendous significance of what these fathers of modern science were doing, but let us continue with our questions. What further specific metaphysical doctrines was Kepler led to adopt as a consequence of this notion of what constitutes the real world? For one thing, it led him to appropriate in his own way the distinction between primary and secondary qualities, which had been noted in the ancient world by the atomist and skeptical schools, and which was being revived in the sixteenth century in varied form by such miscellaneous thinkers as Vives, Sanchez, Montaigne, and Campanella. Knowledge as it is immediately offered the mind through the senses is obscure, confused, contradictory, and hence

untrustworthy; only those features of the world in terms of which we get certain and consistent knowledge open before us what is indubitably and permanently real. Other qualities are not real qualities of things, but only signs of them. For Kepler, of course, the real qualities are those caught up in this mathematical harmony underlying the world of the senses, and which, therefore, have a causal relation to the latter. *The real world is a world of quantitative characteristics only; its differences are differences of number alone.*

I couldn't get the distinction that was being made between primary and secondary qualities, and I certainly didn't have the background that would enable me to make sense of Burtt's brief historical survey: from "atomist and skeptical schools [to] . . . Campanella." It is clear from the author's italics that the last sentence of the passage is important, so I underlined it, but because Burtt's discussion is built on a rich intellectual history that I didn't know, I was reading words but not understanding text. I was the human incarnation of language-recognition computer programs: able to record the dictionary meanings of individual words but unable to generate any meaning out of them.

"What," I asked in class, "are primary and secondary qualities? I don't get it." And here Don Johnson was very good. "The answer," he said, "can be found in the passage itself. I'll go back through it with you. Let's start with primary and secondary qualities. If some qualities are primary and others secondary, which do you think would be most important?"

"Primary?"

"Right. Primary qualities. Whatever they are. Now let's turn to Kepler, since Kepler's the subject of this passage. What is it that's more important to Kepler?"

I pause and say tentatively, "Math." Another student speaks up, reading from the book: "Quantitative characteristics."

"All right. So primary qualities, for Kepler, are mathematical, quantitative. But we still don't know what this primary and secondary opposition really refers to, do we? Look right in the middle of the paragraph. Burtt is comparing mathematical knowledge to the immediate knowledge provided by — what?"

My light bulb goes on: "The senses."

"There it is. The primary-secondary opposition is the opposition between knowledge gained by pure mathematical reasoning versus knowledge gained through our five senses."

We worked with *The Metaphysical Foundations of Modern Science* for some time, and I made my way slowly through it. Mr. Johnson was helping me develop an ability to read difficult texts — I was learning how to reread critically, how to tease out definitions and basic arguments. And I was also gaining confidence that if I stayed with material long enough and kept asking questions, I would get it. That assurance proved to be more valuable than any particular body of knowledge I learned that year.

For my second semester, I had to take Philosophy of Man, and it was during that course that Mr. Johnson delivered his second gift. We read Gabriel Marcel and Erich Fromm, learning about phenomenology and social criticism. We considered the human animal from an anthropological as well as philosophical perspective. And we read humanistic psychologist Abraham Maslow's *Toward a Psychology of Being.* Maslow wrote about "the 'will to health,' the urge to grow, the pressure of self-actualization, the quest for one's identity." The book had a profound effect on me. Six months before, Lou Minton's jaw quivered as if to speak the race's deepest sorrow, and through the rest of that summer I could only feel in my legs and chest some fleeting assurance that the world wasn't a thin mask stretched over nothingness. Now I was reading an articulation of that vague, hopeful feeling. Maslow was giving voice to some delicate possibility within me, and I was powerfully drawn to it. Every person is, in part, "'his own project' and makes himself." I had to know more, so I called Mr. Johnson up and asked if I could visit with him. "Sure," he said, and invited me to campus. So one Saturday morning I took a series of early buses and headed west.

Mr. Johnson and the other initiates to the priesthood lived in an old   *15*
white residence hall on the grassy east edge of campus, and the long walk up Loyola Boulevard was quiet and meditative: Birds were flying tree to tree and a light breeze was coming in off Playa del Rey. I walked up around the gym, back behind Math-Engineering to his quarters, a simple one-story building with those Spanish curves that seem simultaneously thick and weightless. The sun had warmed the stucco. A window by the door was open, and a curtain had fluttered out. I rang the bell and heard steps on a hardwood floor. Mr. Johnson opened the door and stepped out. He was smiling and his eyes were attentive in the light . . . present . . . there. They said, "Come, let's talk."

Dr. Frank Carothers taught what is generally called the sophomore survey, a yearlong sequence of courses that introduces the neophyte English major to the key works in English literary history. Dr. Carothers was tall and robust. He wore thick glasses and a checkered bow tie and his hairline was male Botticelli, picking up somewhere back beyond his brow. As the year progressed, he spread English literary history out in slow time across the board, and I was introduced to people I'd never heard of: William Langland, a medieval acolyte who wrote the dream-vision *Piers Plowman;* the sixteenth-century poet Sir Thomas Wyatt; Elizabethan lyricists with peculiar names like Orlando Gibbons and Tobias Hume (the author of the wondrous suggestion that tobacco "maketh lean the fat men's tumour"); the physician Sir Thomas Browne; the

essayist Joseph Addison; the biographer James Boswell; the political philosopher Edmund Burke, whose prose I could not decipher; and poets
Romantic and Victorian (Shelley and Rossetti and Algernon Charles
Swinburne). Some of the stuff was invitingly strange ("Pallid and pink
as the palm of the flag-flower . . ."), some was awfully hard to read, and
some was just awful. But Dr. Carothers laid it all out with his reserved
passion, drew for us a giant conceptual blueprint onto which we could
place other courses, other books. He was precise, thorough, and rigorous. And he started his best work once class was over.

Being a professor was, for Frank Carothers, a profoundly social
calling: He enjoyed the classroom, and he seemed to love the more
informal contacts with those he taught, those he once taught, and those
who stopped by just to get a look at this guy. He stayed in his office
until about four each afternoon, leaning back in his old swivel chair,
hands clasped behind his head, his bow tie tight against his collar. He
had strong opinions, and he'd get irritated if you missed class, and he
sometimes gave quirky advice — but there he'd be shaking his head sympathetically as students poured out their troubles. It was pure and primary for Frank Carothers: Teaching allowed him daily to fuse the joy he
got from reading literature — poetry especially — with his deep pleasure
in human community. What I saw when I was around him — and I hung
out in his office from my sophomore year on — was very different from
the world I had been creating for myself, a far cry from my withdrawal
into an old house trailer with a silent book.

One of Dr. Carothers's achievements was the English Society. The
English Society had seventy-eight members, and that made it just about
the biggest organization on campus: jocks, literati, C-plus students, frat
boys, engineers, mystics, scholars, profligates, bullies, geeks, Republicans — all stood side by side for group pictures. The English Society
sponsored poetry readings, lectures, and card games, and best of all,
barbecues in the Carotherses' backyard. We would caravan out to Manhattan Beach to be greeted by Betsy, the youngest of the seven Carothers
children, and she'd walk us back to her father who, wrapped now in an
apron, was poking coals or unscrewing the tops from jugs of red wine.

Vivian Carothers, a delicate, soft-spoken woman, would look after
us and serve up trays of cheese and chips and little baked things. Students
would knock on the redwood gate all through the late afternoon, more
and more finding places for themselves among flowers and elephant ears,
patio furniture, and a wizened pine. We would go on way past sunset,
talking to Dr. Carothers and to each other about books and sports and
currently despised professors, sometimes letting off steam and sometimes learning something new. And Frank Carothers would keep us fed,
returning to the big, domed barbecue through the evening to lift the lid
and add hamburgers, the smoke rising off the grill and up through the

telephone lines stretching like the strings of Shelley's harp over the sub-
urbs of the South Bay.

When I was learning my craft at Jack MacFarland's knee, I contin-   20
ually misused words and wrote fragments and run-on sentences and had
trouble making my pronouns agree with whatever it was that preceded
them. I also produced sentences like these:

> Some of these modern-day Ramses are inherent of their wealth,
> others are self-made.

> An exhibition of will on the part of the protagonist enables him to
> accomplish a subjective good (which is an element of tragedy,
> namely: the protagonist does not fully realize the objective wrong
> that he is doing. He feels objectively justified if not completely
> right.)

I was struggling to express increasingly complex ideas, and I couldn't
get the language straight: Words, as in my second sentence on tragedy,
piled up like cars in a serial wreck. I was encountering a new language—
the language of the academy—and was trying to find my way around in
it. I have some more examples, written during my first year and a half
at Loyola. There was inflated vocabulary:

> I conjectured that he was the same individual who had arrested my
> attention earlier.

> In his famed speech, "The American Scholar," Ralph Waldo Emer-
> son posed several problems that are particularly germane to the
> position of the young author.

There were clichés and mixed and awkward metaphors:

> In 1517, when Luther nailed his 95 theses to the door of Wittenburg
> Cathedral, he unknowingly started a snowball rolling that was to
> grow to tremendous reprocussions.

And there was academic melodrama:

> The vast realm of the cosmos or the depths of a man's soul hold
> questions that reason flounders upon, but which can be probed by
> the peculiar private insight of the seer.

Pop grammarians and unhappy English teachers get a little strange
around sentences like these. But such sentences can be seen as marking a
stage in linguistic growth. Appropriating a style and making it your
own is difficult, and you'll miss the mark a thousand times along the
way. The botched performances, though, are part of it all, and developing writers will grow through them if they are able to write for people
who care about language, people who are willing to sit with them and

help them as they struggle to write about difficult things. That is what Ted Erlandson did for me.

Dr. Erlandson was one of the people who agreed to teach me and my Mercy High companions a seminar — a close, intensive course that would substitute for a larger, standard offering like Introduction to Prose Literature. He was tall and lanky and had a long reddish brown beard and lectured in a voice that was basso and happy. He was a strong lecturer and possessed the best memory for fictional detail I'd ever witnessed. And he cared about prose. The teachers I had during my last three years at Loyola assigned a tremendous amount of writing. But it was Ted Erlandson who got in there with his pencil and worked on my style. He would sit me down next to him at his big desk, sweep books and pencils across the scratched veneer, and go back over the sentences he wanted me to revise.

He always began by reading the sentence out loud: "Camus ascented to a richer vision of life that was to characterize the entirety of his work." Then he would fiddle with the sentence, talking and looking up at me intermittently to comment or ask questions: "'Ascent'. That sounds like 'assent', I know, but look it up, Mike." He'd wait while I fluttered the dictionary. "Now, 'the entirety of his work' . . . try this instead: 'his entire work.' Let's read it. 'Camus assented to a richer vision of life that would characterize his entire work.' Sounds better, doesn't it?"

And another sentence. "'Irregardless of the disastrous ending of *Bread and Wine,* it must be seen as an affirmative work.' 'Irregardless' . . . people use it all the time, but 'regardless' will do just fine. Now, I think this next part sounds a little awkward; listen: 'Regardless of the disastrous ending of *Bread and Wine,* it . . . 'Hear that? Let's try removing the 'of' and the 'it': 'Regardless of the disastrous ending, *Bread and Wine* must be seen as an affirmative work.' Hmmm. Better, I think."

And so it would go. He rarely used grammatical terms, and he   25
never got technical. He dealt with specific bits of language: "Try this here" or "Here's another way to say it." He worked as a craftsman works, with particulars, and he shuttled back and forth continually between print and voice, making me breathe my prose, making me hear the language I'd generated in silence. Perhaps he was more directive than some would like, but, to be truthful, direction was what I needed. I was easily frustrated, and it didn't take a lot to make me doubt myself. When teachers would write "no" or "awkward" or "rewrite" alongside the sentences I had worked so hard to produce, I would be peeved and disappointed. "Well, what the hell *do* they want?" I'd grumble to no one in particular. So Ted Erlandson's linguistic parenting felt just right: a modeling of grace until it all slowly, slowly began to work itself into the way I shaped language.

When Father Albertson lectured, he would stand pretty much in one spot slightly to the left or right of center in front of us. He tended to hold his notes or a play or a critical study in both hands, releasing one to emphasize a point with a simple gesture. He was tall and thin, and his voice was soft and tended toward monotone. When he spoke, he looked very serious, but when one of us responded with any kind of intelligence, a little smile would come over his face. Jack MacFarland had told me that it was Clint Albertson's Shakespeare course that would knock my socks off.

For each play we covered, Father Albertson distributed a five- to ten-page list of questions to ask ourselves as we read. These study questions were of three general types.

The first type was broad and speculative and was meant to spark reflection on major characters and key events. Here's a teaser on *Hamlet:*

> Would you look among the portrait-paintings by Raphael, or Rembrandt, or Van Gogh, or El Greco, or Rouault for an ideal representation of Hamlet? Which painting by which of these men do you think most closely resembles your idea of what Hamlet should look like?

The second type focused on the details of the play itself and were very specific. Here are two of the thirty-eight he wrote for *As You Like It:*

ACT I, SCENE 2

> How is Rosalind distinguished from Celia in this scene? How do you explain the discrepancy between the Folio version of lines 284–287 and Act I, scene 3, line 117?

ACT II, SCENES 4–6:

> It has been said these scenes take us definitely out of the world of reality into a world of dream. What would you say are the steps of the process by which Shakespeare brings about this illusion?

The third kind of question required us to work with some historical or critical study. This is an example from the worksheet on *Romeo and Juliet:*

> Read the first chapter of C. S. Lewis's *Allegory of Love,* "Courtly Love." What would you say about Shakespeare's concept of love in relation to what Lewis presents as the traditional contradictory concepts in medieval literature of "romantic love" vs. "marriage."

Father Albertson had placed over 150 books on the reserve shelf in the library, and they ranged from intellectual history to literary criticism to handbooks on theater production. I had used a few such "secondary sources" to quote in my own writing since my days with Jack MacFarland, but this was the first time a teacher had so thoroughly woven them into a course. Father Albertson would cite them during lectures as naturally as though he were recalling a discussion he had overheard. He would add his own opinions and, since he expected us to form opinions, would ask us for ours.

I realize that this kind of thing — the close, line-by-line examination, the citing of critical opinion — has given rise to endless parodies of the academy: repressed schoolmen clucking along in the land of lost language. It certainly can be that way. But with Clint Albertson, all the learning furthered my comprehension of the play. His questions forced me to think carefully about Shakespeare's choice of words, about the crafting of a scene, about the connections between language and performance. I had to read very, very closely, leaning over the thin Formica desk in the trailer, my head cupped in my hands with my two index fingers in my ears to blot out the noise from the alley behind me. There were times when no matter how hard I tried, I wouldn't get it. I'd close the book, feeling stupid to my bones, and go find John. Over then to the liquor store, out into the night. The next day I would visit Father Albertson and tell him I was lost, ask him why this stuff was so damned hard. He'd listen and ask me to tell him why it made me so angry. I'd sputter some more, and then he'd draw me to the difficult passage, slowly opening the language up, helping me comprehend a distant, stylized literature, taking it apart, touching it.

I would then return to a classroom where a historically rich con- *30*
versation was in progress. Other readers of Shakespeare — from Samuel Johnson to the contemporary literary critic Wylie Sypher — were given voice by Father Albertson, and we were encouraged to enter the dialogue, to consider, to take issue, to be seated amid all that potentially intimidating shoptalk. We were shown how to summarize an opinion, argue with it, weave it into our own interpretations. Nothing is more exclusive than the academic club: its language is highbrow, it has fancy badges, and it worships tradition. It limits itself to a few participants who prefer to talk to each other. What Father Albertson did was bring us inside the circle, nudging us out into the chatter, always just behind us, whispering to try this step, then this one, encouraging us to feel the moves for ourselves.

Those four men collectively gave me the best sort of liberal education, the kind longed for in the stream of blue-ribbon reports on the humanities that now cross my desk. I developed the ability to read closely, to persevere in the face of uncertainty and ask questions of what I was reading — not with downcast eyes, but freely, aloud, realizing there is no such thing as an open book. My teachers modeled critical inquiry and linguistic precision and grace, and they provided various cognitive maps for philosophy and history and literature. They encouraged me to make connections and to enter into conversations — present and past — to see what talking a particular kind of talk would enable me to do with a thorny philosophical problem or a difficult literary text. And it was all alive. It transpired in backyards and on doorsteps and inside offices as well as in the classroom. I could smell their tobacco and see the nicks left by their razors. They liked books and ideas, and they liked to talk about them in ways that fostered growth rather than established dominance. They lived their knowledge. And maybe because of that their knowledge grew in me in ways that led back out to the world. I was developing a set of tools with which to shape a life.

FOR DISCUSSION AND WRITING

1. Explain what Mike Rose learned about close reading from Don Johnson.

2. The chapter from which this selection comes is entitled "Entering the Conversation," which means the acquisition or cultivation of the knowledge, intellectual abilities, and language skills a person needs to participate fully in the educated community. In what ways did Dr. Carothers help Mike Rose enter the conversation? (What did Rose learn from Dr. Carothers?)

3. What did Rose learn from Dr. Erlandson? Explain why you think it was or was not an important lesson.

4. Rose tells us that Erlandson "rarely used grammatical terms, and he never got technical" (par. 25). In your opinion, would grammar lessons have helped Rose? Explain.

5. Father Albertson asked three types of questions. Explain those types, and discuss how such questions would help students become critical readers.

6. The section on Don Johnson ends with these sentences (par. 15):

   > I rang the bell and heard steps on a hardwood floor. Mr. Johnson opened the door and stepped out. He was smiling and his eyes were attentive in the light . . . present . . . there. They said, "Come, let's talk."

   What is the meaning of these sentences? What do they tell you about Mike Rose's educational experiences? What do they tell you about his concept of teaching?

7. As Mike Rose characterizes it, "Nothing is more exclusive than the academic club: its language is highbrow, it has fancy badges, and it worships tradition. It limits itself to a few participants who prefer to talk to each other" (par. 30). How do you feel about this club? Are its effects on society positive or negative? Explain why you would or would not want to belong.

FROM OUTSIDE, IN

Barbara Mellix

In 1987, when this essay was published in *The Georgia Review,* Barbara Mellix was an assistant professor at the University of Pittsburgh at Greensburg. She holds a master of fine arts in creative writing.

"From Outside, In" is an essay about the relationship of language to class, race, and one's view of oneself, and it is closely related in theme to the readings by Richard Rodriguez and Mike Rose. As you read, you should keep these questions in mind: What can I learn about language from the essay? How does Mellix's experience relate to my own background?

Two years ago, when I started writing this paper, trying to bring order out of chaos, my ten-year-old daughter was suffering from an acute attack of boredom. She drifted in and out of the room complaining that she had nothing to do, no one to "be with" because none of her friends were at home. Patiently I explained that I was working on something special and needed peace and quiet, and I suggested that she paint, read, or work with her computer. None of these interested her. Finally, she pulled up a chair to my desk and watched me, now and then heaving long, loud sighs. After two or three minutes (nine or ten sighs), I lost my patience. "Looka here, Allie," I said, "you too old for this kinda carryin' on. I done told you this is important. You wronger than dirt to be in here haggin' me like this and you know it. Now git on outta here and leave me off before I put my foot all the way down."

I was at home, alone with my family, and my daughter understood that this way of speaking was appropriate in that context. She knew, as a matter of fact, that it was almost inevitable; when I get angry at home, I speak some of my finest, most cherished black English. Had I been speaking to my daughter in this manner in certain other environments, she would have been shocked and probably worried that I had taken leave of my sense of propriety.

Like my children, I grew up speaking what I considered two distinctly different languages — black English and standard English (or as I thought of them then, the ordinary everyday speech of "country" coloreds and "proper" English) — and in the process of acquiring these languages, I developed an understanding of when, where, and how to use them. But unlike my children, I grew up in a world that was primarily black. My friends, neighbors, minister, teachers — almost everybody I associated with every day — were black. And we spoke to one another in our own special language: *That sho is a pretty dress you got on. If she don' soon leave me off I'm gon tell her head a mess. I was so mad I could'a pissed a blue nail. He all the time trying to low-rate somebody. Ain't that just about the nastiest thing you ever set ears on?*

Then there were the "others," the "proper" blacks, transplanted relatives and one-time friends who came home from the city for weddings, funerals, and vacations. And the whites. To these we spoke standard English. "Ain't?" my mother would yell at me when I used the term in the presence of "others." "You *know* better than that." And I would hang my head in shame and say the "proper" word.

I remember one summer sitting in my grandmother's house in   5 Greeleyville, South Carolina, when it was full of the chatter of city relatives who were home on vacation. My parents sat quietly, only now and then volunteering a comment or answering a question. My mother's face took on a strained expression when she spoke. I could see that she was being careful to say just the right words in just the right way. Her voice sounded thick, muffled. And when she finished speaking, she would lapse into silence, her proper smile on her face. My father was more articulate, more aggressive. He spoke quickly, his words sharp and clear. But he held his proud head higher, a signal that he, too, was uncomfortable. My sisters and brothers and I stared at our aunts, uncles, and cousins, speaking only when prompted. Even then, we hesitated, formed our sentences in our minds, then spoke softly, shyly.

My parents looked small and anxious during those occasions, and I waited impatiently for our leave-taking when we would mock our relatives the moment we were out of their hearing. "Reeely," we would say to one another, flexing our wrists and rolling our eyes, "how dooo you stan' this heat? Chile, it just too hy*ooo*-mid for words." Our relatives had made us feel "country," and this was our way of regaining pride in ourselves while getting a little revenge in the bargain. The words bubbled in our throats and rolled across our tongues, a balming.

As a child I felt this same doubleness in uptown Greeleyville where the whites lived. "Ain't that a pretty dress you're wearing!" Toby, the town policeman, said to me one day when I was fifteen. "Thank you very much," I replied, my voice barely audible in my own ears. The words felt wrong in my mouth, rigid, foreign. It was not that I had never spoken that phrase before — it was common in black English, too — but I was extremely conscious that this was an occasion for proper English. I had taken out my English and put it on as I did my church clothes, and I felt as if I were wearing my Sunday best in the middle of the week. It did not matter that Toby had not spoken grammatically correct English. He was white and could speak as he wished. I had something to prove. Toby did not.

Speaking standard English to whites was our way of demonstrating that we knew their language and could use it. Speaking it to standard-English-speaking blacks was our way of showing them that we, as well as they, could "put on airs." But when we spoke standard English, we acknowledged (to ourselves and to others — but primarily to ourselves) that our customary way of speaking was inferior. We felt foolish, embarrassed, somehow diminished because we were ashamed to be our real selves. We were reserved, shy in the presence of those who owned and/or spoke *the* language.

My parents never set aside time to drill us in standard English. Their forms of instruction were less formal. When my father was feeling particularly expansive, he would regale us with tales of his exploits in the outside world. In almost flawless English, complete with dialogue and flavored with gestures and embellishment, he told us about his attempt to get a haircut at a white barbershop; his refusal to acknowledge one of the town merchants until the man addressed him as "Mister"; the time he refused to step off the sidewalk uptown to let some whites pass; his airplane trip to New York City (to visit a sick relative) during which the stewardesses and porters — recognizing that he was a "gentleman" — addressed him as "Sir." I did not realize then — nor, I think, did my father — that he was teaching us, among other things, standard English and the relationship between language and power.

My mother's approach was different. Often, when one of us said,   *10* "I'm gon wash off my feet," she would say, "And what will you walk on if you wash them off?" Everyone would laugh at the victim of my mother's "proper" mood. But it was different when one of us children was in a proper mood. "You think you are so superior," I said to my oldest sister one day when we were arguing and she was winning. "Superior!" my sister mocked. "You mean I am acting 'biggidy'?" My sisters and brothers sniggered, then joined in teasing me. Finally, my mother said, "Leave your sister alone. There's nothing wrong with using proper English." There was a half-smile on her face. I had gotten "uppity," had "put on airs" for no good reason. I was at home, alone with the family, and I hadn't been prompted by one of my mother's proper moods. But there was also a proud light in my mother's eyes; her children were learning English very well.

Not until years later, as a college student, did I begin to understand our ambivalence toward English, our scorn of it, our need to master it, to own and be owned by it — an ambivalence that extended to the public-school classroom. In our school, where there were no whites, my teachers taught standard English but used black English to do it. When my grammar-school teachers wanted us to write, for example, they usually said something like, "I want y'all to write five sentences that make a statement. Anybody git done before the rest can color." It was probably almost those exact words that led me to write these sentences in 1953 when I was in the second grade:

> The white clouds are pretty.
> There are only 15 people in our room.
> We will go to gym.
> We have a new poster.
> We may go out doors.

Second grade came after "Little First" and "Big First," so by then I knew the implied rules that accompanied all writing assignments. Writing was an occasion for proper English. I was not to write in the way we spoke to one another: The white clouds pretty; There ain't but 15 people in our room; We going to gym. We got a new poster; We can go out in the yard. Rather I was to use the language of "other": clouds *are, there are,* we *will,* we *have,* we *may.*

My sentences were short, rigid, perfunctory, like the letters my mother wrote to relatives:

> Dear Papa,
> How are you? How is Mattie? Fine I hope. We are fine. We will come to see you Sunday. Cousin Ned will give us a ride.
>
> > Love,
> > Daughter

The language was not ours. It was something from outside us, something we used for special occasions.

But my coloring on the other side of that second-grade paper is different. I drew three hearts and a sun. The sun has a smiling face that radiates and envelops everything it touches. And although the sun and its world are enclosed in a circle, the colors I used—red, blue, green, purple, orange, yellow, black—indicate that I was less restricted with drawing and coloring than I was with writing standard English. My valentines were not just red. My sun was not just a yellow ball in the sky.

By the time I reached the twelfth grade, speaking and writing standard English had taken on new importance. Each year, about half of the newly graduated seniors of our school moved to large cities—particularly in the North—to live with relatives and find work. Our English teacher constantly corrected our grammar: "Not 'ain't,' but "isn't.'" We seldom wrote papers, and even those few were usually plot summaries of short stories. When our teacher returned the papers, she usually lectured on the importance of using standard English: "I *am;* you *are;* he, she, or it *is,*" she would say, writing on the chalkboard as she spoke. "How you gon git a job talking about 'I is,' or 'I isn't' or 'I ain't'?"

In Pittsburgh, where I moved after graduation, I watched my aunt   15
and uncle—who had always spoken standard English when in Greeleyville—switch from black English to standard English to a mixture of the two, according to where they were or who they were with. At home and with certain close relatives, friends, and neighbors, they spoke black English. With those less close, they spoke a mixture. In public and with strangers, they generally spoke standard English.

In time, I learned to speak standard English with ease and to switch smoothly from black to standard or a mixture, and back again. But no matter where I was, no matter what the situation or occasion, I continued to write as I had in school:

Dear Mommie,
How are you? How is everybody else? Fine I hope. I am fine. So are
Aunt and Uncle. Tell everyone I said hello. I will write again soon.

Love,
Barbara

At work, at a health insurance company, I learned to write letters to
customers. I studied form letters and letters written by co-workers,
memorizing the phrases and the ways in which they were used. I
dictated:

Thank you for your letter of January 5. We have made the changes
in your coverage you requested. Your new premium will be $150
every three months. We are pleased to have been of service to you.

In a sense, I was proud of the letters I wrote for the company: they were
proof of my ability to survive in the city, the outside world—an indication of my growing mastery of English. But they also indicate that
writing was still mechanical for me, something that didn't require much
thought.

Reading also became a more significant part of my life during those
early years in Pittsburgh. I had always liked reading, but now I devoted
more and more of my spare time to it. I read romances, mysteries,
popular novels. Looking back, I realize that the books I liked best were
simple, unambiguous: good versus bad and right versus wrong with
right rewarded and wrong punished, mysteries unraveled and all set
right in the end. It was how I remembered life in Greeleyville.

Of course I was romanticizing. Life in Greeleyville had not been so
very uncomplicated. Back there I had been—first as a child, then as a
young woman with limited experience in the outside world—living in a
relatively closed-in society. But there were implicit and explicit principles
that guided our way of life and shaped our relationships with one another
and the people outside—principles that a newcomer would find elusive
and baffling. In Pittsburgh, I had matured, become more experienced:
I had worked at three different jobs, associated with a wider range of
people, married, had children. This new environment with different
prescripts for living required that I speak standard English much of the
time, and slowly, imperceptibly, I had ceased seeing a sharp distinction
between myself and "others." Reading romances and mysteries, characterized by dichotomy, was a way of shying away from change, from the
person I was becoming.

But that other part of me—that part which took great pride in my
ability to hold a job writing business letters—was increasingly drawn to
the new developments in my life and the attending possibilities, opportunities for even greater change. If I could write letters for a nationally

known business, could I not also do something better, more challenging, more important? Could I not, perhaps, go to college and become a school teacher? For years, afraid and a little embarrassed, I did no more than imagine this different me, this possible me. But sixteen years after coming north, when my younger daughter entered kindergarten, I found myself unable — or unwilling — to resist the lure of possibility. I enrolled in my first college course: Basic Writing, at the University of Pittsburgh.

For the first time in my life, I was required to write extensively   20
about myself. Using the most formal English at my command, I wrote these sentences near the beginning of the term:

> One of my duties as a homemaker is simply picking up after others. A day seldom passes that I don't search for a mislaid toy, book, or gym shoe, etc. I change the Ty-D-Bol, fight "ring around the collar," and keep our laundry smelling "April fresh." Occasionally, I settle arguments between my children and suggest things to do when they're bored. Taking telephone messages for my oldest daughter is my newest (and sometimes most aggravating) chore. Hanging the toilet paper roll is my most insignificant.

My concern was to use "appropriate" language, to sound as if I belonged in a college classroom. But I felt separate from the language — as if it did not and could not belong to me. I couldn't think and feel genuinely in that language, couldn't make it express what I thought and felt about being a housewife. A part of me resented, among other things, being judged by such things as the appearance of my family's laundry and toilet bowl, but in that language I could only imagine and write about a conventional housewife.

For the most part, the remainder of the term was a period of adjustment, a time of trying to find my bearings as a student in a college composition class, to learn to shut out my black English whenever I composed, and to prevent it from creeping into my formulations; a time for trying to grasp the language of the classroom and reproduce it in my prose; for trying to talk about myself in that language, reach others through it. Each experience of writing was like standing naked and revealing my imperfection, my "otherness." And each new assignment was another chance to make myself over in language, reshape myself, make myself "better" in my rapidly changing image of a student in a college composition class.

But writing became increasingly unmanageable as the term progressed, and by the end of the semester, my sentences sounded like this:

> My excitement was soon dampened, however, by what seemed like a small voice in the back of my head saying that I should be careful with my long awaited opportunity. I felt frustrated and this seemed to make it difficult to concentrate.

There is a poverty of language in these sentences. By this point, I knew that the clichéd language of my Housewife essay was unacceptable, and I generally recognized trite expressions. At the same time, I hadn't yet mastered the language of the classroom, hadn't yet come to see it as belonging to me. Most notable is the lifelessness of the prose, the apparent absence of a person behind the words. I wanted those sentences — and the rest of the essay — to convey the anguish of yearning to, at once, become something more and yet remain the same. I had the sensation of being split in two, part of me going into a future the other part didn't believe possible. As that person, the student writer at that moment, I was essentially mute. I could not — in the process of composing — use the language of the old me, yet I couldn't imagine myself in the language of "others."

I found this particularly discouraging because at midsemester I had been writing in a much different way. Note the language of this introduction to an essay I had written then, near the middle of the term:

> Pain is a constant companion to the people in "Footwork." Their jobs are physically damaging. Employers are insensitive to their feelings and in many cases add to their problems. The general public wounds them further by treating them with disgrace because of what they do for a living. Although the workers are as diverse as they are similar, there is a definite link between them. They suffer a great deal of abuse.

The voice here is stronger, more confident, appropriating terms like "physically damaging," "wounds them further," "insensitive," "diverse" — terms I couldn't have imagined using when writing about my own experience — and shaping them into sentences like "Although the workers are as diverse as they are similar, there is a definite link between them." And there is the sense of a personality behind the prose, someone who sympathizes with the workers. "The general public wounds them further by treating them with disgrace because of what they do for a living."

What caused these differences? I was, I believed, explaining other people's thoughts and feelings, and I was free to move about in the language of "others" so long as I was speaking *of* others. I was unaware that I was transforming into my best classroom language my own thoughts and feelings about people whose experiences and ways of speaking were in many ways similar to mine.

The following year, unable to turn back or to let go of what had become something of an obsession with language (and hoping to catch and hold the sense of control that had eluded me in Basic Writing), I enrolled in a research writing course. I spent most of the term learning how to prepare for and write a research paper. I chose sex education as

25

my subject and spent hours in libraries, searching for information, reading, taking notes. Then (not without messiness and often-demoralizing
frustration) I organized my information into categories, wrote a thesis
statement, and composed my paper — a series of paraphrases and quotations spaced between carefully constructed transitions. The process and
results felt artificial, but as I would later come to realize I was passing
through a necessary stage. My sentences sounded like this:

> This reserve becomes understandable with examination of who the
> abusers are. In an overwhelming number of cases, they are people
> the victims know and trust. Family members, relatives, neighbors
> and close family friends commit seventy-five percent of all reported
> sex crimes against children, and parents, parent substitutes and rel-
> atives are the offenders in thirty to eighty percent of all reported
> cases.[12] While assault by strangers does occur, it is less common,
> and is usually a single episode.[13] But abuse by family members,
> relatives and acquaintances may continue for an extended period of
> time. In cases of incest, for example, children are abused repeatedly
> for an average of eight years.[14] In such cases, "the use of physical
> force is rarely necessary because of the child's trusting, dependent
> relationship with the offender. The child's cooperation is often facil-
> itated by the adult's position of dominance, an offer of material
> goods, a threat of physical violence, or a misrepresentation of moral
> standards."[15]

The completed paper gave me a sense of profound satisfaction, and
I read it often after my professor returned it. I know now that what I
was pleased with was the language I used and the professional voice it
helped me maintain. "Use better words," my teacher had snapped at me
one day after reading the notes I'd begun accumulating from my research, and slowly I began taking on the language of my sources. In my
next set of notes, I used the word "vacillating"; my professor applauded.
And by the time I composed the final draft, I felt at ease with terms like
"overwhelming number of cases," "single episode," and "reserve," and
I shaped them into sentences similar to those of my "expert" sources.

If I were writing the paper today, I would of course do some things
differently. Rather than open with an anecdote — as my teacher suggested — I would begin simply with a quotation that caught my interest
as I was researching my paper (and which I scribbled, without its source,
in the margin of my notebook): "Truth does not do so much good in
the world as the semblance of truth does evil." The quotation felt right
because it captured what was for me the central idea of my essay — an
idea that emerged gradually during the making of my paper — and expressed it in a way I would like to have said it. The anecdote, a hypothetical situation I invented to conform to the information in the paper,
felt forced and insincere because it represented — to a great degree — my

teacher's understanding of the essay, *her* idea of what in it was most significant. Improving upon my previous experiences with writing, I was beginning to think and feel in the language I used, to find my own voices in it, to sense that how one speaks influences how one means. But I was not yet secure enough, comfortable enough with the language to trust my intuition.

Now that I know that to seek knowledge, freedom, and autonomy means always to be in the concentrated process of becoming — always to be venturing into new territory, feeling one's way at first, then getting one's balance, negotiating, accommodating, discovering one's self in ways that previously defined "others" — I sometimes get tired. And I ask myself why I keep on participating in this highbrow form of violence, this slamming against perplexity. But there is no real futility in the question, no hint of that part of the old me who stood outside standard English, hugging to herself a disabling mistrust of a language she thought could not represent a person with her history and experience. Rather, the question represents a person who feels the consequence of her education, the weight of her possibilities as a teacher and writer and human being, a voice in society. And I would not change that person, would not give back the good burden that accompanies my growing expertise, my increasing power to shape myself in language and share that self with "others."

"To speak," says Frantz Fanon, "means to be in a position to use a certain syntax, to grasp the morphology of this or that language, but it means above all to assume a culture, to support the weight of a civilization."[1] To write means to do the same, but in a more profound sense. However, Fanon also says that to achieve mastery means to "get" in a position of power, to "grasp," to "assume." This, I have learned both as a student and subsequently as a teacher — can involve tremendous emotional and psychological conflict for those attempting to master academic discourse. Although as a beginning student writer I had a fairly good grasp of ordinary spoken English and was proficient at what Labov calls "code-switching" (and what John Baugh in *Black Street Speech* terms "style shifting"), when I came face to face with the demands of academic writing, I grew increasingly self-conscious, constantly aware of my status as a black and a speaker of one of the many black English vernaculars — a traditional outsider. For the first time, I experienced my sense of doubleness as something menacing, a built-in enemy. Whenever I turned inward for salvation, the balm so available during my childhood, I found instead this new fragmentation which spoke to me in many voices. It was the voice of my desire to prosper, but at the same time it spoke of what I had relinquished and could not regain: a safe way of being, a state of powerlessness which exempted me from responsibility for who I was

[1] *Black Skin, White Masks* (1952; rpt. New York: Grove Press, 1967), pp. 17–18.

and might be. And it accused me of betrayal, of turning away from blackness. To recover balance, I had to take on the language of the academy, the language of "others." And to do that, I had to learn to imagine myself a part of the culture of that language, and therefore someone free to manage that language, to take liberties with it. Writing and rewriting, practicing, experimenting, I came to comprehend more fully the generative power of language. I discovered—with the help of some especially sensitive teachers—that through writing one can continually bring new selves into being, each with new responsibilities and difficulties, but also with new possibilities. Remarkable power, indeed. I write and continually give birth to myself.

FOR DISCUSSION AND WRITING

1. In contemporary American society, what might have been some possible consequences if Mellix had not mastered standard English?

2. Do you have two "languages"—one that you use at home and with friends and one that you use in other situations (such as your classes in college)? How do the two languages differ? Why are the two languages necessary? Does everyone have several "languages" for use in different situations?

3. What are your reactions to the following passage (par. 29)? What are its implications? Do you agree or disagree with Mellix's point?

    "To speak," says Frantz Fanon, "means to be in a position to use a certain syntax, to grasp the morphology of this or that language, but it means above all to assume a culture, to support the weight of a civilization." To write means to do the same, but in a more profound sense.

4. Do you think the title "From Outside, In" would be appropriate for the selections by Richard Rodriguez and Mike Rose? Why, or why not?

5. Why do you think it was easier for Mellix to write about other people's thoughts and feelings rather than her own?

THE INVISIBLE DISCOURSE OF THE LAW: REFLECTIONS ON LEGAL LITERACY AND GENERAL EDUCATION

James Boyd White

Almost everyone who is not trained in the law has struggled to understand legal documents, such as contracts and guarantees — not because they read poorly but because they lack legal knowledge and experience with legal language. Readers can experience the same difficulty in other fields such as philosophy, literary theory, or economics; it takes time to gain the knowledge required to become an expert reader in these areas. However, between the extremes of the trained legal expert and the complete novice is "another possible meaning of legal literacy: the degree of competence in legal discourse that is required for meaningful and active life in our increasingly legalistic and litigious culture" (par. 2). It is this degree of competence that the author discusses in the following essay.

James Boyd White is a professor of law at the University of Chicago. His interests and knowledge extend beyond the law to the history of civilization; he is a member of a faculty group that focuses on the ancient Mediterranean World. He is the author of *The Legal Imagination* and coauthor of *Constitutional Criminal Procedure*.

As you read, try to answer the following question in relation to the essay: What general principles about language can I learn from the essay?

The subject of this essay is legal literacy, but to put it that way requires immediate clarification for that phrase has a wide range of possible meanings. At one end of its spectrum of significance, for example, legal literacy means full competence in legal discourse, both as reader and as writer. This kind of literacy is the object of a professional education, and it requires not only a period of formal schooling but years of practice as well. Indeed, as with other real languages, the ideal of perfect competence in legal language can never be attained: practitioners are always learning about their language and about the world, they are in a sense always remaking both, and these processes never come to an end. What this sort of professional literacy entails and how it is to be talked about are matters of interest to lawyers and law teachers, but this meaning of legal literacy will not be discussed here. At the other end of the spectrum of legal literacy are people who recognize legal words and locutions as foreign to themselves, as part of the world of law. A person who is literate in this sense knows that there is a world of language and action called "law," but little more about it: certainly not enough to have any real access to it.

Between these extremes is another possible meaning of legal literacy: the degree of competence in legal discourse that is required for meaningful and active life in our increasingly legalistic and litigious culture. Citizens who are ideally literate in this sense are not expected to know how to draft deeds and wills or to try cases or to manage the bureaucratic maze, but they do know when and how to call upon the specialists who can do these things. More important, they are able to protect and advance their own interests: for example in dealing with a landlord or a tenant or in their interactions with the police, with the zoning commission, or with the Social Security Administration. People with this type of literacy are able not only to follow but to evaluate news reports and periodical literature dealing with legal matters—from Supreme Court decisions to House Committee reports. They know how to function effectively in positions of responsibility and leadership (say as an elected member of a school board or as chair of a neighborhood association or as a member of a zoning board or police commission). This sense of the term legal literacy embodies the ideal of a fully competent and engaged citizen, and that ideal is a wholly proper one to keep before us.

But this ideal is for our purposes far too inclusive, for however one defines "legal literacy," one who possesses such literacy also has a great deal in addition: a complete set of social, intellectual, and political relations and capacities. But perhaps we can meaningfully ask, What is the legal literacy that such an ideal figure would have? How could this sort of competence be taught? What seem to be the natural barriers to its acquisition? In the first part of this paper I deal with these questions, but in reverse order. I begin by identifying those features of legal discourse that make it peculiarly difficult for the nonlawyer to understand and use. I then suggest some ways in which those features might be made comprehensible and manageable, and how their value and function might be appreciated. This discussion in turn will constitute my answer to the first question, that is, what kind of legal literacy should an ordinary citizen have, and how can it contribute not only to the development of social competence but to a true education of the mind and self?

THE INVISIBLE DISCOURSE OF THE LAW

It is a common experience for a nonlawyer to feel that legal language is in a deep sense foreign: not only are its terms incomprehensible, but its speakers seem to have available to them a repertoire of moves denied to others. Nonlawyers neither understand the force of legal arguments nor know how to answer them. But the language is, if possible, worse than merely foreign. It is an unpredictable, exasperating, and shifting mixture of the foreign and the familiar. Much of what lawyers say and write is, after all, intelligible to the nonlawyer, and one can sometimes speak in legally competent ways. But at any moment things can change without notice: the language slides into the incomprehensible, and the nonlawyer has no idea how or why the shift occurred. This is powerfully frustrating, to say the least.

But legal illiteracy is more than frustrating, for it entails an increasingly important disability, almost a disenfranchisement. At one time in our history a citizen did not need to have any specialized knowledge of law, for our law was a common law that reflected the customs and expectations of the people to such a degree that ordinary social competence was normally enough for effectiveness in the enterprises of life. No special legal training was required. But in our increasingly bureaucratic and legalistic world, this assumption seems less and less realistic. Frustrated citizens are likely to feel that their lives are governed by language that they cannot understand—in leases, in form contracts, or in federal and state regulations. Who, for example, can read and understand an insurance contract or a pension plan? An OSHA or IRS regulation? Yet these documents govern our lives and are even said in some sense to have the standing of our own acts, either directly, as in the contracts we sign, or indirectly, as in the laws promulgated by officials who represent us. In a democracy this unintelligibility is doubly intolerable, for the people are supposed to be competent both as voters who elect the lawmakers and as jurors who apply the laws. They cannot do these things if they cannot understand the law.

What can explain this flickering pattern of intelligibility and unintelligibility, the stroboscopic alternation of the familiar with the strange? The most visible and frequently denounced culprits are the arcane vocabulary of the law and the complicated structure of its sentences and paragraphs. Thus, people ask why lawyers cannot be made to speak in words they recognize and in sentences they can understand. If lawyers would do so, the ordinary citizen could become competent as a reader of law and even as a legal speaker. Our political method of democracy and its moral premise of equality demand no less. It may be indeed that the only actual effect of this obfuscating legal jargon is to maintain the mystique of the legal profession, and if that mystique is destroyed so much the better.

Impulses such as these have given rise to what is known as the plain English movement, which aims at a translation of legal language into comprehensible English. This movement has had practical effects. At the federal level, for example, one of President Carter's first actions was to order that all regulations be cast in language intelligible to the ordinary citizen, and New York and other states have passed laws requiring that state regulations and certain form contracts meet a similar standard.

If such directives were seriously regarded, they might indeed reduce needless verbosity and obscurity and streamline unwieldy legal sentences. But even if they succeeded in these desirable goals, they would not solve the general problem they address, for, as I try to show, the most serious obstacles to comprehensibility are not the vocabulary and sentence structure employed in the law but the unstated conventions by which the language operates — what I call the "invisible discourse" of the law. Behind the words, that is, are expectations about the ways in which they will be used, expectations that do not find explicit expression anywhere but are part of the legal culture that the surface language simply assumes. These expectations are constantly at work, directing argument, shaping responses, determining the next move, and so on; their effects are everywhere but they themselves are invisible. These conventions, not the diction, primarily determine the mysterious character of legal speech and literature: not the "vocabulary" of the law but what might be called its "cultural syntax."

In what follows I identify those features of the cultural syntax of legal language that seem most radically to differentiate it from ordinary speech. I then outline some methods by which I think students can be taught to become at least somewhat literate in a language that works in these ways. Finally I suggest that this kind of literacy not only entails an important increase in social competence but itself contributes to the development of mind and attitude that is the proper object of a general education.

The Language of Rules

Many of the special difficulties of legal language derive from the fact that at the center of most legal conversations there is a form we call "the legal rule." Not so general as to be a mere maxim or platitude (though we have those in law, too) or so specific as to be a mere order or command (though there are legal versions of these), the legal rule is a directive of intermediate generality. It establishes relations among classes of objects, persons, and events: "All A are [or: shall be] B"; or, "If A, then B." Examples would include the following:

(1) Burglary consists of breaking and entering a dwelling house in the nighttime with intent to commit a felony therein. A person convicted of burglary shall be punished by imprisonment not to exceed 5 years.
(2) Unless otherwise ordered by the court or agreed by the parties, a former husband's obligation to pay alimony terminates upon the remarriage of his former wife.

Legal conversations about rules such as these have three major characteristics that tend to mystify and confuse nonlawyers.

The Invisible Shift from a Language of Description to a Language of Judgment

The form of the legal rule misleads ordinary readers into expecting that once it is understood, its applications will be very simple. The rules presented above, for example, have a plain and authoritative air and seem to contemplate no difficulty whatever in their application. (Notice that with the possible exception of the word "felony," there is nothing legal-istic in their diction.) One will simply look to the facts and determine whether or not the specified conditions exist; if so, the consequence declared by the rule will follow; if not, it will not. "Did she remarry? Then the alimony stops." Nothing to it, the rule seems to say: just look at the world and do what we tell you. It calls for nothing more than a glance to check the name against the reality and obedience to a plain directive.

In practice, of course, the rule does not work so simply — or not always. Is it "breaking and entering" if the person pushes open a screen door but has not yet entered the premises? Is a garage with a loft used as an apartment a "dwelling house"? Is dusk "nighttime"? Is a remarriage that is later annulled a "remarriage" for the purpose of terminating prior alimony? What if there is no formal remarriage but the ex-wife has a live-in boyfriend? These questions do not answer themselves but require thought and conversation of a complex kind, of which no hint is ex-pressed in the rule itself.

Of course there will be some cases so clear that no one could rea-sonably argue about the meaning of the words, and in these cases the rule will work in a fairly simple and direct fashion. Most of our experi-ence with rules, in fact, works this way: we can find out what to do to get a passport or a driver's license, we know what the rules of the road require, we can figure out when we need a building permit, and so on. But these are occasions of rule obedience for which no special social or intellectual competence is involved.

One way to identify what is misleading about the form of a legal   *15* rule might be to say that it appears to be a language of description, which works by a simple process of comparison, but in cases of any difficulty it is actually a language of judgment, which works in ways that find no expression in the rule itself. In such cases the meaning of its terms is not obvious, as the rule seems to assume, but must be deter-mined by a process of interpretation and judgment to which the rule gives no guidance whatever. The discourse by which it works is in this sense invisible.

The False Appearance of Deductive Rationality

If one does recognize that there may be difficulties in understanding and applying a rule, one may still be misled by its form into thinking that the kind of reasoning it requires (and makes possible) is deductive in character. A legal rule looks rather like a rule of geometry, and we naturally expect it to work like one. For example, when the meaning of a term in a rule is unclear — say "dwelling house" or "nighttime" in the burglary statute — we expect to find a stipulative definition elsewhere (perhaps in a special section of the statute) that will define it for us, just as Euclid tells us the meaning of his essential terms. Or if there is no explicit definition, we expect there to be some other rule, general in form, that when considered in connection with our rule will tell us what it must mean. But it is often in vain that we look for such definitions and rules, and when we do find them they often prove to be of little help.

Suppose, for example, the question is whether a person who is caught breaking into a garage that has a small apartment in the loft can be convicted of burglary: does a statutory definition of "dwelling house" as "any residential premises" solve the problem? Or suppose one finds in the law dealing with mortgages a definition of "dwelling house" that plainly does (or does not) cover the garage with the loft: does that help? Upon reflection about the purpose of the burglary statute, which is to punish a certain kind of wrongdoing, perhaps "dwelling house" will suddenly be seen to have a subjective or moral dimension, and properly mean "place where the actor knows that people are living" or, if that be thought too lenient, "place where he has reason to believe that people are living."

Or consider the annulment example. Suppose one finds a statutory statement that "an annulled marriage is a nullity at law." Does that mean that the alimony payment revives upon the annulment of the wife's second marriage? Even if the annulment takes place fifteen years after the date of that marriage? Or suppose that there is another statute, providing that "alimony may be awarded in an annulment proceeding to the same extent as in a divorce proceeding"? This would mean that the wife could get alimony from her second husband, and if the question is seen in terms of fairness among the parties, this opportunity would be highly relevant to whether or not her earlier right to alimony has expired.

The typical form of the legal rule thus seems to invite us to think that the important intellectual operations involved in our use of it will be those of deduction and entailment, as in geometry: that our main concern will be with the relations among propositions, as one rule is related to others by the logical rules of noncontradiction and the like, and that the end result of every intellectual operation will be determined by the rules of deduction.

In fact the situation could hardly be more different. Instead of each *20* term in a legal rule having a meaning of the sort necessary for deductive operations to go on in the first place, each term has a range of possible meanings, among which choices will have to be made. There is no one right answer to the question whether this structure is a "dwelling house" or that relationship a "remarriage"; there are several linguistically and logically tolerable possibilities, and the intellectual process of law is one of arguing and reasoning about which of them is to be preferred. Of course the desirability of internal consistency is a factor (though we shall soon see that the law tolerates a remarkable degree of internal contradiction), and of course in some cases some issues will be too plain for argument. But the operations that lawyers and judges engage in with respect to legal rules are very different from what we might expect from the form of the rule itself. They derive their substance and their shape from the whole world of legal culture and draw upon the most diverse materials, ranging from general maxims to particular cases and regulations. The discourse of the law is far less technical, far more purposive and sensible, than the nonlawyer is likely to think. Argument about the meaning of words in the burglary statute, for example, would include argument about the reasons for having such a statute, about the kind of harm it is meant to prevent or redress, and about the degree and kind of blame-worthiness it should therefore require. Legal discourse is continuous at some points with moral or philosophic discourse, at others with history or anthropology or sociology; and in its tension between the particular and the general, in its essentially metaphorical character, it has much in common with poetry itself. The substantive constitution of legal discourse is of course too complex a subject for us at present; what is important now is to see that this discourse is invisible to the ordinary reader of the legal rules.

These characteristics of legal language convert what looks like a discourse connected with the world by the easy process of naming, and rendered internally coherent by the process of deduction, into a much more complex linguistic and cultural system. The legal rule seems to foreclose certain questions of fact and value, and of course in the clear cases it does so. But in the uncertain cases, which are those that cause trouble, it can better be said to open than to close a set of questions: it gives them definition, connection with other questions, and a place in a rhetorical universe, thus permitting their elaboration and resolution in a far more rich and complex way than could otherwise be the case. Except in the plainest cases, the function of the ordinary meanings of terms used in legal rules is not to determine a necessary result but to establish the uncertain boundaries of permissible decision: the function of logic is not to require a particular result by deductive force but to limit the range of possibilities by prohibiting (or making difficult) contradictory uses of the same terms in the same sentences.

But you have perhaps noticed an odd evasion in that last sentence and may be wondering: Does not the law absolutely prohibit inconsistent uses of the same terms in the same rules? Indeed it does not, or not always, and this is the last of the three mystifying features of legal discourse about which I wish to speak.

The Systematic Character of Legal Discourse
and the Dilemma of Consistency

I have thus far suggested that while the legal rule appears to operate by a simple process of looking at the world to see whether a named object can be found (the "dwelling house" or the "remarriage"), this appearance is highly misleading, for in fact the world does not often present events in packages that are plainly within the meaning of a legal label (or plainly outside of it). Behind the application of the label is a complex world of reasoning, which is in fact the real life of the law but to which the rule makes no overt allusion and for which it gives no guidance. To the extent that the form of the rule suggests that the controlling mode of reason will be deductive, it gives rise to expectations that are seriously misleading. The real discourse of the law is invisible.

This feature of the law may seem bad enough, but in practice things are even worse, and for two reasons. First, however sophisticated and complex one's reasoning may in fact be, at the end of the process the legal speaker is required after all to express his or her judgment in the most simple binary terms: either the label in the rule fits or it does not. No third possibility is admitted. All the richness and complexity of legal life seem to be denied by the kind of act in which the law requires it to be expressed. For example, while we do not know precisely how the "dwelling house" or "remarriage" questions would in fact be argued out, we can see that the process would be complex and challenging, with room both for uncertainty and for invention. But at the end of the process the judge or jury will have to make a choice between two alternatives and express it by the application (or nonapplication) of the label in question: this is or is not a "dwelling house." In this way the legal actors are required to act as if the legal world really were as simple as the rule misleadingly pretends it is. Everything is reduced to a binary choice after all.

Second, it seems that the force of this extreme reductionism cannot ²⁵ be evaded by giving the terms of legal rules slightly different meanings in different contexts, for the rudiments of logic and fairness alike require that the term be given the same meaning each time it is used, or the system collapses into incoherence and injustice. The most basic rule of logic (the rule of noncontradiction) and the most basic rule of justice (like results in like cases) both require consistency of meaning.

A familiar example demonstrating the requirement of internal consistency in systematic talk about the world is this: "However you define 'raining' the term must be used for the purposes of your system such that it is always true that it either is or is not "raining.'" Any other principle would lead to internal incoherence and would destroy the regularity of the discourse as a way of talking about the world. To put the principle in terms of the legal example we have been using: however one defines "dwelling house" for purposes of the burglary statute, it must be used in such a manner that everything in the world either is or is not a "dwelling house"; and because the law is a system for organizing experience coherently across time and space, it must be given the same meaning every time it is used. Logic and fairness alike require no less.

The trouble is that these principles of discourse are very different from those employed in ordinary conversations. Who in real life would ever take the view that it must be the case that it either is or is not "raining"? Suppose it is just foggy and wet? If someone in ordinary life asked you whether it was raining out, you would not expect that person to insist upon an answer cast in categorical terms, let alone in categorical terms that were consistent over a set of conversations. The answer to the question would depend upon the reason it was asked: Does your questioner want to know whether to wear a raincoat? Whether to water the garden? to call off a picnic? to take a sunbath? In each case the answer will be different, and the speaker will in no case feel required to limit the response to an affirmation or negation of the condition "raining." One will speak to the situation as a whole, employing all of one's resources. And one will not worry much about how the word "raining" has been used in other conversations, on other occasions, for the convention of ordinary speech is that critical terms are defined anew each time for the purposes of a particular conversation, not as part of a larger system.

What is distinctive about conversations concerning the meaning of rules is their systematic character. Terms are defined not for the purposes of a particular conversation but for a class of conversations, and the principle of consistency applies across the class. And this class of conversations has, as we have just seen, a peculiar form: in the operation of the rule, all experience is reduced to a single set of questions — say, whether the elements of burglary exist in this case — each of which must be answered "yes" or "no." We are denied what would be the most common response in our ordinary life, which would be to say that the label fits in this way and not in that or that it depends on why you ask. The complex process of argument and judgment that is involved in understanding a legal rule and relating it to the facts of a particular case is at the end forced into a simple statement of application or nonapplication of a label, under a requirement of noncontradiction over time.

But there is still another layer to the difficulty. We may talk about the requirement of consistency as a matter of logic or justice, but how is it to be achieved? Can we for example ensure that "dwelling house" will be used exactly the same way in every burglary case? Obviously we cannot, for a number of reasons. First, different triers of fact will resolve conflicts of testimony in different ways — one judge or jury would believe one side, a second the other — and this builds inconsistency into the process at the most basic level, that of descriptive fact. Second, while the judge may be required to give the same instruction to the jury in every case, the statement of that instruction will to some extent be cast in general terms and admit a fair variation of interpretation even where the historical facts are settled (e.g., a judicial definition of "dwelling house" as "premises employed as a regular residence by those entitled to possession thereof"). Third, if the instruction includes, as well it might, a subjective element (saying for example that the important question is whether the defendant *knew* he was breaking into a place where people were living), there will be an even larger variation in application of what is on the surface the same language.

In short, the very generality of legal language, which constitutes 30 for us an important part of its character as rational and as fair, means that some real variation in application must be tolerated. As the language becomes more general, the delegation of authority to the applier of the language, and hence the toleration of inconsistency in result, becomes greater. As the language becomes more specific, this delegation is reduced, and with it the potential inconsistency. But increasing specificity has its costs, and they too can be stated in terms of consistency. Consider a sentencing statute, for example, that authorizes the punishment of burglars by sentences ranging from probation to five years in prison. This delegation of sentencing authority (usually to a judge) seems to be a toleration of wide variation in result. But it all depends upon how the variation is measured. For to insist that all burglars receive the same sentence, say, three years in jail, is to treat the hardened repeater and the inexperienced novice as if they were identical. That treatment is "consistent" on one measure (burglars are treated alike) but "inconsistent" on another (an obvious difference among offenders is not recognized).

For our purposes the point is this: the requirements (1) that terms be defined not for a single conversation but for the class of conversation established by the rule in question and (2) that the meaning given words be consistent through the system are seriously undercut in practice by a wide toleration of inconsistency in result and in meaning. I do not mean to suggest, however, that either the requirement of consistency or its qualifications are inappropriate — quite the reverse. It seems to me that we have here identified a dilemma central to the life of any discourse that purports to be systematic, rational, and just. My purpose has simply been to describe a structural tension in legal discourse that differentiates it sharply from most ordinary speech.

In addition to the foregoing I wish to mention one other quality of legal discourse that radically distinguishes it from ordinary language: its procedural character.

Procedural Character of Legal Speech

In working with a rule, one must not only articulate substantive questions of definition — is "dusk" "nighttime"? is a "bicycle" a "vehicle"? etc. — one must also ask a set of related procedural questions. Every question of interpretation involves these related questions: Who shall decide what this language means? under what conditions or circumstances, and subject to what limits or controls? Why? And in what body of discourse are these questions to be thought about, argued out, and decided? The answers to such questions are rarely found in the rule itself.

Suppose, for example, the question is what the word "nighttime" should mean in the burglary statute or, to begin not with a rule but with a difficulty in ordinary life, whether the development of a shopping center should be permitted on Brown's farm. It is the professional habit of lawyers to think not only about the substantive merits of the question and how they would argue it but also about (a) the person or agency who ought to decide it and (b) the procedure by which it ought to be decided. Is the shopping-center question a decision for the zoning commission, for the neighbors, for the city as a whole, for Brown, or for the county court? Is the "nighttime" question one for the judge to decide, for the jury, or — if you think what matters is the defendant's intent in that respect — in part for the defendant? Every legal rule, however purely substantive in form, is also by implication a procedural and institutional statement as well, and the lawyers who read it will realize this and start to argue about its meaning in this dimension too. The function of the rule is thus to define not only substantive topics but also procedures of argument and debate and questions about the definition and allocation of competencies to act. The rule does so either expressly or by implication, but in either event it calls upon discourse that is largely invisible to the reader not legally trained.

To sum up my point, what characterizes legal discourse is that it is in a double sense (both substantively and procedurally) constitutive in nature: it creates a set of questions that define a world of thought and action, a set of roles and voices by which experience will be ordered and meanings established and shared, a set of occasions and methods for public speech that constitute us as a community and as a polity. In all of this, legal discourse has its own ways of working, which are to be found not in the rules that are at its center of the structure but in the culture that determines how these rules are to be read and talked about.

I have identified some of the special ways of thinking and talking that characterize legal discourse. Far more than any technical vocabulary, it is these conventions that are responsible for the foreignness of legal speech. To put it slightly differently, there is a sense in which one creates technical vocabulary whenever one creates a rule of the legal kind, for the operation of the rule in a procedural system itself necessarily entails an artificial way of giving meaning both to words and to events. These characteristics of legal discourse mean that the success of any movement to translate legal speech into plain English will be severely limited. For if one replaces a legal word with an ordinary English word, the sense of increased normalcy will be momentary at best: the legal culture will go immediately to work, and the ordinary word will begin to lose its shape, its resiliency, and its familiarity and become, despite the efforts of the drafter, a legal word after all. The reason for this is that the word will work as part of the legal language, and it is the way this language works that determines the meaning of its terms. This is what I meant when I said that it is not the vocabulary of the legal language that is responsible for its obscurity and mysteriousness, but its cultural syntax, the invisible expectations governing the way the words are to be used.

FOR DISCUSSION AND WRITING

1. Explain the "invisible discourse" of the law.

2. What is "the plain English movement" (par. 7)? Why would its objectives have limited effect on legal literacy?

3. Explain the shift from a language of description to a language of judgment.

4. In what ways does the following summary apply to the discourse of other groups with which you are familiar (par. 35)? Reread the summary, substituting for *legal* such terms as *fraternity, sorority, family, baseball,* and *CB.*

   > [W]hat characterizes legal discourse is that it is in a double sense (both substantively and procedurally) constitutive in nature: it creates a set of questions that define a world of thought and action, a set of roles and voices by which experience will be ordered and meanings established and shared, a set of occasions and methods for public speech that constitute us as a community and as a polity. In all of this, legal discourse has its own ways of working, which are to be found not in the rules that are at its center of the structure but in the culture that determines how these rules are to be read and talked about.

5. Does the process of discerning the meaning of legal writing seem more like discovering meaning (mining) or recovering meaning (detecting) to you?

6. Technical terms such as *felony, writ,* and *mandamus* are very common. Do you feel that when lawyers are writing for the general public, they should substitute everyday language for such terminology? Explain.

7. White's notion of literacy is more involved and extensive than most people's notions. How would White determine whether a person is completely literate in legal discourse?

8. Does White present a convincing case for the need to increase legal literacy? Explain.

9. Explain "the false appearance of deductive rationality" (pars. 16–22).

THE LANGUAGE OF THE BUREAUCRACY

Janice C. Redish

Dr. Janice C. Redish is a vice president of American Institutes for Research in Washington, D.C. and director of the Document Design Center. She is a graduate of Bryn Mawr College and holds a doctorate in linguistics from Harvard University. She has worked with many federal agencies, including the Department of Education, the General Accounting Office, and the Internal Revenue Service, as well as with many corporations including AT&T, Hewlett-Packard, IBM, Northern Telecom, and Sony.

Redish developed the model of the document design process that the Document Design Center uses in all its training materials and as the framework for document design projects. A critical aspect of this model is evaluating documents as they are developed. Redish also helped establish the American Institute of Research's first Usability Test Laboratory, where specialists observe users as they try to work with products and documents. Her research focuses on understanding the process of creating useful documents, writing in organizations, testing usability, and exploring new approaches to training and to documentation using advanced technology.

This selection, which is somewhat longer and more complicated than other readings in this book, is an example of how skillful writing can make a technical subject understandable to the nonspecialist. The essay also explains principles of clear, effective prose that you can apply to your own writing. "The Language of the Bureaucracy" is a reference source that might well be valuable to you when you are drafting documents in the "real world" after you leave the institution you are now attending.

For many years, the media have poked fun at the pomposity and incomprehensibility of much of the writing that our government produces. Egregious examples of gobbledygook are easy to find; try, for instance, to make sense of these two passages:

Example 1: From a Department of Agriculture regulation

¶928.310 Papaya Regulation 10.

Order. (a) *No* handler shall ship any container of papayas (*except* immature papayas handled pursuant to ¶928.152 of this part):

(1) During the period January 1 through April 15, 1980, to any destination within the production area *unless* said papayas grade at least Hawaii No. 1, *except* that allowable tolerances for defects may total 10 percent: *Provided,* That *not* more than 5 percent shall be for serious damage, *not* more than 1 percent for immature fruit, and *not* more than 1 percent for decay: *Provided further,* That such papayas shall individually weigh not less than 11 ounces each.

Example 2: From an Immigration and Naturalization Service form.
If you are the spouse or unmarried minor child of a person who has been granted preference classification by the Immigration and Naturalization Service or has applied for preference classification, and you are claiming the same preference classification, or if you are claiming special immigrant classification as the spouse or unmarried child of a minister of religion who has been accorded or is seeking classification as a special immigrant, submit the following. . . . (INS Form I-485)

You may find yourself shaking your head in dismay, as I did when I first read these sentences. Shaking our heads, however, won't improve bureaucratic writing.

For the language of bureaucracy to change, the system and the people in it must relinquish the pervasive philosophy and style of writing. In the 1970s, bureaucratic writing did begin to change. A small but growing body of well-written, direct, personal, and understandable bureaucratic documents has been developed. Although these examples are less often quoted by the media, they exist. For instance:

Example 3: From a Federal Communications Commission regulation.
CB Rule 5. How do I apply for a CB license?
(a) You apply for a CB license by filling out an application (FCC Form 505) and sending it to the FCC, Gettysburg, Pa. 17326.
(b) You can get applications from the FCC, Washington, D.C. 20554 or from any FCC field office. (A list of FCC field offices is contained in CB Rule 45.) Many CB equipment dealers also have application forms.
(c) If you have questions about your application, you should write to the Personal Radio Division, Washington, D.C. 20554.

Example 4: From a Department of Education form.
You can use the form in this booklet to apply for a 1980-81 Basic Educational Opportunity Grant (Basic Grant). A Basic Grant is money to help you pay for your education after high school. It is not a loan, so you do not have to repay it. To get a Basic Grant, you have to meet certain requirements.

The FCC example was written by a lawyer and a program specialist (who has since become a lawyer). I helped write example 4 (and the document from which it was taken) as a consultant to the Department of Education. Both these documents went through the extensive reviews that are characteristic of the government, and both were eventually accepted. Many other examples exist, but most bureaucratic documents have not been rewritten into clear English. Why? And what can English teachers do to foster a change in the language of the bureaucracy?

In this paper, I want to explore the status and future of bureaucratic language by addressing four questions:

(1) What are the characteristics of bureaucratic writing?
(2) How did bureaucratic writing develop and what encourages it not to change?
(3) Where do the pressures for change come from?
(4) What can be done to foster greater literacy in bureaucratic writing among both writers and users of government documents?

CHARACTERISTICS OF TRADITIONAL BUREAUCRATIC LANGUAGE

What characterizes the traditional bureaucratic language that becomes a candidate for a column on gobbledygook? I am going to limit this discussion to prose (as distinct from forms). And I am going to look first at style (the sentences and words).

One of the points I want to make is that style is only part (and perhaps not the most important part) of the problem in bureaucratic language. Style, however, is the most obvious feature of any piece of writing. Most clear writing guidelines focus on style, and readability formulas (which purport to measure comprehensibility of documents) count only stylistic features.

Style

Bureaucratic writing that is difficult to understand has three major stylistic problems. It is nominal, full of jargon, and legalistic.

BUREAUCRATIC WRITING OVERUSES NOUNS. Nouns replace pronouns, verbs, and adjectives. Traditional bureaucratic style does not directly address the reader. If a human subject is mentioned at all, a generic or class term is used.

> Example 5: All employees shall submit to the Director of Personnel within 30 days after their entrance on duty. . . .
> Example 6: Interested persons may . . . submit . . . written comments regarding this proposal.

The effect is both formal and abstract. Readers have to make the connection between themselves and the generic class.

The nominal style of bureaucratic writing is also reflected in the way writers focus on the inanimate object of the action rather than on the actor. Things are more important than people. Thus, bureaucratic writers overuse the passive voice because passive sentences focus on the object.

> Example 7: Proposals must be received no later than 4:00 p.m.
> June 2, 1981.

The government doesn't care who is submitting the proposal; it only
insists that the proposal arrive by a certain time. Most readers can understand a simple sentence, such as this one, even when it is in the
passive. They have trouble, however, when they have to read entire
passages that involve no human agents.

> Example 8: From a Small Business Administration regulation.
> ¶124.1-3 Advance payments.
> (a) *Definitions.* Advance payments are disbursements of
> money made by SBA to a section 8(a) business concern
> prior to the completion of performance of a specific section
> 8(a) subcontract for the purpose of assisting the said 8(a)
> business concern in meeting financial requirements perti-
> nent to the performance of said sub-contract. Advance
> payments must be liquidated from proceeds derived from
> the performance of the specific section 8(a) sub-contract.
> However, this does not preclude repayment of such ad-
> vance payments from other revenues of the business except
> from other advance payments.

Research shows that readers have great difficulty understanding this type
of bureaucratic writing. In trying to make sense out of a passage such as
this one, readers create actor-action scenarios. When they explain the
passage, they put the pronouns in and make the sentences active (Flower,
Hayes, and Swarts).

Another characteristic of bureaucratic writing is the overuse of   10
nouns made out of verbs. The preceding sentence, in fact, is an example
of this problem. I should have written: bureaucratic writing uses too
many nouns that are made out of verbs. The first sentence has no human
actor. The subject is the inanimate noun "characteristic." The sentence
has no action verb, only the linking verb "is." The implied action ("use")
is buried in a derived noun, "the overuse of."

The following example has two derived nouns:

> Example 9: *Failure* to follow these directions will result in *disquali-
> fication* of the applicant.

Again the effect is both formal and abstract. Do applicants realize that
they are being addressed?

When bureaucrats write in the nominal style they tend to use all the
features of the style together. Look again at example 8. How many
derived nouns do you find?

The three features of the nominal style that I have mentioned —
nouns instead of pronouns, passive sentences focusing on inanimate
nouns, and nouns instead of verbs — characterize both bureaucratic and

legal writing. The fourth feature of the nominal style is characteristic of both bureaucratic and academic writing but is less often found in non-bureaucratic legal writing. Government writers frequently use nouns to modify nouns. (We call these "noun strings.")

> Example 10:
> consumer information service
> health maintenance organization
> host area crisis shelter production planning workbook

Noun strings can become acronyms, which can then be used in other noun strings.

> Example 11: Nonbusiness FWREI expenses incurred by the taxpayer are limited to $5,000 per year.
> (Author's note: FWREI stands for Federal Welfare Recipient Employment Incentive.)

Acronyms serve to separate "in" people, who know what they mean (or, at least, what they refer to) from "out" people, who do not have that information.

Noun strings are a shorthand; they take less space to write, but they are difficult for laypeople to understand. A reader who is not familiar with the material must figure out how the nouns relate to each other in order to understand the concepts being discussed. Take this sentence as an example:

> Example 12: Four major characteristics influence *consumer information seeking and utilization behavior.*

The italicized words are a string of nouns. Two of the nouns ("seeking," "utilization") are derived from verbs. The phrase means: "the *behavior of consumers* as they *seek* and *use information.*"

Noun strings obscure connections, make concrete actions into abstract nouns, and move the human actors into subordinate positions. Because noun strings often become frozen units, they are like jargon — meaningful to certain people, obscure to others. 15

BUREAUCRATIC WRITING IS FULL OF JARGON. A specialized vocabulary serves a dual purpose for any professional group. It permits clear communication within the group, and it indicates to both insiders and outsiders who belongs to the group and who does not.

Some jargon is both useful and necessary. For example, the government promulgates laws and regulations. "Promulgate" is a word that is not used in everyday English; it has a meaning understood by legislators and bureaucrats; we cannot easily find an everyday English equivalent for it. "Promulgate" is bureaucratic jargon in a nonpejorative sense of the word "jargon."

But problems arise with bureaucratic jargon in at least three situations. The first is when bureaucratic writers use words that serve only one of the two purposes. These are words that don't have clear and special meanings; they only say, "I know the 'in' terms." Examples include "prioritize," "finalize," "impact" (as a verb), and "implement" (as a verb). Clear everyday English equivalents exist for each of these words. They mark a piece of writing as bureaucratic and as fair game for ridicule in the media.

The second situation in which bureaucratic jargon becomes a problem is when it is combined with the jargon of another professional discipline. Most bureaucratic writers must, in fact, address at least two audiences who do not share jargons (agency contract specialists and engineers, e.g., or lawyers and nursing-home operators). Bureaucratic writers in this situation must control several jargons; many don't, and they misuse words frequently.

In the third place, bureaucratic jargon becomes a problem when *20* government writers have to communicate with a general audience. The general audience, by definition, doesn't share the jargon. (If everyone knew what all the special terms meant, there wouldn't be any "in" language.) The writer may be caught in a bind. The internal audience (peers and supervisors) may demand an internally acceptable style and jargon. The external audience (the general public) may demand a clear and direct writing style. Academic and business writers share this dilemma, but perhaps it is less of a problem to them than to the bureaucratic writer, who is now supposed to be responsible and responsive to the people.

BUREAUCRATIC LANGUAGE IS HIGHLY LEGALISTIC. Jargon is supposed to facilitate communication within the group that shares a specialized vocabulary, but aspects of traditional bureaucratic writing hinder communication even within the "in" group. Because many government documents are also legal documents, bureaucratic writing often includes archaisms and long, overly inclusive, and convoluted sentences that are typical of legalese.

> Example 13: (a) *General.* (1) Every application for Federal financial assistance to carry out a program to which this part applies, except a program to which paragraph (b) of this section applies, and every application for Federal financial assistance to provide a facility shall, as a condition to its approval and the extension of any Federal financial assistance pursuant to the application, contain or be accompanied by an assurance that the program will be conducted or the facility operated in compliance with all requirements imposed by or pursuant to this part.

Furthermore, many of these documents must be read and followed by nonlawyers. Local police officials may be the primary audience for this sentence from the pre-1978 version of the Citizens Band radio rules:

Example 14: Applications, amendments, and related statements of fact filed on behalf of eligible government entities, such as states and territories of the United States and political subdivisions thereof, the District of Columbia, and units of local government, including incorporated municipalities, shall be signed by such duly elected or appointed officials as may be competent to do so under the laws of the applicable jurisdiction.

This is not an extreme example. Sentences of 120–150 words are common in bureaucratic documents. Research in psychology and linguistics shows that long convoluted sentences overtax people's capacity to process information.

Bureaucratic documents written in a highly legalistic style are not necessarily comprehensible to lawyers. When our team at the Document Design Center sits down with a group of government lawyers to rewrite a bureaucratic document, we often find that they disagree on what the document is saying; often, they cannot explain what the bureaucratic language means.

Legal language is the subject of the essay by James Boyd White in this volume and already has a literature of its own (see, e.g., Mellinkoff and Charrow, Crandall, and Charrow). Therefore, I will not dwell here on the stylistic characteristics of legal language except to note that many of the features that are thought of as bureaucratic are the legacies of the intertwined history of legal and bureaucratic language.

Pragmatics

In discussing the language of the bureaucracy so far, I have quoted only short passages from bureaucratic documents. I have used these sentences to illustrate features of traditional bureaucratic style. The solution to stylistic problems is fairly easy. We could recommend a clear writing guideline to remedy each of these problems, and, if the guidelines were applied appropriately, the result would be likely to be a much more readable document.

But that's not the whole picture. Understanding a document requires more than just being able to read the separate sentences. The document as a whole must make sense. The organization must be useful, the purpose clear. If there are procedures to be followed, they must be laid out logically.

A major problem with bureaucratic documents is the lack of attention paid to pragmatics—to the context in which the document will be used, to the audience, and to the rhetorical situation. Perhaps because bureaucratic language derives in large measure from legal language, many bureaucratic documents have traditionally served a denotative rather than a communicative function. The existence of the document and the statement of the facts in writing are of primary importance. Comprehensibility is secondary, if it is considered at all.

H. P. Grice, a philosopher of language, has pointed out that successful communication is based on a principle of cooperation between the parties involved. Each person must be trying to communicate and must believe that the other is also trying to communicate. Readers of a document written in traditional bureaucratic language may be frustrated because they believe the document is trying to communicate when, in fact, the writer had no such intention. Bureaucratic writers have told me that the purpose of their documents — usually regulations and notices — is to set down the rules, not to tell people what to do (even though people outside the agency have to perform according to the rules).

The lack of attention to pragmatics in bureaucratic writing can be seen in poor organization, uninformative headings and tables of contents, a lack of concern for what the audience needs to know, and lack of coordination along the chain from writer to final product.

BUREAUCRATIC DOCUMENTS ARE POORLY ORGANIZED. Much of what the government has to tell people is procedural information — how to go about doing something. Even documents that seem to be about rights and obligations are often procedural. They describe events and actions that occur in a certain order. Government writers are sometimes more concerned with getting down all the nuances of the law (the exceptions and the special cases) than with explaining logically, step by step, what to do. They tend to focus on and to write section by section instead of first outlining the entire document and organizing the sections in a way that makes sense to the person who has to use the document to perform some action.

In addition to being procedural, many bureaucratic documents are primarily used for reference. Although the users may read a regulation from start to finish once to become familiar with it, after that they are likely to need the regulation only when a specific problem arises. At that point, the reader has a question and wants an answer to it as quickly and easily as possible. The same is true for contracts, manuals, and even requests for proposals. Reference documents require a different organization from narratives, persuasive memos, or committee reports.

BUREAUCRATIC HEADINGS AND TABLES OF CONTENTS ARE UNINFORMATIVE. For a document to serve well as a reference, it is not enough for the writer to organize it well. It is also necessary to give the reader clues to the organization. A characteristic trait of difficult bureaucratic documents is that the table of contents and the section headings are often useless to the reader. Example 15 is the table of contents of one agency's rules governing a set of grants programs. The writer could not possibly have developed this table of contents with the readers in mind.

Recent research by Swarts, Flower, and Hayes on a different set of regulations shows that poorly conceived headings are often misleading. Given the heading of a section, participants in the study could not accurately predict the content of that section, nor could they accurately match sentences taken from the regulations with the headings used in the regulation.

Useful headings and tables of contents can be written for bureaucratic documents. Compare this table of contents from another agency's grants program with example 15.

> Example 16:
> Part 161e — Financial Assistance for Consumers' Education Projects
> Subpart A — General
> Sec.
> 161e.1 What is the Consumers' Education Program?
> 161e.2 Who is eligible to receive an award?
> 161e.3 What regulations apply to the Consumers' Education Program?
> 161e.4 What definitions apply specifically to this program?
> Subpart B — What Kinds of Projects Does the Office of Education Assist under This Program?
> 161e.10 What are the purposes of the projects?
> 161e.11 What categories of activities are supported?
> 161e.12 What subject matter may be included?
> 161e.13 Will particular program subject matter be emphasized?
> Subpart C — How Does One Apply for a Grant?

When bureaucratic writers are concerned with helping their audience through a document, they can begin by stating what the document is for and what the document covers.

> Example 17: Federal Communications Commission Rules for Recreational Boaters.
> Subpart CC — How to Use Your VHF Marine Radio
> General
> VHF Marine Rule 1. Who are these rules for?
> These rules are for recreational boaters who have put VHF (Very High Frequency) marine radios on their boats. A VHF marine radio is a two-way radio for boaters. VHF marine radios operate on channels in the very high frequency band between 156 and 162 MHz.
> VHF Marine Rule 2. What do these rules tell me?
> Rules 3 through 9 tell you how to get a license for your radio.
> Rules 10 through 20 tell you how to operate your radio.

Poor organization and lack of useful headings are not unique to the language of the bureaucracy. They are common failings of weak or untrained writers in every sector. But the tradition of noncommunicative documents in law and in the bureaucracy has meant that until recently government writers have had few well-organized and well-presented models to follow.

Table of Contents

BUREAUCRATIC DOCUMENTS LACK CONCERN FOR WHAT THE AUDIENCE NEEDS TO KNOW. Bureaucratic documents are traditionally written from the writer's perspective, not from the reader's perspective. In legal-bureaucratic documents, the lawyer's concern that all contingencies be covered often takes precedence over selecting appropriate and necessary content for the readers.

Even when a bureaucratic writer wants to focus on an audience, the task is difficult. In many government agencies, information brochures are written by trained writers who know about the importance of keeping the reader in mind, but the writer can only imagine who the reader is. Time and funds are rarely available for interviewing a sample of prospective readers. The bureaucracy often isolates writers from their audiences, and there is seldom feedback to tell a writer that the information in a booklet is at the wrong level or answers the wrong questions. If there is feedback, it may be routed to the wrong department and never reach the writer at all.

BUREAUCRATIC DOCUMENTS LACK COORDINATION. The division of responsibility in the bureaucracy discourages people from using writing as a means of communication. For example, my colleagues and I at the Document Design Center recently agreed to help the information services division of an agency evaluate how well readers understood one of its brochures. Our first discovery was that no one at the field offices we had selected as research sites had read the booklet. In fact, no one had seen it. The distribution system had somehow failed. Imagine the devastating effect on the agency's writers when they learned that their brochure had never even reached the clients. Many such experiences lead writers to the belief that "no one will read it anyway."

Complexified, Complex, and Simple Language

In the past five years, an effort to simplify the language of bureaucratic documents (and of consumer contracts in the private sector) has gained significant momentum. The purpose of this effort is to make the language of the bureaucracy communicative and comprehensible — but not necessarily super simple. The term most commonly associated with the effort has been "plain English." New York's Sullivan Act and the similar statutes in Connecticut, Hawaii, New Jersey, and Maine are called "plain language laws."[1] The Practising Law Institute has twice run courses "Plain Language in Public Documents." The Document Design Center publishes a monthly newsletter with the title *Simply Stated.*[2]

[1] New York: General Obligations Law S5-702, effective 1 Nov. 1978; Connecticut: Pub. Act. No. 79-532, Laws 1979, effective 1 Oct. 1979; Hawaii: Act 36, Hawaii Legislature 1980, effective 1 July 1981; New Jersey: Ch. 125, Laws 1980, effective 16 Oct. 1980; Maine: Title 10, Ch. 202, effective 15 Sept. 1979.

[2] *Simply Stated,* newsletter available from Document Design Center, American Institutes for Research, 1055 Thomas Jefferson St., N.W., Washington, DC 20007.

Perhaps "plain English" and "simply stated" are misleading terms. *40*
Bureaucratic writers (and lawyers in the private sector) are concerned
that they are being asked to oversimplify — to write in all cases to a
hypothetical "person on the street," to reduce everything to a "Dick and
Jane" style of writing. Some early versions of the "plain language" bills
specified that all consumer contracts had to be written at the eighth- or
ninth-grade reading level. (Not one of these bills has become law.)

The notion that simplifying the language of bureaucracy must necessarily result in simple language is mistaken. The bureaucratic language
that is being attacked is a highly complexified language with features of
style and pragmatics that set it apart from mature, complex writing that
college composition teachers expect of their students. The purpose of the
"plain language" movement is not so much to simplify as to "decomplexify" bureaucratic documents.

President Carter's executive order requiring a change in the language of the bureaucracy did speak of both simple and "plain English,"
but it also emphasized the level necessary to reach the reader.[3] It said that
"Regulations shall be as simple and clear as possible" and that "The
official [approving regulations] should determine that . . . the regulation
is written in plain English and is understandable to those who must
comply with it." We can take this last statement to be the most critical
one. The order required that writers pay attention to the full rhetorical
situation, to the purpose and the audience, of what they were writing.

Sometimes a highly simplified vocabulary and style are appropriate
and necessary in the new language of bureaucracy. The Citizens Band
radio regulations, addressed to 15 million CB owners, must reach many
people who do not read on a college level. But other bureaucratic documents do not have such broad or general audiences and do not need so
simple a vocabulary.

If you look again at the features of bureaucratic language that I have
described, you will see that the language of the bureaucracy (and the
language of the law) is not just ordinary English with hard words and
long sentences. As Charrow suggests, even highly educated people who
can control the formal registers of written and spoken English do not
understand bureaucratic and legal language.

Distinguishing complexified language from complex language and *45*
both from simple language is important for two reasons. It helps us deal
with the fears (and correspondingly the attitudes and motivations) of
writers in the bureaucracy. It helps us to understand the origins of (at
least some of) the worst gobbledygook in bureaucratic documents.

I would like to hypothesize that poor writers who do not control
the mature style of formal written English do even more poorly when
they try to write in the complexified language of bureaucracy. They

[3]EO12044, March 1978, revoked by President Reagan in EO12291, Feb. 1981.

follow the models without understanding and produce what Joseph Williams calls the "perplexed style," a hypercorrected bureaucratese. For example, the following sentence, the opening statement in a request for proposal, shows a writer trying to sound "bureaucratic" without understanding how to write.

> Example 18: The purpose of this project is to create an awareness on the behalf of the consumer as to how one must proceed to effectively impact upon regulatory agency policymaking processes.

The three-tiered characterization of bureaucratic language and the distinction between control of complex versus complexified styles have implications for how we train (or retrain) bureaucratic writers. I will return to that topic, but before we get there, I want to add to my characterization some thoughts on why bureaucratic documents are written the way they are.

HOW DID THE LANGUAGE OF BUREAUCRACY BECOME SO COMPLEXIFIED?

From a historical perspective, there seem to be two major explanations for the features of bureaucratic language. One is the legal tradition. The other is an earlier attitude that government should represent itself as formal and impersonal.

The Legal Tradition
The domain of the language of bureaucracy overlaps significantly the domain of legal language. Legal language retains its frozen forms of medieval English for a number of reasons. Lawyers believe the rigidity of language is necessary for accuracy. Mellinkoff effectively destroys this argument, but in trying to change the language of bureaucracy, we must deal directly with the lawyer's perception that clear language and legal accuracy are incompatible concepts. Danet and Charrow, Crandall, and Charrow have described the ritualistic and "magical" aspects of complexified legal language. Many lawyers feel that if lay readers were to understand legal language, it would lose some of its magic; and the resistance to changing legal language rubs off onto bureaucratic language as well.

The Government as Impersonal Guardian of the Public Welfare
In a workshop I gave to a group of government writers in 1980, *50* one of the lawyers expressed dismay at my suggestion that he use personal pronouns and active sentences in his bureaucratic documents. "But we were taught to write in the passive," he said. Whether or not he was explicitly taught the impersonal passive (not just passive sentences, but passive sentences with no agents), the models he was given to follow were certainly written that way. The traditional bureaucratic style is

called "the public passive" and is meant to indicate a strong, impersonal, and therefore impartial, institution.

The change to plain English represents a radical philosophical departure from the tradition of the bureaucracy. The call for a new style rests on a belief that the impersonal government has not been impartial and has not been responsive to the people. The demand for a new style is also a demand for a government that is open to public inspection and to public participation. In part, a resistance to the new style of plain English may be an unwillingness to accept this philosophical shift.

In addition to the two historical traditions that I have just discussed, there are many other forces that work against change in the language of the bureaucracy. Let me briefly mention six: institutional inertia, the models that writers have to follow, the social prestige of a special language, time pressures, the review process, and the lack of training to understand and therefore change the style.

Institutional Inertia

The federal bureaucracy is a gigantic institution, and even a small agency is inextricably part of this large organization. In the government, people move from agency to agency following paths of specialization (contract officer, personnel specialist, program analyst, legal counsel). Although personnel changes across agencies can be a vehicle for the spread of new ideas, they can also be a leveling force. If you want to expand your possibilities for promotion to include agencies beyond the one you are in, you have to play the game as it is defined in the overall organization, not just in your own agency.

In any institution it is easier and safer to do things as they have always been done. Change requires taking risks, and if there are no rewards for risk-taking, there are no incentives to do so. The bureaucracy as an institution probably offers less incentive for taking risks than do other large institutions such as private industry or academia. Look at what happened to people who "blew the whistle" on budget overruns.

Higher-ranking people in an institution, however, have more con- 55
trol over the way things are done and consequently are freer to take risks. In the government, in particular, top-level executives move frequently among the business, academic, and public sectors. They have options beyond the institution they are currently in and therefore are not as constrained to play it safe as lower-echelon people might be. This fact suggests that the best path to change is to convince top-level people, who would then reduce the level of risk that change would entail for lower-level people.

Traditional Models

We don't yet know much about how writers acquire institutional literacy—how they learn to write job-related documents. A few process studies are now under way, by Odell and Goswami: ("Nature and Functions"), Scribner and Jacobs, and Mikulecky, but more work needs to be done in this area. We do know that few courses are available to prospective government employees on how to write in the language of bureaucracy. We can assume that writers learn by imitating the style of existing documents, and it is clear that more models are available in the traditional language of the bureaucracy than in a communicative, comprehensible style.

Social Prestige

The specialized features of any complexified language emerge at least in part from a desire among members of a group to be seen as separate. Group members and outsiders can tell who belongs by the way they write and speak. Despite the fact that we laugh at examples of bureaucratic writing, the bureaucracy is a prestigious place to work. The language of the bureaucracy, however infelicitous it may be, is adopted by news commentators and the public when they want to sound as if they too are "in the know." For months, we all discussed the "hostage crisis situation."

Time Pressures

It takes longer to do things a new way, and, in any institution, time is money. Although you may believe that the government is an extremely inefficient and costly institution and that government documents take forever to appear, bureaucratic writers usually feel that they are under unreasonable time pressures. Congress sometimes mandates that a law be turned into regulations in a few months. The OSHA (Occupational Safety and Health Administration) rules that were published under very quick deadlines are an example of how time pressures help produce gobbledygook.

We may argue that communicative, comprehensible English is easier and faster to write than is gobbledygook (and I think that is true), but changing styles and creating new models take time. Instead of being instructed to revise and rethink a form or a regulation when Congress changes the law, writers are only given the time to amend an existing document to account for the changes. The result over time is often to add to the disorganization, inconsistency, and incomprehensibility of the original document.

The Review Process

An institutional review process can benefit both writers and users   *60*
of documents. Problems arise, however, when the review process becomes as cumbersome as it is in many government agencies.

A federal regulation may require as many as ten or twenty levels of review for one document. Although the staff of a program will write it, the agency's general counsel must approve it; OMB (the Office of Management and Budget) may review it; and people at all levels in the organization — from the program supervisors to the secretary — must sign off on it. The effect can be devastating. Compromises in policy and language may obscure rather than clarify. The writer may get fed up with trying to keep the style clear. We do not teach our students how to write by committee, how to deal with reviewers, or even to expect to have to revise what they write.

Institutions, particularly ones as hierarchically arranged as government agencies are, tend to isolate writers from their real (final, external) audience. Mechanisms for feedback from the people who use bureaucratic documents are weak. Direct feedback comes haphazardly (e.g., letters and calls of complaint); types of indirect feedback (such as error rates on forms) are, in theory, available but are seldom used.

Without feedback from the audience, writers do not know when they have fallen into the trap of being too familiar with the vocabulary and style of their profession. The vocabulary and concepts of any field become commonplace to those who use them repeatedly. The shared jargon and style serve an important communicative function within the profession, but it is easy to forget that others may not immediately understand what you are saying. Over time as I work with government regulations, I become more and more used to bureaucratese. Material that shocked me three years ago seems ordinary now. Staying attuned to an audience one does not regularly meet requires an extraordinary expenditure of time and energy.

In a system with many layers of review, writers may also lose a sense of responsibility for the documents. By the time a federal regulation appears in print, the author may well have a different job and other concerns. Of course there are some very stable offices in the government, where a cadre of people have remained for several years building strong programs. There are offices that take public testimony seriously and try to communicate effectively with an external audience despite the inconveniences and counterpressures of a cumbersome review process. But when the chain that joins writer and user has as many links as it does for most bureaucratic documents, the writer may not even know that it is knotted or broken somewhere along its length.

Research on writing in work settings shows that writers are highly 65 attuned to their immediate audiences (Odell and Goswami, "Writing in a Non-Academic Setting," and Goswami). For writers in the bureaucracy, the immediate audience is the internal one — the reviewers. Government writers perceive that their supervisors want to see the traditional language of the bureaucracy. This perception is a major deterrent to change. We have tried to combat both the perception and the reality it may reflect. Whenever we train a group of writers, we give a half-day workshop for their supervisors. We foster communication between writers and reviewers at the beginning of a project.

The issue of the writer's perception versus the reviewer's reality, however, raises some interesting questions about how any systematic change occurs in institutions (not just changes in acceptable style). Is change most effective when it comes down from the top? What signals of change are most likely to be taken seriously? Are the perceptions of staff writers accurate reflections of institutional reality? Do perceptions of what is acceptable lag behind changes in the attitudes of upper-echelon reviewers? How does the bureaucracy, where policy at the top is highly political and may shift drastically every four years, differ in its writer-reviewer relationships from other institutions? It seems to me that if we want to change the language of bureaucracy, we have to have a better understanding of the process of institutional change.

Lack of Training

The final reason I want to offer for why bureaucratic documents are so difficult to understand is that few people who write the language of bureaucracy were ever trained to be writers. Regulations are written by lawyers, engineers, and policy analysts. Requests for proposals are written by program specialists. IRS forms, instructions, and publications are developed by tax-law specialists. Writers and editors, employed by the agencies to help, have far less prestige and clout than do the experts in the subject matter.

When we examine university-level curricula in this country, we still find few courses that might prepare future bureaucrats to understand the principles of clear document design and the realities and possibilities for writing in institutional settings. The programs at the University of Michigan and the University of Maryland are unusual. Technical writing courses for engineers are an appropriate model, but the content is not applicable to most bureaucratic documents. The effect of a lack of training is that even professionals who write well in other contexts are too easily co-opted into using the poor models of the institution, while poor writers do even more poorly with the complex demands of institutional writing.

I have tried to answer the question "How did the language of bureaucracy become so complexified?" by pointing to the forces that shaped that language and that pressure it to remain uncommunicative and incomprehensible. I have suggested these eight factors:
- the legal tradition
- a philosophy that government should be impersonal
- institutional inertia
- traditional models
- social prestige
- time pressures
- the review process
- lack of training

I have ended each of these first two sections with a point that has   70
direct implications for educators. Let us, however, again postpone that
discussion until we have reviewed our third major topic. Let us look now
at pressures for changes in bureaucratic language.

WHY SHOULD WE CHANGE THE LANGUAGE OF THE BUREAUCRACY?

In the 1970s Americans began to realize that the bureaucracy had
grown to enormous size and was influencing the lives of more people in
more ways than ever before. Pressures came from many sources for the
government to reduce the burden of its paperwork both for institutions
and for the public.

Although it has never been more than a minor issue, the clear-
language movement received support from both industry and consumers. On the one hand, it became part of Carter's deregulation package — which was what industry wanted. On the other hand, it was part
of the general rise of consumerism — of the effort to make government
open, responsive, and communicative.

What reasons can we cite for the need to change the language of
bureaucracy? For the sake of brevity, I will keep this discussion to four
critical reasons:

- The growth of government does place a paperwork burden on us all.
- Reorganizing and rewriting bureaucratic documents can significantly reduce that burden.
- Reorganizing and rewriting bureaucratic documents can increase
  compliance with government rules and save the government money.
- Bureaucratic documents can be improved and still be legally accurate and sufficient.

The Paperwork Burden

The expansion of government and the burden of its paperwork
requirements often present serious problems. In its report on rulemaking, the Commission on Federal Paperwork wrote (54) that in the mid-
1970s the number of pages in the *Federal Register,* where notices and
regulations are presented to the public, was growing by more than ten
percent a year — 45,422 pages in 1974, 57,072 pages in 1976. The Commission on Federal Paperwork began its final summary report (3 Oct.
1977) by estimating that government paperwork costs $100 billion a year
or about $500 for each person in this country (5). *U.S. News and World
Report* in 1978 reported that Americans spend 785 million hours each year
filling out 4,987 different federal forms.

Poorly written and poorly designed documents cost us time and   *75*
money both as individuals and as taxpayers. A few years ago, thirty-four
percent of the students applying for federal financial aid had to go
through the process at least twice (sometimes three or four times) because they did not understand how to complete the form accurately. The
students paid in time and frustration — and sometimes in not getting
money they were entitled to. The taxpayers paid in processing costs,
paper and mailing for extra forms, maintaining toll-free telephone lines,
and hiring people to answer questions.

Making Documents Easier Can Significantly
Reduce the Burden on the User

Bureaucratic documents can be changed so that readers find them
easier to understand and use. In one year, with minor changes on the
form and major changes in the information and instructions, we reduced
the error rate on the financial aid applications by about seven percent.

Take as another example the recently revised marine radio regulations for recreational boaters (47 CFR 83). Before the Federal Communications Commission revised these rules, recreational boaters who have
two-way radios on their boats had to buy a copy of a regulation that was
several hundred pages long, find the rules and parts of rules that applied
to them, and understand long and complex explanations in legal language in order to comply with the law. The same rules also regulated
use to two-way radios on ocean liners and merchant ships.

By selecting only the rules that apply to recreational boaters, the
FCC was able to reduce the relevant information to just four pages in
the *Federal Register* (which the FCC now publishes as an eleven-page
question-and-answer booklet). In an empirical evaluation of the old and
new versions of these rules made by Felker and Rose, both experienced
boaters and people interested in boating who had never seen the rules
before performed significantly better with the new rules than with the
old ones. They answered more questions correctly, found the information more quickly, could more often identify the correct section, and
considered the new rules much easier to use.

We *can* write clear and useful bureaucratic documents.

Making Documents Clearer Can Significantly Ease
the Government's Job and Save the Government Money

Writing clear and useful bureaucratic documents helps the agencies   *80*
that produce them as well as the citizens that use them. Many poorly
written bureaucratic documents are rewritten in other forms in an attempt to make them clearer. Thus, from regulations we get guidelines,

manuals, explanatory memos, letters of interpretation, and so on. All these restatements take time and money (for people, paper, and printing). Moreover, something is liable to get lost in the translation, and discrepancies between, for example, the regulation and the manual can be the cause of time-consuming and costly further work.

Multiple documents are not necessary. The Department of Education, for example, has rewritten the regulations for some of its grants programs in a well-organized question-and-answer format with clear language. The regulations are so straightforward that they are now used as the guidelines that go directly to people who want to apply for a grant.

Bureaucratic agencies are charged not only with deciding on the policies and rules for carrying out the law but also with monitoring and enforcing compliance with their rules. Monitoring and enforcement are costly, so the agency must seek ways to increase voluntary compliance. (Obviously, industry and individuals have many reasons for not complying with government rules. Ignorance or misunderstanding may not be the most significant cause of noncompliance.)

When the number of CB radio owners in the United States increased dramatically in the mid-1970s, the Federal Communications Commission decided that the most cost-effective way to increase compliance with the rules was to rewrite them so that CB users could understand them. The revised CB rules (47 CFR 95) are well organized, clearly written, and available as an attractive booklet. Before the new rules went into effect, the FCC had an office of five people who spent all day answering telephone questions about the CB radio rules from people who were trying to comply with them. After the clear-English version of the rules was distributed, the calls stopped. All five employees were transferred to other jobs.

Bureaucratic Documents Can Be Improved and Still Be Legally Accurate and Sufficient

The bureaucratic writer worries about the tension between clarity of language and legal accuracy and sufficiency. It is an important concern. But, for all the reasons given earlier in this paper, the growing body of clear-English legal documents attests to the possibility that a document can meet both the lawyer's and the writer's criteria.

All the clear-English documents I have referred to in this section are legal documents. The agencies' legal counsels have accepted them. Litigation has not ensued. Furthermore, activity on the state level and in the private sector supports the change from traditional bureaucratic language to clear, communicative English. As of August 1979, Pressman writes, twenty-five states had laws or regulations requiring readability in at least some types of insurance policies. By 1980, five states had plain language laws requiring comprehensible consumer contracts. As banks, insurance companies, realtors, and department stores rewrite their documents, the exempted federal notices stand out as outdated monuments to the uncommunicative bureaucratic tradition.[4] They look and sound like what they are—legalese that few consumers understand. But the necessity of writing in the traditional bureaucratic style is belied by the surrounding clear-English text.

Similarly, the irony of writing incomprehensible laws and regulations that require others to write clearly may someday catch up with federal writers. Warrantors regulated by the Magnuson-Moss Act (which requires comprehensible product warranties) and bankers governed by the Federal Reserve Board's Regulation Z (which requires truth in lending and therefore sets standards for many credit documents) are quick to point out that the legislative drafters and regulation writers do not follow their own requirements.

IMPLICATIONS FOR EDUCATORS

What can we do to foster change to a clearer, more communicative language of the bureaucracy? The problem obviously needs to be attacked on several levels at the same time. Each factor contributing to the maintenance of traditional, noncommunicative language must be addressed. We must:

- increase on-the-job training in document design for writers, forms designers, and supervisors;
- develop more models of clear legal and bureaucratic documents; influence decision makers, supervisors, and reviewers to reduce the time pressure on writers, to support effort within their agencies to write well, to appreciate the need for clear communication, the benefits of clear communication, and the fact that it can be done;
- support research on job-related reading and writing skills and on translating that knowledge into educational practice; and
- develop college courses that are directed toward the skills and knowledge students will need in their professions.

[4]For example, the Federal Trade Commission requires that this notice be printed in this manner on the front of consumer credit contracts:
NOTICE: ANY HOLDER OF THIS CONSUMER CREDIT CONTRACT IS SUBJECT TO ALL CLAIMS AND DEFENSES WHICH THE DEBTOR COULD ASSERT AGAINST THE SELLER OF GOODS OR SERVICES OBTAINED PURSUANT HERETO OR WITH THE PROCEEDS HEREOF. RECOVERY HEREUNDER BY THE DEBTOR SHALL NOT EXCEED AMOUNTS PAID BY THE DEBTOR HEREUNDER.

Clearly, the development of more focused advanced composition courses is only one of many strands in the fabric that must be woven to improve legal and bureaucratic writing, but such courses are appropriate to discuss in this book.[5]

What can instructors do in advanced composition courses to better prepare students for professional schools (in law or management) and for the professional writing they will do on the job? First of all, to attract these students, we must offer advanced composition courses that reflect the situations for which they are preparing themselves. Courses in technical writing and business writing do not fill this need. The topics, rhetorical situations, and document types are not relevant.

Within an advanced composition course on document design, an important early goal is to give students both an appreciation for the amount of time that professionals spend in writing, whether they are lawyers, administrators, policy analysts, or technical specialists, and an appreciation of how important writing skills are in getting promotions and in succeeding in managerial roles. We can accomplish this goal by presenting case studies of people at work or, even better, by having the students go out of the classroom to do the case studies themselves. Furthermore, training in an advanced composition class should include discussion of the problems of writing in an organizational setting such as a bureaucracy so that students are equipped to deal with the social context of their work as well as with the basic skills of composing clear sentences.

Another important aspect of training is to make the writing tasks resemble those in the workplace. Writing in college classes is usually an individual endeavor, while writing in organizations is often collaborative. We can make some of the longer writing assignments in an advanced course collaborative and discuss the interactions that facilitate and that hinder arriving at a well-organized, well-written product. College writing is seldom reviewed by many people with different perspectives, and even less often must it be revised to meet the criticisms of multiple reviewers. We can make review and revision part of each assignment, and again we can discuss how different interactions with reviewers hinder or facilitate a good final product.

Although composition teachers and texts speak of different audiences and different purposes, exercises in most classrooms reflect neither

90

---

[5]In this section, as in the rest of the paper, I concentrate on those who write the language of the bureaucracy. In developing instruction in the 1980s, we must also be concerned with literacy for consumers of bureaucratic documents. No matter how much we decomplexify the language of the bureaucracy, government documents (especially forms) will require literacy skills that are different from reading novels or textbooks, as Holland and I point out.

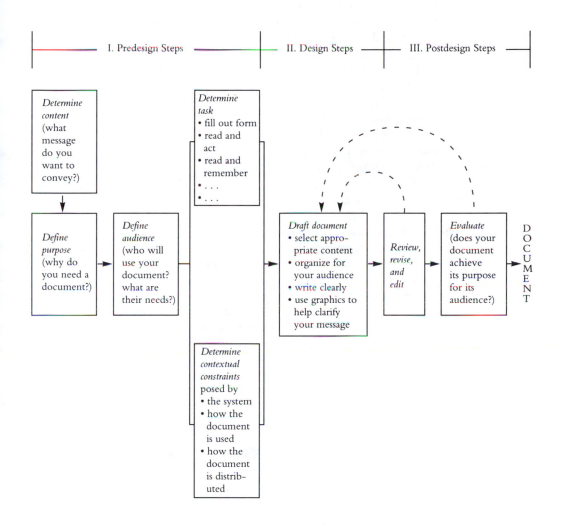

I. Predesign Steps | II. Design Steps | III. Postdesign Steps

Determine content (what message do you want to convey?)

Determine task
• fill out form
• read and act
• read and remember
• . . .
• . . .

Define purpose (why do you need a document?)

Define audience (who will use your document? what are their needs?)

Determine contextual constraints posed by
• the system
• how the document is used
• how the document is distrib-uted

Draft document
• select appro-priate content
• organize for your audience
• write clearly
• use graphics to help clarify your message

Review, revise, and edit

Evaluate (does your document achieve its purpose for its audience?)

D O C U M E N T

the types of documents nor the range of rhetorical situations that students will meet in institutional settings like the federal bureaucracy. Advanced composition courses should include writing and rewriting real documents for different, real audiences. And the students should take their writing to members of the audience to find out if it meets their needs, if they understand it, if they can use it.

All these things can be done in an advanced composition course. For example, my colleagues and I at the Document Design Center are developing a junior-senior level course in document design based on the model on page 87 of this book. In a tryout at Carnegie-Mellon University, students working in small groups selected documents that they thought would be difficult, and, following each step in the model, they interviewed responsible officials and users, analyzed the document, and then reorganized, revised, and retested it. They worked with

- the student government rules,
- a student loan form,
- consent forms,
- credit card agreements,
- descriptions of graduate programs, and
- instructions for using equipment.

All these were documents in use in campus or in the community. In most cases, students on campus were an appropriate audience, and other students or administrators were reviewers representing the official point of view on the document. In the process of this course, the students learned a great deal about different audiences and purposes as they honed their writing skills. They learned about themselves as writers, and they enjoyed the course.

WORKS CITED

Charrow, Veda R. "Linguistic Theory and Legal or Bureaucratic Language." In *Linguistic Theory and Exceptional Languages*. Ed. L. Obler and L. Menn. New York: Academic Press, 1982, 81–102.

——, JoAnn Crandall, and Robert P. Charrow. "Characteristics and Functions of Legal Language." In *Sublanguage: Studies of Language in Restricted Semantic Domains*. Ed. R. Kittredge and J. Lehrberger. Berlin: Walter de Gruyter, 1982, 175–90.

Commission on Federal Paperwork. *Final Summary Report*. 3 Oct. 1977.

——. *Report on Rulemaking*. 15 July 1977.

Danet, Brenda. "Language in the Legal Process." *Law and Society Review* 14.3(1980):445–564.

Felker, Daniel, and Andrew M. Rose. *The Evaluation of a Public Document: The Case of FCC's Marine Radio Rules for Recreational Boaters.* Washington, D.C.: American Institutes for Research, 1981. ED 213 026.

Flower, Linda, John R. Hayes, and Heidi Swarts. *Revising Functional Documents: The Scenario Principle.* Pittsburgh: Carnegie–Mellon Univ., 1980. ED 192 345.

Givens, R. A. *Drafting Documents in Plain Language 1981.* New York: Practising Law Institute, 1981. A4–3093.

Goswami, Dixie. "Naturalistic Studies of Nonacademic Writing." In *Moving between Practice and Research in Writing: Proceedings of the NIE-FIPSE Grantee Workshop.* Los Alamitos, Calif.: SWRL Educational Research and Development, 1981.

Grice, H. Paul. "Logic and Conversation." In vol. 3 of *Syntax and Semantics.* Ed. Peter Cole and Jerry L. Morgan. New York: Academic Press, 1975, 41–58.

Harley, James, Mark Trueman, and Peter Burnhill. "Some Observations on Producing and Measuring Readable Writing." *PLET* 17 (1980):164–74.

Holland, V. Melissa. *Psycholinguistic Alternatives to Readability Formulas.* Washington, D.C.: American Institutes for Research, 1981. ED 214 370.

————, and Janice C. Redish. "Strategies for Understanding Forms — and other Public Documents." In *Analyzing Discourse: Text and Talk.* Ed. Deborah Tannen. Washington, D.C.: Georgetown Univ. Press, 1982, 205–18.

MacDonald, D. A., ed. *Drafting Documents in Plain Language.* New York: Practising Law Institute, 1979. A4–3034.

Mellinkoff, David. *The Language of the Law.* Boston: Little, Brown, 1963.

Mikulecky, L. Indiana Univ. "Literacy Requirements in Industry." Paper presented at NIE Conference on Basic Skills, Washington, D.C., May 1978.

Odell, Lee, and Dixie Goswami. "The Nature and Functions of Writing." Unpublished MS.

————. "Writing in a Non-Academic Setting." *Research in the Teaching of English* 16(Oct. 1982): 201–24.

Pressman, Rebecca. *Legislative and Regulatory Progress on the Readability of Insurance Policies.* Washington, D.C.: American Institutes for Research, 1979.

Redish, Janice C. "How to Draft More Understandable Legal Documents." In *Drafting Documents in Plain Language.* Ed. Duncan A. MacDonald. New York: Practising Law Institute, 1979, 121–56.

————. "Readability." In *Document Design: A Review of the Relevant Literature.* Ed. D. Felker. Washington, D.C.: American Institutes for Research, 1980, 69–94.

————. "Understanding the Limitations of Readability Formulas." *IEEE Transactions on Professional Communication* PC–24 (March 1981): 46–48.

Scribner, S., and E. Jacobs. Center for Applied Linguistics. "Naturalistic Study of Literacy in the Workplace." Paper presented in NIE Conference on Basic Skills, Washington, D.C., May 1978.

Swarts, Heidi, Linda S. Flower, and John R. Hayes. *How Headings in Documents Can Mislead Readers.* Pittsburgh: Carnegie-Mellon Univ., 1980. ED 192 344.

"Ways Federal Forms Eat Away Your Time." *U.S. News and World Report,* 26 June 1978, 58.

Williams, Joseph. *Style: Ten Lessons in Clarity and Grace.* Glenview, Ill.: Scott Foresman, 1981.

FOR DISCUSSION AND WRITING

1. What sorts of readers do you think Redish has in mind? (What are their levels of education? Their socioeconomic status? Their interests?) Explain your opinion.

2. Which details in the selection did you find particularly interesting or useful? In what ways do these details contribute to the meaning and effect of the piece?

3. Why is Example 1 so difficult to read? Does it consist of words or concepts that you are not familiar with? Is its grammar unduly complex?

4. The author states that regulations that are difficult to read are often the result of a conflict between the writer's intention and the purported reason for publishing the regulations. Explain.

5. Did you have to look up the definition of *nominal* in order to understand the point made about nominal writing (par. 8)? Why, or why not? Would you classify the term *nominal writing* as jargon? Why, or why not?

6. How does the organization of this article assist you in understanding its main points? Can you use these techniques in your own writings for school?

7. What organizational characteristics of a bureaucracy contribute to bad writing?

8. Explain the distinction made between the words *simplify* and *decomplexify*. How does this relate to document writing?

9. What, according to the author, is the intention of *the public passive* style? What is the intention of *plain English?*

10. The 1970s saw the rise in the plain English movement. What events during that decade affected the movement's development?

11. Do you feel that college instruction in bureaucratic writing is appropriate? Why, or why not? Why do you think that so few colleges offer such courses?

OF STUDIES

Francis Bacon

Francis Bacon was a most quotable writer, as this often repeated sentence from his essay "Of Studies" indicates: "Some books are to be tasted, others to be swallowed, and some few to be chewed and digested. . . ." Bacon wrote fifty-eight essays on such subjects as education, friendship, riches, ambition, beauty, and anger. However, his major contribution to intellectual history was not his essays—though they have always been widely read and admired—but his philosophical works, particularly *The Advancement of Learning*.

Born in 1561, Bacon studied at Cambridge University. When he was but fifteen, he began to prepare for the law at Gray's Inn. During the reign of Elizabeth I, Bacon was instrumental in convicting the Earl of Essex of treason. After Elizabeth's death in 1603, Bacon advanced rapidly under the reign of James I, ultimately becoming Lord Chancellor. In 1618 James I created him Lord Verulam and, in 1621, Viscount St. Albans. However, in 1621 Bacon was charged with bribery and confessed to neglect of duty. In disgrace, he retired to his family's home at Gorhambury, Hertfordshire, and spent the remainder of his life in philosophical and literary work. He died in 1626.

As you read the essay, keep the following question in mind: Why have Bacon's essays been so highly honored for nearly 400 years?

Studies serve for delight, for ornament, and for ability.° Their chief use for delight, is in privateness and retiring;° for ornament, is in discourse; and for ability, is in the judgement and disposition of business. For expert men° can execute, and perhaps judge of particulars, one by one; but the general counsels, and the plots and marshalling of affairs come best from those that are learned. To spend too much time in studies is sloth; to use them too much for ornament is affectation; to make judgement wholly by their rules is the humour of a scholar. They perfect nature, and are perfected by experience, for natural abilities are like natural plants that need proyning° by study; and studies themselves do give forth directions too much at large, except they be bounded in by experience. Crafty° men contemn studies, simple men admire them, and wise men use them; for they teach not their own use; but that is a wisdom without them and above them, won by observation. Read not to contradict and confute; nor to believe and take for granted; nor to find talk and discourse; but to weigh and consider. Some books are to be tasted, others to be swallowed, and some few to be chewed and digested:

for ability: To make man able.
retiring: Seclusion.
expert men: Men who have learned only from experience, not study.
proyning: Cultivating.
crafty: Practical (but also, cunning).

that is, some books are to be read only in parts; others to be read, but not curiously;° some few to be read wholly and with diligence and attention. Some books also may be read by deputy, and extracts made of them by others, but that would be only in the less important arguments, and the meaner sort of books; else distilled books are like common distilled waters, flashy° things. Reading maketh a full man; conference a ready man; and writing an exact man. And therefore, if a man write little, he had need have a great memory; if he confer little, he had need have a present wit;° and if he read little, he had need have much cunning, to seem to know that he doth not. Histories make men wise, poets witty,° the mathematics subtle, natural philosophy deep, moral grave, logic and rhetoric able to contend. *Abeunt studia in mores.*° Nay, there is no stond° or impediment in the wit° but may be wrought out by fit studies, like as diseases of the body may have appropriate exercises. Bowling is good for the stone and reins;° shooting° for the lungs and breast; gentle walking for the stomach; riding for the head; and the like. So if a man's wit be wandering, let him study the mathematics; for in demonstrations, if his wit be called away never so little, he must begin again. If his wit be not apt to distinguish or find differences, let him study the Schoolmen,° for they are *cymini sectores.*° If he be not apt to beat over matters,° and to call up one thing to prove and illustrate another, let him study the lawyers' cases. So every defect of the mind may have a special receipt.°

not curiously: With great care.
flashy: Insipid.
present wit: Ready mind.
witty: Ingenious.
Abeunt studia in mores: Studies go to make up a man's character (Ovid, *Heroides,* XV. 83).
stond: Obstacle.
wit: Mind.

Bowling is good for the stone and reins: Playing bowls is good for the bladder and kidneys.
shooting: Archery.
Schoolmen: Medieval theologians and academics. See Essay 17, note 7.
cymini sectores: Hair-splitters.
beat over matters: Cover the ground thoroughly.
receipt: Prescription (for remedy).

FOR DISCUSSION AND WRITING

1. As a critical reader, what is your opinion of Bacon's views of the uses of learning in the essay? For example, do you believe, as Bacon says, that "histories make men wise"?

2. Explain why Bacon's characterization of books — those that are "tasted," those that are "swallowed," and those that are "chewed and digested" — does or does not fit your own reading patterns. If these categories do fit your own reading patterns, provide specific examples of books for each category.

3. Some essays analyze their subjects (for example, "The Invisible Discourse of the Law," by James Boyd White, on pages 53–64). Other essays are speculative, discussing what might have been or what might be (for example, the one by Lewis Thomas on pages 415–17). Still other essays are interpretive, explaining a problem, an experience, or a belief (for example, "The Achievement of Desire," by Richard Rodriguez, on pages 12–32). Is this essay analytic, speculative, or interpretive? Given the subject matter, what topics might the author cover if he were to slant the essay toward one of the other two possibilities.

4. Do you think the essay is meant to persuade the reader? Why, or why not?

5. The following sentence is, in important ways, like some other sentences in the essay: "Reading maketh a full man; conference a ready man; and writing an exact man." What characteristic of this sentence stands out prominently? What is the effect of this characteristic on you, the reader? In your opinion, is this sentence effective or ineffective?

6. What type of studies do you think the author might prescribe for someone who was attempting to become learned? Cite parts of the text that support your opinion.

7. If you had written "Of Studies" for your composition class, would your instructor have remarked that your discussion was too general, that you needed to supply more detail and examples? Why, or why not?

8. Explain your reaction to the following "Poetical Essay" by Bacon. Is it in your opinion a good poem? Why, or why not? Is it a good essay? Why, or why not? Besides having meter and rhyme, in what other ways does the "Poetical Essay" differ from "Of Studies"? Which of the two is easier to read? Which is easier to understand? Why?

The world's a bubble, and the life of man less than a span;
In his conception wretched, from the womb so to the tomb:
Curst from the cradle, and brought up to years with cares and fears.
Who then to frail mortality shall trust,
But limns the water, or but writes in dust.

Domestic cares afflict the husband's bed, or pains his head.
Those that live single take it for a curse, or do things worse.
Some would have children; those that have them moan, or wish them
    gone.
What is it then to have or have no wife,
But single thraldom, or a double strife?

Yet since with sorrow here we live opprest, what life is best?
Courts are but only superficial schools to dandle fools.

The rural parts are turned into a den of savage men.
And where's the city from all vice so free,
But may be term'd the worst of all the three?

Our own affections still at home to please is a disease:
To cross the seas to any foreign soil perils and toil.
Wars with their noise affright us: when they cease, we are worse in
    peace.
What then remains, but that we still should cry
Not to be born, or being born to die.

THE LITERATURE OF KNOWLEDGE AND THE LITERATURE OF POWER

Thomas DeQuincey

The essay that follows, which is the first pages of a longer essay on the poet Alexander Pope, first published in 1848, is frequently reprinted under various titles, the most common being the one we are using here. Thomas DeQuincey advances the common argument that there are two kinds of texts: those that satisfy our need for information and those that arouse our emotional responses. Of the two categories, he clearly values the latter over the former.

DeQuincey's best-known work is a lurid account of his addiction, *Confessions of an English Opium Eater,* first published in 1822. His life was filled with tragedy. He was born in Manchester, England, in 1785, the son of a moderately well-to-do merchant. As a child, Thomas was deeply affected by the death of his younger sister Jane and then, when he was seven, by the death of his beloved older sister Elizabeth. A year later his father died of tuberculosis. In 1803 he realized one of his great ambitions when he entered Oxford University, but his life there was grim; he stayed very much to himself, eking out an existence on a small allowance. In 1804 he began to take opium and was addicted for the rest of his life. He married and had six children, but in 1837 his wife died, leaving him with the entire responsibility for the family. Fortunately, his daughters Margaret and Emily cared for the family and for their father until his death in 1859.

On the basis of your own reading experience, do you think the division between the literature of knowledge and the literature of power is valid? Can a piece of literature be *both* powerful and informative? How does the distinction between knowledge and power relate to your own reading preferences?

What is it that we mean by *literature?* Popularly, and amongst the thoughtless, it is held to include everything that is printed in a book. Little logic is required to disturb *that* definition. The most thoughtless person is easily made aware that in the idea of *literature* one essential element is some relation to a general and common interest of man, so that what applies only to a local, or professional, or merely personal interest, even though presenting itself in the shape of a book, will not belong to literature. So far the definition is easily narrowed; and it is as easily expanded. For not only is much that takes a station in books not literature; but inversely, much that really *is* literature never reaches a station in books. The weekly sermons of Christendom, that vast pulpit literature which acts so extensively upon the popular mind — to warn, to uphold, to renew, to comfort, to alarm — does not attain the sanctuary of libraries in the ten thousandth part of its extent. The drama, again — as, for instance, the finest of Shakespeare's plays in England, and all leading

Athenian plays in the noontide of the Attic stage—operated as a literature on the public mind, and were (according to the strictest letter of that term) *published* through the audiences that witnessed* their representation some time before they were published as things to be read; and they were published in this scenical mode of publication with much more effect than they could have had as books during ages of costly copying or of costly printing.

Books, therefore, do not suggest an idea coextensive and interchangeable with the idea of literature; since much literature, scenic, forensic, or didactic (as from lecturers and public orators), may never come into books, and much that *does* come into books may connect itself with no literary interest.[†] But a far more important correction, applicable to the common vague idea of literature, is to be sought not so much in a better definition of literature as in a sharper distinction of the two functions which it fulfills. In that great social organ which, collectively, we call literature, there may be distinguished two separate offices that may blend and often *do* so, but capable, severally, of a severe insulation, and naturally fitted for reciprocal repulsion. There is, first, the literature of *knowledge;* and, secondly, the literature of *power*. The function of the first is—to *teach;* the function of the second is—to *move:* the first is a rudder, the second an oar or a sail. The first speaks to the *mere* discursive understanding; the second speaks ultimately, it may happen, to the higher understanding or reason, but always *through* affections of pleasure and sympathy. Remotely, it may travel towards an object seated in what Lord Bacon calls *dry* light; but, proximately, it does and must operate—else it ceases to be a literature of *power*—on and through that *humid* light which clothes itself in the mists and glittering *iris* of human passions, desires, and genial emotions. Men have so little reflected on the higher functions of literature as to find it a paradox if one should describe it as a mean or subordinate purpose of books to give information. But this is a paradox only in the sense which makes it honorable to be paradoxical. Whenever we talk in ordinary language of seeking information or gaining knowledge, we understand the words as connected with something of absolute novelty. But it is the grandeur of all truth which *can* occupy a very high

---

*Charles I, for example, when Prince of Wales, and many others in his father's court, gained their known familiarity with Shakespeare not through the original quartos, so slenderly diffused, nor through the first folio of 1623, but through the court representations of his chief dramas at Whitehall.

†What are called The *Blue Books*—by which title are understood the folio reports issued every session of Parliament by committees of the two houses, and stitched into blue covers—though often sneered at by the ignorant as so much waste paper, will be acknowledged gratefully by those who have used them diligently as the main wellheads of all accurate information as to the Great Britain of this day. As an immense depository of faithful *(and not superannuated)* statistics, they are indispensable to the honest student. But no man would therefore class the *Blue Books* as literature.

place in human interests that it is never absolutely novel to the meanest of minds: it exists eternally by way of germ or latent principle in the lowest as in the highest, needing to be developed, but never to be planted. To be capable of transplantation is the immediate criterion of a truth that ranges on a lower scale. Besides which, there is a rarer thing than truth — namely, *power*, or deep sympathy with truth. What is the effect, for instance, upon society, of children? By the pity, by the tenderness, and by the peculiar modes of admiration which connect themselves with the helplessness, with the innocence, and with the simplicity of children, not only are the primal affections strengthened and continually renewed, but the qualities which are dearest in the sight of heaven — the frailty, for instance, which appeals to forbearance, the innocence which symbolizes the heavenly, and the simplicity which is most alien from the worldly — are kept up in perpetual remembrance, and their ideals are continually refreshed. A purpose of the same nature is answered by the higher literature, viz., the literature of power. What do you learn from *Paradise Lost?* Nothing at all. What do you learn from a cookery book? Something new, something that you did not know before, in every paragraph. But would you therefore put the wretched cookery book on a higher level of estimation than the divine poem? What you owe to Milton is not any knowledge, of which a million separate items are still but a million of advancing steps on the same earthly level; what you owe is *power* — that is, exercise and expansion to your own latent capacity of sympathy with the infinite, where every pulse and each separate influx is a step upwards, a step ascending as upon a Jacob's ladder from earth to mysterious altitudes above the earth. *All* the steps of knowledge, from first to last, carry you further on the same plane but could never raise you one foot above your ancient level of earth, whereas the very *first* step in power is a flight — is an ascending movement into another element where earth is forgotten.

Were it not that human sensibilities are ventilated and continually called out into exercise by the great phenomena of infancy, or of real life as it moves through chance and change, or of literature as it recombines these elements in the mimicries of poetry, romance, etc., it is certain that, like any animal power or muscular energy falling into disuse, all such sensibilities would gradually droop and dwindle. It is in relation to these great *moral* capacities of man that the literature of power, as contradistinguished from that of knowledge, lives and has its field of action. It is concerned with what is highest in man, for the Scriptures themselves never condescend to deal by suggestion or cooperation with the mere discursive understanding: when speaking of man in his intellectual capacity, the Scriptures speak not of the understanding, but of *"the understanding heart,"* making the heart, i.e. the great *intuitive* (or nondiscursive) organ, to be the interchangeable formula for man in his highest state of capacity for the infinite. Tragedy, romance, fairy tale, or epopee, all alike restore to man's mind the ideals of justice, of hope, of truth, of mercy, of retribution, which else (left to the support of daily life in its realities) would languish for want of sufficient illustration. What is meant, for instance, by *poetic justice?* It does not mean a justice that differs by its object from the ordinary justice of human jurisprudence, for then it must be confessedly a very bad kind of justice; but it means a justice that differs from common forensic justice by the degree in which it *attains* its object, a justice that is more omnipotent over its own ends, as dealing not with the refractory elements of earthly life, but with the elements of its own creation and with materials flexible to its own purest preconceptions. It is certain that, were it not for the literature of power, these ideals would often remain amongst us as mere arid notional forms, whereas by the creative forces of man put forth in literature they gain a vernal life of restoration and germinate into vital activities. The commonest novel, by moving in alliance with human fears and hopes, with human instincts of wrong and right, sustains and quickens those affections. Calling them into action, it rescues them from torpor. And hence the pre-eminency over all authors that merely *teach* of the meanest that *moves,* or that teaches, if at all, indirectly *by* moving. The very highest work that has ever existed in the literature of knowledge is but a *provisional* work — a book upon trial and sufferance, and *quamdiu bene se gesserit.*° Let its teaching be even partially revised, let it be but expanded — nay, even let its teaching be but placed in a better order — and instantly it is superseded. Whereas the feeblest works in the literature of power, surviving at all, survive as finished and unalterable amongst men. For instance, the *Principia* of Sir Isaac Newton was a book *militant* on earth from the first. In all stages of its progress it would have to fight for its existence: first, as regards absolute truth; secondly, when that combat was over, as regards its form or mode of presenting the truth. And as soon as a La Place, or anybody else, builds higher upon the foundations laid by this book, effectually he throws it out of the sunshine into decay and darkness; by weapons won from this book he superannuates and destroys this book, so that soon the name of Newton remains as a mere *nominis umbra,*° but his book, as a living power, has transmigrated into other forms. Now, on the contrary, the *Iliad,* the *Prometheus* of Aeschylus, the *Othello* or *King Lear,* the *Hamlet,* or *Macbeth,* and the *Paradise Lost* are not militant, but triumphant forever as long as the languages exist in which they speak or can be taught to speak. They never *can* transmigrate into new incarnations. To reproduce *these* in new forms, or variations, even in some things they should be improved, would be to plagiarize. A good steam engine is properly superseded by a better. But one lovely pastoral valley is not superseded by another, nor a statue of Praxiteles by a statue of

quamdiv bene se gesserit: Did it last well?
nominis umbra: shadow of a name

Michelangelo. These things are separated not by imparity but by disparity. They are not thought of as unequal under the same standard but as different in *kind,* and if otherwise equal, as equal under a different standard. Human works of immortal beauty and works of nature in one respect stand on the same footing: they never absolutely repeat each other, never approach so near as not to differ; and they differ not as better and worse, or simply by more and less: they differ by undecipherable and incommunicable differences that cannot be caught by mimicries, that cannot be reflected in the mirror of copies, that cannot become ponderable in the scales of vulgar comparison.

All the literature of knowledge builds only ground nests that are swept away by floods or confounded by the plow, but the literature of power builds nests in aerial altitudes of temples sacred from violation or of forests inaccessible to fraud. *This* is a great prerogative of the *power* literature, and it is a greater which lies in the mode of its influence. The *knowledge* literature, like the fashion of this world, passeth away. An encyclopedia is its abstract, and in this respect it may be taken for its speaking symbol — that before one generation has passed an encyclopedia is superannuated, for it speaks through the dead memory and unimpassioned understanding, which have not the repose of higher faculties but are continually enlarging and varying their phylacteries. But all literature properly so called — literature κατ' ἐξοχηνζ* — for the very same reason that it is so much more durable than the literature of knowledge, is (and by the very same proportion it is) more intense and electrically searching in its impressions. The directions in which the tragedy of this planet has trained our human feelings to play, and the combination into which the poetry of this planet has thrown our human passions of love and hatred, of admiration and contempt, exercise a power for bad or good over human life that cannot be contemplated, when stretching through many generations, without a sentiment allied to awe.† And of this let everyone be assured — that he owes to the impassioned books which he has read many a thousand more of emotions than he can consciously trace back to them. Dim by their origination, these emotions yet arise in him and mold him through life like forgotten incidents of his childhood.

---

*[Par excellence.]

†The reason why the broad distinctions between the two literatures of power and knowledge so little fix the attention lies in the fact that a vast proportion of books — history, biography, travels, miscellaneous essays, etc. — lying in a middle zone, confound these distinctions by interblending them. All that we call "amusement" or "entertainment" is a diluted form of the power belonging to passion, and also a mixed form; and, where threads of direct *instruction* intermingle in the texture with these threads of *power,* this absorption of the duality into one representative *nuance* neutralizes the separate perception of either. Fused into a *tertium quid,* or neutral state, they disappear to the popular eye as the repelling forces which, in fact, they are.

FOR DISCUSSION AND WRITING

1. According to DeQuincey, what is the essential characteristic of litera-ture? What qualities or characteristics must a text have for *you* to view it as literature?

2. "What do you learn from *Paradise Lost?*" asks DeQuincey. His answer, "Nothing at all. What do you learn from a cookery book? Something new, something that you did not know before, in every paragraph" (par. 2). Why does DeQuincey claim that we learn nothing from *Paradise Lost?* What seems to be his conception of knowledge?

3. What does one gain from the literature of power?

4. Is it possible for one reader to view *Paradise Lost* as literature of knowl-edge and another reader to take it as literature of power? Explain.

5. Can a piece of literature be both powerful and informative? How does the distinction between knowledge and power relate to your own reading preferences?

THE LIBRARY OF BABEL

Jorge Luis Borges

"The Library of Babel" is an *allegory,* a symbolic tale in which the places, characters, and events connote secondary meanings. Thus, the Library itself stands for the universe, and the books represent knowledge. One might say that the story is Borges's statement concerning humankind's quest for understanding. In this tale, Borges implies that all literate people are trapped in the Library of Babel. One book suggests another, which leads us to yet another, which leads us to yet another, and so on. Thus, we are in an endless search for the Truth.

An Argentinian, Borges was born in 1899 and was educated in Switzerland. He returned to Argentina in 1921 and began to write fiction that portrayed the desperate, hopeless life of the slums. He also wrote avant garde poetry. He was professor of English at the University of Buenos Aires and, after the fall of dictator Juan Peron in 1955, became director of the National Library of Argentina. Blinded by an inherited illness, Borges continued to write, dictating to his mother. "Once the outside world interfered too much," he has said. "Now the world is all inside me. And I see better, for I can see all the things I dream." Borges died in 1986.

As you read this fascinating story, think about this question: Am I forever trapped in the Library of Babel?

By this art you may contemplate
the variations of the 23 letters . . .
— The Anatomy of Melancholy,
Part 2, Sect. II, Mem. IV.

The universe (which others call the Library) is composed of an indefinite, perhaps an infinite, number of hexagonal galleries, with enormous ventilation shafts in the middle, encircled by very low railings. From any hexagon the upper or lower stories are visible, interminably. The distribution of the galleries is invariable. Twenty shelves — five long shelves per side — cover all sides except two; their height, which is that of each floor, scarcely exceeds that of an average librarian. One of the free sides gives upon a narrow entrance way, which leads to another gallery, identical to the first and to all the others. To the left and to the right of the entrance way are two miniature rooms. One allows standing room for sleeping; the other, the satisfaction of fecal necessities. Through this section passes the spiral staircase, which plunges down into the abyss and rises up to the heights. In the entrance way hangs a mirror, which faithfully duplicates appearances. People are in the habit of inferring from this mirror that the Library is not infinite (if it really were, why this illusory duplication?); I prefer to dream that the polished surfaces feign and promise infinity. . . .

Light comes from some spherical fruits called by the name of lamps. There are two, running transversally, in each hexagon. The light they emit is insufficient, incessant.

Like all men of the Library, I have traveled in my youth. I have journeyed in search of a book, perhaps of the catalogue of catalogues; now that my eyes can scarcely decipher what I write, I am preparing to die a few leagues from the hexagon in which I was born. Once dead, there will not lack pious hands to hurl me over the banister; my sepulchre shall be the unfathomable air: my body will sink lengthily and will corrupt and dissolve in the wind engendered by the fall, which is infinite. I affirm that the Library is interminable. The idealists argue that the hexagonal halls are a necessary form of absolute space or, at least, of our intuition of space. They contend that a triangular or pentagonal hall is inconceivable. (The mystics claim that to them ecstasy reveals a round chamber containing a great book with a continuous back circling the walls of the room; but their testimony is suspect; their words, obscure. That cyclical book is God.) Let it suffice me, for the time being, to repeat the classic dictum: *The Library is a sphere whose consummate center is any hexagon, and whose circumference is inaccessible.*

Five shelves correspond to each one of the walls of each hexagon; each shelf contains thirty-two books of a uniform format; each book is made up of four hundred and ten pages; each page, of forty lines; each line, of some eighty black letters. There are also letters on the spine of each book; these letters do not indicate or prefigure what the pages will say. I know that such a lack of relevance, at one time, seemed mysterious. Before summarizing the solution (whose disclosure, despite its tragic implications, is perhaps the capital fact of this history), I want to recall certain axioms.

The first: The Library exists *ab aeterno.*° No reasonable mind can doubt this truth, whose immediate corollary is the future eternity of the world. Man, the imperfect librarian, may be the work of chance or of malevolent demiurges; the universe, with its elegant endowment of shelves, of enigmatic volumes, of indefatigable ladders for the voyager, and of privies for the seated librarian, can only be the work of a god. In order to perceive the distance which exists between the divine and the human, it is enough to compare the rude tremulous symbols which my fallible hand scribbles on the end pages of a book with the organic letters inside: exact, delicate, intensely black, inimitably symmetric.

The second: *The number of orthographic symbols is twenty-five.** This bit of evidence permitted the formulation, three hundred years ago, of a general theory of the Library and the satisfactory resolution of the

ab aeterno: from eternity

*The original manuscript of the present note does not contain digits or capital letters. The punctuation is limited to the comma and the period. These two signs, plus the space sign and the twenty-two letters of the alphabet, make up the twenty-five sufficient symbols enumerated by the unknown author.

problem which no conjecture had yet made clear: the formless and chaotic nature of almost all books. One of these books, which my father saw in a hexagon of the circuit number fifteen ninety-four, was composed of the letters MCV perversely repeated from the first line to the last. Another, very much consulted in this zone, is a mere labyrinth of letters, but on the next-to-the-last page, one may read *O Time your pyramids*. As is well known: for one reasonable line or one straightforward note there are leagues of insensate cacaphony, of verbal farragoes and incoherencies. (I know of a wild region whose librarians repudiate the vain superstitious custom of seeking any sense in books and compare it to looking for meaning in dreams or in the chaotic lines of one's hands. . . . They admit that the inventors of writing imitated the twenty-five natural symbols, but they maintain that this application is accidental and that books in themselves mean nothing. This opinion — we shall see — is not altogether false.)

For a long time it was believed that these impenetrable books belonged to past or remote languages. It is true that the most ancient men, the first librarians, made use of a language quite different from the one we speak today; it is true that some miles to the right the language is dialectical and that ninety stories up it is incomprehensible. All this, I repeat, is true; but four hundred and ten pages of unvarying MCVs do not correspond to any language, however dialectical or rudimentary it might be. Some librarians insinuated that each letter could influence the next, and that the value of MCV on the third line of page 71 was not the same as that of the same series in another position on another page; but this vague thesis did not prosper. Still other men thought in terms of cryptographs; this conjecture has come to be universally accepted, though not in the sense in which it was formulated by its inventors.

Five hundred years ago, the chief of an upper hexagon* came upon a book as confusing as all the rest but which contained nearly two pages of homogeneous lines. He showed his find to an ambulant decipherer, who told him the lines were written in Portuguese. Others told him they were in Yiddish. In less than a century the nature of the language was finally established: it was a Samoyed-Lithuanian dialect of Guaraní, with classical Arabic inflections. The contents were also deciphered: notions of combinational analysis, illustrated by examples of variations with unlimited repetition. These examples made it possible for a librarian of genius to discover the fundamental law of the Library. This thinker observed that all the books, however diverse, are made up of uniform elements: the period, the comma, the space, the twenty-two letters of the alphabet. He also adduced a circumstance confirmed by all travelers:

---

*Formerly, for each three hexagons there was one man. Suicide and pulmonary diseases have destroyed this proportion. My memory recalls scenes of unspeakable melancholy: there have been many nights when I have ventured down corridors and polished staircases without encountering a single librarian.

There are not, in the whole vast Library, two identical books. From all these incontrovertible premises he deduced that the Library is total and that its shelves contain all the possible combinations of the twenty-odd orthographic symbols (whose number, though vast, is not infinite); that is, everything which can be expressed, in all languages. Everything is there: the minute history of the future, the autobiographies of the archangels, the faithful catalogue of the Library, thousands and thousands of false catalogues, a demonstration of the fallacy of these catalogues, a demonstration of the fallacy of the true catalogue, the Gnostic gospel of Basilides, the commentary on this gospel, the commentary on the commentary of this gospel, the veridical account of your death, a version of each book in all languages, the interpolations of every book in all books.

When it was proclaimed that the Library comprised all books, the first impression was one of extravagant joy. All men felt themselves lords of a secret, intact treasure. There was no personal or universal problem whose eloquent solution did not exist — in some hexagon. The universe was justified, the universe suddenly expanded to the limitless dimensions of hope. At that time there was much talk of the Vindications: books of apology and prophecy, which vindicated for all time the actions of every man in the world and established a store of prodigious arcana for the future. Thousands of covetous persons abandoned their dear natal hexagons and crowded up the stairs, urged on by the vain aim of finding their Vindication. These pilgrims disputed in the narrow corridors, hurled dark maledictions, strangled each other on the divine stairways, flung the deceitful books to the bottom of the tunnels, and died as they were thrown into space by men from remote regions. Some went mad. . . .

The Vindications do exist. I have myself seen two of these books, which were concerned with future people, people who were perhaps not imaginary. But the searchers did not remember that the calculable possibility of a man's finding his own book, or some perfidious variation of his own book, is close to zero.

The clarification of the basic mysteries of humanity — the origin of the Library and of time — was also expected. It is credible that those grave mysteries can be explained in words: if the language of the philosophers does not suffice, the multiform Library will have produced the unexpected language required and the necessary vocabularies and grammars for this language.

It is now four centuries since men have been wearying the hexagons. . . .

There are official searchers, *inquisitors.* I have observed them carrying out their functions: they are always exhausted. They speak of a staircase without steps where they were almost killed. They speak of galleries and stairs with the local librarian. From time to time they will pick up the nearest book and leaf through its pages, in search of infamous words. Obviously, no one expects to discover anything.

10

The uncommon hope was followed, naturally enough, by deep depression. The certainty that some shelf in some hexagon contained precious books and that these books were inaccessible seemed almost intolerable. A blasphemous sect suggested that all searches be given up and that men everywhere shuffle letters and symbols until they succeeded in composing, by means of an improbable stroke of luck, the canonical books. The authorities found themselves obliged to issue severe orders. The sect disappeared, but in my childhood I still saw old men who would hide out in the privies for long periods of time, and, with metal disks in a forbidden dicebox, feebly mimic the divine disorder.

Other men, inversely, thought that the primary task was to elimi-   *15* nate useless works. They would invade the hexagons, exhibiting credentials which were not always false, skim through a volume with annoyance, and then condemn entire bookshelves to destruction: their ascetic, hygienic fury is responsible for the senseless loss of millions of books. Their name is execrated; but those who mourn the "treasures" destroyed by this frenzy, overlook two notorious facts. One: the Library is so enormous that any reduction undertaken by humans is infinitesimal. Two: each book is unique, irreplaceable, but (inasmuch as the Library is total) there are always several hundreds of thousands of imperfect facsimiles—of works which differ only by one letter or one comma. Contrary to public opinion, I dare suppose that the consequences of the depredations committed by the Purifiers have been exaggerated by the horror which these fanatics provoked. They were spurred by the delirium of storming the books in the Crimson Hexagon: books of a smaller than ordinary format, omnipotent, illustrated, magical.

We know, too, of another superstition of that time: the Man of the Book. In some shelf of some hexagon, men reasoned, there must exist a book which is the cipher and perfect compendium of *all the rest:* some librarian has perused it, and it is analogous to a god. Vestiges of the worship of that remote functionary still persist in the language of this zone. Many pilgrimages have sought Him out. For a century they trod the most diverse routes in vain. How to locate the secret hexagon which harbored it? Someone proposed a regressive approach: in order to locate book A, first consult book B which will indicate the location of A; in order to locate book B, first consult book C, and so on ad infinitum. . . .

I have squandered and consumed my years in adventures of this type. To me, it does not seem unlikely that on some shelf of the universe there lies a total book.* I pray the unknown gods that some man—even

---

*I repeat: it is enough that a book be possible for it to exist. Only the impossible is excluded. For example: no book is also a stairway, though doubtless there are books that discuss and deny and demonstrate this possibility and others whose structure corresponds to that of a stairway.

if only one man, and though it have been thousands of years ago! — may have examined and read it. If honor and wisdom and happiness are not for me, let them be for others. May heaven exist, though my place be in hell. Let me be outraged and annihilated, but may Thy enormous Library be justified, for one instant, in one being.

The impious assert that absurdities are the norm in the Library and that anything reasonable (even humble and pure coherence) is an almost miraculous exception. They speak (I know) of "the febrile Library, whose hazardous volumes run the constant risk of being changed into others and in which everything is affirmed, denied, and confused as by a divinity in delirium." These words, which not only denounce disorder but exemplify it as well, manifestly demonstrate the bad taste of the speakers and their desperate ignorance. Actually, the Library includes all verbal structures, all the variations allowed by the twenty-five orthographic symbols, but it does not permit of one absolute absurdity. It is pointless to observe that the best book in the numerous hexagons under my administration is entitled *Combed Clap of Thunder;* or that another is called *The Plaster Cramp;* and still another *Axaxaxas Mlö.* Such propositions as are contained in these titles, at first sight incoherent, doubtless yield a cryptographic or allegorical justification. Since they are verbal, these justifications already figure, *ex hypothesi,* in the Library. I can not combine certain letters, as *dhcmrlchtdj,* which the divine Library has not already foreseen in combination, and which in one of its secret languages does not encompass some terrible meaning. No one can articulate a syllable which is not full of tenderness and fear, and which is not, in one of those languages, the powerful name of some god. To speak is to fall into tautologies. This useless and wordy epistle itself already exists in one of the thirty volumes of the five shelves in one of the uncountable hexagons — and so does its refutation. (An *n* number of possible languages makes use of the same vocabulary; in some of them, the symbol *library* admits of the correct definition *ubiquitous and everlasting system of hexagonal galleries,* but *library* is *bread* or *pyramid* or anything else, and the seven words which define it possess another value. You who read me, are you sure you understand my language?)

Methodical writing distracts me from the present condition of men. But the certainty that everything has been already written nullifies or makes phantoms of us all. I know of districts where the youth prostrate themselves before books and barbarously kiss the pages, though they do not know how to make out a single letter. Epidemics, heretical disagreements, the pilgrimages which inevitably degenerate into banditry, have decimated the population. I believe I have mentioned the suicides, more frequent each year. Perhaps I am deceived by old age and fear, but I suspect that the human species — the unique human species — is on the road to extinction, while the Library will last on forever: illuminated, solitary, infinite, perfectly immovable, filled with precious volumes, useless, incorruptible, secret.

Infinite I have just written. I have not interpolated this adjective *20* merely from rhetorical habit. It is not illogical, I say, to think that the world is infinite. Those who judge it to be limited, postulate that in remote places the corridors and stairs and hexagons could inconceivably cease — a manifest absurdity. Those who imagined it to be limitless forget that the possible number of books is limited. I dare insinuate the following solution to this ancient problem: *The Library is limitless and periodic.* If an eternal voyager were to traverse it in any direction, he would find, after many centuries, that the same volumes are repeated in the same disorder (which, repeated, would constitute an order: Order itself). My solitude rejoices in this elegant hope.*

Mar del Plata
1941

— *Translated by* ANTHONY KERRIGAN

FOR DISCUSSION AND WRITING

1. Here is the biblical account of the Tower of Babel. Explain how Borges's story relates to it.

> Now the whole world had one language and a common speech. As men moved eastward, they found a plain in Shinar and settled there.
> They said to each other, "Come, let's make bricks and bake them thoroughly." They used brick instead of stone, and tar instead of mortar. Then they said, "Come, let us build ourselves a city, with a tower that reaches to the heavens, so that we may make a name for ourselves and not be scattered over the face of the whole earth."
> But the Lord came down to see the city and the tower that the men were building. The Lord said, "If as one people speaking the same language they have begun to do this, then nothing they plan to do will be impossible for them. Come, let us go down and confuse their language so they will not understand each other."
> So the Lord scattered them from there over the all the earth, and they stopped building the city.
> —11 Genesis, New International Version

2. If we are in the Library of Babel and the library is infinite, what consequences might we suffer in regard to our search for understanding?

*Letizia Alvarez de Toledo has observed that the vast Library is useless. Strictly speaking, *one single volume* should suffice: a single volume of ordinary format, printed in nine or ten type body, and consisting of an infinite number of infinitely thin pages. (At the beginning of the seventeenth century, Cavalieri said that any solid body is the superposition of an infinite number of planes.) This silky vade mecum would scarcely be handy: each apparent leaf of the book would divide into other analogous leaves. The inconceivable central leaf would have no reverse.

3. Is there some order, some system, in the library? Explain. (For example, can there be order when possibilities are infinite?)

4. Give the literal meaning of the following allegorical passage (par. 15).

   > Other men, inversely, thought that the primary task was to eliminate useless works. They would invade the hexagons, exhibiting credentials which were not always false, skim through a volume with annoyance, and then condemn entire bookshelves to destruction: their ascetic, hygienic fury is responsible for the senseless loss of millions of books. Their name is execrated; but those who mourn the "treasures" destroyed by this frenzy, overlook two notorious facts. One: the Library is so enormous that any reduction undertaken by humans is infinitesimal. Two: each book is unique, irreplaceable, but (inasmuch as the Library is total) there are always several hundreds of thousands of imperfect fascimiles—of works that differ only by one letter or one comma.

5. What is "the total book" (par. 17)?

6. Borges warns, "You who read me, are you sure you understand my language?" (par. 18). In light of this warning, do you think Borges views readers as miners or detectives?

7. The light in the library is "insufficient, incessant" (par. 2). Allegorically, what does the light stand for?

8. Why are the library rooms hexagonal? (What other common structure is made up of hexagonal cells?)

9. Does Borges believe in God? Explain. Since he is forever confined to the Library, could he learn the ultimate truth about God?

10. What is Borges's opinion of most books? How do you know?

11. What are the "Vindications" in the following quote: "Thousands of covetous persons abandoned their dear natal hexagons and crowded up the stairs, urged on by the vain aim of finding their Vindication" (par. 9).

12. Did you find "The Library of Babel" interesting? Intriguing? Enjoyable? Uninteresting? Overly difficult? Obscure? Explain your answer.

2

Thinking Critically
about Narratives

Narratives are stories, either fictional (novels, folk tales, and epics) or factual (histories, biographies, autobiographies, and news reports). Writers use both factual and fictional narratives to explain, to argue, and to persuade. Understanding narrative, therefore, is important to critical reading.

NARRATIVE AS EXPLANATION

Writers often use narrative to explain complex ideas. Any history is a narrative, for example, but a history does not merely list events one after another; it tries to explain the past in terms of processes, causes, and effects.

Concepts as well as events can be explored and clarified by the use of narrative examples. For instance, the philosopher Robert Nozick uses narratives to help explain the concept of identity. Since a human being changes continuously from minute to minute, hour to hour, day to day, and year to year, Nozick wonders how it is logically possible for you to say that you are the same person now as you were ten years ago or on the day of your birth. To explore this problem, Nozick constructs several alternative stories, three of which follow. After reading each one, ask yourself whether individual identity has been maintained from one state of being to the other or whether one identity has been discontinued and an entirely new identity created. Note how the implications of the problem of identity become clearer as you read each story.

You are dying after a heart attack, and your healthy brain is transferred into another body, perhaps one cloned from yours and so very similar though healthier. After the operation, the "old body" expires and the new body-person continues on with all your previous plans, activities, and personal relationships. (38)

As you are dying, your brain patterns are transferred to another (blank) brain in another body, perhaps one cloned from yours. The patterns in the new brain are produced by some analogue process that simultaneously removes these patterns from the old one. . . . Upon completion of the transfer, the old body expires. (39)

Half of an ill person's brain is removed and transplanted into another body, but the original body plus half-brain does not expire when this is being done; it lingers on for one hour, or two days, or two weeks. Had this died immediately, the original person would survive in the new body, via the transplanted half-brain which carries with it psychological similarity and continuity. However, in the intervening hours or days or weeks, the old body lives on, perhaps unconscious or perhaps in full consciousness, alongside the new implanted body. (43)

NARRATIVE AS ARGUMENT

Narrative is useful not only as a means of explaining but also as an instrument for argumentation, the attempt to convince readers that the author's opinions are correct. A good example is an article from the *Washington Post National Weekly Edition*, in which Douglas B. Feaver argues that relying too heavily on technology causes disasters in the airline industry. To establish his point, he tells the stories of three recent crashes. Here is one of those stories. As you read it, consider why it does or does not provide effective backing for the argument.

On Aug. 16, 1987, Northwest Flight 255 started to taxi toward the runway at Detroit Metropolitan Wayne County Airport. The plane was a McDonnell Douglas MD80, one of the new generation of easy-to-fly, highly computerized jets that have turned the deregulated domestic airline business into the nation's bus company.

Twenty years ago a plane this size, with this power, capable of carrying this many passengers, would have needed a flight crew of at least three people to get in the air and stay there. Now it's a two-pilot crew looking at a computer-driven video display terminal. What you see is what you need. The takeoff warning horn—the thing that used to sound like a truck horn bellowing if you tried to take off without everything just so—has been supplanted by a machine that makes a much more pleasant noise suggesting it might be a good idea to check things out before proceeding and also telling you just exactly what to check. Flying is no longer mystical; flying is a learnable skill.

So we're bouncing along the taxiway going through the check-list, and because of weather or traffic or whatever, we get a change of runway and drop an item or two from the checklist. And pretty soon we're right where we're supposed to be, ready for takeoff, and we get a clearance, and we start the takeoff roll. And we roll and roll. And we reach the speed where the computer tells us it's time to lift the nose wheel off the ground; we pull back on the stick, and the nosewheel comes up, but the damn plane won't fly because there aren't any flaps extended on the wings because we missed that part during the checklist and the warning horn didn't go off because somebody pulled the switch.

A little child lives while 154 people die, and it's awful and every-body wonders how such a thing could happen.

"The National Transportation Safety Board determines that the probable cause of the accident was the flight crew's failure to use the taxi checklist to ensure that the flaps . . . were extended for takeoff. Contributing to the accident was the absence of electrical power to the airplane takeoff warning system which thus did not warn . . . ."

How could the pilot be that stupid?

We've all been that stupid. We trust our technology too much. It's an outrage. (23)

NARRATIVE AS PERSUASION

Narrative can also be a useful tool in persuading readers. Though it is impossible to make a sharp distinction, the purpose of argument is to convince your reader that your viewpoint or opinion is correct; the purpose of persuasion is to cause your reader to act. Thus, through argument you might convince your reader that Jones is the best candidate for a political office without persuading the reader to take the trouble to go out and vote for Jones. Many people are convinced that a high-fat diet is unhealthy, yet they have not been persuaded to change their eating habits. On the other hand, millions of people know that there is little difference among certain products, such as brands of toothpaste, yet they can be persuaded by advertising to purchase a given brand.

As you know, the most common purpose of advertisements is per-suasion, as in the case of the ad reproduced on page 113. In spite of its apparent childishness, this advertisement is a complex attempt to make readers act: although the intended audience is adults, the ad conveys its message ironically by telling a story in a way that might appeal to a child.

Exercise: Narrative as Persuasion

1. *Specifically, what action does the Lands' End ad persuade readers to take?*

2. *In your opinion, what are the advantages of using the story "Tim Falls in Love" to persuade readers? What are the disadvantages?*

3. *To persuade a person to take action, the writer must give reasons. What reasons for action does the advertisement give readers?*

4. *Do you think that the advertisement purposely relates itself to the "Peanuts" strip? Explain. What advantages does such a relationship confer?*

CRITICAL QUESTIONS ABOUT NARRATIVES

To read narratives critically, you need to ask a number of questions and also think about the relationships between them: What happened (the act)? Who or what performed the action (the agent)? In what setting or circumstances (the scene)? By what means (the agency)? And with what motive or intention (the purpose)?

Act: What Happened?

A classic example of a narrative in which we want to learn all we can about an act is the murder mystery. We want to know what happened, but we want to know more. "Whodunit?" we ask ourselves. And we are not satisfied merely to find the murderer; we also want to know the motive, or purpose — why the murderer committed the crime. The scene of the crime and the means (gun, knife, poison, overdose of sleeping pills) are also critical: the death of a handsome playboy in the bedroom of his mansion by an overdose of sleeping pills is a story radically different from the machine-gun killing of a gangster in a sleazy nightclub. In other words, when we try to understand the events in a story we think about the kinds of people involved, the scene, the purposes or motives, and the means used to carry out the acts.

Exercise: Questions about Narratives

Survey the stories for one day in your local newspaper or in a national newspaper such as the New York Times. *As you examine each story, consider what it emphasizes. Do any stories simply chronicle an event without analyzing it? Do some focus on the reasons for acts or events? Do others emphasize the people involved? Are some stories especially interesting because of the time or place in which the action occurred? Be prepared to suggest the possible reasons for each writer's choice of focus and to discuss what you have learned about narratives from this investigation.*

Agent: Who Performed the Action?

The people who perform the acts in a narrative are the characters, or agents. To try to determine what sort of person the agent is, critical readers pay careful attention to what the text reveals about the agent's beliefs, values, educational and cultural background, family ties, and so on. Understanding the agent often is crucial to the reader's overall understanding of the text: only after determining the answers to questions about the people involved is the critical reader able to draw reliable conclusions about the events themselves.

For example, is Hamlet indecisive, or is his slowness to take action the result of cunning? Was General Grant a drunkard, or is his legendary consumption of alcohol a myth? Is Lady Macbeth completely evil, or is she a tormented soul? Was Mary Todd Lincoln a cold, domineering woman, or is her portrayal in popular history as such a person a distortion of the real woman?

Exercise: Agent

In The Pine Barrens, *John McPhee writes about a sparsely populated, primitive area located, surprisingly, almost within sight of New York City and equidistant from Richmond, Virginia, and Boston, Massachusetts. One of the inhabitants of the Pine Barrens is Fred Brown. As you read the selection, think about the following questions.*

1. Before McPhee introduces the character, he sets the scene. In what ways does this scene help us to understand Fred Brown?

2. What would be the effect if the specific details were removed from the passage? For instance, McPhee writes, "I walked through a vestibule that had a dirt floor, stepped up into a kitchen, and went on into another room that had several overstuffed chairs in it and a porcelain-topped table, where Fred Brown was seated, eating a pork chop." Here is that same passage with the specific details removed: "I walked through a vestibule, stepped up into a kitchen, and went on into another room that had several chairs in it and a table, where Fred Brown was seated, eating."

3. What sort of person is Fred Brown? For instance, what social class does he apparently belong to? Which details help you begin to understand him?

> Fred Brown's house is on the unpaved road that curves along the edge of a wide cranberry bog. What attracted me to it was the pump that stands in his yard. It was something of a wonder that I noticed the pump, because there were, among other things, eight automobiles in the yard, two of them on their sides and one of them upside down, all ten years old or older. Around the cars were old refrigerators, vacuum cleaners, partly dismantled radios, cathode-ray tubes, a short wooden ski, a large wooden mallet, dozens of cranberry pickers' boxes, many tires, an orange crate dated 1946, a cord or so of firewood, mandolins, engine heads, and maybe a thousand other things. The house itself, two stories high, was covered with tarpaper that was peeling away in some places, revealing its original shingles, made of Atlantic white cedar from the stream courses of the surrounding forest. I called out to ask if anyone was home, and a voice called back, "Come in. Come in. Come on the hell in."
>
> I walked through a vestibule that had a dirt floor, stepped up into a kitchen, and went on into another room that had several overstuffed chairs

in it and a porcelain-topped table, where Fred Brown was seated, eating a pork chop. He was dressed in a white sleeveless shirt, ankle-top shoes, and undershorts. He gave me a cheerful greeting and, without asking why I had come or what I wanted, picked up a pair of khaki trousers that had been tossed onto one of the overstuffed chairs and asked me to sit down. He set the trousers on another chair, and he apologized for being in the middle of his breakfast, explaining that he seldom drank much but the night before he had had a few drinks and this had caused his day to start slowly. "I don't know what's the matter with me, but there's got to be something the matter with me, because drink don't agree with me anymore," he said. He had a raw onion in one hand, and while he talked he shaved slices from the onion and ate them between bites of the chop. He was a muscular and well-built man, with short, bristly white hair, and he had bright, fast-moving eyes in a wide-open face. His legs were trim and strong, with large muscles in the calves. I guessed that he was about sixty, and for a man of sixty he seemed to be in remarkably good shape. He was actually seventy-nine. "My rule is: Never eat except when you're hungry," he said, and he ate another slice of the onion. (83–84)

Scene: Where and When Did the Action Occur?

Scene includes both "when" and "where," the time and the place of the action. The scene at the beginning of *Macbeth* is a blasted heath, where three witches perform their unholy rites. The *Star Trek* episodes are set at an indefinite time in the future, somewhere in space. The typical American Western on film or television takes place toward the end of the nineteenth century, somewhere west of the Mississippi.

Scene can be metaphorical or symbolic as well as literal. For instance, we can say that we live during the Atomic Age in the Land of Opportunity, and are thankful that the Founding Fathers of our nation were products of the Age of Reason. Franklin Roosevelt initiated the era of the New Deal, and Harry Truman's years in the White House were the period of the Fair Deal.

Scene is a key element in any narrative. In a fictional work, the author very carefully sets the scene to create a certain mood or to hint at actions to come. And no biographer or historian would overlook the influence of scene—the time and the place—on the characters or events that he or she is attempting to understand.

Exercise: Scene

Here is the scene that Truman Capote sets in In Cold Blood, *his account of a particularly senseless and grisly murder of a Kansas family by two ex-convict drifters. As you read this vivid descriptive prose, think about the following questions.*

1. Capote gives us both a panoramic and a close-up view of the scene. Why does he give us two perspectives?

2. What does Capote do to characterize the people who inhabit the scene?

3. *What use does Capote make of details of sound?*

The village of Holcomb stands on the high wheat plains of western Kansas, a lonesome area that other Kansans call "out there." Some seventy miles east of the Colorado border, the countryside, with its hard blue skies and desert-clear air, has an atmosphere that is rather more Far West than Middle West. The local accent is barbed with a prairie twang, a ranch-hand nasalness, and the men, many of them, wear narrow frontier trousers, Stetsons, and high-heeled boots with pointed toes. The land is flat, and the views are awesomely extensive; horses, herds of cattle, a white cluster of grain elevators rising as gracefully as Greek temples are visible long before a traveler reaches them.

Holcomb, too, can be seen from great distances. Not that there is much to see — simply an aimless congregation of buildings divided in the center by the main-line tracks of the Santa Fe Railroad, a haphazard hamlet bounded on the south by a brown stretch of the Arkansas (pronounced "Ar-kan-sas") River, on the north by a highway, Route 50, and on the east and west by prairie lands and wheat fields. After rain, or when snowfalls thaw, the streets, unnamed, unshaded, unpaved, turn from the thickest dust into the direst mud. At one end of town stands a stark old stucco structure, the roof of which supports an electric sign — Dance — but the dancing has ceased and the advertisement has been dark for several years. . . .

Until one morning in mid-November of 1959, few Americans — in fact, few Kansans — had ever heard of Holcomb. . . . But then, in the earliest hours of that morning in November, a Sunday morning, certain foreign sounds impinged on the normal nightly Holcomb noises — on the keening hysteria of coyotes, the dry scrape of tumbleweed, the racing, receding wail of locomotive whistles. At the time not a soul in Holcomb heard them — four shotgun blasts that, all told, ended six human lives. (3–5)

Agency: What Means Were Used to Perform the Act?

The agency is the means through which or by which the act is performed. In a mystery story, the murder weapon is the agency. For a financier, money is the agency. Sherlock Holmes's agency is logic, which he employs to solve the most baffling crimes. An agency can even be a person: when Character A uses Character B without B's realization that he is being used, B is the agency.

Anyone who has read a murder mystery knows how important it is to find out what agency was used. Agency is just as important — though not as obviously — in other types of narrative as well. To understand American history, for example, a critical reader must be aware of the impact of such agencies as the Declaration of Independence, the six-shooter, the railroad, television, and the jet airplane.

Exercise: Agency

1. *Give an example of a story — factual or fictional — in which money is the most important agency.*

2. Has anyone ever "used" you? That is, has anyone ever treated you as if you were an agency, not an agent? Explain.

3. In what sense is a computer language or mathematics an agency? Explain how ordinary language can be viewed as an agency.

Purpose: What Was the Motive for the Act?

In trying to understand narratives, we ask what the agents (that is, characters) intend by their acts. What do they want their acts to accomplish? Why did they do what they did? Only a reader who understands the purposes of the acts in a narrative can make valid critical judgments.

For example, the difference between manslaughter and murder depends on the purpose or motive of the person who commits the crime. Manslaughter is the killing of a human being, but without malice; murder is the crime of killing with, as the law puts it, "malice aforethought." Thus, manslaughter can result from negligence (as when a drunk driver causes a fatal accident), but murder cannot; the act of murder always involves a malicious purpose. Thus, juries must determine the motive before they can decide whether a homicide is manslaughter or murder.

Our assessment of candidates' motives influences the way we vote; our judgment of authors' motives determines the credibility of the text for us as readers. If we do not understand a speaker's motives, we cannot grasp the full meaning of what he or she is saying. For example, if someone says to you, "Boy, do you look great today!" you don't know whether the statement is a compliment or an insult until you determine the speaker's motives, for the intention could be sarcastic, in which case the sentence would mean something like, "Boy, do you look terrible today!"

Exercise: Purpose

In the great American classic Walden, *Henry David Thoreau directly explains his purpose for going to live alone by Walden Pond. What is that purpose? How would you paraphrase Thoreau's explanation?*

I went to the woods because I wished to live deliberately, to front only the essential facts of life, and see if I could not learn what it had to teach, and not, when I came to die, discover that I had not lived. I did not wish to live what was not life, living is so dear; nor did I wish to practise resignation, unless it was quite necessary. I wanted to live deep and suck out all the marrow of life, to live so sturdily and spartan-like as to put to rout all that was not life, to cut a broad swath and shave close, to drive life into a corner, and reduce it to its lowest terms, and, if it proved to be mean, why then to get the whole and genuine meanness of it, and publish its meanness to the world; or if it were sublime, to know it by experience, and be able to give a true account of it in my next excursion. For most men, it appears to me, are in a strange uncertainty about it, whether it is of the devil or of God, and have somewhat hastily concluded that it is the chief end of man here to "glorify God and enjoy him forever."

RELATING THE QUESTIONS TO ONE ANOTHER

Here, from the *New Columbia Encyclopedia,* is a brief account of one of the most grisly events in American history:

> *Donner Party,* group of emigrants to California who in the winter of 1846–47 met with one of the most famous tragedies in Western history. The California-bound families were mostly from Illinois and Iowa, and most prominent among them were the two Donner families and the Reed family. In going West they took a little-used route after leaving Fort Bridger and were delayed. They suffered severely in crossing the salt flats W of Great Salt Lake, and dissensions and ill feelings in the party arose when they reached what is today Donner Lake in the Sierra Nevada. They paused (Oct., 1846) to recover their strength, and early snow caught them, falling deep in the passes and trapping them. Their limited food gave out, the cold continued, and the suffering of the group, camped on Alder Creek and Donner Lake, grew intense. A party that attempted to make its way through the snow-choked passes in December suffered horribly.
>
> The surviving members of the Donner Party were driven to cannibalism. Finally, expeditions from the Sacramento Valley made their way through the snowdrifts to rescue the hunger-maddened migrants. Only about half of the original party of 87 reached California. The survivors later disagreed violently as to the details of (and particularly the blame for) the disaster. (783–84)

If you decided to write a full-scale history of the Donner Party, you might take what happened — the *act,* from the beginning of the trek to its conclusion — as the center or pivot of your concern. You would want, of course, to understand the act in terms of the *scene:* time and place. You would be interested not only in the topography of the Great Salt Lake desert, the Sierra Nevada Mountains, and the area around Donner Lake, but also in the larger scene: the United States of America during the period of westward migration. What was it about the American scene (economics, politics, philosophies) that motivated such expeditions as the one undertaken by the Donner Party? In other words, you would be viewing the act in terms of the scene in which it took place.

You would also find out all you could about the people *(agents)* and their motives *(purposes).* Who were they? Why did they do what they did? Furthermore, you would pay careful attention to means *(agencies).* What sort of equipment did the party have? What about its provisions? In a broader sense, did some person or group of people finance the expedition?

In other words, to write the history of the Donner Party you would put the act itself (the bare chronicle of events) in the context of its scene, the people involved, their motives, and the means they used to carry out the act.

You might choose any of the five questions as your starting point or pivot. For example, your interest might focus on the people (agents) and you would explain them in terms of what they did (acts), the scenes in which the acts took place, their purposes, and their means (agencies). That, of course, is exactly what the biographer does. The historian, by contrast, focuses primarily on acts rather than on agents. The writer's intent thus determines which narrative element he or she chooses as the text's focal point.

Exercise: Applying the Questions

"Barbara Allan," which appears below, is an anonymous Scottish ballad (a ballad is a kind of poem that tells a story). The story of Barbara and her lover, however, is puzzling.

Using act *as the key term, develop a theory about unexplained events in the story. What actually happened? What were the causes or motives? The questions following the ballad may help you develop your theory.*

It was in and about the Martinmas time,
    When the green leaves were a-falling,
That Sir John Graeme, in the West Country,
    Fell in love with Barbara Allan.

He sent his men down through the town
    To the place where she was dwelling:
"O haste and come to my master dear,
    If ye be Barbara Allan."

O slowly, slowly rose she up,
    To the place where he was lying,
And when she drew the curtain by,
    "Young man, I think you're dying."

"O it's I'm sick, and very sick,
    And 'tis all for Barbara Allan."
"O the better for me you'll never be
    Though your heart's blood were a-spilling.

"O dinna ye mind, young man," said she,
    "When ye was in the tavern a-drinking,
That ye made the healths go round and round,
    And slighted Barbara Allan?"

And slowly, slowly rose she up,
    And slowly, slowly left him,
And sighing said, she could not stay,
    Since death of life had reft him.

She had not gone a mile but two
  When she heard the dead-bell ringing,
And every stroke the dead-bell gave
  It cried, Woe to Barbara Allan!

"O Mother, Mother, make my bed!
  O make it soft and narrow!
Since my love died for me today,
  I'll die for him tomorrow."

1. *Questions concerning* act *(what happened): Outline the story, the events in their chronological sequence. Are there any aspects of the story that are not stated directly, forcing you to guess what happened? Explain.*

2. *Questions concerning* agents *(the characters in the story): What sort of people do Sir John Graeme and Barbara Allan seem to be? What evidence do you have for your characterization? Does your characterization of the agents help you reconstruct that act? Explain.*

3. *Questions concerning* agency *(the means used to accomplish the act): What did Sir John Graeme die of? What did Barbara Allan die of? (A broken heart? Smallpox?)*

4. *Questions concerning* scene *(the time and place of the act): In what geographical location did the act take place? At what time in history did the act take place? (The Classical age before the Christian era? The Middle Ages? The twentieth century?) What is Martinmas time? Does it have any symbolic significance?*

5. *Questions concerning* purpose *(why the acts took place, motivation): Does what you know about the agents help you to understand the purpose? Does scene help you understand the purpose? Can you be really sure about the purpose, or will your conclusions always be tentative and speculative? Explain.*

REVIEW

In your own words, explain the following concepts:

narrative
act
agent
scene
agency
purpose
relating the questions to one another

SUGGESTIONS FOR WRITING

1. *Explain* something, using a story as the basis for the explanation (for example, how you learned to do something; why you believe something to be true; how you discovered the pleasure of a certain activity).

2. *Argue* in favor of an opinion, using a story as the basis for the argument.

3. *Persuade* a well-defined audience (for example, your classmates, the members of your family, the student body of your college) to take some action that you think will improve the condition of the group. Use a story as the basis for your persuasive essay.

THE INTERIOR LIFE

Annie Dillard

Annie Dillard's book *Pilgrim at Tinker Creek* has often been compared with Henry David Thoreau's *Walden*. Both provide meditations on the meaning of nature based on the authors' solitary existence in the wilds. Dillard, however, offers a modern outlook by recording the daily horrors that occur in the natural world. She details the predatory and parasitic existences of much of the life around Tinker Creek, so much so that morbid curiosity often overcomes the natural joy that is also expressed. *Pilgrim at Tinker Creek* was awarded a Pulitzer Prize for general nonfiction in 1974.

In addition to writing, Dillard has taught creative writing at Western Washington State University, Wesleyan University, and elsewhere, and has been a contributing editor to *Harper's* since 1973. She has published a book of poetry, *Tickets for a Prayer Wheel,* and an autobiography, *An American Childhood,* from which the following selection is taken.

Like all good stories, this one uses significant details to convey to the reader the texture of the writer's life. From this sketch, you can learn how to use detail in your own writing.

The interior life is often stupid. Its egoism blinds it and deafens it; its imagination spins out ignorant tales, fascinated. It fancies that the western wind blows on the Self, and leaves fall at the feet of the Self for a reason, and people are watching. A mind risks real ignorance for the sometimes paltry prize of an imagination enriched. The trick of reason is to get the imagination to seize the actual world—if only from time to time.

When I was five, growing up in Pittsburgh in 1950, I would not go to bed willingly because something came into my room. This was a private matter between me and it. If I spoke of it, it would kill me.

Who could breathe as this thing searched for me over the very corners of the room? Who could ever breathe freely again? I lay in the dark.

My sister Amy, two years old, was asleep in the other bed. What did she know? She was innocent of evil. Even at two she composed herself attractively for sleep. She folded the top sheet tidily under her prettily outstretched arm; she laid her perfect head lightly on an unwrinkled pillow, where her thick curls spread evenly in rays like petals. All night long she slept smoothly in a series of pleasant and serene, if artificial-looking, positions, a faint smile on her closed lips, as if she were posing for an ad for sheets. There was no messiness in her, no roughness for things to cling to, only a charming and charmed innocence that seemed then to protect her, an innocence I needed but couldn't muster. Since Amy was asleep, furthermore, and since when I needed someone most I was afraid to stir enough to wake her, she was useless.

I lay alone and was almost asleep when the damned thing entered   *5*
the room by flattening itself against the open door and sliding in. It was
a transparent, luminous oblong. I could see the door whiten at its touch;
I could see the blue wall turn pale where it raced over it, and see the
maple headboard of Amy's bed glow. It was a swift spirit; it was an
awareness. It made noise. It had two joined parts, a head and a tail, like
a Chinese dragon. It found the door, wall, and headboard; and it swiped
them, charging them with its luminous glance. After its fleet, searching
passage, things looked the same, but weren't.

I dared not blink or breathe; I tried to hush my whooping blood.
If it found another awareness, it would destroy it.

Every night before it got to me it gave up. It hit my wall's corner
and couldn't get past. It shrank completely into itself and vanished like a
cobra down a hole. I heard the rising roar it made when it died or left. I
still couldn't breathe. I knew — it was the worst fact I knew, a very hard
fact — that it could return again alive that same night.

Sometimes it came back, sometimes it didn't. Most often, restless,
it came back. The light stripe slipped in the door, ran searching over
Amy's wall, stopped, stretched lunatic at the first corner, raced wailing
toward my wall, and vanished into the second corner with a cry. So I
wouldn't go to bed.

It was a passing car whose windshield reflected the corner street-
light outside. I figured it out one night.

Figuring it out was as memorable as the oblong itself. Figuring it   *10*
out was a long and forced ascent to the very rim of being, to the membrane of skin that both separates and connects the inner life and the outer
world. I climbed deliberately from the depths like a diver who releases
the monster in his arms and hauls himself hand over hand up an anchor
chain till he meets the ocean's sparkling membrane and bursts through
it; he sights the sunlit, becalmed hull of his boat, which had bulked so
ominously from below.

I recognized the noise it made when it left. That is, the noise it
made called to mind, at last, my daytime sensations when a car passed —
the sight and noise together. A car came roaring down hushed Edgerton
Avenue in front of our house, stopped at the corner stop sign, and passed
on shrieking as its engine shifted up the gears. What, precisely, came into
the bedroom? A reflection from the car's oblong windshield. Why did it
travel in two parts? The window sash split the light and cast a shadow.

Night after night I labored up the same long chain of reasoning, as
night after night the thing burst into the room where I lay awake and
Amy slept prettily and my loud heart thrashed and I froze.

There was a world outside my window and contiguous to it. If I
was so all-fired bright, as my parents, who had patently no basis for
comparison, seemed to think, why did I have to keep learning this same
thing over and over? For I had learned it a summer ago, when men with

jackhammers broke up Edgerton Avenue. I had watched them from the yard; the street came up in jagged slabs like floes. When I lay to nap, I listened. One restless afternoon I connected the new noise in my bedroom with the jackhammer men I had been seeing outside. I understood abruptly that these worlds met, the outside and the inside. I traveled the route in my mind: You walked downstairs from here, and outside from downstairs. "Outside," then, was conceivably just beyond my windows. It was the same world I reached by going out the front or the back door. I forced my imagination yet again over this route.

The world did not have me in mind; it had no mind. It was a coincidental collection of things and people, of items, and I myself was one such item — a child walking up the sidewalk, whom anyone could see or ignore. The things in the world did not necessarily cause my overwhelming feelings; the feelings were inside me, beneath my skin, behind my ribs, within my skull. They were even, to some extent, under my control.

I could be connected to the outer world by reason, if I chose, or I could yield to what amounted to a narrative fiction, to a tale of terror whispered to me by the blood in my ears, a show in light projected on the room's blue walls. As time passed, I learned to amuse myself in bed in the darkened room by entering the fiction deliberately and replacing it by reason deliberately.   15

When the low-roar drew nigh and the oblong slid in the door, I threw my own switches for pleasure. It's coming after me; it's a car outside. It's after me. It's a car. It raced over the wall, lighting it blue wherever it ran; it bumped over Amy's maple headboard in a rush, paused, slithered elongate over the corner, shrank, flew my way, and vanished into itself with a wail. It was a car.

FOR DISCUSSION AND WRITING

1. Explain why agent could be considered the most important element in this selection.

2. What does the scene in this autobiographical sketch tell us about the agent (Annie Dillard)? Which aspects of the scene are most important? Why?

3. What do the agent's acts tell us about her?

4. Is the purpose of the narrative to explain, to argue, to persuade, or something else? How do you know?

5. As a reader, do you need any specialized background information to understand the selection? Explain.

6. In your own words, state the main point of the selection.

7. Why doesn't the author immediately explain what the apparition was?

8. Explain what Dillard means when she says that "the trick of reason is to get the imagination to seize the actual world" (par. 1). Explain how the following metaphors help clarify the statement: (a) "a long and forced ascent to the very rim of being, to the membrane of skin that both separates and connects the inner life and the outer world" (par. 10); (b) "like a diver who releases the monster in his arms and hauls himself hand over hand up an anchor chain till he meets the ocean's sparkling membrane and bursts through it" (par. 10); (c) "'Outside,' then, was conceivably just beyond my windows" (par. 13).

9. Dillard says, "A mind risks real ignorance for the sometimes paltry prize of an imagination enriched" (par. 1). Explain her view of the relationship between imagination and reason. (Think about the last two paragraphs of the selection.)

10. Dillard contrasts her tormented nights of apparitions with the untroubled sleep of her younger sister. What was her attitude then? What do you think it would be now?

11. This and the next two selections, Frank Conroy's "White Days and Red Nights" and Katherine Anne Porter's "St. Augustine and the Bullfight," are autobiographical. The two selections that follow — from Scott Berg's *Goldwyn* and Elizabeth Salter's *Daisy Bates* — are biographical. As sources for reliable information — facts — about a person's life, what are the advantages and disadvantages of autobiography over biography and of biography over autobiography?

WHITE DAYS AND RED NIGHTS

Frank Conroy

When *Stop-Time,* Frank Conroy's autobiography, was published, the *New York Times* hailed it as a triumph; the novelist William Styron said that "*Stop-Time* is in every way a distinguished book"; and a review in the magazine *Commentary* predicted that the book "will be lasting and significant." The selection that follows is one of the most memorable chapters from that autobiography.

Born in 1936, Conroy graduated from Haverford College in 1958 and has taught at the University of Iowa, George Mason University, the Massachusetts Institute of Technology, and Brandeis University. In 1981 he was appointed director of the literature program at the National Endowment for the Arts. His collection of short stories, *Midair,* was published in 1985.

You will undoubtedly find this autobiographical narrative both fascinating and disturbing. As you read, pay attention to the way Conroy uses both detail and direct authorial commentary to create the effect of this extraordinary piece of writing.

Jean and my mother had weekend jobs as wardens at the Southbury Training School, a Connecticut state institution for the feeble-minded. Every Friday afternoon we drove out deep in the hills to an old cabin they had bought for a few hundred dollars on the installment plan.

The first dirt road was always plowed for the milk truck, but never the second, and in the snow you could see the tracks of wagon wheels and two narrow trails where the horses had walked. A mile down the road was the Green's farm. Every morning they hauled milk to the pick-up station, a full silent load up to the hill, and then back, the empty returns from the previous day clanging raucously behind the horses as if in melancholic celebration. No one else ever used the road. If it was passable we drove to the cabin, if not, we walked, single file, in the horses' tracks, our arms full of food.

Every Friday the cheap padlock was opened, every Friday I stepped inside. A room so dim my blood turned gray, so cold I knew no human heart had ever beaten there—every line, every article of furniture, every scrap of paper on the floor, every burned-out match in a saucer filling me with desolation, depopulating me. A single room, twelve feet by eighteen. A double bed, a bureau, a round table to eat on, and against the wall a counter with a kerosene cooker. In the exact center of the room, a potbellied coal stove. All these objects had been watched by me in a state of advanced terror, watched so many long nights that even in the daytime they seemed to be whispering bad messages.

My mother would make a quick meal out of cans. Corned-beef hash or chili. Conversation was usually sparse.

"I have a good cottage tonight."

5

"I can't remember where I am. We'd better stop at the administration building."

Outside, the lead-gray afternoon slipped almost imperceptibly into twilight. Very gradually the earth moved toward night and as I sat eating I noted every darkening shadow. Jean sipped his coffee and lighted a Pall Mall. My mother arranged the kerosene lamp so she could see to do the dishes.

"Frank, get me some water."

Through the door and into the twilight, the bucket against my thigh. There was a path beaten through the snow, a dark line curving through the drifts to the well. The low sky was empty, uniformly leaden. Strands of trees spread pools of darkness, as if night came up from their sunken roots. At the well I tied a rope to the handle of the bucket and dropped it into the darkness upside down, holding the line. The trick was not to hit the sides. I heard a muffled splash. Leaning over the deep hole, with the faintest hint of warmer air rising against my face, I hauled the bucket hand over hand until it rose suddenly into view, the dim sky shimmering within like some luminous oil. Back to the house with the water. Absolute silence except for the sounds of my own movement, absolute stillness except for a wavering line of smoke from the stovepipe.

While Mother did the dishes Jean and I sat at the table. He sipped   10
at his second cup of coffee. I fished a dime out of my pocket. "Could you get me a couple of Baby Ruth bars?"

Jean sucked his teeth and reached for a wooden pick. "The stuff is poison. It rots your teeth."

"Oh Jean, I know. It won't take you a second. There's a stand in the administration building."

"You're so finicky about food and you go and eat that stuff. Can you imagine the crap in those mass-produced candy bars? Dead roaches and mouse shit and somebody's nose-pickings."

"Jean, for heaven's sake!" My mother laughed.

"Well, he won't touch a piece of perfectly good meat and then he'll   15
eat that junk."

"It'll only take you a second." I pushed the dime across the table.

"I know the trouble with you. You're too lazy to chew your food. You wash everything down with milk." He glanced at the coin, his eyes flicking away. "All right. If you want to kill yourself. Keep the dime." He finished his coffee and cigarette slowly, savoring the mixed flavors and the moment of rest. Since he'd stopped using the holder his smoking style had changed. He'd take a quick drag, blow out about a third of the smoke immediately, inhale the rest, and let it come out as he talked. I often made it a point to sit in such a way that a strong light source behind him showed up the smoke. It was amazing how long it came out, a fine, almost invisible blue stream, phrase after phrase, changing direction smoothly as he clipped off the words. For some reason I admired this phenomenon tremendously. I could sit watching for hours.

Jean pushed back his chair and stood up, stretching his arms and yawning exaggeratedly. Even this he did gracefully. Like a cat, he was incapable of making an awkward move. Looking out the window he sucked his teeth noisily. "Well," he said slowly, "the lions and tigers seem to be under control tonight."

I felt my face flush and quickly turned away. It was a complicated moment. My fear of staying alone in the house had been totally ignored for weeks. For Jean to mention it at all was somehow promising, and I was grateful despite the unfairness of his phrasing. He knew of course that it wasn't lions and tigers I was afraid of—by using that image he was attempting to simplify my fear into the realm of childishness (which he could then ignore in good conscience) as well as to shame me out of it. Jean was telling me, with a smile, that my behavior was irrational and therefore he could do nothing to help me, something I would never have expected in any case. I knew perfectly well that no one could help me. The only possible solution would have been for me to stay in the city on weekends with Alison, but that battle had been lost. Jean and Mother wanted me with them. Not because they felt they had to look after me but because I was useful. I drew the water. I tended the fire so the house would be warm in the morning when they returned.

"We'd better go," Mother said, lifting the last dripping dish from the plastic basin. "Frank, you dry the dishes and put them away." 20

I watched their preparations with a sense of remoteness. It was as if they were already gone. Mother dried her hands carefully and put on her heavy coat. Jean bent over the row of paperback books and pulled out an Erskine Caldwell. "I won't be able to read tonight but I'll take it anyway."

"All right?" Mother asked. They stood for a last moment, waiting, making sure they hadn't forgotten anything, sensing in each other the precise moment to leave. Then they were through the door and away. I followed a few moments later, stepping in their footprints to the road. I watched them walk into the darkness underneath the trees. My mother turned at the top of a rise and called back to me over the snow. "Don't forget to set the alarm!" She hurried to catch up with Jean. As they moved down the hill it was as if they sank deeper and deeper into the snow. Dimly I could make out the top halves of their bodies, then only their shoulders, their heads, and they were gone.

I went back to the house. After an initial surge of panic my mind turned itself off. Thinking was dangerous. By not thinking I attained a kind of inner invisibility. I knew that fear attracted evil, that the uncontrolled sound of my own mind would in some way delineate me to the forces threatening me, as the thrashing of a fish in shallow water draws the gull. I tried to keep still, but every now and then the fear escalated up into consciousness and my mind would stir, readjusting itself like the body of a man trying to sleep in an uncomfortable position. In those moments I felt most vulnerable, my eyes widening and my ears straining to catch the sound of approaching danger.

I dried the dishes slowly and put them away, attempting to do the whole job without making a sound. Occasionally a floorboard creaked under my weight, sending a long, lingering charge up my spine, a white thrill at once delicious and ominous. I approached the stove nervously. The coal rattled and the cast-iron grate invariably banged loudly despite my precautions. I had to do it quickly, holding my breath, or I wouldn't do it at all. Once finished I checked the window latches. There was nothing to be done about the door; it couldn't be locked from the inside and mother refused to lock it from the outside because of the danger of my getting trapped in a fire.

By the yellow light of the kerosene lamp I sat on the edge of the 25 bed and removed my shoes, placing them carefully on the floor. The Big Ben alarm clock ticked off the seconds on a shelf above my head, and every now and then a puff of coal gas popped in the stove as the fuel shifted. I got under the covers fully clothed and surveyed the stillness of the room, trying to slow my breathing. For an hour or more I lay motionless in a self-induced trance, my eyes open but seldom moving, my ears listening to the sounds of the house and the faint, inexplicable, continuous noises from outside. (In this state my ears seemed rather far away. I was burrowed somewhere deep in my skull, my ears advance outposts sending back reports to headquarters.) As I remember it the trance must have been close to the real thing. It was an attempt to reach an equipoise of fear, a state in which the incoming fear signals balanced with some internal process of dissimulation. At best it worked only temporarily, since fear held a slight edge. But for an hour or two I avoided what I hated most, the great noisy swings up and down. The panic and the hilarity.

At the first flashing thought of the Southbury Training School I sat up and took a book from the shelf. Escaped inmates were rare, and supposedly harmless, but I knew that a runaway had ripped the teats from one of the Greens' cows with a penknife, and that another had strangled four cats in a barnyard. I read quickly, skimming the pages for action and dialogue while most of my mind stood on guard. Book after book came down from the shelf, piling up on the bed beside me as I waited for sleep. I knew that if I left the lamp on I would stay awake most of the night, so when the pages began to go out of focus I set the alarm clock, cupped my hand over the mouth of the lamp chimney and blew myself into darkness.

Being sleepy and being scared do not cancel each other out. After hours of waiting the mind insists and slips under itself into unconsciousness. The sleeping body remains tense, the limbs bent as if poised for flight, adrenalin oozing steadily into the blood. Every few minutes the mind awakens, listens, and goes back to sleep. Fantastic dreams attempt to absorb the terror, explaining away the inexplicable with lunatic logic, twisting thought to a mad, private vision so that sleep can go on for another few seconds.

I wake up in the dark, a giant hand squeezing my heart. All around me a tremendous noise is splitting the air, exploding like a continuous chain of fireworks. The alarm clock! My God, the clock! Ringing all this time, calling, calling, bringing everything evil. I reach out and shut it off. The vibrations die out under my fingers and I listen to the silence, wondering if anything has approached under the cover of the ringing bell. (Remember a children's game called Giant Steps?)

I sit up cautiously. My body freezes. Rising before me over the foot of the bed is a bright, glowing, cherry-red circle in the darkness, a floating globe pulsating with energy, wavering in the air like the incandescent heart of some dissected monster, dripping sparks and blood. I throw myself backward against the wall behind the bed. Books tumble around me from the shelves, an ashtray falls and smashes on the floor. My hands go out, palms extended, towards the floating apparition, my voice whispering "Please . . ." Impossibly a voice answers, a big voice from all around me. "FRANK! FRANK!" My knees give out and I fall off the bed to the floor. I can feel the pieces of broken ashtray under my hands.

From the corner of my eye I see the red circle. I keep quite still, and the circle doesn't move. If I turn my head I seem to sense a corresponding movement, but I can't be sure. In the blackness there is nothing to relate to. Step by step I begin to understand. My body grows calmer and it's as if a series of veils were being whisked away from my eyes. I see clearly that the circle is only the red-hot bottom of the stove—a glowing bowl, its surface rippling with color changes from draughts of cool air. The last veil lifts and reveals an image of magic beauty, a sudden miracle in the night. I fall asleep watching it, my shoulder against the bed.

Hours later the cold wakes me and I climb up under the covers. When dawn comes my limbs relax. I can tell when dawn has come even though I'm asleep.

I woke up when the wagon went by, creaking like a ship, passing close, just on the other side of the wall by my head. Chip would be driving, I knew, with Toad in back watching the cans. They never spoke as they went by. Sometimes Chip would murmur to the horses, "Hee,

gee-aw." The traces rang quietly and the tall iron-rimmed wheels splintered rocks under the snow.

It was hard to get out of bed. The air was cold. Water froze in the
bucket and the windows were coated with ice. The light was gray, exactly the same quality as the twilight of the night before, devoid of
meaning. I cleaned out the stove, laid paper, a few sticks of kindling and
some coal, splashed kerosene over everything, and struck a match. With
a great whoosh the stove filled with flames. My teeth chattering, I rushed
back under the covers. I fell asleep waiting to get warm.

When Jean and my mother came through the door I woke up. They
seemed tremendously alive, bustling with energy, their voices strangely
loud.

"It's freezing in here. What happened to the fire?" I sat up in bed. *35*
The fire had gone out, or more likely had never caught after the kerosene
had burned.

"You forgot to set the alarm," my mother said.

"No I didn't."

She knelt and relit the fire. Jean stood in the open doorway, knocking snow off his galoshes. He closed the door and sat on the edge of the
bed, bending over to open the buckles. "My God, it's cold. We should
have stayed in Florida."

"I vote for that," I said.

"Just get your ass out of that bed." He rubbed his stocking feet and *40*
twisted up his face. "How about some coffee?"

"Just a second," my mother said, still fussing with the stove.

Jean stood up and undid his belt. "Okay. Let's go." He waited till I
was out of bed, took off his trousers, and climbed in. The heavy black
and red flannel shirt he wore in cold weather was left on, buttoned tight
over his narrow chest. He ran a finger over his mustache and waited for
his cup of coffee.

Mother made it for him while I fixed myself a bowl of cornflakes.

"It's not very much to ask to keep the stove going," my mother
said. "I never ask you to do anything."

I ate my cornflakes. The stove was beginning to give off a little heat *45*
and I pulled my chair closer, arranging it so my back was to the bed. I
heard Mother undressing, and then the creak of the rusty springs as she
got in beside Jean. From that moment on I was supposed to keep quiet
so they could sleep.

There was no place else to go. Outside the land was hidden under
two and a half feet of snow. The wind was sharp and bitter (I found out
later that locals considered it the worst winter in forty years) and in any
case I didn't have the proper clothes. Even indoors, sitting in the chair
with the stove going, I kept a blanket wrapped around me Indian style.
The time dragged slowly. There was nothing to do. I tried to save the
few books for nighttime, when my need of them was greater. I drew

things with a pencil — objects in the room, my hand, imaginary scenes — but I was no good and quickly lost interest. Usually I simply sat in the chair for six or seven hours. Jean snored softly, but after the first hour or so I stopped hearing it.

Midway through the morning I remembered the candy bars. Certain Jean had forgotten them, I looked anyway, getting up from the chair carefully, tiptoeing to his clothes and searching through the pockets. Nothing. I watched him in bed, his face gray with sleep, his open mouth twitching at the top of each gentle snore. My mother turned to the wall. Jean closed his mouth and rolled over. The room was absolutely silent. I went back to the chair.

They awoke in the early afternoon and stayed in bed. Although the small stove was working it was still the warmest place. Freed from the necessity of keeping quiet, I walked around the room aimlessly, getting a drink of water, rubbing the haze off the windows to look outside. My mother raised her voice and I realized she was talking to me.

"Take some money from my purse and go down to the Greens' and get a dozen eggs."

The trip to the Greens' would take an hour each way. Outside the temperature was five or ten degrees above zero and it was windy. I didn't want to go. My heart sank because I knew I had to.

Children are in the curious position of having to do what people tell them, whether they want to or not. A child knows that he must do what he's told. It matters little whether a command is just or unjust since the child has no confidence in his ability to distinguish the difference. Justice for children is not the same as justice for adults. In effect all commands are morally neutral to a child. Yet because almost every child is consistently bullied by older people he quickly learns that if in some higher frame of reference all commands are equally just, they are not equally easy to carry out. Some fill him with joy, others, so obviously unfair that he must paralyze himself to keep from recognizing their quality, strike him instantly deaf, blind, and dumb. Faced with an order they sense is unfair children simply stall. They wait for more information, for some elaboration that will take away the seeming unfairness. It's a stupid way of defending oneself, but children are stupid compared to adults, who know how to get what they want.

"Couldn't we wait until they come up in the wagon?"

"No. The walk will do you good. You can't sit around all day, it's unhealthy."

"Oh Mother, it'll take hours."

Suddenly Jean sat up, his voice trembling with anger. "Look, this time just go. No arguments this time."

I looked at him in amazement. He'd never even raised his voice to me before. It was against the unwritten rules — my mother was the disciplinarian. I could see he was angry and I had no idea why. Even my mother was surprised. "Take it easy," she said to him softly. "He's going."

Jean's anger should have tipped me off, but it didn't. Wearing his galoshes and his overcoat I went to the Greens' without realizing why they had sent me.

It was no secret that I wanted to go along to the training school at night, to sleep on an extra bed somewhere. For months Mother put me off, but when she realized I would never get accustomed to staying alone she gave in. She was tired of dealing with me, tired of my complaints and my silences. (Alternative unconscious motivations for her change of heart: one, she felt guilty about me; two, she decided to show me something that was worth being afraid of—namely, the worst men's cottage, to which Jean was assigned the night I tagged along.)

We drove slowly down the steep, twisting road to Southbury, our headlight beams traversing back and forth across the snow. Jean leaned over the wheel, craning his neck to watch for the cutoff through the black truncated trees. "It's along here somewhere."

"We have to pass that boarded-up farmhouse," my mother said.   60

"Here it is." He applied the brakes slowly and the tires pulled against the sanded road. We were entering the grounds through the back, saving a mile. The car bumped along through the woods for a few hundred yards and then emerged at the top of a hill.

The Southbury Training School spread below us like a toy village in a Christmas display. Small dormitories disguised to look like suburban homes were spread evenly over a square mile of stripped and graded hillside. Halfway down, the two administrative buildings rose into the air, their white cupolas lighted by floodlights. Weaving across the hillside in every direction were the lines and curves of a network of private roads, described in the darkness by chains of street lights, winking on slender poles.

Jean edged the Ford over the lip of the hill and the bumpy dirt road changed immediately to a smooth, carefully plowed asphalt ribbon. We rolled along silently, watching the powdered snow drift across the surface of the road under the headlights.

"There it is," my mother said as we approached one of the dormitories. "Number Twelve."

Jean pulled up in the driveway. There was a brass knocker on the   65
front door, and a mailbox, and a green metal tube on a stand with *"Danbury Times"* written in elaborate lettering. I caught some movement out of the corner of my eye. The blinds were raised in one of the ground-floor windows and a girl stood combing her hair with long, even strokes. She saw the lights of the car and smiled. Half her teeth were gone. I looked away quickly.

My mother rang the bell and stood close to the door to be out of the wind. Almost immediately it swung open, spilling a long bar of yellow light across the snow. She lifted her hand in a signal that could just as easily have meant we should wait a moment as to wave goodbye, and was gone.

We drove slowly across the hill toward the boys' side of the school. In the bad weather the roads were empty.

"It looks deserted," I said.

"It isn't. Wait till you get inside."

The tires spun on a patch of ice as we climbed the driveway to Cottage Eight. We stopped next to a black Chevy, the only car in the parking area. Its windshield was coated with snow.

"That's Olsen's car. He has the shift before mine."

"It's brand new."

"Some of these guys work two shifts. They make a lot of money."

"Why don't you?"

He laughed. We sat for a moment, watching the building. Jean took out a cigarette. "The smell is pretty bad at first but after a couple of hours you don't notice it."

I could see small ways in which the building differed from the one my mother had entered. There was no box for the newspaper, no potted evergreens at the edge of the drive. Even in the darkness one could see that the front door needed painting. Some of the shutters were closed.

"None of these people are dangerous, are they?"

Jean finished his cigarette. "They're just feeble-minded. They can't take care of themselves."

We stepped out of the car. The air was cold and gusts of wind seemed to pass uninterrupted through my clothes. After a few steps the smell began, like a tangible line in space. Smells are hard to describe. This was a combination of pine, vomit, licorice, old urine, sweat, soap, and wet hair. Jean rang the bell and after a few moments the door opened.

I was prepared, of course, but prepared through my imagination, and I couldn't possibly have imagined the reality. First of all it was hot, really hot, like a furnace room. I began to sweat immediately. The smell was overpowering. It was useless to breathe carefully as I'd done outside; here the smell was so pungent and thick it seemed to have taken the place of air—a hot substitute filling my lungs, seeping into my blood, and making me its own creature. With the first deep breath I was no longer an air breather. I'd changed to another species.

It was noisy. A noise that raised the hair on the back of my neck. Far-out throats, tongues, and lips forming sounds that wound their independent way up and down the scale with no relation to anything. Whispering, mumbling, fake laughter and true laughter, bubbling sounds, short screams, bored humming, weeping, long roller-coaster yells — all of it in random dynamic waves like some futuristic orchestra. In this meaningless music were sudden cries of such intense human significance that I stood paralyzed.

It was as if all the saints, martyrs, and mystics of human history were gathered into a single building, each one crying out at the moment of revelation, each one truly *there* at his extreme of joy or pain, crying out with the purity of total selflessness. There was no arguing with these sudden voices above the general clamor, they rang true. All around me were men in a paroxysm of discovery, seeing lands I had never known existed, calling me with a strength I had never known existed. But they called from every direction with equal power, so I couldn't answer. I stood balanced on the pinpoint of my own sanity, a small, cracked tile on the floor.

"They're a little noisy now. It's just before bedtime and we let them blow off some steam."

I looked up and discovered a huge man standing in front of me, smiling. Involuntarily I took a step backward. He was all eyes, immense white eyes impossibly out of his head, rushing at me. No, he was wearing his eyes like glasses. Two bulbous eyes in steel frames. He turned his head and the illusion disappeared. Thick lenses, that was all. His bald head gleamed with sweat. His arm was as big as my leg.

"I'm Olsen," he said.

"Where's Jean?"

"He'll be back in a minute."

85

There was movement behind his back. I watched from the corner of my eye, afraid to look directly. A naked man slipping into the room, hunched over like a beaten dog, a shiny thread of spittle hanging from his jaw. He cruised silently along the wall, limp fingers touching the plaster, turned, and stopped, his shaggy head facing the blank wall one inch away. Without even looking Olsen raised his voice and said, "Back to bed."

The creature lifted one leg and touched his toes to the surface of the wall as if it was a ladder he was about to climb. Below the tangle of black hair in his crotch, his veined penis and scrotum hung limply almost halfway to the knee, against the inside of his thigh. It was as if they'd been grabbed and stretched like soft taffy. His toes scratched the wall. Olsen took a step toward him, leaning over slightly, and clapped his hands smartly. "Back to bed!" The creature scurried along the wall and disappeared through an open doorway. For the first time I noticed there were no doors. Doorways without doors. From each darkened passageway the noises rushed at us. Suddenly, the sound of a crash. Olsen knew just where it came from. "Back in a second," he said.

Alone in the room, I stood by the door, my hand touching the knob. I could hear Olsen shouting in another part of the building. Far

90

back in the corridors half-visible figures were moving in the dim light. I supposed that Jean was with them.

An old man appeared, hesitating at the edge of the room. When he saw me he froze instantly, like a highly trained hunting animal. His watery blue eyes were fuzzy spirals and his cheeks sank into his head, making hollows the size of ping-pong balls. He wore a kind of diaper from which his skinny legs, all tendon and finely wrinkled skin, emerged, half bent with age. He took a step forward.

"Back to bed!" I said. "Back to bed!" For a moment he didn't move, then, leaning his head back, he opened his mouth and revealed two gleaming pink gums, toothless, looking like wet rubber. His thin shoulders shook with laughter. When his fuzzy eyes found me he shouted across the room.

"Sonny, I've been here since before you were born. I don't even belong here. I belong in a mental hospital. Everybody knows that." He turned and left the room.

I wanted to wait outside until Jean came back. There was a large brass lock high on the door. I turned what seemed to be the appropriate knob but the bolt didn't move. Examining the mechanism more closely, I heard a noise behind me.

Something was rushing down one of the corridors, something low *95* and fast. No bullfighter ever waited for his foe more apprehensively. To my amazement I found myself giving a short, nervous laugh, a desperate guffaw in the teeth of my predicament. Zooming into the room was a flash of chrome-man, a monstrous human machine blurred with speed, bearing down on me like a homicidal hot-rodder. A man in a wheelchair, but what kind of man? His body was tiny, like a child's, his head impossibly huge, the size of a watermelon. Flailing at the wheels of his chair like a berserk rowboat enthusiast, he backed me into a corner and threw his hands into my face.

"See my pretty 'racelet?" he said in a high voice. "See my pretty 'racelet?"

Flinching, twisting to avoid the touch of his wild hands, I tried to slip past. He slammed his chair into the wall and trapped me.

"See my pretty 'racelet?"

"What? What do you want? What?" Reluctantly I looked him in the eye. His bland idiot's features seemed small in the gargantuan hydrocephalic head. All scrunched together in the cavity that was his face they stared out at me like a fish from a goldfish bowl.

"See my pretty 'racelet?" he said, still holding his arms up. In a *100* tantrum of infantile frustration he drummed his heels against the bottom of the chair. "See! See!"

"He wants you to look at his bracelet," Jean said, grabbing the back of his chair and pulling him away. "This is Freddie. His nickname is pinhead."

"Pinhead, pinhead! See!"

"Go ahead," Jean said. "Just look at it."

Around the creature's wrist was a cheap chrome I.D. bracelet. He held his hand motionless when he realized I was looking at it. The word FREDDIE was engraved in block letters. I touched it with my index finger. "It's very pretty. Very nice."

"Pretty 'racelet?" Freddie said, calmer now.   *105*

"Yes. Very pretty."

"Pretty 'racelet?"

Olsen appeared from one of the corridors. His big feet clomped noisily on the tile floor. "Time for lights out?"

"Okay," Jean answered, rolling Freddie away. "Frank, you can go in the office." He pointed to an open doorway.

Freddie rocked back and forth in the chair. "Lice-out. Lice-out.   *110* Lice-out."

Olsen reached out and slapped his immense dome with an open hand. "Shut up, idiot." They rolled him down one of the corridors.

The office was a small room with a desk, a chair, and a cot. There was no door to close. I sat on the cot and watched the blank wall. As Jean and Olsen progressed through the building turning out lights, the screaming gradually subsided, falling to a steady murmur like the crowd noises in a movie. It was less nerve-wracking, but somehow more ominous. The mood in the building was changing from wildness to slyness. Plans were beginning to cook in countless heads, and as a novelty, a break in the routine, it seemed to me that I would be the focus. I jumped up nervously as Olsen came in. He looked down at me, his big white eyes embedded in their surrealistic lenses. "I'm going off now. I want to show you something."

I followed him out of the office, sticking close behind. We took a few steps into a hallway and stopped. In the gloom stray rays of light collected in his glasses like fireflies.

"The boys are harmless. They're scareder of you than you are of them, so you got nothing to worry about. I want to show you this guy so you know what he looks like. A couple of times he's grabbed a broom and snuck up behind somebody and belted them. If he ever tries anything all you got to do is look him in the eye and he backs down."

"Maybe it's better if he doesn't see me."   *115*

"He won't. He can't see past the light."

There was a snapping sound and a powerful flashlight beam showed us a glowing circle of green wall. We took a few steps and the beam spilled into a small room. With a flick of his wrist Olsen found the occupant, sitting on his bed, knees drawn up to his chest, rocking slowly back and forth. (In the South they call it hunkering.) He looked young, and strong—completely normal except for his nakedness and the fixed expression of anger on his face. His eyes blinked in the strong light but he didn't look away. The creaking of the bedsprings stopped as he held himself rigid. He seemed to be looking directly into my eyes in a contest of wills. Suddenly his head jerked forward and a glob of spittle curved through the air and fell at my feet.

"Tough guy," said Olsen. "Once he threw his own shit at me. But he'll never do that again."

My eyes were locked with the inmate's. "Did you punish him?"

"Punish him!" Olsen laughed. "I beat the living daylights out of him. He was in the infirmary for three days." 120

"Did he understand?"

"What?"

"Did he understand why you hit him?"

"He didn't throw no more shit so I guess he did."

"What's his name?" 125

"Gregory."

"Can we go back now?"

"He doesn't know how lucky he is. He's the only one in the building with a room of his own. Look." He flashed his light up the hall. Beds were set up along the walls of the corridor. People were sitting up in them watching us silently. Most of them fell back as the light struck them, like dominoes in a row. To the rest Olsen yelled "Lights out! Bedtime!"

"Can we go back now?"

Olsen had gone off duty and Jean and I were in the office. 130

"Lovely, isn't it," Jean said sitting on the edge of the desk.

"Is there any place with a door? I'd feel better with a door."

"No, but you'll be all right."

"What about that guy named Gregory?"

"He won't do anything. He's probably asleep. They go to sleep like 135 *that*." He snapped his fingers. After a moment he raised his head and stared out the doorway. "Isn't it incredible the way some of them are hung? They've got equipment a horse would be proud of."

"Jean, I don't think I can make it."

"It's perfectly safe." He stood up. "I've got to make the rounds."

"I can't stay here."

"Well I can't take you back. You'll just have to."

"I'll sleep in the car." 140

"It's freezing out there."

"I'll take some blankets. It'll be all right."

He stood for a moment without answering.

"Please, Jean."

"Okay. Suit yourself. I've got to make the rounds." He started out, 145 then looked back. "If it gets too cold out there you'd better come back in."

"I will. Yes. Thanks." Quickly I began to strip the blankets from the cot. Then, remembering, I rushed after him. "Jean! The lock! How do you work the lock?"

So for the rest of the winter I stayed in the cabin at night. I never got used to it, but in some ways the nights were better than the days. The nights were warm fantasies of terror, Technicolor nightmares. I recognized somehow that everything happening to me alone at night in the cabin was a low order of reality. My hallucinations, the fear itself, the entire drama came from inside my own head. I was *making* it all, and although it was terrifying, it was not, as were the days, cosmically threatening.

The days were emptiness, a vast, spacious emptiness in which the fact of being alive became almost meaningless. The first fragile beginnings of a personality starting to collect in my twelve-year-old soul were immediately sucked up in to the silence and the featureless winter sky. The overbearing, undeniable reality of those empty days! The inescapable fact that everything around me was nonhuman, that in terms of snow and sky and rocks and dormant trees I didn't exist, these things rendered me invisible even to myself. I wasn't conscious of what was happening, I lived it. I became invisible. I lost myself.

At night I materialized. The outlines of my body were hot, flushed, sharply defined. My senses were heightened. I knew I was real as I animated the darkness with extensions of myself. If the sky was more real than I was, then I was more real than my phantoms.

But the days predominated. The flat sky. As the winter passed a 150 sense of desolation invaded my mind. I wasn't afraid, it was too nebulous for that, but I was profoundly uneasy. Perhaps in the back of my mind was the fear that everything would go blank, that I would become the sky, without a body, without thought. I remembered the peculiarly impersonal quality of some of the screams in Cottage Eight.

In the spring I started going down to the school just to hang around, walking the four miles with a quarter in my pocket to get a milkshake at the soda fountain in the administration building. I roamed freely through the public rooms. In a scaled-down bowling alley I used to set up the pins for myself after each frame. Sometimes there were movies in the auditorium. I'd wait for a group of boys to come across the lawn behind their counselor and tag along at the end. I remember a conversation I had one day before a Gene Autry picture with a boy who attracted my attention because I thought he looked exactly like me.

"Who're you?" he asked. "Are you new?"

"No. I'm Mr. Fouchet's son."

"He takes our cottage at night sometimes. He's okay. He never hits you."

"Do the others?" 155

"Some of them."

(Whistles and applause as Mr. Miller, the director of the school, climbs on stage to make a few announcements before the picture. I laugh at the wildness of the audience. They're having a great time.)

"I'm going home next week," the boy says. "If you're around you'll see the car. It's a red Buick."

"We have a Ford."

"My pop's a policeman. He carries a gun."   160

(More whistles and cheers as the house lights go down and the picture begins. I watch the boy. There's no way to tell anything is wrong with him.)

The Southbury school affected me more deeply than I realized at the time. Most immediately it was a place in which being different was a good thing — I was different only because I wasn't feeble-minded. My general loneliness in the world was dramatized microcosmically, in terms favorable to myself.

I believed I was intelligent. For a long time that thought had been important to me. At the school I felt for the first time that my intelligence was worth something to someone else besides myself. Here was a huge organization, an immense, powerful world existing for the inmate, but existing for me as well. I was the other extreme! At last I'd found someplace where my only possession would be relevant! To picture myself as being aware of all this would be a misrepresentation. I wasn't vain. I didn't look down on the boys. In some ways I needed the school as much as they did, and I certainly felt closer to them than to the children at conventional schools.

But of course the Southbury school, except for one incident, was as uninterested in me as the world it represented. Which is as it should be. While I passed through the attenuated agonies of growing up, trying to get through to a psychologist in the library of the administration building, there were boys next door who were never going to grow up at all, boys who would starve to death without someone to feed them.

I was alone in the library reading *Life* magazine. A man stopped in   165
the hallway and looked at me through the double glass doors. I watched him come in without raising my head.

"Hi," he said casually. "What are you reading?"

"Just this magazine."

"It's a good issue. I've read it myself." He spoke to me as if we were old friends. "You remember me, don't you?"

It came to me in a flash. He'd mistaken me for one of the boys. Perhaps the boy from the movies who looked so much like me. A bewildering array of emotions exploded simultaneously — confusion, embarrassment, a kind of childish love, apprehensiveness, but behind it all, as steady as the solid bar of sunlight across the polished table, triumph. The moment was at hand.

"Of course you're not really reading it, are you?" he said. "You   170
mean you're looking at the pictures."

"No. I'm reading it."

"Don't you remember me? I'm Dr. Janetello."

I hesitated, trying to think up an answer, but he went on.

"Would you mind reading something for me?"

I looked down at the page. "Members of the Eighty-second air- 175 borne reserves bail out over Colorado. Four thousand men took part in a mock attack . . ."

"That's enough," he said. On the table were two books I'd taken from the shelves. He picked them up. *The Short Stories of de Maupassant* and *Pickwick Papers*. Do you read this too?"

"Yes. I liked *David Copperfield* so I thought I'd try this."

"How did you get in here?" he asked quickly. "Are you from Southbury?"

"My stepfather works here."

"You think it's clever to play me along like that?" 180

I didn't answer. It was going wrong. I looked up at his round face. A few beads of sweat were collected along his upper lip and his eyes suddenly seemed very small.

"Do you have permission to use the library?"

"No. I guess not."

He stood for a moment without saying anything, as if undecided whether to continue. Then he dropped the books on the table with a bang, turned quickly, and left the room. The double doors continued swinging long after he was gone.

FOR DISCUSSION AND WRITING

1. Explain why agent could be considered the most important element in this selection.

2. Which author—Dillard or Conroy—gives us the more fully developed scene? Provide specific examples to back up your choice.

3. Explain how the title of the selection denotes scenes.

4. What do the scenes in this selection tell us about the agent?

5. What are significant acts in the narrative? What are the purposes behind those acts? (For example, what was the purpose of ordering Frank to go for a dozen eggs?)

6. In what sense is Frank merely an agency, something to be used (particularly by Jean), not an agent?

7. Young Frank, like other children, struggles to establish his own identity. What acts and purposes characterize this struggle?

8. Since "White Days and Red Nights" is a chapter from Conroy's autobiography, we can assume that the rest of the book supplies information

that appears to be lacking in the selection. Can you point to instances where the reader lacks sufficient information to understand the selection completely?

9. State the main point of the selection.

10. The first paragraph states that Frank, his mother, and Jean spent only weekends at the cabin and the Southbury Training School. Why doesn't Conroy mention ordinary weekdays, when, like other children, he went to school and had a room of his own at home?

11. Explain why, at the end, Conroy preferred the "red nights" to the "white days."

12. The selection has a nightmare quality, particularly with the red, glowing stove and the residents of Cottage Eight. How does Conroy achieve this effect? What specific images does he present? What sort of language does he use?

13. If you were writing the autobiography of your first five years, what sources would give you the details, the "facts" you need? (People? Legal documents? Books? Would you visit important places to get the "feel" of them?)

ST. AUGUSTINE AND THE BULLFIGHT
Katherine Anne Porter

Significantly, Callie Porter, born in Indian Creek, Texas, in 1890, changed her name to the more dignified Katherine Anne when she decided to become a writer, almost as if she had resolved to live a life different from that to which she was born. In "St. Augustine and the Bullfight," we glimpse something of the intellectual, moral, and physical adventure that made up the life of this American writer.

Some data capture the turbulence of Porter's career: the death of her mother before she was two years old; the extreme poverty of her grandmother's home until the death of the grandmother when Porter was eleven; marriage at sixteen, almost immediate separation from her husband, and a divorce in 1915 when she was twenty-five; three subsequent marriages; work as a journalist and free-lance writer; sudden acclaim with the publication of the story "Flowering Judas" in 1929. Her last triumph was the novel *Ship of Fools,* which appeared when she was over seventy. Katherine Anne Porter died in 1980.

As you read this autobiographical narrative, think about what the author means when she says, "Literary art, at least, is the business of setting human events to rights and giving them meanings that, in fact, they do not possess. . . ."

Adventure. The word has become a little stale to me, because it has been applied too often to the dull physical exploits of professional "adventurers" who write books about it, if they know how to write; if not, they hire ghosts who quite often can't write either.

I don't read them, but rumors of them echo, and re-echo. The book business at least is full of heroes who spend their time, money and energy worrying other animals, manifestly their betters such as lions and tigers, to death in trackless jungles and deserts only to be crossed by the stoutest motorcar; or another feeds hooks to an inedible fish like the tarpon; another crosses the ocean on a raft, living on plankton and seaweed, why ever, I wonder? And always always, somebody is out climbing mountains, and writing books about it, which are read by quite millions of persons who feel, apparently, that the next best thing to going there yourself is to hear from somebody who went. And I have heard more than one young woman remark that, though she did not want to get married, still, she would like to have a baby, for the adventure: not lately though. That was a pose of the 1920s and very early '30s. Several of them did it, too, but I do not know of any who wrote a book about it — good for them.

W. B. Yeats remarked — I cannot find the passage now, so must say it in other words — that the unhappy man (unfortunate?) was one whose adventures outran his capacity for experience, capacity for experience being, I should say, roughly equal to the faculty for understanding what has happened to one. The difference then between mere adventure and a real experience might be this? That adventure is something you seek for pleasure, or even for profit, like a gold rush or invading a country; for the illusion of being more alive than ordinarily, the thing you will to occur; but experience is what really happens to you in the long run; the truth that finally overtakes you.

Adventure is sometimes fun, but not too often. Not if you can remember what really happened; all of it. It passes, seems to lead nowhere much, is something to tell friends to amuse them, maybe. "Once upon a time," I can hear myself saying, for I once said it, "I scaled a cliff in Boulder, Colorado, with my bare hands, and in Indian moccasins, bare-legged. And at nearly the top, after six hours of feeling for toe- and fingerholds, and the gayest feeling in the world that when I got to the top I should see something wonderful, something that sounded awfully like a bear growled out of a cave, and I scuttled down out of there in a hurry." This is a fact. I had never climbed a mountain in my life, never had the least wish to climb one. But there I was, for perfectly good reasons, in a hut on a mountainside in heavenly sunny though sometimes stormy weather, so I went out one morning and scaled a very minor cliff; alone, unsuitably clad, in the season when rattlesnakes are casting their skins; and if it was not a bear in that cave, it was some kind of unfriendly animal who growls at people; and this ridiculous escapade, which was nearly six hours of the hardest work I ever did in my life, toeholds and fingerholds on a cliff, put me to bed for just nine days with a complaint the local people called "muscle poisoning." I don't know exactly what they meant, but I do remember clearly that I could not turn over in bed without help and in great agony. And did it teach me anything? I think not, for three years later I was climbing a volcano in Mexico, that celebrated unpronounceably named volcano, Popocatepetl which everybody who comes near it climbs sooner or later; but was that any reason for me to climb it? No. And I was knocked out for weeks, and that finally did teach me: I am not supposed to go climbing things. Why did I not know in the first place? For me, this sort of thing must come under the head of Adventure.

I think it is pastime of rather an inferior sort; yet I have heard men   *5* tell yarns like this only a very little better: their mountains were higher, or their sea was wider, or their bear was bigger and noisier, or their cliff was steeper and taller, yet there was no point whatever to any of it except that it had happened. This is not enough. May it not be, perhaps, that experience, that is, the thing that happens to a person living from day to day, is anything at all that sinks in? is, without making any claims, a part of your growing and changing life? what it is that happens in your mind, your heart?

Adventure hardly ever seems to be that at the time it is happening: not under that name, at least. Adventure may be an afterthought, something that happens in the memory with imaginative trimmings if not downright lying, so that one should suppress it entirely, or go the whole way and make honest fiction of it. My own habit of writing fiction has provided a wholesome exercise to my natural, incurable tendency to try to wangle the sprawling mess of our existence in this bloody world into some kind of shape: almost any shape will do, just so it is recognizably made with human hands, one small proof the more of the validity and reality of the human imagination. But even within the most limited frame what utter confusion shall prevail if you cannot take hold firmly, and draw the exact line between what really happened, and what you have since imagined about it. Perhaps my soul will be saved after all in spite of myself because now and then I take some unmanageable, indigestible fact and turn it into fiction; cause things to happen with some kind of logic — my own logic, of course — and everything ends as I think it should end and no back talk, or very little, from anybody about it. Otherwise, and except for this safety device, I should be the greatest liar unhung. (When was the last time anybody was hanged for lying?) What is Truth? I often ask myself. Who knows?

A publisher asked me a great while ago to write a kind of autobiography, and I was delighted to begin; it sounded very easy when he said, "Just start, and tell everything you remember until now!" I wrote about a hundred pages before I realized, or admitted, the hideous booby trap into which I had fallen. First place, I remember quite a lot of stupid and boring things: there were other times when my life seemed merely an endurance test, or a quite mysterious but not very interesting and often monotonous effort at survival on the most primitive terms. There are dozens of things that might be entertaining but I have no intention of telling them, because they are nobody's business; and endless little gossipy incidents that might entertain indulgent friends for a minute, but in print they look as silly as they really are. Then, there are the tremendous, unmistakable, life-and-death crises, the scalding, the bone-breaking events, the lightnings that shatter the landscape of the soul — who would write that by request? No, that is for a secretly written manuscript to be left with your papers, and if your executor is a good friend, who has probably been brought up on St. Augustine's *Confessions,* he will read it with love and attention and gently burn it to ashes for your sake.

Yet I intend to write something about my life, here and now, and so far as I am able without one touch of fiction, and I hope to keep it as shapeless and unforeseen as the events of life itself from day to day. Yet, look! I have already betrayed my occupation, and dropped a clue in what would be the right place if this were fiction, by mentioning St. Augustine when I hadn't meant to until it came in its right place in life, not in art. Literary art, at least, is the business of setting human events to rights and giving them meanings that, in fact, they do not possess, or not obviously, or not the meanings the artist feels they should have—we do understand so little of what is really happening to us in any given moment. Only by remembering, comparing, waiting to know the consequences can we sometimes, in a flash of light, see what a certain event really meant, what it was trying to tell us. So this will be notes on a fateful thing that happened to me when I was young and did not know much about the world or about myself. I had been reading St. Augustine's *Confessions* since I was able to read at all, and I thought I had read every word, perhaps because I did know certain favorite passages by heart. But then, it was something like having read the Adventures of Gargantua by Rabelais when I was twelve and enjoying it; when I read it again at thirty-odd, I was astounded at how much I had overlooked in the earlier reading, and wondered what I thought I had seen there.

So it was with St. Augustine and my first bullfight. Looking back nearly thirty-five years on my earliest days in Mexico, it strikes me that, for a fairly serious young woman who was in the country for the express purpose of attending a Revolution, and studying Mayan people art, I fell in with a most lordly gang of fashionable international hoodlums. Of course I had Revolutionist friends and artist friends, and they were gay and easy and poor as I was. This other mob was different: they were French, Spanish, Italian, Polish, and they all had titles and good names: a duke, a count, a marquess, a baron, and they were all in some flashy money-getting enterprise like importing cognac wholesale, or selling sports cars to newly rich politicians; and they all drank like fish and played fast games like polo or tennis or jai alai; they haunted the wings of theaters, drove slick cars like maniacs, but expert maniacs, never missed a bullfight or a boxing match; all were reasonably young and they had ladies to match, mostly imported and all speaking French. These persons stalked pleasuure as if it were big game—they took their fun exactly where they found it, and the way they liked it, and they worked themselves to exhaustion at it. A fast, tough, expensive, elegant, high lowlife they led, for the ladies and gentlemen each in turn had other friends you would have had to see to believe; and from time to time, without being in any way involved or engaged, I ran with this crowd of shady characters and liked their company and ways very much. I don't like gloomy sinners, but the merry ones charm me. And one of them introduced me to Shelley. And Shelley, whom I knew in the most superficial way, who remained essentially a stranger to me to the very end, led me, without in the least ever knowing what he had done, into one of the most important and lasting experiences of my life.

He was British, a member of the poet's family; said to be authentic great-great-nephew; he was rich and willful, and had come to Mexico young and wild, and mad about horses, of course. Coldly mad—he bred them and raced them and sold them with the stony detachment and

10

merciless appraisal of the true horse lover — they call it love, and it could be that: but he did not like them. "What is there to like about a horse but his good points? If he has a vice, shoot him or send him to the bullring; that is the only way to work a vice out of the breed!"

Once, during a riding trip while visiting a ranch, my host gave me a stallion to ride, who instantly took the bit in his teeth and bolted down a steep mountain trail. I managed to stick on, held an easy rein, and he finally ran himself to a standstill in an open field. My disgrace with Shelley was nearly complete. Why? Because the stallion was not a good horse. I should have refused to mount him. I said it was a question how to refuse the horse your host offered you — Shelley thought it no question at all. "A lady," he reminded me, "can always excuse herself gracefully from anything she doesn't wish to do." I said, "I wish that were really true," for the argument about the bullfight was already well started. But the peak of his disapproval of me, my motives, my temperament, my ideas, my ways, was reached when, to provide a diversion and end a dull discussion, I told him the truth: that I had liked being run away with, it had been fun and the kind of thing that had to happen unexpectedly, you couldn't arrange for it. I tried to convey to him my exhilaration, my pure joy when this half-broken, crazy beast took off down that trail with just a hoofhold between a cliff on one side and a thousand-foot drop on the other. He said merely that such utter frivolity surprised him in some- one whom he had mistaken for a well-balanced, intelligent girl; and I remember thinking how revoltingly fatherly he sounded, exactly like my own father in his stuffier moments.

He was a stocky, red-faced, muscular man with broad shoulders, hard-jowled, with bright blue eyes glinting from puffy lids; his hair was a grizzled tan, and I guessed him about fifty years old, which seemed a great age to me then. But he mentioned that his Mexican wife had "died young" about three years before, and that his eldest son was only eleven years old. His whole appearance was so remarkably like the typical horsy, landed-gentry sort of Englishman one meets in books by French- men or Americans, if this were fiction I should feel obliged to change his looks altogether, thus falling into one stereotype to avoid falling into another. However, so Shelley did look, and his clothes were magnificent and right beyond words, and never new-looking and never noticeable at all except one could not help observing sooner or later that he was beyond argument the best-dressed man in America, North or South; it was that kind of typical British inconspicuous good taste: he had it, superlatively. He was evidently leading a fairly rakish life, or trying to, but he was of a cast-iron conventionality even in that. We did not fall in love — far from it. We struck up a hands-off, quaint, farfetched, tetchy kind of friendship which consisted largely of good advice about wordly things from him, mingled with critical marginal notes on my charac- ter — a character of which I could not recognize a single trait; and if I said, helplessly, "But I am not in the least like that," he would answer, "Well, you should be!" or "Yes, you are, but you don't know it."

This man took me to my first bullfight. I'll tell you later how St. Augustine comes into it. It was the first bullfight of that season; Covadonga Day; April; clear, hot blue sky; and a long procession of women in flower-covered carriages; wearing their finest lace veils and highest combs and gauziest fans; but I shan't describe a bullfight. By now surely there is no excuse for anyone who can read or even hear or see not to know pretty well what goes on in a bullring. I shall say only that Sánchez Mejías and Rudolfo Gaona each killed a bull that day; but before the Grand March of the toreros, Hattie Weston rode her thoroughbred High School gelding into the ring to thunders of shouts and brassy music.

She was Shelley's idol. "Look at that girl, for God's sake," and his voice thickened with feeling, "the finest rider in the world," he said in his dogmatic way, and it is true I have not seen better since.

She was a fine buxom figure of a woman, a highly colored blonde with a sweet, childish face; probably forty years old, and perfectly rounded in all directions; a big round bust, and that is the word, there was nothing plural about it, just a fine, warm-looking bolster straight across her front from armpit to armpit; fine firm round hips — again, why the plural? It was an ample seat born to a side-saddle, as solid and undivided as the bust, only more of it. She was tightly laced and her waist was small. She wore a hard-brimmed dark gray Spanish sailor hat, sitting straight and shallow over her large golden knot of hair; a light gray bolero and a darker gray riding skirt — not a Spanish woman's riding dress, nor yet a man's, but something tight and fit and formal and appropriate. And there she went, the most elegant woman in the saddle I have ever seen, graceful and composed in her perfect style, with her wonderful, lightly dancing, learned horse, black and glossy as shoe polish, perfectly under control — no, not under control at all, you might have thought, but just dancing and showing off his paces by himself for his own pleasure. 15

"She makes the bullfight seem like an anticlimax," said Shelley, tenderly.

I had not wanted to come to this bullfight. I had never intended to see a bullfight at all. I do not like the slaughtering of animals as sport. I am carnivorous, I love all the red juicy meats and all the fishes. Seeing animals killed for food on the farm in summers shocked and grieved me sincerely, but it did not cure my taste for flesh. My family for as far back as I know anything about them, only about 450 years, were the huntin', shootin', fishin' sort: their houses were arsenals and their dominion over the animal kingdom was complete and unchallenged. When I was older, my father remarked on my tiresome timidity, or was I just pretending to finer feelings than those of the society around me? He hardly knew which was the more tiresome. But that was perhaps only a personal matter. Morally, if I wished to eat meat I should be able to kill the animal — otherwise it appeared that I was willing to nourish myself on other people's sins? For he supposed I considered it a sin. Otherwise why bother about it? Or was it just something unpleasant I wished to avoid? Maintaining my own purity — and a very doubtful kind of purity he found it, too — at the expense of the guilt of others? Altogether, my father managed to make a very sticky question of it, and for some years at intervals I made it a matter of conscience to kill an animal or bird, something I intended to eat. I gave myself and the beasts some horrible times, through fright and awkwardness, and to my shame, nothing cured me of my taste for flesh. All forms of cruelty offend me bitterly, and this repugnance is inborn, absolutely impervious to any arguments, or even insults, at which the red-blooded lovers of blood sports are very expert; they don't admire me at all, any more than I admire them. . . . Ah, me, the contradictions, the paradoxes! I was once perfectly capable of keeping a calf for a pet until he outgrew the yard in the country and had to be sent to the pastures. His subsquent fate I leave you to guess. Yes, it is all revoltingly sentimental and, worse than that, confused. My defense is that no matter whatever else this world seemed to promise me, never once did it promise to be simple.

So, for a great tangle of emotional reasons I had no intention of going to a bullfight. But Shelley was so persistently unpleasant about my cowardice, as he called it flatly, I just wasn't able to take the thrashing any longer. Partly, too, it was his natural snobbery: smart people of the world did not have such feelings; it was to him a peculiarly provincial if not downright Quakerish attitude. "I have some Quaker ancestors," I told him. "How absurd of you!" he said, and really meant it.

The bullfight question kept popping up and had a way of spoiling other occasions that should have been delightful. Shelley was one of those men, of whose company I feel sometimes that I have had more than my fair share, who simply do not know how to drop a subject, or abandon a position once they have declared it. Constitutionally incapable of admitting defeat, or even its possibility, even when he had not the faintest shadow of right to expect a victory — for why should he make a contest of my refusal to go to a bullfight? — he would start an argument during the theater intermissions, at the fronton, at a street fair, on a stroll in the Alameda, at a good restaurant over coffee and brandy; there was no occasion so pleasant that he could not shatter it with his favorite gambit: "If you would only see one, you'd get over this nonsense."

So there I was, at the bullfight, with cold hands, trembling innerly, *20* with painful tinglings in the wrists and collarbone: yet my excitement was not altogether painful; and in my happiness at Hattie Weston's performance I was calmed and off guard when the heavy barred gate to the corral burst open and the first bull charged through. The bulls were from the Duke of Veragua's° ranch, as enormous and brave and hand-some as any I ever saw afterward. (This is not a short story, so I don't have to maintain any suspense.) This first bull was a beautiful monster of brute courage: his hide was a fine pattern of black and white, much enhanced by the goad with fluttering green ribbons stabbed into his shoulder as he entered the ring; this in turn furnished an interesting design in thin rivulets of blood, the enlivening touch of scarlet in his sober color scheme, with highly aesthetic effect.

He rushed at the waiting horse, blindfolded in one eye and standing at the proper angle for the convenience of his horns, the picador making only the smallest pretense of staving him off, and disemboweled the horse with one sweep of his head. The horse trod in his own guts. It happens at least once every bullfight. I could not pretend not to have expected it; but I had not been able to imagine it. I sat back and covered my eyes. Shelley, very deliberately and as inconspicuously as he could, took both my wrists and held my hands down on my knees. I shut my eyes and turned my face away, away from the arena, away from him, but not before I had seen in his eyes a look of real, acute concern and almost loving anxiety for me — he really believed that my feelings were the sign of a grave flaw of character, or at least an unbecoming, unworthy weak-ness that he was determined to overcome in me. He couldn't shoot me, alas, or turn me over to the bullring; he had to deal with me in human terms, and he did it according to his lights. His voice was hoarse and fierce: "Don't you dare come here and then do this! You must face it!"

Part of his fury was shame, no doubt, at being seen with a girl who would behave in such a pawky way. But at this point he was, of course, right. Only he had been wrong before to nag me into this, and I was altogether wrong to have let him persuade me. Or so I felt then. "You have got to face this!" By then he was right; and I did look and I did face it, though not for years and years.

During those years I saw perhaps a hundred bullfights, all in Mex-ico City, with the finest bulls from Spain and the greatest bullfighters — but not with Shelley — never again with Shelley, for we were not com-fortable together after that day. Our odd, mismatched sort of friendship declined and neither made any effort to revive it. There was bloodguilt between us, we shared an evil secret, a hateful revelation. He hated what he had revealed in me to himself, and I hated what he had revealed to me about myself, and each of us for entirely opposite reasons; but there was nothing more to say or do, and we stopped seeing each other.

I took to the bullfights with my Mexican and Indian friends. I sat with them in the cafés where the bullfighters appeared; more than once went at two o'clock in the morning with a crowd to see the bulls brought

Duke of Veragua: Lineal descendant of Christopher Columbus.

into the city; I visited the corral back of the ring where they could be seen before the corrida. Always, of course, I was in the company of impassioned adorers of the sport, with their special vocabulary and mannerisms and contempt for all others who did not belong to their charmed and chosen cult. Quite literally there were those among them I never heard speak of anything else; and I heard then all that can be said—the topic is limited, after all, like any other—in love and praise of bullfighting. But it can be tiresome, too. And I did not really live in that world, so narrow and so trivial, so cruel and so unconscious; I was a mere visitor. There was something deeply, irreparably wrong with my being there at all, something against the grain of my life; except for this (and here was the falseness I had finally to uncover): I loved the spectacle of the bullfights, I was drunk on it, I was in a strange, wild dream from which I did not want to be awakened. I was now drawn irresistibly to the bullring as before I had been drawn to the race tracks and the polo fields at home. But this had death in it, and it was the death in it that I loved. . . . And I was bitterly ashamed of this evil in me, and believed it to be in me only—no one had fallen so far into cruelty as this! These bullfight buffs I truly believed did not know what they were doing—but I did, and I knew better because I had once known better; so that spiritual pride got in and did its deadly work, too. How could I face the cold fact that at heart I was just a killer, like any other, that some deep corner of my soul consented not just willingly but with rapture? I still clung obstinately to my flattering view of myself as a unique case, as a humane, blood-avoiding civilized being, somehow a fallen angel, perhaps? Just the same, what was I doing there? And why was I beginning secretly to abhor Shelley as if he had done me a great injury, when in fact he had done me the terrible and dangerous favor of helping me to find myself out?

In the meantime I was reading St. Augustine; and if Shelley had   25
helped me find myself out, St. Augustine helped me find myself again. I read for the first time then his story of a friend of his, a young man from the provinces who came to Rome and was taken up by the gang of clever, wellborn young hoodlums Augustine then ran with; and this young man, also wellborn but severely brought up, refused to go with the crowd to the gladiatorial combats; he was opposed to them on the simple grounds that they were cruel and criminal. His friends naturally ridiculed such dowdy sentiments; they nagged him slyly, bedeviled him openly, and, of course, finally some part of him consented—but only to a degree. He would go with them, he said, but he would not watch the games. And he did not, until the time for the first slaughter, when the howling of the crowd brought him to his feet, staring: and afterward he was more bloodthirsty than any.

Why, of course: oh, it might be a commonplace of human nature, it might be it could happen to anyone! I longed to be free of my uniqueness, to be a fellow-sinner at least with someone: I could not bear my guilt alone — and here was this student, this boy at Rome in the fourth century, somebody I felt I knew well on sight, who had been weak enough to be led into adventure but strong enough to turn it into experience. For no matter how we both attempted to deceive ourselves, our acts had all the earmarks of adventure: violence of motive, events taking place at top speed, at sustained intensity, under powerful stimulus and a willful seeking for pure sensation; willful, I say, because I was not kidnapped and forced, after all, nor was that young friend of St. Augustine's. We both proceeded under the power of our own weakness. When the time came to kill the splendid black and white bull, I who had pitied him when he first came into the ring stood straining on tiptoe to see everything, yet almost blinded with excitement, and crying out when the crowd roared, and kissing Shelley on the cheekbone when he shook my elbow and shouted in the voice of one justified: "Didn't I tell you? Didn't I?"

FOR DISCUSSION AND WRITING

1. Explain why agent could be considered the most important element in this selection.

2. Which author — Porter or Conroy — gives us the more fully developed scene? Give specific examples to substantiate your choice. Why is scene important in the selection by Porter?

4. What do the scenes in this selection tell us about the agent?

5. What are significant acts in the narrative? What are the purposes behind those acts? (For example, why did Porter attend the bullfight?)

6. In what sense is Porter merely an agency, something to be used (particularly by Shelley), not an agent?

7. Porter suggests a reason for a writer's interest in writing fiction. What is it?

8. Explain Porter's distinction between adventure and experience.

9. Why did Porter finally stop writing her autobiography? Is the reason at all related to her distinction between adventure and experience?

10. What do the similarities between the following two passages suggest about Porter's view of the relationship between art and life?

> Literary art, at least, is the business of setting human events to rights and giving them meanings that, in fact, they do not possess, or not obviously, or not the meanings the artist feels they should

have — we do understand so little of what is really happening to us in any given moment. (par. 8)

We struck up a hands-off, quaint, farfetched, tetchy kind of friendship which consisted largely of good advice about worldly things from him, mingled with critical marginal notes on my character — a character of which I could not recognize a single trait; and if I said, helplessly, "But I am not in the least like that," he would answer, "Well, you should be!" or "Yes, you are, but you don't know it." (par. 12)

11. Was Porter's attendance at a bullfight an adventure, in the special way in which she defines adventure? Why, or why not?

12. Explain the importance of the St. Augustine episode to Porter.

13. Does Porter ever explain what she learned from her experience at the bullring? In your own words, explain what she learned.

14. Porter's description of her climb in Boulder, Colorado, has the potential to be either an exciting or a comic story. How would you describe the narrative tone? How does Porter achieve the effect, and for what reason?

15. Porter writes, "Yet I intend to write something about my life, here and now, and so far as I am able without one touch of fiction, and I hope to keep it as shapeless and unforeseen as the events of life itself from day to day" (par. 8). Does she fulfill this intention? Point out passages in which Porter does not simply set forth the facts but evaluates them as well. Even if the author gave only the facts without background or interpretation, would it be as "shapeless and unforeseen" as life itself? Why, or why not?

THE GOLDEN AGE OF THE BROADWAY MUSICAL

A. Scott Berg

In 1895, Schmuel Gelbfisz—who later changed his name to Samuel Goldwyn—made his way, on foot, from his native Poland to Hamburg; from there he went to London and, via steerage, to New York City. He began his career as a sweeper in a glove factory and then became a star traveling salesman for the firm. His meeting with vaudevillian Jesse Lasky and the then unknown Cecil B. DeMille changed his career—and the nature of American entertainment. With these two pioneers, Goldwyn entered the movie business. As a producer, he was responsible for such classics as *Wuthering Heights, Stella Dallas, The Little Foxes, The Secret Life of Walter Mitty,* and *The Best Years of Our Lives.*

The selection that follows tells of Goldwyn's negotiations with Marlon Brando to take the role of Sky Masterson in *Guys and Dolls.* At that time, both Brando and Goldwyn were legendary figures on the Hollywood scene, Brando as an actor whose influence in the 1950s was unequaled and Goldwyn as a monument in the film industry.

A. Scott Berg is a gifted biographer. His *Max Perkins: Editor of Genius* was highly praised, and his biography of Samuel Goldwyn, from which the following selection is taken, very quickly became a best-seller. Berg graduated from Princeton in 1971, and in 1984 he received a Guggenheim Fellowship to enable him to research the life of Samuel Goldwyn.

The selections by Dillard, Conroy, and Porter, you will recall, are autobiographical. As you read this selection from Berg's biography, think about the differences in points of view between autobiographical and biographical works. How does the autobiographer achieve intimacy without embarrassing the reader, and how does the biographer achieve objectivity while creating a rounded portrait of the subject?

A golden age of the Broadway musical was climaxing—a decade and a half in which the art form's leading practitioners were creating the greatest works of their careers. Hollywood's recent success in enhancing size, sound, and spectrum made motion pictures feel they were at last fully able to do those works justice. Between 1955 and 1958, four Rodgers and Hammerstein classics reached the screen—*Oklahoma!, Carousel, The King and I,* and *South Pacific* (which Goldwyn called "Southern Pacific"). Invigorated by the success of *An American in Paris,* MGM attacked the genre in the fifties with all the artillery the big studio could muster. They filmed Cole Porter's *Kiss Me, Kate* in 3-D in 1953, Lerner and Loewe's *Brigadoon* in CinemaScope the following year, *Kismet* the year after that. When Hollywood ran out of recent Broadway hits, it turned out original musicals and revived old favorites by Berlin, the Gershwins, and Jerome Kern.

Frank Loesser's *Guys and Dolls* had opened at the 46th Street Theater on November 24, 1950. Before the second-act curtain had fallen that night, Samuel Goldwyn later noted, "I made up my mind to bring that show to the motion picture screen." Unfortunately, so did practically every other Hollywood producer there. After its three-year run, the show's owners auctioned the property. On March 3, 1954, Sam Goldwyn found himself bidding against MGM, Paramount, and Columbia. He won with an offer of one million dollars (against 10 percent of the picture's worldwide box-office gross) — the highest figure yet paid for a story property in motion picture history.

Guys and Dolls was based on a Damon Runyon short story, "The Idyll of Sarah Brown," with several of his other touts and tinhorn characters thrown in. Screenwriter Jo Swerling laid the groundwork for the play, and Abe Burrows (formerly a radio gag writer) finished it; Frank Loesser wrote a dozen original songs. The musical tells two love stories — one between Nathan Detroit (proprietor of "the oldest established permanent floating crap game in New York") and Miss Adelaide, a nightclub performer with a persistent "bad, bad cold," the psychosomatic result of their fourteen-year engagement. The other lovers are Sky Masterson, a freewheeling smoothie who will bet on anything, and Sarah Brown, a volunteer at the Save-a-Soul Mission. All of them take a chance and wind up winners at a double wedding ceremony in Times Square.

It was a peculiar moment to produce *Guys and Dolls*. Hollywood, in its attempts to attract crowds, had split itself along generational lines. The old guard believed in making pictures bigger still, more fantastic. (Such new box-office champions as *Quo Vadis, Cinerama Holiday,* and *The Robe* supported their case.) The Young Turks saw the effectiveness of realism on the silver screen, using the camera as a kind of microscope. Mumbling young men in black leather jackets (*The Wild One* and *Rebel Without a Cause*) were fast becoming the screen's heroes of preference; gritty slums *(The Blackboard Jungle)* proved exciting screen locations. Smaller, psychological works full of sexual tension — William Inge's *Come Back, Little Sheba, Picnic,* and *Splendor in the Grass* and Tennessee Williams's *The Rose Tattoo* and *Suddenly Last Summer* — spoke to a new generation of moviegoers. Even in directing *Oklahoma!* Fred Zinnemann strove for realism, shooting much of the action outside the confines of the soundstage, in actual cornfields. For Goldwyn, these trends were ill winds. As his son noted, "Now he was living in a world he didn't like."

"One day, around 1954," Mrs. William Wyler later observed, "there was a whole crowd of new faces in town." Many were a breed of young television executives who saw their medium as the dominant communication and entertainment force of the future. Other Hollywood tenderfoots made up a new generation of movie executives, men with little stake of their own in the industry. Directors, actors, agents, and new independent producers were building businesses from chips of the crumbling studios. The very concept of an independent producer would soon seem outmoded — and a misnomer. As studios begain to phase out their supervisors (executive producers), "independent" came to designate anyone with an idea who went to a studio in search of backing — making him, in fact, an extremely dependent producer. Those few, like Goldwyn, who still financed themselves, struck most of the industry as archaic. Hollywood was falling into the hands of men who had no passion for the "garments" they manufactured, no feel for the material.

Sam Goldwyn was one primordial producer not ready to trudge into extinction. He drew strength from Cecil B. DeMille, who was just then moving heaven and earth to produce the greatest spectacle of his career, a remake of his 1923 *The Ten Commandments*. (Jesse Lasky, the third in that triumvirate of Hollywood pioneers, was reduced to writing his memoirs to pay his bills.) Goldwyn grew determined to produce *Guys and Dolls* as the ultimate film musical, an epic. He would demonstrate for the world that none of his powers had diminished, the cost be damned. Every element of the film was "special ordered," to the extent that the handiwork drew attention to itself. Goldwyn spent $5.5 million overproducing the movie.

He started by hiring one of Hollywood's most prodigious talents to write and direct *Guys and Dolls,* even though the twenty-five-year veteran of motion pictures had never made a musical. Joseph L. Mankiewicz had, however, won back-to-back pairs of Oscars — for writing and directing *A Letter to Three Wives* in 1949 and for *All About Eve* in 1950. Mankiewicz was one of the most intellectual moviemakers ever to succeed in Hollywood. He felt the libretto of *Guys and Dolls* was thin, and so he wrote an entire script that could have played without any music at all. "My primary, almost only, objective in this writing," he explained to Goldwyn, "has been to tell the story as warmly and humanly as possible — and to characterize our four principals as fully as if their story were going to be told in purely dramatic terms." With songs, the film would have run four hours. Goldwyn knew the script was long but liked Mankiewicz's deepening of the characters and creation of more "romantic interest." He told him, "You write with great warmth and charmth."

Goldwyn and Mankiewicz considered almost every leading man in Hollywood for both male leads. The roles had been rendered practically indistinguishable, different only in Sky's being required to sing the show's serious songs while Nathan had to play the more comic scenes. They thought first of Gene Kelly, but MGM refused to loan him out. Then they discussed Tony Martin, Kirk Douglas, Robert Mitchum, and Burt Lancaster. Bing Crosby wanted the role of Sky so much that he sent his attorney to plead his case before Goldwyn. Clark Gable's agent pushed hard for his client. In a moment of wild inspiration, Goldwyn thought of a team that had proved unusually successful in the last five years, Dean Martin and Jerry Lewis. Mankiewicz put the kibosh on that idea.

Although nobody knew if he could even carry a tune, one name kept surfacing in every casting session for the role of Sky—Marlon Brando. The hottest actor in films, since his 1950 debut in *The Men,* he had been nominated for four Best Actor Oscars in his next five roles; he won for *On the Waterfront.* Because of Brando's strong aversion to the press, he had been vilified as a "bad boy"; but Mankiewicz, who had directed him in *Julius Caesar,* considered him the consummate actor. When Goldwyn heard that Brando's hestitation in taking the part was not his ability to sing so much as the size of the role, he urged Mankie- wicz to win him over. "WANT VERY MUCH TO HAVE YOU PLAY SKY MASTERSON," the director wired. "IN ITS OWN WAY ROLE AS I WOULD WRITE IT FOR YOU OFFERS CHALLENGE ALMOST EQUAL OF MARK AN- TONY. YOU HAVE NEVER DONE A MUSICAL NEITHER HAVE I. WE NEVER DID SHAKESPEARE EITHER. I AM CONFIDENT THIS WOULD BE EXCITING GRATIFYING AND REWARDING EXPERIENCE FOR BOTH OF US."

In the midst of negotiations, Frank Sinatra's agent got hold of the   10 script. His client insisted on being in the picture. There would be no conflict in the fact that Goldwyn was about to sign Brando; Sinatra was desperate to play Nathan Detroit. Mankiewicz thought Sinatra was all wrong for the part; in fact, he still hoped to talk Goldwyn into signing Sam Levene, who had created the role on Broadway. But he met the singer at the Beverly Hills Hotel and found that "Frank was just in love with it." Even though Brando and Sinatra were better suited for each other's roles, Goldwyn liked the ring of the stars' names. Brando received top billing and $200,000 for fourteen weeks. Thinking of MGM's adver- tising on Garbo's first talking picture, Goldwyn thought they might promote *Guys and Dolls* with two words: "Brando Sings." When Harry Cohn, who was then working with Abe Burrows, heard this casting news, he said, "Good for Goldwyn, bad for the picture."

Goldwyn wanted Grace Kelly for Sarah Brown, the missionary. In the three years since he had first heard about her, she had made two films for Hitchcock, played Gary Cooper's leading lady in *High Noon,* and won an Academy Award for her performance in *The Country Girl.* She would make but a few more films before playing in *The Swan* (a remake of Frances Howard's farewell to the silent screen before marrying her "prince"). When she turned this part down becauuse of prior commit- ments, Goldwyn tried Deborah Kerr, who was also booked. The third choice was Jean Simmons, who had just played Desiree to Brando's Napoleon.

With Betty Grable unavailable to play Miss Adelaide, Goldwyn hired Vivian Blaine, who had originated the role onstage. A chorus of new Goldwyn Girls was recruited. Michael Kidd was asked to re-create his original choreography, and Goldwyn rounded up several members of the Broadway cast—including Stubby Kaye (whom Goldwyn called "Stubby Toe").

A septuagenarian producing his seventy-ninth film, Sam Goldwyn had the enthusiasm of a neophyte. No detail of the production escaped his Argus eyes. One afternoon, Mankiewicz and Loesser were supposed to discuss with Goldwyn the placement of a new song in the picture. "We didn't want to argue in front of him," the director later recounted; "it's better to be a unified front." So on their way to his office, they stopped at a supply closet and hid inside. "We were discussing the situation," said Mankiewicz, "when suddenly the door opened. There was Sam. We both felt awful. A couple of shits. Like we were stealing from him or something. Sam just looked at us with a look of hurt dignity and said, 'I want you to know—I'm not the kind of producer who shoves the money under the door.'"

Irene Sharaff, who designed the costumes, discovered Goldwyn's basic passion for his work as well. She would long remember the day she quietly laughed behind Goldwyn's back when she overheard him tell Mankiewicz he wanted a "close-up" of Brando in one of the dance numbers, "with his feet"; but she also never forgot the day just before they were to film the wedding finale. He and the director had already approved of the dress Jean Simmons was to wear, but as Goldwyn and Sharaff were walking along, he suddenly grabbed her arm and said, "How about the uniform and holding the bouquet instead of the wedding dress?" Ordinarily, the designer later said, "I would have put such a query down to his shrewd budget-paring, but in this instance he was absolutely right. The incident, brief and beyond the film of no consequence, won me over."

Despite the public's new taste for slice-of-life realism, Goldwyn still believed movies should make magic. "People don't want to pay good money," he told Alfred Crown, "to see somebody else's kitchen." So the sets of *Guys and Dolls* were nothing like the streets of New York—not even as Stanley Donen had colorfully captured them in *On the Town.* Keeping his films stage-bound, Miss Sharaff suggested, was "his way of maintaining control." In this case, Oliver Smith's sets were a vivid mixture of scenery both realistic and stylized. "As a result," wrote Stephen Sondheim in *Films in Review,* "they have the disadvantages of both, and these disadvantages work against the very special nature of Runyonesque story-telling." They added a dimension of phoniness to the proceedings, offering little wit or irony.

Joseph Mankiewicz's direction did not help. Sam Goldwyn, Jr., suggested that the director had become so taken with the spectacle of production numbers that he was inclined to keep the camera still, often producing a static quality. Furthermore, the film felt padded, its songs often proving redundant alongside the protracted nonmusical scenes.

Orson Welles told Abe Burrows, "They put a tiny turd on every one of your lines."

Vivian Blaine and Stubby Kaye (particularly in his rousing rendition of "Sit Down, You're Rockin' the Boat") recaptured the essence of the show. Nobody found Frank Sinatra noteworthy, but with the addition of a new song, "Adelaide," he sang enough to satisfy his fans. For Goldwyn, the most unexpected surprise proved to be the beautiful Jean Simmons, whose sweet voice and strong acting made him think the love story worked better in the film than onstage. "I'm so happy," he said, bustling toward her after seeing the rushes one day, "that I couldn't get Grace Kelly."

The first time the Goldwyns heard the recording of Brando's songs, Frances tried to make the best of a painful moment. "He sounds like . . . a young Astaire." she offered. Frank Loesser rolled his eyes skyward. Gordon Sawyer and his crew of sound engineers worked hard to patch together respectable versions of his numbers. In the end, Goldwyn was so pleased with Brando's performance onscreen and off that he rewarded him with a white Ford Thunderbird. Seeing no strings attached, Brando accepted it.

"Faithful in detail, the picture is false to the original in its feeling," read the November 14, 1955, *Time* review of *Guys and Dolls,* stating the objections of practically every other critic.

Predictably, Goldwyn ordered his biggest promotional push ever. *20* Richard Avedon took publicity photographs, Ed Sullivan featured numbers on his show, and even the reclusive Brando (feeling indebted to Goldwyn for the new car) gave interviews and attended the film's premieres. When he finally had enough, he announced at one press conference that the film was "nothing to get on your tricycle about."

After more than a decade of profitably releasing his films through RKO, Goldwyn changed distributors. The Howard Hughes film enterprise was in a corporate tailspin, and by 1958 would be run into the ground. Goldwyn found the best terms for himself at MGM, which, since the expulsion of Louis B. Mayer, had been nosediving as well. Nicholas Schenck, the president of Lowe's, Inc., the studio's parent company, made much of Goldwyn's at last joining the organization that had long borne his name. Goldwyn privately delighted in the fact that after all those years, he could make that claim and the exiled Mayer could not. *Guys and Dolls* did over thirteen million dollars in business, becoming the number one box-office attraction of the year.

The film also received Oscar nominations in the three visual categories—sets, costumes, and cinematography—but it won no awards. For the third year in a row, the Academy's grand prize went to a smaller-screen, black-and-white $350,000 production, *Marty*—the story of a lonely butcher that had originated as a live television drama. "It is neither high, wide, nor handsome, and it has been photographed with a camera designed to present films of the type we used to know and love before

CinemaScope opened new and lunatic vistas for enjoyment," said *The New Yorker* review. *Marty* also won trophies for Best Director, Best Screenplay, and Best Actor, and it grossed in the millions.

Goldwyn continued to back his style of Hollywood entertainment. He sent the Goldwyn Girls on a world tour, from Australia to South America; and *Guys and Dolls* became a huge international hit, rivaling MGM's overseas records set by *Gone With the Wind*. Sam and Frances resumed their globe-trotting, to preside at as many foreign openings of the picture as possible, traveling as far as Tokyo. When he learned that Marlon Brando was in Japan filming *Teahouse of the August Moon* at the time of the *Guys and Dolls* premiere there, Goldwyn asked him to attend. Brando refused, saying, "I've done enough for that white Thunderbird." The film grossed almost half a million dollars in that country alone, twenty thousand dollars in Venezuela, over one million dollars in England.

FOR DISCUSSION AND WRITING

1. Explain why agent might well be the most important element in this selection.

2. Characterize the central agent, Samuel Goldwyn, in this selection. What acts help you understand the man?

3. What agencies does Goldwyn use to achieve his purposes?

4. Berg devotes a great deal of attention to purpose. Explain the purposes behind the following acts: (a) Goldwyn's decision to produce *Guys and Dolls;* (b) Goldwyn's decision to hire Marlon Brando and Frank Sinatra; (c) Mankiewicz's decision to hire Marlon Brando and Frank Sinatra; and (d) Goldwyn's decision to film within a studio though the trend, even in musicals, was toward location shooting.

5. The scene (the time and place in history) in which Goldwyn resolved to make *Guys and Dolls* is very important. His son said of him, "Now he was living in a world he didn't like" (par. 4). What kind of world was that? "People don't want to pay good money," [Goldwyn] told Alfred Crown, "to see somebody else's kitchen" (par. 15). In what sense can it be said that scene creates the purpose for the act (producing *Guys and Dolls*)?

6. What kind of scene did Goldwyn create in *Guys and Dolls?* Do you find that scene ironic? Explain.

7. Explain this metaphor: "Hollywood was falling into the hands of men who had no passion for the 'garments' they manufactured, no feel for the material" (par. 5).

8. *Guys and Dolls* was not a critical success. Develop an explanation for this failure by considering the agents involved (producer, director, actors), the scene of filming (on a sound stage), the film script as an agency, and the purpose in filming the play.

9. In "The Interior Life" and "White Days and Red Nights," the primary agent, as in any autobiography, is the author himself. In "The Golden Age of the Broadway Musical," a biography, the central agent is not the author. What are some of the advantages and disadvantages for authors of autobiographies? For authors of biographies?

10. Does the reader need any particular background knowledge to understand the selection? Be specific.

11. In his biography of the American novelist Thomas Wolfe, David Herbert Donald explains his theory of biography as follows:

> In telling Wolfe's story I have so far as possible avoided intruding my own comments on the events of his life. I believe that present-day readers no more desire moral judgments or psychoanalytical diagnoses from an author of a biography than they want heavy-handed moralizing and editorial pronouncements from a novelist. I am not persuaded that anything would be gained if I interrupted my account of Wolfe's attitudes toward Jews to announce that such bigotry is intolerable and uncivilized — as of course it is. Nor am I convinced that my portrait of Julia Wolfe would be more credible if I characterized her as an anal-retentive type.
>
> This does not mean, of course, that I have simply let the facts speak for themselves. The record of Wolfe's actions is so full that his biographer has constantly to make choices. Every quotation or incident included reflects my judgment of what is important and what is inconsequential in Wolfe's life. Throughout, I have inter-woven interpretation with narrative. But I have tried not to stress an interpretive structure that would reduce Wolfe to a case study, whether psychological, literary, or sociological. My purpose has, instead, been to present him as a man, like all men full of contra-dictions and ambiguities.

In your own words, state Donald's criteria for biography. Are they "rules of thumb" for writing successful biographies? Explain your answer. In your opinion, does the selection from Berg's *Goldwyn* meet these crite-ria? Explain.

A TENT AT MAAMBA

Elizabeth Salter

Born in 1863 in County Tipperary, Ireland, to a family of landed gentry, Daisy May O'Dwyer was a child of privilege. Her mother died when Daisy was a young girl, and Daisy was brought up by her father and her maternal grandmother. In 1884, Daisy sailed for Australia at the invitation of a family friend, Bishop G. H. Stanton, who had emigrated to the island continent. In Australia she married a drover, Jack Bates, and had a son by him. However, the marriage was a failure; Daisy, too independent to be a wife and mother, abandoned husband and child to return to England, where she worked as a journalist. After five years, she returned to Australia and began her study of the Aborigines.

Elizabeth Salter, descendant of a pioneer Australian family, became fascinated at a young age with the life of Daisy Bates. Before writing the story of Daisy Bates's life, Salter was secretary to the British literary lioness Dame Edith Sitwell, about whom she wrote a highly acclaimed memoir, *The Last Years of a Rebel*.

Of her native land, Salter says,

> The settlement of Australia is a tale of two colours. Historically, the white invasion is a mere ripple on the surface of a bottomless well. Soundings have been taken that carbon-date the black Australians back to twenty-five or even thirty thousand years. But these are according to white technology that measures black history in its own terms. The Aboriginal is wiser. He allows his ancestry to melt into the "dreaming" as the desert horizon melts into mirage. (xii)

"A Tent at Maamba" gives a vivid picture of Daisy Bates's life in the bush. One might view the selection as a perfect example of how the scene and the agent interrelate.

Her new home was surprisingly comfortable. Commissioned from "Adams the tentmaker", her tent was fourteen feet in diameter, supported by a central pole of Oregon pine, with flaps that opened out at back and front. Protected by a lattice work of tea-trees and mallee bushes that she called her "breakwind", the interior had been designed with the economy of experience.

"Along one side of the tent are my hold-all and tucker box and some odd aluminum plates and sundries; under my table, placed across the open 'back door' and covered by study books, tea cups and looking glass, is my portmanteau, which, with the hold-all, carries all the wardrobe I require for a year. The other side is occupied with my Coolgardie stretcher, at the foot of which are the kerosene supply and medicine chest for the natives."

As a carpet, blackboy tops were strewn over the ground and covered by bagging as a protection against snakes. Around her table were pockets in which she put "everything hangable".

Her "kitchen" was outside in the breakwind. Here was her fire-place, an upturned case to serve as table, and inside it, her gridiron and pans. Nails hammered into the trunk of a tree were used to hang tea-towels, washing-up dish and other odds and ends. She liked to write outside and, by placing a packing case against the trunk of a tree, she was provided with a chair. Not, perhaps, the most comfortable of sup-ports, but then, "I wasn't allowed to lean back when I was little and so I do not miss an easy chair."

Her routine was spartan. As six hours sleep was all she ever needed,   *5* it usually began before the dawn. In her own account, written for the *Western Mail,* she leaves a vivid picture of the early morning:

"The sun has another half hour before he shows his clear cold face over the horizon. . . . A keen strong wind blows, making sweet music amongst the karugu trees. Out into the bright cool air I come from my tent and probe the ashes of my open fireplace in the hope that some embers have remained alight. I am usually rewarded as I cover my big fire with soft white ash as I have often seen my compatriots cover theirs with turf ash in Ireland."

Careful to readjust her stones to leeward of the morning wind, she set the billy to boil.

Breakfast consisted of a boiled egg, bacon grilled on the gridiron, bread and butter and the inevitable tea. It was, in fact, the most substan-tial of her meals, partly because of her limitations as a cook and partly because "like Toddie I don't want to be bothered with lots of things."

Much more important to her was the aesthetic beauty of her sur-roundings. As she ate, she watched the rising of the sun transform her "white canvas wall . . . into the most exquisite frescoed patterning, far surpassing the finest of Grinling Gibbons' handiwork".

No matter how busy her day, these early mornings were peaceful,   *10* given to contemplation of "the slow sweet living ways of old time". The bush was an endless fascination. Although commenting that "the adjec-tives of scenic description are exhausted and moreover the coinage has been too long debased," her notebooks are scattered with her attempts to put down what she saw. Descriptions such as "the elfin fabrics of iridescent gossamer in beaded spider webs of morning", are interwoven with observations about "the marvellous bird the mallee fowl who . . . never knows his parents but can fly as soon as he is hatched"; or about the "vivid wattle that permits the clinging embrace of the clematis and so courts its own undoing, for here and there I notice a dead tree hugged round and round by the soft and subtle tendrils of the vine."

Everywhere she saw evidence of an implacable Nature that "is ever making and breaking with infinitely slow process. She fits her verdure to the soil, her trees to their surroundings, her plants to their environ-ment and no sooner has she accomplished this work than she proceeds to disintegrate [it]."

The breaking up of the native groups she saw as part of this inexorable process. Her certainty of their eventual extinction provided the incentive for the enormous effort she put into the next fews years. It was also her reason for risking the disapproval of the Government, believing that it was necessary to give all that she could of care and comfort in order to "mitigate the guilt of one's race", as she put it.

Her neighbours on the reserve were, in the main, a pathetic group. She called them "the remnants of the once mighty Bibbulmuns", reduced by age and frailty to dependence on the white man's bounty.

Daisy behaved with politeness in their midst, never crossing the dividing hundred yards unless invited; because, she said, "you must not go indiscriminately into a native camp if the friendship of the occupants is valued." They returned courtesy for courtesy and answered her questions. Her informants were old men and women, often the last of their groups. One was Fanny Balbuk, and the other, Jubytch, a native trooper and last of the Guildford line.

Stead's° influence was beginning to show. Daisy took down all that they told her, used the material for her book and turned their personal histories into stories for the newspapers, "Fanny Balbuk-Yooreel" and "Policeman Jubytch" being two of the more successful. 15

Balbuk, an aggressive character, remained noisily resentful of her loss of property and prestige and turned towards the white man's drink for compensation. Jubytch, on the other hand, kept his dignity to the end, retaining the beliefs that had fortified the community into which he had been born. Nor did he compete with his friends Monnop and Dool for the favours of Ngilgee, the "rich widow" of the camp.

Ngilgee, one-time nurse of John Forrest,° was an old friend of Daisy's. She had been a domestic at the Fairbairn household and was valued as a gossip who entertained the family with the peccadilloes of Perth society. On the Maamba reserve she had been given a Government hut complete with a double bed which she shared, successively or at once, with her "thirty-two dogs, seven goats, a dozen fowls, four aboriginal suitors and one half caste aspirant".

Brought up in a white family, she had been married at an early age to a half-caste called Whitey Brown George and found herself deserted by him for another of his colour.

For Daisy, Ngilgee was proof of the adage that, where a man was concerned, women, black or white, were sisters under the skin. From then on, she wrote, Ngilgee became a wanderer, choosing her own "acting husbands" as she called them. These she got rid of when the time came by the effective method of emptying a bucket of water over their

---

Stead: W. T. Stead, editor of *The Review of Reviews,* gave Daisy her start in journalism.
John Forrest: The governor of Australia.

heads. An Aboriginal beauty, she was possessed of a "shapely form, beautiful teeth and eyes, and skin smooth as burnished bronze". Though already sixty years old when Daisy moved into the reserve, she was the source of rivalry among the four elderly "bachelors" who sought for her attentions.

One morning Daisy saw one of these emerging from Ngilgee's hut   20
to the accompaniment of the contents of a bucket and asked what the trouble was. Ngilgee, whose English was perfect, confided in her that, a few months beforehand, she had taken unto herself a new lover, young enough to be her grandson, with whom she had fallen in love. Unknown to her, the jealous four had threatened him with their magic unless he left the camp and Ngilgee woke up one morning to find him gone. She tried in vain to "sing him back". When this didn't work she had consoled herself with old Baabur, one of her suitors.

It was no good. Ngilgee's heart remained with her young lover and old Baabur had been given his marching orders.

Through Ngilgee, Daisy learnt an important lesson in native manners.

One day she called at her tent with a present of a somewhat soggy damper.° Daisy thanked her and noticed that Ngilgee's departure was a trifle crestfallen.

Next day she arrived with a second damper. This time she lingered. "Wangallin", as Daisy was called, put down her pen and paper, prepared for the inevitable.

"Wangallin learning all our customs now?" Ngilgee asked conver-   25
sationally.

"Coming along, Ngilgee."

"Not know all customs yet. When we give a present we get one back."

Daisy registered this. She went on talking for a minute or two longer and then said, as though the idea had just occurred to her:

"Would you like a tin of fish, Ngilgee?"

"Thank you Wangallin," Ngilgee answered, with polished cour-   30
tesy. "You are kind."

The lesson learned, Daisy's larder, never plentiful, became seriously threatened. Fortunately she found that her neighbours would gladly exchange fresh native fruits for the tinned variety, and that illustrated magazines were much in demand. This was just as well because, even if camp life solved her accommodation problems, eight shillings a day did not go far. By now the papers accepted everything she sent them, but for two articles in the *West Australian* she received only £10.10s. and for one of six columns in length in the *Western Mail* she received £6, reasonable recompense for the period but inadequate for her needs.

damper: Unleavened bread.

Medicines were a constant expense. Like her first teacher, Father Nicholas, she bound up cuts and sores while asking questions. Fortunately she needed only the simplest of remedies, bandages, antiseptics, fruit salts, olive oil; brandy in emergencies. Her patients responded to psychological rather than medical cures. Dominated as they were by their belief in the supernatural, a *mobburn* or magic doctor could cure them or kill them. Daisy graduated to their ranks after she came into possession of her *nowinning,* or magic stick.

Her explanation for it was that she had been called to the bedside of a dying *mobburn* doctor who had placed his stick between his body and hers and died after pronouncing her the official recipient of his *mobburn*. The stick, four inches long and carved with the figure of a woman, became her "passport". The southern natives believed that there was fire in it. When she left the camp for Perth, she would be told on her return that a light had shone all night from her tent from the *nowinning*. While she possessed it, no native would come near her without permission. She could go anywhere, ask anything. If there was trouble she had only to produce it.

A visit to the Ashburton district added to her reputation as a "sorceress".

Although her headquarters remained for two years at the Maamba reserve, she spent some time visiting the different camps. In the Northwest, a signal honour was conferred on her. She was included as a member of the "rain totem". According to traditional belief, Aboriginal ancestry could be traced back to the natural world that surrounded them. A dreamtime ancestor might have been a kangaroo, an emu, a tree, or in this case, rain. Whichever it was, it became the totem of its group. Totem boards were sacred. Ceremonies were held to encourage increase. When Daisy was made a member of the rain totem, she went with the group carrying a wooden bowl of water to the top of a nearby hill. Arrived at the crown, one chosen amongst them filled his mouth from the bowl and squirted himself and his companions. During this rite a "rain song" was sung which, she said, was both plaintive and catchy. One day she was heard "thoughtlessly singing the rain song" and that same night a cloudburst descended on the camp.

"After that," she told reporter Gwen Sargent White, "my reputation was established for ever."

She could never resist making a good story out of her experiences, but in fact she was less contemptuous of Aboriginal magic than she had been of Stead's experiments in spiritualism. Like Grant Watson,° she saw evidence of its power. Seldom if ever did she rely on it for protection, for the reason that she never felt the need for any.

Grant Watson: A member, along with Daisy, of an anthropological team led by A. R. Radcliffe-Brown.

"Not one native felt like a stranger to me," she explained. "I seem to have known them ages ago. They are my kin. My poor relations, if you like."

At the Katanning camp, at which she was a regular visitor, her confidence was tested.

One twilight evening, seated beside her fire dreaming dreams of   40
northern gloamings in which she wandered through English rose gardens with her former lover Carrick Hoare, she became aware of a silence that had settled over the camp. Looking up, she saw a group of figures in full war array, watching her. Moving without sound, as only Aborigines can, they had crept close. At the same time she noticed that all the campfires had been extinguished, a bad sign, as fire is a token of welcome.

It was evident that this was no friendly visit. Daisy remained where she was, returning their interest. After a moment she called out to them:

"I don't know who you are but will you come and have tucker with me?"

They accepted her offer, though with some caution, sitting on the ground beside her fire, spears ready in case of emergency. Daisy ignored the spears, set the women to making damper for them all and gave them supper. Turning their backs on each other, as was camp etiquette, they devoured the damper and drank the tea. She said they "spent a pleasant evening together, chatting like friends." Next morning they were gone. Danger had been averted.

Although she was provided with a revolver as part of her equipment, she told Hurst that she never used it except to kill a rabbit and then "only when I was sure of hitting my target".

The one time when she produced it for disciplinary purposes was   45
for the benefit of white and not black offenders.

For some reason her account of this episode was never published and remains, as she wrote it, in her notebooks:

> One night after a full day I was getting ready for my night's rest. I heard some drunken voices and, putting on my kimono and slippers, took my revolver and went out.
>
> Three drunken men with a sugar bag full of bottles of drink were calling for black gins.
>
> I went over to them and said: "Get up at once and go before me."
>
> The lantern showed my revolver. They got up, staggering, and I called out in native dialect:
>
> "Go into town, one of you, and tell Sergeant Perkins I will guard these bad men and wait for you."

Hoping that she would not have to walk into Katanning in kimono and slippers, she began to march them in the direction of the town. In due course Kaka, the Aboriginal who had done as she asked, appeared out of the darkness with the sergeant.

"The Sergeant touched his cap and went off with the men. Not a word was spoken by him or by me."

Next morning was Sunday and Daisy, who was in the habit of walking to church when she was near a town, passed unrecognized as the sergeant headed the three men out of Katanning.

"I rewarded Kaka with a new pair of trousers," she noted. "They   50 do so hate the dark."

It was while she was at Katanning that she dealt, single-handed, with an outbreak of measles. This arduous and at times distressing experience she transformed into an amusing article which was published first in the *West Australian* in November 1907, and later in *Science of Man*.

Her first invalid was Notuman, an elderly "sister" "who embodied in her bulky form all the cunning and devilment of her race . . . whether it hailed, rained, or the sun shone, I being the 'younger sister' was at her beck and call at all hours." After her came Daddel, a thirteen-year-old boy, Togur his friend, and so on from one to the other as the disease spread through the camp. The Katanning doctor broke the sad news to her that there was no hospital space and recommended "gruel, milk, soup, tea, or any other liquid foods for a few days".

"To begin with I can't cook," Daisy wrote, "cooking and washing having been left out of my itinerary. I had never made gruel and the only soup I could manage was Liebig's extract of Bovril. I had, however, either heard or read somewhere that properly made gruel took four hours in the making. I wish I could put all the native magic I possess into the fiend who made that statement! My fire was an open one, and the winter winds of Katanning are not faithful two minutes, running to any one point of the compass. I sat down by the fire on a kerosene case to make my first billycan of gruel. . . . The wind shifted suddenly and the fire caught a handful of my hair and singed it. I changed my seat but the wind changed too, and blew smoke and flames against my scorching face. I stirred the gruel steadily, discarded the kerosene case and walked round the fire and billycan to the forty-eight points of the compass with which the wind was flirting that dreadful afternoon. I had started gruel making at 2 p.m. and at 6 exactly I took it off the fire. By this time I had recited FitzGerald's *Omar* at least six times . . . it wasn't the words of the poem that brought relief but the way they could be uttered."

Daddel had no sooner recovered than his mother and seven brothers and sisters caught the infection. Living in a *mia* (hut) divided into two, the entire family was housed in a space of not more than five feet in diameter.

"They lay with their heads within the mia, their feet towards the   55 open fireplace between the two huts. To reach one I had to lean over the others, huddled up at either side . . . like peas in a rounded pod. What with the odour, the smoke, and the bodily contortions necessary to reach each patient and spoon feed him or her, it became a matter of constant appeal to emulate Mark Tapley and to be jolly and cheerful during the process."

All but one of her patients got better and her account ends with a paean of approval for the cheerfulness that was her birthright.

"Oh! I do think cheerfulness more than cleanliness is next to god-liness and down in that miserable camp where not a single convenience helped to lighten the troubles of sickness for those poor natives, I often thanked Heaven for the light Irish heart I was born with, which went all the way with me and helped them to bear their troubles more easily."

FOR DISCUSSION AND WRITING

1. Why is it possible to view agent as the main element in this selection?

2. The selection starts with a detailed account of Daisy Bates's camp. What does this scene tell you about the agent who inhabits it?

3. What was Daisy Bates's purpose? What evidence do you have for your conclusion?

4. What character traits seem to have contributed to Daisy's success? Be specific.

5. What part do agencies play in the narrative (for example, damper, the pistol)? In what sense is the rain ceremony an agency?

6. What sort of person (agent) is Ngilgee? How do her purposes clash or coincide with those of Daisy?

7. The last question regarding Berg's biography of Samuel Goldwyn (p. 162) quotes David Herbert Donald's theory of biography. Does his theory seem to characterize Salter's biography of Daisy Bates? Explain.

8. In your own words, state the main point of the selection.

THE FIRE

John Hersey

Hersey was born in Tientsin, China, in 1914 to American parents. He obtained his bachelor's degree from Yale University before becoming a writer and editor for *Time* magazine, for which he was a World War II correspondent covering the South Pacific and Mediterranean theaters of conflict.

Since 1945, Hersey has had an ongoing publishing relationship with *The New Yorker.* In fact, *Hiroshima,* from which "The Fire" is excerpted, was first published in that magazine in 1946 before being issued in book form. *Hiroshima* has become a landmark work in a field that has since been labeled the New Journalism, a reporting style in which actual events are arranged and presented in much the same ways as works of fiction. Writes Hersey,

> Palpable "facts" are mortal. Like certain moths and flying ants, they lay their eggs and die overnight. The important "flashes" and "bulletins" are already forgotten by the time yesterday morning's paper is used to line the trash can. . . . The things we remember for longer periods are emotions and impressions and illusions and images and characters: the elements of fiction. . . .

Although Hersey is primarily a writer, he has been actively involved in the field of education, serving as a member of the Westport, Connecticut, School Study Council; of the Westport Board of Education; of the Yale University Council Committee on the Humanities; of the Fairfield, Connecticut, Citizens School Study Council; and as a trustee for both the National Citizens' Council for the Public Schools and the National Committee for Support of the Public Schools.

Perhaps Hersey's best-known work of fiction is *A Bell for Adano,* a novel of World War II.

There's an old saying: Let the facts speak for themselves. In *Hiroshima,* the facts do eloquently and shatteringly speak for themselves. As you read, notice the power that factual details give the text.

Immediately after the explosion, the Reverend Mr. Kiyoshi Tanimoto, having run wildly out of the Matsui estate and having looked in wonderment at the bloody soldiers at the mouth of the dugout they had been digging, attached himself sympathetically to an old lady who was walking along in a daze, holding her head with her left hand, supporting a small boy of three or four on her back with her right, and crying. "I'm hurt! I'm hurt! I'm hurt!" Mr. Tanimoto transferred the child to his own back and led the woman by the hand down the street, which was darkened by what seemed to be a local column of dust. He took the woman to a grammar school not far away that had previously been designated for use as a temporary hospital in case of emergency. By this solicitous behavior, Mr. Tanimoto at once got rid of his terror. At the school, he was much surprised to see glass all over the floor and fifty or sixty injured people already waiting to be treated. He reflected that, although the all-clear had sounded and he had heard no planes, several bombs must have been dropped. He thought of a hillock in the rayon man's garden from which he could get a view of the whole of Koi—of the whole of Hiroshima, for that matter—and he ran back up to the estate.

From the mound, Mr. Tanimoto saw an astonishing panorama. Not just a patch of Koi, as he had expected, but as much of Hiroshima as he could see through the clouded air was giving off a thick, dreadful miasma. Clumps of smoke, near and far, had begun to push up through the general dust. He wondered how such extensive damage could have been dealt out of a silent sky; even a few planes, far up, would have been audible. Houses nearby were burning, and when huge drops of water the size of marbles began to fall, he half thought that they must be coming from the hoses of firemen fighting the blazes. (They were actually drops of condensed moisture falling from the turbulent tower of dust, heat, and fission fragments that had already risen miles into the sky above Hiroshima.)

Mr. Tanimoto turned away from the sight when he heard Mr. Matsuo call out to ask whether he was all right. Mr. Matsuo had been safely cushioned within the falling house by the bedding stored in the front hall and had worked his way out. Mr. Tanimoto scarcely answered. He had thought of his wife and baby, his church, his home, his parishioners, all of them down in that awful murk. Once more he began to run in fear—toward the city.

Mrs. Hatsuyo Nakamura, the tailor's widow, having struggled up from under the ruins of her house after the explosion, and seeing Myeko, the youngest of her three children, buried breast-deep and unable to move, crawled across the debris, hauled at timbers, and flung tiles aside, in a hurried effort to free the child. Then, from what seemed to be caverns far below, she heard two small voices crying, *"Tasukete! Tasukete!* Help! Help!"

She called the names of her ten-year-old son and eight-year-old *5* daughter: "Toshio! Yaeko!"

The voices from below answered.

Mrs. Nakamura abandoned Myeko, who at least could breathe, and in a frenzy made the wreckage fly above the crying voices. The children had been sleeping nearly ten feet apart, but now their voices seemed to come from the same place. Toshio, the boy, apparently had some freedom to move, because she could feel him undermining the pile of wood and tiles as she worked from above. At last she saw his head, and she hastily pulled him out by it. A mosquito net was wound intricately, as if it had been carefully wrapped, around his feet. He said he had been blown right across the room and had been on top of his sister Yaeko under the wreckage. She now said, from underneath, that she could not move, because there was something on her legs. With a bit more digging, Mrs. Nakamura cleared a hole above the child and began to pull her arm. *"Itai!* It hurts!" Yaeko cried. Mrs. Nakamura shouted, "There's no time now to say whether it hurts or not," and yanked her whimpering daughter up. Then she freed Myeko. The children were filthy and bruised, but none of them had a single cut or scratch.

Mrs. Nakamura took the children out into the street. They had nothing on but underpants, and although the day was very hot, she worried rather confusedly about their being cold, so she went back into the wreckage and burrowed underneath and found a bundle of clothes she had packed for an emergency, and she dressed them in pants, blouses, shoes, padded-cotton air-raid helmets called *bokuzuki,* and even, irrationally, overcoats. The children were silent, except for the five-year-old, Myeko, who kept asking questions: "Why is it night already? Why did our house fall down? What happened?" Mrs. Nakamura, who did not know what had happened (had not the all-clear sounded?), looked around and saw through the darkness that all the houses in her neighborhood had collapsed. The house next door, which its owner had been tearing down to make way for a fire lane, was now very thoroughly, if crudely, torn down; its owner, who had been sacrificing his home for the community's safety, lay dead. Mrs. Nakamoto, wife of the head of the local air-raid-defense Neighborhood Association, came across the street with her head all bloody, and said that her baby was badly cut; did Mrs. Nakamura have any bandage? Mrs. Nakamura did not, but she crawled into the remains of her house again and pulled out some white cloth that she had been using in her work as a seamstress, ripped it into strips, and gave it to Mrs. Nakamoto. While fetching the cloth, she noticed her sewing machine; she went back in for it and dragged it out. Obviously, she could not carry it with her, so she unthinkingly plunged her symbol of livelihood into the receptacle which for weeks had been her symbol of safety—the cement tank of water in front of her house, of the type every household had been ordered to construct against a possible fire raid.

A nervous neighbor, Mrs. Hataya, called to Mrs. Nakamura to run away with her to the woods in Asano Park—an estate, by the Kyo River not far off, belonging to the wealthy Asano family, who once owned the Toyo Kisen Kaisha steamship line. The park had been designated as an evacuation area for their neighborhood. Seeing fire breaking out in a nearby ruin (except at the very center, where the bomb itself ignited some fires, most of Hiroshima's citywide conflagration was caused by inflammable wreckage falling on cook stoves and live wires), Mrs. Nakamura suggested going over to fight it. Mrs. Hataya said "Don't be foolish. What if planes come and drop more bombs?" So Mrs. Nakamura started out for Asano Park with her children and Mrs. Hataya, and she carried her rucksack of emergency clothing, a blanket, an umbrella, and a suitcase of things she had cached in her air-raid shelter. Under many ruins, as they hurried along, they heard muffled screams for help. The only building they saw standing on their way to Asano Park was the Jesuit mission house, alongside the Catholic kindergarten to which Mrs. Nakamura had sent Myeko for a time. As they passed it, she saw Father Kleinsorge, in bloody underwear, running out of the house with a small suitcase in his hand.

Right after the explosion, while Father Wilhelm Kleinsorge, S.J., was 10 wandering around in his underwear in the vegetable garden, Father Superior LaSalle came around the corner of the building in the darkness. His body, especially his back, was bloody; the flash had made him twist away from his window, and tiny pieces of glass had flown at him. Father Kleinsorge, still bewildered, managed to ask, "Where are the rest?" Just then, the two other priests living in the mission house appeared—Father Cieslik, unhurt, supporting Father Schiffer, who was covered with blood that spurted from a cut above his left ear and who was very pale. Father Cieslik was rather pleased with himself, for after the flash he had dived into a doorway, which he had previously reckoned to be the safest place inside the building, and when the blast came, he was not injured. Father LaSalle told Father Cieslik to take Father Schiffer to a doctor before he bled to death, and suggested either Dr. Kanda, who lived on the next corner, or Dr. Fujii, about six blocks away. The two men went out of the compound and up the street.

The daughter of Mr. Hoshijima, the mission catechist, ran up to Father Kleinsorge and said that her mother and sister were buried under the ruins of their house, which was at the back of the Jesuit compound, and at the same time the priests noticed that the house of the Catholic-kindergarten teacher at the front of the compound had collapsed on her. While Father LaSalle and Mrs. Murata, the mission housekeeper, dug the teacher out, Father Kleinsorge went to the catechist's fallen house and began lifting things off the top of the pile. There was not a sound underneath; he was sure the Hoshijima women had been killed. At last, under what had been a corner of the kitchen, he saw Mrs. Hoshijima's head. Believing her dead, he began to haul her out by the hair, but suddenly she screamed, "*Itai! Itai!* It hurts! It hurts!" He dug some more and lifted her out. He managed, too, to find her daughter in the rubble and free her. Neither was badly hurt.

A public bath next door to the mission house had caught fire, but since there the wind was southerly, the priests thought their house would be spared. Nevertheless, as a precaution, Father Kleinsorge went inside to fetch some things he wanted to save. He found his room in a state of weird and illogical confusion. A first-aid kit was hanging undisturbed on a hook on the wall, but his clothes, which had been on other hooks nearby, were nowhere to be seen. His desk was in splinters all over the room, but a mere papier-mâché suitcase, which he had hidden under the desk, stood handle-side up, without a scratch on it, in the doorway of the room, where he could not miss it. Father Kleinsorge later came to regard this as a bit of Providential interference, inasmuch as the suitcase contained his breviary, the account books for the whole diocese, and a considerable amount of paper money belonging to the mission, for which he was responsible. He ran out of the house and deposited the suitcase in the mission air-raid shelter.

At about this time, Father Cieslik and Father Schiffer, who was still spurting blood, came back and said that Dr. Kanda's house was ruined and that fire blocked them from getting out of what they supposed to be the local circle of destruction to Dr. Fujii's private hospital, on the bank of the Kyo River.

Dr. Masakazu Fujii's hospital was no longer on the bank of the Kyo River; it was in the river. After the overturn, Dr. Fujii was so stupefied and so tightly squeezed by the beams gripping his chest that he was unable to move at first, and he hung there about twenty minutes in the darkened morning. Then a thought which came to him—that soon the tide would be running in through the estuaries and his head would be submerged—inspired him to fearful activity; he wriggled and turned and exerted what strength he could (though his left arm, because of the pain in his shoulder, was useless), and before long he had freed himself from the vise. After a few moments' rest, he climbed onto the pile of timbers and, finding a long one that slanted up to the riverbank, he painfully shinnied up it.

Dr. Fujii, who was in his underwear, was now soaking and dirty. His undershirt was torn, and blood ran down it from bad cuts on his chin and back. In this disarray, he walked out onto Kyo Bridge, beside which his hospital had stood. The bridge had not collapsed. He could see only fuzzily without his glasses, but he could see enough to be amazed at the number of houses that were down all around. On the bridge, he encountered a friend, a doctor named Machii, and asked in bewilderment, "What do you think it was?"

Dr. Machii said, "It must have been a *Molotoffano banakago*"—a Molotov flower basket, the delicate Japanese name for the "bread basket," or self-scattering cluster of bombs.

At first, Dr. Fujii could see only two fires, one across the river from his hospital site and one quite far to the south. But at the same time, he and his friend observed something that puzzled them, and which, as doctors, they discussed: although there were as yet very few fires, wounded people were hurrying across the bridge in an endless parade of misery, and many of them exhibited terrible burns on their faces and arms. "Why do you suppose it is?" Dr. Fujii asked. Even a theory was comforting that day, and Dr. Machii stuck to his. "Perhaps because it was a Molotov flower basket," he said.

There had been no breeze earlier in the morning when Dr. Fujii had walked to the railway station to see his friend off, but now brisk winds were blowing every which way; here on the bridge the wind was easterly. New fires were leaping up, and they spread quickly, and in a very short time terrible blasts of hot air and showers of cinders made it impossible to stand on the bridge any more. Dr. Machii ran to the far side of the river and along a still unkindled street. Dr. Fujii went down into the water under the bridge, where a score of people had already taken refuge, among them his servants, who had extricated themselves from the wreckage. From there, Dr. Fujii saw a nurse hanging in the timbers of his hospital by her legs, and then another painfully pinned across the breast. He enlisted the help of some of the others under the bridge and freed both of them. He thought he heard the voice of his niece for a moment, but he could not find her; he never saw her again. Four of his nurses and the two patients in the hospital died, too. Dr. Fujii went back into the water of the river and waited for the fire to subside.

The lot of Drs. Fujii, Kanda, and Machii right after the explosion — and, as these three were typical, that of the majority of the physicians and surgeons of Hiroshima — with their offices and hospitals destroyed, their equipment scattered, their own bodies incapacitated in varying degrees, explained why so many citizens who were hurt went untended and why so many who might have lived died. Of a hundred and fifty doctors in the city, sixty-five were already dead and most of the rest were wounded. Of 1,780 nurses, 1,654 were dead or too badly hurt to work. In the biggest hospital, that of the Red Cross, only six doctors out of thirty were able to function, and only ten nurses out of more than two hundred. The sole uninjured doctor on the Red Cross Hospital staff was Dr. Sasaki. After the explosion, he hurried to a storeroom to fetch bandages. This room, like everything he had seen as he ran through the hospital, was chaotic — bottles of medicines thrown off shelves and broken, salves spattered on the walls, instruments strewn everywhere. He grabbed up some bandages and an unbroken bottle of mercurochrome, hurried back to the chief surgeon, and bandaged his cuts. Then he went out into the corridor and began patching up the wounded patients and the doctors and nurses there. He blundered so without his glasses that he took a pair off the face of a wounded nurse, and although they only approximately compensated for the errors of his vision, they were better than nothing. (He was to depend on them for more than a month.)

Dr. Sasaki worked without method, taking those who were nearest him first, and he noticed soon that the corridor seemed to be getting

20

more and more crowded. Mixed in with the abrasions and lacerations which most people in the hospital had suffered, he began to find dreadful burns. He realized then that casualties were pouring in from outdoors. There were so many that he began to pass up the lightly wounded; he decided that all he could hope to do was to stop people from bleeding to death. Before long, patients lay and crouched on the floors of the wards and the laboratories and all the other rooms, and in the corridors, and on the stairs, and in the front hall, and under the portecochère, and on the stone front steps, and in the driveway and courtyard, and for blocks each way in the streets outside. Wounded people supported maimed people; disfigured families leaned together. Many people were vomiting. A tremendous number of schoolgirls—some of those who had been taken from their classrooms to work outdoors, clearing fire lanes—crept into the hospital. In a city of two hundred and forty-five thousand, nearly a hundred thousand people had been killed or doomed at one blow; a hundred thousand more were hurt. At least ten thousand of the wounded made their way to the best hospital in town, which was altogether unequal to such a trampling, since it had only six hundred beds, and they had all been occupied. The people in the suffocating crowd inside the hospital wept and cried, for Dr. Sasaki to hear, "*Sensei!* Doctor!," and the less seriously wounded came and pulled at his sleeve and begged him to go to the aid of the worse wounded. Tugged here and there in his stockinged feet, bewildered by the numbers, staggered by so much raw flesh, Dr. Sasaki lost all sense of profession and stopped working as a skillful surgeon and a sympathetic man; he became an automaton, mechanically wiping, daubing, winding, wiping, daubing, winding.

Some of the wounded in Hiroshima were unable to enjoy the questionable luxury of hospitalization. In what had been the personnel office of the East Asia Tin Works, Miss Sasaki lay doubled over, unconscious, under the tremendous pile of books and plaster and wood and corrugated iron. She was wholly unconscious (she later estimated) for about three hours. Her first sensation was of dreadful pain in her left leg. It was so black under the books and debris that the borderline between awareness and unconsciousness was fine; she apparently crossed it several times, for the pain seemed to come and go. At the moments when it was sharpest, she felt that her leg had been cut off somewhere below the knee. Later, she heard someone walking on top of the wreckage above her, and anguished voices spoke up, evidently from within the mess around her: "Please help! Get us out!"

Father Kleinsorge stemmed Father Schiffer's spurting cut as well as he could with some bandage that Dr. Fujii had given the priests a few days before. When he finished, he ran into the mission house again and found the jacket of his military uniform and an old pair of gray trousers. He put them on and went outside. A woman from next door ran up to him and shouted that her husband was buried under her house and the house was on fire; Father Kleinsorge must come and save him.

Father Kleinsorge, already growing apathetic and dazed in the presence of the cumulative distress, said, "We haven't much time." Houses all around were burning, and the wind was now blowing hard. "Do you know exactly which part of the house he is under?" he asked.

"Yes, yes," she said. "Come quickly."

They went around to the house, the remains of which blazed violently, but when they got there, it turned out that the woman had no idea where her husband was. Father Kleinsorge shouted several times, "Is anyone there?" There was no answer. Father Kleinsorge said to the woman, "We must get away or we will all die." He went back to the Catholic compound and told the Father Superior that the fire was coming closer on the wind, which had swung around and was now from the north; it was time for everybody to go.   *25*

Just then, the kindergarten teacher pointed out to the priests Mr. Fukai, the secretary of the diocese, who was standing in his window on the second floor of the mission house, facing in the direction of the explosion, weeping. Father Cieslik, because he thought the stairs unusable, ran around to the back of the mission house to look for a ladder. There he heard people crying for help under a nearby fallen roof. He called to passers-by running away in the street to help him lift it, but nobody paid any attention, and he had to leave the buried ones to die. Father Kleinsorge ran inside the mission house and scrambled up the stairs, which were awry and piled with plaster and lathing and called to Mr. Fukai from the doorway of his room.

Mr. Fukai, a very short man of about fifty, turned around slowly, with a queer look, and said, "Leave me here."

Father Kleinsorge went into the room and took Mr. Fukai by the collar of his coat and said, "Come with me or you'll die."

Mr. Fukai said, "Leave me here to die."

Father Kleinsorge began to shove and haul Mr. Fukai out of the room. Then the theological student came up and grabbed Mr. Fukai's feet, and Father Kleinsorge took his shoulders, and together they carried him downstairs and outdoors. "I can't walk!" Mr. Fukai cried. "Leave me here!" Father Kleinsorge got his paper suitcase with the money in it and took Mr. Fukai up pickaback, and the party started for the East Parade Ground, their district's "safe area." As they went out of the gate, Mr. Fukai, quite childlike now, beat on Father Kleinsorge's shoulders and said, "I won't leave. I won't leave." Irrelevantly, Father Kleinsorge turned to Father LaSalle and said, "We have lost all our possessions but not our sense of humor."   *30*

The street was cluttered with parts of houses that had slid into it, and with fallen telephone poles and wires. From every second or third house came the voices of people buried and abandoned, who invariably screamed, with formal politeness, "*Tasukete kure!* Help, if you please!" The priests recognized several ruins from which these cries came as the homes of friends, but because of the fire it was too late to help. All the way, Mr. Fukai whimpered, "Let me stay." The party turned right when they came to a block of fallen houses that was one flame. At Sakai Bridge, which would take them across to the East Parade Ground, they saw that the whole community on the opposite side of the river was a sheet of fire; they dared not cross and decided to take refuge in Asano Park, off to their left. Father Kleinsorge, who had been weakened for a couple of days by his bad case of diarrhea, began to stagger under his protesting burden, and as he tried to climb up over the wreckage of several houses that blocked their way to the park, he stumbled, dropped Mr. Fukai, and plunged down, head over heels, to the edge of the river. When he picked himself up, he saw Mr. Fukai running away. Father Kleinsorge shouted to a dozen soldiers, who were standing by the bridge, to stop him. As Father Kleinsorge started back to get Mr. Fukai, Father LaSalle called out, "Hurry! Don't waste time!" So Father Kleinsorge just requested the soldiers to take care of Mr. Fukai. They said they would, but the little, broken man got away form them, and the last the priests could see of him, he was running back toward the fire.

Mr. Tanimoto, fearful for his family and church, at first ran toward them by the shortest route, along Koi Highway. He was the only person making his way into the city; he met hundreds and hundreds who were fleeing, and every one of them seemed to be hurt in some way. The eyebrows of some were burned off and skin hung from their faces and hands. Others, because of pain, held their arms up as if carrying something in both hands. Some were vomiting as they walked. Many were naked or in shreds of clothing. On some undressed bodies, the burns had made patterns — of undershirt straps and suspenders and, on the skin of some women (since white repelled the heat from the bomb and dark clothes absorbed it and conducted it to the skin), the shapes of flowers they had had on their kimonos. Many, although injured themselves, supported relatives who were worse off. Almost all had their heads bowed, looked straight ahead, were silent, and showed no expression whatever.

After crossing Koi Bridge and Kannon Bridge, having run the whole way, Mr. Tanimoto saw, as he approached the center, that all the houses had been crushed and many were afire. Here the trees were bare and their trunks were charred. He tried at several points to penetrate the ruins, but the flames always stopped him. Under many houses, people screamed for help, but no one helped; in general, survivors that day assisted only their relatives or immediate neighbors, for they could not comprehend or tolerate a wider circle of misery. The wounded limped past the screams, and Mr. Tanimoto ran past them. As a Christian he was filled with compassion for those who were trapped, and as a Japanese he was overwhelmed by the shame of being unhurt, and he prayed as he ran, "God help them and take them out of the fire."

He thought he would skirt the fire, to the left. He ran back to Kannon Bridge and followed for a distance one of the rivers. He tried several cross streets, but they all were blocked, so he turned far left and ran out to Yokogawa, a station on a railroad line that detoured the city in a wide semicircle, and he followed the rails until he came to a burning train. So impressed was he by this time by the extent of the damage that he ran north two miles to Gion, a suburb in the foothills. All the way, he overtook dreadfully burned and lacerated people, and in his guilt he turned to right and left as he hurried and said to some of them, "Excuse me for having no burden like yours." Near Gion, he began to meet country people going toward the city to help, and when they saw him, several exclaimed, "Look! There is one who is not wounded." At Gion, he bore toward the right bank of the main river, the Ota, and ran down it until he reached fire again. There was no fire on the other side of the river, so he threw off his shirt and shoes and plunged into it. In midstream, where the current was fairly strong, exhaustion and fear finally caught up with him — he had run nearly seven miles — and he became limp and drifted in the water. He prayed, "Please, God, help me to cross. It would be nonsense for me to be drowned when I am the only uninjured one." He managed a few more strokes and fetched up on a spit downstream.

Mr. Tanimoto climbed up the bank and ran along it until, near a large Shinto shrine, he came to more fire, and as he turned left to get around it, he met, by incredible luck, his wife. She was carrying their infant son. Mr. Tanimoto was now so emotionally worn out that nothing could surprise him. He did not embrace his wife; he simply said, "Oh, you are safe." She told him that she had got home from her night in Ushida just in time for the explosion; she had been buried under the parsonage with the baby in her arms. She told how the wreckage had pressed down on her, how the baby had cried. She saw a chink of light, and by reaching up with a hand, she worked the hole bigger, bit by bit. After about half an hour, she heard the crackling noise of wood burning. At last the opening was big enough for her to push the baby out, and afterward she crawled out herself. She said she was now going out to Ushida again. Mr. Tanimoto said he wanted to see his church and take care of the people of his Neighborhood Association. They parted as casually — as bewildered — as they had met.

35

Mr. Tanimoto's way around the fire took him across the East Parade Ground, which being an evacuation area, was now the scene of a gruesome review: rank on rank of the burned and bleeding. Those who were burned moaned, "*Mizu, mizu!* Water, water!" Mr. Tanimoto found a basin in a nearby street and located a water tap that still worked in the crushed shell of a house, and he began carrying water to the suffering strangers. When he had given drink to about thirty of them, he realized he was taking too much time. "Excuse me," he said loudly to those nearby who were reaching out their hands to him and crying their thirst. "I have many people to take care of." Then he ran away. He went to the river again, the basin in his hand, and jumped down onto a sandspit. There he saw hundreds of people so badly wounded that they could not get up to go farther from the burning city. When they saw a man erect and unhurt, the chant began again: "*Mizu, mizu, mizu.*" Mr. Tanimoto could not resist them; he carried them water from the river—a mistake, since it was tidal and brackish. Two or three small boats were ferrying hurt people across the river from Asano Park, and when one touched the spit, Mr. Tanimoto again made his loud, apologetic speech and jumped into the boat. It took him across to the park. There, in the underbrush, he found some of his charges of the Neighborhood Association, who had come there by his previous instructions, and saw many acquaintances, among them Father Kleinsorge and the other Catholics. But he missed Fukai, who had been a close friend. "Where is Fukai-*san?*" he asked.

"He didn't want to come with us," Father Kleinsorge said. "He ran back."

When Miss Sasaki heard the voices of the people caught along with her in the dilapidation at the tin factory, she began speaking to them. Her nearest neighbor, she discovered, was a high-school girl who had been drafted for factory work, and who said her back was broken. Miss Sasaki replied, "I am lying here and I can't move. My left leg is cut off."

Some time later, she again heard somebody walk overhead and then move off to one side, and whoever it was began burrowing. The digger released several people, and when he had uncovered the high-school girl, she found that her back was not broken, after all, and she crawled out. Miss Sasaki spoke to the rescuer, and he worked toward her. He pulled away a great number of books, until he had made a tunnel to her. She could see his perspiring face as he said, "Come out, Miss." She tried. "I can't move," she said. The man excavated some more and told her to try with all her strength to get out. But books were heavy on her hips, and the man finally saw that a bookcase was leaning on the books and that a heavy beam pressed down on the bookcase. "Wait," he said. "I'll get a crowbar."

The man was gone a long time, and when he came back, he was   40
ill-tempered, as if her plight were all her fault. "We have no men to help
you!" he shouted in through the tunnel. "You'll have to get out by
yourself."

"That's impossible," she said. "My left leg . . ." The man went
away.

Much later, several men came and dragged Miss Sasaki out. Her
left leg was not severed, but it was badly broken and cut and it hung
askew below the knee. They took her out into a courtyard. It was raining. She sat on the ground in the rain. When the downpour increased,
someone directed all the wounded people to take cover in the factory's
air-raid shelters. "Come along," a torn-up woman said to her. "You can
hop." But Miss Sasaki could not move, and she just waited in the rain.
Then a man propped up a large sheet of corrugated iron as a kind of
lean-to, and took her in his arms and carried her to it. She was grateful
until he brought two horribly wounded people—a woman with a whole
breast sheared off and a man whose face was all raw from a burn—to
share the simple shed with her. No one came back. The rain cleared and
the cloudy afternoon was hot; before nightfall the three grotesques under
the slanting piece of twisted iron began to smell quite bad.

The former head of the Nobori-cho Neighborhood Association to
which the Catholic priests belonged was an energetic man named Yoshida. He had boasted, when he was in charge of the district air-raid
defenses, that fire might eat away all of Hiroshima but it would never
come to Nobori-cho. The bomb blew down his house, and a joist pinned
him by the legs, in full view of the Jesuit mission house across the way
and of the people hurrying along the street. In their confusion as they
hurried past, Mrs. Nakamura, with her children, and Father Kleinsorge,
with Mr. Fukai on his back, hardly saw him; he was just part of the
general blur of misery through which they moved. His cries for help
brought no response from them; there were so many people shouting for
help that they could not hear him separately. They and all the others
went along. Nobori-cho became absolutely deserted, and the fire swept
through it. Mr. Yoshida saw the wooden mission house—the only erect
building in the area—go up in a lick of flame, and the heat was terrific
on his face. Then flames came along his side of the street and entered his
house. In a paroxysm of terrified strength, he freed himself and ran
down the alleys of Nobori-cho, hemmed in by the fire he had said would
never come. He began at once to behave like an old man; two months
later his hair was white.

As Dr. Fujii stood in the river up to his neck to avoid the heat of
the fire, the wind blew stronger and stronger, and soon, even though the
expanse of water was small, the waves grew so high that the people

under the bridge could no longer keep their footing. Dr. Fujii went close to the shore, crouched down, and embraced a large stone with his usable arm. Later it became possible to wade along the very edge of the river, and Dr. Fujii and his two surviving nurses moved about two hundred yards upstream, to a sandspit near Asano Park. Many wounded were lying on the sand. Dr. Machii was there with his family; his daughter, who had been outdoors when the bomb burst, was badly burned on her hands and legs but fortunately not on her face. Although Dr. Fujii's shoulder was by now terribly painful, he examined the girl's burns curiously. Then he lay down. In spite of the misery all around, he was ashamed of his appearance, and he remarked to Dr. Machii that he looked like a beggar, dressed as he was in nothing but torn and bloody underwear. Later in the afternoon, when the fire began to subside, he decided to go to his parental house, in the suburb of Nagatsuka. He asked Dr. Machii to join him, but the Doctor answered that he and his family were going to spend the night on the spit, because of his daughter's injuries. Dr. Fujii, together with his nurses, walked first to Ushida, where, in the partially damaged house of some relatives, he found first-aid materials he had stored there. The two nurses bandaged him and he them. They went on. Now not many people walked in the streets, but a great number sat and lay on the pavement, vomited, waited for death, and died. The number of corpses on the way to Nagatsuka was more and more puzzling. The Doctor wondered: Could a Molotov flower basket have done all this?

Dr. Fujii reached his family's house in the evening. It was five miles   *45* from the center of town, but its roof had fallen in and the windows were all broken.

All day, people poured into Asano Park. This private estate was far enough away from the explosion so that its bamboos, pines, laurel, and maples were still alive, and the green place invited refugees — partly because they believed that if the Americans came back, they would bomb only buildings; partly because the foliage seemed a center of coolness and life, and the estate's exquisitely precise rock gardens, with their quiet pools and arching bridges, were very Japanese, normal, secure; and also partly (according to some who were there) because of an irresistible, atavistic urge to hide under leaves. Mrs. Nakamura and her children were among the first to arrive, and they settled in the bamboo grove near the river. They all felt terribly thirsty, and they drank from the river. At once they were nauseated and began vomiting, and they retched the whole day. Others were also nauseated; they all thought (probably because of the strong odor of ionization, an "electric smell" given off by the bomb's fission) that they were sick from a gas the Americans had dropped. When Father Kleinsorge and the other priests came into the park, nodding to their friends as they passed, the Nakamuras were all sick and prostrate. A woman named Iwasaki, who lived in the neighbor-hood of the mission and who was sitting near the Nakamuras, got up and asked the priests if she should stay where she was or go with them. Father Kleinsorge said, "I hardly know where the safest place is." She stayed there, and later in the day, though she had no visible wounds or burns, she died. The priests went farther along the river and settled down in some underbrush. Father LaSalle lay down and went right to sleep. The theological student, who was wearing slippers, had carried with him a bundle of clothes, in which he had packed two pairs of leather shoes. When he sat down with the others, he found that the bundle had broken open and a couple of shoes had fallen out and now he had only two lefts. He retraced his steps and found one right. When he rejoined the priests, he said, "It's funny, but things don't matter any more. Yes-terday, my shoes were my most important possessions. Today, I don't care. One pair is enough."

Father Cieslik said, "I know. I started to bring my books along, and then I thought, 'This is no time for books.'"

When Mr. Tanimoto, with his basin still in his hand, reached the park, it was very crowded, and to distinguish the living from the dead was not easy, for most of the people lay still, with their eyes open. To Father Kleinsorge, an Occidental, the silence in the grove by the river, where hundreds of gruesomely wounded suffered together, was one of the most dreadful and awesome phenomena of his whole experience. The hurt ones were quiet; no one wept, much less screamed in pain; no one complained; none of the many who died did so noisily; not even the children cried; very few people even spoke. And when Father Kleinsorge gave some water to some whose faces had been almost blotted out by flash burns, they took their share and then raised themselves a little and bowed to him, in thanks.

Mr. Tanimoto greeted the priests and then looked around for other friends. He saw Mrs. Matsumoto, wife of the director of the Methodist School, and asked her if she was thirsty. She was, so he went to one of the pools in the Asano's rock gardens and got water for her in his basin. Then he decided to try to get back to his church. He went into Nobori-cho by the way the priests had taken as they escaped, but he did not get far; the fire along the streets was so fierce that he had to turn back. He walked to the river bank and began to look for a boat in which he might carry some of the most severely injured across the river from Asano Park and away from the spreading fire. Soon he found a good-sized pleasure punt drawn up on the bank, but in and around it was an awful tableau—five dead men, nearly naked, badly burned, who must have expired more or less all at once, for they were in attitudes which suggested that they had been working together to push the boat down into the river. Mr. Tanimoto lifted them away from the boat, and as he did so, he experienced such horror at disturbing the dead—preventing them, he momentarily felt, from launching their craft and going on their ghostly way—that he said out loud, "Please forgive me for taking this boat. I must use it for others, who are alive." The punt was heavy, but he managed to slide it into the water. There were no oars, and all he could find for propulsion was a thick bamboo pole. He worked the boat upstream to the most crowded part of the park and began to ferry the wounded. He could pack ten or twelve into the boat for each crossing, but as the river was too deep in the center to pole his way across, he had to paddle with the bamboo, and consequently each trip took a very long time. He worked several hours that way.

Early in the afternoon, the fire swept into the woods of Asano *50* Park. The first Mr. Tanimoto knew of it was when, returning in his boat, he saw that a great number of people had moved toward the riverside. On touching the bank, he went up to investigate, and when he saw the fire, he shouted, "All the young men who are not badly hurt come with me!" Father Kleinsorge moved Father Schiffer and Father LaSalle close to the edge of the river and asked people there to get them across if the fire came too near, and then joined Tanimoto's volunteers. Mr. Tanimoto sent some to look for buckets and basins and told others to beat the burning underbrush with their clothes; when utensils were at hand, he formed a bucket chain from one of the pools in the rock gardens. The team fought the fire for more than two hours, and gradually defeated the flames. As Mr. Tanimoto's men worked, the frightened people in the park pressed closer and closer to the river, and finally the mob began to force some of the unfortunates who were on the very bank into the water. Among those driven into the river and drowned were Mrs. Matsumoto, of the Methodist School, and her daughter.

When Father Kleinsorge got back after fighting the fire, he found Father Schiffer still bleeding and terribly pale. Some Japanese stood around and stared at him, and Father Schiffer whispered, with a weak smile, "It is as if I were already dead." "Not yet," Father Kleinsorge said. He had brought Dr. Fujii's first-aid kit with him, and he had noticed Dr. Kanda in the crowd, so he sought him out and asked him if he would dress Father Schiffer's bad cuts. Dr. Kanda had seen his wife and daughter dead in the ruins of his hospital; he sat now with his head in his hands. "I can't do anything," he said. Father Kleinsorge bound more bandage around Father Schiffer's head, moved him to a steep place, and settled him so that his head was high, and soon the bleeding diminished.

The roar of approaching planes was heard about this time. Someone in the crowd near the Nakamura family shouted, "It's some Grummans coming to strafe us!" A baker named Nakashima stood up and commanded, "Everyone who is wearing anything white, take it off." Mrs. Nakamura took the blouses off her children, and opened her umbrella and made them get under it. A great number of people, even badly burned ones, crawled into bushes and stayed there until the hum, evidently of a reconnaissance or weather run, died away.

It began to rain. Mrs. Nakamura kept her children under the umbrella. The drops grew abnormally large, and someone shouted, "The Americans are dropping gasoline. They're going to set fire to us!" (This alarm stemmed from one of the theories being passed through the park as to why so much of Hiroshima had burned: it was that a single plane had sprayed gasoline on the city and then somehow set fire to it in one flashing moment.) But the drops were palpably water, and as they fell, the wind grew stronger and stronger, and suddenly—probably because of the tremendous convection set up by the blazing city—a whirlwind ripped through the park. Huge trees crashed down; small ones were uprooted and flew into the air. Higher, a wild array of flat things revolved in the twisting funnel—pieces of iron roofing, papers, doors, strips of matting. Father Kleinsorge put a piece of cloth over Father Schiffer's eyes, so that the feeble man would not think he was going crazy. The gale blew Mrs. Murata, the mission housekeeper, who was sitting close by the river, down the embankment at a shallow, rocky place, and she came out with her bare feet bloody. The vortex moved out onto the river, where it sucked up a waterspout and eventually spent itself.

After the storm, Mr. Tanimoto began ferrying people again, and Father Kleinsorge asked the theological student to go across and make his way out to the Jesuit Novitiate at Nagatsuka, about three miles from the center of town, and to request the priests there to come with help for Fathers Schiffer and LaSalle. The student got into Mr. Tanimoto's boat and went off with him. Father Kleinsorge asked Mrs. Nakamura if she would like to go out to Nagatsuka with the priests when they came. She said she had some luggage and her children were sick—they were still vomiting from time to time, and so, for that matter, was she—and therefore she feared she could not. He said he thought the fathers from the Novitiate could come back the next day with a pushcart to get her.

Late in the afternoon, when he went ashore for a while, Mr. Tanimoto, upon whose energy and initiative many had come to depend, heard people begging for food. He consulted Father Kleinsorge, and they decided to go back into town to get some rice from Mr. Tanimoto's Neighborhood Association shelter and from the mission shelter. Father Cieslik and two or three others went with them. At first, when they got among the rows of prostrate houses, they did not know where they were; the change was too sudden, from a city of two hundred and forty-five thousand that morning to a mere pattern of residue in the afternoon. The asphalt of the streets was still so soft and hot from the fires that walking was uncomfortable. They encountered only one person, a woman, who said to them as they passed, "My husband is in those ashes." At the mission, where Mr. Tanimoto left the party, Father Kleinsorge was dismayed to see the building razed. In the garden, on the way to the shelter, he noticed a pumpkin roasted on the vine. He and Father Cieslik tasted it and it was good. They were surprised at their hunger, and they ate quite a bit. They got out several bags of rice and gathered up several other cooked pumpkins and dug up some potatoes that were nicely baked under the ground, and started back. Mr. Tanimoto rejoined them on the way. One of the people with him had some cooking utensils. In the park, Mr. Tanimoto organized the lightly wounded women of his neighborhood to cook. Father Kleinsorge offered the Nakamura family some pumpkin, and they tried it, but they could not keep it on their stomachs. Altogether, the rice was enough to feed nearly a hundred people.

Just before dark, Mr. Tanimoto came across a twenty-year-old girl, Mrs. Kamai, the Tanimotos' next-door neighbor. She was crouching on the ground with the body of her infant daughter in her arms. The baby had evidently been dead all day. Mrs. Kamai jumped up when she saw Mr. Tanimoto and said, "Would you please try to locate my husband?"

Mr. Tanimoto knew that her husband had been inducted into the Army just the day before; he and Mrs. Tanimoto had entertained Mrs. Kamai in the afternoon, to make her forget. Kamai had reported to the Chugoku Regional Army Headquarters—near the ancient castle in the middle of town—where some four thousand troops were stationed. Judging by the many maimed soldiers Mr. Tanimoto had seen during the day, he surmised that the barracks had been badly damaged by whatever it was that had hit Hiroshima. He knew he hadn't a chance of finding Mrs. Kamai's husband, even if he searched, but he wanted to humor her. "I'll try," he said.

"You've got to find him," she said. "He loved our baby so much. I want him to see her once more."

FOR DISCUSSION AND WRITING

1. Explain why the relationship between the scene and the people in the narrative is important in "The Fire."

2. How would each of the following interpretations of scene influence your understanding of "The Fire": (a) Hiroshima, (b) Japan, (c) Asia, (d) World War II, and (e) the dawn of the Atomic Age?

3. If you were to choose agency (the bomb) as your pivotal term, how would your interpretation of the selection change?

4. As a source of knowledge about the atomic bombing of Hiroshima, is Hersey's book reliable? Explain your judgment.

5. What are some of the ways in which Hersey makes his work easy to read and to understand?

6. Hersey's account of the chaos in Hiroshima is tightly structured. What structural principle does Hersey employ? Do you find the contrast between the chaos of the subject and the "neatness" of the account ironic? Explain.

7. Hersey tells us that the magnitude of the catastrophe in Hiroshima inured many of the survivors to the horror. How does he try to avoid inuring his readers to the horrors?

THE LONG EGYPTIAN NIGHT
Alan Moorehead

Born in Melbourne, Australia, Alan Moorehead began his literary career as a World War II correspondent for the *London Daily Express*. His coverage of the fighting in Africa and the Mediterranean served as the basis for his first three books: *Mediterranean Front, Don't Blame the Generals,* and *The End in Africa.*

His most famous book, *Gallipoli,* is also concerned with war. It is a study of the ill-fated World War I campaign waged by the Allied forces of Britain, Australia, New Zealand, and France against the Turks along the Gallipoli peninsula in an attempt to gain control of the Dardanelles and the Bosporus straits. The book is unanimously regarded as a classic work of history. In 1983, Moorehead died of a stroke in London, England.

"The Long Egyptian Night" is taken from *The Blue Nile,* which, with its companion volume, *The White Nile,* is an account of the nineteenth-century exploration of the Nile River. In these two books, Moorehead presents a great quantity of information in a very clear fashion while telling a good story at the same time.

For readers not familiar with the history of Egypt, the information in this chapter from *The Blue Nile* is stunning, even startling. The selection demonstrates that history can be as luridly interesting as any best-selling novel or popular television program.

Egypt was not easy to defend. The great deserts to the west of the Nile offered a formidable barrier, and no one attempted to penetrate the country that way, but a landing could be made at any place on the low flat shoreline of the delta, and there was a safe anchorage at Alexandria. Once Alexandria fell and the Rosetta mouth of the Nile was taken, no mountains impeded the advance of the invader inland, and he was certain to find food and water nearly all the way to Cairo, over one hundred miles to the south. Two other routes had been successfully exploited since prehistoric times — the one that came down the Nile itself from central Africa, and the other that led in from the east across the isthmus of Suez — but these were not available to an invader from the west.

The delta was a great prize. Here in this artificial garden where rain hardly ever fell but where fresh water was plentiful, two or even three crops were gathered every year, and the annual flooding of the Nile provided a rich layer of silt several inches deep. With comparatively little labour every good thing in life sprang up in abundance, rice and sugar-cane, coffee and tobacco, cotton and flax, lentils and dates, flowers and vines. So long as the water was distributed through the flat land by canals there was no limit to this fertility. Frosts and storms were almost unknown, and most plagues and pests succumbed eventually in the dry antiseptic air of the desert. Except for occasional sandstorms and a muggy, soporific quality in the air during the floods in September, the heat was not excessive, and the winter months were very nearly perfect.

At the time of Bonaparte's landing the population of Egypt was about two and a half million, which was a third of what it was estimated to have been in the days of the Pharaohs and hardly more than a tenth of what it is at present. The people were a mixed lot. Far away in Upper Egypt the Nubian tribes clung to their strips of vegetation along the river bank and in the cultivated oases. Provincial governors sent out from Cairo gathered taxes from them and maintained a rough and ready sort of administration, but for the most part life went by on the Upper Nile in ignorance and solitude. The Bedouin who roamed the intervening deserts that formed fourteen-fifteenths of Egypt were also very largely a law unto themselves, and cannot have numbered more than a few tens of thousands. By far the largest part of the population was huddled into the delta. Apart from the Mamelukes, whom we must consider in a moment, the delta population consisted of about 1,750,000 fellaheen, the indigenous natives who cultivated the soil and formed the labouring population of the cities; about 150,000 Copts — Egyptians who wor-shipped Christ and fulfilled more or less the role of the Parsees in India, as money-lenders, traders and government officials — and finally the for-eigners. These last numbered perhaps 200,000 and lived almost entirely in the cities. They included Turks (the great majority), Greeks, Arme-nians, Jews, Syrians and a handful of French traders who, at the first news of Bonaparte's landing, were interned.

The only two cities of any consequence were Cairo and Alexandria, and Alexandria at this time had sunk to the nadir of its fortunes. Of its ancient glory — of its reputed 4,000 palaces, its theatres, temples and monuments that had once made it second only to Rome in the Roman Empire — hardly anything remained. Pompey's Pillar still stood, and the walls still rose to a height of forty feet in some places, but for the rest all had sunk into dust and rubble, the canal from the Nile had silted up, and the inhabitants, decimated by repeated plagues, had dwindled to less than 10,000. Browne, the English traveller who visited the city in 1792, says 'Heaps of rubbish are on all sides visible, whence every shower of rain, not to mention the industry of the natives in digging, discovers pieces of precious marble, and sometimes ancient coins and fragments of sculpture.' Denon, who got into the city on the heels of the French assault, says he found the houses shut up, the streets deserted except for a few ragged women trailing about like ghosts among the ruins, and a universal silence broken only by the cries of the kites. Even Pompey's Pillar seen from close to was not very impressive.

Cairo, on the other hand, was a flourishing place; after Constanti-nople it was the most important city in the Near East, with a population of about 250,000 people. Since it was first founded over a thousand years before it had been rebuilt several times, and the present city (variously

5

known as Masr, Misr, El-Kahira or Grand Cairo) stood on the site of an ancient Roman fortress. It lay a little distance from the right bank of the river under the cover of the Mokattam Hills, and was ringed by high walls and dominated by a citadel.

The skyline, seen from a distance, had romantic aspects: the domes and minarets of 300 mosques rose from the smoke of cooking fires, and the palm trees and cultivated fields along the river bank gave the place a placid and rather rural air. The citadel, built by Saladin in the twelfth century, was a fine complex of dun-coloured battlements, and in the desert beyond, on the opposite side of the river, one descried the pyramids. Seen from closer at hand, however, these noble prospects disintegrated. Except for the large open squares such as the Esbekiah, which were flooded and thronged with boats during the annual inundation of the Nile, the city was a warren of narrow unpaved streets and nondescript Turkish houses covering about three square miles. Rubbish lay about on every side, the haunt of scavenging dogs and cats, and in the worst slums it was hard to say which were the ruins of fallen buildings and which the hovels of the present generation. 'Not a single fine street,' Denon cries in despair, 'not a single beautiful building. . . . They build as little as they can help; they never repair anything.'

The mosques, crowded with pilgrims living in their outer courtyards, cannot have been very sanitary places, and the bazaars, roofed over with canopies of straw or linen, were both hot and smelly. Browne speaks of 'the polluted dust'.

Yet no one with any love for oriental life could resist this place. The day began before dawn when the mueddins (many of them chosen because they were blind and thus unable to see down into the private houses) roused the people with their first call to the mosques: 'Come to prayer. Come to security. God is most great.' Within an hour—that first fresh hour of the Egyptian morning—the life of the city spilled itself out into the streets, the bazaars and the coffee-houses, and at every turn the passer-by was bound to come on a spectacle of some kind: a marriage or a funeral, an impromptu performance of strolling players in the square, a well-to-do merchant trotting along on his ass with a slave running in front to clear the way, a string of camels thrusting through the crowds with their heads held high and disdainfully in the air. There was a constant passage of street-vendors shouting up to the balconies overhead, and of water-carriers with goatskins slung round their shoulders, and a hullabaloo of shouts and cries filled the air: '*Ya bint; dahrak,*' 'Watch thy back, daughter,' '*Ya efendee,*' 'Take care,' 'O consoler of the embarrassed, my supper must be thy gift'—this last from the innumerable beggars whom one refused by replying with some such phrase as 'God will sustain'.

Craftsmen did their work in their shops under the customer's eye; there was one street for gold- and silversmiths and jewellers, another for leatherworkers and brass-founders, others for potters, silk-spinners, makers of weapons, dyers and perfumers. There was no appetite, no refinement of the senses, that could not be satisifed somewhere in the bazaars, and if the city was squalid it was also very much alive.

Nightfall and darkness (there were no street lights) put an end to the hubbub. Soon after the mueddins' fifth and final call the gates of the city were locked, and many of the streets with large wooden doors at either end were shut up for the night as well. 'One might pass through the whole length of the metropolis,' Lane says, 'and scarcely meet more than a dozen or twenty persons, excepting the watchmen and guards, and the porters at the gates of the bye-streets and quarters. The sentinel, or guard, calls out to the approaching passenger in Turkish "Who is that?", and is answered in Arabic, "A citizen". The private watchman, in same case, exclaims, "Attest the unity of God!" or merely, "Attest the unity!" The reply given to this is, "There is no deity but God!"'

The Nile was the all-provider of this existence. It grew every ounce of food, it supplied water to the wells which were dug in each quarter of the city, and it was the main highway to the outside world. The ceremony of the opening of the canals when the flood rose in August was one of the great occasions of the year. The river at Cairo was about half a mile wide, but it was divided by two islands, Bulaq and Rhoda, where crops were grown and where some of the wealthier people had their pleasure-gardens. Memphis, the ancient capital a little further up the river, had decayed to nothing. In the desert at Gizeh the Sphinx lay buried up to its neck in sand, its nose already broken.

There was one other aspect of the city which gave it a special importance, and which made travellers think of it not simply as Cairo but Grand Cairo: it was the great terminal of the caravan routes that spread out over northern Africa and the Near East. No one dreamed of travelling alone through the desert any more than one would dream of crossing the Atlantic in a canoe. You waited until a caravan was being formed in Cairo, and then applied to the sheikh in command for permission to accompany it. Sometimes months would go by before all was ready, and then on a certain day the order to march would be given, and a long straggling procession of camels, mules, donkeys and men on foot would set off into the desert. Incoming caravans signalled their arrival at the pyramids and were then told where to cross the Nile and encamp. The distances covered were prodigious. One route—and of course there were no clearly defined tracks in the desert, merely a general line of march that led on from one waterhole or oasis to the next—took you north-east to Damascus, where the traveller could join other caravans headed for Aleppo and Baghdad; another carried the pilgrims down to Mecca and the Red Sea; another followed the general course of the Nile to Sennar and Darfur in the Sudan; still another led off to Fezzan in the west. Every journey was an adventure, and the traders, like migratory birds, were controlled by the seasons and beset at every stage by unpredictable hazards such as civil wars, Bedouin raids, drought, floods and sickness. A year, two years on the road — this was nothing to an experienced merchant. Taking with him his wives, his children and his slaves, he would go on and on wherever the markets offered a profit, and in the end nomadism became an object in itself, and many of these men could endure no other way of life. No one knew the extent of this vast, haphazard network. It was quite possible for a man to travel from Egypt to Timbuktu on the other side of Africa, and it is certain that Indian and even Chinese goods appeared in the bazaars in Cairo.

The merchants dealt in kind rather than in money. In Cairo they obtained grain, rice, cotton, flax, and the thousand and one products of the bazaars. These things, increasing in value with every mile they travelled, would be bartered for other goods in the Near East and in the primitive villages in the far interior of Africa. The Sudan trade was particularly profitable. It produced black slaves, gold, ivory, ostrich feathers, rhinoceros horn, gum arabic, ebony, coffee (brought from Ethiopia) and spices (from the Red Sea). Petroleum was also brought in small quantities from the Arabian Gulf; it was either drunk as a medicine or rubbed on the body. Thus there was a continual interchange at Cairo, a constant ebb and flow of strange faces and of strange goods displayed for sale, a commotion of arrivals and departures.

In our time a thousand travellers' books and a spate of illustrated magazines and moving pictures have made a cliché of the East, but in 1798 nothing in Egypt was familiar to the Europeans. Travellers marvelled at everything they saw, and what they did not understand they tended to dismiss as decadent, superstitious and uncouth. It seemed ridiculous, for example, that the Egyptians, on the occasion of a death in the family, should turn their furniture upside down; and that they should believe that, with music, they could charm snakes out of their houses. The music itself was a cacophony to European ears, and the Moslem prayers a grovelling on the ground. The sheikh, sitting cross-legged by the hour on his divan, appeared to be merely apathetic and dull.

Yet the Egyptians were not quite so decadent as the West has liked to imagine, either before or since. The French now, and the English later on, were to exclaim about the lasciviousness of the public dancing girls in Cairo, the prevalence of brothels, the abomination of the slave trade, the shiftlessness and deceit of the orientals, their hopeless indolence. But in fact there were strict rules in the midst of this apparent *laissez-faire*. The majority of Egyptian women were not dancing girls but wives who behaved with much more decorum than women of the West. Divorce was easy, but marriage while it lasted was usually sacrosanct, and family ties were very strong. Drunkenness hardly existed, drug-taking and sodomy were not common vices, and slaves in Cairo were too valuable to

15

be maltreated. As for the sheikhs, they were very far from being apathetic and dull: they were the men of law and religion in the community and they were greatly respected. The Koran which they expounded put the strongest strictures upon everybody's life, and in the main they were obeyed. Lane lists the seven deadly sins in Egypt, and very interesting they are: disobedience to parents, murder, desertion during an expedition against infidels, usury, falsely accusing a woman of adultery, idolatry and the wasting of the property of orphans.

It would be absurd, of course, to make out that the Egyptians were paragons of virtue compared, say, with the invading French — they lied, they stole, they were superstitiously ignorant, they were always lazy when they had the chance, and were probably cowards as well, but they also had a certain dignity in their lives, they knew patience and quietude (which the French did not), and they were graceful, even beautiful, people. Lane describes the women as follows:

'The forms of womenhood begin to develop themselves about the ninth and tenth year; at the age of 15 or 16 they generally attain their highest degree of perfection. . . . They are characterized, like the men, by a fine oval countenance, though in some instances it is rather broad. The eyes, with very few exceptions, are black, large and of a long almond-form, with long and beautiful lashes and an exquisitely soft, bewitching expression — eyes more beautiful can hardly be conceived: their charming effect is heightened by the concealment of the other features (however pleasing the latter may be), and is rendered still more striking by a practice universal among the females of the higher and middle classes, and very common among those of the lower orders, which is that of blackening the edge of the eylids both above and below the eye, with a black powder called Kohl.'

The other practice of the women — that of tattooing eyelids, lips and chin with a kind of purple ink — was not so pleasant.

The extreme modesty of the respectable women — outside the harem they went swathed from head to foot in black — made a strange contrast to the licence of the dancing girls who were often called in after a banquet. Denon, like most of the European travellers who were soon to follow him up the Nile, affected to be appalled. 'Their dance,' he says, 'began voluptuously and soon became lascivious, displaying nothing but a gross and indecent expression of the ectasy of the senses; and what rendered these pictures still more disgusting, was that at the moment in which they kept the least bounds, the two (female) musicians, with the bestiality of the lowest women in the streets of Europe disturbed with a coarse laugh the sense of intoxication that terminated the dance.'

Lane makes a distinction between the *almehs,* the singers and musicians who would be admitted into a respectable house, and the *ghazeeyehs,* or common dancing girls. 'Some of them,' he says, 'when they exhibit before a private party of men, wear nothing but the *shinityán* (or 20 trousers) and a *tób* (or very full shirt or gown) of semi-transparent, coloured gauze, open nearly halfway down the front. To extinguish the least spark of modesty which they may yet sometimes affect to retain, they are plentifully supplied with brandy or some other intoxicating liquor. The scenes that ensue cannot be described.' But he adds, rather unexpectedly: 'Upon the whole I think they are the finest women in Egypt. . . . Women, as well as men, take delight in witnessing their performances. . . .'

It was a question of taboos, of course. To the Egyptians of ancient as well as modern times it was quite normal for the sexual act to be sublimated in a dance, and no doubt there were many things about the French, their impiety, their acceptance of adultery, their aggressiveness, which seemed to these conservative people both vulgar and vile. And in the midst of so much apparent looseness of behaviour, of so much materialism and cynical indulgence in the weakness of human nature, the Egyptians were, in fact, extremely conservative, as conservative as only a subject-race can ever be. Mentally they lived in a kind of fatalistic torpor and they had no will for change. There was indeed something about the very nature of the country, the preservative properties of its dry air and dry sand, its absence of strong contrasts in the way of mountains and valleys, storms and high winds, and the unfailing rise and fall of the Nile, that disposed them to think that all change was futile and improvement an impossibility. The Moslem religion, with its absolute rules, suited them perfectly and they never dreamed of questioning it. They never even thought of revolting against their rulers, the Mamelukes.

In this shut-in, hothouse atmosphere, where the people were absorbed to the limit in their own parochial affairs, the energetic proselytizing spirit of the French made no sense at all, and all their revolutionary talk of liberty, equality and fraternity was merely rhetoric. This was a truth Bonaparte had still to learn. The Egyptian imams and sheikhs who were confused about so much else were not taken in for two minutes by his declaration that he had come to rescue them from the Mamelukes. They knew that he wanted the power for himself and (unlike the Mamelukes) they suspected that it was useless to resist him. He could come to Cairo as a successful general, as a substitute for the Mamelukes, as one more new tyrant (and an infidel at that) to be added to the rest, or not at all; he could never hope to enter into partnership with the Egyptians. It was at the very core of their nature to resist all governments in a passive and dissembling way, to defeat the tax-gatherer, to cheat the magistrates and to avoid military service. Behind the locked doors of their houses and in their mosques they had their own brand of equality, fraternity and liberty, and it had nothing to do with their rulers.

The Mamelukes themselves were hardly less conservative than their subjects; indeed, they were an anachronism only to be compared with the Turkish janissaries in Constantinople or the Manchus in eighteenth-century China. A stranger group of men it is hardly possible to conceive.

The word Mameluke means male slave, more especially a white male slave, but they were slaves of a special kind. They were purchased as children from impoverished peasant families in Georgia and the Caucasus, and then imported into Egypt, where they were brought up by their masters (who had also been slaves in their time) with the express purpose of ruling the country upon the lines of a military oligarchy. War was the Mamelukes' trade. From their earliest years they were trained as horsemen and warriors, as a military clique, and they went to fantastic lengths to keep their caste intact. The natural instinct of philoprogenitiveness did not apply; the Mameluke boy was taught that marriage and family were fatal to his profession — it was certainly a loss of caste to marry an Egyptian — and in point of fact they produced few male offspring; each new generation of Mamelukes preferred instead to purchase white Christian slave-children from southern Russia, convert them to Islam, and then bring them up as their heirs. Hitler, it will be remembered, had a somewhat similar notion when he proposed to set up a sort of human stud-farm for the creation of perfect men and women in Nazi Germany. The Mamelukes, however, tended not to live very long, and no doubt their addiction to homosexuality was another reason why they had so few children of their own.

Through the years the Mamelukes had steadily increased in numbers. When Browne was in Egypt in 1792 he was told that 16,000 had been imported in the preceding eleven years, and the total Mameluke population with its dependants now in 1798 numbered nearly 100,000. The great majority of them lived in Cairo.

These supermen saw to it that they looked and behaved like supermen. Many of them were tall and strikingly handsome, and their costume was a wonder to behold: a green cap wreathed with a large yellow turban, a coat of chain-mail beneath a long robe that was bound at the waist by an embroidered shawl, voluminous red pantaloons, leather gauntlets and red, pointed slippers. Each man's armament consisted of a brace of pistols, a mace, a long curved sword, a sheaf of arrows and an English carbine, all with handles and blades chased in silver and copper designs of fine workmanship and sometimes studded with precious stones. Thus encumbered they were mounted upon an enormous saddle of wood and iron — each of the copper stirrups alone weighed thirteen pounds — and it was nothing for a man to pay the equivalent of several hundred pounds for a mount. Their horses were the finest Arabs, and probably as cavalry the Mamelukes had no equal in the world; they charged with utter recklessness and fought with a ferocity that was a byword in the East. 'They start,' says one observer, 'like lightning and arrive like thunder.' Once unhorsed, however, they were heavily encumbered by their arms, and it was left to their irregular Bedouin infantry to save the day.

25

Lane describes the Mamelukes thus: 'A band of lawless adventurers, slaves in origin, butchers by choice, turbulent, bloodthirsty and too often treacherous, these slave-kings had a keen appreciation of the arts . . . a taste and refinement which would have been hard to parallel in western countries. . . .' One can observe something of this even at the present time. The Ibn Tulun mosque in Cairo, the first pure mosque to be built in the world, and possibly the most beautiful building in Africa, was the work of a Tartar Mameluke. The huge domed and min-areted tombs of the Mameluke beys, standing in the desert outside the walls of Cairo, are also an architectural triumph of their kind, and not even the dust and squalor of the slums that now surround them, or the hordes of ragged children who haunt this city of the dead, can quite obscure the revelation that there was a vision here that rose above a barbarous and material life.

As for the houses which the Mamelukes inhabited within the city walls, they were rather disappointing on the outside: rickety-looking structures of wood and stone with balconies that projected so far they almost formed a roof over the narrow streets below. But inside their houses the wealthier men indulged themselves in great splendour: a foun-tain playing in the courtyard fell into a pool lined with black and white marble, mosaics and wooden lattice-work decorated the walls, and Per-sian carpets were spread upon the floor. In place of chairs there were divans with silken cushions and coverings. No room, not even the harem upstairs, was specifically designed as a bedroom — the bedding was put away in a cupboard by day and laid out at any convenient place at night; very often, in hot weather, one slept on the roof. The general object inside the house was to exclude the hot sunlight, and thus the Mameluke sat with his friends in a fine cool gloom eating his three daily meals (one before dawn, another at 10 a.m. and a third at 5 p.m.), sipping his coffee and sherbet, or puffing at the carved and jewelled ivory mouthpiece of his water-pipe while, sometimes, he watched a performance of musicians and dancers. Some of the leading men maintained pleasure boats on the Nile, and in their country estates they lived in kiosks surrounded by gardens of sycamore, jasmine and orange. Needless to say, their retinues of slaves were very large: one man to guard the door, another to carry water, a third to run before his master and clear a way through the crowded streets, and many others to staff the house. The establishments of the more powerful men were tremendous; it was nothing for a bey to have several hundred Circassian slaves, all armed and mounted, and each of these slaves would be attended by two or three Egyptian servants of his own.

Ghorbal says of the Mamelukes: 'Without relations, without chil-dren, their past was a blank. . . . Power had no other end than procuring women, horses, jewels and retainers.' Yet they were abstemious; their meals were reasonably simple, no wine was served, and the fast of Ram-adan was strictly observed.

Their wealth came mostly from customs dues. The merchant cara- *30*
vans that picked up goods from the Red Sea ships and transported them
to the Mediterranean were charged enormous sums. £10,000 worth of
Indian spices would pay up to £8,000 or £9,000 on the passage through
Egypt (which was one reason why the British had developed the trade
round the Cape of Good Hope), and the desert caravans were taxed as
well. Upon the income from this trade, as well as upon plunder and
the ruthless exploitation of the Egyptians, the Mamelukes lived the full,
rich life.

To rule, if not by the sword, then by bribery and treachery—this
was the mainspring of their existence. And despite murderous quarrels
among themselves, endless intrigues and a morality that made a virtue
of broken faith, they had succeeded in ruling for something over five
hundred years at the time of Bonaparte's arrival. Generation after generation of Egyptians had succumbed to these gorgeous butchers, and between pogroms, invasions and civil wars, the fellaheen tried to eke out
some sort of living by remaining inconspicuous and servile. 'Obscurity,'
says Browne, 'under the falcon eye of power always a blessing, is here
[in Egypt] sought with peculiar avidity.' In short, the Mamelukes lorded
it over the land very much as the Pharaohs had done in ancient times.

In theory the Mamelukes were still subject to the Sultan in Constantinople; they were bound to pay him an annual bounty and to accept
a Viceroy appointed by the Porte. In fact, it was many years since the
bounty had been paid, and the present Viceroy, Abu Bekir Pasha, was
hardly more than a puppet of the twenty-three Mameluke beys who
composed the government. In recent years two of these beys, Ibrahim
and Murad, had formed an uneasy and mutually suspicious partnership
in Cairo, and it was they who exercised the real power. In 1798 Ibrahim,
a tall, thin figure with an aquiline nose and a reputation for meanness,
had reached his sixties, and Murad, the man with whom we are chiefly
concerned was gaining the ascendancy. Browne tells us that Murad Bey
could neither read nor write; the engravings made of him at the time
reveal a patriarchal figure, rather plump, his face wreathed with a fringe
of beard, and he sits complacently on his divan smoking his pipe. Nothing could less reveal the real nature of this formidable man. He was in
his late forties at this time, and his life had been one long struggle for
power. Eight years before, when he had seemed at the summit of success,
a Turkish army had landed and driven him into Upper Egypt. But he
had returned and had been reinstated, and it was no small part of his
powers of survival that he had married a woman named Fatima who was
older than himself (she was about 50), and the daughter of Ali Bey, the
leading Mameluke of the previous reign. She had great wealth, intelligence and influence—all very valuable attributes for a man who was by
nature an impetuous and ambitious soldier, an adventurer who was physically tough and energetic even by the standards of the Mamelukes.

Murad Bey had a flotilla of boats on the Nile, a pleasure garden at Gizeh close to the pyramids, and a personal bodyguard of about four hundred men. It was accepted that in a crisis he was the general who would lead the Mamelukes into battle, and at this moment very few of his followers doubted that he would succeed.

He felt strong. With his 10,000 cavalry and his 30,000 irregular infantry he believed that he was more than equal to any invasion of 'Franks', however numerous they might be. We are told by a Turkish observer that when the news of the landing first reached Murad in Cairo 'his eyes became red and fire devoured his entrails'. He summoned Carlo Rossetti, the Venetian consul, and sounded him out about the French. It was in vain that Rossetti tried to make Murad realize who Bonaparte was, and to explain the power of modern arms; Murad ridiculed the French, calling them 'donkey-boys' whom he did not wish to hurt; they should be given a present and sent away; it was absurd to think that they might conquer Egypt.

Murad was not alone in suffering delusions; for centuries, ever since the Crusades in fact, it had been an article of faith in the Ottoman Empire that the Western Christians were poor soldiers, inexpertly led. Professor Toynbee has summed up the matter very clearly: 'The piquancy of the situation lay in the fact that the French had descended on Egypt before — in the twelfth and thirteenth centuries — at a time when they had been the inferiors of the Orientals in general civilization, not excluding the art of war. The medieval French knight had been a clumsier and less expert version of the Mameluke; and accordingly, when he tried conclusions with the Mameluke, he had been badly beaten and had abandoned the attempt to conquer Egypt as a total failure. For five and a half centuries the Mamelukes remained as they were (except that they abandoned their Central Asian bows for English carbines), and they naturally assumed that the French had changed as little as they had changed themselves. Consequently, when they heard that Napoleon had had the temerity to land at Alexandria, they proposed to deal with him as they had dealt with St Louis. Light-heartedly they rode out to trample his little army under their horses' hoofs. . . .'

And so one finds here all the makings of a major tragedy, a genuine clash of ignorant armies. Cut off from the mainstream of Mediterranean civilization for a thousand years or more, caught up in the long, slow cycle of Moslem life that turned over and over on itself, advancing nowhere, permitting no new ideas, Egypt was absolutely unprepared for the shock of the French landing. She had no means of knowing that this invasion was quite unlike any other invasion in the past, that it meant the collapse at last of the Middle Ages in the Near East — in Ghorbal's phrase, 'the ending of the long Egyptian night'.

And the French on their side had their delusions too, for they had no knowledge of campaigning in the desert, no hope of maintaining their conquest without command of the sea, and no real prospect of consolidating their rule in a country that was hostile to nearly everything they stood for. Once the first devastating clash was over the best that could be hoped for was that each side would learn something from the other, that a bridge of a sort would be established between the East and the West, and that then the French would be willing to depart.

Ibrahim, the older and wiser man of the two reigning beys, may have had an inkling of all this, for he is said to have demurred when resistance was proposed during the Mameluke council of war in Cairo. But he was overruled. The army was called out, and Murad himself rode north, at the head of some four thousand cavalry, to meet the invader on the coast.

FOR DISCUSSION AND WRITING

1. What are the primary scenes that Moorehead portrays in this selection? What does each of them tell you about Egyptian society during the Napoleonic era?

2. What does "the long Egyptian night" refer to?

3. As Moorehead says, thousands of books have been written on the exotic East; this scene, as a result, has become a cliché. Does Moorehead's own account of Egypt add to the cliché, or is it original and informative? Explain. (What new aspects of Egyptian history and culture did you learn from the selection?)

4. The author makes a number of value judgments concerning the Egyptian character during the late eighteenth century. What virtues does he find? What faults? Do you think it is fair or appropriate to judge as Moorehead does?

5. Moorehead identifies two major influences on the Egyptians' fatalistic attitude. What were they, and how did they influence the character of the people?

6. Even if the reader does not have any knowledge of Egyptian history, the fate of the Mamelukes' campaign against Napoleon is foretold at the end of the chapter, with Murad riding north to meet the French army on the Mediterranean coast. How does Moorehead foreshadow the outcome, and why does he do so?

7. Viewing the Mamelukes from the standpoint of purpose, explain their values and their way of life.

8. Does Moorehead believe that Denon and Lane are sincere in their statements regarding Egyptian dancers? Explain.

9. In the foreword to *A Distant Mirror,* Barbara Tuchman's magnificent history of the fourteenth century, the author tells of the problems a historian faces regarding sources. As a reader, what lessons about history do you learn from Tuchman's statement? In your opinion, can we ever know the "truth" about such a distant era? Explain your answer.

I come now to the hazards of the enterprise. First are uncertain and contradictory data with regard to dates, numbers, and hard facts. Dates may seem dull and pedantic to some, but they are fundamental because they establish sequence — what precedes and what follows — thereby leading toward an understanding of cause and effect. Unfortunately, medieval chronology is extremely hard to pin down. The year was considered to begin at Easter and since this could fall any time between March 22 and April 22, a fixed date of March 25 was generally preferred. The change over to New Style took place in the 16th century but was not everywhere accepted until the 18th, which leaves the year to which events of January, February, and March belong in the 14th century a running enigma — further complicated by use of the regnal year (dating from the reigning King's accession) in official English documents of the 14th century and use of the papal year in certain other cases. Moreover, chroniclers did not date an event by the day of the month but by the religious calendar — speaking, for example, of two days before the Nativity of the Virgin, or the Monday after Epiphany, or St. John the Baptist's Day, or the third Sunday in Lent. The result is to confuse not only the historian but the inhabitants of the 14th century themselves, who rarely if ever agree on the same date for any event.

Numbers are no less basic because they indicate what proportion of the population is involved in a given situation. The chronic exaggeration of medieval numbers — of armies, for example — when accepted as factual, has led in the past to a misunderstanding of medieval war as analogous to modern war. . . . J. C. Russell puts the pre-plague population of France at 21 million, Ferdinand Lot at 15 or 16 million, and Edouard Perroy at a lowly 10 to 11 million. Size of population affects studies of everything else — taxes, life expectancy, commerce and agriculture, famine or plenty — and here are figures by modern authorities which differ by 100 percent. . . .

Discrepancies of supposed fact were often due to mistakes of oral transmission or later misreading of a manuscript source, as when the Dame de Coucy, subject of an international scandal, was mistaken by an otherwise careful 19th century historian for Coucy's second wife, at a cost, for a while, of devastating confusion to the present author. . . .

Isabeau of Bavaria, Queen of France, is described by one historian as a tall blonde and by another as a "dark, lively, little woman." The Turkish Sultan Bajazet, reputed by his contemporaries to be bold, enterprising, and avid for war, and surnamed Thunderbolt for the rapidity of his strikes, is described by a modern Hungarian historian as "effeminate, sensual, irresolute and vacillating." (xv–xvii)

10. Since many of the "facts" and interpretations of history are problematic, how can you, as a reader, make a judgment about the reliability of a historical text?

11. Does Moorehead provide all the information you need to understand "The Long Egyptian Night"?

THE PLATTE AND THE DESERT

Francis Parkman

The Oregon Trail, from which the following selection was taken, is an American classic. As A. B. Guthrie, Jr., says,

> The reasons for its popularity aren't far to seek. The first of them is that it communicates . . . it brings to sight and sound and feeling the great and barren valley of the Platte River, where wolves slink and antelopes circle and buffalo lumber. . . . [I]t shows us old Fort Laramie, that way point on the road to empire, and the traders, fur hunters, Canadian French, half-breeds, and full-bloods who frequented it. It recreates the camps of the Sioux, whom Parkman called "Dahcotahs," the wild and risky camps, bloody with butchered buffalo, solemn with ceremony, mean with little grievances, formal with a designing hospitality that at its most gracious included on the menu the item of boiled pup. It excites us with the chase and alarms us with dangers. It fills us with admiration for the young easterner who would let neither illness nor peril stand in the way of his purpose, which was not amusement but knowledge. (ix)

The "young easterner," Francis Parkman, was a Bostonian, born in 1823. After graduating from Harvard in 1844, he made his famous trek on the Oregon Trail in 1846 and published his account of the journey in 1849. He continued to write, publishing the last of an eight-volume history of France and England in North America in 1892. In his later years, Parkman, though plagued by ill health, became a leading authority on horticulture and was professor of that subject in the agriculture school of Harvard. He died in 1893.

This selection, like "The Long Egyptian Night" from Alan Moorehead's *The Blue Nile* and "The Fire" from John Hersey's *Hiroshima,* are examples of excellent historical writing. History presents a special challenge to critical readers, for they must evaluate both historical facts and the judgments the historian bases on those facts.

We were now at the end of our solitary journeyings along the St. Joseph trail. On the evening of the twenty-third of May we encamped near its junction with the old legitimate trail of the Oregon emigrants. We had ridden long that afternoon, trying in vain to find wood and water, until at length we saw the sunset sky reflected from a pool encircled by bushes and rocks. The water lay in the bottom of a hollow, the smooth prairie gracefully rising in ocean-like swells on every side. We pitched our tents by it; not however before the keen eye of Henry Chatillon had discerned some unusual object upon the faintly defined outline of the distant swell. But in the moist, hazy atmosphere of the evening, nothing could be clearly distinguished. As we lay around the fire after supper, a low and distant sound, strange enough amid the loneliness of the prairie, reached our ears — peals of laughter, and the faint voices of men and women. For eight days we had not encountered a human being, and this singular warning of their vicinity had an effect extremely impressive.

About dark a sallow-faced fellow descended the hill on horseback, and splashing through the pool, rode up to the tents. He was enveloped in a huge cloak, and his broad felt hat was weeping about his ears with the drizzling moisture of the evening. Another followed, a stout, square-built, intelligent-looking man, who announced himself as leader of an emigrant party, encamped a mile in advance of us. About twenty wagons, he said, were with him; the rest of his party were on the other side of the Big Blue, waiting for a woman who was in the pains of child birth, and quarrelling meanwhile among themselves.

These were the first emigrants that we had overtaken, although we had found abundant and melancholy traces of their progress throughout the course of the journey. Sometimes we passed the grave of one who had sickened and died on the way. The earth was usually torn up, and covered thickly with wolf-tracks. Some had escaped this violation. One morning, a piece of plank, standing upright on the summit of a grassy hill, attracted our notice, and riding up to it, we found the following words very roughly traced upon it, apparently with a redhot piece of iron: —

MARY ELLIS.

DIED MAY 7th, 1845.

AGED TWO MONTHS.

Such tokens were of common occurrence.

We were late in breaking up our camp on the following morning, and scarcely had we ridden a mile when we saw, far in advance of us, drawn against the horizon, a line of objects stretching at regular intervals along the level edge of the prairie. An intervening swell soon hid them from sight, until, ascending it a quarter of an hour after, we saw close before us the emigrant caravan, with its heavy white wagons creeping on in slow procession, and a large drove of cattle following behind. Half a dozen yellow-visaged Missourians, mounted on horseback, were cursing and shouting among them, their lank angular proportions enveloped in brown homespun, evidently cut and adjusted by the hands of a domestic female tailor. As we approached, they called out to us: "How are ye, boys? Are ye for Oregon or California?"

As we pushed rapidly by the wagons, children's faces were thrust out from the white coverings to look at us; while the care-worn, thin-featured matron, or the buxom girl, seated in front, suspended the knitting on which most of them were engaged to stare at us with wondering curiosity. By the side of each wagon stalked the proprietor, urging on

5

his patient oxen, who shouldered heavily along, inch by inch, on their interminable journey. It was easy to see that fear and dissension prevailed among them; some of the men—but these, with one exception, were bachelors—looked wistfully upon us as we rode lightly and swiftly by, and then impatiently at their own lumbering wagons and heavy-gaited oxen. Others were unwilling to advance at all, until the party they had left behind should have rejoined them. Many were murmuring against the leader they had chosen, and wished to depose him; and this discontent was fomented by some ambitious spirits, who had hopes of succeeding in his place. The women were divided between regrets for the homes they had left and fear of the deserts and savages before them.

We soon left them far behind, and hoped that we had taken a final leave; but our companions' wagon stuck so long in a deep and muddy ditch, that before it was extricated the van of the emigrant caravan appeared again, descending a ridge close at hand. Wagon after wagon plunged through the mud; and as it was nearly noon, and the place promised shade and water, we saw with satisfaction that they were resolved to encamp. Soon the wagons were wheeled into a circle: the cattle were grazing over the meadow, and the men, with sour, sullen faces, were looking about for wood and water. They seemed to meet but indifferent success. As we left the ground, I saw a tall, slouching fellow, with the nasal accent of "down east," contemplating the contents of his tin cup, which he had just filled with water.

"Look here, you," said he; "it's chock-full of animals!"

The cup, as he held it out, exhibited in fact an extraordinary variety of profusion of animal and vegetable life.

Riding up the little hill, and looking back on the meadow, we could   10
easily see that all was not right in the camp of the emigrants. The men were crowded together, and an angry discussion seemed to be going forward. R—— was missing from his wonted place in the line, and the Captain told us that he had remained behind to get his horse shod by a blacksmith attached to the emigrant party. Something whispered in our ears that mischief was on foot; we kept on, however, and coming soon to a stream of tolerable water, we stopped to rest and dine. Still the absentee lingered behind. At last, at the distance of a mile, he and his horse suddenly appeared, sharply defined against the sky on the summit of a hill; and close behind, a huge white object rose slowly into view.

"What is that blockhead bringing with him now?"

A moment dispelled the mystery. Slowly and solemnly, one behind the other, four long trains of oxen and four emigrant wagons rolled over the crest of the hill and gravely descended, while R——rode in state in the van. It seems, that during the process of shoeing the horse, the smothered dissensions among the emigrants suddenly broke into open rupture. Some insisted on pushing forward, some on remaining where they were, and some on going back. Kearsley, their captain, threw up his command in disgust. "And now, boys," said he, "if any of you are for going ahead, just you come along with me."

Four wagons, with ten men, one woman, and one small child, made up the force of the "go-ahead" faction, and R——, with his usual proclivity toward mischief, invited them to join our party. Fear of the Indians — for I can conceive no other motive — must have induced him to court so burdensome an alliance. At all events, the proceeding was a cool one. The men who joined us, it is true, were all that could be desired; rude indeed in manners, but frank, manly, and intelligent. To tell them we could not travel with them was out of the question. I merely reminded Kearsley that if his oxen could not keep up with our mules he must expect to be left behind, as we could not consent to be farther delayed on the journey; but he immediately replied, that his oxen "*should* keep up; and if they couldn't, why, he allowed, he'd find out how to make 'em."

On the next day, as it chanced, our English companions broke the axle-tree of their wagon, and down came the whole cumbrous machine lumbering into the bed of a brook. Here was a day's work cut out for us. Meanwhile our emigrant associates kept on their way, and so vigorously did they urge forward their powerful oxen that, what with the broken axle-tree and other mishaps, it was full a week before we overtook them; when at length we discovered them, one afternoon, crawling quietly along the sandy brink of the Platte. But meanwhile various incidents occurred to ourselves.

It was probable that at this stage of our journey the Pawnees would   15 attempt to rob us. We began therefore to stand guard in turn, dividing the night into three watches, and appointing two men for each. Deslauriers and I held guard together. We did not march with military precision to and fro before the tents: our discipline was by no means so strict. We wrapped ourselves in our blankets and sat down by the fire; and Deslauriers, combining his culinary functions with his duties as sentinel, employed himself in boiling the head of an antelope for our breakfast. Yet we were models of vigilance in comparison with some of the party; for the ordinary practice of the guard was to lay his rifle on the ground, and, enveloping his nose in his blanket, meditate on his mistress, or whatever subject best pleased him. This is all well enough when among Indians who do not habitually proceed further in their hostility than robbing travellers of their horses and mules, though, indeed, a Pawnee's forbearance is not always to be trusted; but in certain regions farther to the west, the guard must beware how he exposes his person to the light of the fire, lest some keen-eyed skulking marksman should let fly a bullet or an arrow from the darkness.

Among various tales that circulated around our campfire was one told by Boisverd, and not inappropriate here. He was trapping with several companions on the skirts of the Blackfoot country. The man on guard, knowing that it behooved him to put forth his utmost precaution, kept aloof from the firelight, and sat watching intently on all sides. At length he was aware of a dark, crouching figure, stealing noiselessly into the circle of the light. He hastily cocked his rifle, but the sharp click of the lock caught the ear of the Blackfoot, whose senses were all on the alert. Raising his arrow, already fitted to the string, he shot in the direction of the sound. So sure was his aim, that he drove it through the throat of the unfortunate guard, and then, with a loud yell, bounded from the camp.

As I looked at the partner of my watch, puffing and blowing over his fire, it occurred to me that he might not prove the most efficient auxiliary in time of trouble.

"Deslauriers," said I, "would you run away if the Pawnees should fire at us?"

"Ah! oui, oui, Monsieur!" he replied very decisively.

At this instant a whimsical variety of voices, — barks, howls, yelps, and whines, — all mingled together, sounded from the prairie, not far off, as if a conclave of wolves of every age and sex were assembled there. Deslauriers looked up from his work with a laugh, and began to imitate this medley of sounds with a ludicrous accuracy. At this they were repeated with redoubled emphasis, the musician being apparently indignant at the successful efforts of a rival. They all proceeded from the throat of one little wolf, not larger than a spaniel, seated by himself at some distance. He was of the species called the prairie-wolf: a grimvisaged, but harmless little brute, whose worst propensity is creeping among horses and gnawing the ropes of raw hide by which they are picketed around the camp. Other beasts roam the prairies, far more formidable in aspect and in character. These are the large white and gray wolves, whose deep howl we heard at intervals from far and near.

At last I fell into a doze, and awaking from it, found Deslauriers fast asleep. Scandalized by this breach of discipline, I was about to stimulate his vigilance by stirring him with the stock of my rifle; but, compassion prevailing, I determined to let him sleep a while, and then arouse him to administer a suitable reproof for such forgetfulness of duty. Now and then I walked the rounds among the silent horses, to see that all was right. The night was chill, damp, and dark, the dank grass bending under the icy dew-drops. At the distance of a rod or two the tents were invisible, and nothing could be seen but the obscure figures of the horses, deeply breathing, and restlessly starting as they slept, or still slowly champing the grass. Far off, beyond the black outline of the prairie, there was a ruddy light, gradually increasing, like the glow of a conflagration; until at length the broad disk of the moon, blood-red, and vastly magnified by the vapors, rose slowly upon the darkness, flecked by one or two little clouds, and as the light poured over the gloomy plain, a fierce and stern howl, close at hand, seemed to greet it as an unwelcome intruder. There was something impressive and awful in the place and the hour; for I and the beasts were all that had consciousness for many a league around.

Some days elapsed, and brought us near the Platte. Two men on horseback approached us one morning, and we watched them with the curiosity and interest that, upon the solitude of the plains, such an encounter always excites. They were evidently whites, from their mode of riding, though, contrary to the usage of that region, neither of them carried a rifle.

"Fools!" remarked Henry Chatillon, "to ride that way on the prairie; Pawnee find them — then they catch it."

Pawnee *had* found them, and they had come very near "catching it"; indeed, nothing saved them but the approach of our party. Shaw and I knew one of them, — a man named Turner, whom we had seen at Westport. He and his companion belonged to an emigrant party encamped a few miles in advance, and had returned to look for some stray oxen, leaving their rifles, with characteristic rashness or ignorance, behind them. Their neglect had nearly cost them dear; for, just before we came up, half a dozen Indians approached, and, seeing them apparently defenseless, one of the rascals seized the bridle of Turner's horse and ordered him to dismount. Turner was wholly unarmed; but the other jerked a pistol out of his pocket, at which the Pawnee recoiled; and just then some of our men appearing in the distance, the whole party whipped their rugged little horses and made off. In no way daunted, Turner foolishly persisted in going forward.

Long after leaving him, and late that afternoon, in the midst of a   25
gloomy and barren prairie, we came suddenly upon the great trail of the Pawnees, leading from their villages on the Platte to their war and hunting grounds to the southward. Here every summer passes the motley concourse: thousands of savages, men, women, and children, horses and mules, laden with their weapons and implements, and an innumerable multitude of unruly wolfish dogs, who have not acquired the civilized accomplishment of barking, but howl like their wild cousins of the prairie.

The permanent winter villages of the Pawnees stand on the lower Platte, but throughout the summer the greater part of the inhabitants are wandering over the plains, — a treacherous, cowardly banditti, who, by a thousand acts of pillage and murder, have deserved chastisement at the hands of government. Last year a Dahcotah warrior performed a notable exploit at one of these villages. He approached it alone, in the middle of a dark night, and clambering up the outside of one of the lodges, which are in the form of a half-sphere, looked in at the round hole made at the top for the escape of smoke. The dusky light from the embers showed him the forms of the sleeping inmates; and dropping lightly through the opening, he unsheathed his knife, and, stirring the fire, coolly selected his victims. One by one, he stabbed and scalped them; when a child suddenly awoke and screamed. He rushed from the lodge, yelled a Sioux war-cry, shouted his name in triumph and defiance, and darted out upon the dark prairie, leaving the whole village behind him in a tumult, with the howling and baying of dogs, the screams of women, and the yells of the enraged warriors.

Our friend Kearsley, as we learned on rejoining him, signalized himself by a less bloody achievement. He and his men were good woodsmen, well skilled in the use of the rifle, but found themselves wholly out of their element on the prairie. None of them had ever seen a buffalo; and they had very vague conceptions of his nature and appearance. On the day after they reached the Platte, looking towards a distant swell, they beheld a multitude of little black specks in motion upon its surface.

"Take your rifles, boys," said Kearsley, "and we'll have fresh meat for supper." This inducement was quite sufficient. The ten men left their wagons, and set out in hot haste, some on horseback and some on foot, in pursuit of the supposed buffalo. Meanwhile a high, grassy ridge shut the game from view; but mounting it after half an hour's running and riding, they found themselves suddenly confronted by about thirty mounted Pawnees. Amazement and consternation were mutual. Having nothing but their bows and arrows, the Indians thought their hour was come, and the fate that they were conscious of richly deserving about to overtake them. So they began, one and all, to shout forth the most cordial salutations, running up with extreme earnestness to shake hands with the Missourians, who were as much rejoiced as they were to escape the expected conflict.

A low, undulating line of sand-hills bounded the horizon before us. That day we rode ten hours, and it was dusk before we entered the hollows and gorges of these gloomy little hills. At length we gained the summit, and the long-expected valley of the Platte lay before us. We all drew rein, and sat joyfully looking down upon the prospect. It was right welcome; strange, too, and striking to the imagination, and yet it had not one picturesque or beautiful feature; nor had it any of the features of grandeur, other than its vast extent, its solitude, and its wildness. For league after league, a plain as level as a lake was outspread beneath us; here and there the Platte, divided into a dozen thread-like sluices, was traversing it, and an occasional clump of wood, rising in the midst like a shadowy island, relieved the monotony of the waste. No living thing was moving throughout the vast landscape, except the lizards that darted over the sand and through the rank grass and prickly pears at our feet.

We had passed the more tedious part of the journey; but four hundred miles still intervened between us and Fort Laramie; and to reach that point cost us the travel of three more weeks. During the whole of this time we were passing up the middle of a long, narrow, sandy plain, reaching like an outstretched belt nearly to the Rocky Mountains. Two

30

lines of sand-hills, broken often into the wildest and most fantastic forms, flanked the valley at the distance of a mile or two on the right and left; while beyond them lay a barren, trackless waste, extending for hundreds of miles to the Arkansas on the one side, and the Missouri on the other. Before and behind us, the level monotony of the plain was unbroken as far as the eye could reach. Sometimes it glared in the sun, an expanse of hot, bare sand; sometimes it was veiled by long coarse grass. Skulls and whitening bones of buffalo were scattered everywhere; the ground was tracked by myriads of them, and often covered with the circular indentations where the bulls had wallowed in the hot weather. From every gorge and ravine, opening from the hills, descended deep, well-worn paths, where the buffalo issue twice a day in regular procession to drink in the Platte. The river itself runs through the midst, a thin sheet of rapid, turbid water, half a mile wide, and scarcely two feet deep. Its low banks, for the most part without a bush or a tree, are of loose sand, with which the stream is so charged that it grates on the teeth in drinking. The naked landscape is, of itself, dreary and monotonous enough; and yet the wild beasts and wild men that frequent the valley of the Platte make it a scene of interest and excitement to the traveller. Of those who have journeyed there, scarcely one, perhaps, fails to look back with fond regret to his horse and his rifle.

Early in the morning after we reached the Platte, a long procession of squalid savages approached our camp. Each was on foot, leading his horse by a rope of bull-hide. His attire consisted merely of a scanty cincture, and an old buffalo robe, tattered and begrimed by use, which hung over his shoulders. His head was close shaven, except a ridge of hair reaching over the crown from the middle of the forehead, very much like the long bristles on the back of a hyena, and he carried his bow and arrows in his hand, while his meagre little horse was laden with dried buffalo meat, the produce of his hunting. Such were the first specimens that we met — and very indifferent ones they were — of the genuine savages of the prairie.

They were the Pawnees whom Kearsley had encountered the day before, and belonged to a large hunting party, known to be ranging the prairie in the vicinity. They strode rapidly by, within a furlong of our tents, not pausing or looking towards us, after the manner of Indians when meditating mischief, or conscious of ill desert. I went out to meet them, and had an amicable conference with the chief, presenting him with half a pound of tobacco, at which unmerited bounty he expressed much gratification. These fellows, or some of their companions, had committed a dastardly outrage upon an emigrant party in advance of us. Two men, at a distance from the rest, were seized by them, but, lashing their horses, they broke away and fled. At this the Pawnees raised the yell and shot at them, transfixing the hindmost through the back with several arrows, while his companion galloped away and brought in the news to his party. The panic-stricken emigrants remained for several days in camp, not daring even to send out in quest of the dead body.

Our New-England climate is mild and equable compared with that of the Platte. This very morning, for instance, was close and sultry, the sun rising with a faint oppressive heat; when suddenly darkness gathered in the west, and a furious blast of sleet and hail drove full in our faces, icy cold, and urged with such demoniac vehemence that it felt like a storm of needles. It was curious to see the horses; they faced about in extreme displeasure, holding their tails like whipped dogs, and shivering as the angry gusts, howling louder than a concert of wolves, swept over us. Wright's long train of mules came sweeping round before the storm, like a flight of snowbirds driven by a winter tempest. Thus we all remained stationary for some minutes, crouching close to our horses' necks, much too surly to speak, though once the Captain looked up from between the collars of his coat, his face blood-red, and the muscles of his mouth contracted by the cold into a most ludicrous grin of agony. He grumbled something that sounded like a curse, directed, as we believed, against the unhappy hour when he had first thought of leaving home. The thing was too good to last long; and the instant the puffs of wind subsided we pitched our tents, and remained in camp for the rest of a gloomy and lowering day. The emigrants also encamped near at hand. We being first on the ground, had appropriated all the wood within reach; so that our fire alone blazed cheerily. Around it soon gathered a group of uncouth figures, shivering in the drizzling rain. Conspicuous among them were two or three of the half-savage men who spend their reckless lives in trapping among the Rocky Mountains, or in trading for the Fur Company in the Indian villages. They were all of Canadian extraction; their hard, weather-beaten faces and bushy moustaches looked out from beneath the hoods of their white capotes with a bad and brutish expression, as if their owners might be the willing agents of any villainy. And such in fact is the character of many of these men.

On the day following we overtook Kearsley's wagons, and thenceforward, for a week or two, we were fellow-travellers. One good effect, at least, resulted from the alliance; it materially diminished the fatigues of standing guard; for the party being now more numerous, there were longer intervals between each man's turn of duty.

FOR DISCUSSION AND WRITING

1. Explain why it could be argued that scene is the most important element of "The Platte and the Desert."

2. Think of the various interpretations that you can give scene and how these differing viewpoints will influence your "reading" of the piece. For

example, the scene can be: (a) the area that Parkman describes in "The Platte and the Desert" (What effect does the location have on the acts of the agents? In what way is the "desert" symbolic? What is the region like now?); (b) the area traversed by the Oregon Trail (What was the route of the trail? Why was the trail established? Why were Parkman's group and the emigrant party on the trail?); or (c) mid-nineteenth-century America (In what way was the Oregon Trail related to the opening of the West? What part did the trail play in the history of the period? In what way did the trail represent the spirit of the nation?).

3. Survey the selection from the standpoint of how the actions relate to one another. In your opinion, are any selections irrelevant? Explain.

4. Francis Parkman's historical account of the Oregon Trail is based on firsthand observation: Parkman was there. As a source of historical information, what are the advantages and disadvantages of eyewitness accounts?

5. If you know where the Platte is, you will suspect that the meaning of *desert* has changed since Parkman used the term more than one hundred years ago. Where can you find the mid-nineteenth-century meaning of *desert?* (What specialized dictionaries are in the reference section of your library?)

6. Parkman is obviously prejudiced against the Pawnees. What are his justifications for this dislike?

7. Most American readers come to the Oregon Trail with preconceived notions of the westward migration, conceptions derived largely from motion pictures and television dramas. In what ways does "the wild West" as portrayed in *The Oregon Trail* differ from the version in the popular media?

8. Find two or three examples of anecdotes in the selection, and explain what purpose they serve.

9. Compare and contrast Moorehead's characterization of the Egyptians with Parkman's characterization of the Pawnees. Which is the more objective analysis? Explain.

THE PRUSSIAN OFFICER

D. H. Lawrence

"The Prussian Officer" and the two following readings, "An Outpost of Progress" (p. 232) and "The Yellow Wallpaper" (p. 252), are fiction; therefore, critical readers must approach them differently. When we read history, we expect that the narrative will recount actual events that can be verified by the evidence; however, when we read realistic fiction, we look for a different kind of truth—*verisimilitude,* that is, the appearance of truth. Thus, we judge these three readings on the basis of how true they seem to us, not according to their factuality. Nevertheless, the critical questions discussed in this chapter are just as useful for analyzing and interpreting fictional narratives as they are for autobiography, biography, and history.

Because he dealt frankly with human sexuality, D. H. Lawrence (1885–1930) was considered daring and even scandalous during his lifetime. In our own era, his works are hardly shocking, but they are nonetheless powerful, none more so than "The Prussian Officer." During his relatively brief life, Lawrence was enormously productive, completing such masterpieces as *Sons and Lovers, The Rainbow,* and *Women in Love.* Lawrence married Frieda von Richthofen, cousin of the famous Red Baron, the World War I flying ace. The Lawrences wandered from England to Australia to New Mexico to Italy, never sinking roots in one place for very long. Lawrence's ashes are in a chapel on a small ranch outside Taos, New Mexico.

I

They had marched more than thirty kilometres since dawn, along the white, hot road where occasional thickets of trees threw a moment of shade, then out into the glare again. On either hand, the valley, wide and shallow, glittered with heat; dark-green patches of rye, pale young corn, fallow and meadow and black pine woods spread in a dull, hot diagram under a glistening sky. But right in front the mountains ranged across, pale blue and very still, snow gleaming gently out of the deep atmosphere. And towards the mountains, on and on, the regiment marched between the rye-fields and the meadows, between the scraggy fruit trees set regularly on either side the high road. The burnished, dark-green rye threw off a suffocating heat, the mountains drew gradually nearer and more distinct. While the feet of the soldiers grew hotter, sweat ran through their hair under their helmets, and their knapsacks could burn no more in contact with their shoulders, but seemed instead to give off a cold, prickly sensation.

He walked on and on in silence, staring at the mountains ahead, that rose sheer out of the land, and stood fold behind fold, half earth, half heaven, the heaven, the barrier with slits of soft snow, in the pale, bluish peaks.

He could now walk almost without pain. At the start, he had determined not to limp. It had made him sick to take the first steps, and during the first mile or so, he had compressed his breath, and the cold drops of sweat had stood on his forehead. But he had walked it off. What were they after all but bruises! He had looked at them, as he was getting up: deep bruises on the backs of his thighs. And since he had made his first step in the morning, he had been conscious of them, till now he had a tight, hot place in his chest, with suppressing the pain, and holding himself in. There seemed no air when he breathed. But he walked almost lightly.

The Captain's hand had trembled at taking his coffee at dawn: his orderly saw it again. And he saw the fine figure of the Captain wheeling on horseback at the farmhouse ahead, a handsome figure in pale-blue uniform with facings of scarlet, and the metal gleaming on the black helmet and the sword-scabbard, and dark streaks of sweat coming on the silky bay horse. The orderly felt he was connected with that figure moving so suddenly on horseback: he followed it like a shadow, mute and inevitable and damned by it. And the officer was always aware of the tramp of the company behind, the march of his orderly among the men.

The Captain was a tall man of about forty, grey at the temples. He had a handsome, finely-knit figure, and was one of the best horsemen in the West. His orderly, having to rub him down, admired the amazing riding-muscles of his loins.

For the rest, the orderly scarcely noticed the officer any more than he noticed himself. It was rarely he saw his master's face: he did not look at it. The Captain had reddish-brown, stiff hair, that he wore short upon his skull. His moustache was also cut short and bristly over a full, brutal mouth. His face was rather rugged, the cheeks thin. Perhaps the man was the more handsome for the deep lines in his face, the irritable tension of his brow, which gave him the look of a man who fights with life. His fair eyebrows stood bushy over light-blue eyes that were always flashing with cold fire.

He was a Prussian aristocrat, haughty and overbearing. But his mother had been a Polish countess. Having made too many gambling debts when he was young, he had ruined his prospects in the Army, and remained an infantry captain. He had never married: his position did not allow of it, and no woman had ever moved him to it. His time he spent riding — occasionally he rode one of his own horses at the races — and at the officers' club. Now and then he took himself a mistress. But after such an event, he returned to duty with his brow still more tense, his eyes still more hostile and irritable. With the men, however, he was merely impersonal, though a devil when roused; so that, on the whole, they feared him, but had no great aversion from him. They accepted him as the inevitable.

To his orderly he was at first cold and just and indifferent: he did not fuss over trifles. So that his servant knew practically nothing about him, except just what orders he would give, and how he wanted them obeyed. That was quite simple. Then the change gradually came.

The orderly was a youth of about twenty-two, of medium height, and well built. He had strong, heavy limbs, was swarthy, with a soft, black, young moustache. There was something altogether warm and young about him. He had firmly marked eyebrows over dark, expressionless eyes, that seemed never to have thought, only to have received life direct through his senses, and acted straight from instinct.

Gradually the officer had become aware of his servant's young vigorous, unconscious presence about him. He could not get away from the sense of the youth's person, while he was in attendance. It was like a warm flame upon the older man's tense, rigid body, that had become almost unliving, fixed. There was something so free and self-contained about him, and something in the young fellow's movement, that made the officer aware of him. And this irritated the Prussian. He did not choose to be touched into life by his servant. He might easily have changed his man, but he did not. He now very rarely looked direct at his orderly, but kept his face averted, as if to avoid seeing him. And yet as the young soldier moved unthinking about the apartment, the elder watched him, and would notice the movement of his strong young shoulders under the blue cloth, the bend of his neck. And it irritated him. To see the soldier's young, brown, shapely peasant's hand grasp the loaf or the wine-bottle sent a flash of hate or of anger through the elder man's blood. It was not that the youth was clumsy: it was rather the blind, instinctive sureness of movement of an unhampered young animal that irritated the officer to such a degree.

Once, when a bottle of wine had gone over, and the red gushed out on to the tablecloth, the officer had started up with an oath, and his eyes, bluey like fire, had held those of the confused youth for a moment. It was a shock for the young soldier. He felt something sink deeper, deeper into his soul, where nothing had ever gone before. It left him rather blank and wondering. Some of his natural completeness in himself was gone, a little uneasiness took its place. And from that time an undiscovered feeling had held between the two men.

Henceforward the orderly was afraid of really meeting his master. His subconsciousness remembered those steely blue eyes and the harsh brows, and did not intend to meet them again. So he always stared past his master, and avoided him. Also, in a little anxiety, he waited for the three months to have gone, when his time would be up. He began to feel a constraint in the Captain's presence, and the soldier even more than the officer wanted to be left alone, in his neutrality as servant.

He had served the Captain for more than a year, and knew his duty. This he performed easily, as if it were natural to him. The officer and his commands he took for granted, as he took the sun and the rain, and he served as a matter of course. It did not implicate him personally.

10

But now if he were going to be forced into a personal interchange with his master he would be like a wild thing caught, he felt he must get away.

But the influence of the young soldier's being had penetrated   15
through the officer's stiffened discipline, and perturbed the man in him. He, however, was a gentleman, with long, fine hands and culti-vated movements, and was not going to allow such a thing as the stirring of his innate self. He was a man of passionate temper, who had always kept himself suppressed. Occasionally there had been a duel, an outburst before the soldiers. He knew himself to be always on the point of breaking out. But he kept himself hard to the idea of the Ser-vice. Whereas the young soldier seemed to live out his warm, full nature, to give it off in his very movements, which had a certain zest, such as wild animals have in free movement. And this irritated the officer more and more.

In spite of himself, the Captain could not regain his neutrality of feeling towards his orderly. Nor could he leave the man alone. In spite of himself, he watched him, gave him sharp orders, tried to take up as much of his time as possible. Sometimes he flew into a rage with the young soldier, and bullied him. Then the orderly shut himself off, as it were out of earshot, and waited, with sullen, flushed face, for the end of the noise. The words never pierced to his intelligence, he made himself, protectively, impervious to the feelings of his master.

He had a scar on his left thumb, a deep seam going across the knuckle. The officer had long suffered from it, and wanted to do some-thing to it. Still it was there, ugly and brutal on the young, brown hand. At last the Captain's reserve gave way. One day, as the orderly was smoothing out the tablecloth, the officer pinned down his thumb with a pencil, asking:

"How did you come by that?"

The young man winced and drew back at attention.

"A wood axe, Herr Hauptmann," he answered.   20

The officer waited for further explanation. None came. The orderly went about his duties. The elder man was sullenly angry. His servant avoided him. And the next day he had to use all his will-power to avoid seeing the scarred thumb. He wanted to get hold of it and — A hot flame ran in his blood.

He knew his servant would soon be free, and would be glad. As yet, the soldier had held himself off from the elder man. The Captain grew madly irritable. He could not rest when the soldier was away, and when he was present, he glared at him with tormented eyes. He hated those fine, black brows over the unmeaning, dark eyes, he was infuriated by the free movement of the handsome limbs, which no military disci-pline could make stiff. And he became harsh and cruelly bullying, using contempt and satire. The young soldier only grew more mute and expressionless.

"What cattle were you bred by, that you can't keep straight eyes? Look me in the eyes when I speak to you."

And the soldier turned his dark eyes to the other's face, but there was no sight in them: he stared with the slightest possible cast, holding back his sight, perceiving the blue of his master's eyes, but receiving no look from them. And the elder man went pale, and his reddish eyebrows twitched. He gave his order, barrenly.

Once he flung a heavy military glove into the young soldier's face. *25* Then he had the satisfaction of seeing the black eyes flare up into his own, like a blaze when straw is thrown on a fire. And he had laughed with a little tremor and a sneer.

But there were only two months more. The youth instinctively tried to keep himself intact: he tried to serve the officer as if the latter were an abstract authority and not a man. All his instinct was to avoid personal contact, even definite hate. But in spite of himself the hate grew, responsive to the officer's passion. However, he put it in the background. When he had left the Army he could dare acknowledge it. By nature he was active, and had many friends. He thought what amazing good fellows they were. But, without knowing it, he was alone. Now this solitariness was intensified. It would carry him through his term. But the officer seemed to be going irritably insane, and the youth was deeply frightened.

The soldier had a sweetheart, a girl from the mountains, independent and primitive. The two walked together, rather silently. He went with her, not to talk, but to have his arm round her, and for the physical contact. This eased him, made it easier for him to ignore the Captain; for he could rest with her held fast against his chest. And she, in some unspoken fashion, was there for him. They loved each other.

The Captain perceived it, and was mad with irritation. He kept the young man engaged all the evenings long, and took pleasure in the dark look that came on his face. Occasionally, the eyes of the two men met, those of the younger sullen and dark, doggedly unalterable, those of the elder sneering with restless contempt.

The officer tried hard not to admit the passion that had got hold of him. He would not know that his feeling for his orderly was anything but that of a man incensed by his stupid, perverse servant. So, keeping quite justified and conventional in his consciousness, he let the other thing run on. His nerves, however, were suffering. At last he slung the end of a belt in his servant's face. When he saw the youth start back, the pain-tears in his eyes and the blood on his mouth, he had felt at once a thrill of deep pleasure and of shame.

But this, he acknowledged to himself, was a thing he had never *30* done before. The fellow was too exasperating. His own nerves must be going to pieces. He went away for some days with a woman.

It was a mockery of pleasure. He simply did not want the woman. But he stayed on for his time. At the end of it, he came back in an agony of irritation, torment, and misery. He rode all the evening, then came straight in to supper. His orderly was out. The officer sat with his long, fine hands lying on the table, perfectly still, and all his blood seemed to be corroding.

At last his servant entered. He watched the strong, easy young figure, the fine eyebrows, the thick black hair. In a week's time the youth had got back his old well-being. The hands of the officer twitched and seemed to be full of mad flame. The young man stood at attention, unmoving, shut off.

The meal went in silence. But the orderly seemed eager. He made a clatter with the dishes.

"Are you in a hurry?" asked the officer, watching the intent, warm face of his servant. The other did not reply.

"Will you answer my question?" said the Captain.   35

"Yes sir," replied the orderly, standing with his pile of deep Army plates. The Captain waited, looked at him, then asked again:

"Are you in a hurry?"

"Yes, sir," came the answer, that sent a flash through the listener.

"For what?"

"I was going out, sir."   40

"I want you this evening."

There was a moment's hesitation. The officer had a curious stiffness of countenance.

"Yes, sir," replied the servant, in his throat.

"I want you to-morrow evening also — in fact you may consider your evenings occupied, unless I give you leave."

The mouth with the young moustache set close.   45

"Yes, sir," answered the orderly, loosening his lips for a moment.

He again turned to the door.

"And why have you a piece of pencil in your ear?"

The orderly hesitated, then continued on his way without answering. He set the plates in a pile outside the door, took the stump of pencil from his ear, and put it in his pocket. He had been copying a verse for his sweetheart's birthday card. He returned to finish clearing the table. The officer's eyes were dancing, he had a little, eager smile.

"Why have you a piece of pencil in your ear?" he asked.   50

The orderly took his hands full of dishes. His master was standing near the great green stove, a little smile on his face, his chin thrust forward. When the young soldier saw him his heart suddenly ran hot. He felt blind. Instead of answering, he turned dazedly to the door. As he was crouching to set down the dishes, he was pitched forward by a kick from behind. The pots went in a stream down the stairs, he clung to the pillar of the banisters. And as he was rising he was kicked heavily again and again, so that he clung sickly to the post for some moments. His master had gone swiftly into the room and closed the door. The maidservant downstairs looked up the staircase and made a mocking face at the crockery disaster.

The officer's heart was plunging. He poured himself a glass of wine, part of which he spilled on the floor, and gulped the remainder, leaning against the cool, green stove. He heard his man collecting the dishes from the stairs. Pale, as if intoxicated, he waited. The servant entered again. The Captain's heart gave a pang, as of pleasure, seeing the young fellow bewildered and uncertain on his feet with pain.

"Schöner!" he said.

The soldier was a little slower in coming to attention.

"Yes, sir!"

The youth stood before him, with pathetic young moustache, and fine eyebrows very distinct on his forehead of dark marble.

"I asked you a question."

"Yes, sir."

The officer's tone bit like acid.

"Why had you a pencil in your ear?"

Again the servant's heart ran hot, and he could not breathe. With dark, strained eyes, he looked at the officer, as if fascinated. And he stood there sturdily planted, unconscious. The withering smile came into the Captain's eyes, and he lifted his foot.

"I forgot it—sir," panted the soldier, his dark eyes fixed on the other man's dancing blue ones.

"What was it doing there?"

He saw the young man's breast heaving as he made an effort for words.

"I had been writing."

"Writing what?"

Again the soldier looked him up and down. The officer could hear him panting. The smile came into the blue eyes. The soldier worked his dry throat, but could not speak. Suddenly the smile lit like a flame on the officer's face, and a kick came heavily against the orderly's thigh. The youth moved sideways. His face went dead, with two black, staring eyes.

"Well?" said the officer.

The orderly's mouth had gone dry, and his tongue rubbed in it as on dry brown-paper. He worked his throat. The officer raised his foot. The servant went stiff.

"Some poetry, sir," came the crackling, unrecognisable sound of his voice.

"Poetry, what poetry?" asked the Captain, with a sickly smile.

Again there was the working in the throat. The Captain's heart had suddenly gone down heavily, and he stood sick and tired.

"For my girl, sir," he heard the dry, inhuman sound.

"Oh!" he said, turning away. "Clear the table."

"Click!" went the soldier's throat; then again, "click!" and then the   75
half–articulate:

"Yes, sir."

The young soldier was gone, looking old, and walking heavily.

The officer, left alone, held himself rigid, to prevent himself from thinking. His instinct warned him that he must not think. Deep inside him was the intense gratification of his passion, still working powerfully. Then there was a counteraction, a horrible breaking down of something inside him, a whole agony of reaction. He stood there for an hour motionless, a chaos of sensations, but rigid with a will to keep blank his consciousness, to prevent his mind grasping. And he held himself so until the worst of the stress had passed, when he began to drink, drank himself to an intoxication, till he slept obliterated. When he woke in the morning he was shaken to the base of his nature. But he had fought off the realisation of what he had done. He had prevented his mind from taking it in, had suppressed it along with his instincts, and the conscious man had nothing to do with it. He felt only as after a bout of intoxication, weak, but the affair itself all dim and not to be recovered. Of the drunkenness of his passion he successfully refused remembrance. And when his orderly appeared with coffee, the officer assumed the same self he had had the morning before. He refused the event of the past night — denied it had ever been — and was successful in his denial. He had not done any such thing — not he himself. Whatever there might be lay at the door of a stupid insubordinate servant.

The orderly had gone about in a stupor all the evening. He drank some beer because he was parched, but not much, the alcohol made his feeling come back, and he could not bear it. He was dulled, as if nine-tenths of the ordinary man in him were inert. He crawled about disfigured. Still, when he thought of the kicks, he went sick, and when he thought of the threat of more kicking, in the room afterwards, his heart went hot and faint, and he panted, remembering the one that had come. He had been forced to say: "For my girl." He was much too done even to want to cry. His mouth hung slightly open, like an idiot's. He felt vacant, and wasted. So, he wandered at his work, painfully, and very slowly and clumsily, fumbling blindly with the brushes, and finding it difficult, when he sat down, to summon the energy to move again. His limbs, his jaw, were slack and nerveless. But he was very tired. He got to bed at last, and slept inert, relaxed, in a sleep that was rather stupor than slumber, a dead night of stupefaction shot through with gleams of anguish.

In the morning were the manœuvres. But he woke even before the   80
bugle sounded. The painful ache in his chest, the dryness of his throat, the awful steady feeling of misery made his eyes come awake and dreary at once. He knew, without thinking, what had happened. And he knew that the day had come again, when he must go on with his round. The

last bit of darkness was being pushed out of the room. He would have to move his inert body and go on. He was so young, and had known so little trouble, that he was bewildered. He only wished it would stay night, so that he could lie still, covered up by the darkness. And yet nothing would prevent the day from coming, nothing would save him from having to get up and saddle the Captain's horse, and make the Captain's coffee. It was there, inevitable. And then, he thought, it was impossible. Yet they would not leave him free. He must go and take the coffee to the Captain. He was too stunned to understand it. He only knew it was inevitable — inevitable, however long he lay inert.

At last, after heaving at himself, for he seemed to be a mass of inertia, he got up. But he had to force every one of his movements from behind, with his will. He felt lost, and dazed, and helpless. Then he clutched hold of the bed, the pain was so keen. And looking at his thighs he saw the darker bruises on his swarthy flesh, and he knew that if he pressed one of his fingers on one of the bruises, he should faint. But he did not want to faint — he did not want anybody to know. No one should ever know. It was between him and the Captain. There were only the two people in the world now — himself and the Captain.

Slowly, economically, he got dressed and forced himself to walk. Everything was obscure, except just what he had his hands on. But he managed to get through his work. The very pain revived his dull senses. The worst remained yet. He took the tray and went up to the Captain's room. The officer, pale and heavy, sat at the table. The orderly, as he saluted, felt himself put out of existence. He stood still for a moment submitting to his own nullification — then he gathered himself, seemed to regain himself, and then the Captain began to grow vague, unreal, and the younger soldier's heart beat up. He clung to this situation — that the Captain did not exist — so that he himself might live. But when he saw his officer's hand tremble as he took the coffee, he felt everything falling shattered. And he went away, feeling as if he himself were coming to pieces, disintegrated. And when the Captain was there on horseback, giving orders, while he himself stood, with rifle and knapsack, sick with pain, he felt as if he must shut his eyes — as if he must shut his eyes on everything. It was only the long agony of marching with a parched throat that filled him with one single, sleep-heavy intention: to save himself.

II

He was getting used even to his parched throat. That the snowy peaks were radiant among the sky, that the whity-green glacier-river twisted through its pale shoals, in the valley below, seemed almost supernatural. But he was going mad with fever and thirst. He plodded on uncomplaining. He did not want to speak, not to anybody. There were two gulls, like flakes of water and snow, over the river. The scent of

green rye soaked in sunshine came like a sickness. And the march continued, monotonously, almost like a bad sleep.

At the next farmhouse, which stood low and broad near the high
road, tubs of water had been put out. The soldiers clustered round to
drink. They took off their helmets, and the steam mounted from their
wet hair. The Captain sat on horseback, watching. He needed to see his
orderly. His helmet threw a dark shadow over his light, fierce eyes, but
his moustache and mouth and chin were distinct in the sunshine. The
orderly must move under the presence of the figure of the horseman. It
was not that he was afraid, or cowed. It was as if he was disembowelled,
made empty, like an empty shell. He felt himself as nothing, a shadow
creeping under the sunshine. And, thirsty as he was, he could scarcely
drink, feeling the Captain near him. He would not take off his helmet to
wipe his wet hair. He wanted to stay in shadow, not to be forced into
consciousness. Starting, he saw the light heel of the officer prick the
belly of the horse; the Captain cantered away, and he himself could
relapse into vacancy.

Nothing, however, could give him back his living place in the hot,   85
bright morning. He felt like a gap among it all. Whereas the Captain
was prouder, overriding. A hot flash went through the young servant's
body. The Captain was firmer and prouder with life, he himself was
empty as a shadow. Again the flash went through him, dazing him out.
But his heart ran a little firmer.

The company turned up the hill, to make a loop for the return.
Below, from among the trees, the farm-bell clanged. He saw the labour-
ers, mowing bare-foot at the thick grass, leave off their work and go
downhill, their scythes hanging over their shoulders, like long, bright
claws curving down behind them. They seemed like dream-people, as if
they had no relation to himself. He felt as in a blackish dream: as if all
the other things were there and had form, but he himself was only a
consciousness, a gap that could think and perceive.

The soldiers were tramping silently up the glaring hill-side. Gradually his head began to revolve, slowly, rhythmically. Sometimes it was
dark before his eyes, as if he saw this world through a smoked glass, frail
shadows and unreal. It gave him a pain in his head to walk.

The air was too scented, it gave no breath. All the lush green-stuff
seemed to be issuing its sap, till the air was deathly, sickly with the smell
of greenness. There was the perfume of clover, like pure honey and bees.
Then there grew a faint acrid tang — they were near the beeches; and then
a queer clattering noise, and a suffocating, hideous smell; they were
passing a flock of sheep, a shepherd in a black smock, holding his crook.
Why should the sheep huddle together under this fierce sun? He felt that
the shepherd would not see him, though he could see the shepherd.

At last there was the halt. They stacked rifles in a conical stack, put
down their kit in a scattered circle around it, and dispersed a little, sitting

on a small knoll high on the hill-side. The chatter began. The soldiers were steaming with heat, but were lively. He sat still, seeing the blue mountains rising upon the land, twenty kilometres away. There was a blue fold in the ranges, then out of that, at the foot, the broad, pale bed of the river, stretches of whity-green water between pinkish-grey shoals among the dark pine woods. There it was, spread out a long way off. And it seemed to come downhill, the river. There was a raft being steered, a mile away. It was a strange country. Nearer, a red-roofed, broad farm with white base and square dots of windows crouched beside the wall of beech foliage on the wood's edge. There were long strips of rye and clover and pale green corn. And just at his feet, below the knoll, was a darkish bog, where globe flowers stood breathless still on their slim stalks. And some of the pale gold bubbles were burst, and a broken fragment hung in the air. He thought he was going to sleep.

Suddenly something moved into this coloured mirage before his eyes. The Captain, a small, light-blue and scarlet figure, was trotting evenly between the strips of corn, along the level brow of the hill. And the man making flag-signals was coming on. Proud and sure moved the horseman's figure, the quick, bright thing, in which was concentrated all the light of this morning, which for the rest lay fragile, shining shadow. Submissive, apathetic, the young soldier sat and stared. But as the horse slowed to a walk, coming up the last steep path, the great flash flared over the body and soul of the orderly. He sat waiting. The back of his head felt as if it were weighted with a heavy piece of fire. He did not want to eat. His hands trembled slightly as he moved them. Meanwhile the officer on horseback was approaching slowly and proudly. The tension grew in the orderly's soul. Then again, seeing the Captain ease himself on the saddle, the flash blazed through him. *90*

The Captain looked at the patch of light blue and scarlet, and dark head, scattered closely on the hill-side. It pleased him. The command pleased him. And he was feeling proud. His orderly was among them in common subjection. The officer rose a little on his stirrups to look. The young soldier sat with averted, dumb face. The Captain relaxed on his seat. His slim-legged, beautiful horse, brown as a beech nut, walked proudly uphill. The Captain passed into the zone of the company's atmosphere: a hot smell of men, of sweat, of leather. He knew it very well. After a word with the lieutenant, he went a few paces higher, and sat there, a dominant figure, his sweat-marked horse swishing its tail, while he looked down on his men, on his orderly, a nonentity among the crowd.

The young soldier's heart was like fire in his chest, and he breathed with difficulty. The officer, looking downhill, saw three of the young soldiers, two pails of water between them, staggering across a sunny green field. A table had been set up under a tree, and there the slim lieutenant stood, importantly busy. Then the Captain summoned himself to an act of courage. He called his orderly.

The flame leapt into the young soldier's throat as he heard the command, and he rose blindly, stifled. He saluted, standing below the officer. He did not look up. But there was the flicker in the Captain's voice.

"Go to the inn and fetch me . . ." the officer gave his commands. "Quick!" he added.

At the last word, the heart of the servant leapt with a flash, and he   95 felt the strength come over his body. But he turned in mechanical obedience, and set off at a heavy run downhill, looking almost like a bear, his trousers bagging over his military boots. And the officer watched this blind, plunging run all the way.

But it was only the outside of the orderly's body that was obeying so humbly and mechanically. Inside had gradually accumulated a core into which all the energy of that young life was compact and concentrated. He executed his commission, and plodded quickly back uphill. There was a pain in his head as he walked that made him twist his features unknowingly. But hard there in the centre of his chest was himself, himself, firm, and not to be plucked to pieces.

The Captain had gone up into the wood. The orderly plodded through the hot, powerfully smelling zone of the company's atmosphere. He had a curious mass of energy inside him now. The Captain was less real than himself. He approached the green entrance to the wood. There, in the half-shade, he saw the horse standing, the sunshine and the flickering shadow of leaves dancing over his brown body. There was a clearing where timber had lately been felled. Here, in the gold-green shade beside the brilliant cup of sunshine, stood two figures, blue and pink, the bits of pink showing out plainly. The Captain was talking to his lieutenant.

The orderly stood on the edge of the bright clearing, where great trunks of trees, stripped and glistening, lay stretched like naked, brown-skinned bodies. Chips of wood littered the trampled floor, like splashed light, and the bases of the felled trees stood here and there, with their raw, level tops. Beyond was the brilliant, sunlit green of a beech.

"Then I will ride forward," the orderly heard his Captain say. The lieutenant saluted and strode away. He himself went forward. A hot flash passed through his belly, as he tramped towards his officer.

The Captain watched the rather heavy figure of the young soldier   100 stumble forward, and his veins, too, ran hot. This was to be man to man between them. He yielded before the solid, stumbling figure with bent head. The orderly stooped and put the food on a level-sawn tree-base. The Captain watched the glistening, sun-inflamed, naked hands. He wanted to speak to the young soldier, but could not. The servant propped a bottle against his thigh, pressed open the cork, and poured out the beer into the mug. He kept his head bent. The Captain accepted the mug.

"Hot!" he said, as if amiably.

The flame sprang out of the orderly's heart, nearly suffocating him. "Yes, sir," he replied between shut teeth.

And he heard the sound of the Captain's drinking, and he clenched his fists, such a strong torment came into his wrists. Then came the faint clang of the closing of the pot-lid. He looked up. The Captain was watching him. He glanced swiftly away. Then he saw the officer stoop and take a piece of bread from the tree-base. Again the flash of flame went through the young soldier, seeing the stiff body stoop beneath him, and his hands jerked. He looked away. He could feel the officer was nervous. The bread fell as it was being broken. The officer ate the other piece. The two men stood tense and still, the master laboriously chewing his bread, the servant staring with averted face, his fist clenched.

Then the young soldier started. The officer had pressed open the lid of the mug again. The orderly watched the lip of the mug, and the white hand that clenched the handle, as if he were fascinated. It was raised. The youth followed it with his eyes. And then he saw the thin, strong throat of the elder man moving up and down as he drank, the strong jaw working. And the instinct which had been jerking at the young man's wrists suddenly jerked free. He jumped, feeling as if it were rent in two by a strong flame. 105

The spur of the officer caught in a tree root, he went down backwards with a crash, the middle of his back thudding sickeningly against a sharp-edged tree-base, the pot flying away. And in a second the orderly, with serious, earnest young face, and underlip between his teeth, had got his knee in the officer's chest and was pressing the chin backward over the farther edge of the tree-stump, pressing, with all his heart behind in a passion of relief, the tension of his wrists exquisite with relief. And with the base of his palms he shoved at the chin, with all his might. And it was pleasant, too, to have that chin, that hard jaw already slightly rough with beard, in his hands. He did not relax one hair's breadth, but, all the force of all his blood exulting in his thrust, he shoved back the head of the other man, till there was a little "cluck" and a crunching sensation. Then he felt as if his head went to vapour. Heavy convulsions shook the body of the officer, frightening and horrifying the young soldier. Yet it pleased him, too, to repress them. It pleased him to keep his hands pressing back the chin, to feel the chest of the other man yield in expiration to the weight of his strong, young knees, to feel the hard twitchings of the prostrate body jerking his own whole frame, which was pressed down on it.

But it went still. He could look into the nostrils of the other man, the eyes he could scarcely see. How curiously the mouth was pushed out, exaggerating the full lips, and the moustache bristling up from them. Then, with a start, he noticed the nostrils gradually filled with blood. The red brimmed, hesitated, ran over, and went in a thin trickle down the face to the eyes.

It shocked and distressed him. Slowly, he got up. The body twitched and sprawled there, inert. He stood and looked at it in silence. It was a pity *it* was broken. It represented more than the thing which had kicked and bullied him. He was afraid to look at the eyes. They were hideous now, only the whites showing, and the blood running to them. The face of the orderly was drawn with horror at the sight. Well, it was so. In his heart he was satisfied. He had hated the face of the Captain. It was extinguished now. There was a heavy relief in the orderly's soul. That was as it should be. But he could not bear to see the long, military body lying broken over the tree-base, the fine fingers crisped. He wanted to hide it away.

Quickly, busily, he gathered it up and pushed it under the felled tree trunks, which rested their beautiful, smooth length either end on the logs. The face was horrible with blood. He covered it with the helmet. Then he pushed the limbs straight and decent, and brushed the dead leaves off the fine cloth of the uniform. So, it lay quite still in the shadow under there. A little strip of sunshine ran along the breast, from a chink between the logs. The orderly sat by it for a few moments. Here his own life also ended.

Then, through his daze, he heard the lieutenant, in a loud voice, *110* explaining to the men outside the wood, that they were to suppose the bridge on the river below was held by the enemy. Now they were to march to the attack in such and such a manner. The lieutenant had no gift of expression. The orderly, listening from habit, got muddled. And when the lieutenant began it all again he ceased to hear.

He knew he must go. He stood up. It surprised him that the leaves were glittering in the sun, and the chips of wood reflecting white from the ground. For him a change had come over the world. But for the rest it had not—all seemed the same. Only he had left it. And he could not go back. It was his duty to return with the beer-pot and the bottle. He could not. He had left all that. The lieutenant was still hoarsely explaining. He must go, or they would overtake him. And he could not bear contact with anyone now.

He drew his fingers over his eyes, trying to find out where he was. Then he turned away. He saw the horse standing in the path. He went up to it and mounted. It hurt him to sit in the saddle. The pain of keeping his seat occupied him as they cantered through the wood. He would not have minded anything, but he could not get away from the sense of being divided from the others. The path led out of the trees. On the edge of the wood he pulled up and stood watching. There in the spacious sunshine of the valley soldiers were moving in a little swarm. Every now and then, a man harrowing on a strip of fallow shouted to his oxen, at the turn. The village and the white-towered church was small in the sunshine. And he no longer belonged to it—he sat there, beyond, like a man outside in the dark. He had gone out from everyday life into the unknown and he could not, he even did not want to go back.

Turning from the sun-blazing valley, he rode deep into the wood. Tree trunks, like people standing grey and still, took no notice as he went. A doe, herself a moving bit of sunshine and shadow, went running through the flecked shade. There were bright green rents in the foliage. Then it was all pine wood, dark and cool. And he was sick with pain, and had an intolerable great pulse in his head, and he was sick. He had never been ill in his life. He felt lost, quite dazed with all this.

Trying to get down from the horse, he fell, astonished at the pain and his lack of balance. The horse shifted uneasily. He jerked its bridle and sent it cantering jerkily away. It was his last connection with the rest of things.

But he only wanted to lie down and not be disturbed. Stumbling through the trees, he came on a quiet place where beeches and pine trees grew on a slope. Immediately he had lain down and closed his eyes, his consciousness went racing on without him. A big pulse of sickness beat in him as if it throbbed through the whole earth. He was burning with dry heat. But he was too busy, too tearingly active in the incoherent race of delirium to observe.

III

He came to with a start. His mouth was dry and hard, his heart beat heavily, but he had not the energy to get up. His heart beat heavily. Where was he? — the barracks — at home? There was something knocking. And, making an effort, he looked round — trees, and litter of greenery, and reddish, bright, still pieces of sunshine on the floor. He did not believe he was himself, he did not believe what he saw. Something was knocking. He made a struggle towards consciousness, but relapsed. Then he struggled again. And gradually his surroundings fell into relationship with himself. He knew, and a great pang of fear went through his heart. Somebody was knocking. He could see the heavy, black rags of a fir tree overhead. Then everything went black. Yet he did not believe he had closed his eyes. He had not. Out of the blackness sight slowly emerged again. And someone was knocking. Quickly, he saw the blood-disfigured face of his Captain, which he hated. And he held himself still with horror. Yet, deep inside him, he knew that it was so, the Captain should be dead. But the physical delirium got hold of him. Someone was knocking. He lay perfectly still, as if dead, with fear. And he went unconscious.

When he opened his eyes again he started, seeing something creeping swiftly up a tree trunk. It was a little bird. And the bird was whistling overhead. Tap-tap-tap — it was the small, quick bird rapping the tree trunk with its beak, as if its head were a little round hammer. He watched it curiously. It shifted sharply, in its creeping fashion. Then, like a mouse, it slid down the bare trunk. Its swift creeping sent a flash of revulsion through him. He raised his head. It felt a great weight. Then, the little bird ran out of the shadow across a still patch of sunshine, its little head bobbing swiftly, its white legs twinkling brightly for a moment. How neat it was in its build, so compact, with piece of white on its wings. There were several of them. They were so pretty — but they crept like swift, erratic mice, running here and there among the beech-mast.

He lay down again exhausted, and his consciousness lapsed. He had a horror of the little creeping birds. All his blood seemed to be darting and creeping in his head. And yet he could not move.

He came to with a further ache of exhaustion. There was the pain in his head, and the horrible sickness, and his inability to move. He had never been ill in his life. He did not know where he was or what he was. Probably he had got sunstroke. Or what else? — he had silenced the Captain for ever — some time ago — oh, a long time ago. There had been blood on his face, and his eyes had turned upwards. It was all right, somehow. It was peace. But now he had got beyond himself. He had never been here before. Was it life, or not life? He was by himself. They were in a big, bright place, those others, and he was outside. The town, all the country, a big bright place of light: and he was outside, here, in the darkened open beyond, where each thing existed alone. But they would all have to come out there sometime, those others. Little, and left behind him, they all were. There had been father and mother and sweetheart. What did they all matter? This was the open land.

He sat up. Something scuffled. It was a little brown squirrel running in lovely undulating bounds over the floor, its red tail completing the undulation of its body — and then, as it sat up, furling and unfurling. He watched it, pleased. It ran on again, friskily, enjoying itself. It flew wildly at another squirrel, and they were chasing each other, and making little scolding, chattering noises. The soldier wanted to speak to them. But only a hoarse sound came out of his throat. The squirrels burst away — they flew up the trees. And then he saw the one peeping round at him, half-way up a tree trunk. A start of fear went through him, though in so far as he was conscious, he was amused. It still stayed, its little keen face staring at him half-way up the tree trunk, its little ears pricked up, its clawey little hands clinging to the bark, its white breast reared. He started from it in panic.

Struggling to his feet, he lurched away. He went on walking, walking, looking for something — for a drink. His brain felt hot and inflamed for want of water. He stumbled on. Then he did not know anything. He went unconscious as he walked. Yet he stumbled on, his mouth open.

When, to his dumb wonder, he opened his eyes on the world again, he no longer tried to remember what it was. There was thick, golden light behind golden-green glitterings, and tall, grey-purple shafts, and darknesses farther off, surrounding him, growing deeper. He was conscious of a sense of arrival. He was amid the reality, on the real, dark bottom. But there was the thirst burning in his brain. He felt lighter, not so heavy. He supposed it was newness. The air was muttering with

120

thunder. He thought he was walking wonderfully swiftly and was coming straight to relief—or was it to water?

Suddenly he stood still with fear. There was a tremendous flare of gold, immense—just a few dark trunks like bars between him and it. All the young level wheat was burnished gold glaring on its silky green. A woman, full-skirted, a black cloth on her head for head-dress, was passing like a block of shadow through the glistening, green corn, into the full glare. There was a farm, too, pale blue in shadow, and the timber black. And there was a church spire, nearly fused away in the gold. The woman moved on, away from him. He had no language with which to speak to her. She was the bright, solid unreality. She would make a noise of words that would confuse him, and her eyes would look at him without seeing him. She was crossing there to the other side. He stood against a tree.

When at last he turned, looking down the long, bare grove whose flat bed was already filling dark, he saw the mountains in a wonder-light, not far away, and radiant. Behind the soft grey ridge of the nearest range the farther mountains stood golden and pale grey, the snow all radiant like pure, soft gold. So still, gleaming in the sky, fashioned pure out of the ore of the sky, they shone in their silence. He stood and looked at them, his face illuminated. And like the golden, lustrous gleaming of the snow he felt his own thirst bright in him. He stood and gazed, leaning against a tree. And then everything slid away into space.

During the night the lightning fluttered perpetually, making the whole sky white. He must have walked again. The world hung livid round him for moments, fields a level sheen of grey-green light, trees in dark bulk, and the range of clouds black across a white sky. Then the darkness fell like a shutter, and the night was whole. A faint flutter of a half-revealed world, that could not quite leap out of the darkness!—Then there again stood a sweep of pallor for the land, dark shapes looming, a range of clouds hanging overhead. The world was a ghostly shadow, thrown for a moment upon the pure darkness, which returned ever whole and complete. *125*

And the mere delirium of sickness and fever went on inside him— his brain opening and shutting like the night—then sometimes convulsions of terror from something with great eyes that stared round a tree—then the long agony of the march, and the sun decomposing his blood—then the pang of hate for the Captain, followed by a pang of tenderness and ease. But everything was distorted, born of an ache and resolving into an ache.

In the morning he came definitely awake. Then his brain flamed with the sole horror or thirstiness! The sun was on his face, the dew was steaming from his wet clothes. Like one possessed, he got up. There, straight in front of him, blue and cool and tender, the mountains ranged across the pale edge of the morning sky. He wanted them—he wanted them alone—he wanted to leave himself and be identified with them.

They did not move, they were still and soft, with white, gentle markings of snow. He stood still, mad with suffering, his hands crisping and clutching. Then he was twisting in a paroxysm on the grass.

He lay still, in a kind of dream of anguish. His thirst seemed to have separated itself from him, and to stand apart, a single demand. Then the pain he felt was another single self. Then there was the clog of his body, another separate thing. He was divided among all kinds of separate things. There was some strange, agonised connection between them, but they were drawing farther apart. Then they would all split. The sun, drilling down on him, was drilling through the bond. Then they would all fall, fall through the everlasting lapse of space. Then again, his consciousness reasserted itself. He roused on to his elbow and stared at the gleaming mountains. There they ranked, all still and wonderful between earth and heaven. He stared till his eyes went black, and the mountains, as they stood in their beauty, so clean and cool, seemed to have it, that which was lost in him.

IV

When the soldiers found him, three hours later, he was lying with his face over his arm, his black hair giving off heat under the sun. But he was still alive. Seeing the open, black mouth the young soldiers dropped him in horror.

He died in the hospital at night, without having seen again.   *130*

The doctors saw the bruises on his legs, behind, and were silent.

The bodies of the two men lay together, side by side, in the mortuary, the one white and slender, but laid rigidly at rest, the other looking as if every moment it must rouse into life again, so young and unused, from a slumber.

FOR DISCUSSION AND WRITING

1. Explain why the agent-purpose relationship could be considered the most important element in this story.

2. One part of the scene, the mountains, is very important. What do the mountains symbolize for the young soldier?

> He walked on and on in silence, staring at the mountains ahead, that rose sheer out of the land, and stood fold behind fold, half earth, half heaven, the heaven, the barrier with slits of soft snow, in the pale, bluish peaks. (par. 2)

> He was getting used even to his parched throat. That the snowy peaks were radiant among the sky, that the whity-green glacier-river twisted through its pale shoals, in the valley below, seemed almost supernatural. (par. 83)

> There, straight in front of him, blue and cool and tender, the mountains ranged across the pale edge of the morning sky. (par. 127)

3. From one point of view, the captain — an educated, cultured aristocrat — represents civilization, whereas Schöner — an uneducated peasant — represents nature. Does Lawrence seem to value civilization or nature more highly? Explain. You might think of this question in terms of an agent-scene relationship. What happens when the captain and Schöner are put into scenes that are not their natural habitat?

4. In what sense is Schöner merely an agency?

5. Might the scene in this story have *believably* been the United States of approximately 1900? Why or why not?

6. Some scenes in the story are described in realistic detail. For example:

> At the next farmhouse, which stood low and broad near the high road, tubs of water had been put out. The soldiers clustered round to drink. They took off their helmets, and the steam mounted from their wet hair. (par. 84)

Some scenes, by contrast, are misty and almost dreamlike. For example:

> When, to his dumb wonder, he opened his eyes on the world again, he no longer tried to remember what it was. There was thick, golden light behind golden-green glitterings, and tall, grey-purple shafts, and darknesses farther off, surrounding him, growing deeper. (par. 122)

How do these scenes help us understand the agents and their acts?

7. In what ways do the acts of the agents reveal their thoughts and feelings?

8. What do you think is the main point of the story?

9. The overall scene for the story is Prussia before World War I. What sort of place was Prussia? What kind of symbolic value does the term *Prussian* have? (If I were to call a government official a Prussian, what would I mean?) What reliable and easily accessible sources would you consult to find out about Prussia?

10. The young soldier's name is *Schöner,* which in German means "more beautiful." What are the implications of that name for the story?

11. Does Lawrence have an opinion of Prussia and Prussianism? If so, what is that opinion? How does Lawrence express it?

12. Explain why a spilled bottle of wine marks the turning point, or *peripeteia,* in the story.

AN OUTPOST OF PROGRESS

Joseph Conrad

Conrad is the author of enough novels and tales to occupy several feet of space on one's book shelves. Particular favorites of many readers are the novels *Lord Jim,* a study of the moral and psychological consequences of cowardice when a ship sinks; *Nostromo,* a tale of colonialism and revolution in a fictional South American country; *The Secret Agent,* a story of spying and intrigue set in London; and *Victory,* about a nineteenth-century Adam and Eve whose Paradise is invaded by sinisterly comic agents of evil.

Josef Teodor Konrad Walecz Korzeniowski — who took the pen name Joseph Conrad — was born in Poland in 1857, the son of landed gentry. Improbably, he chose a career as a sailor on French ships; after four years he shifted to the English merchant marine. Before he was thirty, he had achieved his master's license and captained sailing ships that visited South America, Africa, and other far-flung parts of the globe.

In 1890, Conrad gained command of a Congo River steamer and went into the heart of Africa on that great waterway. The journey broke his health but gave him material for literary masterpieces, particularly *Heart of Darkness* (1902), which is a companion piece to "An Outpost of Progress."

In 1894, Conrad resigned from the merchant marine and began his career as a professional writer. His first novel, *Almayer's Folly,* appeared in 1895. His first major work was *Lord Jim* (1900).

In 1898, he married Jessie George, and the couple had two sons. The family lived in various rural homes in England, in 1919 moving to a spacious house near Canterbury. Conrad died in 1924, one of the honored literary artists of his age. It is remarkable that a man whose first language was *not* English should have become one of the most admired writers in the English language.

I

There were two white men in charge of the trading station. Kayerts, the chief, was short and fat; Carlier, the assistant, was tall, with a large head and a very broad trunk perched upon a long pair of thin legs. The third man on the staff was a Sierra Leone nigger, who maintained that his name was Henry Price. However, for some reason or other, the natives down the river had given him the name of Makola, and it stuck to him through all his wanderings about the country. He spoke English and French with a warbling accent, wrote a beautiful hand, understood bookkeeping, and cherished in his innermost heart the worship of evil spirits. His wife was a Negress from Loanda, very large and very noisy. Three children rolled about in sunshine before the door of his low, shed-like dwelling. Makola, taciturn and impenetrable, despised the two white men. He had charge of a small clay storehouse with a dried-grass roof, and pretended to keep a correct account of beads, cotton cloth, red kerchiefs, brass wire, and other trade goods it contained. Besides the storehouse and Makola's hut, there was only one large building in the cleared ground of the station. It was built neatly of reeds, with a verandah on all the four sides. There were three rooms in it. The one in the middle was the living room, and had two rough tables and a few stools in it. The other two were the bedrooms for the white men. Each had a bedstead and a mosquito net for all furniture. The plank floor was littered with the belongings of the white men; open half-empty boxes, torn wearing apparel, old boots; all the things dirty, and all the things broken, that accumulate mysteriously round untidy men. There was also another dwelling place some distance away from the buildings. In it, under a tall cross much out of the perpendicular, slept the man who had seen the beginning of all this; who had planned and had watched the construction of this outpost of progress. He had been, at home, an unsuccessful painter who, weary of pursuing fame on an empty stomach, had gone out there through high protections. He had been the first chief of that station. Makola had watched the energetic artist die of fever in the just finished house with his usual kind of "I told you so" indifference. Then, for a time, he dwelt alone with his family, his account books, and the Evil Spirit that rules the lands under the equator. He got on very well with his god. Perhaps he had propitiated him by a promise of more white men to play with, by and by. At any rate the director of the Great Trading Company, coming up in a steamer that resembled an enormous sardine box with a flat-roofed shed erected on it, found the station in good order, and Makola as usual quietly diligent. The director had the cross put up over the first agent's grave, and appointed Kayerts to the post. Carlier was told off as second in charge. The director was a man ruthless and efficient, who at times, but very imperceptibly, indulged in grim humour. He made a speech to Kayerts and Carlier, pointing out to them the promising aspect of their station. The nearest trading post was about three hundred miles away. It was an exceptional opportunity for them to distinguish themselves and to earn percentages on the trade. This appointment was a favour done to beginners. Kayerts was moved almost to tears by his director's kindness. He would, he said, by doing his best, try to justify the flattering confidence, &c., &c. Kayerts had been in the Administration of the Telegraphs, and knew how to express himself correctly. Carlier, an ex-noncommissioned officer of cavalry in an army guaranteed from harm by several European powers, was less impressed. If there were commissions to get, so much the better; and, trailing a sulky glance over the river, the forests, the impenetrable bush that seemed to cut off the station from the rest of the world, he muttered between his teeth, "We shall see, very soon."

Next day, some bales of cotton goods and a few cases of provisions having been thrown on shore, the sardine-box steamer went off, not to return for another six months. On the deck the director touched his cap to the two agents, who stood on the bank waving their hats, and turning to an old servant of the Company on his passage to headquarters, said, "Look at those two imbeciles. They must be mad at home to send me such specimens. I told those fellows to plant a vegetable garden, build new storehouses and fences, and construct a landing stage. I bet nothing will be done! They won't know how to begin. I always thought the station on this river useless, and they just fit the station!"

"They will form themselves there," said the old stager with a quiet smile.

"At any rate, I am rid of them for six months," retorted the director.

The two men watched the steamer round the bend, then, ascending 5 arm in arm the slope of the bank, returned to the station. They had been in this vast and dark country only a very short time, and as yet always in the midst of other white men, under the eye and guidance of their superiors. And now, dull as they were to the subtle influences of surroundings, they felt themselves very much alone, when suddenly left unassisted to face the wilderness; a wilderness rendered more strange, more incomprehensible by the mysterious glimpses of the vigorous life it contained. They were two perfectly insignificant and incapable individuals, whose existence is only rendered possible through the high organization of civilized crowds. Few men realize that their life, the very essence of their character, their capabilities and their audacities, are only the expression of their belief in the safety of their surroundings. The courage, the composure, the confidence; the emotions and principles; every great and every insignificant thought belongs not to the individual but to the crowd: to the crowd that believes blindly in the irresistible force of its institutions and of its morals, in the power of its police and of its opinion. But the contact with pure unmitigated savagery, with primitive nature and primitive man, brings sudden and profound trouble into the heart. To the sentiment of being alone of one's kind, to the clear perception of the loneliness of one's thoughts, of one's sensations — to the negation of the habitual, which is safe, there is added the affirmation of the unusual, which is dangerous; a suggestion of things vague, uncontrollable, and repulsive, whose discomposing intrusion excites the imagination and tries the civilized nerves of the foolish and the wise alike.

Kayerts and Carlier walked arm in arm, drawing close to one another as children do in the dark; and they had the same, not altogether unpleasant, sense of danger which one half suspects to be imaginary. They chatted persistently in familiar tones. "Our station is prettily situated," said one. The other assented with enthusiasm, enlarging volubly on the beauties of the situation. Then they passed near the grave. "Poor devil!" said Kayerts. "He died of fever, didn't he?" muttered Carlier, stopping short. "Why," retorted Kayerts, with indignation, "I've been told that the fellow exposed himself recklessly to the sun. The climate here, everybody says, is not at all worse than at home, as long as you keep out of the sun. Do you hear that, Carlier? I am chief here, and my orders are that you should not expose yourself to the sun!" He assumed his superiority jocularly, but his meaning was serious. The idea that he would, perhaps, have to bury Carlier and remain alone, gave him an inward shiver. He felt suddenly that this Carlier was more precious to him here, in the centre of Africa, than a brother could be anywhere else. Carlier, entering into the spirit of the thing, made a military salute and answered in a brisk tone, "Your orders shall be attended to, Chief!" Then he burst out laughing, slapped Kayerts on the back and shouted, "We shall let life run easily here! Just sit still and gather in the ivory those savages will bring. This country has its good points, after all!" They both laughed loudly while Carlier thought: "That poor Kayerts; he is so fat and unhealthy. It would be awful if I had to bury him here. He is a man I respect." . . . Before they reached the verandah of their house they called one another "my dear fellow."

The first day they were very active, pottering about with hammers and nails and red calico, to put up curtains, make their house habitable and pretty; resolved to settle down comfortably to their new life. For them an impossible task. To grapple effectually with even purely material problems requires more serenity of mind and more lofty courage than people generally imagine. No two beings could have been more unfitted for such a struggle. Society, not from any tenderness, but because of its strange needs, had taken care of those two men, forbidding them all independent thought, all initiative, all departure from routine; and forbidding it under pain of death. They could only live on condition of being machines. And now, released from the fostering care of men with pens behind the ears, or of men with gold lace on the sleeves, they were like those lifelong prisoners who, liberated after many years, do not know what use to make of their freedom. They did not know what use to make of their faculties, being both, through want of practice, incapable of independent thought.

At the end of two months Kayerts often would say, "If it was not for my Melie, you wouldn't catch me here." Melie was his daughter. He had thrown up his post in the Administration of the Telegraphs, though he had been for seventeen years perfectly happy there, to earn a dowry for his girl. His wife was dead, and the child was being brought up by his sisters. He regretted the streets, the pavements, the cafés, his friends of many years; all the things he used to see, day after day; all the thoughts suggested by familiar things — the thoughts effortless, monotonous, and soothing of a Government clerk; he regretted all the gossip, the small enmities, the mild venom, and the little jokes of Government offices. "If I had had a decent brother-in-law," Carlier would remark, "a fellow with a heart, I would not be here." He had left the army and had made himself so obnoxious to his family by his laziness and impudence, that an exasperated brother-in-law had made superhuman efforts to procure him an appointment in the Company as a second-class agent. Having not a penny in the world he was compelled to accept this means of livelihood as soon as it became quite clear to him that there was nothing more to squeeze out of his relations. He, like Kayerts, regretted his old life. He regretted the clink of sabre and spurs on a fine afternoon, the barrack room witticisms, the girls of garrison towns; but, besides, he had also a sense of grievance. He was evidently a much ill-used man. This made him moody, at times. But the two men got on well together in the fellowship of their stupidity and laziness. Together they did nothing, absolutely nothing, and enjoyed the sense of the idleness for which they were paid. And in time they came to feel something resembling affection for one another.

They lived like blind men in a large room, aware only of what came in contact with them (and of that only imperfectly), but unable to see the general aspect of things. The river, the forest, all the great land throbbing with life, were like a great emptiness. Even the brilliant sunshine disclosed nothing intelligible. Things appeared and disappeared before their eyes in an unconnected and aimless kind of way. The river seemed to come from nowhere and flow nowhither. It flowed through a void. Out of that void, at times, came canoes, and men with spears in their hands would suddenly crowd the yard of the station. They were naked, glossy black, ornamented with snowy shells and glistening brass wire, perfect of limb. They made an uncouth babbling noise when they spoke, moved in a stately manner, and sent quick, wild glances out of their startled, never-resting eyes. Those warriors would squat in long rows, four or more deep, before the verandah, while their chiefs bargained for hours with Makola over an elephant tusk. Kayerts sat on his chair and looked down on the proceedings, understanding nothing. He stared at them with his round blue eyes, called out to Carlier, "Here, look! look at that fellow there — and that other one, to the left. Did you ever see such a face? Oh, the funny brute!"

Carlier, smoking native tobacco in a short wooden pipe, would   10 swagger up twirling his moustaches, and surveying the warriors with haughty indulgence, would say:

"Fine animals. Brought any bone? Yes? It's not any too soon. Look at the muscles of that fellow — third from the end. I wouldn't care to get a punch on the nose from him. Fine arms, but legs no good below the knee. Couldn't make calvary men of them." And after glancing down complacently at his own shanks, he always concluded: "Pah! Don't they stink! You, Makola! Take that herd over to the fetish" (the storehouse was in every station called the fetish, perhaps because of the spirit of civilization it contained) "and give them up some of the rubbish you keep there. I'd rather see it full of bone than full of rags."

Kayerts approved.

"Yes, yes! Go and finish that palaver over there, Mr. Makola. I will come round when you are ready, to weigh the tusk. We must be careful." Then turning to his companion: "This is the tribe that lives down the river; they are rather aromatic. I remember, they had been once before here. D'ye hear that row? What a fellow has got to put up with in this dog of a country! My head is split."

Such profitable visits were rare. For days the two pioneers of trade and progress would look on their empty courtyard in the vibrating brilliance of vertical sunshine. Below the high bank, the silent river flowed on glittering and steady. On the sands in the middle of the stream, hippos and alligators sunned themselves side by side. And stretching away in all directions, surrounding the insignificant cleared spot of the trading post, immense forests, hiding fateful complications of fantastic life, lay in the eloquent silence of mute greatness. The two men understood nothing, cared for nothing but for the passage of days that separated them from the steamer's return. Their predecessor had left some torn books. They took up these wrecks of novels, and, as they had never read anything of the kind before, they were surprised and amused. Then during long days there were interminable and silly discussions about plots and personages. In the centre of Africa they made acquaintance of Richelieu and of d'Artagnan, of Hawk's Eye and of Father Goriot, and of many other people. All these imaginary personages became subjects for gossip as if they had been living friends. They discounted their virtues, suspected their motives, decried their successes; were scandalized at their duplicity or were doubtful about their courage. The accounts of crimes filled them with indignation, while tender or pathetic passages moved them deeply. Carlier cleared his throat and said in a soldierly voice, "What nonsense!" Kayerts, his round eyes suffused with tears, his fat cheeks quivering, rubbed his bald head, and declared, "This is a splendid book. I had no idea there were such clever fellows in the world." They also found some old copies of a home paper. That print discussed what it was pleased to call "Our Colonial Expansion" in high-flown language. It spoke much of the rights and duties of civilization, of the sacredness of the civilizing work, and extolled the merits of those who went about bringing light and faith and commerce to the dark places of the earth. Carlier and Kayerts read, wondered, and began to think better of themselves. Carlier said one evening, waving his hand about, "In a hundred years, there will be perhaps a town here. Quays, and warehouses, and barracks, and — and — billiard-rooms. Civilization, my boy, and virtue — and all. And then, chaps will read that two good fellows, Kayerts and Carlier, were the first civilized men to live in this very spot!" Kayerts nodded, "Yes, it is a consolation to think of that." They seemed to forget their dead predecessor; but, early one day, Carlier went out and replanted the cross firmly. "It used to make me squint whenever I walked that way," he explained to Kayerts over the morning coffee. "It made me squint, leaning over so much. So I just planted it upright. And solid, I promise you! I suspended myself with both hands to the crosspiece. Not a move. Oh, I did that properly."

At times Gobila came to see them. Gobila was the chief of the neighbouring villages. He was a grey-headed savage, thin and black, with a white cloth round his loins and a mangy panther skin hanging over his back. He came up with long strides of his skeleton legs, swinging a staff as tall as himself, and, entering the common room of the station, would squat on his heels to the left of the door. There he sat, watching Kayerts, and now and then making a speech which the other did not understand. Kayerts, without interrupting his occupation, would from time to time say in a friendly manner: "How goes it, you old image?" and they would smile at one another. The two whites had a liking for that old and incomprehensible creature, and called him Father Gobila. Gobila's manner was paternal, and he seemed really to love all white men. They all appeared to him very young, indistinguishably alike (except for stature), and he knew that they were all brothers, and also immortal. The death of the artist, who was the first white man whom he knew intimately, did not disturb this belief, because he was firmly convinced that the white stranger had pretended to die and got himself buried for some mysterious purpose of his own, into which it was useless to inquire. Perhaps it was his way of going home to his own country? At any rate, these were his brothers, and he transferred his absurd affection to them. They returned it in a way. Carlier slapped him on the back, and recklessly struck off matches for his amusement. Kayerts was always ready to let him have a sniff at the ammonia bottle. In short, they behaved just like that other white creature that had hidden itself in a hole in the ground. Gobila considered them attentively. Perhaps they were the same being with the other—or one of them was. He couldn't decide—clear up that mystery; but he remained always very friendly. In consequence of that friendship the women of Gobila's village walked in single file through the reedy grass, bringing every morning to the station, fowls, and sweet potatoes, and palm wine, and sometimes a goat. The Company never provisions the stations fully, and the agents required those local supplies to live. They had them through the goodwill of Gobila, and lived well. Now and then one of them had a bout of fever, and the other nursed him with gentle devotion. They did not think much of it. It left them weaker, and their appearance changed for the worse. Carlier was hollow-eyed and irritable. Kayerts showed a drawn, flabby face above the rotundity of his stomach, which gave him a weird aspect. But being constantly together, they did not notice the change that took place gradually in their appearance, and also in their dispositions.

Five months passed in that way.

Then, one morning, as Kayerts and Carlier, lounging in their chairs under the verandah, talked about the approaching visit of the steamer, a

15

knot of armed men came out of the forest and advanced towards the station. They were strangers to that part of the country. They were tall, slight, draped classically from neck to heel in blue fringed cloths, and carried percussion muskets over their bare right shoulders. Makola showed signs of excitement, and ran out of the storehouse (where he spent all his days) to meet these visitors. They came into the courtyard and looked about them with steady, scornful glances. Their leader, a powerful and determined looking Negro with bloodshot eyes, stood in front of the verandah and made a long speech. He gesticulated much, and ceased very suddenly.

There was something in his intonation, in the sounds of the long sentences he used, that startled the two whites. It was like a reminiscence of something not exactly familiar, and yet resembling the speech of civilized men. It sounded like one of those impossible languages which sometimes we hear in our dreams.

"What lingo is that?" said the amazed Carlier. "In the first moment I fancied the fellow was going to speak French. Anyway, it is a different kind of gibberish to what we ever heard."

"Yes," replied Kayerts. "Hey, Makola, what does he say? Where do they come from? Who are they?" 20

But Makola, who seemed to be standing on hot bricks, answered hurriedly, "I don't know. They come from very far. Perhaps Mrs. Price will understand. They are perhaps bad men."

The leader, after waiting for a while, said something sharply to Makola, who shook his head. Then the man, after looking round, noticed Makola's hut and walked over there. The next moment Mrs. Makola was heard speaking with great volubility. The other strangers—they were six in all—strolled about with an air of ease, put their heads through the door of the storeroom, congregated round the grave, pointed understandingly at the cross, and generally made themselves at home.

"I don't like those chaps—and, I say, Kayerts, they must be from the coast; they've got firearms," observed the sagacious Carlier.

Kayerts also did not like those chaps. They both, for the first time, became aware that they lived in conditions where the unusual may be dangerous, and that there was no power on earth outside of themselves to stand between them and the unusual. They became uneasy, went in and loaded their revolvers. Kayerts said, "We must order Makola to tell them to go away before dark."

The strangers left in the afternoon, after eating a meal prepared for them by Mrs. Makola. The immense woman was excited, and talked much with the visitors. She rattled away shrilly, pointing here and there at the forests and at the river. Makola sat apart and watched. At times he got up and whispered to his wife. He accompanied the strangers across the ravine at the back of the station ground, and returned slowly looking 25 very thoughtful. When questioned by the white men he was very strange, seemed not to understand, seemed to have forgotten French — seemed to have forgotten how to speak altogether. Kayerts and Carlier agreed that the nigger had had too much palm wine.

There was some talk about keeping a watch in turn, but in the evening everything seemed so quiet and peaceful that they retired as usual. All night they were disturbed by a lot of drumming in the villages. A deep, rapid roll near by would be followed by another far off — then all ceased. Soon short appeals would rattle out here and there, then all mingle together, increase, become vigorous and sustained, would spread out over the forest, roll through the night, unbroken and ceaseless, near and far, as if the whole land had been one immense drum booming out steadily an appeal to heaven. And through the deep and tremendous noise sudden yells that resembled snatches of songs from a madhouse darted shrill and high in discordant jets of sound which seemed to rush far above the earth and drive all peace from under the stars.

Carlier and Kayerts slept badly. They both thought they had heard shots fired during the night — but they could not agree as to the direction. In the morning Makola was gone somewhere. He returned about noon with one of yesterday's strangers, and eluded all Kayerts' attempts to close with him: had become deaf apparently. Kayerts wondered. Carlier, who had been fishing off the bank, came back and remarked while he showed his catch, "The niggers seem to be in a deuce of a stir; I wonder what's up. I saw about fifteen canoes cross the river during the two hours I was there fishing." Kayerts, worried, said, "Isn't this Makola very queer today?" Carlier advised, "Keep all our men together in case of some trouble."

II

There were ten station men who had been left by the Director. Those fellows, having engaged themselves to the Company for six months (without having any idea of a month in particular and only a very faint notion of time in general), had been serving the cause of progress for upwards of two years. Belonging to a tribe from a very distant part of the land of darkness and sorrow, they did not run away, naturally supposing that as wandering strangers they would be killed by the inhabitants of the country; in which were right. They lived in straw huts on the slope of a ravine overgrown with reedy grass, just behind the station buildings. They were not happy, regretting the festive incantations, the sorceries, the human sacrifices of their own land; where they also had parents, brothers, sisters, admired chiefs, respected magicians, loved friends, and other ties supposed generally to be human. Besides, the rice rations served out by the Company did not agree with them, being a food unknown to their land, and to which they could not get used. Consequently they were unhealthy and miserable. Had they been of any other tribe they would have made up their minds to die—for nothing is easier to certain savages than suicide—and so have escaped from the puzzling difficulties of existence. But belonging, as they did, to a warlike tribe with filed teeth, they had more grit, and went on stupidly living through disease and sorrow. They did very little work, and had lost their splendid physique. Carlier and Kayerts doctored them assiduously without being able to bring them back into condition again. They were mustered every morning and told off to different tasks—grass cutting, fence building, tree felling, &c., &c., which no power on earth could induce them to execute efficiently. The two whites had practically very little control over them.

In the afternoon Makola came over to the big house and found Kayerts watching three heavy columns of smoke rising above the forests. "What is that?" asked Kayerts. "Some villages burn," answered Makola, who seemed to have regained his wits. Then he said abruptly: "We have got very little ivory; bad six months' trading. Do you like get a little more ivory?"

"Yes," said Kayerts, eagerly. He thought of percentages which were low.   30

"Those men who came yesterday are traders from Loanda who have got more ivory than they can carry home. Shall I buy? I know their camp."

"Certainly," said Kayerts. "What are those traders?"

"Bad fellows," said Makola, indifferently. "They fight with people, and catch women and children. They are bad men, and got guns. There is a great disturbance in the country. Do you want ivory?"

"Yes," said Kayerts. Makola said nothing for a while. Then: "Those workmen of ours are no good at all," he muttered, looking round. "Station in very bad order, sir. Director will growl. Better get a fine lot of ivory, then he say nothing."

"I can't help it; the men won't work," said Kayerts. "When will   35
you get that ivory?"

"Very soon," said Makola. "Perhaps tonight. You leave it to me, and keep indoors, sir. I think you had better give some palm wine to our men to make a dance this evening. Enjoy themselves. Work better to-morrow. There's plenty palm wine—gone a little sour."

Kayerts said "yes," and Makola, with his own hands carried big calabashes to the door of his hut. They stood there till the evening, and Mrs. Makola looked into every one. The men got them at sunset. When Kayerts and Carlier retired, a big bonfire was flaring before the men's huts. They could hear their shouts and drumming. Some men from Gobila's village had joined the station hands, and the entertainment was a great success.

In the middle of the night, Carlier waking suddenly, heard a man shout loudly; then a shot was fired. Only one. Carlier ran out and met Kayerts on the verandah. They were both startled. As they went across the yard to call Makola, they saw shadows moving in the night. One of them cried, "Don't shoot! It's me, Price." Then Makola appeared close to them. "Go back, go back, please," he urged, "you spoil all," "There are strange men about," said Carlier. "Never mind; I know," said Makola. Then he whispered, "All right. Bring ivory. Say nothing! I know my business." The two white men reluctantly went back to the house, but did not sleep. They heard footsteps, whispers, some groans. It seemed as if a lot of men came in, dumped heavy things on the ground, squabbled a long time, then went away. They lay on their hard beds and thought: "This Makola is invaluable." In the morning Carlier came out, very sleepy, and pulled at the cord of the big bell. The station hands mustered every morning to the sound of the bell. That morning nobody came. Kayerts turned out also, yawning. Across the yard they saw Makola come out of his hut, a tin basin of soapy water in his hand. Makola, a civilized nigger, was very neat in his person. He threw the soapsuds skilfully over a wretched little yellow cur he had, then turning his face to the agent's house, he shouted from the distance, "All the men gone last night!"

They heard him plainly, but in their surprise they both yelled out together: "What!" Then they stared at one another. "We are in a proper fix now," growled Carlier. "It's incredible!" muttered Kayerts. "I will go to the huts and see,' said Carlier, striding off. Makola coming up found Kayerts standing alone.

"I can hardly believe it," said Kayerts, tearfully. "We took care of   40
them as if they had been our children."

"They went with the coast people," said Makola after a moment of hesitation.

"What do I care with whom they went—the ungrateful brutes!" exclaimed the other. Then with sudden suspicion, and looking hard at Makola, he added: "What do you know about it?"

Makola moved his shoulders, looking down on the ground. "What do I know? I think only. Will you come and look at the ivory I've got there? It is a fine lot. You never saw such."

He moved towards the store. Kayerts followed him mechanically, thinking about the incredible desertion of the men. On the ground before the door of the fetish lay six splendid tusks.

"What did you give for it?" asked Kayerts, after surveying the lot   45
with satisfaction.

"No regular trade," said Makola. "They brought the ivory and gave it to me. I told them to take what they most wanted in the station. It is a beautiful lot. No station can show such tusks. Those traders wanted carriers badly, and our men were no good here. No trade, no entry in books; all correct."

Kayerts nearly burst with indignation. "Why!" he shouted, "I believe you have sold our men for these tusks!" Makola stood impassive and silent. "I—I—will—I," stuttered Kayerts. "You fiend!" he yelled out.

"I did the best for you and the Company," said Makola, imperturbably. "Why you shout so much? Look at this tusk."

"I dismiss you! I will report you—I won't look at the tusks. I forbid you to touch them. I order you to throw them into the river. You—you!"

"You very red, Mr. Kayerts. If you are so irritable in the sun,   *50* you will get fever and die—like the first chief!" pronounced Makola impressively.

They stood still, contemplating one another with intense eyes, as if they had been looking with effort across immense distances. Kayerts shivered. Makola had meant no more than he said, but his words seemed to Kayerts full of ominous menace! He turned sharply and went away to the house. Makola retired into the bosom of his family; and the tusks, left lying before the store, looked very large and valuable in the sunshine.

Carlier came back on the verandah. "They're all gone, hey?" asked Kayerts from the far end of the common room in a muffled voice. "You did not find anybody?"

"Oh, yes," said Carlier, "I found one of Gobila's people lying dead before the huts—shot through the body. We heard that shot last night."

Kayerts came out quickly. He found his companion staring grimly over the yard at the tusks, away by the store. They both sat in silence for a while. Then Kayerts related his conversation with Makola. Carlier said nothing. At the midday meal they ate very little. They hardly exchanged a word that day. A great silence seemed to lie heavily over the station and press on their lips. Makola did not open the store; he spent the day playing with his children. He lay full length on a mat outside his door, and the youngsters sat on his chest and clambered all over him. It was a touching picture. Mrs. Makola was busy cooking all day as usual. The white men made a somewhat better meal in the evening. Afterwards, Carlier smoking his pipe strolled over to the store; he stood for a long time over the tusks, touched one or two with his foot, even tried to lift the largest one by its small end. He came back to his chief, who had not stirred from the verandah, threw himself in the chair, and said:

"I can see it! They were pounced upon while they slept heavily after   *55* drinking all that palm wine you've allowed Makola to give them. A put-up job! See? The worst is, some of Gobila's people were there, and got carried off too, no doubt. The least drunk woke up, and got shot for his sobriety. This is a funny country. What will you do now?"

"We can't touch it, of course," said Kayerts.

"Of course not," assented Carlier.

"Slavery is an awful thing," stammered out Kayerts in an unsteady voice.

"Frightful—the sufferings," grunted Carlier with conviction.

They believed their words. Everybody shows a respectful deference   *60* to certain sounds that he and his fellows can make. But about feelings people really know nothing. We talk with indignation or enthusiasm; we talk about oppression, cruelty, crime, devotion, self-sacrifice, virtue, and we know nothing real beyond the words. Nobody knows what suffering or sacrifice mean—except, perhaps, the victims of the mysterious purpose of these illusions.

Next morning they saw Makola very busy setting up in the yard the big scales used for weighing ivory. By and by Carlier said: "What's that filthy scoundrel up to?" and lounged out into the yard. Kayerts followed. They stood watching. Makola took no notice. When the balance was swung true, he tried to lift a tusk into the scale. It was too heavy. He looked up helplessly without a word, and for a minute they stood round that balance as mute and still as three statues. Suddenly Carlier said: "Catch hold of the other end, Makola—you beast!" and together they swung the tusk up. Kayerts trembled in every limb. He muttered, "I say! O! I say!" and putting his hand in his pocket found there a dirty bit of paper and the stump of a pencil. He turned his back on the others, as if about to do something tricky, and noted stealthily the weights which Carlier shouted out to him with unnecessary loudness. When all was over Makola whispered to himself: "The sun's very strong here for the tusks." Carlier said to Kayerts in a careless tone: "I say, Chief, I might just as well give him a lift with this lot into the store."

As they were going back to the house Kayerts observed with a sigh: "It had to be done." And Carlier said: "It's deplorable, but, the men being Company's men the ivory is Company's ivory. We must look after it." "I will report to the Director, of course," said Kayerts. "Of course; let him decide," approved Carlier.

At midday they made a hearty meal. Kayerts sighed from time to time. Whenever they mentioned Makola's name they always added to it an opprobrious epithet. It eased their conscience. Makola gave himself a half-holiday, and bathed his children in the river. No one from Gobila's villages came near the station that day. No one came the next day, and the next, nor for a whole week. Gobila's people might have been dead and buried for any sign of life they gave. But they were only mourning for those they had lost by the witchcraft of white men, who had brought wicked people into their country. The wicked people were gone, but fear remained. Fear always remains. A man may destroy everything within himself, love and hate and belief, and even doubt; but as long as he clings to life he cannot destroy fear: the fear, subtle, indestructible, and terrible, that pervades his being; that tinges his thoughts; that lurks in his heart; that watches on his lips the struggle of his last breath. In his fear, the mild old Gobila offered extra human sacrifices to all the Evil Spirits that had taken possession of his white friends. His heart was heavy. Some warriors spoke about burning and killing, but the cautious old savage dissuaded them. Who could foresee the woe those mysterious creatures, if irritated, might bring? They should be left alone. Perhaps in time they would disappear into the earth as the first one had disappeared. His people must keep away from them, and hope for the best.

Kayerts and Carlier did not disappear, but remained above on this earth, that, somehow, they fancied had become bigger and very empty. It was not the absolute and dumb solitude of the post that impressed them so much as an inarticulate feeling that something from within them was gone, something that worked for their safety, and had kept the wilderness from interfering with their hearts. The images of home; the memory of people like them, of men that thought and felt as they used to think and feel, receded into distances made indistinct by the glare of unclouded sunshine. And out of the great silence of the surrounding wilderness, its very hopelessness and savagery seemed to approach them nearer, to draw them gently, to look upon them, to envelop them with a solicitude irresistible, familiar, and disgusting.

Days lengthened into weeks, then into months. Gobila's people   65
drummed and yelled to every new moon, as of yore, but kept away from the station. Makola and Carlier tried once in a canoe to open communications, but were received with a shower of arrows, and had to fly back to the station for dear life. That attempt set the country up and down the river into an uproar that could be very distinctly heard for days. The steamer was late. At first they spoke of delay jauntily, then anxiously, then gloomily. The matter was becoming serious. Stores were running short. Carlier cast his lines off the bank, but the river was low, and the fish kept out in the stream. They dared not stroll far away from the station to shoot. Moreover, there was no game in the impenetrable forest. Once Carlier shot a hippo in the river. They had no boat to secure it, and it sank. When it floated up it drifted away, and Gobila's people secured the carcass. It was the occasion for a national holiday, but Carlier had a fit of rage over it and talked about the necessity of exterminating all the niggers before the country could be made habitable. Kayerts mooned about silently; spent hours looking at the portrait of his Melie. It represented a little girl with long bleached tresses and a rather sour face. His legs were much swollen, and he could hardly walk. Carlier, undermined by fever, could not swagger any more, but kept tottering about, still with a devil-may-care air, as became a man who remembered his crack regiment. He had become hoarse, sarcastic, and inclined to say unpleasant things. He called it "being frank with you." They had long ago reckoned their percentages on trade, including in them that last deal of "this infamous Makola." They had also concluded not to say anything about it. Kayerts hesitated at first — was afraid of the Director.

"He has seen worse things done on the quiet," maintained Carlier, with a hoarse laugh. "Trust him! He won't thank you if you blab. He is no better than you or me. Who will talk if we hold our tongues? There is nobody here."

That was the root of the trouble! There was nobody there; and being left there alone with their weakness, they became daily more like a pair of accomplices than like a couple of devoted friends. They had heard nothing from home for eight months. Every evening they said, "Tomorrow we shall see the steamer." But one of the Company's steamers had been wrecked, and the Director was busy with the other, relieving very distant and important stations on the main river. He thought that the useless station, and the useless men, could wait. Meantime Kayerts and Carlier lived on rice boiled without salt, and cursed the Company, all Africa, and the day they were born. One must have lived on such diet to discover what ghastly trouble the necessity of swallowing one's food may become. There was literally nothing else in the station but rice and coffee; they drank the coffee without sugar. The last fifteen lumps Kayert had solemnly locked away in his box, together with a half-bottle of Cognâc, "in case of sickness," he explained. Carlier approved. "When one is sick," he said, "any little extra like that is cheering."

They waited. Rank grass began to sprout over the courtyard. The bell never rang now. Days passed, silent, exasperating, and slow. When the two men spoke, they snarled; and their silences were bitter, as if tinged by the bitterness of their thoughts.

One day after a lunch of boiled rice, Carlier put down his cup untasted, and said: "Hang it all! Let's have a decent cup of coffee for once. Bring out that sugar, Kayerts!"

"For the sick," muttered Kayerts, without looking up.   70

"For the sick," mocked Carlier. "Bosh! . . . Well! I am sick."

"You are no more sick than I am, and I go without," said Kayerts in a peaceful tone.

"Come! Out with that sugar, you stingy old slave-dealer."

Kayerts looked up quickly. Carlier was smiling with marked insolence. And suddenly it seemed to Kayerts that he had never seen that man before. Who was he? He knew nothing about him. What was he capable of? There was a surprising flash of violent emotion within him, as if in the presence of something undreamt-of, dangerous, and final. But he managed to pronounce with composure:

"That joke is in very bad taste. Don't repeat it."   75

"Joke!" said Carlier, hitching himself forward on his seat. "I am hungry — I am sick — I don't joke! I hate hypocrites. You are a hypocrite. You are a slave-dealer. I am a slave-dealer. There's nothing but slave-dealers in this cursed country. I mean to have sugar in my coffee today, anyhow!"

"I forbid you to speak to me in that way," said Kayerts with a fair show of resolution.

"You! — What?" shouted Carlier, jumping up.

Kayerts stood up also. "I am your chief," he began, trying to master the shakiness of his voice.

"What?" yelled the other. "Who's chief? There's no chief here.   80
There's nothing here: there's nothing but you and I. Fetch the sugar —
you potbellied ass."

"Hold your tongue. Go out of this room," screamed Kayerts. "I dismiss you — you scoundrel!"

Carlier swung a stool. All at once he looked dangerously in earnest. "You flabby, good-for-nothing civilian — take that!" he howled.

Kayerts dropped under the table, and the stool struck the grass inner wall of the room. Then, as Carlier was trying to upset the table, Kayerts in desperation made a blind rush, head low, like a cornered pig would do and, overturning his friend, bolted along the verandah, and into his room. He locked the door, snatched his revolver, and stood panting. In less than a minute Carlier was kicking at the door furiously, howling, "If you don't bring out that sugar, I will shoot you at sight, like a dog. Now then — one — two — three. You won't? I will show you who's the master."

Kayerts thought the door would fall in, and scrambled through the square hole that served for a window in his room. There was then the whole breadth of the house between them. But the other was apparently not strong enough to break in the door, and Kayerts heard him running round. Then he also began to run laboriously on his swollen legs. He ran as quickly as he could, grasping the revolver, and unable yet to understand what was happening to him. He saw in succession Makola's house, the store, the river, the ravine, and the low bushes; and he saw all those things again as he ran for the second time round the house. Then again they flashed past him. That morning he could not have walked a yard without a groan.

And now he ran. He ran fast enough to keep out of sight of the other man.

Then as, weak and desperate, he thought, "Before I finish the next round I shall die," he heard the other man stumble heavily, then stop. He stopped also. He had the back and Carlier the front of the house, as before. He heard him drop into a chair cursing, and suddenly his own legs gave way, and he slid down into a sitting posture with his back to the wall. His mouth was as dry as a cinder, and his face was wet with perspiration — and tears. What was it all about? He thought it must be a horrible illusion; he thought he was dreaming; he thought he was going mad! After a while he collected his senses. What did they quarrel about? That sugar! How absurd! He would give it to him — didn't want it himself. And he began scrambling to his feet with a sudden feeling of security. But before he had fairly stood upright, a commonsense reflection occurred to him and drove him back into despair. He thought: "If I give way now to that brute of a soldier, he will begin this horror again tomorrow — and the day after — every day — raise other pretensions, trample on me, torture me, make me his slave — and I will be lost! Lost! The steamer may not come for days — may never come." He shook so that he had to sit down on the floor again. He shivered forlornly. He felt he could not, would not move any more. He was completely distracted by the sudden perception that the position was without issue—that death and life had in a moment become equally difficult and terrible.

All at once he heard the other push his chair back; and he leaped to his feet with extreme facility. He listened and got confused. Must run again! Right or left? He heard footsteps. He darted to the left, grasping his revolver, and at the very same instant, as it seemed to him, they came into violent collision. Both shouted with surprise. A loud explosion took place between them; a roar of red fire, thick smoke; and Kayerts, deafened and blinded, rushed back thinking: "I am hit—it's all over." He expected the other to come round—to gloat over his agony. He caught hold of an upright of the roof—"All over!" Then he heard a crashing fall on the other side of the house, as if somebody had tumbled headlong over a chair—then silence. Nothing more happened. He did not die. Only his shoulder felt as if it had been badly wrenched, and he had lost his revolver. He was disarmed and helpless! He waited for his fate. The other man made no sound. It was a stratagem. He was stalking him now! Along what side? Perhaps he was taking aim this very minute!

After a few moments of an agony frightful and absurd, he decided to go and meet his doom. He was prepared for every surrender. He turned the corner, steadying himself with one hand on the wall; made a few paces, and nearly swooned. He had seen on the floor, protruding past the other corner, a pair of turned-up feet. A pair of white naked feet in red slippers. He felt deadly sick, and stood for a time in profound darkness. Then Makola appeared before him, saying quietly: "Come along, Mr. Kayerts. He is dead." He burst into tears of gratitude; a loud, sobbing fit of crying. After a time he found himself sitting in a chair and looking at Carlier, who lay stretched on his back. Makola was kneeling over the body.

"Is this your revolver?" asked Makola, getting up.

"Yes," said Kayerts; then he added very quickly, "He ran after me   90
to shoot me—you saw!"

"Yes, I saw," said Makola. "There is only one revolver; where's his?"

"Don't know," whispered Kayerts in a voice that had become suddenly very faint.

"I will go and look for it," said the other, gently. He made the round along the verandah, while Kayerts sat still and looked at the corpse. Makola came back empty-handed, stood in deep thought, then stepped quietly into the dead man's room, and came out directly with a revolver, which he held up before Kayerts. Kayerts shut his eyes. Everything was going round. He found life more terrible and difficult than death. He had shot an unarmed man.

After meditating for a while, Makola said softly, pointing at the dead man who lay there with his right eye blown out:

"He died of fever." Kayerts looked at him with a stony stare. "Yes," ⁹⁵
repeated Makola, thoughtfully, stepping over the corpse, "I think he died
of fever. Bury him tomorrow."

And he went away slowly to his expectant wife, leaving the two
white men alone on the verandah.

Night came, and Kayerts sat unmoving on his chair. He sat quiet as
if he had taken a dose of opium. The violence of the emotions he had
passed through produced a feeling of exhausted serenity. He had
plumbed in one short afternoon the depths of horror and despair, and
now found repose in the conviction that life had no more secrets for him:
neither had death! He sat by the corpse thinking; thinking very actively,
thinking very new thoughts. He seemed to have broken loose from
himself altogether. His old thoughts, convictions, likes and dislikes,
things he respected and things he abhorred, appeared in their true light
at last! Appeared contemptible and childish, false and ridiculous. He
revelled in his new wisdom while he sat by the man he had killed. He
argued with himself about all things under heaven with that kind of
wrong-headed lucidity which may be observed in some lunatics. Incidentally he reflected that the fellow dead there had been a noxious beast
anyway; that men died every day in thousands; perhaps in hundreds of
thousands — who could tell? — and that in the number, that one death
could not possibly make any difference; couldn't have any importance,
at least to a thinking creature. He, Kayerts, was a thinking creature. He
had been all his life, till that moment, a believer in a lot of nonsense like
the rest of mankind — who are fools; but now he thought! He knew!
He was at peace; he was familiar with the highest wisdom! Then he
tried to imagine himself dead, and Carlier sitting in his chair watching
him; and his attempt met with such unexpected success, that in a very
few moments he became not at all sure who was dead and who was
alive. This extraordinary achievement of his fancy startled him, however, and by a clever and timely effort of mind he saved himself just
in time from becoming Carlier. His heart thumped, and he felt hot
all over at the thought of that danger. Carlier! What a beastly thing!
To compose his now disturbed nerves — and no wonder! — he tried
to whistle a little. Then, suddenly, he fell asleep, or thought he had
slept; but at any rate there was a fog, and somebody had whistled in
the fog.

He stood up. The day had come, and a heavy mist had descended
upon the land: the mist penetrating, enveloping, and silent; the morning
mist of tropical lands; the mist that clings and kills; the mist white and
deadly, immaculate and poisonous. He stood up, saw the body, and
threw his arms above his head with a cry like that of a man who, waking from a trance, finds himself immured forever in a tomb. *"Help! . . .
My God!"*

A shriek inhuman, vibrating and sudden, pierced like a sharp dart the white shroud of that land of sorrow. Three short, impatient screeches followed, and then, for a time, the fog-wreaths rolled on, undisturbed, through a formidable silence. Then many more shrieks, rapid and piercing, like the yells of some exasperated and ruthless creature, rent the air. Progress was calling to Kayerts from the river. Progress and civilization and all the virtues. Society was calling to its accomplished child to come, to be taken care of, to be instructed, to be judged, to be condemned; it called him to return to that rubbish heap from which he had wandered away, so that justice could be done.

Kayerts heard and understood. He stumbled out of the verandah,   100
leaving the other man quite alone for the first time since they had been thrown there together. He groped his way through the fog, calling in his ignorance upon the invisible heaven to undo its work. Makola flitted by in the mist, shouting as he ran:

"Steamer! Steamer! They can't see. They whistle for the station. I go ring the bell. Go down to the landing, sir. I ring."

He disappeared. Kayerts stood still. He looked upwards; the fog rolled low over his head. He looked round like a man who has lost his way; and he saw a dark smudge, a cross-shaped stain, upon the shifting purity of the mist. As he began to stumble towards it, the station bell rang in a tumultuous peal its answer to the impatient clamour of the steamer.

The Managing Director of the Great Civilizing Company (since we know that civilization follows trade) landed first, and incontinently lost sight of the steamer. The fog down by the river was exceedingly dense; above, at the station, the bell rang unceasing and brazen.

The Director shouted loudly to the steamer:

"There is nobody down to meet us; there may be something   105
wrong, though they are ringing. You had better come, too!"

And he began to toil up the steep bank. The captain and the engine driver of the boat followed behind. As they scrambled up the fog thinned, and they could see their Director a good way ahead. Suddenly they saw him start forward, calling to them over his shoulder: "Run! Run to the house! I've found one of them. Run, look for the other!"

He had found one of them! And even he, the man of varied and startling experience, was somewhat discomposed by the manner of this finding. He stood and fumbled in his pockets (for a knife) while he faced Kayerts, who was hanging by a leather strap from the cross. He had evidently climbed the grave, which was high and narrow, and after tying the end of the strap to the arm, had swung himself off. His toes were only a couple of inches above the ground; his arms hung stiffly down; he seemed to be standing rigidly at attention, but with one purple cheek playfully posed on the shoulder. And, irreverently, he was putting out a swollen tongue at his Managing Director.

FOR DISCUSSION AND WRITING

1. What sort of people are Kayerts and Carlier? What do you learn about them from the scene in the first paragraph? What are their attitudes toward (a) their assignment, (b) each other, and (c) the natives and the land?

2. What is the turning point in the story (peripeteia)? How do the attitudes and actions of Kayerts and Carlier change after the peripeteia?

3. During the nineteenth century, Europeans "invaded" Africa in force, colonializing, exploiting, and "modernizing." (The slave trade is just one aspect of the impact of "civilization" on the "Dark Continent.") How is Makola symbolic of nineteenth-century Africa? How does the agent represent the vast scene?

4. Is Makola the perfect "company man"? Explain.

5. Give specific examples of background knowledge the reader must have to understand this story.

6. What is the main idea of the story? How does the title relate to the main idea?

7. What is Conrad's attitude toward European civilization? Cite specific evidence for your opinion.

8. The story conveys Joseph Conrad's opinions about nineteenth-century colonialism in Africa, among other subjects. Give examples of passages in which he directly states his opinions. How do the characters and their actions further develop the author's opinions about his theme?

9. In what ways does the author withhold information to build suspense?

10. Conrad frequently uses irony to convey his meaning. Point out some instances, and explain them.

THE YELLOW WALLPAPER

Charlotte Perkins Gilman

This very "modern" story was first published in the *New England Magazine* in 1892, but, with minor changes, it would not appear anachronistic in *The New Yorker* in 1992. "The Yellow Wallpaper" is a fascinating tale of man–woman relationships and of mental breakdown.

Gilman's mother was Mary A. Fitch, whose family had lived in Rhode Island for two centuries; her father was Frederic Beecher Perkins, nephew of the great American preacher Henry Ward Beecher and of Harriet Beecher Stowe, author of *Uncle Tom's Cabin*. Shortly after Gilman's birth in 1860, her father deserted the family.

Before her marriage in 1884 to the artist Charles Stetson, Charlotte supported herself by working as a governess, art teacher, and designer of greeting cards. Nine months after her marriage, her daughter, Katherine, was born, and Charlotte began to suffer the depression that is the theme of "The Yellow Wallpaper." Believing that marriage to Stetson would ultimately drive her mad, Charlotte left him in 1884 and moved with Katherine to Pasadena, California. In 1892, she was granted a divorce from Stetson, and after he remarried she sent Katherine east to live with him, an action that brought about much criticism of her values and way of life. Nonetheless, she continued to work as a writer and lecturer and in 1898 published her influential *Women and Economics,* which was followed by, among other works, *Man-Made World* (1911) and *His Religion and Hers* (1923).

In 1900, Charlotte married her cousin, George Houghton Gilman, and lived happily with him until his death in 1934. In 1935 — bereaved, convinced that her productive life was over, and wracked by breast cancer — she took her own life.

Although "The Yellow Wallpaper" is fiction, it is a good example of how stories can explain, argue, and persuade. From one point of view, it can be interpreted as Charlotte Perkins Gilman's explanation of her own mental problems; a reader can also view it as an argument in favor of feminism; and, to the extent that we accept its verisimilitude (its trueness to life), it is forceful persuasion.

It is very seldom that mere ordinary people like John and myself secure ancestral halls for the summer.

A colonial mansion, a hereditary estate, I would say a haunted house, and reach the height of romantic felicity — but that would be asking too much of fate!

Still I will proudly declare that there is something queer about it.

Else, why should it be let so cheaply? And why have stood so long untenanted?

John laughs at me, of course, but one expects that in marriage.   5

John is practical in the extreme. He has no patience with faith, an intense horror of superstition, and he scoffs openly at any talk of things not to be felt and seen and put down in figures.

John is a physician, and *perhaps*—(I would not say it to a living soul, of course, but this is dead paper and a great relief to my mind—) *perhaps* that is one reason I do not get well faster.

You see he does not believe I am sick!

And what can one do?

If a physician of high standing, and one's own husband, assures   10 friends and relatives that there is really nothing the matter with one but temporary nervous depression—a slight hysterical tendency—what is one to do?

My brother is also a physician, and also of high standing, and he says the same thing.

So I take phosphates or phosphites—whichever it is, and tonics, and journeys, and air, and exercise, and am absolutely forbidden to "work" until I am well again.

Personally, I disagree with their ideas.

Personally, I believe that congenial work, with excitement and change, would do me good.

But what is one to do?   15

I did write for a while in spite of them; but it *does* exhaust me a good deal—having to be so sly about it, or else meet with heavy opposition.

I sometimes fancy that in my condition if I had less opposition and more society and stimulus—but John says the very worst thing I can do is to think about my condition, and I confess it always makes me feel bad.

So I will let it alone and talk about the house.

The most beautiful place! It is quite alone, standing well back from the road, quite three miles from the village. It makes me think of English places that you read about, for there are hedges and walls and gates that lock, and lots of separate little houses for the gardeners and people.

There is a *delicious* garden! I never saw such a garden—large and   20 shady, full of box-bordered paths, and lined with long grape-covered arbors with seats under them.

There were greenhouses, too, but they are all broken now.

There was some legal trouble, I believe, something about the heirs and coheirs; anyhow, the place has been empty for years.

That spoils my ghostliness, I am afraid, but I don't care—there is something strange about the house—I can feel it.

I even said so to John one moonlight evening, but he said what I felt was a *draught,* and shut the window.

I get unreasonably angry with John sometimes. I'm sure I never   25
used to be so sensitive. I think it is due to this nervous condition.

But John says if I feel so, I shall neglect proper self-control; so I
take pains to control myself—before him, at least, and that makes me
very tired.

I don't like our room a bit. I wanted one downstairs that opened on
the piazza and had roses all over the window, and such pretty old-fashioned chintz hangings! but John would not hear of it.

He said there was only one window and not room for two beds,
and no near room for him if he took another.

He is very careful and loving, and hardly lets me stir without
special direction.

I have a schedule prescription for each hour in the day; he takes all   30
care from me, and so I feel basely ungrateful not to value it more.

He said we came here solely on my account, that I was to have
perfect rest and all the air I could get. "Your exercise depends on your
strength, my dear," said he, "and your food somewhat on your appetite;
but air you can absorb all the time." So we took the nursery at the top
of the house.

It is a big, airy room, the whole floor nearly, with windows that
look all ways, and air and sunshine galore. It was nursery first and then
playroom and gymnasium, I should judge; for the windows are barred
for little children, and there are rings and things in the walls.

The paint and paper look as if a boys' school had used it. It is
stripped off—the paper—in great patches all around the head of my bed,
about as far as I can reach, and in a great place on the other side of the
room low down. I never saw a worse paper in my life.

One of those sprawling flamboyant patterns committing every artistic sin.

It is dull enough to confuse the eye in following, pronounced   35
enough to constantly irritate and provoke study, and when you follow
the lame uncertain curves for a little distance they suddenly commit
suicide—plunge off at outrageous angles, destroy themselves in unheard
of contradictions.

The color is repellant, almost revolting; a smouldering unclean yellow, strangely faded by the slow-turning sunlight.

It is a dull yet lurid orange in some places, a sickly sulphur tint in
others.

No wonder the children hated it! I should hate it myself if I had to
live in this room long.

There comes John, and I must put this away,—he hates to have me
write a word.

We have been here two weeks, and I haven't felt like writing before,   40
since that first day.

I am sitting by the window now, up in this atrocious nursery, and there is nothing to hinder my writing as much as I please, save lack of strength.

John is away all day, and even some nights when his cases are serious.

I am glad my case is not serious!

But these nervous troubles are dreadfully depressing.

John does not know how much I really suffer. He knows there is   45
no *reason* to suffer, and that satisfies him.

Of course it is only nervousness. It does weigh on me so not to do my duty in any way!

I mean to be such a help to John, such a real rest and comfort, and here I am a comparative burden already!

Nobody would believe what an effort it is to do what little I am able, — to dress and entertain, and order things.

It is fortunate Mary is so good with the baby. Such a dear baby!

And yet I *cannot* be with him, it makes me so nervous.   50

I suppose John never was nervous in his life. He laughs at me so about this wallpaper!

At first he meant to repaper the room, but afterwards he said that I was letting it get the better of me, and that nothing was worse for a nervous patient than to give way to such fancies.

He said that after the wallpaper was changed it would be the heavy bedstead, and then the barred windows, and then that gate at the head of the stairs, and so on.

"You know the place is doing you good," he said, "and really, dear, I don't care to renovate the house just for a three months' rental."

"Then do let us go downstairs," I said, "there are such pretty   55
rooms there."

Then he took me in his arms and called me a blessed little goose, and said he would go down cellar, if I wished, and have it whitewashed into the bargain.

But he is right enough about the beds and windows and things.

It is an airy and comfortable room as any one need wish, and, of course, I would not be so silly as to make him uncomfortable just for a whim.

I'm really getting quite fond of the big room, all but that horrid paper.

Out of one window I can see the garden, those mysterious deep-   60
shaded arbors, the riotous old-fashioned flowers, and bushes and gnarly trees.

Out of another I get a lovely view of the bay and a little private wharf belonging to the estate. There is a beautiful shaded lane that runs down there from the house. I always fancy I see people walking in these numerous paths and arbors, but John has cautioned me not to give way to fancy in the least. He says that with my imaginative power and habit of story-making, a nervous weakness like mine is sure to lead to all manner of excited fancies, and that I ought to use my will and good sense to check the tendency. So I try.

I think sometimes that if I were only well enough to write a little it would relieve the press of ideas and rest me.

But I find I get pretty tired when I try.

It is so discouraging not to have any advice and companionship about my work. When I get really well, John says we will ask Cousin Henry and Julia down for a long visit; but he says he would as soon put fireworks in my pillowcase as to let me have those stimulating people about now.

I wish I could get well faster.   65

But I must not think about that. This paper looks to me as if it *knew* what a vicious influence it had!

There is a recurrent spot where the pattern lolls like a broken neck and two bulbous eyes stare at you upside down.

I get positively angry with the impertinence of it and the everlastingness. Up and down and sideways they crawl, and those absurd, unblinking eyes are everywhere. There is one place where two breadths didn't match, and the eyes go all up and down the line, one a little higher than the other.

I never saw so much expression in an inanimate thing before, and we all know how much expression they have! I used to lie awake as a child and get more entertainment and terror out of blank walls and plain furniture than most children could find in a toy-store.

I remember what a kindly wink the knobs of our big, old bureau   70
used to have, and there was one chair that always seemed like a strong friend.

I used to feel that if any of the other things looked too fierce I could always hop into that chair and be safe.

The furniture in this room is no worse than inharmonious, however, for we had to bring it all from downstairs. I suppose when this was used as a playroom they had to take the nursery things out, and no wonder! I never saw such ravages as the children have made here.

The wallpaper, as I said before, is torn off in spots, and it sticketh closer than a brother — they must have had perseverance as well as hatred.

Then the floor is scratched and gouged and splintered, the plaster itself is dug out here and there, and this great heavy bed which is all we found in the room, looks as if it had been through the wars.

But I don't mind it a bit — only the paper.   75

There comes John's sister. Such a dear girl as she is, and so careful of me! I must not let her find me writing.

She is a perfect and enthusiastic housekeeper, and hopes for no better profession. I verily believe she thinks it is the writing which made me sick!

But I can write when she is out, and see her a long way off from these windows.

There is one that commands the road, a lovely shaded winding road, and one that just looks off over the country. A lovely country, too, full of great elms and velvet meadows.

This wallpaper has a kind of sub-pattern in a different shade, a *80* particularly irritating one, for you can only see it in certain lights, and not clearly then.

But in the places where it isn't faded and where the sun is just so— I can see a strange, provoking, formless sort of figure, that seems to skulk about behind that silly and conspicuous front design.

There's sister on the stairs!

Well, the Fourth of July is over! The people are all gone and I am tired out. John thought it might do me good to see a little company, so we just had mother and Nellie and the children down for a week.

Of course I didn't do a thing. Jennie sees to everything now.

But it tired me all the same. *85*

John says if I don't pick up faster he shall send me to Weir Mitchell° in the fall.

But I don't want to go there at all. I had a friend who was in his hands once, and she says he is just like John and my brother, only more so!

Besides, it is such an undertaking to go so far.

I don't feel as if it was worth while to turn my hand over for anything, and I'm getting dreadfully fretful and querulous.

I cry at nothing, and cry most of the time. *90*

Of course I don't when John is here, or anybody else, but when I am alone.

And I am alone a good deal just now. John is kept in town very often by serious cases, and Jennie is good and lets me alone when I want her to.

So I walk a little in the garden or down that lovely lane, sit on the porch under the roses, and lie down up here a good deal.

I'm getting really fond of the room in spite of the wallpaper. Per- haps *because* of the wallpaper.

It dwells in my mind so! *95*

I lie here on this great immovable bed—it is nailed down, I be- lieve—and follow that pattern about by the hour. It is as good as gym- nastics, I assure you. I start, we'll say, at the bottom, down in the corner over there where it has not been touched, and I determine for the thou- sandth time that I *will* follow that pointless pattern to some sort of conclusion.

I know a little of the principle of design, and I know this thing was

Weir Marshall: A noted physician and specialist in nervous disorders.

not arranged on any laws of radiation, or alternation, or repetition, or symmetry, or anything else that I ever heard of.

It is repeated, of course, by the breadths, but not otherwise.

Looked at in one way each breadth stands alone, the bloated curves and flourishes — a kind of "debased Romanesque"° with *delirium tremens* — go waddling up and down in isolated columns of fatuity.

But, on the other hand, they connect diagonally, and the sprawling   100 outlines run off in great slanting waves of optic horror, like a lot of wallowing seaweeds in full chase.

The whole thing goes horizontally, too, at least it seems so, and I exhaust myself in trying to distinguish the order of its going in that direction.

They have used a horizontal breadth for a frieze, and that adds wonderfully to the confusion.

There is one end of the room where it is almost intact, and there, when the crosslights fade and the low sun shines directly upon it, I can almost fancy radiation after all, — the interminable grotesque seem to form around a common center and rush off in headlong plunges of equal distraction.

It makes me tired to follow it. I will take a nap I guess.

I don't know why I should write this.   105

I don't want to.

I don't feel able.

And I know John would think it absurd. But I *must* say what I feel and think in some way — it is such a relief!

But the effort is getting to be greater than the relief.

Half the time now I am awfully lazy, and lie down ever so much.   110

John says I mustn't lose my strength, and has me take cod liver oil and lots of tonics and things, to say nothing of ale and wine and rare meat.

Dear John! He loves me very dearly, and hates to have me sick. I tried to have a real earnest reasonable talk with him the other day, and tell him how I wish he would let me go and make a visit to Cousin Henry and Julia.

But he said I wasn't able to go, nor able to stand it after I got there; and I did not make out a very good case for myself, for I was crying before I had finished.

It is getting to be a great effort for me to think straight. Just this nervous weakness I suppose.

And dear John gathered me up in his arms, and just carried me   115 upstairs and laid me on the bed, and sat by me and read to me till it tired my head.

He said I was his darling and his comfort and all he had, and that I must take care of myself for his sake, and keep well.

Romanesque: An ornate architectural style.

He says no one but myself can help me out of it, that I must use my will and self-control and not let any silly fancies run away with me.

There's one comfort, the baby is well and happy, and does not have to occupy this nursery with the horrid wallpaper.

If we had not used it, that blessed child would have! What a fortunate escape! Why, I wouldn't have a child of mine, an impressionable little thing, live in such a room for worlds.

I never thought of it before, but it is lucky that John kept me here   120
after all, I can stand it so much easier than a baby, you see.

Of course I never mention it to them any more — I am too wise, — but I keep watch of it all the same.

There are things in that paper that nobody knows but me, or ever will.

Behind that outside pattern the dim shapes get clearer every day.

It is always the same shape, only very numerous.

And it is like a woman stooping down and creeping about behind   125
that pattern. I don't like it a bit. I wonder — I begin to think — I wish John would take me away from here!

It is so hard to talk with John about my case, because he is so wise, and because he loves me so.

But I tried it last night.

It was moonlight. The moon shines in all around just as the sun does.

I hate to see it sometimes, it creeps so slowly, and always comes in by one window or another.

John was asleep and I hated to waken him, so I kept still and   130
watched the moonlight on that undulating wallpaper till I felt creepy.

The faint figure behind seemed to shake the pattern, just as if she wanted to get out.

I got up softly and went to feel and see if the paper *did* move, and when I came back John was awake.

"What is it, little girl?" he said. "Don't go walking about like that — you'll get cold."

I thought it was a good time to talk, so I told him that I really was not gaining here, and that I wished he would take me away.

"Why, darling!" said he, "our lease will be up in three weeks, and   135
I can't see how to leave before.

"The repairs are not done at home, and I cannot possibly leave town just now. Of course if you were in any danger, I could and would, but you really are better, dear, whether you can see it or not. I am a doctor, dear, and I know. You are gaining flesh and color, your appetite is better, I feel really much easier about you."

"I don't weigh a bit more," said I, "nor as much; and my appetite may be better in the evening when you are here, but it is worse in the morning when you are away!"

"Bless her little heart!" said he with a big hug, "she shall be as sick as she pleases! But now let's improve the shining hours by going to sleep, and talk about it in the morning!"

"And you won't go away?" I asked gloomily.

"Why, how can I, dear? It is only three weeks more and then we will take a nice little trip of a few days while Jennie is getting the house ready. Really dear you are better!" 140

"Better in body perhaps—" I began, and stopped short, for he sat up straight and looked at me with such a stern, reproachful look that I could not say another word.

"My darling," said he, "I beg of you, for my sake and for our child's sake, as well as for your own, that you will never for one instant let that idea enter your mind! There is nothing so dangerous, so fascinating, to a temperament like yours. It is a false and foolish fancy. Can you not trust me as a physician when I tell you so?"

So of course I said no more on that score, and we went to sleep before long. He thought I was asleep first, but I wasn't, and lay there for hours trying to decide whether that front pattern and the back pattern really did move together or separately.

On a pattern like this, by daylight, there is a lack of sequence, a defiance of law, that is a constant irritant to a normal mind.

The color is hideous enough, and unreliable enough, and infuriat- 145 ing enough, but the pattern is torturing.

You think you have mastered it, but just as you get well underway in following, it turns a back-somersault and there you are. It slaps you in the face, knocks you down, and tramples upon you. It is like a bad dream.

The outside pattern is a florid arabesque, reminding one of a fungus. If you can imagine a toadstool in joints, an interminable string of toadstools, budding and sprouting in endless convolutions—why, that is something like it.

That is, sometimes!

There is one marked peculiarity about this paper, a thing nobody seems to notice but myself, and that is that it changes as the light changes.

When the sun shoots in through the east window—I always watch 150 for that first long, straight ray—it changes so quickly that I never can quite believe it.

That is why I watch it always.

By moonlight—the moon shines in all night when there is a moon—I wouldn't know it was the same paper.

At night in any kind of light, in twilight, candlelight, lamplight, and worst of all by moonlight, it becomes bars! The outside pattern I mean, and the woman behind it is as plain as can be.

I didn't realize for a long time what the thing was that showed behind, that dim sub-pattern, but now I am quite sure it is a woman.

By daylight she is subdued, quiet. I fancy it is the pattern that keeps 155 her so still. It is so puzzling. It keeps me quiet by the hour.

I lie down ever so much now. John says it is good for me, and to sleep all I can.

Indeed he started the habit by making me lie down for an hour after each meal.

It is a very bad habit I am convinced, for you see I don't sleep.

And that cultivates deceit, for I don't tell them I'm awake — O no!

The fact is I am getting a little afraid of John. 160

He seems very queer sometimes, and even Jennie has an inexplicable look.

It strikes me occasionally, just as a scientific hypothesis, — that perhaps it is the paper!

I have watched John when he did not know I was looking, and come into the room suddenly on the most innocent excuses, and I've caught him several times *looking at the paper!* And Jennie too. I caught Jennie with her hand on it once.

She didn't know I was in the room, and when I asked her in a quiet, a very quiet voice, with the most restrained manner possible, what she was doing with the paper — she turned around as if she had been caught stealing, and looked quite angry — asked me why I should frighten her so!

Then she said that the paper stained everything it touched, that she 165 had found yellow smooches on all my clothes and John's, and she wished we would be more careful!

Did not that sound innocent? But I know she was studying that pattern, and I am determined that nobody shall find it out but myself!

Life is very much more exciting now than it used to be. You see I have something more to expect, to look forward to, to watch. I really do eat better, and am more quiet than I was.

John is so pleased to see me improve! He laughed a little the other day, and said I seemed to be flourishing in spite of my wallpaper.

I turned it off with a laugh. I had no intention of telling him it was *because* of the wallpaper — he would make fun of me. He might even want to take me away.

I don't want to leave now until I have found it out. There is a week 170 more, and I think that will be enough.

I'm feeling ever so much better! I don't sleep much at night, for it is so interesting to watch developments; but I sleep a good deal in the daytime.

In the daytime it is tiresome and perplexing.

There are always new shoots on the fungus, and new shades of yellow all over it. I cannot keep count of them, though I have tried conscientiously.

It is the strangest yellow, that wallpaper! It makes me think of all the yellow things I ever saw — not beautiful ones like buttercups, but old foul, bad yellow things.

But there is something else about that paper — the smell! I noticed   175
it the moment we came into the room, but with so much air and sun it was not bad. Now we have had a week of fog and rain, and whether the windows are open or not, the smell is here.

It creeps all over the house.

I find it hovering in the dining-room, skulking in the parlor, hiding in the hall, lying in wait for me on the stairs.

It gets into my hair.

Even when I go to ride, if I turn my head suddenly and surprise it — there is that smell!

Such a peculiar odor, too! I have spent hours in trying to analyze   180
it, to find what it smelled like.

It is not bad — at first, and very gentle, but quite the subtlest, most enduring odor I ever met.

In this damp weather it is awful, I wake up in the night and find it hanging over me.

It used to disturb me at first. I thought seriously of burning the house — to reach the smell.

But now I am used to it. The only thing I can think of that it is like is the *color* of the paper! A yellow smell.

There is a very funny mark on this wall, low down, near the   185
mopboard. A streak that runs round the room. It goes behind every piece of furniture, except the bed, a long, straight, even *smooch,* as if it had been rubbed over and over.

I wonder how it was done and who did it, and what they did it for. Round and round and round — round and round and round — it makes me dizzy!

I really have discovered something at last.

Through watching so much at night, when it changes so, I have finally found out.

The front pattern *does* move — and no wonder! The woman behind shakes it!

Sometimes I think there are a great many women behind, and   190
sometimes only one, and she crawls around fast, and her crawling shakes it all over.

Then in the very bright spots she keeps still, and in the very shady spots she just takes hold of the bars and shakes them hard.

And she is all the time trying to climb through. But nobody could climb through that pattern — it strangles so; I think that is why it has so many heads.

They get through, and then the pattern strangles them off and turns them upside down, and makes their eyes white!

If those heads were covered or taken off it would not be half so bad.

I think that woman gets out in the daytime! 195

And I'll tell you why — privately — I've seen her!

I can see her out of every one of my windows!

It is the same woman, I know, for she is always creeping, and most women do not creep by daylight.

I see her in that long shaded lane, creeping up and down. I see her in those dark grape arbors, creeping all around the garden.

I see her on that long road under the trees, creeping along, and 200 when a carriage comes she hides under the blackberry vines.

I don't blame her a bit. It must be very humiliating to be caught creeping by daylight!

I always lock the door when I creep by daylight. I can't do it at night, for I know John would suspect something at once.

And John is so queer now, that I don't want to irritate him. I wish he would take another room! Besides, I don't want anybody to get that woman out at night but myself.

I often wonder if I could see her out of all the windows at once.

But, turn as fast as I can, I can only see out of one at one time. 205

And though I always see her, she *may* be able to creep faster than I can turn!

I have watched her sometimes away off in the open country, creeping as fast as a cloud shadow in a high wind.

If only that top pattern could be gotten off from the under one! I mean to try it, little by little.

I have found out another funny thing, but I shan't tell it this time! It does not do to trust people too much.

There are only two more days to get this paper off, and I believe 210 John is beginning to notice. I don't like the look in his eyes.

And I heard him ask Jennie a lot of professional questions about me. She had a very good report to give.

She said I slept a good deal in the daytime.

John knows I don't sleep very well at night, for all I'm so quiet!

He asked me all sorts of questions, too, and pretended to be very loving and kind.

As if I couldn't see through him! 215

Still, I don't wonder he acts so, sleeping under this paper for three months.

It only interests me, but I feel sure John and Jennie are secretly affected by it.

Hurrah! This is the last day, but it is enough. John to stay in town over night, and won't be out until this evening.

Jennie wanted to sleep with me — the sly thing! but I told her I should undoubtedly rest better for a night all alone.

That was clever, for really I wasn't alone a bit! As soon as it was 220 moonlight and that poor thing began to crawl and shake the pattern, I got up and ran to help her.

I pulled and she shook, I shook and she pulled, and before morning we had peeled off yards of that paper.

A strip about as high as my head and half around the room.

And then when the sun came and that awful pattern began to laugh at me, I declared I would finish it to-day!

We go away to-morrow, and they are moving all my furniture down again to leave things as they were before.

Jennie looked at the wall in amazement, but I told her merrily that 225 I did it out of pure spite at the vicious thing.

She laughed and said she wouldn't mind doing it herself, but I must not get tired.

How she betrayed herself that time!

But I am here, and no person touches this paper but me, — not *alive!*

She tried to get me out of the room — it was too patent! But I said it was so quiet and empty and clean now that I believed I would lie down again and sleep all I could; and not to wake me even for dinner — I would call when I woke.

So now she is gone, and the servants are gone, and the things are 230 gone, and there is nothing left but that great bedstead nailed down, with the canvas mattress we found on it.

We shall sleep downstairs to-night, and take the boat home to-morrow.

I quite enjoy the room, now it is bare again.

How those children did tear about here!

This bedstead is fairly gnawed!

But I must get to work.   235

I have locked the door and thrown the key down into the front path.

I don't want to go out, and I don't want to have anybody come in, till John comes.

I want to astonish him.

I've got a rope up here that even Jennie did not find. If that woman does get out, and tries to get away, I can tie her!

But I forgot I could not reach far without anything to stand on! *240*
This bed will *not* move!

I tried to lift and push it until I was lame, and then I got so angry I bit off a little piece at one corner—but it hurt my teeth.

Then I peeled off all the paper I could reach standing on the floor. It sticks horribly and the pattern just enjoys it! All those strangled heads and bulbous eyes and waddling fungus growths just shriek with derision!

I am getting angry enough to do something desperate. To jump out of the window would be admirable exercise, but the bars are too strong even to try.

Besides I wouldn't do it. Of course not. I know well enough that a *245* step like that is improper and might be misconstrued.

I don't like to *look* out of the windows even—there are so many of those creeping women, and they creep so fast.

I wonder if they all come out of that wallpaper as I did?

But I am securely fastened now by my well-hidden rope—you don't get *me* out in the road there!

I suppose I shall have to get back behind the pattern when it comes night, and that is hard!

It is so pleasant to be out in this great room and creep around as I *250* please!

I don't want to go outside. I won't, even if Jennie asks me to.

For outside you have to creep on the ground, and everything is green instead of yellow.

But here I can creep smoothly on the floor, and my shoulder just fits in that long smooch around the wall, so I cannot lose my way.

Why there's John at the door!

It is no use, young man, you can't open it! *255*

How he does call and pound!

Now he's crying for an axe.

It would be a shame to break down that beautiful door!

"John dear!" said I in the gentlest voice, "the key is down by the front steps, under a plantain leaf!"

That silenced him for a few moments. *260*

Then he said—very quietly indeed, "Open the door, my darling!"

"I can't," said I. "The key is down by the front door under a plantain leaf!"

And then I said it again, several times, very gently and slowly, and said it so often that he had to go and see, and he got it of course, and came in. He stopped short by the door.

"What is the matter?" he cried. "For God's sake, what are you doing!"

I kept on creeping just the same, but I looked at him over my *265* shoulder.

"I've got out at last," said I, "in spite of you and Jane? And I've pulled off most of the paper, so you can't put me back!"

Now why should that man have fainted? But he did, and right across my path by the wall, so that I had to creep over him every time!

FOR DISCUSSION AND WRITING

1. Do a thumbnail sketch of the husband. Cite the parts of the story that reveal his traits to you. Are they opinions expressed by the narrator/ wife, are they the actions or reactions of the husband, or are they some other aspect of the narrative? What acts does the husband perform? What is his relationship to the scenes? Is some agency important? What are the purposes of the husband's acts?

2. Now do a thumbnail sketch of the wife.

3. In doing your characterizations of the husband and the wife, did you find that some relationships among the critical questions were more useful than others? Explain.

4. The primary scene of the story, the room with the ugly yellow wallpaper, is unusual. What other strange elements are there about the room? Do you believe that these features actually exist, or are they figments of the wife's imagination? Explain your reasoning. Explain how these details of scene enhance the story.

5. Was any of your world knowledge about the era during which the story takes place useful (or essential) in evaluating the relationship between the husband and wife? Explain.

6. Does the story itself provide you with essential background information? What is this information?

7. What clues in the story, besides references to historical personalities, tell you that it was not written recently?

8. The story is told by a character who is mentally ill. At what point in the story do you realize that the wife is seriously ill and not just suffering from a slight nervous disorder? What clues and foreshadowing are presented before this point of revelation? How does the unreliability of the narrator affect your interpretation of the story?

3

Thinking Critically
about Exposition

In this chapter, you will learn to ask critical questions about texts that explain ideas, processes, concepts, and opinions. A text whose purpose is to explain is called *exposition* or *expository writing*. (As the previous chapter pointed out, narratives can be used to explain. Some narratives, then, are expository.) The instruction manuals that come with new appliances are expository, as are textbooks (this one, for example) and many essays (for example, "The Invisible Discourse of the Law," by James Boyd White, in Chapter 1).

CRITICAL QUESTIONS ABOUT EXPOSITION

To comprehend a text, we must have the background information (world knowledge) necessary for understanding the subjects that the text deals with. For example, the following text would be incomprehensible to a reader who is unfamiliar with modern linguistics: "The concept 'phoneme' belongs to *langue,* whereas the concept 'allophone' belongs to *parole.*" To go beyond mere comprehension — that is, to read critically — we must also know about the author or authors of the text; the circumstances (past or current) in which the text originated; the influence of the medium of publication (magazine, book, newspaper) and publisher on the text; and the purpose of the text. In other words, we need answers to the four questions that follow.

How Can Knowledge about the Author(s)
Help Me Read Critically?

To read critically, one must, as much as possible, understand the author of the text:

1. What is her or his background? What credentials — diplomas, positions of importance, awards — does he or she hold? For example, you can probably place confidence in the opinions of an author writing about the latest cancer treatments if he or she has a medical degree from a respectable university and holds a responsible position in some health organization, such as a major hospital or research institute.
2. What else has the author written? If she or he has written widely on the subject, you can check to find out how the other books or articles have been received by reviewers and experts in the field.
3. What do peers say about the author's work? If respected authorities pay serious attention to the work, then you have evidence that the author is not merely a crackpot.
4. What are the author's obvious political or ethical commitments? Conservative, liberal, radical? Republican, Democrat, Socialist? Atheist? Roman Catholic? Orthodox Jew? Hindu? Religious beliefs and political philosophies obviously influence one's opinions.

In *The Coming Battle for the Media,* William Rusher, publisher of the conservative *National Review,* argues that the news media are controlled by people who have a liberal view of politics and human nature. It follows, according to Rusher, that Americans do not get a balanced view of the news. In reviewing Rusher's book for the *Washington Post National Weekly Edition* (27 June 1988:35), Timothy Foote writes, "As a Galahad of the right, he [Rusher] strikes some shrewd blows; but as the combined gadfly and ombudsman he ought to be, he seems too scrappy and too ideological." In other words, according to Foote, Rusher's ideological bias prevents him from giving a balanced view of the media. Knowing the author's ideologies allows Foote to make his claim about the text.

Exercise: Author

1. *Name one national figure whose opinion on a current issue is obviously influenced by religious beliefs. Explain the issue and the influence.*

2. *Name a national figure whose opinion on a current issue is obviously influenced by a political philosophy. Explain the issue and the influence.*

3. *Name a national figure whose viewpoint on a current issue is, in your opinion, merely a prejudice. Explain why you think the figure is prejudiced.*

How Can Knowledge about the Time and Place in Which the Text Was Written or Published Help Me Read Critically?

Both time and place influence authors and publishers in many ways, both obvious and subtle. For example, the Declaration of Independence was written at a time (now often called the Age of Reason) in which thinkers believed the universe was rational and orderly and that humans had the intellectual capability to perceive and understand this order. (You will recall that the second paragraph of the Declaration begins with these words: "We hold these truths to be self-evident . . . .") To read the Declaration critically, one must know that its author, Thomas Jefferson, lived at a time when people had great faith in human rationality; in the Declaration, Jefferson expresses the spirit of his times.

On the other hand, think of what writers could *not* say if they lived in certain places at certain times: Germany during the Hitler era, the China of Mao Tse-tung, the Russia of Stalin, or the United States during the McCarthy era.

Frequently, it is impossible to render a fair judgment of a text — or even to understand it — without knowing about the time and place in which it was created. For example, *The Armies of the Night,* a modern American classic by Norman Mailer, gives a personal account of the 1967 protests against the Vietnam War, but unless the reader knows about the Vietnam era (time) in the United States (place), the book will be largely meaningless.

Writing in the *Los Angeles Times Magazine,* Paddy Calistro provides an interesting example of the relationship of time and place to a text:

> Picture a surfer, his hair just about shoulder length, his skin glowing that California glow, his body cultivated to ripple in just the right places. Now take him off the beach and dress him in a business suit and necktie.
>
> Sound like a contradiction? Not at all. This is California style, circa 1990. In its formative stages, this pseudo-surfer mien was restricted to artsy types in oversize suits. But today the look is cropping up on Yale-bred attorneys practicing L.A. law; on doctors in swank Beverly Hills offices, and on executives back East who rarely visit Los Angeles. (37)

The author identifies the style with a place — Los Angeles sunshine and beaches — and implies that the place created the style. The critical reader would question this implication. Did the southern California scene create the style, or did other factors, such as advertisers who promote fashions for economic gain, play a role?

Exercise: Time and Place

1. *Explain how time and place have influenced your own writing (or what you say in public). Be specific rather than general.*

2. *In a current issue of a national magazine such as* Time *or* Newsweek, *find an example of the influence of time and place on the publication of some text and explain that influence. (If you prefer, you might explain the influence of time and place on a film or television program.)*

How Can Knowledge about the Medium Help Me Read Critically?

When we read critically, knowledge about the *medium* (for example, book, newspaper, advertisement) is often essential, because to a greater or lesser extent, the medium influences the message, as the following statements from *Writer's Market for 1988* demonstrate. As you read these statements, notice that publishers have their own philosophies and policies that may predetermine the content, values, and attitudes to be expressed in the books they issue. This shows that writers must conform to certain restrictions and guidelines proposed by the particular medium in which their work will be published.

> BETHANY HOUSE PUBLISHERS. *Nonfiction:* Publishes reference (lay oriented); devotional (evangelical, charismatic); and personal growth books. . . . Looks for "provocative subject, quality writing style, authoritative presentation, unique approach, sound Christian truth." *Fiction:* Well-written stories with a Christian message. . . . *Tips:* "The writer has the best chance of selling our firm a book that will market well in the Christian bookstore. In your query, list other books in this category (price, length, main thrust), and tell how yours is better or unique." (34)

> SIERRA CLUB BOOKS. *Nonfiction:* Animals; health; history (natural); how-to (outdoors); and travel (by foot or bicycle). "The Sierra Club was founded to help people explore, enjoy and preserve the nation's forests, waters, wildlife and wilderness. The books program looks to publish quality trade books about the outdoors and the protection of natural resources. Specifically, we are interested in nature, environmental issues such as nuclear power, self-sufficiency, natural history, politics and the environment, and juvenile books with an ecological theme." *Fiction:* Adventure, historical, mainstream and ecological science fiction. "We do very little fiction, but will consider a fiction manuscript if its theme fits our philosophical aims: the enjoyment and protection of the environment." (151)

A critical reader understands that publications from Bethany House will have a definite Christian bias and that books published by the Sierra Club will be unlikely to advocate, for example, further logging in the redwood forests of the Pacific coast. Since it influences the message, critical readers must be aware of medium as they interpret and evaluate texts.

Exercise: Medium

Discuss one of the following magazines as a medium. What sorts of articles does it publish? What sorts would it not publish? How might its readers be classified (for instance, lowbrow, middlebrow, highbrow — though many other classifications and schemes are possible)? Does it seem to have a political bias? Explain.

Alaska Outdoors	B'Nai B'Rith International Jewish Monthly
Child Life Discoveries Esquire Family Circle	
Good Housekeeping Harper's Magazine Insight	
Jack and Jill Mademoiselle Ms. National Review	
Outdoor Life Paris Review People Road and Track	

How Can Knowledge about Purpose Help Me Read Critically?

What is the actual purpose of the text? The stated purpose may be different from the actual purpose—excellent examples of such discrepancies can often be found in advertisements. The stated purpose of an ad for patent medicine may be to relieve human pain and suffering, but the actual purpose is to sell more products and hence accrue profits.

Writers sometimes communicate purpose by using irony. Consider the famous opening sentence of Jane Austen's *Pride and Prejudice:* "It is a truth universally acknowledged, that a single man in possession of a good fortune must be in want of a wife." It is certainly not a universal truth that wealthy bachelors need (or want) a wife, but it is the case that many single women aspire to capture such a husband (just as some men seek wealthy women). Without irony, a statement of the idea is uninteresting and lacks emotional shading: "Many women try to capture wealthy men as husbands." This sentence would make the novel that follows much less rich and interesting.

Exercise: Purpose

The mysteries of purpose are often more difficult to unravel than they are in most advertisements. For example, Ernest Hemingway wrote The Torrents of Spring, *a parody of the work of his friend Sherwood Anderson. If you read carefully and think about what is* not *said as well as what is said, Hemingway's explanation of why he wrote this book illustrates the complexity of motives that underlie some texts. After you have carefully read the selection, discuss your perceptions of Hemingway's motives. (Explain how knowledge of Hemingway's life would help you determine his purpose in the selection.)*

I wrote it because I was righteous which is the worst thing you can be. And I thought he was going to pot the way he was writing and that I could kid him out of it by showing him how awful it was. I wrote 'The Torrents of Spring' to poke fun at him. It was cruel to do and it didn't do any good and he just wrote worse and worse. What the hell business of mine was it if he wanted to write badly. None. He had written good and then lost it. But then I was more righteous and more loyal to writing than to my friend. (qtd. in Plimpton 36)

THE WRITER-READER CONTRACT

When you begin to analyze a text to determine its strengths and weaknesses — that is, when you read critically — you will find it useful to consider, as the philosopher H. P. Grice has demonstrated, that the writer has entered into an unwritten contract with you, the reader, guaranteeing

1. to give you all of the information you need to gain his or her complete meaning but no more than is necessary *(quantity)*;
2. to tell the truth and not write or talk about subjects concerning which he or she is not knowledgeable *(quality)*;
3. to be as clear as possible *(manner)*; and
4. to stick to the point *(relation)*.

Exercise: The Writer-Reader Contract

Before you read the examples, explanations, and analyses that follow in this chapter, explain your initial reaction to these "terms" of the writer-reader contract. Might not some writers intentionally give more information than is necessary? Don't some writers lie? Do writers always stick to the point? Do you know of texts that you think are intentionally written to violate one or more of these rules? In light of these questions, does the writer-reader contract seem valid to you?

The Terms of the Writer-Reader Contract

THE QUANTITY OF INFORMATION IN A TEXT Both of the following sets of instructions will no doubt seem strange to you:

1. If you want to review the concept of "world knowledge," turn to page 30 of this book. Page 30 is the one with a three and a zero in the upper left-hand corner.
2. If you want to review the concept of "world knowledge," turn to a page in this book.

One of these gives you too much information, whereas the other gives you too little. You hardly need the explanation about the numbering system for the pages of the book, and you certainly want to know more than that the material is to be found on "a page in this book."

In short, the writers of the two passages have violated the principle of quantity, which can be stated directly like this:

> *quantity:* Readers can assume that the writer will give them all they need in order to understand the writer's intention, and no more than is necessary.

Exercise: Quantity

Discuss the quantity of information in the following brief texts. For what sort of reader are they apparently intended? For example, an article in a general encyclopedia is intended for nonspecialists. In your opinion, do the texts provide enough information for those readers? Do they contain more information than is necessary? For example, an ichthyologist would not need the nonitalicized information in the following sentence:

> *Last year, I caught a fifteen-pound steelhead,* a trout that, like a salmon, spends its life in the ocean, but returns to its native stream to spawn.

However, an ichthyologist probably would need the nonitalicized information in the following sentence:

> *Last year, I caught a fifteen-pound brown trout in Rock Creek,* a tributary of the Clark Fork of the Columbia, which flows into the Clark Fork about thirty miles west of Missoula, Montana.

1. *Mercury, the nearest planet to the sun, is the second smallest of the nine planets known to be orbiting the sun. Its diameter is 3,100 miles and its mean distance from the sun is 36,000,000 miles.* (The World Almanac and Book of Facts, 1991)

2. *The Flesch scale does not give grade level equivalents. You end up instead with a number between 0 and 100. The higher your text rates on the Flesch scale, the easier it should be. A Flesch score of 40 is called "difficult," while 75 is fairly easy. The FOG index and the Dale-Chall formula do give grade level equivalents.* (*Janice Redish,* Readability)

3. *To us, layman and scholar alike, writing is* written language. *Ask a man in the street and he will not even hesitate about giving his answer. The same definition is expressed poetically by Voltaire: "L'écriture est la peinture de la voix; plus elle est ressemblante, meilleure elle est," and by Brébeuf: "Cet art ingénieux de piendre la parole et de parler aux yeux." The French authors are in good company here because they can back their opinion with the authority of the reliable Aristotle, who centuries ago, in the introductory chapter of* De Interpretatione *of his* Logic, *said: "Spoken words are symbols of mental experience and written words are the symbols of spoken words.* (*I. J. Gelb,* A Study of Writing)

4. *More than a hundred million years ago there were some kinds of ants scurrying about on the earth much as they do today. A hundred million years! In this great length of time many other kinds of animals came into being, flourished for a while, then died away leaving only fossil remains as evidence that they ever existed. It is not surprising, therefore, that we sometimes wonder about the success of these little insects.*

> *In general, people are apt to think that ants thrive because they are constantly busy. Certainly their reputation for industry is widespread, being noted even in Biblical times when King Solomon gave the advice, 'Go to the ant, O sluggard, consider her ways and be wise.' Because the quotation often is ended here, it may be thought that the mere hustle and bustle of ants were the only 'ways' Solomon had in mind. But the words that follow concern a harvest, and indicate that the King was thinking of an ability to provide for the future during fair-weather months. However, it is not likely*

that he really had an understanding of all the remarkable ways of ants. Did he know that some kinds do not harvest but eat only meat, while others keep plant lice as 'cows,' obtaining nourishment through them? Did he realize that certain ants enslaved others? Did he know of the fine cooperation between the members of an ant colony and of their talents in constructing homes and caring for them? (Dorothy Shuttlesworth and Su Zan Noguchi Swain, The Story of Ants)

THE QUALITY OF INFORMATION IN A TEXT At the very least, readers must believe that the writer (1) is honest and (2) knows what he or she is talking about. Writers, like all people, can be liars yet know their subject matter thoroughly. Conversely, they can be completely honest yet not understand or know much about their subject matter.

History is studded with enormous lies that were exposed only after masses were duped. One famous case is that of the Piltdown man. In 1912, Charles Dawson, an amateur archeologist, claimed to have discovered skull fragments of a humanlike creature in a gravel pit in Piltdown, England. Dawson alleged that his "Piltdown man" was the earliest human inhabitant of the British Isles yet discovered. For thirty or more years, Piltdown man had a place on the tree of human evolution. Finally, however, scientists concluded that Dawson had managed to dupe the experts. (Stephen Jay Gould tells the story in "Piltdown Revisited," on pages 491–502 of this book.)

The big liar, however, often doesn't present as great a danger as the writer who, in perfectly good faith, deals with subjects in which he or she is unqualified. (The paradox, of course, is that you cannot know what you do not know! Though we are not experts in, for instance, endocrinology, we have no idea what we would need to learn in order to become experts. In other words, we cannot know what we do not know.) Writers who believe they know a subject but in fact do not are a menace.

The principle with which we are dealing can be stated directly like this:

quality: Readers can assume that the writer will not lie and that he or she is knowledgeable about the subject of the text.

Exercise: Quality

This is the first sentence in the preface to the New International Version *of the Bible, copyrighted in 1978:*

The New International Version is a completely new translation of the Holy Bible made by over a hundred scholars working directly from the best available Hebrew, Aramaic and Greek texts. (vii)

1. *Why did the editors feel that such a statement was necessary?*

2. *Explain why the quality of the New International Version depends on other texts.*

3. *Explain how judging the quality of the New International Version or any other version of the Bible is similar to judging the quality of a secular convenant such as the United States Constitution. Another way of looking at the question is this: In what way or ways are theologians who study the Bible like the members of the United States Supreme Court?*

THE MANNER IN WHICH A TEXT IS WRITTEN Which sentence in the following pairs is easier to read?

> The horse raced around the track dropped dead.
> The horse that was raced around the track dropped dead.

> That Melvin told Marcia that Mervin thought that Mary is odd is strange.
> It is strange that Melvin told Marcia that Mervin thought that Mary is odd.

> The woman took the picture that her husband had hung up down.
> The woman took down the picture that her husband had hung up.

In each case, the second version is easier to read, even though the two versions convey the same information. Obviously, the same basic ideas can be expressed in harder-to-read and easier-to-read versions. And this leads us to another term of the writer-reader contract:

> *manner:* Readers can assume that the writer will be as clear as possible in conveying his or her intention.

In the examples above, the writer violates this term of the contract by using poor sentence structure. Writers can violate this term in other ways, as well. Here are a few of them.

Ambiguity is one of the more common violations. Consider this sentence:

> Visiting relatives can be tiring.

Does the writer mean that it can be tiring to visit relatives *or* that relatives who visit can be tiring?

A lack of specifics leaves the reader without a real understanding of what the author is trying to say:

> If you want a liberal education, you must take courses from several different fields.

What fields is the writer referring to? What courses? This text is too vague to be meaningful.

Misplaced modifiers are another source of murkiness in texts:

> Wanting to get the best seats available, I was astounded that some fans were willing to pay as much as $150 for tickets to the game.

At first glance, it appears that it was the writer, not the fans, who wanted the best seats. Here is the correct placement of the modifier:

> I was astounded that some fans, wanting to get the best seats available, were willing to pay as much as $150 for tickets to the game.

Using nouns instead of verbs can make a text less clear.

> *The writer's use* of nouns where *the use* of verbs is possible leads to *the creation* of problems for readers since *the interpretation* of nominal constructions is more difficult than that of verbal constructions. Thus, a general principle for *the writing* of readable prose is *the use* of verbs instead of nouns.

Changing the italicized nouns to verbs creates a much more readable passage:

> A writer who *uses* nouns where he could *use* verbs *creates* problems for readers, since it is more difficult *to get* the meaning from nominal constructions than from verbal constructions. Thus, a general principle for *writing* readable prose is to *use* verbs instead of nouns.

You do not need technical knowledge to recognize and diagnose unclarity. First, recognize that you don't understand what the writer is trying to say. Then refer to the text to determine where the problem lies. The following exercise will give you some practice.

Exercise: Manner

Without worrying about technical language, explain how the following examples violate the principle of manner. If possible, rewrite the examples so that they are easier to understand.

1. *"The system of 'hearing (understanding) oneself speak' through the phonic substance — which presents itself as the nonexterior, nonmundane, therefore non-empirical or noncontingent signifier — has necessarily dominated the history of the world during an entire epoch, and has even produced the idea of the world, the idea of world-origin, that arises from the difference between the worldly and nonworldly, the outside and the inside, ideality and nonideality, universal and nonuniversal, transcendental and empirical, etc."* (Jacques Derrida, Of Grammatology, *translated by Gayatri Chakrovorty Spivak*).

2. *"Dr. Lisa Eichler, my psychology professor, criticized Susanne Langer's concept of symbolism. She said that she did not adequately differentiate verbal knowledge from nonverbal"* (Advanced Composition student).

3. *"Of the exercises which the rules of the University required, some were published by him in his maturer years. They had been undoubtedly applauded; for they were such as few can perform: yet there is reason to suspect that he was regarded in his college with no great fondness. That he obtained no fellowship is certain; but the unkindness with which he was treated was not merely negative. I*

am ashamed to relate what I fear is true, that Milton was the last student in either university that suffered the public indignity of corporal correction" (*Samuel Johnson*, Milton).

4. *"When a man teaches something he does not know to somebody else who has no aptitude for it, and gives him a certificate of proficiency, the latter has completed the education of a gentleman" (George Bernard Shaw).*

THE RELATION OF MATERIAL IN THE TEXT TO THE WRITER'S POINT AND PURPOSE A *coherent* text is one in which all of the parts relate to the main point and the writer's purpose. Nothing is beside the point or irrelevant. This principle can be stated thus:

> *relation:* Readers can assume that the writer will not include irrelevant material.

At first glance, this appears to be a simple principle. Surely a reader can easily pick out information that is irrelevant in a text. However, information that is irrelevant for one group of readers might be essential for others. If someone who is familiar with a campus asks a student for the location of a professor's office, the response will be something like this: "He's on the second floor of Whitman Hall." But if the questioner is unfamiliar with the campus, the response might be something like this: "He's on the second floor of Whitman Hall. That's the building at the corner of Emerson Way and Dickinson Lane, just across from the gymnasium. You can see the roof of the gymnasium from here, the one with red tiles." In short, relevance must be judged in relation both to the writer's purpose and the intended audience.

Exercise: Relation

Below is a "doctored" version of the first paragraph of an enigmatically titled book that you would probably enjoy, The Dancing Wu Li Masters, *by Gary Zukav. Point out the irrelevancies in the paragraph, the material that has no relation or only a tenuous relation to the point of the text. Don't consult the original paragraph, which follows the "doctored" version, until after you have made your decision.*

> *My first exposure to quantum physics occurred a few years ago when a friend invited me to an afternoon conference at the Lawrence Laboratory in Berkeley, California. At that time, I had no connections with the scientific community, so I went to see what physicists were like. To my great surprise, I discovered that Chinese restaurants in Berkeley are just as good as those across the Bay in San Francisco, and I discovered also that (1), I understood everything the physicists said, and (2), their discussion sounded very much like a theological discussion. When I was in college, I was very religious and talked theology to my roommates for hours. I scarcely could believe*

what I had discovered. Physics was not the sterile, boring discipline that I had assumed it to be. It was as interesting as history, my favorite subject. (Since I was in high school, I have been a Civil War buff.) It was a rich, profound venture which had become inseparable from philosophy. Incredibly, no one but physicists seemed to be aware of this remarkable development. As my interest in and knowledge of physics grew, I resolved to share this discovery with others. This book is a gift of my discovery. It is one of a series.

My first exposure to quantum physics occurred a few years ago when a friend invited me to an afternoon conference at the Lawrence Laboratory in Berkeley, California. At that time, I had no connections with the scientific community, so I went to see what physicists were like. To my great surprise, I discovered that (1), I understood everything the physicists said, and (2), their discussion sounded very much like a theological discussion. I scarcely could believe what I had discovered. Physics was not the sterile, boring discipline that I had assumed it to be. It was a rich, profound venture which had become inseparable from philosophy. Incredibly, no one but physicists seemed to be aware of this remarkable development. As my interest in and knowledge of physics grew, I resolved to share this discovery with others. This book is a gift of my discovery. It is one of a series. (23)

VIOLATING THE WRITER-READER CONTRACT

Violations of the terms of the writer-reader contract, like those of any contract, can be either intentional or unintentional. Unintentional violations result either from carelessness or from ignorance; the writer either forgets to carry out the terms of the contract or doesn't understand those terms and therefore cannot carry them out. A writer might unintentionally include either more or less information than the reader needs (quantity); include false information (quality); write snarled sentences or use vague terms (manner); and include irrelevant information (relation).

On the other hand, good writers sometimes violate the terms of the contract on purpose, to make a point. In such instances, the writer expects the readers to understand that a violation has occurred and to recognize that the violation is purposeful and therefore significant. Let's look at specific examples.

1. *Quality.* Writers create figures of speech by intentionally violating the principle of quality. *Irony,* you will recall, is the figure of speech in which the writer's intention contradicts the literal meaning. A famous example of this device is "A Modest Proposal," by Jonathan Swift, eighteenth-century man of letters and clergyman. (This work appears on pages 540–46.) He "proposes" that Ireland could solve its economic problems by using children as food.

> I have been assured by a very knowing American of my acquaintance in London, that a young healthy child well nursed is at a year old a most delicious, nourishing, and wholesome food, whether stewed, roasted, baked, or boiled; and I make no doubt that it will equally serve in a fricassee or ragout.

A reader who takes the "proposal" at face value must conclude that Swift is a monster. But a reader who perceives the intentional violation of the principle of quality is alerted to recognize that Swift is really a compassionate and passionate advocate for humanity, purposely using an outrageous "argument" to shock British readers into awareness of the poverty and hardship of the Irish people in the eighteenth century.

Other figures of speech that result from intentional violation of the quality principle include overstatement, or *hyperbole* ("I'm so hungry I could eat a ton of spaghetti"), and understatement, or *litotes* ("Uncle Eldon barely touched the spaghetti last night; he ate only four heaping platesful").

2. *Quantity.* Massive amounts of detail—more than necessary for the literal meaning that the author intends—can make a text both enjoyable and memorable, as in the following passage from *Pilgrim at Tinker Creek,* by Annie Dillard:

> The pond is popping with life. Midges are swarming over the center, and the edges are clotted with the jellied egg masses of snails. One spring I saw a snapping turtle lumber from the pond to lay her eggs. Now a green heron picks around in the pondweed and bladderwort; two muskrats at the shallow end are stock-piling cattails. Diatoms, which are algae that look under a microscope like crystals, multiply so fast you can practically watch a submersed green leaf transform into a brown fuzz. In the plankton, single-cell algae, screw fungi, bacteria, and water mold abound. Insect larvae and nymphs carry on their eating business everywhere in the pond. Stillwater caddises, alderfly larvae, and damselfly and dragonfly nymphs stalk on the bottom debris; mayfly nymphs hide in the weeds, mosquito larvae wriggle near the surface, and red-tailed maggots stick their breathing tubes up from between decayed leaves along the shore. Also at the pond's muddy edges it is easy to see the tiny red tubifex worms and bloodworms; the convulsive jerking of hundreds and hundreds together catches my eye. (121)

Conversely, an author might withhold information in order to arouse the reader's curiosity and thus encourage him or her to read further. For example, the following text is the opening paragraph of a *New Yorker* profile. Notice how the author, Caroline Alexander, arouses your curiosity by withholding the most important bit of information, the identity of her subject:

> The guest speaker at a recent dinner for Oxford and Cambridge alumni, held at the Harvard Club in Manhattan, was introduced by the master of ceremonies as possessing a résumé that read like a James Bond thriller: after working in North Africa for Britain's Special Operations Executive during the Second World War, the speaker had entered the Foreign Office and held diplomatic postings in places as diverse as Moscow, in the immediate post-Stalin years, and Ulan Bator, in Outer Mongolia. A latecomer who had not heard the speaker's name might have been surprised to see that the person approaching the podium was not one of the urbane, sleek-haired gentlemen dotted around the dining hall but a white-haired woman in her late sixties, who smiled genially at the company as she made her way forward in a somewhat heavy, rocking gait. One couldn't help thinking she would make a very good Miss Marple. (57–71)

Only after having kept us in suspense through this recitation of background does the author finally reveal that her subject is Daphne Margaret Sybil Désirée Park, the principal of a college at Oxford University.

3. *Manner.* Writers can intentionally violate the principle of manner for several reasons. For example, writers generally try to avoid repetition because it distracts the reader and makes texts more difficult to read, as this example illustrates:

> The economist predicted a recession. This economist, though highly respected, is one of the most conservative economists in America. Most liberal economists predict an economic upturn.

However, in the following passage, the intentional repetition of one word effectively conveys Ian Frazier's mood, his longing for and love of the wide open spaces of the Great Plains:

> Away to the Great Plains of America, to that immense Western shortgrass prairie now mostly plowed under! Away to the still empty land beyond newsstands and malls and velvet restaurant ropes! Away to the headwaters of the Missouri, now quelled by many impoundment dams, and to the headwaters of the Platte, and to the almost invisible headwaters of the slurped-up Arkansas! Away to the land where TV used to set its most popular dramas, but not anymore! Away to the land beyond the hundredth meridian of longitude, where sometimes it rains and sometimes it doesn't, where agriculture stops and does a double take! Away to the skies of sparrow hawks sitting on telephone wires, thinking of mice and flaring their tail feathers suddenly, like a card trick! Away to the airshaft of the continent, where weather fronts from two hemispheres meet and the wind blows almost all the time. Away to the fields of wheat and milo and Sudan grass and flax and alfalfa and nothing! Away to parts of Montana and South Dakota and Wyo-

ming and Nebraska and Kansas and Colorado and New Mexico and Oklahoma and Texas. Away to the high plains rolling in waves to the rising final chord of the Rocky Mountains! (49–88)

Intentional misuse of language is frequently a source of humor. In *The Devil's Dictionary,* Ambrose Bierce gives his own *mis*definitions of common terms that we normally define quite differently:

admiration, n. Our polite recognition of another's resemblance to ourselves.
Christian, n. One who believes that the New Testament is a divinely inspired book admirably suited to the spiritual needs of his neighbor. One who follows the teaching of Christ in so far as they are not inconsistent with a life of sin.
logic, n. The art of thinking and reasoning in strict accordance with the limitations and incapacities of the human misunderstanding. The basis of logic is the syllogism, consisting of a major and a minor premise and a conclusion — thus:
    Major Premise: Sixty men can do a piece of work sixty times as quickly as one man.
    Minor Premise: One man can dig a post-hole in sixty seconds; therefore —
    Conclusion: Sixty men can dig a post-hole in one second.
This may be called the syllogism arithmetical, in which, by combining logic and mathematics, we obtain a certainty and are twice blessed.

4. *Relation:* A brilliant flouting of the principle of relation is Woody Allen's course description, which is full of irrelevant information:

Fundamental Astronomy: A detailed study of the universe and its care and cleaning. The sun, which is made of gas, can explode at any moment, sending our entire planetary system hurtling to destruction; students are advised what the average citizen can do in such a case. They are also taught to identify various constellations, such as the Big Dipper, Cygnus the Swan, Sagittarius the Archer, and the twelve stars that form Lumides the Pants Salesman.

Writers, then, use the principles of *quality, quantity, manner,* and *relation* to achieve their ends, just as readers use them to interpret the writers' intentions.

THE READER VARIABLE

Because readers are diverse, the writer must be constantly aware of who the intended readers are. The *reader variable* guides the writer in determining the right quantity of information for those readers, convincing them of the text's *quality,* ensuring clarity, and adjusting the manner to their needs and expectations.

You can take this whole chapter as an example of the authors' attempt to fulfill all of the terms of the writer-reader contract. We have tried to provide enough information to enable you to understand the concepts, but not so much that the discussion becomes overwhelming or tedious. We have written in a manner quite different from the one we would use if we were writing about these ideas for, say, specialists in the philosophy of language. We assume that you believe we are truthful and know what we are talking about, and we have excluded irrelevancies from the chapter.

THE WRITER-READER CONTRACT AND CRITICAL READING

Stated as questions, the terms of the writer-reader contract become powerful instruments for critically analyzing texts:

1. *Quantity:* Does the text supply all that I need to know about its subject? Does it contain more than I need to know? What is lacking? What is excessive?
2. *Quality:* Can I trust the information in the text? Is the writer being honest? Does the writer know what he or she is talking about? How do *I* know that the writer knows?
3. *Manner:* In relation to the author's purpose, is the text as clear and as easy to read as possible? Is the style appropriate to the subject matter and the author's intention, or does the style distract me?
4. *Relation:* Is everything in the text relevant to the writer's point? Does anything unnecessarily sidetrack me from the point?

The answers to these questions depend, of course, on the reader variable. An explanation of the human endocrine system intended for elementary school children will necessarily differ from an explanation intended for college physiology students, but each can be excellent for its audience. Instructions for getting to a destination will be less detailed for natives of the area than for strangers to the region.

It is really quite amazing that a principle so simply elegant as the writer-reader contract can reveal so much about the texts that we try to understand and evaluate.

REVIEW

1. Explain the importance of the following questions for critical reading:
   How can knowledge about the author or authors help me read critically?
   How can knowledge about the time and place in which the text was written or published help me read critically?

How can knowledge about the medium help me read critically?
How can knowledge about the purpose help me read critically?

2. Explain the writer-reader contract and its terms: quantity, quality, manner, and relation.

3. Explain the reader variable.

4. Explain intentional and unintentional violations of the writer-reader contract. Give examples.

SUGGESTIONS FOR WRITING

1. Using the four questions above as a guide, write an interpretation and analysis of any one of the essays that follow in this chapter.

2. Arguments concerning texts such as the United States Constitution or the Bible frequently concern *interpretation*. For example, in July of 1988, the United States Supreme Court rendered a decision in a case involving both the interpretation of the concept of "cruel and unusual punishment" and the justices' values. Here is an account of that decision.

> The Supreme Court has decided a case that was supposed to answer with some finality the question of whether execution of children is constitutional. William Wayne Thompson, an Oklahoma 15-year-old, had been convicted of the particularly brutal murder of his brother-in-law and was sentenced to death. Four justices ruled that the Eighth Amendment prohibition against cruel and unusual punishment must be interpreted by considering the "evolving standards of decency that mark the progress of a maturing society." Finding a growing national consensus against executing persons under 16 — 14 states allow no capital punishment at all, and 18 others have a minimum age of at least 16 — and citing the many circumstances in which such youngsters are treated differently from adults, these justices found that under the Eighth Amendment, it is cruel and unusual punishment to apply the death penalty for crimes committed before 16. Three other justices saw no such evolving consensus — in fact, they cited examples of a trend in the other direction — and found no clear-cut age bar to execution, preferring individualized assessments of each defendant. Justice O'Connor concurred with the plurality, but only as to penalties imposed on those under 16 in cases where state statutes did not set a minimum age at all. Justice Kennedy did not participate in deciding the case. ("Children and the Court," *Washington Post National Weekly Edition* 11 July 1988:25)

All of the justices who participated in the decision agreed that the meaning of "cruel and unusual punishment" is not stable but depends upon the time and place of its use. (Acceptable punishment in the late eighteenth century, which included pressing criminals to death with heavy weights and burning them at the stake, would today be "cruel and unusual.") However, the justices disagreed on the current interpretation of the "cruel and unusual" provision.

In other words, even the "experts" did not agree on an interpretation. In such a case, you have two choices: (1) to disengage from the argument, since even the experts cannot reach a consensus or (2) to develop an argument on the basis of your own knowledge and value system. The first alternative would isolate you from virtually all of the important issues of the day, for most of them concern questions of value and interpretation about which the experts disagree. If you choose the second alternative, you enter the ongoing debate regarding the conduct of society and thus become a participant in establishing the norms, meanings, and value systems that guide and govern.

Using the four questions as a guide, be prepared to discuss your own interpretation of a disputed text. You might choose a passage from the Bible, a poem (such as John Keats's "Ode on a Grecian Urn"), or a law that is currently being debated in the courts and the media. You will probably want to do some background research on your topic (and you will find suggestions about using the library on pages 577–83).

3. For an educated adult reader, write an explanation of *anything* on which you are an expert. Then rewrite your explanation for a fourth- or fifth-grader. You are, of course, an expert on many subjects: an aspect of local, state, or national politics? A hobby, such as woodworking? Some historical event, such as the Battle of Shiloh? A sport? Sporting equipment, such as skis? Your own religious beliefs? Sports cars? The social system in your neighborhood? A category of food — e.g., Chinese, Italian, junk? A scholarly subject, such as the phenomenologists in philosophy? Your reasons for attending college? Your career goals?

4. Using the principles of quantity, quality, manner, and relation as guides, write a paper analyzing the ways in which you revised your explanation so that a fourth- or fifth-grader could easily understand it. Or *compare* and *contrast* the version that you wrote for an educated adult with the version for a child.

5. Write an explanation of a typical American holiday — Thanksgiving, the Fourth of July, Labor Day — for a newcomer to this country, specifically, a Chinese student. You can assume that this person has a general knowledge of American history but is unfamiliar with details.

6. Write a humorous essay about education (e.g., the college or university that you are attending, your major, a textbook, the cafeteria, the dormitory, the athletic program). You can base the essay on something that actually happened, or you can create an imaginary situation. In any case, your awareness of the principles of quality, quantity, manner, and relation should help you.

POPULAR AND SCHOLARLY VIEWS OF "GOOD ENGLISH"

Edward Finegan

Edward Finegan teaches at the University of Southern California, where he formerly chaired the Linguistics Department. His research interests focus on legal language and the development of other professional and folk styles of English and on attitudes toward correctness in language use. He is editor of *Oxford Studies in Sociolinguistics* and coauthor of *Language: Its Structure and Use,* an introductory linguistics textbook. He has written several short stories about his two-year stint in prerevolutionary Iran as director of an English language teaching program.

A set of related questions runs through this essay and the two that follow it, John Simon's "U, Non-U, and You" and George Orwell's "Politics and the English Language": What is good English? Indeed, is there any such thing as "good English"? If there is, what is it like? How might we characterize it? Who determines what is good and what isn't?

"Winston tastes good, like a cigarette should."

"As, damn it!" — A FIRST-GRADE BOY

". . . anyone who complains that its use as a conjunction is a corruption introduced by Winston cigarettes ought, in all fairness, to explain how Shakespeare, Keats, and the translators of the Authorized Version of the Bible came to be in the employ of the R. J. Reynolds Tobacco Company." — BERGEN EVANS, 1960

At its peak of popularity in the mid-sixties, the advertising slogan "Winston tastes good, like a cigarette should" was denounced by *Saturday Review* magazine. *SR*'s communications editor claimed that, despite its frequent occurrence, *like* "still offends us" when used as a conjunction. The passing of a few weeks saw the editor's words pale beside the flushed enthusiasm in the applauding letters that swamped his desk. For months afterwards readers wrote in to condemn detested expressions like "Drive Slow" and "I'll try and go." Their sentiments ranged from plain gratitude to ecstatic "love" over *Saturday Review*'s "good grammar" campaign.[1]

Readers called Winston's jingle "a cause of shame to its creator," "an abiding object of scorn," "a constant reproach," even a "sin." A woman from Florida wrote that "Our educable young people need not be demoralized at every turn." And abstainers found Winston's grammar "as irritating as tobacco smoke." It was reported with obvious approval

---

[1] Richard L. Tobin, "Like Your Cigarette Should" (1966), p. 59. Letters appeared in 1966 in the June 11, July 9, and August 13 issues of *Saturday Review*.

that a posse of vigilantes had torn down and destroyed a *Drive Slow* sign in one American town, while grammatical guardians all across the country were boycotting both Winstons and Tareytons ("Us Tareyton smokers would rather fight than switch"). Some extremists even claimed to have quit smoking altogether—not because of the Surgeon General's hazard warning on every pack, but to punish the R. J. Reynolds Tobacco Company for flaunting bad grammar!

Some sixty years earlier a similar flood of letters had inundated the American press with objections to Rudyard Kipling's "Recessional"; grammatical sensibilities were aroused by the poet's use of a singular verb with a compound subject: "The tumult and the shouting dies!"[2] Across the Atlantic, earlier still, the British government in certain treaty negotiations with the United States made concessions on weighty matters like the Alabama claims and the Canadian fisheries but "telegraphed that in the wording of the treaty it would under no circumstances endure the insertion of an adverb between the preposition *to,* the sign of the infinitive, and the verb."[3] The faded might of the split infinitive has yielded to the intemperate wrath aroused by *like* as a conjunction. When polled for his opinion on this point of grammar, *New York Times* writer John Kieran replied, "Such things . . . persuade me that the death penalty should be retained."[4] And poet John Ciardi confessed that he'd rather hear his first-grade son swearing "*As,* damn it!" than using *like* as a conjunction.[5] More recently, *hopefully* (in the sense "I hope that . . . ") has drawn fire from writers in *Newsweek* (February 13, 1978) and *Time* (January 1, 1979) and from Edwin Newman on NBC's "Today" show (November 17, 1978). And *Time* reported on March 26, 1979, that three grammatical hot lines were available to Americans troubled about particular points of usage. (Ironically, only the Arkansas dial-a-grammarian scored a perfect 3 on *Time's* disguised quiz. The other two hot lines—one of which is provided toll free to Kansans—disappointed *Time's* reporter with "wrong" answers!) Thus the sometimes sanctimonious support that readers gave to *SR*'s grammatical campaign reflects a common conviction among English speakers on both sides of the Atlantic that of the several ways to say a thing, there is only one right way—and that the wrong ways can be sinfully bad.

Speakers of English have been preoccupied with correct linguistic usage since before our earliest grammars and dictionaries were composed. Some of them call to mind Shakespeare's pedant Holofernes, who railed against pronouncing *doubt* and *debt* as if they had no *b:* "I abhor

---

[2]Reported by Brander Matthews in *Parts of Speech* (1901), p. 217.
[3]Thomas R. Lounsbury, *The Standard of Usage in English* (1908), p. 242; cited also in W. H. Mittins et al., *Attitudes to English Usage* (1970), p. 70.
[4]Reported in *Time* (August 22, 1969), p. 50.
[5]"Manner of Speaking" (1961), p. 30.

such fanatical phantasimes, such insociable and point-device companions; such rackers of orthography. . . . This is abhominable—which he would call abbominable" (*Love's Labour's Lost,* V, i).

Holofernes first uttered his futile detestations a decade before America had its earliest permanent English settlement. Four centuries later, on this side of the Atlantic, a truly extraordinary reaction against "fanatical phantasimes" burst forth, and it shook the literate world. In 1961, shortly after the G. & C. Merriam Company published *Webster's Third New International Dictionary,* the editorial staff must have feared they had fired a fatal shot through the English-speaking world; for the frenzy of journalists, educators, and book reviewers conveyed the impression that the English language had been mortally wounded. I will discuss this development in detail in a later section; here I merely indicate how incendiary the dictionary's treatment of a small number of contested entries was.

Mario Pei, a professor of Italian and well-known author, accused *Webster's* editors of blurring "to the point of obliteration the older distinction between standard, substandard, colloquial, vulgar, and slang." As he interpreted the new dictionary, "Good and bad, right and wrong, correct and incorrect no longer exist."[6]

Across the nation editors and educators rallied in support of Pei's judgment. A few hinted that the good old red-white-and-blue American dictionary was now mostly pink. "Small wonder that our English-speaking world . . . is having trouble with creatures like beatniks—not to mention Nikita Khrushchev and his kind," lamented the Washington *Sunday Star* (September 10, 1961). The *Detroit News* (February 10, 1962) found the dictionary motivated by a "bolshevik spirit" and called it "a kind of Kinsey Report in linguistics."[7]

Through the pen of Wilson Follett, *The Atlantic* (January 1962) accused the dictionary of a "sort of theoretical improvement that in practice impairs. . . ." As Follett assessed it, "we have seen the gates propped wide open in enthusiastic hospitality to miscellaneous confusions and corruptions." And "Worse yet," he said, the *Third* "plumes itself on its faults and parades assiduously cultivated sins as virtues without precedent."

English professor A. M. Tibbetts called the three-and-a-half-million-dollar investment an "inelegant, five-and-dime store approach to language . . . as democratic and mechanical as a bean picker."[8]

5

---

[6]Mario Pei, "The Dictionary as a Battlefront: English Teachers' Dilemma" (1962), p. 45.
[7]Reviews of *Webster's Third* appearing originally before June 1962 are cited from James Sledd and Wilma R. Ebbitt, eds., *Dictionaries and THAT Dictionary* (1962). Reviews published after May 1962 are cited from the original sources.
[8]A. M. Tibbetts, "The Real Issues in the Great Language Controversy" (1966), p. 36.

Much of the criticism heaped on the new *Webster's* represented   10
straightforward opposition to the impartial recording of language customs in a dictionary. Many reviewers maintained that in lieu of an official
national academy to preserve the purity of the mother tongue, reputable
American dictionaries, successors to the original "Webster's" (i.e., Noah
Webster's, 1828), must assume the role of guardian of good grammar.
They must carefully elect the words and meanings they list, rigorously
weeding out every questionable usage. "The Custodians of Language,"
Pei told his fellow Americans, "hold that there is a right and a wrong
way of expressing yourself, and that the right way should be prescribed
by works of a certain description, chief among them the dictionaries of
the language."⁹ Most language custodians in America felt that in the new
dictionary an already indiscriminate linguistic democracy had yielded to
anarchy. Even *The New York Times* — the *Third's* most often cited source
of usage examples — lamented that the Merriam editors had not lived up
to their public responsibility in the new "say-as-you-go dictionary."

Opposed to the position of these reviewers, of course, were the
compilers of the dictionary. The *Third's* editor in chief believed that
lexicography "should have no traffic with guesswork, prejudice, or bias,
or with artificial notions of correctness and superiority. . . . If a
dictionary should neglect the obligation to act as a faithful recorder and
interpreter of usage, it cannot expect to be any longer appealed to as an
authority."¹⁰ *Webster's* lexicographers took the function of a dictionary to
be the faithful and scrupulous recording of actual language usage, which
they identified as whatever language forms appropriate groups of people
use in speaking and writing. This is a view in which descriptive linguists
concur. They claim that the setting of value on linguistic forms is a
social, not a lexicographic, matter. They maintain that lexicographers
should record what society *does* with language, not what society says
should be done or what society *thinks* it does. Linguists and lexicographers espousing this view, often considered liberal or even leftist, regard the proper function of grammars and dictionaries as exclusively
descriptive: their books describe actual language practice.

Descriptive linguists do not recommend that a grammar of nonstandard English be taught in schools and colleges, where a command of
standard English is assumed as the accepted goal. But if it were desirable
to have descriptions of particular varieties of *spoken* English — English
spoken on the Bowery, for example, or by United States Senators, or
eleven-year-old Hopi Indians, or atomic physicists — then such grammars should accurately reflect the customary usage and pronunciation of
those speakers. A hypothetical illustration: If atomic physicists ordinarily
speak of the "nuculus" of an atom and of "nucular" energy, then a gram-

⁹Mario Pei, "A Loss for Words" (1964), p. 82.
¹⁰Philip B. Gove, "Linguistic Advances and Lexicography" (1961), p. 8.

mar of their English has an obligation to say so. In recording such a usage linguists would not be making a value judgment; they would be saying not that "nucular" is as good as or better than "nuclear" but merely that it is the form physicists ordinarily use.[11] A factual illustration: Quite a few educated American house hunters of my acquaintance seek assistance these days from a "*real*-a-tor" rather than a "*re*-al-tor"; descriptivists think it would be misleading for a dictionary to ignore this usage or to label it restrictively — assuming, of course, that its citation files for a wider sample of educated speakers validated my own observations. (As a matter of interest, *Webster's Third* — on the basis of mammoth citation files — labeled the pronunciation "*real*-a-tor" *substandard* and the pronunciation "nu-cu-lar" *chiefly substandard*. Whether or not the intervening two decades have witnessed sufficient spread of these pronunciations to warrant different labels is difficult for an individual to tell.)

The linguists' concern has been that school grammar, in stressing and continually testing disputed usages, has given the impression that nonstandard *spoken* varieties of English (and sometimes merely informal standard ones) are "bad" or "ungrammatical" English and has failed to distinguish the functions of these varieties and those customary in more formal communication, especially in writing. They have also quarreled with too-narrow and too-rigid definitions of "standard English" itself, definitions that reject the usages of many educated and cultured speakers and writers.

Different linguists would doubtless have different answers to questions about particular disputed usages. (Is "nucular" standard spoken English? Should students be taught not to write "different than" and not to say "It's me"? Should they be taught to say or write "Whom did you see?" Are *through* and *thru* equally good?) But the linguists' answers would be alike in not being absolutely Yes or No; and in most cases they would probably begin with "It depends" — on the social and linguistic background of the speaker or writer *and* of the person or persons addressed; on the topic of discussion and its setting; on the nature and context of the usage in question; and so on. And they would insist that students should learn the *differences* between standard varieties of English and other varieties *without* being made to feel the other varieties are "inferior." Linguists think students should understand that all varieties of English — including standard written English — have evolved to meet communicative or social needs of the linguistic communities using them. (Additionally, linguists want teachers to be aware of the similarities among all the varieties of English, so that its underlying systematic

---

[11]"Nucular" is a fairly common pronunciation throughout the States (though probably *not* among physicists); it is the form President Eisenhower employed in his television broadcasts to the American public.

nature will be better understood; and many of them would like to see students become familiar with the outlines of the historical growth and development of their language. But these features of a full-scale program of language study are beyond the scope of my concern with ideas about "good usage.") For my purposes here, the view of descriptive linguists may be summarized thus: the correctness of "grammar" or "English usage" is relative.

Obviously this relativist view is not universally shared. Wilson Follett, a distinguished editor and teacher, could hardly contain his rage when he heard usage so defined. "Let those who choose define usage as what a swarm of folk say or write by reason of laziness, shiftlessness, or ignorance; the tenable definition is still what the judicious do as a result of all that they can muster of conscious determination."[12] The absolutist view of correctness is also represented by Edwin Newman, who in *Strictly Speaking* (1974) cites hundreds of "wrong" and "impossible" usages culled from *The New York Times, Esquire* magazine, and other periodicals. For example: "'Different than,' rather than different from, is wrong. So is 'augur for.' Augur does not take for after it. It cannot take for after it." That *augur* has in fact taken *for* after it in the pages he cites does not shake Newman's faith in his index of impossible usages. Unlike these rigid custodians of language, descriptive linguists do define what a swarm of folk say or write—by reason of laziness, shiftlessness, ignorance, or anything else—as *their* usage, and what the judicious speak and write, for whatever reasons, as *their* usage. They maintain that different usages are appropriate to the different uses and users of English.

Follett believed that linguistic scholarship, using such definitions, was "dedicating itself to the abolition of standards" and that "the new rhetoric evolved under its auspices is an organized assumption that language good enough for anybody is good enough for everybody." He called for a "philosophy of usage grounded in the steadfast conviction that the best, whether or not we have it in us to attain it, is not too good to be aspired to."[13] Language guardians like Follett prefer basing grammars and dictionaries on standards other than current custom. The rules they favor would delimit what they regard as the best possible English; and insofar as such rules portray a potential rather than an actual state of affairs, they are properly called linguistic exhortations or prescriptive rules.

The position taken by Follett, Pei, Newman, certain critics of *Webster's Third,* and *Saturday Review*'s letter writers, has often been referred

---

[12]Wilson Follett, "Grammar Is Obsolete" (1960), p. 76. In permitting a reprinting of this article, Follett changed the title to "Bargain Basement English"; see Anderson and Stageberg, eds., *Introductory Readings on Language* (1962). Follett (1887–1963) had taught English at Texas A and M, Dartmouth, and Brown before turning to a career in editing.

[13]"Grammar Is Obsolete," pp. 73, 76.

to as a "doctrine of correctness," while the view of most modern linguists and the lexicographers who compiled the *Third* has been termed a "doctrine of usage."

Adherents of a doctrine of correctness strive to mold linguistic practice according to selected patterns of grammar; they attempt to retard the pace of language change or halt it altogether; they are idealistic and prescriptive; some are elitist; they make explicit value judgments about English locutions. As the editor of *The American Heritage Dictionary* acknowledged about its panel of prescriptive usage consultants, "They have eschewed the 'scientific' delusion that a dictionary should contain no value judgments."[14] Another prescriber, former *Fortune* magazine editor Dwight Macdonald, appearing on the "Today" show in 1975, told host Edwin Newman that he considered one of his editorial duties to be slowing down of the acceptance of new usages. On the same broadcast Theodore M. Bernstein of *The New York Times* agreed with Macdonald and with writer Jean Stafford that their position with respect to linguistic correctness is and should be "elitist." Stafford, winner of a Pulitzer Prize, remarked that a usage must be accepted by the "educated," not merely "widely accepted," in order to be correct.

Supporters of a doctrine of usage, on the other hand, attempt to base rules of grammar and lexical entries in dictionaries on actual language practice. It is their goal to be realistic and descriptive. They make no explicit value judgments about the logic, utility, or esthetics — i.e., the "correctness" — of particular lexical or grammatical items, but report the known facts about the ways in which a given form, meaning, or pronunciation is actually used and in what circumstances.

The word *grammar* has a variety of meanings in America. Almost any book about a particular language can be called a "grammar." To most professional grammarians "grammar" means a relatively complete and systematic description of the language in a community, however large or small, rural or urban, technologically advanced or primitive. Among linguists of the transformational-generative school, a "grammar" describes the internalized, psychological system of elements and rules underlying the use of one's native language. And there are other related senses of the word. But to most Americans "grammar" suggests a code of good conduct regulating spoken and especially written English. For violation of its precepts we are said not to know grammar or to have bad grammar; and, as with other codes of etiquette, disregard of this one can elicit judgments of educational, social, and even personal inferiority. Like other etiquettes, this one too has intricate and subtle applications, though most of us are unaware of their complexity. A word or phrase that goes unnoticed in one set of circumstances may brand a speaker as boorish if used on another occasion.

[14]Morris Bishop, "Good Usage, Bad Usage, and Usage," in *The American Heritage Dictionary of the English Language,* ed. William Morris (1969), p. xxiii.

Because we customarily think of preschoolers as knowing little or   20
no grammar in this last sense, we can call this linguistic etiquette "school
grammar." Great effort is expended teaching this protocol, and it is this
kind of grammar that is talked about in schools and in newspaper discussions. The linguistic punctilios that constitute school grammar are often
taught as absolutes: *ain't* is wrong; *as* is the right conjunction, *like* is
wrong; *whom* is correct in this structure but not in that one; use *I,* not
me, in this phrase; *infer* cannot mean "imply"; and so on. Embracing
perhaps several hundred generally unrelated linguistic usages, such a
code of fashion must be taught in the schools because it is not much
observed in ordinary spoken communication and therefore cannot be
acquired the way a child absorbs the vast bulk of his internalized linguistic system — without conscious effort or formal instruction. This grammatical *savoir faire* covers just a portion of our English language and
draws attention to itself only when we venture outside our immediate
familial and social milieu. Like other codes of convention school grammar is a social artifact, though not unimportant; indeed, in the United
States (as in some other countries) its traditional importance is un-
matched by any other academic subject, reading and perhaps arithmetic
excepted.

Not everyone agrees that school grammar should play a major role
in education; fewer still approve the influence wielded by its nice distinctions in socioeconomic advancement. Because many recent debunkers of
this absolute code of conduct have in fact been professional students of
language, I shall for convenience group supporters of a relativistic view
of correct English under the label *linguist.* Of course, many linguists
have expressed little or no interest in the correctness controversy or in
the debate over the role that the mastery of particular items of English
usage should play in the schools. Most linguists have directed their energies instead to historical or descriptive problems in the grammar and
phonology of English or to analysis of other languages. They have taken
their transcriptions of speech as given, much as historical linguists and
philologists accept the language forms of extant texts. Linguists afford
the spoken word primacy over the written; they regard writing as a
sometimes pallid reflection of speech. For descriptive and historical linguists of all persuasions, a relativist view of correctness and the primacy
of speech over writing are working assumptions.

But how shall I characterize Pei, Follett, Macdonald, Newman, the
writers of *SR*'s letters, and their company? It is difficult to choose a fair
and telling designation for the various antagonists of the relativistic approach. *Purist* and *absolutist* are harsh and too rigid to encompass many
who ought to be included. *Conservative* is too broad, perhaps too political. *Rhetorician* is narrow and too professional. *Traditional grammarian,*
sometimes shortened to *traditionalist,* fits more comfortably, and I shall

use it, though it is perhaps not so well tailored as *linguist* is to its wearers. The truth is that many of those I shall call traditional grammarians have not been professional grammarians at all. Some are authors, editors, and teachers of composition; some are professors of history, rhetoric, and literature; some are social critics, journalists, television and radio commentators; in the past there were many clergymen and amateur philosophers among them. What they share is the belief that acceptance and practice of their principles and preferences would improve the English language and the lives of its users.

Because they understand and propagate the orthodox rules about *who* and *whom, shall* and *will, like* and *as,* various traditionalists are popularly considered grammarians, and it will serve my purpose to follow custom in this regard. And because traditional grammarians have been concerned with protecting the English language from what they take to be degeneration and debasement, it will be appropriate at times to refer to them as *language guardians.* And, taking a cue from the form of their guidance, I shall on occasion call them *prescriptivists* and *prescribers,* in contrast with the linguists, who are *descriptivists* and *describers.*

It must be admitted that none of these labels is ideal! Readers should bear in mind, as they come across generalizations about *linguists* or *traditional grammarians,* that the terms have been chosen to characterize two warring factions — the supporters and opponents of a relativistic view of language correctness. Often I will have need to refer to both groups and so I will sometimes use "grammarians" as an umbrella term for all writers about English.

The term *usage* also needs a word of explanation, though my employment of it is in keeping with customary interpretations over the past fifty years. "Usage" sometimes refers to the complete set of lexical, grammatical, and phonological or orthographical occurrences in speech and writing (that is, to everything that people say or write, with special reference to the way they do it). Often, however, the term's reference is limited to that subset of linguistic items whose social or functional status is debatable (that is, to locutions whose "correctness" is in question). For each debatable item or questionable "usage," there is another that language guardians consider better or worse and hence to be preferred or avoided (*whom/who;* "that thing"/"dat ting"; *different from/different than;* "nucular"/"nuclear"; and so forth).

There has been disagreement between the advocates of actual usage and the proponents of correctness since grammars and dictionaries were first compiled. Linguists and traditional grammarians have quarreled for generations about what is correct English, what the standards for correctness should be, and who should set them.

The appearance of *Webster's Third,* in 1961, crystallized the issues. More than that, it politicized them and gave diverse tractarians occasion to cloud the debate and lobby for their views in the ensuing storm. The depth and character of the convictions threatened by the *Third's* treatment of usage can be highlighted by noting that *The New York Times* in its editions of November 30, 1961, dubbed the new dictionary "Webster's Third (or Bolshevik) International." Further, the president of a respectable publishing firm sought to buy out the Merriam Company and scuttle the *Third,* alleging that the world of scholarship was "horrified" at its permissive standards.[15] Finally, the hint of linguistic promiscuity latent in the already cited comparison between the *Third* and the somewhat notorious "Kinsey Report" is a reminder of the moral and puritanical overtones that often surround discussion of English usage. Clearly, the tug of war between description and prescription in English lexicography and grammar, though four hundred years in the waging, remained taut and unresolved in 1961.

And so it continues. While the doctrine of usage is gaining support in some school books and already dominates lexicography, many teachers of English still favor a form of the centuries-old doctrine of correctness for dictionaries, handbooks, and school grammars; and in general both educated and uneducated opinion agrees with them. Indeed, traditionalists blame much that is wrong in our schools and public places on the rise of structural, descriptive linguistics and the alleged easing of language standards. Television commentator Edwin Newman has linked the decline of public confidence in government with the looser language standards of politicians; he has placed two such indictments on the best-seller lists since 1974. In the last month of 1978 and the first month or so of 1979 I happened upon discussions of the poor state of the language in *Saturday Review, Newsweek,* and *Time* magazines, as well as on television—on the "Today" show, on a local Los Angeles news broadcast, and (for an entire week!) on the Dick Cavett show. "All Things Considered," a syndicated news program on National Public Radio, has reported that the most "irate" mail received from listeners deals with the "improper" use of English by the broadcasters. And a New Jersey professor of English has been receiving nationwide attention for his newsletter, *The Underground Grammarian,* which details the decline and fall of the English language with illustrations from memoranda issued on his campus. Finally, even *Esquire* magazine now publishes a monthly column on English usage. Ironically, as gracefully as it is written, its author learned

---

[15]The publisher was James Parton, president of the American Heritage Publishing Company. His attempt to wrest control of the *Third* from the G. & C. Merriam Company was widely reported at the time. See, e.g., *The New York Times* for February 20, 1962, p. 32 (from which Parton is here quoted) and October 4, 1964; *Newsweek* also reported the attempted takeover in its edition of March 12, 1962, pp. 104–105.

English not as a native language from family and friends but from grammar books as a foreign language (his fifth in fact!); quite understandably he takes a consistently conservative and sometimes unnaturally rigid view of correctness. Uneasiness, then, over the state of the language is not limited to a few Americans in publishing houses or on university campuses nor even to teachers of English. It is a matter of deep and widespread and continuing concern.

It was late in the sixteenth century, after English had started to replace Latin as a medium of learned discussion in Britain, that Englishmen first complained about the absence in their use of the vernacular of the kind of regularity and certainty to which they were accustomed in the classical language. They began writing handbooks to supply this want, and since then Englishmen and Americans have continued publishing grammars and lexicons of their language. While some grammarians and dictionary makers lamented linguistic alteration and tended to regard the descriptions and strictures of their predecessors as nearly immutable, others strenuously objected to analyses based on anything but actual current usage. As usage changes, these latter argued, grammars and lexicons must also change; the rules are dependent, not primary, and cannot be considered sacrosanct. But the more conservative codifiers, noting the variety of English and American dialects and the natural tendency of tongues to change, were convinced that without powerful safeguards English speakers would find themselves unable to read the literature and written records of earlier periods and unable to communicate across countries (or possibly even counties). Dwight Macdonald expressed this fear in 1962, saying that without "brakes applied by those who know and care about the language, . . . the change will be so fast and so dominated by the great majority who have other things to do besides worrying about good English that the result will be a jargon as cut off from the race's culture and traditions as the Pidgin English of the South Seas."[16] To further complicate things, the relationship between speech and writing has confounded nearly all literate English speakers; and the linguists' focus on spoken systems has not helped. In 1975, *Newsweek* warned that, with speech taking priority over writing, a second tower of Babel was building![17]

Continued struggle over four centuries has dragged to the surface   *30* several underlying causes of disagreement and misunderstanding. Changing social and educational conditions have demanded clearer expositions of each viewpoint. In America, especially, dramatic increases in the numbers of students from lower socioeconomic levels and from

[16]"Three Questions for Structural Linguists; Or, Webster 3 Revisited" (Postscript to Sledd and Ebbitt), p. 258.
[17]"Why Johnny Can't Write," *Newsweek* (December 8, 1975), p. 65.

foreign cultures have forced educators to reconsider the linguistic needs of students and the purposes and means of teaching them English grammar and spelling. Supporters of the idea that usage determines correctness in language began abandoning a right-or-wrong approach in favor of a relativistic one that distinguished varieties of English according to level and function. But as they groped their way toward objective analysis of what this might mean in terms of linguistic correctness, they met resistance from traditional grammarians who found their objective criteria irrelevant.

In this century, grammar has provided a battering ram both for supporters and for opponents of progressive education. Liberals claimed that objectives for language instruction have not remained consonant with the changing social situations of students, while conservatives, generally cool to universal education at all levels, deplored the diluting of traditional ideals. Language guardians feared that the permissiveness associated with progressive education was infecting the teaching of grammar and would ultimately contaminate the language itself if left unchecked.

Besides straightforward differences of opinion, we find that misunderstanding, hostility, and bigotry have contributed at times in this century — as before — to the confusion surrounding the composition of dictionaries and grammars and the teaching of English usage. Philosophical differences over the nature of language, the purposes of education, the function of science (especially its role in language studies), the value of democracy, and ultimately the character of human society have obscured discussions ostensibly about English usage.

Beginning with early British views, the chapters that follow examine the opinions that scholars and laymen from various walks of life have expressed about correct English in grammars, dictionaries, and handbooks. A look at the development of a doctrine of correctness and of opposition to it in the nineteenth and twentieth centuries reveals that the chasm separating these views goes far deeper than mere technical disagreement about the status of specific items of usage. A historical survey of American views of linguistic propriety helps uncover certain veiled assumptions embodied in the letters to *Saturday Review,* in the imbroglio surrounding *Webster's Third,* and in the attitudes of countless Americans toward the proper use of the national tongue. It also subjects to scrutiny the linguists' assumptions and the successive refinements of their position resulting from the vigorous opposition of traditional grammarians.

Since a good deal of the antagonism between descriptivists and language guardians stems from a bilateral misunderstanding of intentions and aspirations, a historical overview provides a perspective for evaluating the two opposing views of propriety in lexicography and grammar. The Danish linguist Otto Jespersen, perhaps the world's most distinguished student of the English language (and sometimes affectionately referred to as "the great Dane"), has identified seven kinds of standards commonly applied in classroom and newspaper discussions of linguistic correctness. Besides the standard of authority, he noted appeal to geographical, literary, aristocratic, democratic, logical, and esthetic standards.[18] We shall find these same criteria and others learnedly discussed throughout our historical search.

FOR DISCUSSION AND WRITING

1. Regarding the principle of quantity: At any points in this essay, does Finegan fail to give you enough information for you to understand him? Does he ever give you more than necessary? (Be specific in your answers.)

2. Regarding the principle of quality: What reasons do you have for trusting (or distrusting) Finegan's knowledge of his subject or his honesty?

3. Regarding the principle of manner: If you think the essay is sometimes unclear, indicate where, and explain the difficulty.

4. Regarding the principle of relation: Are any parts of the essay irrelevant to the topic? Explain.

5. The controversy over *Webster's Third New International Dictionary* had to do with its purpose. Contrast the publisher's purpose with what Mario Pei and the other "traditionalists" believe the purpose should have been.

6. State the main point of "Popular and Scholarly Views of 'Good English.'"

7. Should dictionaries try to describe language as it is used, or should they attempt to set standards?

8. Explain "doctrine of correctness" and "doctrine of usage" (pars. 16–17).

9. Explain "school grammar" (par. 20).

10. Explain your reaction to "bad grammar" such as "Me and him played on the same team," "Louella don't have no time for extracurricular activities," and "George ain't been here since May."

11. Why do many people value "correct" grammar so highly?

12. What are your own opinions about "correct" grammar? Do you believe that there is an absolute standard of correctness to which one should

[18]*Mankind, Nation and Individual* (1925; repr. 1964), p. 83.

aspire? Explain the ways in which you agree or disagree with Finegan's viewpoint.

13. How would a linguist determine whether a disputed word or phrase should be used or avoided? Relate your answer to critical questions that readers of texts should ask themselves. For example, a critical reader considers the *scene* in which a text was written and in which it is read; a linguist also considers scene. Think about other questions regarding critical reading, and apply them to the problem of word usage.

U, NON-U, AND YOU

John Simon

John Simon's command of languages is remarkable. Born in Subotica, Yugoslavia, in 1925, he was able to speak Serbo-Croatian, Hungarian, and German fluently by the age of six. He first learned English at the age of thirteen, when he was sent to boarding school in Cambridge, England, and became fluent while attending college in the United States. He earned his bachelor's, master's, and doctoral degrees at Harvard University.

Simon has held positions both in the academic world and in the publishing world. He has taught at Harvard, the Massachusetts Institute of Technology, and Bard College, and has been drama critic for the *Hudson Review, Commonweal,* and *New York* magazine and film critic for *Esquire, New Leader,* and *New York.*

Simon has earned the reputation of being a snob, an accusation to which he admits in the following essay. While reading "U, Non-U, and You," think of how Simon's rather late introduction to English might have influenced the ideas expressed in this essay.

Virtually nothing is so feared and hated in this allegedly egalitarian country of ours as snobbishness. There is no more detested creature anywhere — unless it be the elitist or the intellectual — than the snob, who cannot even enjoy the semifavorable publicity accorded bank robbers, necrophiliacs, and starters of forest fires. And yet H. B. Brooks-Baker, the publisher of *Debrett's Peerage* and, with the Viking Press, of *U and Non-U Revisited,* claims that England, the reputed cradle of snobbism, "is among the least snobbish and class-conscious countries. Far less so," he continues in the Foreword to *U and Non-U Revisited,* "than America, for example, which basks in the reputation of being the most democratic of nations."

As the jacket copy explains, the present tome is a kind of sequel to *Noblesse Oblige,* a book edited in 1956 by the late Nancy Mitford that "hit the world like a bombshell. Profiting from the researches of the philologist Professor Alan C. Ross, who had coined the expressions 'U' and 'non-U' — that is 'Upper-class' and 'non-Upper-class' — [Nancy Mitford] set about telling the man in the street just how common he was." I remember the immense sensation the book caused twenty-three years ago even in "classless" America, and the only reason I myself did not read it when everybody else did was snobbishness.

Just to show you how promiscuously and hostilely the word *snob* is bandied about, let me quote from an article on drag queens in the June 25, 1979, *Village Voice* by Edmund White, a respected novelist and a coauthor of *The Joy of Gay Sex:* "Disdain for drag is, I would contend, often concealed snobbism. Most gay transvestites, especially street drags, are either black or Puerto Rican. Discrimination against them may be both elitist and racist." First, I am surprised that a homosexual writer of White's talent and literacy espouses the dreadful abuse of the word *gay;* second, I am appalled at his subscribing to that bugbear of gutter radicals, the three-headed monster Snob-Elitist-Racist. Obviously the distaste of heterosexuals for drag queens — leaving aside the question of whether it is justifiable or not — stems from sexual sources: sexuality is so ingrained, so elemental a thing with us that the person whose sexual practices are antithetical to ours and who flaunts this antithesis becomes more resented than a mere religious, political, or social adversary. But whenever heavy demagogic weaponry is needed, *snob, elitist,* and *racist* get hauled out.

The origins of the word *snob* remain uncertain.* The late, sorely missed Eric Partridge, in his splendid etymological dictionary *Origins,* writes: "*Snob,* cobbler, hence (slang) a townee, a plebeian, hence a toady and a superior person: o.o.o." ("O.o.o." means of obscure origin.) Ernest Weekley, whose *Concise Etymological Dictionary* Partridge goes on to cite, argues that *snob* is related to *snip,* a tailor, suggesting kinship with *snub,* to cut short. Notice the implication that a snob is an inferior person trying to climb the social ladder, hence he is both "a toady" to those above and "a superior person" to those beside and below him.

What concerns me here, however, is whether there is such a thing   5
as linguistic snobbery: the use of language to achieve or assert social superiority. Such language, though correct from the linguistic point of view, might be reprehensible in a larger, humanistic context and thus a good thing to avoid. As *Noblesse Oblige* made crystal clear, there existed an Upper-class English and a non–Upper-class one. The differences still exist, though *U and Non-U Revisited* makes them only plastic, not crystal, clear. What the little book makes manifest, though, is that snobbery goes on and on, even if Thackeray, as long ago as 1846, wrote an entire book castigating the snob as one who "meanly admires mean things." As the new book demonstrates, however, distinctions between U and non-U in language are getting fuzzier, what with the non-U people trying to sound U, and the U ones, out of reverse snobbery, espousing non-U terminology.

Which brings me back to the question of snobbishness in the U.S.A., which does indeed flourish in various forms. For example, in Los Angeles you are mercilessly classed according to what make of car you drive. This kind of snobbery is the accepted thing there and has even spawned an appropriate reverse snobbery, whereby a beat-up old Chevy is considered in some circles more prestigious than the latest Jaguar, Mercedes, Porsche, or Rolls. Similarly, there is a plutocratic snobbery

*I can find no evidence for the frequent assertion that *snob* derives from *s. nob.,* for *sine nobilitate,* as a designation for commoners on certain British rosters.

rampant from coast to coast; for instance, when country clubs can no longer discriminate along racial and religious lines, they resort to admitting members according to their income tax bracket.

Such things are, by and large, accepted as matters of course. Not so, however, linguistic snobbery, which is considered totally heinous and to be expunged by hook, crook, or napalm. There are, clearly, two possible places for linguistic snobbishness: in pronunciation and in vocabulary. Your linguistic snob (or U speaker) still tends to say de-*cay*-dence rather than *dek*-a-dence, even though current dictionaries usually list the former as a secondary and less desirable pronunciation. De-*cay*-dence makes more sense in terms of the word's Latin provenance and pronunciation; but who nowadays knows anything about Latin?

Likewise, the correct American pronunciation of *squalor* used to rhyme with *tailor* and was so given in *Funk & Wagnalls Standard Dictionary,* which in matters of pronunciation was ranked above even the good second edition of *Webster's.* Some thirty-five years ago, I heard of someone's not getting a job teaching in the New York public-school system because he made *squalor* rhyme with *holler*—though in England this was always the accepted pronunciation. Nowadays, I suppose, you don't need to know even the meaning of *squalor* to teach English anywhere; the assumption may be that you'll learn the meaning from experiencing it on the job.

Pronunciations change, and we change with them. There is an interesting discussion of language in *U and Non-U Revisited* among Professor Ross, Richard Buckle (author, ballet critic, and the book's editor), and Philip Howard (the language columnist of the London *Times.*) As an example of non-U speech, Ross adduces the tendency for the accent to shift from the first to the middle (actually the second) syllable in words of three or four syllables; he and Buckle cite and deplore, among others, *laméntable, preférable, exquísite,* and *marítal.* But Howard, who is more permissive, points out that there is something called the progressive accent, which evolves in the course of time "because we dislike a rapid succession of light syllables and find them hard to pronounce." He notes that *commendable* was once accented on the first syllable—thus in Shakespeare: "'Tis sweet and cómmendable in thy nature, Hamlet"—but has since become *comméndable.* And he makes the usual defense for change: language is a living thing, we foolishly want the pronunciations of our childhood frozen for all time, and more of the like.

Buckle responds to this with an admirable *non serviam* hurled at the   10 collective ignorance of the unwashed:

> You may be right that I am "frozen" in the customs of my childhood but I do think—or rather, feel—that to pronounce "exquisite" or "lamentable," and particularly "marital," with the accent on the middle syllable is vile. It is aesthetically offensive. I

know the laws of beauty change, like everything else, but I should fight against that to the end of my days. Incidentally, can you imagine the French or Italians changing the pronunciation of a word like "formidable" or "amabile"?

Here, bless him, is the linguistic snob — or, as I prefer to call him, purist — speaking. When I hear, as I often do these days, *influence* pronounced by ignoramuses with the accent on the second syllable, it makes my blood freeze — and not in the customs of my childhood. What makes *inflúence* so ghastly is not necessarily its sound (though I think it is ugly) but its demonstration of the existence of people so uneducated, so deaf to what others are saying, so unable to learn the obvious that they are bound to be a major source of verbal pollution, linguistic corruption, cultural erosion. Their bad offices clearly won't stop at this single egregious error. When Howard cheerfully accepts this sort of thing, only to go on to bemoan the "vexing" loss of discrimination between *disinterested* and *uninterested,* does he not realize that it is the same persons who are guilty of both?

The point, as any snob can tell you, is that the melody of the English language is being ruined. Make the accent (´ denotes stressed syllable, ˘ unstressed) fall regularly on the second syllable in trisyllabic words, and you get what is called in scansion an amphibrach (˘ ´˘) where before there might have been a dactyl (´ ˘ ˘). This and similar changes would reduce English to a much more boring melodic pattern, such as that of, say, Finnish and Hungarian, with their monotonous stress on initial syllables.

Of course, it is British English that truly lends itself to snobbery. When, as Buckle claims, the U pronounce *garage* in the French manner, whereas "the middle-class pronounce it to rhyme with 'barrage' [that is, *bear*-azh]" while the "lower-class is 'garridge,'" you have a perfect spectrum: language as a total class indicator. Except that Ross disagrees and finds the alleged U pronunciation merely old-fashioned. Which is precisely what linguistic snobbery or purism is: old-fashionedness. Or take Ross's statement that the non-U pronunciation of *fiancé* rhymes with "pie fancy," whereupon Buckle contends that he thought the "usual non-U . . . was 'feonn-say.' U people wouldn't use the word anyway." Better yet: lower class, fie-*an*-cy; middle class, fee-*on*-say; upper class — no such word. One has just a one-night stand, an affair, or a marriage.

Well, we are a bit closer to classlessness in America, but there *are* differences, especially in vocabulary. As the "American Section" of the book indicates, there exist, for example, the non-U *chaise lounge, drapes, folks, hose, home,* for which the U words are *chaise longue, curtains, parents* or *relations, stockings, house.* (Though the list is not always accurate: thus *trousers* is not the non-U for *pants* but vice versa.) If you are the sort of person who thinks that to sound well brought up, educated, fastidious, and perhaps even old-fashioned is not shameful but distinguished, go ahead and be a linguistic snob. You may not want to be the last by whom the old is laid aside, but you certainly don't want to be the first to try the illiterate new.

FOR DISCUSSION AND WRITING

1. Regarding the principle of quantity: At any points in this essay, does Simon fail to give you enough information? Does he ever give you more than necessary? (Be specific in your answers.)

2. Regarding the principle of quality: What reasons do you have for trusting (or distrusting) Simon's knowledge of his subject or his honesty?

3. Regarding the principle of manner: If you think the essay is sometimes unclear, indicate where, and explain the difficulty.

4. Regarding the principle of relation: Are any parts of the essay irrelevant to the topic? Explain.

5. Explain your reaction to Simon's advice: "If you are the sort of person who thinks that to sound well brought up, educated, fastidious, and perhaps even old-fashioned is not shameful but distinguished, go ahead and be a linguistic snob."

6. Explain why Simon considers Edmund White's use of the word *gay* a "dreadful abuse" (par. 3).

7. In the argument between Richard Buckle and Philip Howard, whose side are you on? Explain.

8. Explain instances of snobbery in a group with whom you are associated (e.g., a sports team, social organization, your family).

9. State the main point of "U, Non-U, and You."

POLITICS AND THE ENGLISH LANGUAGE

George Orwell

George Orwell, the pseudonym of Eric Blair, was born in India in 1903 to British parents. After attending Eton College in England, Orwell worked five years for the Indian Imperial Police in Burma, after which he returned to Europe, where he lived in poverty for several years. In 1936, he fought with the Republicans in the Spanish civil war and was seriously wounded. Orwell wrote several autobiographical books concerned with this period in his life, including *Down and Out in Paris and London* (1933), *Burmese Days* (1934), and *Homage to Catalonia* (1938).

Orwell's ardent opposition to totalitarianism is evident in his two most famous novels, *Animal Farm* (1945) and *Nineteen Eighty-Four* (1949). *Animal Farm* is an adult fable in which barnyard animals form a collective, communal organization that eventually deteriorates into tyrannical rule. *Nineteen Eighty-Four* envisions a world of the future run by a totalitarian government able to follow the lives of each of its citizens by electronic surveillance. In *Nineteen Eighty-Four,* Orwell calls attention to the way in which language can be abused and distorted for unethical purposes. For example, to pacify the population, the government constantly uses slogans whose meanings are exactly the opposite of the words they employ: "War is Peace," "Freedom is Slavery," and "Ignorance is Strength."

Many critics consider Orwell an even better essayist than novelist. The following selection, one of Orwell's best-known essays, is also concerned with the corruption of language, although the reasons Orwell advances for such a decline are less insidious than those in *Nineteen Eighty-Four.*

Most people who bother with the matter at all would admit that the English language is in a bad way, but it is generally assumed that we cannot by conscious action do anything about it. Our civilization is decadent and our language—so the argument runs—must inevitably share in the general collapse. It follows that any struggle against the abuse of language is a sentimental archaism, like preferring candles to electric light or hansom cabs to aeroplanes. Underneath this lies the half-conscious belief that language is a natural growth and not an instrument which we shape for our own purposes.

Now, it is clear that the decline of a language must ultimately have political and economic causes: it is not due simply to the bad influence of this or that individual writer. But an effect can become a cause, reinforcing the original cause and producing the same effect in an intensified form, and so on indefinitely. A man may take to drink because he feels himself to be a failure, and then fail all the more completely because he drinks. It is rather the same thing that is happening to the English language. It becomes ugly and inaccurate because our thoughts are foolish, but the slovenliness of our language makes it easier for us to have foolish thoughts. The point is that the process is reversible. Modern English, especially written English, is full of bad habits which spread by imitation and which can be avoided if one is willing to take the necessary trouble. If one gets rid of these habits one can think more clearly, and to think clearly is a necessary first step towards political regeneration: so that the fight against bad English is not frivolous and is not the exclusive concern of professional writers. I will come back to this presently, and I hope that by that time the meaning of what I have said here will have become clearer. Meanwhile, here are five specimens of the English language as it is now habitually written.

These five passages have not been picked out because they are especially bad—I could have quoted far worse if I had chosen—but because they illustrate various of the mental vices from which we now suffer. They are a little below the average, but are fairly representative samples. I number them so that I can refer back to them when necessary:

(1) "I am not, indeed, sure whether it is not true to say that the Milton who once seemed not unlike a seventeenth-century Shelley had not become, out of an experience ever more bitter in each year, more alien [*sic*] to the founder of that Jesuit sect which nothing could induce him to tolerate."
> Professor Harold Laski (Essay in *Freedom of Expression*)

(2) "Above all, we cannot play ducks and drakes with a native battery of idioms which prescribes such egregious collocations of vocables as the Basic *put up with* for *tolerate* or *put at a loss* for *bewilder.*"
> Professor Lancelot Hogben (*Interglossa*)

(3) "On the one side we have the free personality: by definition it is not neurotic, for it has neither conflict nor dream. Its desires, such as they are, are transparent, for they are just what institutional approval keeps in the forefront of consciousness; another institutional pattern would alter their number and intensity; there is little in them that is natural, irreducible, or culturally dangerous. But *on the other side,* the social bond itself is nothing but the mutual reflection of these self-secure integrities. Recall the definition of love. Is not this the very picture of a small academic? Where is there a place in this hall of mirrors for either personality or fraternity?"
> Essay on psychology in *Politics* (New York)

(4) "All the 'best people' from the gentlemen's clubs, and all the frantic fascist captains, united in common hatred of Socialism and bestial horror of the rising tide of the mass revolutionary movement, have turned to acts of provocation, to foul incendiarism, to medieval legends of poisoned wells, to legalize their

own destruction of proletarian organizations, and rouse the ag-
itated petty-bourgeoisie to chauvinistic fervour on behalf of the
fight against the revolutionary way out of the crisis."

Communist pamphlet

(5) "If a new spirit *is* to be infused into this old country, there is
one thorny and contentious reform which must be tackled, and
that is the humanization and galvanization of the B.B.C.
Timidity here will bespeak cancer and atrophy of the soul. The
heart of Britain may be sound and of strong beat, for instance,
but the British lion's roar at present is like that of Bottom in
Shakespeare's *Midsummer Night's Dream*—as gentle as any suck-
ing dove. A virile new Britain cannot continue indefinitely to
be traduced in the eyes or rather ears, of the world by the effete
languors of Langham Place, brazenly masquerading as 'standard English.' When the Voice of Britain is heard at nine
o'clock, better far and infinitely less ludicrous to hear aitches
honestly dropped than the present priggish, inflated, inhibited,
school-ma'amish arch braying of blameless bashful mewing
maidens!"

Letter in *Tribune*

Each of these passages has faults of its own, but, quite apart from
avoidable ugliness, two qualities are common to all of them. The first is
staleness of imagery: the other is lack of precision. The writer either has
a meaning and cannot express it, or he inadvertently says something else,
or he is almost indifferent as to whether his words mean anything or not.
This mixture of vagueness and sheer incompetence is the most marked
characteristic of modern English prose, and especially of any kind of
political writing. As soon as certain topics are raised, the concrete melts
into the abstract and no one seems able to think of turns of speech that
are not hackneyed: prose consists less and less of *words* chosen for the
sake of their meaning, and more and more of *phrases* tacked together like
the sections of a prefabricated hen-house. I list below, with notes and
examples, various of the tricks by means of which the work of prose-
construction is habitually dodged:

DYING METAPHORS

A newly invented metaphor assists thought by evoking a visual   5
image, while on the other hand a metaphor which is technically "dead"
(e.g. *iron resolution*) has in effect reverted to being an ordinary word and
can generally be used without loss of vividness. But in between these
two classes there is a huge dump of worn-out metaphors which have lost
all evocative power and are merely used because they save people the
trouble of inventing phrases for themselves. Examples are: *Ring the
changes on, take up the cudgels for, toe the line, ride roughshod over, stand*

shoulder to shoulder with, play into the hands of, no axe to grind, grist to the mill, fishing in troubled waters, on the order of the day, Achilles' heel, swan song, hotbed. Many of these are used without knowledge of their meaning (what is a "rift," for instance?), and incompatible metaphors are frequently mixed, a sure sign that the writer is not interested in what he is saying. Some metaphors now current have been twisted out of their original meaning without those who use them even being aware of the fact. For example, *toe the line* is sometimes written *tow the line*. Another example is *the hammer and the anvil,* now always used with the implication that the anvil gets the worst of it. In real life it is always the anvil that breaks the hammer, never the other way about: a writer who stopped to think what he was saying would be aware of this, and would avoid perverting the original phrase.

OPERATORS OR VERBAL FALSE LIMBS

These save the trouble of picking out appropriate verbs and nouns, and at the same time pad each sentence with extra syllables which give it an appearance of symmetry. Characteristic phrases are: *render inoperative, militate against, make contact with, be subjected to, give rise to, give grounds for, have the effect of, play a leading part (role) in, make itself felt, take effect, exhibit a tendency to, serve the purpose of, etc., etc.* The keynote is the elimination of simple verbs. Instead of being a single word, such as *break, stop, spoil, mend, kill,* a verb becomes a *phrase,* made up of a noun or adjective tacked on to some general-purposes verb such as *prove, serve, form, play, render.* In addition, the passive voice is wherever possible used in preference to the active, and noun constructions are used instead of gerunds (*by examination of* instead of *by examining*). The range of verbs is further cut down by means of the *-ize* and *de-* formation, and the banal statements are given an appearance of profundity by means of the *not un-* formation. Simple conjunctions and prepositions are replaced by such phrases as *with respect to, having regard to, the fact that, by dint of, in view of, in the interests of, on the hypothesis that;* and the ends of sentences are saved from anticlimax by such resounding commonplaces as *greatly to be desired, cannot be left out of account, a development to be expected in the near future, deserving of serious consideration, brought to a satisfactory conclusion,* and so on and so forth.

PRETENTIOUS DICTION

Words like *phenomenon, element, individual* (as noun), *objective, categorical, effective, virtual, basic, primary, promote, constitute, exhibit, exploit, utilize, eliminate, liquidate,* are used to dress up simple statements and give an air of scientific impartiality to biased judgments. Adjectives like *epoch-making, epic, historic, unforgettable, triumphant, age-old, inevitable, inexorable, veritable,* are used to dignify the sordid processes of international politics, while writing that aims at glorifying war usually takes on an archaic colour, its characteristic words being: *realm, throne, chariot, mailed fist, trident, sword, shield, buckler, banner, jackboot, clarion.* Foreign words and expressions such as *cul de sac, ancien régime, deus ex machina, mutatis mutandis, status quo, gleichschaltung, weltanschauung,* are used to give an air of culture and elegance. Except for the useful abbreviations *i.e., e.g.,* and *etc.,* there is no real need for any of the hundreds of foreign phrases now current in English. Bad writers, and especially scientific, political and sociological writers, are nearly always haunted by the notion that Latin or Greek words are grander than Saxon ones, and unnecessary words like *expedite, ameliorate, predict, extraneous, deracinated, clandestine, subaqueous* and hundreds of others constantly gain ground from their Anglo-Saxon opposite numbers.[1] The jargon peculiar to Marxist writing (*hyena, hangman, cannibal, petty bourgeois, these gentry, lacquey, flunkey, mad dog, White Guard,* etc.) consists largely of words and phrases translated from Russian, German or French: but the normal way of coining a new word is to use a Latin or Greek root with the appropriate affix and, where necessary, the *-ize* formation. It is often easier to make up words of this kind (*deregionalize, impermissible, extramarital, nonfragmentatory* and so forth) than to think up the English words that will cover one's meaning. The result, in general, is an increase in slovenliness and vagueness.

MEANINGLESS WORDS

In certain kinds of writing, particularly in art criticism and literary criticism, it is normal to come across long passages which are almost completely lacking in meaning.[2] Words like *romantic, plastic, values, human, dead, sentimental, natural, vitality,* as used in art criticism, are strictly meaningless in the sense that they not only do not point to any discoverable object, but are hardly ever expected to do so by the reader. When one critic writes, "The outstanding feature of Mr. X's work is its living quality," while another writes, "The immediately striking thing about Mr. X's work is its peculiar deadness," the reader accepts this as a simple difference of opinion. If words like *black* and *white* were involved, instead

---

[1]An interesting illustration of this is the way in which the English flower names which were in use till very recently are being ousted by Greek ones, *snapdragon* becoming *antirrhinum, forget-me-not* becoming *myosotis,* etc. It is hard to see any practical reason for this change of fashion: it is probably due to an instinctive turning-away from the more homely word and a vague feeling that the Greek word is scientific.

[2]Example: "Comfort's catholicity of perception and image, strangely Whitmanesque in range, almost the exact opposite in aesthetic compulsion, continues to evoke that trembling atmospheric accumulative hinting at a cruel, an inexorably serene timelessness . . . Wrey Gardiner scores by aiming at simple bull's-eyes with precision. Only they are not so simple, and through this contented sadness runs more than the surface bittersweet of resignation." *(Poetry Quarterly.)*

of the jargon words *dead* and *living,* he would see at once that language was being used in an improper way. Many political words are similarly abused. The word *Fascism* has now no meaning except in so far as it signifies "something not desirable." The words *democracy, socialism, freedom, patriotic, realistic, justice,* have each of them several different meanings which cannot be reconciled with one another. In the case of a word like *democracy,* not only is there no agreed definition, but the attempt to make one is resisted from all sides. It is almost universally felt that when we call a country democratic we are praising it: consequently the defenders of every kind of régime claim that it is a democracy, and fear that they might have to stop using the word if it were tied down to any one meaning. Words of this kind are often used in a consciously dishonest way. That is, the person who uses them has his own private definition, but allows his hearer to think he means something quite different. Statements like *Marshal Pétain was a true patriot, The Soviet Press is the freest in the world, The Catholic Church is opposed to persecution,* are almost always made with intent to deceive. Other words used in variable meanings, in most cases more or less dishonestly, are: *class, totalitarian, science, progressive, reactionary, bourgeois, equality.*

Now that I have made this catalogue of swindles and perversions, let me give another example of the kind of writing that they lead to. This time it must of its nature be an imaginary one. I am going to translate a passage of good English into modern English of the worst sort. Here is a well-known verse from *Ecclesiastes:*

> "I returned and saw under the sun, that the race is not to the swift, nor the battle to the strong, neither yet bread to the wise, nor yet riches to men of understanding, nor yet favour to men of skill; but time and chance happeneth to them all."

Here it is in modern English: 10

> "Objective consideration of contemporary phenomena compels the conclusion that success or failure in competitive activities exhibits no tendency to be commensurate with innate capacity, but that a considerable element of the unpredictable must invariably be taken into account."

This is a parody, but not a very gross one. Exhibit (3), above, for instance, contains several patches of the same kind of English. It will be seen that I have not made a full translation. The beginning and ending of the sentence follow the original meaning fairly closely, but in the middle the concrete illustrations — race, battle, bread — dissolve into the vague phrase "success or failure in competitive activities." This had to be so, because no modern writer of the kind I am discussing — no one capable of using phrases like "objective consideration of contemporary phenomena" — would ever tabulate his thoughts in that precise and detailed way. The whole tendency of modern prose is away from concreteness. Now analyse these two sentences a little more closely. The first contains forty-nine words but only sixty syllables, and all its words are those of everyday life. The second contains thirty-eight words of ninety syllables: eighteen of its words are from Latin roots, and one from Greek. The first sentence contains six vivid images, and only one phrase ("time and chance") that could be called vague. The second contains not a single fresh, arresting phrase, and in spite of its ninety syllables it gives only a shortened version of the meaning contained in the first. Yet without a doubt it is the second kind of sentence that is gaining ground in modern English. I do not want to exaggerate. This kind of writing is not yet universal, and outcrops of simplicity will occur here and there in the worst-written page. Still, if you or I were told to write a few lines on the uncertainty of human fortunes, we should probably come much nearer to my imaginary sentence than to the one from *Ecclesiastes*.

As I have tried to show, modern writing at its worst does not consist in picking out words for the sake of their meaning and inventing images in order to make the meaning clearer. It consists in gumming together long strips of words which have already been set in order by someone else, and making the results presentable by sheer humbug. The attraction of this way of writing is that it is easy. It is easier—even quicker, once you have the habit—to say *In my opinion it is a not unjustifiable assumption that* than to say *I think*. If you use ready-made phrases, you not only don't have to hunt about for words; you also don't have to bother with the rhythms of your sentences, since these phrases are generally so arranged as to be more or less euphonious. When you are composing in a hurry—when you are dictating to a stenographer, for instance, or making a public speech—it is natural to fall into a pretentious, Latinized style. Tags like *a consideration which we should do well to bear in mind* or *a conclusion to which all of us would readily assent* will save many a sentence from coming down with a bump. By using stale metaphors, similes and idioms, you save much mental effort, at the cost of leaving your meaning vague, not only for your reader but for yourself. This is the significance of mixed metaphors. The sole aim of a metaphor is to call up a visual image. When these images clash—as in *The Fascist octopus has sung its swan song, the jackboot is thrown into the melting pot*—it can be taken as certain that the writer is not seeing a mental image of the objects he is naming; in other words he is not really thinking. Look again at the examples I gave at the beginning of this essay. Professor Laski (1) uses five negatives in fifty-three words. One of these is superfluous, making nonsense of the whole passage, and in addition there is the slip *alien* for akin, making further nonsense, and several avoidable pieces of clumsiness which increase the general vagueness. Professor Hogben (2) plays ducks and drakes with a battery which is able to write prescriptions, and, while disapproving of the everyday phrase *put up with,* is unwilling to look *egregious* up in the dictionary and see what it means.

(3), if one takes an uncharitable attitude towards it, is simply meaning-less: probably one could work out its intended meaning by reading the whole of the article in which it occurs. In (4), the writer knows more or less what he wants to say, but an accumulation of stale phrases chokes him like tea leaves blocking a sink. In (5), words and meaning have almost parted company. People who write in this manner usually have a general emotional meaning — they dislike one thing and want to express solidarity with another — but they are not interested in the detail of what they are saying. A scrupulous writer, in every sentence that he writes, will ask himself at least four questions, thus: What am I trying to say? What words will express it? What image or idiom will make it clearer? Is this image fresh enough to have an effect? And he will probably ask himself two more: Could I put it more shortly? Have I said anything that is avoidably ugly? But you are not obliged to go to all this trouble. You can shirk it by simply throwing your mind open and letting the ready-made phrases come crowding in. They will construct your sentences for you — even think your thoughts for you, to a certain extent — and at need they will perform the important service of partially concealing your meaning even from yourself. It is at this point that the special connection between politics and the debasement of language becomes clear.

In our time it is broadly true that political writing is bad writing. Where it is not true, it will generally be found that the writer is some kind of rebel, expressing his private opinions and not a "party line." Orthodoxy, of whatever colour, seems to demand a lifeless, imitative style. The political dialects to be found in pamphlets, leading articles, manifestos, White Papers and the speeches of under-secretaries do, of course, vary from party to party, but they are all alike in that one almost never finds in them a fresh, vivid, home-made turn of speech. When one watches some tired hack on the platform mechanically repeating the familiar phrases — *bestial atrocities, iron heel, bloodstained tyranny, free peoples of the world, stand shoulder to shoulder* — one often has a curious feeling that one is not watching a live human being but some kind of dummy: a feeling which suddenly becomes stronger at moments when the light catches the speaker's spectacles and turns them into blank discs which seem to have no eyes behind them. And this is not altogether fanciful. A speaker who uses that kind of phraseology has gone some distance to-wards turning himself into a machine. The appropriate noises are com-ing out of his larynx, but his brain is not involved as it would be if he were choosing his words for himself. If the speech he is making is one that he is accustomed to make over and over again, he may be almost unconscious of what he is saying, as one is when one utters the responses in church. And this reduced state of consciousness, if not indispensable, is at any rate favourable to political conformity.

In our time, political speech and writing are largely the defence of the indefensible. Things like the continuance of British rule in India, the

Russian purges and deportations, the dropping of the atom bombs on Japan, can indeed be defended, but only by arguments which are too brutal for most people to face, and which do not square with the professed aims of political parties. Thus political language has to consist largely of euphemism, question-begging and sheer cloudy vagueness. Defenceless villages are bombarded from the air, the inhabitants driven out into the countryside, the cattle machine-gunned, the huts set on fire with incendiary bullets: this is called *pacification*. Millions of peasants are robbed of their farms and sent trudging along the roads with no more than they can carry: this is called *transfer of population* or *rectification of frontiers*. People are imprisoned for years without trial, or shot in the back of the neck or sent to die of scurvy in Arctic lumber camps: this is called *elimination of unreliable elements*. Such phraseology is needed if one wants to name things without calling up mental pictures of them. Consider for instance some comfortable English professor defending Russian totalitarianism. He cannot say outright, "I believe in killing off your opponents when you can get good results by doing so." Probably, therefore, he will say something like this:

"While freely conceding that the Soviet régime exhibits certain   15
features which the humanitarian may be inclined to deplore, we must, I think, agree that a certain curtailment of the right to political opposition is an unavoidable concomitant of transitional periods, and that the rigours which the Russian people have been called upon to undergo have been amply justified in the sphere of concrete achievement."

The inflated style is itself a kind of euphemism. A mass of Latin words falls upon the facts like soft snow, blurring the outlines and covering up all the details. The great enemy of clear language is insincerity. When there is a gap between one's real and one's declared aims, one turns as it were instinctively to long words and exhausted idioms, like a cuttlefish squirting out ink. In our age there is no such thing as "keeping out of politics." All issues are political issues, and politics itself is a mass of lies, evasions, folly, hatred and schizophrenia. When the general atmosphere is bad, language must suffer. I should expect to find—this is a guess which I have not sufficient knowledge to verify—that the German, Russian and Italian languages have all deteriorated in the last ten or fifteen years, as a result of dictatorship.

But if thought corrupts language, language can also corrupt thought. A bad usage can spread by tradition and imitation, even among people who should and do know better. The debased language that I have been discussing is in some ways very convenient. Phrases like *a not unjustifiable assumption, leaves much to be desired, would serve no good purpose, a consideration which we should do well to bear in mind,* are a continuous temptation, a packet of aspirins always at one's elbow. Look back through this essay, and for certain you will find that I have again and again committed the very faults I am protesting against. By this morning's post I have received a pamphlet dealing with conditions in Germany. The author tells me that he "felt impelled" to write it. I open it at random, and here is almost the first sentence that I see: "(The Allies) have an opportunity not only of achieving a radical transformation of Germany's social and political structure in such a way as to avoid a nationalistic reaction in Germany itself, but at the same time of laying the foundations of a co-operative and unified Europe." You see, he "feels impelled" to write — feels, presumably, that he has something new to say — and yet his words, like cavalry horses answering the bugle, group themselves automatically into the familiar dreary pattern. This invasion of one's mind by ready-made phrases *(lay the foundations, achieve a radical transformation)* can only be prevented if one is constantly on guard against them, and every such phrase anaesthetizes a portion of one's brain.

I said earlier that the decadence of our language is probably curable. Those who deny this would argue, if they produced an argument at all, that language merely reflects existing social conditions, and that we cannot influence its development by any direct tinkering with words and constructions. So far as the general tone or spirit of a language goes, this may be true, but it is not true in detail. Silly words and expressions have often disappeared, not through any evolutionary process but owing to the conscious action of a minority. Two recent examples were *explore every avenue* and *leave no stone unturned,* which were killed by the jeers of a few journalists. There is a long list of flyblown metaphors which could similarly be got rid of if enough people would interest themselves in the job; and it should also be possible to laugh the *not un-* formation out of existence,[1] to reduce the amount of Latin and Greek in the average sentence, to drive out foreign phrases and strayed scientific words, and, in general, to make pretentiousness unfashionable. But all these are minor points. The defence of the English language implies more than this, and perhaps it is best to start by saying what it does *not* imply.

To begin with it has nothing to do with archaism, with the salvaging of obsolete words and turns of speech, or with the setting up of a "standard English" which must never be departed from. On the contrary, it is especially concerned with the scrapping of every word or idiom which has outworn its usefulness. It has nothing to do with correct grammar and syntax, which are of no importance so long as one makes one's meaning clear, or with the avoidance of Americanisms, or with having what is called a "good prose style." On the other hand it is not concerned with fake simplicity and the attempt to make written English colloquial. Nor does it even imply in every case preferring the Saxon word to the Latin one, though it does imply using the fewest and

---

[1]One can cure oneself of the *not un-* formation by memorizing this sentence: A not unblack dog was chasing a not unsmall rabbit across a not ungreen field.

shortest words that will cover one's meaning. What is above all needed is to let the meaning choose the word, and not the other way about. In prose, the worst thing one can do with words is to surrender to them. When you think of a concrete object, you think wordlessly, and then, if you want to describe the thing you have been visualizing you probably hunt about till you find the exact words that seem to fit. When you think of something abstract you are more inclined to use words from the start, and unless you make a conscious effort to prevent it, the existing dialect will come rushing in and do the job for you, at the expense of blurring or even changing your meaning. Probably it is better to put off using words as long as possible and get one's meaning as clear as one can through pictures or sensations. Afterwards one can choose — not simply *accept* — the phrases that will best cover the meaning, and then switch round and decide what impression one's words are likely to make on another person. This last effort of the mind cuts out all stale or mixed images, all prefabricated phrases, needless repetitions, and humbug and vagueness generally. But one can often be in doubt about the effect of a word or a phrase, and one needs rules that one can rely on when instinct fails. I think the following rules will cover most cases:

(i)   Never use a metaphor, simile or other figure of speech which you are used to seeing in print.
(ii) Never use a long word where a short one will do.
(iii) If it is possible to cut a word out, always cut it out.
(iv) Never use the passive where you can use the active.
(v)   Never use a foreign phrase, a scientific word or a jargon word if you can think of an everyday English equivalent.
(vi) Break any of these rules sooner than say anything outright barbarous.

These rules sound elementary, and so they are, but they demand a deep change of attitude in anyone who has grown used to writing in the style now fashionable. One could keep all of them and still write bad English, but one could not write the kind of stuff that I quoted in those five specimens at the beginning of this article.

I have not here been considering the literary use of language, but   *20* merely language as an instrument for expressing and not for concealing or preventing thought. Stuart Chase and others have come near to claiming that all abstract words are meaningless, and have used this as a pretext for advocating a kind of political quietism. Since you don't know what Fascism is, how can you struggle against Fascism? One need not swallow such absurdities as this, but one ought to recognize that the present political chaos is connected with the decay of language, and that one can probably bring about some improvement by starting at the verbal end. If you simplify your English, you are freed from the worst follies of orthodoxy. You cannot speak any of the necessary dialects, and when you make a stupid remark its stupidity will be obvious, even to yourself. Political language — and with variations this is true of all political parties, from Conservatives to Anarchists — is designed to make lies sound truthful and murder respectable, and to give an appearance of solidity to pure wind. One cannot change this all in a moment, but one can at least change one's own habits, and from time to time one can even, if one jeers loudly enough, send some worn-out and useless phrase — some *jackboot, Achilles' heel, hotbed, melting pot, acid test, veritable inferno* or other lump of verbal refuse — into the dustbin where it belongs.

FOR DISCUSSION AND WRITING

1. Regarding the principle of quantity: At any points in this essay, does Orwell fail to give you enough information? Does he ever give you more than necessary? (Be specific in your answers.)

2. Regarding the principle of quality: What reasons do you have for trusting (or distrusting) Orwell's knowledge of his subject or his honesty? (Remember that Orwell is one of the most respected writers in English.)

3. Regarding the principle of manner: If you think the essay is sometimes unclear, indicate where, and explain the difficulty.

4. Regarding the principle of relation: Are any parts of the essay irrelevant to the topic? Explain.

5. In the second paragraph of the essay, Orwell explains his view of the decline of English. What specifically does he do to help the reader understand his point?

6. Use the terms of the writer-reader contract to explain the point of paragraph 4, beginning, "Each of these passages has faults of its own."

7. Use the terms of the writer-reader contract to explain why you agree or disagree with each of the six rules that Orwell sets forth in paragraph 19.

8. What is Orwell's purpose in "Politics and the English Language"? Is he trying to persuade, explain, amuse, horrify, convince?

9. Reread the quotation from Ecclesiastes and Orwell's corruption thereof. Which version is more difficult to understand? To answer this question, ask yourself, Are there words whose definitions I don't know? Are there greater gaps to be filled in one version or the other?

10. Does the fact that the essay was written four decades ago in a foreign country (the United Kingdom) make the piece less relevant today? Explain. Are the examples that Orwell cites less relevant today?

11. State the main point of the selection.

12. Explain why Finegan would disagree with Orwell's first sentence. What is your own opinion?

13. In what ways do Orwell and Simon agree in their attitudes toward language?

14. Give examples of overused dying metaphors.

15. Give examples of language usages that annoy you. For example, many find the repeated use of "ya know" in conversation to be objectionable.

16. Is Orwell's argument merely one of aesthetics? Explain.

17. Explain how politics enters into Orwell's discussion.

18. Orwell says that political speeches often "mechanically repeat familiar phrases" (par. 13). Might politicians have valid reasons for repeating familiar phrases over and over again? Explain.

THE COUNTRY OF THE MIND

Barry Lopez

In the poem "Desert Places," Robert Frost writes,

> Snow falling and night falling fast, oh, fast
> In a field I looked into going past,
> And the ground almost covered smooth in snow,
> But a few weeds and stubble showing last.
>
> The woods around it have it — it is theirs.
> All animals are smothered in their lairs.
> I am too absent-spirited to count;
> The loneliness includes me unawares.
>
> And lonely as it is that loneliness
> Will be more lonely ere it will be less —
> A blanker whiteness of benighted snow
> With no expression, nothing to express.
>
> They cannot scare me with their empty spaces
> Between stars — on stars where no human race is.
> I have it in me so much nearer home
> To scare myself with my own desert places.

As you read the three selections that follow ("The Country of the Mind," by Barry Lopez; a journal entry from *The Snow Leopard,* by Peter Matthiessen; and "The Angry Winter," by Loren Eiseley), ask yourself how this poem relates to them. In what ways are the selections "poetic" even though they are written in prose? In the poem, snowy fields become symbols of the poet's "own desert places." What are the symbolic values of the scenes in the four selections? Frost obviously chooses language that not only conveys the plain sense of his message but also displays beauty of sound and imagery. Do Lopez, Matthiessen, and Eiseley also use language in these "poetic" ways?

The success of "Desert Places" is not based on the information it provides about winter in the country. If the poem is not especially informative in the practical sense, what is it that gives the poem its merit? Do the three prose selections succeed in some of the same ways?

As I step out of our small cabin on Pingok Island, the undistinguished plain of tundra spreads before me to the south and east. A few glaucous gulls rise from the ground and drop back, and I feel the cold, damp air, like air from a refrigerator, against my cheeks. A few yards from the door, stark and alone on the tundra, a female common eider lies dead. A few more yards to the west, a bearded-seal skin has been expertly stretched between short wooden stakes to dry. A few yards beyond, a northern phalarope spins wildly on the surface of a freshwater pond, feeding on zooplankton.

A southwest wind has been blowing for two days; it's the reason we are ashore today. The sky threatens squalls and snow. I head south across the tundra toward the lagoon, wondering if I will find ducks there. In my mind is a vague plan: to go there, then east along the coast to a place where the tundra is better drained, easier walking, then back across the island, and to come home along the seaward coast.

In such flat terrain as this, even with the lowering skies, I brood on the vastness of the region. The vastness is deceptive, however. The journals of arctic explorers are full of examples of messages stashed out there with a high expectation of their discovery, because the prominent places in such a featureless landscape are so obvious. They are the places a human eye notices right away. And there is something, too, about the way the landscape funnels human movement, such that encounters with strangers are half expected, as is the case in a desert crossing. Human beings are so few here and their errands such a part of the odd undercurrent of knowledge that flows in a remote region that you half expect, too, to know of the stranger. Once, camped on the upper Yukon, I saw a man in a distant canoe. When he raised his field glasses to look at a cliff where peregrine falcons were nesting, I surmised who he was (a biological consultant working on a peregrine census) from a remark I had overheard a week before in a small restaurant in Fairbanks. He probably knew of my business there, too. Some of the strangeness went out of the country in that moment.

If the mind releases its fiduciary grip on time, does not dole it out in a fretful way like a valued commodity but regards it as undifferentiated, like the flatness of the landscape, it is possible to transcend distance — to travel very far without anxiety, to not be defeated by the great reach of the land. If one is dressed well and carrying a little food, and has the means to secure more food and to construct shelter, the mind is that much more free to work with the senses in an appreciation of the country. The unappealing tundra plain, I recall, is to its denizens a storehouse of food and instant tools.

As I thread my way southwest, along the margins of frost polygons, I am aware of the movement of birds. A distant speck moves across the sky with a loon's trajectory. A Savannah sparrow flits away over the ground. The birds come and go — out to sea to feed or to the lagoon to rest — on a seemingly regular schedule. Scientists say the pattern of coming and going, of feeding and resting, repeats itself every twenty-four hours. But a description of it becomes more jagged and complex than the experience, like any parsing of a movement in time.

The sound of my footfall changes as I step from damp ground to wet, from wet to dry. Microhabitats. I turn the pages of a mental index to arctic plants and try to remember which are the ones to distinguish these borders: which plants separate at a glance mesic tundra from hydric, hydric from xeric? I do not remember. Such generalities, in any case, would only founder on the particulars at my feet. One is better off with a precise and local knowledge, and a wariness of borders. These small habitats, like the larger landscapes, merge imperceptibly with each other. Another, remembered landscape makes this one seem familiar; and the habits of an animal in one region provoke speculation about behavior among its relatives in another region. But no country, finally, is just like another. The generalities are abstractions. And the lines on our topographic maps reveal not only the scale at which we are discerning, but our tolerance for discrepancies in nature.

A tundra botanist once described to me her patient disassembly of a cluster of plants on a tussock, a tundra mound about 18 inches high and a foot or so across. She separated live from dead plant tissue and noted the number and kind of the many species of plants. She examined the insects and husks of berries, down to bits of things nearly too slight to see or to hold without crushing. The process took hours, and her concentration and sense of passing time became fixed at that scale. She said she remembered looking up at one point, at the tundra that rolled away in a hundred thousand tussocks toward the horizon, and that she could not return her gaze because of that sight, not for long minutes.

My route across Pingok seems rich, but I am aware that I miss much of what I pass, for lack of acuity in my senses, lack of discrimination, and my general unfamiliarity. If I knew the indigenous human language, it would help greatly. A local language discriminates among the local phenomena, and it serves to pry the landscape loose from its anonymity.

I know how much I miss—I have only to remember the faces of the Eskimos I've traveled with, the constant flicker of their eyes over the countryside. Even inside their houses men prefer to talk while sitting by a window. They are always looking away at the land or looking up to the sky, the coming weather. As I near the lagoon, pondering the identity of something I saw a flock of ptarmigan eating, I smile wryly at a memory: it was once thought that scurvy was induced in the Arctic by the bleakness of its coasts.

There are no ducks nearby in the lagoon. With my field glasses I can just make out the dark line of their rafts on the far side of the water, a lee shore. I settle myself in a crease in the tundra, out of the wind, arrange my clothing so nothing binds, and begin to study the far shore with the binoculars. After ten or fifteen minutes I have found two caribou. Stefansson was once asked by an Eskimo to whom he was showing a pair of binoculars for the first time whether he could "see into tomorrow" with them. Stefansson took the question literally and was amused. What the *inuk* probably meant was, Are those things powerful enough to see something that will not reach you for another day, like migrating caribou? Or a part of the landscape suitable for a campsite, which you yourself will not reach for another day? Some Eskimo hunters have

10

astounding natural vision; they can point out caribou grazing on a slope three or four miles away. But the meticulous inspection of the land that is the mark of a good hunter becomes most evident when he uses a pair of field glasses. Long after the most inquiring nonnative has grown weary of glassing the land for some clue to the movement of animals, a hunter is still scouring its edges and interstices. He may take an hour to glass 360° of the apparently silent tundra, one section at a time.

You can learn to do this; and such scrutiny always turns up a ground squirrel, an itinerant wolverine, a nesting bird — something that tells you where you are and what's going on. And when you fall into the habit, find some way like this to shed your impatience, you feel less conspicuous in the land.

I walk a long ways down the beach before arriving at the place where the tundra dries out, and turn inland. Halfway across I find the skull of a goose, as seemingly random in this landscape as the dead eider in the grass by the cabin. A more thoughtful inquirer, someone dependent upon these bits of information in a way that I am not, would find out why. To the southwest I can see a snow squall — I want to reach the seaward side of the island before it arrives, in case there is something worse behind it. The shoreline is my way home. I put the paper-thin skull back on the ground. Far to the east I see a dilapidated spire of driftwood, a marker erected in 1910 by Ernest Leffingwell when he was mapping these coasts. Leaning slightly askew, it has the aspect of an abandoned building, derelict and wind-punished. It is a monument to the desire to control vastness. It is a referent for the metes and bounds that permit a proper division and registry of the countryside, an assignment of ownership.

I move the glasses off Leffingwell's tower. On the ridge of sand dune along the beach to the north I spot an arctic fox. A great traveler in winter, like the polar bear and the wolf. In summer, when water intervenes in the fox's coastal habitat, he may stay in one place — an island like this, for example. The fox always seems to be hurrying somewhere, then stopping suddenly to sit down and rest. He runs up on slight elevations and taps the air all over with his nose.

The arctic fox's fur runs to shades of brown in summer, which blend with ivory whites on its underparts. (In winter the coat is gleaming white or a grayish blue to pale beige, which is called "blue.") As with any animal, the facets of its life are complexly engaging. The extent and orderliness of its winter caches and its ability to withstand very cold weather are striking. Also its tag-along relationship with the polar bear. It is the friendliest and most trusting of the North American foxes, although it is characterized in many expedition journals as "impudent," derided for its "persistent cheekiness," and disparaged as a "parasite" and a scavenger. Arctic foxes are energetic and persistent in their search for food. They thoroughly scour the coastlines over which they travel and, like polar bears, will gather from miles around at a source of carrion. If it's a cook tent they choose instead, and thirty or forty of them are racing around, tearing furiously into everything, an expedition's initial sense of amusement can easily turn sour or violent. Arctic foxes so pestered Vitus Bering's shipwrecked second Kamchatka expedition that the men tortured and killed the ones they caught with the unrestrained savagery one would expect of men driven insane by hordes of insects.

In his encounter with modern man in the Arctic, then, the fox's efficient way of life has sometimes gone fatally against him. (His dealings with modern Eskimos have fit more perfectly, though also fatally, with human enterprise. Once largely ignored, he became the most relentlessly pursued fur-bearer in the Arctic with the coming of the fur trade and the advent of the village trading post.) 15

I watch the fox now, traveling the ridge of the sand dune, the kinetic blur of its short legs. I have seen its (or another's) tracks at several places along the beach. I think of it traveling continuously over the island, catching a lemming here, finding part of a seal there, looking for a bird less formidable than a glaucous gull to challenge for its eggs. I envision the network of its trails as though it were a skein of dark lines over the island, anchored at slight elevations apparent to the eye at a distance because of their dense, rich greens or clusters of wildflowers.

Because the fox is built so much closer to the ground and is overall so much smaller than a human being, the island must be "longer" in its mind than four and a half miles. And traveling as it does, trotting and then resting, trotting and then resting, and "seeing" so much with its black nose — what is Pingok like for it? I wonder how any animal's understanding of the island changes over the year; and the difference in its shape to a gyrfalcon, a wolf spider, or a bowhead echolocating along its seashore. What is the island to the loon, who lives on the water and in the air, stepping awkwardly ashore only at a concealed spot at the edge of a pond, where it nests? What of the bumblebee, which spends its evening deep in the corolla of a summer flower that makes its world 8°F warmer? What is the surface of the land like for a creature as small but as adroit as the short-tailed weasel? And how does the recollection of such space guide great travelers like the caribou and the polar bear on their journeys?

A friend working one summer near Polar Bear Pass on Bathurst Island once spotted a wolf running off with a duck in its mouth. He saw the wolf bury the duck, and when the wolf left he made for the cache. He couldn't find it. It was open, uncomplicated country. He retraced his steps, again took his bearings, and tried a second time. A third time. He never found it. The wolf, he thought, must have a keener or at least a different way of holding that space in its mind and remembering the approach. The land appeared to him more complicated.

One day, out on the sea ice, I left the protection of a temporary building and followed a bundle of electric cables out into a blizzard. The winds were gusting to 40 knots; it was −20°F. I stood for a long time with my back to the storm, peering downwind into the weak January light, fearful of being bowled over, of losing touch with the umbilical under which I had hooked a boot. Both its ends faded away in that swirling whiteness. In the 40-foot circle of visibility around me I could see only ice hummocks. I wondered what notions of "direction" a fox would have standing here, how the imperatives for food and shelter would affect us differently.

One can only speculate about how animals organize land into meaningful expanses for themselves. The worlds they perceive, their *Umwelten,** are all different. The discovery of an animal's *Umwelt* and its elucidation require great patience and experimental ingenuity, a free exchange of information among different observers, hours of direct observation, and a reluctance to summarize the animal. This, in my experience, is the Eskimo hunter's methodology. Under ideal circumstances it can also be the methodology of Western science.† 20

Many Western biologists appreciate the mystery inherent in the animals they observe. They comprehend that, objectively, what they are watching is deceptively complex and, subjectively, that the animals themselves have nonhuman ways of life. They know that while experiments can be designed to reveal aspects of the animal, the animal itself will always remain larger than the sum of any set of experiments. They know they can be very precise about what they do, but that that does not guarantee they will be accurate. They know the behavior of an individual animal may differ strikingly from the generally recognized behavior of its species; and that the same species may behave quite differently from place to place, from year to year.

It is very hard to achieve a relatively complete and accurate view of

---

*The world we perceive around an animal is its *environment;* what it sees is its *Umwelt,* or self-world. A specific environment contains many *Umwelten,* no two of which are the same. The concept, developed by Jakob von Uexküll in 1934, assumes that the structure of the organs of perception, the emphasis each receives, the level of their sensitivity, and the ability of each to discriminate, are different in all animals.

†In practice, the two methodologies usually differ. The Eskimo's methods are less formal than those of the scientist, but not necessarily less rigorous. By comparison, Western scientists often fall far short on hours of observation; and they usually select only a few aspects of an animal's life to study closely. The Eskimo's ecological approach, however, his more broad-based consideration of an animal's interaction with many, some seemingly insignificant, aspects of its environment, increasingly becoming a Western approach. Western science is better informed about the life history of migratory animals, especially distribution and movement. Eskimos, on the other hand, show a marked reluctance to extrapolate from the individual to include all other animals of that type, as Western scientists do. In recent years some scientists have come to learn more than many Eskimos about specific animals. The last generation of highly informed, broadly experienced native hunters is passing away.

an animal's life, especially in the Arctic, where field conditions present so many problems, limiting observation. Many biologists studying caribou, muskoxen, wolves, and polar bear in the North are more distressed by this situation than they otherwise might be. Industry, which pays much of the bill for this arctic research, is less interested in the entire animal than it is in those aspects of its life that might complicate or hinder development—or to be fair, how in some instances industry might disrupt the animal's way of life. What bothers biologists is the narrowness of the approach, the haste with which the research must be conducted, and, increasingly, the turning of an animal's life into numbers. The impersonality of statistics masks both the complexity and the ethics inherent in any wildlife situation. Biologists are anxious about "the tyranny of statistics" and "the ascendency of the [computer] modeler," about industry's desire for a "standardized animal," one that always behaves in predictable ways.

A Canadian scientist told me, "I hate as a biologist having to reduce the behavior of animals to numbers. I hate it. But if we are going to stand our ground against [head-long development] we must produce numbers, because that's all they will listen to. I am spending my whole *life* to answer these questions—they want an answer in two months. And anything a native says about animals, well, that counts for nothing with them. Useless anecdotes."

A belief in the authority of statistics and the dismissal of Eskimo narratives as only "anecdotal" is a dichotomy one encounters frequently in arctic environmental assessment reports. Statistics, of course, can be manipulated—a whale biologist once said to me, "If you punish the data enough, it will tell you anything." And the *Umwelt* of a statistician, certainly, plays a role in developing the "statistical picture" of a landscape. The Eskimos' stories are politely dismissed not because Eskimos are not good observers or because they lie, but because the narratives cannot be reduced to a form that is easy to handle or lends itself to summary. Their words are too hard to turn into numbers.

What the uninitiated scientist in the Arctic lacks is not ideas about how the land works, or a broad theoretical knowledge of how the larger pieces fit together, but time in the field, prolonged contact with the specific sources of an understanding. Several Western scientists, including anthropologist Richard Nelson, marine mammal biologists John Burns, Francis Fay, and Kerry Finley, and terrestrial mammal biologist Robert Stephenson, have sought out Eskimo hunters as field companions in order to get a better understanding of arctic ecology. Nelson, who arrived in Wainwright in the early 1960s quite skeptical about the kinds of animal behavior the hunters had described to him, wrote a line any one of the others might have written after a year of traveling through the country with these people: "[Their] statements which seem utterly incredible at first almost always turn out to be correct."

I walk on toward the dune where the fox has disappeared. The inconspicuous plants beneath my feet, I realize, efficiently harbor minerals and nutrients and water in these acidic, poorly drained soils. They are compact; they distribute the weight of snow, of passing caribou and myself, so it does not crush them. The stems of these willows are shorter than those of their southern counterparts, with many more leaves to take advantage of the light. It may take years for a single plant to produce a seed crop. What do these plants murmur in their dreams, what of warning and desire passes between them?

It is beginning to snow a little, on a slant from the southeast. I walk on, my eye to the ground, out to the horizon, back to the ground. And what did Columbus, sailing for Zaiton, the great port of Cathay, think of the reach of the western Atlantic? How did Coronado assess the Staked Plain of Texas, the rawest space he ever knew, on his way to Quivera? Or Mungo Park the landscape of Africa in search of the Niger? What one thinks of any region, while traveling through, is the result of at least three things: what one knows, what one imagines, and how one is disposed.

What one knows is either gathered firsthand or learned from books or indigenous observers. This information, however, is assembled differently by each individual, according to his cultural predispositions and his personality. A Western traveler in the Arctic, for example, is inclined to look (only) for cause-and-effect relationships, or predator-prey relationships; and to be (especially) alert for plants and animals that might fill "gaps" in Western taxonomies. Human beings, further, are inclined to favor visual information over the testimony of their other senses when learning an area, and to be more drawn to animals that approximate their own scale. Our view is from a certain height above the ground. In any new country we want panoramas.

What one imagines in a new landscape consists of conjecture, for example, about what might lie beyond that near horizon of small hills, or the far line of the horizon. Often it consists of what one "hopes to see" during the trip — perhaps a barren-ground grizzly standing up on the tundra, or the tusk of a mammoth in the alluvial silt of a creek. These expectations are based on a knowledge of what has happened in this land for others. At a deeper level, however, imagination represents the desire to find what is unknown, unique, or farfetched — a snowy owl sitting motionless on the hips of a muskox, a flower of a favorite color never before reported, tundra swans swimming in a winter polynya.°

Imagination also poses the questions that give a new land dimension   30
in time. Are these wolverine tracks from *this* summer or the summer before? How old is this orange lichen? Will the caribou feeding placidly in this swale be discovered by those wolves traveling in the distance? Why did the people camped here leave this piece of carved seal bone behind?

polyna: An area of open water in the frozen sea.

The way we are disposed toward the land is more nebulous, harder to define. The reluctant traveler, brooding about events at home, is oblivious to the landscape. And no one is quite as alert as an indigenous hunter who is hungry. If one feels longing or compassion at the sight of something beautiful, or great excitement over some unexpected event, these may effect an optimistic disposition toward the land. If one has lost a friend in the Arctic to exposure after an airplane crash, or gone broke speculating in a northern mine, one might regard the land as antagonistic and be ill-disposed to recognize any value in it.

The individual desire to understand, as much as any difference in acuity of the senses, brings each of us to find something in the land others did not notice.

Over time, small bits of knowledge about a region accumulate among local residents in the form of stories. These are remembered in the community; even what is unusual does not become lost and therefore irrelevant. These narratives comprise for a native an intricate, long-term view of a particular landscape. And the stories are corroborated daily, even as they are being refined upon by members of the community traveling between what is truly known and what is only imagined or unsuspected. Outside the region this complex but easily shared "reality" is hard to get across without reducing it to generalities, to misleading or imprecise abstraction.

The perceptions of any people wash over the land like a flood, leaving ideas hung up in the brush, like pieces of damp paper to be collected and deciphered. No one can tell the whole story.

I must set my face to the wind to head west, back toward the cabin. *35* I drop down to the seaward beach where I will have the protection of the dune. Oldsquaw and eider ducks ride the ocean swell close to shore in the lee of the storm, their beaks into the wind. Between gaps in the dune I catch glimpses of the dark tundra, swept by wind and snow. My thoughts leap ahead to the cabin, to something warm to drink, and then return. I watch the ducks as I walk. Watching animals always slows you down. I think of the months explorers spent locked up in the ice here, some of them trapped in their ships for three or four years. Their prospects for an early departure were never good, but, their journals reveal, they rarely remarked on the animals that came around, beyond their potential as food, as threats or nuisances. These were men far from home, who felt helpless; the landscape hardly registered as they waited, except as an obstacle. Our inattentiveness is of a different order. We insist on living today in much shorter spans of time. We become exasperated when the lives of animals unfold in ways inconvenient to our schedules — when they sit and do "nothing." I search both the featureless tundra to my left and the raft of brown sea ducks to my right for something untoward, something that stands out. Nothing. After hours of walking, the tundra and the ducks recede into the storm, and my mind pulls far back into its own light.

A Lakota woman named Elaine Jahner once wrote that what lies at the heart of the religion of hunting peoples is the notion that a spiritual landscape exists within the physical landscape. To put it another way, occasionally one sees something fleeting in the land, a moment when line, color, and movement intensify and something sacred is revealed, leading one to believe that there is another realm of reality corresponding to the physical one but different.

In the face of a rational, scientific approach to the land, which is more widely sanctioned, esoteric insights and speculations are frequently overshadowed, and what is lost is profound. The land is like poetry: it is inexplicably coherent, it is transcendent in its meaning, and it has the power to elevate a consideration of human life.

The cabin emerges silently up ahead in the flowing snow as the storm closes in. It seems to rest within a white cave or at the far end of a canyon. Sound only comes now from what is immediately around me. The distant voices of birds are gone. I hear the gritty step of my boots in the sand. Splash of wavelets on the beach. Wind rushing over the cones of my ears.

Through a window yellow with light I see a friend at a table, whipping the end of a boat line with waxed thread. I will have hot tea and lie in my bunk, and try to recall what I saw that did not, in those moments, come to mind.

In the 1930s a man named Benjamin Lee Whorf began to clarify an 40 insight he had had into the structure of the Hopi language. Hopi has only limited tenses, noted Whorf, makes no reference to time as an entity distinct from space, and, though relatively poor in nouns, is rich in verbs. It is a language that projects a world of movement and changing relationships, a continuous "fabric" of time and space. It is better suited than the English language to describing quantum mechanics. English divides time into linear segments by making use of many tenses. It is a noun-rich, verb-poor tongue that contrasts fixed space with a flow of time. It is a language of static space, more suited, say, to architectural description. All else being equal, a Hopi child would have little difficulty comprehending the theory of relativity in his own language, while an American child could more easily master history. A Hopi would be confounded by the idea that time flowed from the past into the present.

In 1936 Whorf wrote that many aboriginal languages "abound in finely wrought, beautifully logical discriminations about causation, action, result, dynamic and energetic quality, directness of experience, etc. . . ." He made people see that there were no primitive languages; and that there was no pool of thought from which all cultures drew their metaphysics. "All observers," he cautioned, "are not led by the same physical evidence to the same picture of the universe."

These ideas were anticipated to some extent by the anthropologist Franz Boas, who emphasized the individual integrity of different aboriginal cultures. His was a reaction against the predominant Victorian view that considered all cultures reducible to a set of "true" observations about the world. (Boas's "functionalist" approach has since been replaced by a "structuralist" view, which knowingly imposes abstract and subjective patterns on a culture.)

Whorf, Boas, and others in this tradition urged people after the turn of the century to see human culture as a mechanism for ordering reality. These realities were separate, though they might be simultaneously projected onto the same landscape. And there was no ultimate reality — any culture that would judge the perceptions of another, particularly one outside its own traditions, should proceed cautiously.

In recent years the writing of people like Joseph Campbell and Claude Lévi-Strauss has illuminated the great panorama of human perceptual experience, pointing up not only the different approaches we take to the background that contains us (the landscape) but the similarities we seem to share. For hunting peoples, for example, says Lévi-Strauss, an animal is held in high totemic regard not merely because it is food and therefore good to eat but because it is "good to think." The animal is "good to imagine."

In the Arctic, researchers such as Richard Nelson, Edmund Carpenter, and Hugh Brody, each addressing a different aspect of Eskimo existence, have reiterated these themes in studying the land. Their work has made clear the integrity and coherence of a different vision of the Arctic; misunderstandings that arise when a view of reality similar to our own is assumed to exist; and the ways in which the Eskimo's view of the land presents us with growing ethical, political, and economic problems, because we would prefer that ours was the mind of record in that landscape.

I have already referred to Nelson's work on natural history and hunting. Brody has been influential in the development of land-use-and-occupancy studies. Carpenter has written cogently on Eskimo art and Eskimo perceptions of space. Not surprisingly, each has emphasized that a knowledge of the language, the pertinent regional dialect, is critical to an understanding of what Eskimos are talking about when they talk about the land. Says Nelson, an understanding of the behavior of sea ice off the coast at Wainwright, where the ice is very active, is "difficult to acquire, especially without a full understanding" of Eskimo terminology. Brody, discussing Eskimo concepts of intimacy with the land, says, flatly, "The key terms are not translatable."

Carpenter discerns a correspondence between the Inuktitut language and Eskimo carving: the emphasis in both is on what is dynamic, and on observations made from a variety of viewpoints. In our language, says Carpenter, we lavish attention on concepts of time; Eskimos give their attention to varieties of space. We assume all human beings are oriented similarly in space and therefore regard objects from the same point of view — the top is the top, the bottom the bottom; that direction

45

is north and this south. In describing a distant place, however, says Carpenter, an Eskimo will often make no reference to the mass of the land in between (which would impress us, and which we would describe in terms of distance), but only to geographical points, and not necessarily as seen from the point of one's approach. Thus, to a non-Eskimo observer, the Eskimo might seem to have "no sense of direction." And because he travels somewhat like the arctic fox — turning aside to investigate something unusual, or moving ahead in a series of steps punctuated by short stops for tea, instead of in a straight, relentless dash for a "goal" — the Eskimo might be thought poorly self-disciplined or improvident. But it would only have to do with how the Eskimo saw himself in the fabric of space and time, how he conceived of "proceeding" through the world, where he placed lines or points in the stream of duration.

The Eskimo's different but still sophisticated mind is largely inaccessible without recourse to his language. And, of course, it works the other way around. Each for the other is a kind of primitive.

The Eskimo language reaches its apogee in describing the land and man's activity in it. Young people in modern Eskimo villages, especially in the eastern Arctic, say that when they are out on the land with their parents, they find it much more difficult to speak Inuktitut, though they speak it at home all the time. It is not so much a lack of vocabulary as a difficulty with constructions, with idioms, a lost fluency that confuses them. It is out on the land, in the hunting camps and traveling over the ice, that the language comes alive.* The Eskimo language is seasonal — terms for the many varieties of snow emerge in winter, while those for whaling come into use in the spring. Whole areas of the language are starting to disappear because they refer to activities no longer much practiced, like traveling with dogs; or to the many different parts of an animal like the walrus that are no longer either eaten or used; or to activities that are discouraged, such as the intercession of shamans.

For Whorf, language was something man created in his mind and   50
projected onto reality, something he imposed on the landscape, as though the land were a receptacle for his imagination. I think there are possibly two things wrong with this thought. First, the landscape is not inert; and it is precisely because it is alive that it eventually contradicts the imposition of a reality that does not derive from it. Second, language is not something man imposes on the land. It evolves in his conversation with the land — in testing the sea ice with the toe of a *kamik,* in the eating of a wild berry, in repairing a sled by the light of a seal-oil lamp. A long-

---

*So do some people. It is relatively common in the Arctic to meet a person in a village who seems clumsy, irresponsible, lethargic, barely capable of taking care of himself — and then to find the same person in the bush astoundingly skilled, energetic, and perspicacious.

lived inquiry produces a discriminating language. The very order of the language, the ecology of its sounds and thoughts, derives from the mind's intercourse with the landscape. To learn the indigenous language, then, is to know what the speakers of the language have made of the land.

FOR DISCUSSION AND WRITING

1. Regarding the principle of quantity: At any points in this essay, does Lopez fail to give you enough information? Does he ever give you more than necessary? (Be specific in your answers.)

2. Regarding the principle of quality: What reasons do you have for trusting (or distrusting) Lopez's knowledge of his subject or his honesty? Does the discussion that precedes this selection relate to this question?

3. Regarding the principles of manner: If you think the essay is sometimes unclear, indicate where, and explain the difficulty.

4. Regarding the principle of relation: Are any parts of the essay irrelevant to the topic? Explain. For example, what is the relevance of the long passage regarding the arctic fox?

5. What sorts of readers do you think Lopez has in mind? (Their levels of education? Their socioeconomic status? Their interests?) Explain your answer.

6. Which details in the selection did you find particularly vivid? In what ways do these details contribute to the meaning and effect of the piece?

7. What is the main point of "The Country of the Mind"?

8. What is the most prominent theme of the selection?

9. In your own words, explain Lopez's critique of modern science. (It starts with paragraph 20.)

10. In paragraph 40, Lopez begins a discussion of language. What would Edward Finegan and George Orwell say about his ideas?

11. Lopez writes, "All else being equal, a Hopi child would have little difficulty comprehending the theory of relativity in his own language, while an American child could more easily master history" (par. 40). When we asked Edward Finegan about this statement, he replied, "What was Einstein's native language?" Explain what Finegan meant by his response.

NOVEMBER 6

Peter Matthiessen

Even though Peter Matthiessen was born in New York City (in 1927), much of his writing is set in natural environs far from civilization. His nonfiction works include *Under the Mountain Wall* (an account of the Kurelu tribe of New Guinea), *The Cloud Forest* (about the flora and fauna of South America), *Blue Meridian* (about the great white shark), and, most recently, *African Silences* (a study of the endangered wildlife of Africa). The following selection is from *The Snow Leopard,* Matthiessen's journal of a Himalayan expedition.

Matthiessen wrote the first of his many novels, *Race Rock* (1954), in Paris, where he also co-founded the prestigious *Paris Review* with Harold Humes. *Paris Review* has been instrumental in establishing the reputations of several important authors, among them William Styron, George Plimpton, and James Baldwin. He even spent 1967 on a turtle boat in the Cayman Islands, researching his novel *Far Tortuga* (1975). The author is also a devout follower of Zen, and his combination of inner and outer explorations within a seamless whole, expressed so eloquently in this selection, is part of his genius as a writer.

The nights at Shey are rigid, under rigid stars; the fall of a wolf pad on the frozen path might be heard up and down the canyon. But a hard wind comes before the dawn to rattle the tent canvas, and this morning it is clear again, and colder. At daybreak, the White River, just below, is sheathed in ice, with scarcely a murmur from the stream beneath.

The two ravens come to tritons on the gompa roof. *Gorawk, gorawk,* they croak, and this is the name given to them by the sherpas. Amidst the prayer flags and great horns of Tibetan argali, the gorawks greet first light with an odd musical double note — *a-ho* — that emerges as if by miracle from those ragged throats. Before sunrise every day, the great black birds are gone, like the last tatters of departing night.

The sun rising at the head of the White River brings a suffused glow to the tent canvas, and the robin accentor flits away across the frozen yard. At seven, there is breakfast in the cook hut — tea and porridge — and after breakfast on most days I watch sheep with GS,° parting company with him after a while, when the sheep lie down, to go off on some expedition of my own. Often I scan the caves and ledges on the far side of Black River in the hope of leopard; I am alert for fossils, wolves, and birds. Sometimes I observe the sky and mountains, and sometimes I sit in meditation, doing my best to empty out my mind, to attain that state in which everything is "at rest, free, and immortal. . . . All things

---

George Schaller: The zoologist whom Matthiessen accompanied on a field trip to study the bharal, or Himalayan blue sheep.

abided eternally as they were in their proper places . . . something infinite behind everything appeared." (No Buddhist said this, but a seventeenth-century Briton.) And soon all sounds, and all one sees and feels, take on imminence, an immanence, as if the Universe were coming to attention, a Universe of which one is the center, a Universe that is not the same and yet not different from oneself, even from a scientific point of view: within man as within mountains there are many parts of hydrogen and oxygen, of calcium, phosphorus, potassium, and other elements. "You never enjoy the world aright, till the Sea itself flows in your veins, till you are clothed with the heavens, and crowned with the stars: and perceive yourself to be the sole heir of the whole world, and more than so, because men are in it who are every one sole heirs as well as you."[1]

I have a meditation place on Somdo mountain, a broken rock outcrop like an altar set into the hillside, protected from all but the south wind by shards of granite and dense thorn. In the full sun it is warm, and its rock crannies give shelter to small stunted plants that cling to this desert mountainside — dead red-brown stalks of a wild buckwheat *(Polygonum),* some shrubby cinquefoil, pale edelweiss, and everlasting, and even a few poor wisps of *Cannabis.* I arrange a rude rock seat as a lookout on the world, set out binoculars in case wild creatures should happen into view, then cross my legs and regulate my breath, until I scarcely breathe at all.

Now the mountains all around me take on life; the Crystal Mountain moves. Soon there comes the murmur of the torrent, from far away below under the ice: it seems impossible that I can hear this sound. Even in windlessness, the sound of rivers comes and goes and falls and rises, like the wind itself. An instinct comes to open outward by letting all life in, just as a flower fills with sun. To burst forth from this old husk and cast one's energy abroad, to fly. . . .

Although I am not conscious of emotion, the mind-opening brings a soft mist to my eyes. Then the mist passes, the cold wind clears my head, and body-mind comes and goes on the light air. A sun-filled Buddha. One day I shall meditate in falling snow.

I lower my gaze from the snow peaks to the glistening thorns, the snow patches, the lichens. Though I am blind to it, the Truth is near, in the reality of what I sit on — rocks. These hard rocks instruct my bones in what my brain could never grasp in the Heart Sutra, that "form is emptiness, and emptiness is form" — the Void, the emptiness of blue-black space, contained in everything. Sometimes when I meditate, the big rocks dance.

The secret of the mountains is that the mountains simply exist, as I do myself: the mountains exist simply, which I do not. The mountains

[1]Thomas Traherme, *Centuries of Mediation.*

have no "meaning," they *are* meaning; the mountains *are*. The sun is round. I ring with life, and the mountains ring, and when I can hear it, there is a ringing that we share. I understand all this, not in my mind but in my heart, knowing how meaningless it is to try to capture what cannot be expressed, knowing that mere words will remain when I read it all again, another day.

Toward four, the sun sets fires on the Crystal Mountain. I turn my collar up and put on gloves and go down to Somdo, where my tent has stored the last sun of the day. In the tent entrance, out of the wind, I drink hot tea and watch the darkness rise out of the earth. The sunset fills the deepening blues with holy rays and turns a twilight raven into the silver bird of night as it passes into the shadow of the mountain. Then the great hush falls, and cold descends. The temperature has already dropped well below freezing, and will drop twenty degrees more before the dawn.

At dark, I walk past lifeless houses to the cooking hut where Phu-Tsering will be baking a green loaf; the sherpas have erected two stone tables, and in the evenings, the hut is almost cozy, warmed by the dung and smoking juniper in the clay oven. 10

As usual, GS is there ahead of me, recording data. Eyes watering, we read and write by kerosene lamp. We are glad to see each other, but we rarely speak more than a few words during a simple supper, usually rice of a poor bitter kind, with tomato or soy sauce, salt and pepper, sometimes accompanied by thin lentil soup. After supper I watch the fire for a time, until smoke from the sparking juniper closes my eyes. Bidding goodnight, I bend through the low doorway and go out under the stars and pick my way around the frozen walls to my cold tent, there to remain for twelve hours or more until first light. I read until near asphyxiated by my small wick candle in its flask of kerosene, then lie still for a long time in the very heart of the earth silence, exhilarated and excited as a child. I have yet to use the large packet of *Cannabis* that I gathered at Yamarkhar and dried along the way, to see me through long lightless evenings on this journey: I am high enough.

"Regard as one, this life, the next life, and the life between," wrote Milarepa. And sometimes I wonder into which life I have wandered, so still are the long nights here, and so cold.

FOR DISCUSSION AND WRITING

1. Regarding the principle of quantity: At any points does Matthiessen give you less information than you need? Does he ever give you more than necessary? (Be specific in your answers.)

2. Regarding the principle of quality: What reasons do you have for trusting (or distrusting) Matthiessen's knowledge of his subject or his honesty? (What tests could you apply to determine whether Matthiessen is reliable? The discussions on evaluating the source, in Chapters 3 and 5, relates to this question.)

3. Regarding the principle of manner: If you think the selection is sometimes unclear, indicate where, and explain the difficulty.

4. Regarding the principle of relation: Are any parts of the selection irrelevant to the topic? Explain.

5. Considering the complexity of his intention, do you think that Matthiessen expresses himself as clearly as possible? Explain.

6. No one doubts that Peter Matthiessen did trek into the Himalayas with zoologist George Schaller. Suppose, however, that Matthiessen had taken the journey only in imagination, not in reality. How would that fact affect your judgment of the quality of information in the text?

7. Does one of the following sentences express the main point of the selection? All of them? None of them? Other sentences from the selection? Explain.

> Though I am blind to it, the Truth is near, in the reality of what I sit on — rocks. (par. 7)

> These hard rocks instruct my bones in what my brain could never grasp in the Heart Sutra, that "form is emptiness, and emptiness is form" — the Void, the emptiness of blue-black space, contained in everything. (par. 7)

> The mountains have no "meaning," they *are* meaning; the mountains *are*. (par. 8)

8. Now that you have read a brief selection from *The Snow Leopard,* explain why you would or would not like to read the whole book.

9. What is the principle of structure or organization in a journal such as *The Snow Leopard*? How does this structure compare with that of Barry Lopez's "Country of the Mind"?

10. If you wanted general, reliable information about Zen Buddhism, to what source or sources would you turn?

THE ANGRY WINTER

Loren Eiseley

Loren Eiseley started his writing career while he was still an undergraduate student at the University of Nebraska. The college literary fraternity to which he belonged founded *Prairie Schooner,* a magazine devoted to young western writers. Eiseley soon became one of its editors and contributed stories and poems in its pages even after he graduated in 1933 with a bachelor's degree in anthropology. *Best Short Stories of 1936* included a selection written by Eiseley, and one of his sonnets was chosen for *Best Poems of 1942.*

In 1937, Eiseley received his doctorate in anthropology from the University of Pennsylvania and was associated with that institution until his death in 1977. He served as chair of the Department of Anthropology, as curator of the university museum's early man collection, and as provost of the university.

Eiseley wrote many notable scholarly articles within his field, publishing them in such journals as *American Antiquity, American Anthropologist,* and the *American Journal of Physical Anthropology;* he edited a collection of papers marking the centennial publication of Charles Darwin's *Origin of Species* and coedited *An Appraisal of Anthropology Today.* He was equally comfortable with writing for the lay person, publishing articles in *Harper's, Reader's Digest,* and the *Saturday Evening Post.*

Eiseley's articles have been collected into *The Immense Journey* and *The Firmament of Time.* Critics have praised these books for the eloquence and imagination Eiseley brings to the topic of the evolution of life.

"The Angry Winter," from a collection entitled *The Unexpected Universe,* is a difficult essay but well worth the effort to understand. The key to reading and enjoying the essay is to follow the images, visualizing in your mind the scenes Eiseley describes.

As to what happened next, it is possible to maintain that the hand of heaven was involved, and also possible to say that when men are desperate no one can stand up to them. —XENOPHON

A time comes when creatures whose destinies have crossed somewhere in the remote past are forced to appraise each other as though they were total strangers. I had been huddled beside the fire one winter night, with the wind prowling outside and shaking the windows. The big shepherd dog on the hearth before me occasionally glanced up affectionately, sighed, and slept. I was working, actually, amidst the debris of a far greater winter. On my desk lay the lance points of ice age hunters and the heavy leg bone of a fossil bison. No remnants of flesh attached to these relics. The deed lay more than ten thousand years remote. It was represented here by naked flint and by bone so mineralized it rang when struck. As I worked on in my little circle of light, I absently laid the bone beside me on the floor. The hour had crept toward midnight. A grating noise, a heavy rasping of big teeth diverted me. I looked down.

The dog had risen. That rock-hard fragment of a vanished beast was in his jaws and he was mouthing it with a fierce intensity I had never seen exhibited by him before.

"Wolf," I exclaimed, and stretched out my hand. The dog backed up but did not yield. A low and steady rumbling began to rise in his chest, something out of a long-gone midnight. There was nothing in that bone to taste, but ancient shapes were moving in his mind and determining his utterance. Only fools gave up bones. He was warning me.

"Wolf," I chided again.

As I advanced, his teeth showed and his mouth wrinkled to strike. The rumbling rose to a direct snarl. His flat head swayed low and wickedly as a reptile's above the floor. I was the most loved object in his universe, but the past was fully alive in him now. Its shadows were whispering in his mind. I knew he was not bluffing. If I made another step he would strike.

Yet his eyes were strained and desperate. "Do not," something pleaded in the back of them, some affectionate thing that had followed at my heel all the days of his mortal life, "do not force me. I am what I am and cannot be otherwise because of the shadows. Do not reach out. You are a man, and my very god. I love you, but do not put out your hand. It is midnight. We are in another time, in the snow."

"The *other* time," the steady rumbling continued while I paused, "the other time in the snow, the big, the final, the terrible snow, when the shape of this thing I hold spelled life. I will not give it up. I cannot. The shadows will not permit me. Do not put out your hand."

I stood silent, looking into his eyes, and heard his whisper through. Slowly I drew back in understanding. The snarl diminished, ceased. As I retreated, the bone slumped to the floor. He placed a paw upon it, warningly.

And were there no shadows in my own mind, I wondered. Had I not for a moment, in the grip of that savage utterance, been about to respond, to hurl myself upon him over an invisible haunch ten thousand years removed? Even to me the shadows had whispered—to me, the scholar in his study.

"Wolf," I said, but this time, holding a familiar leash, I spoke from the door indifferently. "A walk in the snow." Instantly from his eyes that other visitant receded. The bone was left lying. He came eagerly to my side, accepting the leash and taking it in his mouth as always.

A blizzard was raging when we went out, but he paid no heed. On his thick fur the driving snow was soon clinging heavily. He frolicked a little—though usually he was a grave dog—making up to me for something still receding in his mind. I felt the snowflakes fall upon my face, and stood thinking of another time, and another time still, until I was moving from midnight to midnight under ever more remote and vaster snows. Wolf came to my side with a little whimper. It was he who was civilized now. "Come back to the fire," he nudged gently, "or you will be lost." Automatically I took the leash he offered. He led me safely home and into the house.

"We have been very far away," I told him solemnly. "I think there is something in us that we had both better try to forget." Sprawled on the rug, Wolf made no response except to thump his tail feebly out of courtesy. Already he was mostly asleep and dreaming. By the movement of his feet I could see he was running far upon some errand in which I played no part.

Softly I picked up his bone — our bone, rather — and replaced it high on a shelf in my cabinet. As I snapped off the light the white glow from the window seemed to augment itself and shine with a deep, glacial blue. As far as I could see, nothing moved in the long aisles of my neighbor's woods. There was no visible track, and certainly no sound from the living. The snow continued to fall steadily, but the wind, and the shadows it had brought, had vanished.

2

Vast desolation and a kind of absence in nature invite the emergence of equally strange beings or spectacular natural events. An influx of power accompanies nature's every hesitation; each pause is succeeded by an uncanny resurrection. The evolution of a lifeless planet eventually culminates in green leaves. The altered and oxygenated air hanging above the continents presently invites the rise of animal apparitions compounded of formerly inert clay.

Only after long observation does the sophisticated eye succeed in labeling these events as natural rather than miraculous. There frequently lingers about them a penumbral air of mystery not easily dispersed. We seem to know much, yet we frequently find ourselves baffled. Humanity itself constitutes such a mystery, for our species arose and spread in a time of great extinctions. We are the final product of the Pleistocene period's millennial winters, whose origin is still debated. Our knowledge of this ice age is only a little over a century old, and the time of its complete acceptance even less. Illiterate man has lost the memory of that huge snowfall from whose depths he has emerged blinking.

"Nature is a wizard," Thoreau once said. The self-styled inspector of snowstorms stood in awe of the six-pointed perfection of a snowflake. The air, even thin air, was full of genius. The poetic naturalist to whom, in our new-found scientism, we grudgingly accord a literary name but whom we dismiss as an indifferent investigator, made a profound observation about man during a moment of shivering thought on a frozen river. "The human brain," meditated the snowbound philosopher, "is the kernel which the winter itself matures." The winter, he thought, tended to concentrate and extend the power of the human mind.

"The winter," Thoreau continued, "is thrown to us like a bone to a famishing dog, and we are expected to get the marrow out of it." In foreshortened perspective Thoreau thus symbolically prefigured man's passage through the four long glacial seasons, from which we have indeed painfully learned to extract the marrow. Although Thoreau had seen the scratches left by the moving ice across Mount Monadnock, even to recording their direction, he was innocent of their significance. What he felt was a sign of his intuitive powers alone. He sensed uncannily the opening of a damp door in a remote forest, and he protested that nature was too big for him, that it was, in reality, a playground of giants.

Nor was Thoreau wrong. Man is the product of a very unusual epoch in earth's history, a time when the claws of a vast dragon, the glacial ice, groped fumbling toward him across a third of the world's land surface and blew upon him the breath of an enormous winter. It was a world of elemental extravagance, assigned by authorities to scarcely one per cent of earth's history and labeled "geo-catastrophic." For over a million years man, originally a tropical orphan, has wandered through age-long snowdrifts or been deluged by equally giant rains.

He has been present at the birth of mountains. He has witnessed the disappearance of whole orders of life and survived the cyclonic dust clouds that blew in the glacial winds off the receding ice fronts. In the end it is no wonder that he himself has retained a modicum of that violence and unpredictability which lie sleeping in the heart of nature. Modern man, for all his developed powers and his imagined insulation in his cities, still lives at the mercy of those giant forces that created him and can equally decree his departure. These forces are revealed in man's simplest stories — the stories in which the orphaned and abused prince evades all obstacles and, through the assistance of some benign sorcerer, slays the dragon and enters into his patrimony.

As the ice age presents a kind of caricature or sudden concentration   20
of those natural forces that normally govern the world, so man, in the development of that awful instrument, his brain, himself partakes of the same qualities. Both his early magic and his latest science have magnified and frequently distorted the powers of the natural world, stirring its capricious and evil qualities. The explosive force of suns, once safely locked in nature, now lies in the hand that long ago dropped from a tree limb into the upland grass.

We have become planet changers and the decimators of life, including our own. The sorcerer's gift of fire in a dark cave has brought us more than a simple kingdom. Like so many magical gifts it has conjured up that which cannot be subdued but henceforth demands unceasing attention lest it destroy us. We are the genuine offspring of the sleeping ice, and we have inherited its power to magnify the merely usual into the colossal. The nature we have known throughout our venture upon earth has not been the stable, drowsy summer of the slow reptilian ages. Instead, we are the final product of a seemingly returning cycle, which comes once in two hundred and fifty million years—about the time, it has been estimated, that it takes our sun to make one full circle of the galactic wheel.

That circle and its recurrent ice have been repeated back into dim pre-Cambrian eras, whose life is lost to us. When our first tentative knowledge of the cold begins, the time is Permian. This glaciation, so far as we can determine, was, in contrast to the ice age just past, confined primarily to the southern hemisphere. Like the later Pleistocene episode, which saw the rise of man, it was an epoch of continental uplift and of a steeper temperature gradient from the poles to the equator. It produced a crisis in the evolution of life that culminated in the final invasion of the land by the reptilian vertebrates. More significantly, so far as our own future was concerned, it involved the rise of those transitional twilight creatures, the mammal-like reptiles whose remote descendants we are.

They were moving in the direction of fur, warm blood, and controlled body temperature, which, in time, would give the true mammals the mastery of the planet. Their forerunners were the first vertebrate responses to the recurrent menace of the angry dragon. Yet so far away in the past, so dim and distant was the breath of that frosty era that the scientists of the nineteenth century, who believed in a constant heat loss from a once fiery earth, were amazed when A. C. Ramsay, in 1854, produced evidence that the last great winter, from which man is only now emerging, had been long preceded in the Permian by a period of equally formidable cold.

Since we live on the borders of the Pleistocene, an ice age that has regressed but not surely departed, it is perhaps well to observe that the older Permian glaciation is the only one of whose real duration we can form a reasonable estimate. Uncertain traces of other such eras are lost in ancient strata or buried deep in the pre-Cambrian shadows. For the Permian glaciation, however, we can derive a rough estimate of some twenty-five to thirty million years, during which the southern continents periodically lay in the grip of glacial ice. Philip King, of the U.S. Geological Survey, has observed that in Australia the period of Permian glaciation was prolonged, and that in eastern Australia boulder beds of glacial origin are interspersed through more than ten thousand feet of geological section. The temperature gradient of that era would never again be experienced until the onset of the cold that accompanied the birth of man.

If the cause of these glacial conditions, with the enormous intervals between them, is directed by recurrent terrestrial or cosmic conditions, 25 then man, unknowingly, is huddling memoryless in the pale sunshine of an interstadial spring. Ice still lies upon the poles; the arctic owl, driven south on winter nights, drifts white and invisible over the muffled countryside. He is a survival from a vanished world, a denizen of the long cold of which he may yet be the returning harbinger.

I have said that the earlier Permian glaciation appears to have fluctuated over perhaps thirty million years. Some two hundred and fifty million years later, the Pleistocene — the ice age we call our own — along with four interglacial summers (if we include the present), has persisted a scant million years.* So recent is it that its two earlier phases yield little evidence of animal adjustment to the cold. "The origin of arctic life," remarks one authority, "is shrouded in darkness." Only the last two ice advances have given time, apparently, for the emergence of a fauna of arctic aspect — the woolly mammoths, white bears, and tundra-grazing reindeer, who shared with man the experience of the uttermost cold.

The arctic, in general, has been the grave of life rather than the place of its primary development. Man is the survivor among many cold-adapted creatures who streamed away at last with the melting glaciers. So far, the Pleistocene, in which geologically we still exist, has been a time of great extinctions. Its single new emergent, man, has himself contributed to making it what Alfred Russel Wallace has called a "zoologically impoverished world." Judging from the Permian record, if we were to experience thirty million more years of alternate ice and sun across a third of the earth's surface, man's temperate-zone cities would be ground to powder, his numbers decimated, and he himself might die in bestial savagery and want. Or, in his newfound scientific cleverness, he might survive his own unpredictable violence and live on as an archaic relic, a dropped pebble from a longer geological drama.

Already our own kind, *Homo sapiens,* with the assistance of the last two ice advances, appears to have eliminated, directly or indirectly, a sizable proportion of the human family. One solitary, if fertile, species, lost in internecine conflict, confronts the future even now. Man's survival record, for all his brains, is not impressive against the cunning patience of the unexpired Great Winter. In fact, we would do well to consider the story of man's past and his kinship with the planetary dragon — for of this there is no doubt at all. "The association of unusual physical conditions with a crisis in evolution is not likely to be pure coincidence,"

---

*Late discoveries have extended the Tertiary time range of the protohuman line. *Homo sapiens* may have existed for a time contemporaneously with the last of the heavy-browed forms of man, well back in the Pleistocene. If so, however, there is suggestive evidence that fertile genetic mixture between the two types existed. The human interminglings of hundreds of thousands of years of prehistory are not to be clarified by a single generation of archaeologists.

George Gaylord Simpson, a leading paleontologist, has declared. "Life and its environment are interdependent and evolve together."

The steps to man begin before the ice age. Just as in the case of the ancestral mammals, however, they are heralded by the oncoming cold of the late Age of Mammals, the spread of grass, the skyward swing of the continents, and the violence of mountain upheaval. The Pleistocene episode, so long unguessed and as insignificant as a pinprick on the earth's great time scale, signifies also, as did the ice of the late Paleozoic, the rise of a new organic world. In this case it marked in polycentric waves, distorted and originally hurled back by the frost, the rise of a creature not only new, but also one whose head contained its own interior lights and shadows and who was destined to reflect the turbulence and beauty of the age in which it was born.

It was an age in which the earth, over a third of its surface, over   *30* millions of square miles of the Northern Hemisphere, wore a mantle of blue ice stolen from the shrinking seas. And as that mantle encased and covered the final strata of earth, so, in the brain of man, a similar superimposed layer of crystalline thought substance superseded the dark, forgetful pathways of the animal brain. Sounds had their origin there, strange sounds that took on meaning in the air, named stones and gods. For the first time in the history of the planet, living men received names. For the first time, also, men wept bitterly over the bodies of their dead.

There was no longer a single generation, which bred blindly and without question. Time and its agonizing nostalgia would touch the heart each season and be seen in the fall of a leaf. Or, most terrible of all, a loved face would grow old. Kronos and the fates had entered into man's thinking. Try to escape as he might, he would endure an interior ice age. He would devise and unmake fables and at last, and unwillingly, comprehend an intangible abstraction called space-time and shiver inwardly before the endless abysses of space as he had once shivered unclothed and unlighted before the earthly frost.

As Thoreau anticipated, man has been matured by winter; he has survived its coming, and has eaten of its marrow. But its cold is in his bones. The child will partake always of the parent, and that parent is the sleeping dragon whose kingdom we hold merely upon sufferance, and whose vagaries we have yet to endure.

3

A few days ago I chanced to look into a rain pool on the walk outside my window. For a long time, because I was dreaming of other things, I saw only the occasional spreading ripple from a raindrop or the simultaneous overlapping circles as the rain fell faster. Then, as the beauty and the strange rhythm of the extending and concentric wavelets entered my mind, I saw that I was looking symbolically upon the whole history of life upon our globe. There, in a wide, sweeping circle, ran the early primates from whom we are descended; here, as a later drop within the rim of the greater circle, emerged the first men. I saw the mammoths pass in a long, slow, world-wide surge, but the little drop of man changed into a great hasty wave that swept them under.

There were sudden little ringlets, like the fauna of isolated islands, that appeared and disappeared with rapidity. Sometimes so slow were the drops that the pool was almost quiet, like the intense, straining silence of a quiescent geological period. Sometimes the rain, like the mutations in animal form, came so fast that the ripples broke, mixed, or kept their shapes with difficulty and did not spread far. Jungles, I read in my mystical water glass, microfaunas changing rapidly but with little spread.

Watch instead, I thought, for the great tides — it is they that contain the planet's story. As the rain hastened or dripped slowly, the pictures in the little pool were taken into my mind as though from the globe of a crystal-gazer. How often, if we learn to look, is a spider's wheel a universe, or a swarm of summer midges a galaxy, or a canyon a backward glance into time. Beneath our feet is the scratched pebble that denotes an ice age, or above us the summer cloud that changes form in one afternoon as an animal might do in ten million windy years. 35

All of these perceptive insights that we obtain from the natural world around us depend upon painfully accumulated knowledge. Otherwise, much as to our ancestors, the pebble remains a pebble, the pool but splashing water, the canyon a deep hole in the ground. Increasingly, the truly perceptive man must know that where the human eye stops, and hearing terminates, there still vibrates an inconceivable and spectral world of which we learn only through devised instruments. Through such instruments measuring atomic decay we have learned to probe the depths of time before our coming and to gauge temperatures long vanished.

Little by little, the orders of life that had characterized the earlier Age of Mammals ebbed away before the oncoming cold of the Pleistocene, interspersed though this cold was by interglacial recessions and the particularly long summer of the second interglacial. There were times when ice accumulated over Britain; in the New World, there were times when it stretched across the whole of Canada and reached southward to the fortieth parallel of latitude, in what today would be Kansas.

Manhattan Island and New Jersey felt its weight. The giant, long-horned bison of the middle Pleistocene vanished before man had entered America. Other now extinct but less colossal forms followed them. By the closing Pleistocene, it has been estimated, some seventy per cent of the animal life of the Western world had perished. Even in Africa, remote from the ice centers, change was evident. Perhaps the devastation was a partial response to the Pluvials, the great rains that in the tropics seem to have accompanied or succeeded the ice advances in the north.

The human groups that existed on the Old World land mass were alternately squeezed southward by advancing ice, contracted into pockets, or released once more to find their way northward. Between the alternate tick and tock of ice and sun, man's very bones were changing. Old species passed slowly away in obscure refuges or fell before the weapons devised by sharper minds under more desperate circumstances. Perhaps, since the rise of mammals, life had been subjected to no more drastic harassment, no more cutting selective edge, no greater isolation and then renewed genetic commingling. Yet we know that something approximating man was on the ground before the ice commenced and that naked man is tropical in origin. What, then, has ice to do with his story?

It has, in fact, everything. The oncoming chill caught him early in   40
his career; its forces converged upon him even in the tropics; its influence can be seen in the successive human waves that edge farther and ever farther north until at last they spill across the high latitudes at Bering Strait and descend the length of the two Americas. Only then did the last southwestern mammoths perish in the shallow mud of declining lakes, the last mastodons drop their tired bones in the New Jersey bogs on the receding drift.

The story can best be seen from the map, as time, ice, and the sorcerer's gift of fire run like the concentric ripples of the falling rain across the zones of temperature. The tale is not confined to ice alone. As one glaciologist, J. K. Charlesworth, has written: "The Pleistocene . . . witnessed earth-movements on a considerable, even catastrophic scale. There is evidence that it created mountains and ocean deeps of a size previously unequalled. . . . The Pleistocene represents one of the crescendi in the earth's tectonic history."

I have spoken of the fact that, save for violent glacial episodes, the world's climate has been genial. The planet has been warmer than to-day — "acryogenic," as the specialists would say. Both earlier and later, warm faunas reached within the Arctic Circle, and a much higher percentage of that fauna represented forest forms. Then in the ice phases, world temperature dipped, even in the tropics; the mountain snowlines crept downward. In the north, summers were "short and false," periods of "dry cold" — again to quote the specialists. Snow blanketed the high ground in winter, and that winter covered half the year and was extremely harsh.

With our short memory, we accept the present climate as normal. It is as though a man with a huge volume of a thousand pages before him — in reality, the pages of earth time — should read the final sentence on the last page and pronounce it history. The ice has receded, it is true, but world climate has not completely rebounded. We are still on the steep edge of winter or early spring. Temperature has reached mid-point. Like refugees, we have been dozing memoryless for a few scant millennia before the windbreak of a sun-warmed rock. In the European

Lapland winter that once obtained as far south as Britain, the temperature lay eighteen degrees Fahrenheit lower than today.

On a world-wide scale this cold did not arrive unheralded. Somewhere in the highlands of Africa and Asia the long Tertiary descent of temperature began. It was, in retrospect, the prelude to the ice. One can trace its presence in the spread of grasslands and the disappearance over many areas of the old forest browsers. The continents were rising. We know that by Pliocene time, in which the trail of man ebbs away into the grass, man's history is more complicated than the simple late descent, as our Victorian forerunners sometimes assumed, of a chimpanzee from a tree. The story is one whose complications we have yet to unravel.

Avoiding complexities and adhering as we can to our rain-pool   45
analogy, man, subman, protoman, the euhominid, as we variously denote him, was already walking upright on the African grasslands more than two million years ago. He appears smaller than modern man, pygmoid and light of limb. Giantism comes late in the history of a type and sometimes foretells extinction. Man is now a giant primate and, where food is plentiful, growing larger, but he is a unique creature whose end is not yet foreseeable.

Three facts can be discerned as we examine the earliest bipedal man-apes known to us. First, they suggest, in their varied dentition and skull structure, a physical diversity implying, as Alfred Russel Wallace theorized long ago, an approach to that vanished era in which protoman was still being molded by natural selective processes unmediated by the softening effect of cultural defenses. He was, in other words, scant in numbers and still responding genetically to more than one ecological niche. Heat and cold were direct realities; hunger drove him, and, on the open savanna into which he had descended, vigilance was the price of life. The teeth of the great carnivores lay in wait for the old, the young, and the unwary.

Second, at the time we encounter man, the long descent of the world's climate toward the oncoming Pleistocene cold had already begun. It is not without interest that all man's most primitive surviving relatives — living fossils, we would call them — are tree dwellers hidden in the tropical rain forests of Africa, Madagascar, and the islands of southeastern Asia. They are the survivors of an older and a warmer world — the incubation time that was finally to produce, in some unknown fashion, the world-encircling coils of the ice dragon.

In the last of Tertiary time, grasslands and high country were spreading even in the tropics. Savanna parkland interspersed with trees clothed the uplands of East Africa; North China grew colder and more arid. Steppe- and plains-loving animals became predominant. Even the seas grew colder, and the tropical zone narrowed. Africa was to remain the least glaciated of the continents, but even here the lowering of temperature drew on, and the mountain glaciations finally began to descend into their valleys. As for Asia, the slow, giant upthrust of the Himalayas had brought with it the disappearance of jungles harboring the old-fashioned tree climbers.

Of the known regions of late-Tertiary primate development, whether African or Asian, both present the spectacle of increasing grasslands and diminishing forest. The latter, as in southeastern Asia, offered a refuge for the arboreal conservatives, such as the gibbon and orang, but the Miocene-Pliocene parklands and savannas must have proved an increasing temptation to an intelligent anthropoid sufficiently unspecialized and agile to venture out upon the grass. Our evidence from Africa is more complete at present, but fragmentary remains that may prove to be those of equally bipedal creatures are known from pre-Pleistocene and less explored regions below the Himalayas.

Third, and last of the points to be touched on here, the man-apes, *50* in venturing out erect upon the grass, were leaving forever the safety of little fruit-filled niches in the forest. They were entering the open sunlight of a one-dimensional world, but they were bringing to that adventure a freed forelimb at the conscious command of the brain, and an eye skillfully adjusted for depth perception. Increasingly they would feed on the rich proteins provided by the game of the grasslands; by voice and primitive projectile weapon, man would eventually become a space leaper more deadly than the giant cats.

In the long, chill breath that presaged the stirring of the world dragon, the submen drifted naked through an autumnal haze. They were, in body, partly the slumbering product of the earth's long summer. The tropical heat had warmed their bones. Thin-furred and hungry, old-fashioned descendants from the forest attic, they clung to the tropical savannas. Unlike the light gazelle, they could neither bound from enemies nor graze on the harsh siliceous grasses. With a minimum of fragmentary chips and stones, and through an intensified group co-operation, they survived.

The first human wave, however, was a little wave, threatening to vanish. A patch in Africa, a hint in the Siwalik beds below the Himalayas—little more. Tremendous bodily adjustments were in process, and, in the low skull vault, a dream animal was in the process of development, a user of invisible symbols. In its beginnings, and ever more desperately, such a being walks the knife-edge of extinction. For a creature who dreams outside of nature, but is at the same time imprisoned within reality, has acquired, in the words of the psychiatrist Leonard Sillman, "one of the cruelest and most generous endowments ever given to a species of life by a mysterious providence."

On that one most recent page of life from which we can still read, it is plain that the second wave of man ran onward into the coming of the ice. In China a pithecanthropine creature with a cranial capacity of some 780 cubic centimeters has been recently retrieved from deposits suggesting a warm grassland fauna of the lower Pleistocene, perhaps over 700,000 years remote from the present. The site lies in Shensi province in about thirty degrees north latitude. Man is moving northward. His brain has grown, but he appears still to lack fire.

4

In the legendary cycles of the Blackfoot Indians there is an account of the early people, who were poor and naked and did not know how to live. Old Man, their maker, said: "Go to sleep and get power. Whatever animals appear in your dream, pray and listen." "And," the story concludes, "that was how the first people got through the world, by the power of their dreams."

Man was not alone young and ignorant in the morning of his world; *55* he also died young. Much of what he grasped of the world around him he learned like a child from what he imagined, or was gleaned from his own childlike parents. The remarks of Old Man, though clothed in myth, have an elemental ring. They tell the story of an orphan — man — bereft of instinctive instruction and dependent upon dream, upon, in the end, his own interpretation of the world. He had to seek animal helpers because they alone remembered what was to be done.

And so the cold gathered and man huddled, dreaming, in the lightless dark. Lightning struck, the living fire ran from volcanoes in the fury of earth's changes, and still man slumbered. Twice the ice ground southward and once withdrew, but no fire glimmered at a cave mouth. Humanly flaked flints were heavier and better-made. Behind that simple observation lies the unknown history of drifting generations, the children of the dreamtime.

At about the forty-fifth parallel of latitude, in the cave vaults at Choukoutien, near Peking, a heavy-browed, paleoanthropic form of man with a cranial capacity as low, in some instances, as 860 cubic centimeters, gnawed marrow bones and chipped stone implements. The time lies 500,000 years remote; the hour is late within the second cold, the place northward and more bleak than Shensi.

One thing strikes us immediately. This creature, with scarcely two-thirds of modern man's cranial capacity, was a fire user. Of what it meant to him beyond warmth and shelter we know nothing; with what rites, ghastly or benighted, it was struck or maintained, no word remains. We know only that fire opened to man the final conquest of the earth.

I do not include language here, in spite of its tremendous significance to humanity, because the potentiality of language is dependent upon the germ plasm. Its nature, not its cultural expression, is written into the motor centers of the brain, into high auditory discrimination and equally rapid neuromuscular response in tongue, lips, and palate. We are biologically adapted for the symbols of speech. We have determined its forms, but its potential is not of our conscious creation. Its mechanisms are written in our brain, a simple gift from the dark powers behind nature. Speech has made us, but it is a human endowment not entirely of our conscious devising.

By contrast, the first fires flickering at a cave mouth are our own   *60* discovery, our own triumph, our grasp upon invisible chemical power. Fire contained, in that place of brutal darkness and leaping shadows, the crucible and the chemical retort, steam and industry. It contained the entire human future.

Across the width of the Old World land mass near what is now Swanscombe, England, a better-brained creature of almost similar dating is also suspected of using fire, though the evidence, being from the open, is not so clear. But at last the sorcerer-priest, the stealer from the gods, the unknown benefactor remembered in a myriad legends around the earth, had done his work. He had supplied man with an overmastering magic. It would stand against the darkness and the cold.

In the frontal and temporal lobes, anatomy informs us, lie areas involved with abstract thought. In modern man the temporal lobes in particular are "hazardously supplied with blood through tenuous arteries. They are protected by a thin skull and crowded against a shelf of bone. They are more commonly injured than any other higher centers." The neurologist Frederick Gibbs goes on to observe that these lobes are attached to the brain like dormer windows, jammed on as an afterthought of nature. In the massive armored cranium of Peking man those lobes had already lit the fires that would knit family ties closer, promote the more rapid assimilation of wild food, and increase the foresight that goes into the tending of fires always. Fire is the only natural force on the planet that can both feed and travel. It is strangely like an animal; that is, it has to be tended and fed. Moreover, it can also rage out of control.

Man, long before he trained the first dog, had learned to domesticate fire. Its dancing midnight shadows and the comfort it gave undoubtedly enhanced the opportunities for brain growth. The fourth ice would see man better clothed and warmed. In our own guise, as the third and last great human wave, man would pursue the trail of mammoths across the Arctic Circle into America. The animal counselors that once filled his dreams would go down before him. Thus, inexorably, he would be forced into a new and profound relationship with plants. If one judges by the measures of civilization, it was all for the best. There are, however, lingering legends that carry a pathetic symbolism: that it was fire that separated man from the animals. It is perhaps a last wistful echo from a time when the chasm between ourselves and the rest of life did not yawn so impassably.

5

They tell an old tale in camping places, where men still live in the open among stones and trees. Always, in one way or another, the tale has to do with messages, messages that the gods have sent to men. The burden of the stories is always the same. Someone, man or animal, is laggard or gets the message wrong, and the error is impossible to correct; thus have illness and death intruded in the world.

Mostly the animals understand their roles, but man, by compari- 65 son, seems troubled by a message that, it is often said, he cannot quite remember, or has gotten wrong. Implied in this is our feeling that life demands an answer from us, that an essential part of man is his struggle to remember the meaning of the message with which he had been entrusted, that we are, in fact, message carriers. We are not what we seem. We have had a further instruction.

There is another story that is sometimes told of the creator in the morning of the world. After he had created the first two beings, which he pronounced to be "people," the woman, standing by the river, asked: "Shall we always live?" Now the god had not considered this, but he was not unwilling to grant his new creations immortality. The woman picked up a stone and, gesturing toward the stream, said: "If it floats we shall always live, but if it sinks, people must die so that they shall feel pity and have compassion." She tossed the stone. It sank. "You have chosen," said the creator.

Many years ago, as a solitary youth much given to wandering, I set forth on a sullen November day for a long walk that would end among the fallen stones of a forgotten pioneer cemetery on the High Plains. The weather was threatening, and only an unusual restlessness drove me into the endeavor. Snow was on the ground and deepening by the hour. There was a rising wind of blizzard proportions sweeping across the land.

Late in a snow-filled twilight, I reached the cemetery. The community that placed it there had long vanished. Frost and snow, season by season, had cracked and shattered the flat, illegible stones till none remained upright. It was as though I, the last living man, stood freezing among the dead. I leaned across a post and wiped the snow from my eyes.

It was then I saw him — the only other living thing in that bleak countryside. We looked at each other. We had both come across a way so immense that neither my immediate journey nor his seemed of the slightest importance. We had each passed over some immeasurably greater distance, but whatever the word we had carried, it had been forgotten between us.

He was nothing more than a western jack rabbit, and his ribs were 70 gaunt with hunger beneath his skin. Only the storm contained us equally. That shrinking, long-eared animal, cowering beside a slab in an abandoned graveyard, helplessly expected the flash of momentary death, but it did not run. And I, with the rifle so frequently carried in that day and time, I also stood while the storm — a real blizzard now — raged over and between us, but I did not fire.

We both had a fatal power to multiply, the thought flashed on me, and the planet was not large. Why was it so, and what was the message that somehow seemed spoken from a long way off beyond an ice field, out of all possible human hearing?

The snow lifted and swirled between us once more. He was going to need that broken bit of shelter. The temperature was falling. For his frightened, trembling body in all the million years between us, there had been no sorcerer's aid. He had survived alone in the blue nights and the howling dark. He was thin and crumpled and small.

Step by step I drew back among the dead and their fallen stones. Somewhere, if I could follow the fence lines, there would be a fire for me. For a moment I could see his ears nervously recording my movements, but I was a wraith now, fading in the storm.

"There are so few tracks in all this snow," someone had once protested. It was true. I stood in the falling flakes and pondered it. Even my own tracks were filling. But out of such desolation had arisen man, the desolate. In essence, he is a belated phantom of the angry winter. He carried, and perhaps will always carry, its cruelty and its springtime in his heart.

FOR DISCUSSION AND WRITING

1. Regarding the principle of quantity: At any points in this essay, does Eiseley give you less information than you need? Does he ever give you more than necessary? (Be specific in your answers.)

2. Regarding the principle of quality: What reasons do you have for trusting (or distrusting) Eiseley's knowledge of his subject or his honesty?

3. Regarding the principle of manner: If you think the essay is sometimes unclear, indicate where, and explain the difficulty. Was it difficult for you to relate the images so that they add up to a coherent whole?

4. Regarding the principle of relation: Are any parts of the essay irrelevant to the topic? Explain.

5. How does Eiseley's method (manner) affect the credibility of his argument (quality)?

6. In "The Country of the Mind," "November 6," and "The Angry Winter," a winter landscape is the setting, or scene. How does this scene contribute to the meaning and effectiveness of Eiseley's essay?

7. Loren Eiseley creates brilliant metaphors, such as this one:

> Every man contains within himself a ghost continent—a place circled as warily as Antarctica was circled two hundred years ago by Captain James Cook. ("The Ghost Continent," in *The Unexpected Universe*)

This metaphor means that all of us are afraid to explore some parts of our psyches. Point out the metaphors in "The Angry Winter" that you think are most striking. Paraphrase them, and explain what you gain or lose with the paraphrase. Is the paraphrase easier to understand than the original metaphor? Is the paraphrase as powerful (vivid, memorable) as the original?

8. Eiseley uses anecdotes (brief stories) to make his points. For example, Eiseley draws this "lesson" from the anecdote about the author and his dog: "I think there is something in us that we had both better try to forget" (par. 12). Point out other anecdotes in the essay. Is this anecdotal method of explaining ideas and establishing points effective or ineffective? Explain your answer.

9. What is the main point of "The Angry Winter"? Could Eiseley have conveyed it more effectively? If you think he could have, explain how.

THE BLEEDERS

Earle Hackett

Blood, the source of the following selection, is a book for laypeople written by an expert. The author, Earle Hackett, is a hematologist who was educated at Trinity College, Dublin. He then moved to Australia, where he became president of the Royal College of Pathologists.

"The Bleeders" is documentary evidence of a good writer's ability to explain specialized subjects in such a way that nonspecialists can understand. As one genial skeptic put the matter: "In fifteen minutes or half an hour, any experts should be able to explain the general nature of their fields to nonexperts. Show me an 'expert' who can't do that, and I'll show you someone who's not an expert."

Notice particularly the diagram that Hackett includes. This "picture" may not be worth a thousand words, but it does show that sometimes a chart, a graph, or an illustration makes understanding much easier for the reader.

If the word 'leukaemia' has come to have alarming connotations, then 'haemophilia' has acquired an aura of romantic intrigue, because of its occurrence in the royal houses of Europe in the nineteenth century, and because it had a bearing on the machinations of Rasputin, the influential monk at the Court of the Czar. The disease has been known for a long time, but only recently, in the early nineteenth century, it received its present name (a bad one, literally meaning 'blood-fondness': in this sense, leeches, fleas, vampires, lice and lady mosquitoes are the real 'haemophiliacs'). It is a hereditary defect in the blood-clotting mechanism, and is inherited in such a way that it can appear only in males.

SEX-LINKED DISEASE

Genetically, as we have seen, the maleness of men is determined by their inheriting two different sex chromosomes, X and Y, while the femaleness of women is the result of a double dose of the X-chromosome. The egg-cells formed in a woman's ovaries each carry one X-chromosome. About half her eggs will have one of her Xs, and half will have the other. In the male, half the sperms carry an X, and half carry a Y. When a sperm unites with an egg, the sex of the baby which will grow from the fusion depends upon whether an X-sperm gives it a female combination (XX) or a Y-sperm gives it a male one (XY).

The inherited defect in haemophilia is 'sex-linked,' being carried on one of the X-chromosomes. That is to say that although the disorder is in the blood-clotting mechanism, the actual genetic 'instruction' which determines it is located on one of the pair of chromosomes which also determines sex. The defect appears by chance—a gene mutating during the formation of an egg or an X-sperm—but once present it can be inherited for generations. In geneticist's language, it is a 'recessive' character. This means that if it is matched by a normal (non-mutated) gene on an accompanying X-chromosome, it will not produce its effects in the person who owns it, who in such a case will always be a female (XX). But a Y-chromosome is a different shape, and its units of inheritance do not match or counter those on the X-chromosome at the gene-slot where the haemophilia mutation is situated. Therefore a male will have the disease if he inherits the one X-chromosome gene determining it. Because the disease is severe enough to prevent many male sufferers from reaching reproductive age (at least until recently), a female child is likely to inherit only one affected X-chromosome (from her mother), and so although she can carry the trait she will not have the disease, because the effects of the gene will be countered by her normal X-chromosome. But half the egg-cells which will form in her ovaries will bear the mutated gene, and so if she ever has a male child, there is a fifty-fifty chance that he will develop from one of the defective egg-cells. Then he will be a haemophiliac, as will (on average) half his brothers also. On average half his sisters will carry the trait, as his mother did, and half will not. If he lives to marry—which is a possibility—then all his daughters, and those of his affected brothers, will also carry it, because these girls must derive one of their Xs from their fathers, who have only an affected one to give them. On the other hand his sons, who derive their Y from him and their X from his wife (who we shall presume is normal), will be entirely free of it.

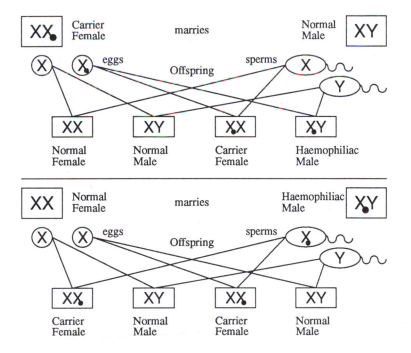

THE BOY BLEEDERS

In haemophilia the blood clots very slowly, taking perhaps fifteen or thirty minutes instead of the usual three to six. Therefore automatic staunching of haemorrhage is defective, and a haemophiliac can bleed to death from a small cut. This is responsible for the folk belief that a 'bleeder' lacks two of the 'seven skins' supposed to cover a normal individual, or alternatively that 'his skin is too small for him.'

Haemophiliacs lack one of the plasma substances which are involved in the very first — prothrombinase — stages of the formation of a blood clot. These stages can be short-circuited by other substances, which can be released from injured tissue cells. An abrasive or lacerating type of injury will release these tissue substances, and in this case a haemophiliac may not suffer abnormal bleeding. On the other hand, a cut from a sharp blade severs blood vessels while causing a minimum of damage to tissue cells, and such a wound may prove dangerous, though bleeding can be prevented where firm pressure or bandaging can be applied, because this pinches the blood-vessel walls together. The greatest constant hazard a haemophiliac has to reckon with is internal bleeding, which often results from quite minor knocks and blows. A frequent disabling event is haemorrhage into a joint. This occurs because the lining membrane of a joint has a folded fringe-like structure, rich in small blood vessels that can get nipped and broken between the bone surfaces in some unexpected fall or strain. This means that blood will flood into the joint cavity, ballooning it and causing inflammation and perhaps permanent damage. Therefore haemophiliacs frequently have stiff joints. Unfortunate though this is, there are other internal parts of the body where the swelling caused by a local haemorrhage can bring about death. This may happen anywhere inside the skull, or in the soft tissues of the neck where the air passages can be compressed by it, causing smothering.

Haemophilia was known to the ancient civilizations, and must have excited much notice in races which practised the rite of male circumcision: Jewish tradition, for example, waived the operation in families known to be 'bleeders.' If a trivial injury causes a young boy's joints to swell, or produces an unexpectedly severe spreading bruise, then haemophilia may be present. If it is, such procedures as tooth extractions and surgical operations become dangerous, and life has to be one of studied care. The disease may be inherited with different degrees of severity, and in some cases the haemorrhagic tendency waxes and wanes from time to time. This has given many a charlatan cause to claim success for some 'treatment,' and it was because of a situation of this kind that the Czarina believed in the monk Rasputin's power to influence her son's disease.

A transfusion of fresh normal blood can temporarily restore the clotting defect in a haemophiliac by replacing the missing plasma substance, and it is also possible to make a concentrated extract from normal plasma that is more effective still. But the benefit lasts only for a short time, and eventually there may be a falling off in the effects of the treatment if it is repeated too often. This means that such treatments must be kept for times of special risk and cannot be constantly used.

The life of a haemophiliac is bound to be difficult, but less so than in the past. A real 'cure' of an hereditary disease like this, where the disorder is inborn in the body structure, is unlikely, unless manipulation of gene material in the individual becomes possible; but increasing knowledge of the chemical mechanisms of blood coagulation may lead in the end to precise chemical identification of the substance lacking in haemophilia, and then to the artificial manufacture of an active substitute which will have a prolonged and reproducible effect.

This raises an important contemporary problem. Those who suffer from certain directly inherited diseases (such as haemophilia or the hereditary haemolytic anaemias, and numerous other conditions not primarily involving the blood) may now live in the shelter of modern medicine sufficiently long and effectively to marry and have children. In times past they were usually not vigorous enough to survive or to raise a family, unless they were sustained in a rich or aristocratic household. But today, with palliative treatment, such diseases are in some cases being passed on by their bearers to an increasing proportion of children in each generation. There may also be inherited physical dispositions towards other sicknesses which respond to elaborate treatment but whose genetic component we are not yet directly aware of. From the medical point of view there is no doubt that at present we should 'treat' all disease in individuals so far as we can, for this relieves much suffering and is the only way practicable in a humanitarian culture in our present incomplete state of knowledge. There is also the probability that a few genes which are disadvantageous or disease-producing in one environment may be of positive advantage in another. But it is becoming increasingly clear to those communities with very high standards of medical knowledge and development that in the long run certain medical policies may be an economic or social disadvantage. This is a problem best assessed by each community in the context of its local situation; wide generalizations cannot and should not be made. From a slightly different point of view it is also obvious that, because many of our medical techniques involve highly developed, expensive scientific teamwork, a population which might normally carry a high proportion of hereditary physical dependants would become very vulnerable in times of national stress if elaborate medical teams became disorganized. However, these problems may not present themselves widely for some generations yet, and meantime more information will have been gained.

A haemophiliac who is enabled to marry is in a special genetic and moral situation. His children will all be outwardly normal and his sons will have no defect at all. But all his daughters will be carriers. Therefore

10

some of his grandsons born to his daughters are likely to have the disease, though these will be a minority of all his grandchildren. Would you say that he should abstain from having children because of this possibility? Perhaps he would feel unwilling to create an individual, no matter how indirectly, who would have to go through the same trials as himself. Artificial insemination of his wife by semen from a non-haemophiliac donor is one possible solution. Another which is still in the future, but maybe not too far off, is a technique for choosing the sex of one's children. But apart from these possibilities, what is essential at present is to make sure that all haemophiliacs, and their wives and daughters, fully understand the chances of the disease reappearing in their descendants. Women whose fathers are not haemophiliacs, and who have had two or more affected sons, must assume that they are carriers in whom the haemophilia mutation is expressing itself for the first time in that line.

CHRISTMAS DISEASE

Some few years ago classical haemophilia was shown to have two forms, inherited in the same way, but distinguished by different blood-clotting factors in their plasmas. The British doctors who first observed this decided that one form should continue to be called 'haemophilia,' but they felt that to give the variant a scientific name before the real nature and chemistry of the missing clotting substances was known would be pretentious. They therefore called it after the person in whom they had first observed the new disorder. His surname was unusual and easy to remember, and 'Christmas disease' was added to the haematologists' list.

Because haemophilia is a chronic disease with definite and dramatic symptoms, we are perhaps more 'aware' of its presence in the community than we are of other rare inherited conditions. There is not in fact much of it around, but, as biologists, we should ask why it has not died out long ago. It seems that just about as often as a haemophiliac line disappears, another appears somewhere else as a result of a fresh, rare, but regularly recurring mutation.

THE ROYAL HAEMOPHILIACS

Such a mutation probably affected Queen Victoria. Her husband, Prince Albert, and her father, the Duke of Kent, were not haemophiliacs, nor were her ancestors on the maternal side. She was an only child and therefore had no brothers or sisters in whom either frank haemophilia or the carrier trait might have been observed if her mother had grown from a cell with a mutated X-chromosome. The mutation must have occurred either in one of her mother's, or her maternal grandmother's egg-cells; or in one of her father's, or her maternal grandfather's X-sperms. Several of the children of Queen Victoria inherited the haemophiliac gene from her. She had four sons, one of whom, Leopold, was a haemophiliac who married. At least two of her daughters, Alice and Beatrice, turned out to be carriers. Alice passed the gene to a son who died young, and to two daughters, Alix and Irene. Irene had three sons, two of whom were haemophiliacs but had no children. Alix married a Romanov and became Czarina of Russia, and her son, Alexis the Czarevitch, was a haemophiliac. All members of this Russian family were reported to have been executed in 1918, but from time to time we hear a rumour that they survived in hiding. For instance, there is a woman claiming to be the Grand Duchess Anastasia, one of the Czarina's daughters, and if she could show she is a carrier of haemophilia it would somewhat strengthen her case. There is even a candidate for the Czarevitch; he, of course, should have frank haemophilia.

Victoria's daughter Beatrice married Prince Henry of Battenberg, a cousin of her sister Alice's husband. Beatrice's daughter, Victoria Eugénie, became Queen of Spain, and two of her sons were haemophiliacs and died without having children. The Battenberg (now Mountbatten) line that continues in England is free of haemophilia because it is descended from one of Alice's unaffected daughters who married another Battenberg, and had a daughter who became Queen of Greece and the mother of Philip, the husband of the present Queen of England.

There are still some great-great-granddaughters of Queen Victoria, *15* descended from her haemophiliac son Leopold, who had a son and a daughter, or from the Queen of Spain. They may be carrying the gene, but it has died out in the rest of the family.

COUSIN MARRIAGES

It is widely believed that cousin marriages are likely to result in offspring with hereditary diseases. This is true in some circumstances, but although European royalty has been closely intermarried, this is not the reason for the preponderance of haemophilia, because a sex-linked disease of this kind appears whenever males inherit the gene, whether their parents are cousins or not. There are nevertheless many other genes which can be inherited on any of the non-sex human chromosomes. All the non-sex chromosomes are present in matching pairs, unlike the non-matching pair of X and Y chromosomes which determine male sex. Recessive genes on non-sex chromosomes will not express their effects in the body unless both members of the chromosome pair have the gene.

Many recessive genes which determine abnormal features amounting to 'disease' are rare, and it is statistically unlikely that two people bearing the same recessive gene will meet and marry. But if they do, then one in four of their children will be born with a double dose of the recessive gene and are likely to have whatever 'defects' are characteristic of the gene action. And in cousin marriages there is already an increased chance that both partners will be carrying the same recessive genes inherited from a common grandparent, and so in that case they are more likely than random partners to have children suffering from hereditary defects. Whatever form the 'defects' take (and of course these vary with the genes involved), their most general biological effect, in spite of medical palliation, would seem at first sight to be a reduction in the children's fertility: that is, fewer survive to maturity, and so on average fewer have children.

But there are inbred human lines, such as those of minority religious groups, or of island or isolated valley peoples, or of royal houses, where cousin marriages are frequent, and these are not always seen to suffer excessively from inherited defects. It seems that in such established inbred societies these defects are revealed quickly in the generations following immediately after their origin by mutation, and are then quickly eliminated from the stock by the lower viability and lower fertility of the individuals bearing them. In fact it is in the outbred communities, where cousin marriages are the exception, that rare genes inherited from a common grandparent continue to come together occasionally in double dose in the offspring of such marriages.

Evidently human stock, like animal stock, adapts itself after a few generations to consistent inbreeding or consistent outbreeding. Really close or incestuous inbreeding has usually been prohibited in human society, but it is not, genetically speaking, an absolutely bad policy. It can establish and maintain seemingly desirable inherited features. Its disadvantage is that it tends to restrict the gene pool, leaving fewer potential variations, which might be of great use to us humans if some remarkable change occurred in our environment necessitating an adaptive evolutionary response in subsequent generations.

DEVIL'S PINCHES

There are other bleeding diseases, some transient, some prolonged   20
in their effects. One due to lack of blood platelets, usually temporary, is *thrombocytopenic purpura*. Another, caused by lack of prothrombin, is the result of malnutrition or of liver disease. Many others are caused by changes in the small blood vessels. The prime indication of a bleeding disease is easy bruising, but some normal people are quite easily bruised, even though their blood-clotting mechanisms are active so that they do not bleed unnaturally after injury. Easy bruising is commoner in women than men, because their skins are more delicate. Inexplicable bruises on the bodies of young women were taken, in medieval times, to be evidence of an incubus having visited them while they slept, and you will still hear such marks called 'devil's pinches.'

FOR DISCUSSION AND WRITING

1. Where could you find out about Earle Hackett, the author (aside from the scant information that precedes the selection)?

2. In your opinion, what might have been Hackett's purposes in writing the book from which "The Bleeders" is taken? On what do you base your opinion?

3. As a "thought experiment," place "The Bleeders" in the following variety of scenes. Does it "fit"? Why, or why not?
    a. Hackett reads the paper to a group of hematologists at a convention of the American Medical Association.
    b. Hacket has been invited to speak about his field at a meeting of the Jefferson High School PTA. He reads "The Bleeders" and uses an overhead projector to display the chart.
    c. Hacket is visiting a faculty member at Utopia University. This faculty member invites Hacket to speak to a freshman class in biology. Hacket reads "The Bleeders."
    d. Hacket has been invited to speak at an anti-abortion rally. Three hundred noisy participants fall silent when he takes the microphone. He reads "The Bleeders."

4. Point out and explain some ways in which Hackett attempts to make his technical subject understandable to nonexperts.

5. Evaluate "The Bleeders" from the standpoint of quantity. At any point, do you need more information? Less information?

6. Hacket violates the principle of relation. Point out where. Do you believe that the violation is justified? Explain.

7. What criteria can you apply to evaluate "The Bleeders"? What do experts in medicine think about the book? What do laypeople think? Where could you find such information?

8. What world knowledge must a reader have in order to understand the technical explanation of the inheritance of hemophilia?

9. Point out ways in which Hackett attempts to make this technical subject interesting to nonexperts.

10. State the main point of "The Bleeders."

THE NATURE OF THEORIES

Stephen Hawking

Considered one of the great minds of our century, Stephen W. Hawking lives a heroic life, fighting Lou Gehrig's disease, which for twenty years has disabled him more and more. Nonetheless, he travels widely to attend scientific conferences and is Lucasian Professor of Mathematics at Cambridge University. His work is directed toward answering awesome questions about the universe.

The following selection is from *A Brief History of Time,* Professor Hawking's best-selling book on cosmology, with the subtitle *From the Big Bang to Black Holes.* Hawking's explanation of the nature of theories is an example of the clarity of both his thought and his writing. As you read this selection, note how the author uses specific examples to clarify abstract concepts.

In order to talk about the nature of the universe and to discuss questions such as whether it has a beginning or an end, you have to be clear about what a scientific theory is. I shall take the simple-minded view that a theory is just a model of the universe, or a restricted part of it, and a set of rules that relate quantities in the model to observations that we make. It exists only in our minds and does not have any other reality (whatever that might mean). A theory is a good theory if it satisfies two requirements: It must accurately describe a large class of observations on the basis of a model that contains only a few arbitrary elements, and it must make definite predictions about the results of future observations. For example, Aristotle's theory that everything was made out of four elements, earth, air, fire, and water, was simple enough to qualify, but it did not make any definite predictions. On the other hand, Newton's theory of gravity was based on an even simpler model, in which bodies attracted each other with a force that was proportional to a quantity called their mass and inversely proportional to the square of the distance between them. Yet it predicts the motions of the sun, the moon, and the planets to a high degree of accuracy.

Any physical theory is always provisional, in the sense that it is only a hypothesis: you can never prove it. No matter how many times the results of experiments agree with some theory, you can never be sure that the next time the result will not contradict the theory. On the other hand, you can disprove a theory by finding even a single observation that disagrees with the predictions of the theory. As philosopher of science Karl Popper has emphasized, a good theory is characterized by the fact that it makes a number of predictions that could in principle be disproved or falsified by observation. Each time new experiments are observed to agree with the predictions the theory survives, and our confidence in it is increased; but if ever a new observation is found to disagree, we have to abandon or modify the theory. At least that is what is supposed to happen, but you can always question the competence of the person who carried out the observation.

In practice, what often happens is that a new theory is devised that is really an extension of the previous theory. For example, very accurate observations of the planet Mercury revealed a small difference between its motion and the predictions of Newton's theory of gravity. Einstein's general theory of relativity predicted a slightly different motion from Newton's theory. The fact that Einstein's predictions matched what was seen, while Newton's did not, was one of the crucial confirmations of the new theory. However, we still use Newton's theory for all practical purposes because the difference between its predictions and those of general relativity is very small in the situations that we normally deal with. (Newton's theory also has the great advantage that it is much simpler to work with than Einstein's!)

The eventual goal of science is to provide a single theory that describes the whole universe. However, the approach most scientists actually follow is to separate the problem into two parts. First, there are the laws that tell us how the universe changes with time. (If we know what the universe is like at any one time, these physical laws tell us how it will look at any later time.) Second, there is the question of the initial state of the universe. Some people feel that science should be concerned with only the first part; they regard the question of the initial situation as a matter for metaphysics or religion. They would say that God, being omnipotent, could have started the universe off any way he wanted. That may be so, but in that case he also could have made it develop in a completely arbitrary way. Yet it appears that he chose to make it evolve in a very regular way according to certain laws. It therefore seems equally reasonable to suppose that there are also laws governing the initial state.

It turns out to be very difficult to devise a theory to describe the universe all in one go. Instead, we break the problem up into bits and invent a number of partial theories. Each of these partial theories describes and predicts a certain limited class of observations, neglecting the effects of other quantities, or representing them by simple sets of numbers. It may be that this approach is completely wrong. If everything in the universe depends on everything else in a fundamental way, it might be impossible to get close to a full solution by investigating parts of the problem in isolation. Nevertheless, it is certainly the way that we have made progress in the past. The classic example again is the Newtonian theory of gravity, which tells us that the gravitational force between two bodies depends only on one number associated with each body, its mass, but is otherwise independent of what the bodies are made of. Thus one does not need to have a theory of the structure and constitution of the sun and the planets in order to calculate their orbits.

Today scientists describe the universe in terms of two basic partial theories — the general theory of relativity and quantum mechanics. They are the great intellectual achievements of the first half of this century. The general theory of relativity describes the force of gravity and the large-scale structure of the universe, that is, the structure on scales from only a few miles to as large as a million million million million (1 with twenty-four zeros after it) miles, the size of the observable universe. Quantum mechanics, on the other hand, deals with phenomena on extremely small scales, such as a millionth of a millionth of an inch. Unfortunately, however, these two theories are known to be inconsistent with each other — they cannot both be correct. One of the major endeavors in physics today, and the major theme of this book, is the search for a new theory that will incorporate them both — a quantum theory of gravity. We do not yet have such a theory, and we may still be a long way from having one, but we do already know many of the properties that it must have. And we shall see, in later chapters, that we already know a fair amount about the predictions a quantum theory of gravity must make.

Now, if you believe that the universe is not arbitrary, but is governed by definite laws, you ultimately have to combine the partial theories into a complete unified theory that will describe everything in the universe. But there is a fundamental paradox in the search for such a complete unified theory. The ideas about scientific theories outlined above assume we are rational beings who are free to observe the universe as we want and to draw logical deductions from what we see. In such a scheme it is reasonable to suppose that we might progress ever closer toward the laws that govern our universe. Yet if there really is a complete unified theory, it would also presumably determine our actions. And so the theory itself would determine the outcome of our search for it! And why should it determine that we come to the right conclusions from the evidence? Might it not equally well determine that we draw the wrong conclusion? Or no conclusion at all?

The only answer that I can give to this problem is based on Darwin's principle of natural selection. The idea is that in any population of self-reproducing organisms, there will be variations in the genetic material and upbringing that different individuals have. These differences will mean that some individuals are better able than others to draw the right conclusions about the world around them and to act accordingly. These individuals will be more likely to survive and reproduce and so their pattern of behavior and thought will come to dominate. It has certainly been true in the past that what we call intelligence and scientific discovery has conveyed a survival advantage. It is not so clear that this is still the case: our scientific discoveries may well destroy us all, and even if they don't, a complete unified theory may not make much difference to our chances of survival. However, provided the universe has evolved in a regular way, we might expect that the reasoning abilities that natural selection has given us would be valid also in our search for a complete unified theory, and so would not lead us to the wrong conclusions.

Because the partial theories that we already have are sufficient to make accurate predictions in all but the most extreme situations, the search for the ultimate theory of the universe seems difficult to justify on practical grounds. (It is worth noting, though, that similar arguments could have been used against both relativity and quantum mechanics, and these theories have given us both nuclear energy and the microelectronics revolution!) The discovery of a complete unified theory, therefore, may not aid the survival of our species. It may not even affect our life-style. But ever since the dawn of civilization, people have not been content to see events as unconnected and inexplicable. They have craved an understanding of the underlying order in the world. Today we still yearn to know why we are here and where we came from. Humanity's deepest desire for knowledge is justification enough for our continuing quest. And our goal is nothing less than a complete description of the universe we live in.

FOR DISCUSSION AND WRITING

1. As a "thought experiment," place the selection in the following variety of scenes. Does it "fit"? Why, or why not?
   a. At a convention of the American Astrophysical Society, Hawking is brought to the platform in a wheelchair. Because of Lou Gehrig's disease he is unable to speak in such a way that the crowd will understand him, so he has one of his associates read the essay to a group of astrophysicists.
   b. Hawking has been invited to speak about his field at a meeting of the Jefferson High School PTA. His associate reads the selection.
   c. Hawking is visiting a faculty member at Utopia University, who invites him to speak to a freshman class in physics. Hawking's associate reads the essay.
   d. Hawking has been invited to speak at an anti-abortion rally. Three hundred noisy participants fall silent when the associate starts to read Hawking's paper on the nature of theories.

2. Regarding author: How does your knowledge of Hawking's physical condition affect your reaction to his essay?

3. On the basis of the following statement, what can you conclude about Hawking's purposes in writing *A Brief History of Time*? Relate those purposes to the author and to the time and place he has chosen for the book.

I decided to try and write a popular book about space and time after I gave the Loeb lectures at Harvard in 1982. There were already a considerable number of books about the early universe and black holes, ranging from the very good, such as Steven Weinberg's book, *The First Three Minutes,* to the very bad, which I will not identify. However, I felt that none of them really addressed the questions that had led me to do research in cosmology and quantum theory: Where did the universe come from? How and why did it begin? Will it come to an end, and if so, how? These are questions that are of interest to us all. But modern science has become so technical that only a very small number of specialists are able to master the mathematics used to describe them. Yet the basic ideas about the origin and fate of the universe can be stated without mathematics in a form that people without a scientific education can understand. That is what I have attempted to do in this book. The reader must judge whether I have succeeded.

Someone told me that each equation I included in the book would halve the sales. I therefore resolved not to have any equations at all. In the end, however, I *did* put in one equation, Einstein's famous equation, $E = mc^2$. I hope that this will not scare off half of my potential readers. (vi–vii)

4. Why should anyone want to find a unified theory?

5. Evaluate the selection from the standpoint of quality.

6. Evaluate the selection from the standpoint of manner. What are some of the ways in which Hawking tries to make his subject understandable?

7. Does Hawking give you enough information about both the general theory of relativity and the theory of quantum mechanics? In other words, do you believe that he violates the principle of quantity? Does he violate the principle elsewhere?

8. State the main point of the selection.

9. What world knowledge does one need in order to understand the selection? (What theological debates relate to the selection?)

10. According to Hawking, what two qualities must a good theory have?

11. What is the easiest way to disprove a theory?

12. Explain what Hawking means by a unified theory of the universe. Would such a theory necessarily invalidate other partial theories, such as the theory of evolution, to which Hawking alludes in the latter part of the essay? To the theory of supply-side economics? To the theory of relativity or quantum mechanics?

13. Explain how Hawking rescues himself from this paradox: "[I]f there really is a complete unified theory, it would also presumably determine our actions. And so the theory itself would determine the outcome of our search for it!" (par. 7).

14. Do you see a certain contradiction in the search for a unified theory and Hawking's statement that "any physical theory is always provisional" (par. 2)? How do you think that Hawking might answer this question? (Before answering this question, reread his comparison of Newton's theory of gravity with Einstein's theory of relativity.)

ICE POND

John McPhee

Any list of the ten best writers of nonfiction in America today would probably contain John McPhee, and many readers and critics would put him at the top of the list.

In his introduction to *The John McPhee Reader,* William L. Howarth gives an interesting and illuminating account of John McPhee's method of composition, which can fairly be summarized as a process of gathering and arranging: taking copious notes (in the field, from interviews, from library resources), arranging the notes, and then writing the successive drafts of his works. McPhee's genius is his ability to use a narrative structure as a vehicle for conveying facts and judgments, a rhetorical technique characteristic of good journalism.

Born in Princeton, New Jersey, in 1931, McPhee is the son of a physician father and a horticulturist mother. He attended both Princeton and Cambridge universities. He is a staff writer for *The New Yorker* and teaches a course, Literature of Fact, at Princeton. He has written about such diverse topics as the Florida orange industry *(Oranges),* rural New Jersey *(The Pine Barrens),* Alaska *(Coming into the Country),* and geology *(Rising from the Plains).*

Summer, 1981

At Princeton University, off and on since winter, I have observed the physicist Theodore B. Taylor standing like a mountaineer on the summit of what appears to be a five-hundred-ton Sno-Kone. Taylor now calls himself a "nuclear dropout." His has been, at any rate, a semicircular career, beginning at Los Alamos Scientific Laboratory, where, as an imaginative youth in his twenties, he not only miniaturized the atomic bomb but also designed the largest-yield fission bomb that had ever been exploded anywhere. In his thirties, he moved on to General Atomic, in La Jolla, to lead a project called Orion, his purpose being to construct a spaceship sixteen stories high and as voluminous as a college dormitory, in which he personally meant to take off from a Nevada basin and set a course for Pluto, with intermediate stops on Ganymede, Rhea, and Dione — ice-covered satellites of Jupiter and Saturn. The spaceship Orion, with its wide flat base, would resemble the nose of a bullet, the head of a rocket, the ogival hat of a bishop. It would travel at a hundred thousand miles an hour and be driven by two thousand fission bombs. Taylor's colleague Freeman Dyson meant to go along, too, extending spectacularly a leave of absence from the Institute for Advanced Study, in Princeton. The project was developing splendidly when the nuclear treaty of 1963 banned explosions in space and the atmosphere. Taylor quelled his dreams, and turned to a sombre subject. Long worried about the possibility of clandestine manufacture of nuclear bombs by individuals or small groups of terrorists, he spent his forties enhancing the protection of weapons-grade uranium and plutonium where it exists in private industries throughout the world. And now, in his fifties—and with the exception of his service as a member of the President's Commission on the Accident at Three Mile Island—he has gone flat-out full-time in pursuit of sources of energy that avoid the use of fission and of fossil fuel, one example of which is the globe of ice he has caused to be made in Princeton. "This isn't Ganymede," he informs me, scuffing big crystals under his feet. "But it's almost as exciting."

Taylor's hair is salt-and-peppery now but still stands in a thick youthful wave above his dark eyebrows and luminous brown eyes. He is tall, and he remains slim. What he has set out to do is to air-condition large buildings or whole suburban neighborhoods using less than ten per cent of the electricity required to cool them by conventional means, thereby saving more than ninety per cent of the oil that might be used to make the electricity. This way and that, he wants to take the "E" out of OPEC. The ice concept is simple. He grins and calls it "simple-minded—putting old and new ideas together in a technology appropriate to our time." You scoop out a depression in the ground, he explains—say, fifteen feet deep and sixty feet across—and line it with plastic. In winter, you fill it with a ball of ice. In summer, you suck ice water from the bottom and pump it indoors to an exchanger that looks something like an automobile radiator and cools air that is flowing through ducts. The water, having picked up some heat from the building, is about forty-five degrees as it goes back outside, where it emerges through shower heads and rains on the porous ice. Percolating to the bottom, the water is cooled as it descends, back to thirty-two degrees. Taylor calls this an ice pond. A modest number of ice ponds could cool, for example, the District of Columbia, saving the energy equivalent of one and a half million barrels of oil each summer.

The initial problem was how to make the ice. Taylor first brooded about this some years ago when he was researching the theoretical possibilities of constructing greenhouses that would aggregately cover tens of millions of acres and solve the pollution problems of modern agriculture. The greenhouses had to be cooled. He thought of making ice in winter and using it in summer. For various regions, he calculated how much ice you would have to make in order to have something left on Labor Day. How much with insulation? How much without insulation? The volumes were small enough to be appealing. How to make the ice? If you were to create a pond of water and merely let it freeze, all you would get, of course, would be a veneer that would break up with the arrival of spring. Ice could be compiled by freezing layer upon layer, but in most places in the United States six or eight feet would be the maximum thickness attainable in an average winter, and that would not be enough. Eventually, he thought of artificial snow. Ski trails were covered with it not only in Vermont and New Hampshire but also in New Jersey and Pennsylvania, and even in North Carolina, Georgia, and Alabama. To make ice, Taylor imagined, one might increase the amount of water moving through a ski-resort snow machine. The product would be slush. In a pondlike receptacle, water would drain away from the slush. It could be pumped out and put back through the machine. What remained in the end would be a ball of ice.

Taylor had meanwhile become a part-time professor at Princeton, and on one of his frequent visits to the university from his home in Maryland he showed his paper ice ponds to colleagues at the university's Center for Energy and Environmental Studies. The Center spent a couple of years seeking funds from the federal government for an ice-pond experiment, but the government was not interested. In 1979, the Prudential Insurance Company of America asked the university to help design a pair of office buildings — to be built just outside Princeton — that would be energy-efficient and innovative in as many ways as possible. Robert Socolow, a physicist who is the Center's director, brought Taylor into the Prudential project, and Taylor soon had funds for his snow machine, his submersible pumps, his hole in the ground.

At Los Alamos, when Taylor got together on paper the components of a novel bomb he turned over his numbers and his ideas to other people, who actually made the device. Had such a job been his to do, there would have been no bombs at all. His mind is replete with technology but innocent of technique. He cannot competently change a tire. He has difficulty opening doors. The university hired Don Kirkpatrick, a consulting solar engineer, to assemble and operate appropriate hardware, while unskilled laborers such as Taylor and Freeman Dyson would spread insulating materials over the ice or just stand by to comment. 5

"The first rule of technology is that no one can tell in advance whether a piece of technology is any good," Dyson said one day. "It will hang on things that are unforeseeable. In groping around, one wants to try things out that are quick and cheap and find out what doesn't work. The Department of Energy has many programs and projects — solar-energy towers and other grandiose schemes — with a common characteristic: no one can tell whether they're any good or not, and they're so big it will take at least five years and probably ten to find out. This ice pond is something you can do cheaply and quickly, and see whether it works."

A prototype pond was tried in the summer of 1980. It was dug beside a decrepit university storage building, leaky with respect to air and water, that had cinder-block walls and a flat roof. Size of an average house, there were twenty-four hundred square feet of space inside. Summer temperatures in the nineties are commonplace in New Jersey, and in musty rooms under that flat roof temperatures before the ice pond were sometimes close to a hundred and thirty. The 1980 pond was square — seventy-five feet across and fifteen feet deep. It contained a thousand tons of ice for a while, but more than half of that melted before insulation was applied: six inches of dry straw between sheets of polyethylene, weighed down with bald tires. Even so, the old building was filled most of the time from June to September with crisp October air. Something under seven tons of ice would melt away on a hot day. Nonetheless, at the end of summer a hundred tons remained. "It's a nice alternative to fossil fuels," Robert Socolow commented. "It has worked too well to be forgotten."

The concept having been successfully tested, the next imperative was to refine the art — technically, economically, and aesthetically. "The point is to make it elegant this time," said Freeman Dyson, and, from its hexagonal concrete skirt to its pure-white reflective cover, "elegant" is the word for the 1981 pond. Concealing the ice is a tentlike Dacron-covered free-span steel structure with six ogival sides — a cryodesic dome — which seems to emerge from the earth like the nose of a bullet, the head of a rocket, the hat of a bishop. Lift a flap and step inside. Look up at the summit of a white tower under insulation. Five hundred tons of ice — fifty-eight feet across the middle — rise to a conical peak, under layers of polyethylene foam, sewn into fabric like enormous quilts. It is as if the tip of the Finsteraarghorn had been wrapped by Christo.

Taylor, up on the foam, completes his inspection of the ice within, whose crystals are jagged when they first fall from the snow machine, and later, like glacier ice, recrystallize more than once into spheres of increasing diameter until the ultimate substance is very hard and resembles a conglomerate of stream gravel. The U.S. Army's Cold Regions Research and Engineering Laboratory has cored it with instruments of the type used on glaciers in Alaska. Suspended from a girder high above Taylor's head and pointing at the summit of the ice is something that appears to be a small naval cannon with a big daisy stuck in its muzzle. This is SMI SnowStream 320, the machine that made the ice. In its days of winter operation, particles plumed away from it like clouds of falling smoke. Unlike many such machines, it does not require compressed air but depends solely on its daisy-petalled propeller blades of varying length for maximum effectiveness in disassembling water. "We are harvesting the cold of winter for use in the summer," Taylor says. "This is natural solar refrigeration, powered by the wind. Wind brings cold air to us, freezes the falling water, and takes the heat away. We are rolling with nature — trying to make use of nature instead of fighting it. That machine cost seven thousand dollars. It can make about eight thousand tons of ice in an average winter here in Princeton — for thirty-five dollars a hundred tons. A hundred tons is enough to air-condition almost any house, spring to fall. In the course of a winter, that machine could make ten thousand tons of ice in Boston, seven thousand in Washington, D.C., fifteen thousand in Chicago, thirty thousand in Casper, Wyoming, fifty thousand in Minneapolis, and, if anybody cares, a hundred thousand tons of ice in Fairbanks. The lower the temperature, the more water you can move through the machine. We don't want dry snow, of course. Snow is too fluffy. We want slop. We want wet sherbet. At twenty degrees Fahrenheit, we can move fifty gallons a minute through the machine. The electricity that drives the snow machine amounts to a very small fraction of the electricity that is saved by the cooling capacity of the ice. In summer, electrical pumps circulate the ice water from the bottom of the pond for a few tenths of a cent a ton. The cost of moving air in ducts through the building is the same as in a conventional system and is negligible in comparison with the electrical cost of cooling air. We're substituting ice water made with winter winds for the cold fluid in a refrigerated-air-conditioner, using less than a tenth as much electrical energy as a conventional air-conditioning system. Our goal is to make the over-all cost lower than the cost of a conventional system and use less than one-tenth of the energy. We're just about there."

The Prudential's new buildings—a hundred and thirty thousand 10 square feet each, by Princeton's School of Architecture and Skidmore, Owings & Merrill—will be started this summer on a site a mile away. They are low, discretionary structures, provident in use of resources, durable, sensible, actuarial—with windows shaded just enough for summer but not to much for winter, with heat developing in a passive solar manner and brought in as well by heat pumps using water from the ground—and incorporating so many other features thrifty with energy that God will probably owe something to the insurance company after the account is totted up. An ice pond occupying less than half an acre can be expected to compound His debt.

A man who could devise atomic bombs and then plan to use them to drive himself to Pluto might be expected to expand his thinking if he were to create a little hill of ice. Taylor has lately been mulling the potentialities of abandoned rock quarries. You could fill an old rock quarry a quarter of a mile wide with several million tons of ice and then pile up more ice above ground as high as the Washington Monument. One of those could air-condition a hundred thousand homes. With all that volume, there would be no need for insulation. You would build pipelines at least ten feet in diameter and aim them at sweltering cities, where heat waves and crime waves would flatten in the water-cooled air. You could make ice reservoirs comparable in size to New York's water reservoirs and pipe ice water to the city from a hundred miles away. After the water had served as a coolant, it would be fed into the city's water supply.

"You could store grain at fifty degrees in India," Taylor goes on. "We're exploring that. The idea is to build an aqueduct to carry an ice slurry from the foothills of the Himalayas down to the Gangetic plain.

With an insulated cover over the aqueduct, the amount of ice lost in, say, two hundred miles would be trivial—if the aqueduct is more than ten feet across. In place of electric refrigeration, dairies could use ice ponds to cool milk. Most cheese factories could use at least fifty thousand tons of ice a year. If all the cheese factories in the United States were to do that, they alone would save annually, about six million barrels of oil. When natural gas comes out of the earth, it often contains too much water vapor to be suitable for distribution. One way to get rid of most of the water is to cool the gas to forty degrees. If ice ponds were used to cool, say, half the natural gas that is produced in this country, they would save the equivalent of ten million barrels of oil each year. Massive construction projects, such as dams, use amazing amounts of electricity to cool concrete while it hardens, sometimes for as much as three years. Ice ponds could replace the electricity. Ice ponds could cool power plants more effectively than environmental water does, and therefore make the power plants more efficient. Ice would also get rid of the waste heat in a manner more acceptable than heating up a river. In places like North Dakota, you can make ice with one of these machines for a few cents a ton—and the coolant would be economically advantageous in all sorts of industrial processing."

Taylor shivers a little, standing on the ice, and, to warm himself, he lights a cigarette. "You could also use snow machines to freeze seawater," he continues. "As seawater freezes, impurities migrate away from it, and you are left with a concentrated brine rich in minerals, and with frozen water that is almost pure—containing so little salt you can't taste it. As seawater comes out of the snow machine and the spray is freezing in the air, the brine separates from the pure frozen water as it falls. To use conventional refrigeration—to use an electric motor to run a compressor to circulate Freon to freeze seawater—is basically too costly. The cost of freezing seawater with a ski-slope machine is less than a hundredth the cost of freezing seawater by the conventional system. There are sixty-six pounds of table salt in a ton of seawater, almost three pounds of magnesium, a couple of pounds of sulphur, nearly a pound of calcium, lesser amounts of potassium, bromine, boron, and so forth. Suppose you had a ship making ice from seawater with snow machines that had been enlarged and adapted for the purpose. You would produce a brine about ten times as concentrated with useful compounds as the original seawater. It would be a multifarious ore. Subsequent extraction of table salt, magnesium, fertilizers, and other useful material from the brine would make all these products cheaper than they would be if they were extracted from unconcentrated seawater by other methods. The table salt alone would pay for the ship. You could separate it out for a dollar a ton. A ship as large as a supertanker could operate most of the year, shuttling back and forth from the Arctic to the Antarctic. At latitudes like that, you can make twenty times as much ice as you can in Princeton."

"What do you do with the ice?"

"Your options are to return it to the sea or to put it in a skirt and   15
haul it as an iceberg to a place where they need fresh water. The Saudis
and the French have been looking into harvesting icebergs in Antarctica
and towing them to the Red Sea. Someone has described this as bringing
the mountain to Muhammad. I would add that if you happen to live in
a place like New York the mountain is right at your doorstep — all you
have to do is make it. The cost of making fresh water for New York
City with snow machines and seawater would be less than the cost of
delivered water there now. Boston looks awfully good — twice as good
as Princeton. Boston could make fresh water, become a major producer
of table salt and magnesium and sulphur, and air-condition itself — in one
operation. All they have to do is make ice. It would renew Boston. More
than a hundred years ago, people cut ice out of ponds there and shipped
it around Cape Horn to San Francisco. When this country was getting
going, one of Boston's main exports was ice."

FOR DISCUSSION AND WRITING

1. What is McPhee's purpose? To provide information about the technology
   of ice ponds? To do a character sketch of Theodore B. Taylor? Are both
   of these statements inadequate? If so, give a better one.

2. What is McPhee's purpose in using vivid descriptive language? Point out
   instances of such language.

3. In regard to author, "The Bleeders" is impersonal; Hackett is almost
   completely in the background. "Sounding" (which you will read later in
   this chapter) is very personal; the author, Mark Twain, is central to the
   piece. Is McPhee, like Hackett, almost invisible in "Ice Pond," or is he,
   like Mark Twain, a central element in the essay? Or does McPhee's
   "authorial presence" fall somewhere between these two poles? Point out
   references that McPhee makes to himself, either overtly or by implication. What is the effect of "authorial presence"?

4. In your opinion, is the quality of the information adequate? Why do you
   think that McPhee is or is not a reliable source of information on this
   subject?

5. In regard to manner, most readers feel that McPhee's prose is exceptionally clear and easy to read. What are some of the ways McPhee
   achieves this clarity? (Sentence structure? Vocabulary? Figures of speech?
   Examples?)

6. With regard to scene, how have the issues of the day shaped Theodore
   Taylor's career?

7. What is some of the world knowledge readers must have in order to
   understand "Ice Pond"?

8. In your opinion, how does Taylor's earlier plan to build a sixteen-story spaceship affect his credibility?

9. In the opening paragraph, McPhee writes, "His [Taylor's] has been, at any rate, a semicircular career." The final paragraph also concerns itself with matters coming back around. In the latter instance, what matters will come back around? Why do you think the piece ends as it does?

10. What images show the semicircular nature of Taylor's career?

11. What do you suppose are the author's qualifications for writing "Ice Pond?" Explain.

THE FIRST CURE

Black Elk

Black Elk, of the Oglala Lakota Sioux, was born in what is now Wyoming in 1863, one year before the Bozeman trail opened the area to white settlement, and died in 1950. The bare chronicle of his life is interesting and instructive. When he was nine, he learned through a vision that he was destined to be holy man and healer. After Custer's defeat in 1876, the Oglala Lakota fled to Canada and did not return to the reservation (in present-day South Dakota) until Black Elk was seventeen. Wanting to learn more about the whites and their ways, he joined Buffalo Bill's Wild West Show in 1886 and traveled through the eastern United States and Europe. After returning to the reservation, Black Elk witnessed the infamous massacre at Wounded Knee in 1890. In 1892 he married, and in 1904 he converted to Catholicism. Thus, Black Elk in a way symbolizes the fate of native Americans through the last half of the nineteenth century and into the twentieth.

The poet John Neihardt met Black Elk and, wanting to learn his history, asked Black Elk's son to interpret. (Black Elk spoke little English, and Neihardt spoke no Sioux.) The result of a long and laborious series of interviews was the book *Black Elk Speaks,* first published in 1932 and reissued in 1961. It has become an important document in the movement to preserve native American culture.

In the following selection, Black Elk explains why Indians do things in circles and how he once cured a child.

After the heyoka ceremony, I came to live here where I am now between Wounded Knee Creek and Grass Creek. Others came too, and we made these little gray houses of logs that you see, and they are square. It is a bad way to live, for there can be no power in a square.

You have noticed that everything an Indian does is in a circle, and that is because the Power of the World always works in circles, and everything tries to be round. In the old days when we were a strong and happy people, all our power came to us from the sacred hoop of the nation, and so long as the hoop was unbroken, the people flourished. The flowering tree was the living center of the hoop, and the circle of the four quarters nourished it. The east gave peace and light, the south gave warmth, the west gave rain, and the north with its cold and mighty wind gave strength and endurance. This knowledge came to us from the outer world with our religion. Everything the Power of the World does is done in a circle. The sky is round, and I have heard that the earth is round like a ball, and so are all the stars. The wind, in its greatest power, whirls. Birds make their nests in circles, for theirs is the same religion as ours. The sun comes forth and goes down again in a circle. The moon does the same, and both are round. Even the seasons form a great circle in their changing, and always come back again to where they were. The life of a man is a circle from childhood to childhood, and so it is in everything where power moves. Our tepees were round like the nests of birds, and these were always set in a circle, the nation's hoop, a nest of many nests, where the Great Spirit meant for us to hatch our children.

But the Wasichus have put us in these square boxes. Our power is gone and we are dying, for the power is not in us any more. You can look at our boys and see how it is with us. When we were living by the power of the circle in the way we should, boys were men at twelve or thirteen years of age. But now it takes them very much longer to mature.

Well, it is as it is. We are prisoners of war while we are waiting here. But there is another world.

It was in the Moon of Shedding Ponies (May) when we had the heyoka ceremony. One day in the Moon of Fatness (June), when everything was blooming, I invited One Side to come over and eat with me. I had been thinking about the four-rayed herb that I had now seen twice — the first time in the great vision when I was nine years old, and the second time when I was lamenting on the hill. I knew that I must have this herb for curing, and I thought I could recognize the place where I had seen it growing that night when I lamented.

After One Side and I had eaten, I told him there was a herb I must find, and I wanted him to help me hunt for it. Of course I did not tell him I had seen it in a vision. He was willing to help, so we got on our horses and rode over to Grass Creek. Nobody was living over there. We came to the top of a high hill above the creek, and there we got off our horses and sat down, for I felt that we were close to where I saw the herb growing in my vision of the dog.

We sat there awhile singing together some heyoka songs. Then I began to sing alone a song I had heard in my first great vision:

> In a sacred manner they are sending voices.

After I had sung this song, I looked down towards the west, and yonder at a certain spot beside the creek were crows and magpies, chicken hawks and spotted eagles circling around and around.

Then I knew, and I said to One Side: "Friend, right there is where the herb is growing." He said: "We will go forth and see." So we got on our horses and rode down Grass Creek until we came to a dry gulch, and this we followed up. As we neared the spot the birds all flew away, and it was a place where four or five dry gulches came together. There right on the side of the bank the herb was growing, and I knew it, although I had never seen one like it before, except in my vision.

It had a root about as long as to my elbow, and this was a little thicker than my thumb. It was flowering in four colors, blue, white, red, and yellow.

We got off our horses, and after I had offered red willow bark to the Six Powers, I made a prayer to the herb, and said to it: "Now we shall go forth to the two-leggeds, but only to the weakest ones, and there shall be happy days among the weak."

It was easy to dig the herb, because it was growing in the edge of the clay gulch. Then we started back with it. When we came to Grass Creek again, we wrapped it in some good sage that was growing there.

Something must have told me to find the herb just then, for the next evening I needed it and could have done nothing without it.

I was eating supper when a man by the name of Cuts-to-Pieces came in, and he was saying: "Hey, hey, hey!" for he was in trouble. I asked him what was the matter, and he said: "I have a boy of mine, and he is very sick and I am afraid he will die soon. He has been sick a long time. They say you have great power from the horse dance and the heyoka ceremony, so maybe you can save him for me. I think so much of him."

I told Cuts-to-Pieces that if he really wanted help, he should go   *15* home and bring me back a pipe with an eagle feather on it. While he was gone, I thought about what I had to do; and I was afraid, because I had never cured anybody yet with my power, and I was very sorry for Cuts-to-Pieces. I prayed hard for help. When Cuts-to-Pieces came back with the pipe, I told him to take it around to the left of me, leave it there, and pass out again to the right of me. When he had done this, I sent for One Side to come and help me. Then I took the pipe and went to where the sick little boy was. My father and my mother went with us, and my friend, Standing Bear, was already there.

I first offered the pipe to the Six Powers, then I passed it, and we all smoked. After that I began making a rumbling thunder sound on the drum. You know, when the power of the west comes to the two-leggeds, it comes with rumbling, and when it has passed, everything lifts up its head and is glad and there is greenness. So I made this rumbling sound. Also, the voice of the drum is an offering to the Spirit of the World. Its sound arouses the mind and makes men feel the mystery and power of things.

The sick little boy was on the northeast side of the tepee, and when we entered at the south, we went around from left to right, stopping on the west side when we had made the circle.

You want to know why we always go from left to right like that. I can tell you something of the reason, but not all. Think of this: Is not the south the source of life, and does not the flowering stick truly come from there? And does not man advance from there toward the setting sun of his life? Then does he not approach the colder north where the white hairs are? And does he not then arrive, if he lives, at the source of light and understanding, which is the east? Then does he not return to where he began, to his second childhood, there to give back his life to all life, and his flesh to the earth whence it came? The more you think about this, the more meaning you will see in it.

As I said, we went into the tepee from left to right, and sat ourselves down on the west side. The sick little boy was on the northeast side, and he looked as though he were only skin and bones. I had the pipe, the drum and the four-rayed herb already, so I asked for a wooden cup, full of water, and an eagle bone whistle, which was for the spotted eagle of my great vision. They placed the cup of water in front of me; and then I had to think awhile, because I had never done this before and I was in doubt.

I understood a little more now, so I gave the eagle bone whistle to One Side and told him how to use it in helping me. Then I filled the pipe with red willow bark, and gave it to the pretty young daughter of Cuts-to-Pieces, telling her to hold it, just as I had seen the virgin of the east holding it in my great vision.

Everything was ready now, so I made low thunder on the drum, keeping time as I sent forth a voice. Four times I cried "Hey-a-a-hey," drumming as I cried to the Spirit of the World, and while I was doing this I could feel the power coming through me from my feet up, and I knew that I could help the sick little boy.

I kept on sending a voice, while I made low thunder on the drum, saying: "My Grandfather, Great Spirit, you are the only one and to no other can any one send voices. You have made everything, they say, and you have made it good and beautiful. The four quarters and the two roads crossing each other, you have made. Also you have set a power where the sun goes down. The two-leggeds on earth are in despair. For them, my Grandfather, I send a voice to you. You have said this to me: The weak shall walk. In vision you have taken me to the center of the world and there you have shown me the power to make over. The water in the cup that you have given me, by its power shall the dying live. The herb that you have shown me, through its power shall the feeble walk upright. From where we are always facing (the south), behold, a virgin shall appear, walking the good red road, offering the pipe as she walks, and hers also is the power of the flowering tree. From where the Giant lives (the north), you have given me a sacred, cleansing wind, and where this wind passes the weak shall have strength. You have said this to me. To you and to all your powers and to Mother Earth I send a voice for help."

You see, I had never done this before, and I know now that only one power would have been enough. But I was so eager to help the sick little boy that I called on every power there is.

I had been facing the west, of course, while sending a voice. Now I walked to the north and to the east and to the south, stopping there where the source of all life is and where the good red road begins. Standing there I sang thus:

20

In a sacred manner I have made them walk.
A sacred nation lies low.
In a sacred manner I have made them walk.
A sacred two-legged, he lies low.
In a sacred manner, he shall walk.

While I was singing this I could feel something queer all through   *25*
my body, something that made me want to cry for all unhappy things,
and there were tears on my face.

Now I walked to the quarter of the west, where I lit the pipe,
offered it to the powers, and, after I had taken a whiff of smoke, I passed
it around.

When I looked at the sick little boy again, he smiled at me, and I
could feel that the power was getting stronger.

I next took the cup of water, drank a little of it, and went around
to where the sick little boy was. Standing before him, I stamped the
earth four times. Then, putting my mouth to the pit of his stomach, I
drew through him the cleansing wind of the north. I next chewed some
of the herb and put it in the water, afterward blowing some of it on the
boy and to the four quarters. The cup with the rest of the water I gave
to the virgin, who gave it to the sick little boy to drink. Then I told the
virgin to help the boy stand up and to walk around the circle with him,
beginning at the south, the source of life. He was very poor and weak,
but with the virgin's help he did this.

Then I went away.

Next day Cuts-to-Pieces came and told me that his little boy was   *30*
feeling better and was sitting up and could eat something again. In four
days he could walk around. He got well and lived to be thirty years old.

Cuts-to-Pieces gave me a good horse for doing this; but of course
I would have done it for nothing.

When the people heard about how the little boy was cured, many
came to me for help, and I was busy most of the time.

This was in the summer of my nineteenth year (1882), in the Moon
of Making Fat.

FOR DISCUSSION AND WRITING

1. Explain why one can argue that the selection resulted from the effect of
   time and place on the author.

2. In this selection, language is presumably spoken. How does this spoken
   language differ from the written language in, for instance, the selection
   by Hawking?

3. Discuss the effect of Black Elk's language on the reader's perception of
   him (the author) and of the time and place that he talks about.

4. Many literature courses now include works by native Americans (such as Black Elk) and black Americans (such as Zora Neale Hurston, whose piece "How It Feels to Be Colored Me" appears later in this chapter), whereas twenty years ago these authors were virtually unknown. In what way have changes in the American scene brought about changes in the literature curriculum?

5. In what ways does the discussion of the circle as a sacred element of Dakota culture violate the principle of relation?

6. Do you trust the quality of the information in the selection? Explain.

7. The literal medium used in "Black Elk Speaks" is, presumably, written transcriptions of interviews. On a less literal level, the medium is an oral history. How do you think each medium influences the other?

8. In your opinion, what is the most important theme in "The First Cure"?

9. Some texts are valuable for the information they contain. For example, the manual that comes with a new computer contains absolutely essential information. Other texts are valuable because of the imaginative experience they provide readers. And some texts, of course, are both informative and imaginative. From your point of view, why is "The First Cure" valuable?

10. The Black Elk and Hawking pieces illustrate the differences between a belief and a theory. Use the two selections to explain this difference.

THE VASSAR GIRL

Mary McCarthy

Mary McCarthy was an "intellectual," a person who spent her life thinking and writing about art, literature, politics, and the American scene in general. In her novel *The Groves of Academe* (1952), she scrutinizes higher education; *The Group* (1963) is a fictional treatment of some of the themes that you will discover in "The Vassar Girl"; another novel, *A Charmed Life* (1955), is largely autobiographical. *Memories of a Catholic Girlhood* (1957) and *How I Grew* (1987) are autobiographical nonfiction. Two books on Italian art and history show the range of her interests: *Venice Observed* (1956) and *The Stones of Florence* (1959). Her reactions to the Vietnam war are expressed in a series of essays collected in *Vietnam* (1967) and *Hanoi* (1968). *The Mask of State: Watergate Portraits* (1974) deals, obviously, with the scandals during the administration of President Richard Nixon.

Born in Seattle in 1912, McCarthy was orphaned and was reared by elderly relatives. After graduating from Vassar in 1933, McCarthy became a book reviewer for two intellectual magazines, *The Nation* and *The New Republic,* and theater critic for the highbrow *Partisan Review*. She and her husband, the extremely influential critic Edmund Wilson, were virtually an institution in American culture until his death in 1972. Mary McCarthy died in 1989.

"Vassar Girl" is a nostalgic, but critical, look at the changes that took place in her alma mater. The graduates in her day, she tells us, thought of themselves as offbeat radicals, whereas the graduates of the class of 1951 (the date of the essay) considered themselves solid citizens working within the community for liberal causes.

The essay, although it appeared forty years ago, deals with issues that never grow old: the values and purposes of education, the relationship of the student to his or her college or university, the struggle for gender equality in the professions, and the attitudes of students. As you read this essay, ask yourself how the issues it raises apply to your own educational experience.

May, 1951

Like Athena, goddess of wisdom, Vassar College sprang in full battle dress from the head of a man. Incorporated at Poughkeepsie, New York, in 1861, the year of Lincoln's inauguration and the emancipation of the serfs in Russia, it was the first woman's college to be conceived as an idea, a manifesto, a declaration of rights, and a proclamation of equality.

It did not evolve, like Mount Holyoke, chartered in 1836, from a female seminary into a college; it came into being at one stroke, so to speak, equipped with a museum of natural history, a library, a main building modeled on the Tuileries, an observatory with a gigantic telescope, a collection of paintings and a course of study. This was to embrace, in the specifications of the Founder, "the English language and its

Literature; other Modern Languages, the Ancient Classics, so far as may be demanded by the spirit of the times; the Mathematics, to such an extent as may be deemed advisable; all the branches of Natural Science . . . Anatomy, Physiology, and Hygiene . . . the elements of Political Economy; some knowledge of Federal and State Constitutions and Laws; Moral Science, particularly as bearing on the filial, conjugal, and parental relations; Aesthetics . . . Domestic Economy . . . last, and most important of all, the daily, systematic Reading and Study of the Holy Scriptures, as the only and all-sufficient Rule of Christian faith and practice. . . ."

The promulgator of this curriculum, which, except for the last proviso, remains the basis of the Vassar education, was not a gentleman of parts or a social reformer, but a self-educated Poughkeepsie brewer, the keeper of an ale and oyster house. Matthew Vassar's farming parents had migrated from England to Dutchess County, New York, when the boy was four years old. He left school at the age of ten to go to work for a neighboring farmer, carrying his few small belongings tied up in a cotton handkerchief. Persistence and hard work had their storied rewards: at forty, he was a successful Poughkeepsie businessman with a good-sized brewery on the river, membership in the Baptist church, an urge toward foreign travel, and strong philanthropic inclinations. Having no children, he determined to attach his name to some lasting benevolent enterprise and settled on woman's education after cautious shopping and advice-seeking. Once, however, he had been fixed in the notion, his plan became clothed in rhetoric and in philosophic axioms: "Woman, having received from her Creator the same intellectual constitution as man, has the same rights as man to intellectual culture and development. . . . The mothers of a country mold the character of its citizens, determine its institutions, and shape its destiny. Next to the influence of the mother is that of the female teacher. . . ." His maiden speech to the Board of Trustees at the initial meeting in February, 1861, had the resonance of a sovereign pronouncement: "I have come to the conclusion, that the establishment and endowment of a College for the education of young women is a work which will satisfy my highest aspirations, and will be, under God, a rich blessing to this city and State, to our country and the world."

The authoritative tone is characteristic; it is as though, speaking through the mouth of the elderly, didactic brewer, were the first, fresh Vassar girl. The stiff, exact provisions evoke the basic architecture of the Vassar campus, different from the colonial republicanism of the early men's colleges and from the collegiate Gothic of the late big philanthropy — something purposive and utilitarian: dark-red brick, plainly set-out buildings in the prevailing factory style of the late nineteenth century. In the phraseology also, candidly revealed, is the first note of Vassar emulation, of the passion for public service coupled with a yearning for the limelight, a wish to play a part in the theatre of world events, to perform some splendid action that will cut one's name in history like a figure eight in ice.

The essence of Vassar is mythic. Today, despite much competition,   *5*
it still figures in the public mind as the archetypal woman's college. Less intellectual than Radcliffe or Bryn Mawr, less social and weekendish than Smith, less athletic than Wellesley, less Bohemian than Bennington, it is nevertheless the stock butt of musical-comedy jokes and night-club wheezes. It has called down thunder from the pulpit, provided heroines for popular ballads; even a girdle bears its name. Like Harvard, it is always good for a knowledgeable smile from members of the population who have scarcely heard the name of another college. It signifies a certain *je ne sais quoi;* a whiff of luxury and the ineffable; plain thinking and high living. If a somehow know-it-all manner is typical of the Vassar student, the public has a way of winking that it knows all about Vassar, though this sly wink only intimates that there is something to know. For different people, in fact, at different periods, Vassar can stand for whatever is felt to be wrong with the modern female: humanism, atheism, Communism, short skirts, cigarettes, psychiatry, votes for women, free love, intellectualism. Pre-eminently among American college women, the Vassar girl is thought of as carrying a banner. The inscription on it varies with the era or with the ideas of the beholder and in the final sense does not matter — the flushed cheek and tensed arm are what count.

I myself was an ardent literary little girl in an Episcopal boarding school on the West Coast, getting up at four in the morning to write a seventeen-page medieval romance before breakfast, smoking on the fire-escape and thinking of suicide, meeting a crippled boy in the woods by the cindery athletic field, composing a novelette in study hall about the life of a middle-aged prostitute ("Her eyes were turbid as dishwater") when the name, *Vassar,* entered my consciousness through the person of an English teacher. She symbolized to me the critical spirit, wit, cool learning, detachment — everything I suddenly wished to have and to be, from the moment I first heard her light, precise, cutting voice score some pretension, slatternly phrase or construction on the part of her pupils. With blond buns over her ears, gold-rimmed glasses and a teacher's taste in dress, Miss A—— was severe and formidable, yet she smoked, as I knew, on the side, read *The American Mercury* and was shocked by nothing. She advised me to send my novelette to H. L. Mencken for criticism. The idea of going to Vassar and becoming like Miss A—— immediately dominated my imagination. I gave up a snap course in domestic science and registered for Latin. I tutored in Caesar during the summer and coaxed my family. To go east to college was quite a step in Seattle.

What Vassar represented at that time to the uninitiated person can be gathered from the attitude of my Catholic grandmother in Minneapolis, whom I stopped to visit on my way east to Poughkeepsie. She sent for the parish priest to armor me against the "heresy" I should be exposed to. The priest was as embarrassed as I was at the task set him. He contented himself with a few rumbling remarks about the efficacy of prayer and the sacraments, and then admonished the old lady that at Vassar I would find the very best of Western thought, contemporary and classical — I ought to be proud to be going there. Listening breathlessly, I hardly knew whether to be more thrilled by the priest's liberal commendation or by my grandmother's conservative disapproval.

For the majority, perhaps, of the freshmen swarming through Taylor Gate that year for their first interview with the dean, Vassar had some such overtones. Its high, iron-runged, Gothic gate, which swung open on this day to receive the stream of cars laden with luggage, tennis rackets, phonographs, lamps, and musical instruments, was for most of us outlanders, still in our neat cloche hats and careful little traveling suits, a threshold to possibility. (It was the autumn, though we could not foresee it, of the Wall Street crash.) Bucolically set in rolling orchard country just outside the town of Poughkeepsie, with the prospect of long walks and rides along curving back roads and cold red apples to bite; framed by two mirror-like lakes, by a lively off-campus street full of dress shops, antique stores, inns, which were brimming now with parents, brothers, and fiancés, Vassar, still warm and summery, gave the impression of a cornucopia overflowing with promises. The bareheaded Yale boys in roadsters parked outside Taylor Gate; the tall, dazzling girls, upperclassmen, in pale sweaters and skirts, impeccable, with pearls at the throat and stately walks, like goddesses; the vaulted library; the catalogue already marked and starred for courses like Psychology and Philosophy ("The Meaning of Morals, Beauty, Truth, God — open to freshmen by special permission"); the trolley tracks running past the spiked fence downtown to further shopping, adventure, the railroad station, New York, plays, concerts, night clubs, Fifth Avenue bus rides — all this seemed to foretell four years of a Renaissance lavishness, in an academy that was a Forest of Arden and a Fifth Avenue department store combined.

The dean, in her opening address, told us that we were the smallest class ever to be admitted (in recent years, I presume) and hence the most highly selected. She spoke to us of the responsibilities that thereby devolved on us, but to this part I hardly listened, being so filled with the pride and glory of belonging to the very best class in the very best college in America. This feeling did not really leave me during four years in college; Vassar has a peculiar power of conveying a sense of excellence.

After October, 1929, some of us had smaller allowances; my room- 10
mate and I no longer went off-campus every night for a dinner beginning

with *canapé* of anchovies and going on to artichokes and mushrooms under glass. More of us were on scholarships or using some form of self-help. Typing papers for others, waking friends in the morning, for the first time became regular industries. Some students' fathers were rumored to have shot themselves or to have had nervous breakdowns, but the off-campus shops still prospered, selling grape lemonade, bacon-and-tomato sandwiches, and later 3.2 beer. New York department stores brought dress exhibitions once or twice a year to the tearooms; we bought more than we could afford and charged it. Yale boys came down weekly for the Saturday-night "J" dance, at which the girls were stags and cut in on them. At these times the more prosperous went out to eat at roadhouses, tearooms, or inns in twos, fours, sixes, or eights. The boys carried whiskey in flasks, and sometimes there were gin picnics. One of my friends had an airplane; another girl kept a pet goat, very white and pretty; in the spring of senior year, when cars were permitted, a few roadsters appeared. In New York, we went to plays, musicals, and speakeasies, two or three girls together on a Saturday day leave; on weekends, alone with our beaux. Many of us were engaged.

During our junior year, the word "Communist" first assumed an active reality: a plain girl who was a science major openly admitted to being one. But most of our radicals were Socialists, and throughout that election year they campaigned for Norman Thomas, holding parades and rallies, though in most cases they were too young to vote. We of the "aesthetic" camp considered them jejune and naïve; we were more impressed when we heard, after a poll, that a plurality (as I recall) of the faculty were voting for Thomas that year.

The inert mass of the student body was, as usual, Republican; we aesthetes did not believe in politics, but slightly favored the Democrats. Then our trustee, Franklin Roosevelt, was elected President. Miss Newcomer of the Economics Department went off to serve on a committee at Albany. Doctor MacCracken, our president, had lunch with Roosevelt off a tray in the White House — and we undergraduates felt more than ever that Vassar was at the center of everything.

With the impetus of the New Deal and memories of the breadlines behind us, even we aesthetes began reading about Sacco and Vanzetti and Mooney. We wrote papers for Contemporary Prose Fiction on Dos Passos. The pretty blue-eyed Republican girls looked troubled when you talked to them about these things; *their* favorite book was *Of Human Bondage,* which we despised. The Socialists made friends with us, though they swore by Miss Lockwood's press course, and we by Miss Sandison's Renaissance or by Miss Rindge's art or by a course in Old English or in verse writing: our group, being aesthetes, was naturally more individualistic. But by the end of our senior year the Socialists, the aesthetes, and the pretty Republican girls had been drawn closer together.

We all drank 3.2 beer at night in Mrs. Cary's tearoom, discussed term papers and politics, sang songs of farewell to each other in half-mocking, half-tender accents. We were happy to be together, our differences of origin and opinion reconciled in the fresh May darkness, but our happiness rested on the sense that all this was provisional and transitory. "Lost now in the wide, wide world," we sang fervently, but actually almost all of us were joyous to be leaving college, precisely because we had loved it, for Vassar had inspired us with the notion that the wide, wide world was our oyster.

A few years later, a census was taken, and it was discovered that   15
the average Vassar graduate had two-plus children and was married to a Republican lawyer.

This finding took by surprise even that section of the alumnae — Vassar Club activists, organizers of benefits and fund-raising drives — who looked upon it as providential. Here, at last, they felt, was something concrete to offset newspaper stories of students picketing during a strike in nearby Beacon, students besieging the state legislature in Albany, that would put an end to the rumors of immorality, faddishness, and Bohemianism that, because of a few undergraduates, had clung to the college's public persona for two decades or more. What these figures proved, the alumnae apologists were really implying, was that the Vassar education had not "taken" or had taken only on a small group who were not at all typical of Vassar and who by their un-Vassarish behavior were getting the college a bad name. And yet the statistical Average herself would have been the first to protest (with that touch of apology so characteristic of Vassar women who have not "done" anything later on) that she was not at all representative of Vassar standards and point to some more unconventional classmate as the real Vassar thing.

A wistful respect for the unorthodox is ingrained in the Vassar mentality. The Vassar freshman still comes through Taylor Gate as I did, with the hope of being made over, redirected, vivified. The daughter of a conservative lawyer, doctor, banker, or businessman, she will have chosen Vassar in all probability with the idea of transcending her background. And if she does not have such plans for herself, her teachers have them for her. If she is, say, a Vassar daughter or a girl from a preparatory school like Chapin or Madeira who chose Vassar because her friends did, her teachers, starting freshman year, will seek to "shake her up," "emancipate" her, make her "think for herself." This dynamic conception of education is Vassar's hallmark.

The progressive colleges have something similar, but there the tendency is to orient the student in some preconceived direction — toward the modern dance or toward "progressive" political thinking, while at Vassar, by and large, the student is almost forbidden to take her direction from the teacher. "What do *you* think?" is the question that ricochets on the student if she asks the teacher's opinion; and the difference between Vassar and the traditional liberal college (where the teacher is also supposed to keep his own ideas in the background) is that at Vassar the student is obliged, every day, to proffer hers.

Thus at a freshman English class I recently visited, the students were discussing Richard Hughes' *The Innocent Voyage,* a book whose thesis is that children are monsters, without moral feeling in the adult sense, insane, irresponsible, incapable of conventional grief or remorse. This idea was very shocking to perhaps half the class, well-brought-up little girls who protested that children were not "like that," indignant hands waved in the air, anguished faces grimaced, while a more detached student in braids testified that her own experience as a baby-sitter bore Mr. Hughes out. The teacher took no sides but merely smiled and encouraged one side and then the other, raising a hand for quiet when the whole class began shouting at once, and interrupting only to ask, "Do you really know children? Are you speaking from what you have seen or remember, or from what you think *ought* to be so?" This book plainly was chosen not because it was a favorite with the professor or even because of its literary merits but because it challenged preconceptions and disturbed set ideas.

The effect of this training is to make the Vassar student, by the time she has reached her junior year, look back upon her freshman self with pity and amazement. When you talk to her about her life in college, you will find that she sees it as a series of before-and-after snapshots: "When I came to Vassar, I thought like Mother and Daddy . . . I was conservative in my politics . . . I had race prejudice . . . I liked academic painting." With few exceptions, among those who are articulate and who feel that the college has "done something" for them, the trend is from the conservative to the liberal, from the orthodox to the heterodox, with stress on the opportunities Vassar has provided for getting to know "different" people, of opposite opinions and from different backgrounds.

Yet the statistical fate of the Vassar girl, thanks to Mother and Dad and the charge account, is already decreed. And the result is that the Vassar alumna, uniquely among American college women, is two persons — the housewife or matron, and the yearner and regretter. The Vassar graduate who has failed to make a name for herself, to "keep up," extend her interests, is, because of her training, more poignantly conscious of backsliding than her contemporary at Barnard or Holyoke. And unlike the progressive-college graduate, on the other hand, who has been catered to and conciliated by her instructors, the Vassar girl who drifts into matronhood or office work is more inclined to blame herself than society for what has happened, and to feel that she has let the college down by not becoming famous or "interesting." The alumnae records are full of housewives, doctors, teachers, educators, social workers, child-welfare specialists, public-health consultants. But the Vassar dream

20

obdurately prefers such figures as Inez Milholland, '09, who rode a white horse down Fifth Avenue campaigning for woman suffrage; Edna St. Vincent Millay, '17, the *révoltée* girl-poet who made herself a byword of sexual love and disenchanted lyricism; Elizabeth Hawes, '25, iconoclastic dress designer, and author of *Fashion Is Spinach*. The Vassar romanticism will pass over a college president in favor of an author or journalist — Constance Rourke, '07, pioneer folklorist and author of *American Humor;* Muriel Rukeyser, ex-'34, Eleanor Clark, Elizabeth Bishop, '34, poets and writers, Jean Poletti, '25, Lois ("Lipstick" of *The New Yorker*) Long, '22, Beatrice Berle, '23, noted for her opinions on marriage and for the twin bathtubs she and her husband, Adolf A. Berle, Jr., shared in their Washington house — and it will recognize as its own even such antipodal curiosities as Elizabeth Bentley, '30, the ex-Communist spy queen, and Major Julia Hamblet, '37, the first woman to enlist in the Marines.

The incongruities on this list are suggestive. An *arresting performance* in politics, fashion, or art is often taken by the Vassar mind to be synonymous with true accomplishment. The Vassar dynamism drives toward money and success and the limelight in a truly Roman fashion, when it is not yoked to their opposite — service. With its alertness, its eagerness to *do* things, it tends, once the academic restraints are removed, to succumb to a rather journalistic notion of what constitutes value.

In the arts, after the first few intransigent gestures, Vassar talent streams into commercial side lines — advertising, fashion writing, publicity, promotion — and here assurance and energy case the Vassar success woman in an elephant-hide of certainties — a sort of proud flesh. This older Vassar career woman is nearly as familiar to American folklore as the intrepid young Portia or Rosalind she may at one time have passed for. Conscious of being set apart by a superior education, confident of her powers in her own field of enterprise, she is impervious to the universe, which she dominates, both mentally and materially. On the campus, she is found at vocational conferences, panel discussions, committee meetings — she is one of those women who are always dominating, in an advisory capacity. In the world, she is met in political-action groups, consumers' leagues, on school boards and in charitable drives, at forums and roundtables. Married, almost professionally so, the mother of children, she is regarded as a force in her community or business, is respected and not always liked. Vassar, of course, has no patent on this model of the American woman, but there is a challenge in the Vassar atmosphere that makes her graduates feel that they owe it as a positive duty to the college and to the human community to be outstanding, aggressive, and secure.

All this is still far away from the current undergraduate. She has heard vaguely through the alumnae magazine that some Vassar graduates are unhappy and frustrated because college did not prepare them for a life of dishwashing and babies, but this prospect for herself appears to have no relevance, though she may be planning to marry immediately on graduation and to begin having children at once. The Vassar career woman she is aware of, without self-identification. Vassar girls today, even more than most young people, seem to live in an ideal present; the alumnae they are heading to become seem as remote to them as the freshmen selves they have transcended. They knit, play bridge, attend classes and lectures, looking decorous and polite, with smooth, soft coiffures and tranquil faces. Their plans are made — one will be a doctor; one will work for the UN; another will take up journalism. There is none of the conflict and indecision that harried us in the thirties; they have decided to help the world, but not to change or destroy it. They prepare their work with competence, recite with poise and credit; in mastery of assigned material, some of it quite difficult, they outdo any group of college students I have had experience with. In the classroom, a serene low voice begs elucidation of a point in a Platonic dialogue: "I'm not sure I understand what Socrates means to say here." The difficulty is explained — "Thank you," and a note is taken. Among the upperclassmen, these nods of illumination and swift scribbles on the note pad are frequent; the college is businesslike.

They read Sartre and Tennessee Williams as part of their work in the drama; a class in Aesthetics is popular; they listen to music in the dormitories; but, despite competence, civility, and even deferential interest, they have an air of placid aloofness from what is currently going on in the world of arts and letters. All that appears distant to them; they ask about the names of current authors in the same tone of dreamy, faraway curiosity as they ask about the Vassar of fifteen or twenty years ago. Has the college changed much, they inquire, certain that it has changed immeasurably because *they* are there. The so-called literary renaissance of Vassar during the thirties is something they now hear of with amazement and for the very first time. Reversing the situation in most colleges, the faculty is ahead of the student body in its awareness of the times. To the student, the immediate Vassar is the planet.

If you ask a Vassar undergraduate today to define what a Vassar girl essentially is, she will repulse the thought of a Vassar *stereotype,* as she calls it, and tell you that Vassar is a collection of very different "individuals." Yet this reply, to the ears of an alumna, is a highly Vassar remark, indicating a certain virtuous superiority of popular error.

In many ways, Vassar *has* changed. The campus remains the same — the two lakes; the walk through the pines; Sunset Hill; the deserted golf course; the six spare buildings of the Quadrangle; the Main Hall with its porte-cochere, busy Message Center and post office, dark parlors, and bright bulletin boards; the old riding academy housing the theatre and the classics department; the old observatory; the hemlocks;

the new gymnasium; the bulging fieldstone Gothic of the Euthenics Building; the Circle with its brilliant rim of spring flowers, where class picnics are held; the two suburbanish faculty dormitories; the Shakespeare Garden; the outdoor theatre, a great green stadium overlooking the lake; the Students' Building, scene of lectures and dances; Taylor Gate. Poughkeepsie and the railroad station by the Hudson are reached by bus along the track where the old trolley once ran, but the burgher town, with its twisting streets, melancholy river light, somber Hudson Valley mansions and tinny store façades, is still held at a distance. Some of the students, as always, do welfare work in the various Community Centers; Luckey-Platt, the serviceable family-style department store, still offers charge accounts to students; Poughkeepsie citizens attend Vassar lectures and plays, and Poughkeepsie matrons hold luncheon parties in the dining room of Alumnae House; but the off-campus life, in the main, centers about a street or two in Arlington, the outlying section in which the campus is located. And this itself is less lively than formerly; a Peck & Peck, a drugstore, an eating place or two, and the Vassar Bank are the principal remains of a once-spirited commercial area, where teashops, inns, and dress shops once flourished on Vassar extravagance.

Today, "off-campus" for the students is mainly represented by Alumnae House, a tall stucco and brown-beamed building that stands on a hill overlooking the college and that plays, significantly, more and more of a part in campus life and politics. Where, in my day, the roadster, the trolley car, and the taxi bore us off the campus and away from the supervisory eye—downtown in groups to a speakeasy, or off with our dates to a roadhouse or a picturesque old inn—today's undergraduates flock up the hill to Alumnae House for beer, Cokes, hamburgers, and Vassar devils (a sort of fudgy cake sundae) in the Pub on week nights; and on weekends, they join their young men in the big lounge-living room for a cocktail or two, under the watchful eyes of the alumnae secretary or her assistants, who see that the young men do not get too much to drink, that there is no necking, that somebody plays the piano or sings during the bigger cocktail parties (thus slowing down the consumption of liquor) and that, on such occasions, the bar is shut down in ample time to speed the girls and their escorts off to an early dinner in the dining halls before the evening dance.

There is no compulsion on the part of the college that off-campus social life should be conducted under these auspices—the students apparently prefer it so. This increasing dependency on the college and its auxiliary agencies to furnish not only education but pleasure, emotional guidance, and social direction is reflected in nearly every sphere of the current Vassar life. Two hundred and sixteen Yale freshmen, for example, were imported last year by the college for a Saturday-night freshman dance—in former years the Vassar neophyte was dependent on her own initiative, the kindness of her brother or her roommate, to get herself "started." For girls from the West or from small-town high schools, this could be a source of misery, yet in my day any attempt on the part of the administration to pair us off with male wallflowers in a similar predicament was met with groans. I well remember, as a freshman member of the Vassar debate squad, being paired off with a poor freshman from Wesleyan (six and a half feet tall and chinless) when their team came to debate us on censorship and how my six roommates followed us about, laughing and drawing satirical caricatures, as we danced, ate, and walked around the campus together.

In the same way, the college's Vocational Bureau has multiplied its   30
activities of mercy, so that the senior now who goes out into the world will be counseled, fortified, and supplied with letters of introduction by a network of Vassar alumnae. The college is a miniature welfare state. During the early thirties, a single psychiatrist, a psychologist, and a visiting consultant from Riggs Institute took care of the emotional problems of 1,250 students. Now Vassar's 1,350 girls have been endowed with a two-million-dollar grant by Paul Mellon (in memory of his wife, an alumna) for a guidance and counseling program under the direction of Dr. Carl Binger, the psychiatrist who testified in the second Alger Hiss trial.

These fresh, pink-cheeked girls in neatly turned-up blue jeans, flannel culottes, tweed jackets, well-cut shirts appear both too well adjusted and too busy to take any more guidance or counseling. The extracurricular side of Vassar life has already expanded to the point where solitude and self-questioning seem regulated out of existence. Lectures, symposia, recitals, dance programs, foreign movies compete with each other and with organized camping trips, bicycle trips, square dances, factory tours, Hall Plays, for the students' spare time. The student is always "signed up" for some activity, afternoons, evenings, weekends. There are two competing newspapers to be got out, plus the usual literary magazine, yearbook and scholarly magazine. Then there is the radio workshop, the Outing Club, the "Swupper" Club, the travel bureau. Every student is required to give four hours a week to the cooperative work program in the kitchens, dining rooms, or Message Center; slackers are put on a "blacklist" and given demerits of additional hours, which are meted out also for improper dress.

There are Student Council Meetings and Student Curriculum Committee meetings, meetings of the United World Federalists, of the Student Liberal Association, and the Students for Democratic Action. Nearly every afternoon and evening, besides the usual athletics, besides the scheduled lectures, forums, and recitals given for the college at large, there are tryouts for something or other: the Hall Play, one of the two newspapers, the literary magazine, the Flora Dora Girls, or the Gold Dusters (all Vassar music makers), the choir, the orchestra, or the Glee

Club. There is scenery to be made for the Theatre (not to be confused with the Hall Plays, which are extracurricular), costumes to be sewed. There are meetings of the Thekla Club, the *Cercle Français,* the Classics Club, the Spanish Club, Philosophers' Holiday, the Psychology Club, the Russian Club, the Science Club, the German Club.

Nehru is speaking at Hyde Park; a New York doctor is discussing "Whither Medicine?" at the Dutchess County Social Planning Council; the Yale Outing Club is visiting; the Senior or Junior Prom Committee must meet; the Daisy Chain has to be chosen from the sophomore class. Founder's Day must be planned for, and the Tree Ceremonies; a note-topic is due. Jeans must be changed for dinner (only skirts are permitted in the dining room). After dinner, if no lecture or recital is impending, if there are no interviews or rehearsals, or last-minute dummying of the newspaper, if there is no reading to be done in the library, no quiz to prepare for or letters to write, there are the endless bridge and knitting in the common rooms or a hurried excursion to the Pub for beer or Cokes and conversation. And in the morning, there is the Mail Rush, the central event of the day, a jostle and scramble for love letters, letters from home, campus mail, bills, in that order of preference.

This intensification of the extracurricular life, in which every hour is planned for and assigned to some scheduled group activity, in which no one is left out or discriminated against (there are no secret societies or sororities), is the most striking feature of the current scene at Vassar. To the returning alumna whose college years were both more snobbish and sectarian, on the one hand, and more Bohemian, rebellious, and lyrical, on the other, the administrative cast, so to speak, of the present Vassar mold is both disquieting and praiseworthy. A uniform, pliant, docile undergraduate seems to be resulting from the stress on the group and the community that prevails at Vassar today. The outcast and the rebel are almost equally known. There has been a leveling-off in the Vassar geography of what was once a series of ranges, peaks, and valleys, so that Vassar, formerly known for the extremities of her climate, is now a moderate plateau. The vivid and extraordinary student, familiar to the old teachers and the alumnae, is, at least temporarily, absent from the scene.

The idea of excellence, the zest for adventure, the fastidiousness of mind and humanistic breadth of feeling that were so noticeable at Vassar during the long reign of the *emeritae* (as its retired female teacher are styled — a name that evokes a wonderful extinct species of butterfly) seem somehow to have abandoned the college, even though many of the courses that used to be given by the senior faculty have been passed on in their classic form to younger women from the graduate schools. What is missing is a certain largeness of mind, an amplitude of style, the mantle of a calling, a sense of historical dignity. I think of old Miss Haight,

35

Elizabeth Hazelton Haight, of the Latin Department — tall, deep-voiced, Sabine, with olive skin and a mass of white hair piled high and a stately classroom delivery: her romantic attachment to Horace and Apuleius, her Augustan lecture style ("When Theseus came to Athens [pause] as it were [pause] *in medias res . . .*") and the letter she wrote the student chief justice when a group of my friends took two statues from the old Music Hall (which, together with Classics, was in the old Riding Academy), to celebrate with wine and garlands the opening of the new Music Building ("I regret to report the rape of Venus and Minerva from the Classics Department"). And robust, flushed, warm-hearted Anna Kitchel with her Middle-Western accent and schoolgirlish way of smoking a cigarette, which she held at a perpendicular to the orifice of her lips, puffing mightily away like a choo-choo in a child's picture book; her sympathy with George Eliot in her common-law marriage with Mr. Lewes; her sympathy with Annette, Wordsworth's abandoned light-of-love and yet her hearty relish for this un-Wordsworthian lapse ("Oh, he was a *rare bird!*"). And slight, gray-haired, pretty Helen Sandison, the Elizabethan specialist, like an Elizabethan heroine herself, with her mettlesome sharpness, her hatred of imprecision and of bowdlerization of texts. . . . At the present Vassar salary level, it is hard to attract young women fired with the ardor of teaching and capable of all the renunciations that the unmarried teacher who lives with a few books and prints in a faculty dormitory must make. For the gifted young woman today, such a life, even with summers off and sabbaticals, is not a destiny but a fate.

The problem posed by the passing of the *emeritae* is not unique, of course, to Vassar; it is felt throughout the teaching profession, wherever fine women of the old liberal school reigned — in private academies and public schools, from the big-city high school to the one-room country schoolhouse. The pioneers are gone, and who is to take their places? Other private colleges have turned to the literary avant-garde and found Abelards to substitute for the Héloïses — young male critics, philosophers, poets, novelists, short-story writers, trained, for the most part, in the New Criticism, a scholastic discipline of its own. But Vassar is committed to the *woman teacher*. That is, it considers women a discriminated-against minority in the college teaching field, and, as a woman's college, believes that it has a duty to hire women in preference to men. This principle, which worked well in the past, today creates a number of dilemmas — among them the dilemma of defining what a woman is or ought to be. Is she a child-bearing animal, as some ultra-modern theorists, represented on the Vassar faculty, now contend? If so, is a spinster a woman? Is a feminist a woman? In its hiring policy, Vassar today has compromised on these questions. The faculty at present has a larger proportion of men and of married women with children than it had in former years, but now for the first time Vassar's president is a woman, and an unmarried woman, Miss Sarah Gibson Blanding, a Kentuckian, former head of the Department of Home Economics at Cornell, an economist and one-time athlete—unconventional, direct, liberal, dynamic, outspoken, hospitable. The choice of Miss Blanding a few years ago seems on the surface a victory for feminism, but at bottom it is probably a defeat. The old humanistic curriculum, which flourished under the paternal administration of President MacCracken, a Chaucerian and a classics scholar who once played Theseus in Greek for a college production of the *Hippolytus,* is slowly yielding to "education-for-living," as literature and the arts give way to the social sciences, and "pure" scholarship cedes to preparation for civic life and marriage.

Miss Blanding has gone on record as saying that college should not be "an ivory tower"; she is noted for her championship of the Negro, both in word and in deed; and Vassar, under her leadership, prides itself on its advances in social democracy. "Field work" among the people of Dutchess County is given prominence in the social sciences. The college points to the fact that, unlike most private colleges, including some progressive ones, it has no Jewish quota or geographical quota (a device for limiting, without acknowledging it, the proportion of Jewish students); it points to the three Negro girls in this year's freshman class and to the unusually high number of students recruited from public high schools, to its interdenominational church using ritual from various faiths, to its student self-government, its fixed room rate, its cooperative work program and new cooperative dormitory, to its interdepartmental course, *The City,* a sort of living documentary, given a few years ago under the spurring of Helen Lockwood, the militant of sociology within the English department.

These, taken together, are indices of progress within the field of private education, yet it must be pointed out that the progress is relative: Vassar, after having been incorporated for more than seventy-five years, has now achieved the degree of democracy that prevails in most free state universities.

That maximum of social protection once afforded by the private college to the daughters of the well-to-do is here being withdrawn in favor of a more "open" environment that will better prepare the student for those realities of modern life that the CCNY or Hunter student faces from birth. Meanwhile, a new questionnaire answered by 7,915 alumnae discloses that 61 per cent of those answering still favor the Republican Party and that 36 per cent think that Vassar could have helped them "to adjust to life" more than it did; 67 per cent, however, would choose Vassar all over again.

The adjustment-to-life question is typical of Vassar and perhaps, more generally, of feminine insularity and self-centeredness—it is impossible to imagine such a question being asked by Harvard or Chicago.

40

But it reflects the preoccupations of the alumnae and of certain powerful faculty figures of the new dispensation; in particular, of Mrs. Dorothy Lee, '27, of Anthropology, the most controversial person on today's campus — dark, short-haired, vibrant, abrupt, boyish, speaking with a slight foreign accent, photographed with her four children by the alumnae magazine making meatballs, a cultural anthropologist of the school that emphasizes childbearing as the crucial activity in woman's life. Careers for women in the old sense are abhorrent to Mrs. Lee and her followers; she believes in a faculty of homemakers, in an extension of the cooperative principle for training in group betterment. She detests institutional living. Her views are dynamic, integralist, and puritanical; she would sacrifice the part to the whole and believes that the one-sided person is the enemy of society. In her own way, she is a pioneer, like the spinsters who preceded her, and an iconoclast, like the suffragettes she spurns.

For the present college mood, her temper is too radical, and she is as far, perhaps, from that element in the alumnae which feels itself cheated by dishwashing and diaper-changing as from the traditionalists on the faculty who fear her influence on the students. The preparation-for-life controversy that rages in the alumnae magazine and in alumnae panel discussions reaches the undergraduate body in a somewhat muted form. The superior students do not yet demand courses in the techniques of home-making or a serious revision of the curriculum. Rather, unlike their rebellious sisters of the twenties and thirties, they look forward to "working within their community" for social betterment, while being married and having babies. As the *Vassar Alumnae Magazine* puts it, speaking of the normative Vassar woman revealed by the new questionnaire:

> She is the woman who changed the local school situation from a political machine to an educational institution. She is the woman behind the League of Women Voters, Planned Parenthood, and, yes, the 4-H Club. She won't very often be found sitting at the luncheon bridge table. She'll be found actively, thoughtfully, even serenely, playing her role as an intelligent citizen.

FOR DISCUSSION AND WRITING

1. The principle of quantity: At any points in this essay, does McCarthy give you less information than you need? Does she ever give you more than necessary? (Be specific in your answers.)

2. The principle of quality: What reasons do you have for trusting (or distrusting) McCarthy's knowledge of her subject or her honesty?

3. The principle of manner: If you think the essay is sometimes unclear, indicate where, and explain the difficulty.

4. The principle of relation: Are any parts of the essay irrelevant to the topic? Explain.

5. What sorts of readers do you think McCarthy has in mind? (Their levels of education? Their socioeconomic status? Their interests?) Explain your answer.

6. Which details in the selection did you find particularly vivid? In what ways do these details contribute to the meaning and effect of the piece?

7. McCarthy notes that Vassar was founded in 1861, the year of Lincoln's inauguration and the emancipation of the Russian serfs. What purpose does the author have in providing this seemingly extraneous information? (Has she violated the principle of relationship?)

8. Explain how differences in the scene at the time of writing this piece and the scene described within the piece have influenced this autobiographical essay.

9. Is the purpose of this essay autobiographical? Or is McCarthy explaining something? Is she arguing? Explain your answer.

10. Do you understand the following? What world knowledge do you need? If you did not understand why, for instance, October 1929 is a significant date, where could you find out about this date?

   > After October, 1929, some of us had smaller allowances . . . . (par. 10)

   > . . . the off-campus shops still prospered, selling grape lemonade, bacon-and-tomato sandwiches, and later 3.2 beer. (par. 10)

   > With the impetus of the New Deal and memories of the breadlines behind us, even we aesthetes began reading about Sacco and Vanzetti and Mooney. We wrote papers for Contemporary Prose Fiction on Dos Passos. (par. 13)

11. Does McCarthy's Vassar College experience represent your own ideas of the role colleges should play in the lives of students? Do you think that the changes at Vassar are for the better? Why, or why not? Which Vassar, that of the late 1920s and early 1930s or that of the early 1950s, do you feel more closely corresponds to the mission of the college, as stated by its founder?

12. Most of McCarthy's readers haven't attended Vassar, nor do they have much knowledge of the institution, yet the essay deals in large part with a discussion of the changes in the campus over the course of two decades.

Briefly list these changes, and explain how the author has given the reader enough information to understand these changes.

13. McCarthy makes repeated allusions both to classical mythology and to classic literary personae. Why? What are the purpose and the effect of these allusions?

14. McCarthy obviously enjoyed her years at Vassar a great deal and has great admiration for the institution, but she also is clear-eyed about its drawbacks. What were they at the time she attended, and what are the drawbacks the author sees in the early 1950s? Do you yourself see these as drawbacks?

15. In typifying the Vassar student, McCarthy writes, ". . . the Vassar girl is thought of as carrying a banner. The inscription on it varies with the era or with the ideas of the beholder and in the final sense does not matter — the flushed cheek and tensed arm are what count" (par. 5). Explain what McCarthy is getting at here.

16. McCarthy notes that Vassar in the 1950s is a hubbub of planned activity. List the activities mentioned. What point is McCarthy emphasizing by itemizing to such a great extent?

HOW IT FEELS TO BE COLORED ME

Zora Neale Hurston

During the 1920s, a group of black Americans in New York City's Harlem district formed a loose alliance to give expression to their cultural heritage, a movement that came to be known as the Harlem Renaissance. The novelist Richard Wright (whose best-known work is *Native Son*), the poet Countee Cullin, and Zora Neale Hurston were among the writers associated with the Harlem Renaissance. These three became symbols of the movement and are its best-known members.

Hurston was born in 1891 in Eatonville, Florida, a black community. Desperately wanting an education, she worked, scrimped, and saved until she had enough money to attend Howard University. She went on to Barnard College, where she studied with the great anthropologist Franz Boas (who also taught Margaret Mead). When Hurston graduated from Barnard in 1927, she received a fellowship to study the oral traditions of her own community, Eatonville, and when the fellowship ran out, she was supported by a wealthy and opinionated white woman, Mrs. R. Osgood Mason, who insisted that Hurston focus her work on the "primitive."

Among Zora Neale Hurston's works are *The Eatonville Anthology,* a collection of tales about the people in her hometown; *Jonah's Gourd Vine* (1934), a novel; and her masterpiece, the novel *Their Eyes Were Watching God* (1937). She is now gaining recognition as one of America's great and original writers, yet when she died in 1960, she was in a welfare home, penniless and forgotten.

The following selection explains the author's feelings and attitudes concerning her race, but it is also a wonderful mixture of bitterness and humor. Hurston gives us knowledge about the black experience and entertains us with her artistry.

I am colored but I offer nothing in the way of extenuating circumstances except the fact that I am the only Negro in the United States whose grandfather on the mother's side was *not* an Indian chief.

I remember the very day that I became colored. Up to my thirteenth year I lived in the little Negro town of Eatonville, Florida. It is exclusively a colored town. The only white people I knew passed through the town going to or coming from Orlando. The native whites rode dusty horses, the Northern tourists chugged down the sandy village road in automobiles. The town knew the Southerners and never stopped cane chewing when they passed. But the Northerners were something else again. They were peered at cautiously from behind the curtains by the timid. The more venturesome would come out on the porch to watch them go past and got just as much pleasure out of the tourists as the tourists got out of the village.

The front porch might seem a daring place for the rest of the town, but it was a gallery seat for me. My favorite place was atop the gate-post. Proscenium box for a born first-nighter. Not only did I enjoy the show, but I didn't mind the actors knowing that I liked it. I usually spoke to them in passing. I'd wave at them and when they returned my salute, I would say something like this: "Howdy-do-well-I-thank-you-where-you-goin'?" Usually automobile or the horse paused at this, and after a queer exchange of compliments, I would probably "go a piece of the way" with them, as we say in farthest Florida. If one of my family happened to come to the front in time to see me, of course negotiations would be rudely broken off. But even so, it is clear that I was the first "welcome-to-our-state" Floridian, and I hope the Miami Chamber of Commerce will please take notice.

During this period, white people differed from colored to me only in that they rode through town and never lived there. They liked to hear me "speak pieces" and sing and wanted to see me dance the parse-me-la, and gave me generously of their small silver for doing these things, which seemed strange to me for I wanted to do them so much that I needed bribing to stop. Only they didn't know it. The colored people gave no dimes. They deplored any joyful tendencies in me, but I was their Zora nevertheless. I belonged to them, to the nearby hotels, to the county—everybody's Zora.

But changes came in the family when I was thirteen, and I was sent   5
to school in Jacksonville. I left Eatonville, the town of the oleanders, as Zora. When I disembarked from the river-boat at Jacksonville, she was no more. It seemed that I had suffered a sea change. I was not Zora of Orange County any more, I was now a little colored girl. I found it out in certain ways. In my heart as well as in the mirror, I became a fast brown—warranted not to rub nor run.

But I am not tragically colored. There is no great sorrow dammed up in my soul, nor lurking behind my eyes. I do not mind at all. I do not belong to the sobbing school of Negrohood who hold that nature some-how has given them a lowdown dirty deal and whose feelings are all hurt about it. Even in the helter-skelter skirmish that is my life, I have seen that the world is to the strong regardless of a little pigmentation more or less. No, I do not weep at the world—I am too busy sharpening my oyster knife.

Someone is always at my elbow reminding me that I am the grand-daughter of slaves. It fails to register depression with me. Slavery is sixty years in the past. The operation was successful and the patient is doing well, thank you. The terrible struggle that made me an American out of a potential slave said "On the line!" The Reconstruction said "Get set!"; and the generation before said "Go!" I am off to a flying start and I must not halt in the stretch to look behind and weep. Slavery is the price I paid for civilization, and the choice was not with me. It is a bully adventure and worth all that I have paid through my ancestors for it. No one on earth ever had a greater chance for glory. The world to be won and nothing to be lost. It is thrilling to think — to know that for any act of mine, I shall get twice as much praise or twice as much blame. It is quite exciting to hold the center of the national stage, with the spectators not knowing whether to laugh or to weep.

The position of my white neighbor is much more difficult. No brown specter pulls up a chair beside me when I sit down to eat. No dark ghost thrusts its leg against mine in bed. The game of keeping what one has is never so exciting as the game of getting.

I do not always feel colored. Even now I often achieve the unconscious Zora of Eatonville before the Hegira. I feel most colored when I am thrown against a sharp white background.

For instance at Barnard. "Besides the waters of the Hudson" I feel   *10* my race. Among the thousand white persons, I am a dark rock surged upon, and over-swept, but through it all, I remain myself. When covered by the waters, I am; and the ebb but reveals me again.

Sometimes it is the other way around. A white person is set down in our midst, but the contrast is just as sharp for me. For instance, when I sit in the drafty basement that is The New World Cabaret with a white person, my color comes. We enter chatting about any little nothing that we have in common and are seated by the jazz waiters. In the abrupt way that jazz orchestras have, this one plunges into a number. It loses no time in circumlocutions, but gets right down to business. It constricts the thorax and splits the heart with its tempo and narcotic harmonics. This orchestra grows rambunctious, rears on its hind legs and attacks the tonal veil with primitive fury, rending it, clawing it until it breaks through to the jungle beyond. I follow those heathen — follow them exultingly. I dance wildly inside myself; I yell within, I whoop; I shake my assegai above my head, I hurl it true to the mark *yeeeeooww!* I am in the jungle and living in the jungle way. My face is painted red and yellow and my body is painted blue. My pulse is throbbing like a war drum. I want to slaughter something — give pain, give death to what, I do not know. But the piece ends. The men of the orchestra wipe their lips and rest their fingers. I creep back slowly to the veneer we call civilization with the last tone and find the white friend sitting motionless in his seat smoking calmly.

"Good music they have here," he remarks, drumming the table with his fingertips.

Music. The great blobs of purple and red emotion have not touched him. He has only heard what I felt. He is far away and I see him but dimly across the ocean and the continent that have fallen between us. He is so pale with his whiteness then and I am *so* colored.

At certain times I have no race, I am *me*. When I set my hat at a certain angle and saunter down Seventh Avenue, Harlem City, feeling as snooty as the lions in front of the Forty-Second Street Library, for instance. So far as my feelings are concerned, Peggy Hopkins Joyce on the Boule Mich with her gorgeous raiment, stately carriage, knees knocking together in a most aristocratic manner, has nothing on me. The cosmic Zora emerges. I belong to no race nor time. I am the eternal feminine with its string of beads.

I have no separate feeling about being an American citizen and colored. I am merely a fragment of the Great Soul that surges within the boundaries. My country, right or wrong.   15

Sometimes, I feel discriminated against, but it does not make me angry. It merely astonishes me. How *can* any deny themselves the pleasure of my company? It's beyond me.

But in the main, I feel like a brown bag of miscellany propped against a wall. Against a wall in company with other bags, white, red and yellow. Pour out the contents, and there is discovered a jumble of small things priceless and worthless. A first-water diamond, an empty spool, bits of broken glass, lengths of string, a key to a door long since crumbled away, a rusty knife-blade, old shoes saved for a road that never was and never will be, a nail bent under the weight of things too heavy for any nail, a dried flower or two still a little fragrant. In your hand is the brown bag. On the ground before you is the jumble it held — so much like the jumble in the bags, could they be emptied, that all might be dumped in a single heap and the bags refilled without altering the content of any greatly. A bit of colored glass more or less would not matter. Perhaps that is how the Great Stuffer of Bags filled them in the first place — who knows?

1928

FOR DISCUSSION AND WRITING

1. It can be argued that time and place are the most important elements of this essay. What are the important scenes that Hurston portrays? Do these scenes symbolize aspects of America? Explain.

2. How does change of scene affect Hurston?

3. Explain the "brown bag" metaphor with which the essay concludes. (Who is the Great Stuffer of Bags?) In regard to manner, what does Hurston gain through using a metaphor to express this idea?

4. What was Hurston's purpose in writing the essay? What evidence do you have for your conclusion?

5. Hurston calls herself "colored." What term do "colored" people now apply to themselves? Why do you think the terminology changed?

6. What forces in contemporary America prompted the editors of the *Norton Anthology of American Literature* to rediscover Zora Neale Hurston and to include her work in their collection?

7. Paraphrase the following passage, making it easier for the casual reader to understand:

> It is quite exciting to hold the center of the national stage, with the spectators not knowing whether to laugh or weep.
>
> The position of my white neighbor is much more difficult. No brown specter pulls up a chair beside me when I sit down to eat. No dark ghost thrusts its leg against mine in bed. The game of keeping what one has is never so exciting as the game of getting. (par. 7–8)

   From the standpoint of manner, would you say that Hurston has expressed herself as clearly as possible? What does your paraphrase gain? What does it lose?

8. Do you believe that Hurston has satisfied the writer-reader contract from the standpoint of quantity when she describes how she feels to be colored? What would you delete or add to the text?

9. Does Hurston's vignette in the jazz club violate the principle of relation? Explain.

10. What world knowledge must the reader have in order to understand the essay?

11. Characterize Hurston's attitude toward her race. How does that attitude compare with the attitudes of blacks today?

ON THE PILGRIM'S PATH TO LOURDES

Eleanor Munro

> In April, says Chaucer at the beginning of *The Canterbury Tales,* "longen folk to goon on pilgrimages" — people long to go on pilgrimages. In this essay, Eleanor Munro explains her view of this longing, and, in particular, she tells about one of the most famous of Christian shrines.
>
> Munro is the author of, among other books, *Originals: American Women Artists, On Glory Roads: A Pilgrim's Book about Pilgrimage,* and *Memoir of a Modernist Daughter.* Her writings, which include critical essays on art, appear in several national journals, including the *New York Times, Art in America,* and *The New Republic.* She and her husband live in New York and on Cape Cod.
>
> As you read this essay, think about Munro's attitude toward her subject. Does she appear to be a skeptic or a true believer? Is she neither of these, but simply a disinterested observer? On what evidence do you base your judgment?

Among sacred pilgrimage sites of the world — far-off snowy peaks on which gods are thought to dance, thronged temples by the Ganges, gold-domed cathedrals or humble country altars — the French shrine of Lourdes in its gloomy mountain setting may be one of the most instructive.

That is to say, if you look beyond the blatant commercialism of the new town and steep yourself instead in the geography, architecture and massed population of the sacred precinct, you may gain an inkling of the meaning of this ancient and universal human practice. For pilgrimage is an enterprise of deep antiquity and powerful psychological appeal, and its associated rites are much the same across all religions, and the same today as in the past.

When a pilgrim arrives at his destination (it can as well be a natural feature, rock, tree or riverbank as a man-made church or temple), he invariably can be seen walking a circular path around or in it, often following the clockwise course of the sun. If by night, he will carry a candle or torch, which, multiplied many times in many hands, becomes a galaxy of stars turning slowly in darkness. The metaphor holds. In these circumambulations, the pilgrim imitates the flight of the stars and planets, which orbit the celestial pole, disappearing and reappearing in a harmonic order we on earth find both beautiful and eternal. So the pilgrim enacts the answer to his longing for immortality.

Indeed, the folklore that has grown up around Lourdes describes its location at "the confluence of seven valleys" — seven being one of those immemorial mystical numbers in scripture and myth referring to the visible planets, the outermost travelers of the solar system. Mystical Lourdes thus is identified as its axis.

Legend in this case enhances geography. Actual Lourdes lies betwixt gorges and bare cliffs, where icy torrents off the high slopes collide

5

in a perpetual tumult of white water, ethereal rainbows and ghostly low-hanging clouds.

A hundred years ago, when its modern history began, Lourdes was no more than a scatter of wretched stone huts wedged along a couple of crooked climbing streets. Perched on an overhanging rock stood the town jail. In one of those freezing dwellings lived a poor miller, sometimes resident in the jail, and his wife and children, all of them suffering from hunger and ill health.

It was a bitter February day in 1858 when Bernadette, the eldest child, went with her sister to the riverbank to gather kindling. And there, as she later recalled with the help of her confessor and other priests of the region, "I heard a noise like a gust of wind. I saw the trees were not swaying. I heard the same noise again. As I lifted my head and looked at the grotto, I saw a lady in white. Fear took hold of me. My hand shook."

What she reported seeing in an "aureole of sunlight" was a woman who much resembled a statue of the Madonna in a church nearby, save that instead of treading on a snake as the plaster woman did, the Beautiful Lady wore on each foot a yellow rose.

Not till her third visit did the Lady explain who she was, adding, "I cannot promise to make you happy in this world, but in *the other*." A skeptic may suppose Bernadette's life history shaped her visions, for she had twice been sent as a boarder to another village, once in infancy and later as a hired shepherdess, where she enjoyed milk and bread in abundance offered by a warm-hearted foster mother. In any case, at her ninth appearance, the Lady spoke words both motherly and rural: "Go drink and wash at the fountain. Eat the grass you will find there."

So strange a suggestion led Bernadette to tear hungrily at the grass   *10*
by the cliff and so to widen the opening over an underground spring which today, some 125 years later, is the most famous water source in the Western world. Over four million pilgrims visit it each summer, and it has become the nexus of a vast ecclesiastical, touristic and economic bureaucracy.

For the Beautiful Lady, who in the end identified herself in terms Bernadette said she had never heard before — "I am the Immaculate Conception" — asked that a chapel be built by the spring and pilgrims attend it "in procession." And so it was done, and so they do, but not by miracle alone.

Four years before the visions, in 1854, the Pope, against stiff opposition from within the church but in response to a centuries-long groundswell of popular faith, had announced the dogma of the Immaculate Conception of the Virgin. Bernadette's visions, tailored and broadcast by her confessors, brought that arcane dogma down to earth and gave it sentimental color.

She herself died at thirty-six, a reclusive nun, leaving only a modest disclaimer: "The Blessed Lady used me. I am nothing without her." In

1925, she was beatified and, eight years later, on the Feast Day of the Immaculate Conception, canonized. The Vatican still maintains a stiffish attitude toward the occasional reported cures at the place, but pastors from all over Europe shepherd their charges there, often in special railroad cars fitted out as hospitals. Even if the cures are dubious or short-lasting, the patients return home, sometimes to institutions that are their lifelong homes, lifted in mind and heart by the experience.

The modern commercial town of Lourdes offers hotels and boarding houses great and small—some four hundred of them—wax museums, audio-visual instructional parlors and shops where you can pick up a cuckoo clock, pine candy, a skein of Pyrenees wool, a set of cowbells, color prints of the Angelus and all sizes of plastic Virgin-shaped water bottles.

Near the sacred precinct stands the Hospice of Our Lady of Seven 15 Sorrows, where bedridden pilgrims are tenderly housed and fed before and after their ritual visit to the shrine. The order was started four years after the visions were officially accepted, by Marie St. Frai, a mountain woman with a mission toward the terminally ill. Her nuns still wear black in bereavement. But the rule of the order is *allegresse,* lightness of heart, and so these sisters' spirit seems to be.

I asked one of them, Sister Stanislaw, a dainty young person with dancing eyes, how she came to the order. She grew up in a secular, bourgeois home, in which she danced and partied and wore pretty clothes. But, she said, "I loved the poor and I followed the thread to the end. When I came into the order, I shut the door behind me. And ever since, it's as if I were in heaven."

The mystical center or axis of heavenly Lourdes is the place by the riverbank where Bernadette knelt to tear at the grass. There bubbles the famous spring, its open mouth protected by plate glass. Its waters are piped off into twice-seven tubs in as many little cold bathrooms where volunteer attendants convey the suffering hopeful. Alternately, in the open air is a row of bright copper taps, through which water is constantly drawn off into gallon tanks, thermoses and bottles to be carried to Christian homes around the world.

Behind that place of holy power, the ground rises sharply toward the cliff top, where great trees fill with mountain wind, bending half-over under the scudding clouds. At the axial summit stands the basilica, a neo-Gothic concoction like a Disneyland castle. In the sanctuary's mosaic-adorned dome, a smiling teenage Bernadette in a golden crown holds out thin arms to her petitioners.

At four each afternoon and again at eight in the evening, a procession takes place in Lourdes. The pilgrims form rows, six abreast, some walking but most wheeled by attendants in chairs or litters.

The lines, also guided by ecclesiastics in full regalia, move gravely, *20*
in perfect order, along the base of the cliff beside the spring and the water
taps, then out along a wide, tree-shaded alley leading toward the commercial town, where they turn as if in orbit to return toward the basilica
and begin again.

I stood there one afternoon watching and asking myself what the
meaning was of what I saw.

I was standing as if on a shore while toward me flowed faces by the
six, by the twelve, by the hundred — peasant faces and faces suggestive
of high station, such a host of sufferers I couldn't have imagined without
being there. I even wished for the power of a Homer to help me describe
that tremendous host — thick fingers twisted in blankets or splayed upon
them, wasted flesh gray as cement, cheeks and noses sharp as cut stone,
black brows bristling over sunken eyes; polio-afflicted children in their
mothers' arms; a handsome woman whose well-combed hair framed
frantic, maniacal eyes; men with barrel chests and legs like rolled towels,
stretching anguished faces back toward the spring even after their litters
had been wheeled on past.

Look, these shapes on their beds seemed to be saying to the
clouds — Look on us: *your handiwork.*

There were still more painful cases to come, reaching with hands
flailing like flags run off their pulleys, crossing themselves with the heels
of those flapping hands. There were beings without legs or arms at all,
with swollen heads too heavy to lift, or shaped like turnips.

The procession moved to amplified music, minor-keyed folk songs, *25*
plaintive chants, wistful children's choirs, until at last, inevitably, came
the cry from loudspeakers all along the way: *Lord . . . heal us.*

That evening I stood on the balcony of my hotel looking down on
thousands of little lights turning in rainy darkness, asking myself
whether it was morbidity that had kept me fixed to the sight of so many
individuals there in extremes of deformity and fear. But I thought it was
not.

I was transfixed at Lourdes because through those imprisoning
bodies, some entangled yet separate *will* to continue living had glinted
out with shocking immediacy — the same I had witnessed elsewhere in
travels to other pilgrimage sites.

In India, you see human suffering in the open, unapologetically
displayed, considered an inevitable feature of the material world. Hindu
religious practice helps you overlook immediate pain and dwell instead
on vast metaphysical abstractions. Western religious thought focuses on
the narrower, more piercing mystery of human consciousness in an inhuman world. And every single person who walked or was rolled before
my eyes at Lourdes was like a plumb-weight pulling the cords of a whole
belief system into alignment.

I went down to the shrine where the lights were still turning among the trees and took a flame from a taper in the hand of a country woman with averted eyes and heavy facial hair who, when I thanked her, replied in the deep stoic timbre of a hermaphrodite.

There came into my mind then the well-known words *Eppur si* 30 *muove:* And still it moves. That there exists some natural law or force that binds such pilgrims into their passionate faith and labor seems to me as unarguable — yet still as mysterious — as was, to Galileo, the turning of the earth around the sun.

FOR DISCUSSION AND WRITING

1. The author states that if you "steep yourself instead in the geography, architecture and massed population of the sacred precinct, you may gain an inkling of the meaning of this ancient and universal human practice [of making pilgrimages]" (par. 2). In short, if you steep yourself in the time and place, you might gain some inkling. Explain the unique characteristics of the geography of Lourdes and the pilgrims who journey there.

2. The author concludes her essay with a comparison of the pilgrims' faith to the orbiting of the earth around the sun. Find another place where the author makes a similar comparison. Do you think that this repetition is effective? What is the author's purpose in the repetition? Explain. ·

3. What is Munro's purpose in the essay?

4. In what sense could we say that "On the Pilgrim's Path to Lourdes" is about the relationship between the time and the place and what occurs at that time and place?

5. Munro writes in the first paragraph, "Among sacred pilgrimage sites of the world . . . the French shrine of Lourdes in its gloomy mountain setting may be one of the most instructive." Do you believe that Munro satisfies the principle of relation throughout the essay in supporting this statement? Why, or why not?

6. Do you trust Munro's statements of fact? Her description of the shrine? Her interpretation of its meaning? Can you disagree with her interpretation and still believe that she has satisfied the principle of quality? Explain.

7. Do you believe that the Lourdes shrine would have less religious significance if it were set in a sunny and warm climate amid flat, fertile farmland? Would it have a different literary significance to Munro? Why, or why not?

8. According to the author, what is the primary difference between Hindu and Western religious thought? How does this difference relate to the significance of Lourdes?

9. What historical incident four years before the occurrence of Saint Bernadette's vision helped to establish the importance of such a miracle?

10. Lourdes is identified as a site at which the Virgin Mary appeared nine times, but how it has become associated with the cure of bodily ills remains unclear. What do you think the connection between the appearance and the pilgrimage reveals about the beliefs of the Catholic congregation? According to the article, do they completely agree with those of the Vatican?

11. Why do you think that the author only incidentally alludes to the great tourist industry that has sprung up around Lourdes?

12. Briefly state the main point of the essay.

ORANGES AND SWEET SISTER BOY

Judy Ruiz

This essay, first published in *Iowa Woman,* was reprinted in *The Best American Essays, 1989*. In this volume is a statement about the author, almost certainly written *by* the author. If Ruiz did indeed write the statement, as we believe she did, here is what she says about herself:

> Judy Ruiz writes and lives in Fayetteville, Arkansas, where she is an assistant professor of English at the University of Arkansas. She teaches creative writing in the Adult Community Education program. Her second book of poetry, *Because the Swans Ballet Is So Hard,* is looking for a home, as is her first, *The Pepper Birds*. She is now working on a collection of essays. She directs a performance arts group called Entourage, which made its debut during the Eureka Springs Arts Festival. Ms. Ruiz will read from her work as part of the Spoken Arts series at the Painted Bride Art Center in Philadelphia in the fall of 1989. (291–92)

Different from the other expository pieces in this chapter, "Oranges and Sweet Sister Boy" does not proceed systematically, step by step, to clarify its topic. Rather, it sets ideas and impressions side by side in an order that could be rearranged without destroying the effectiveness of the essay, the power of which results from the overall impression that the reader gains, not from a logically impeccable chain of reasoning or a stack of data.

As you read, think about the ways in which the image of oranges unifies this piece of writing.

I am sleeping, hard, when the telephone rings. It's my brother, and he's calling to say that he is now my sister. I feel something fry a little, deep behind my eyes. Knowing how sometimes dreams get mixed up with not-dreams, I decide to do a reality test at once. "Let me get a cigarette," I say, knowing that if I reach for a Marlboro and it turns into a trombone or a snake or anything else on the way to my lips that I'm still out in the large world of dreams.

The cigarette stays a cigarette. I light it. I ask my brother to run that stuff by me again.

It is the Texas Zephyr at midnight — the woman in a white suit, the man in a blue uniform; she carries flowers — I know they are flowers. The petals spill and spill into the aisle, and a child goes past this couple who have just come from their own wedding — goes past them and past them, going always to the toilet but really just going past them; and the child could be a horse or she could be the police and they'd not notice her any more than they do, which is not at all — the man's hands high up on the woman's legs, her skirt up, her stockings and garters, the petals and finally all the flowers spilling out into the aisle and his mouth open on her. My mother. My father.

I am conceived near Dallas in the dark while a child passes, a young girl who knows and doesn't know, who witnesses, in glimpses, the creation of the universe, who feels an odd hurt as her own mother, fat and empty, snores with her mouth open, her false teeth slipping down, snores and snores just two seats behind the Creators.

News can make a person stupid. It can make you think you can do something. So I ask The Blade question, thinking that if he hasn't had the operation yet that I can fly to him, rent a cabin out on Puget Sound. That we can talk. That I can get him to touch base with reality.

"Begin with an orange," I would tell him. "Because oranges are mildly intrusive by nature, put the orange somewhere so that it will not bother you — in the cupboard, in a drawer, even a pocket or a handbag will do. The orange, being a patient fruit, will wait for you much longer than say a banana or a peach."

I would hold an orange out to him. I would say, "This is the one that will save your life." And I would tell him about the woman I saw in a bus station who bit right into her orange like it was an apple. She was wild looking, as if she'd been outside for too long in a wind that blew the same way all the time. One of the dregs of humanity, our mother would have called her, the same mother who never brought fruit into the house except in cans. My children used to ask me to "start" their oranges for them. That meant to make a hole in the orange so they could peel the rind away, and their small hands weren't equipped with fingernails that were long enough or strong enough to do the job. Sometimes they would suck the juice out of the hole my thumbnail had made, leaving the orange flat and sad.

The earrings are as big as dessert plates, filigree gold-plated with thin dangles hanging down that touch her bare shoulders. She stands in front of the Alamo while a bald man takes her picture. The sun is absorbed by the earrings so quickly that by the time she feels the heat, it is too late. The hanging dangles make small blisters on her shoulders, as if a centipede had traveled there. She takes the famous river walk in spiked heels, rides in a boat, eats some Italian noodles, returns to the motel room, soaks her feet, and applies small Band-Aids to her toes. She is briefly concerned about the gun on the nightstand. The toilet flushes. She pretends to be sleeping. The gun is just large and heavy. A .45? A .357 magnum? She's never been good with names. She hopes he doesn't try to. Or that if he does, that it's not loaded. But he'll say it's loaded just for fun. Or he'll pull the trigger and the bullet will lodge in her medulla oblongata, ripping through her womb first, taking everything else vital on the way.

In the magazine articles, you don't see this: "Well, yes. The testicles have to come out. And yes. The penis is cut off." What you get is tonsils.

So-and-so has had a "sex change" operation. A sex change operation. How precious. How benign. Doctor, just what do you people do with those penises?

News can make a person a little crazy also. News like, "We regret to inform you that you have failed your sanity hearing."

The bracelet on my wrist bears the necessary information about me, but there is one small error. The receptionist typing the information asked me my religious preference. I said, "None." She typed, "Neon."

Pearl doesn't have any teeth and her tongue looks weird. She says, "Pumpkin pie." That's all she says. Sometimes she runs her hands over my bed sheets and says pumpkin pie. Sometimes I am under the sheets. Marsha got stabbed in the chest, but she tells everyone she fell on a knife. Elizabeth — she's the one who thinks her shoe is a baby — hit me in the back with a tray right after one of the cooks gave me extra toast. There's a note on the bulletin board about a class for the nurses: "How Putting A Towel On Someone's Face Makes Them Stop Banging Their Spoon/OR Reduction of Disruptive Mealtime Behavior By Facial Screening — 7 P.M. — Conference Room." Another note announces the topic for remotivation class: "COWS." All the paranoid schizophrenics will be there.

Here, in the place for the permanently bewildered, I fit right in. Not because I stood at the window that first night and listened to the trains. Not because I imagined those trains were bracelets, the jewelry of earth. Not even because I imagined that one of those bracelets was on my own arm and was the Texas Zephyr where a young couple made love and conceived me. I am eighteen and beautiful and committed to the state hospital by a district court judge for a period of one day to life. Because I am a paranoid schizophrenic.

I will learn about cows.

So I'm being very quiet in the back of the classroom, and I'm peeling an orange. It's the smell that makes the others begin to turn around, that mildly intrusive nature. The course is called "Women and Modern Literature," and the diaries of Virginia Woolf are up for discussion except nobody has anything to say. I, of course, am making a mess with the orange; and I'm wanting to say that my brother is now my sister.

Later, with my hands still orangey, I wander in to leave something on a desk in a professor's office, and he's reading so I'm being very quiet, and then he says, sort of out of nowhere, "Emily Dickinson up there in her room making poems while her brother was making love to her best friend right downstairs on the dining room table. A regular thing. Think of it. And Walt Whitman out sniffing around the boys. Our two great American poets." And I want to grab this professor's arm and say, "Listen. My brother called me and now he's my sister, and I'm having trouble making sense out of my life right now, so would you mind not telling me any more stuff about sex." And I want my knuckles to turn white while the pressure of my fingers leaves imprints right through his jacket, little indentations he can interpret as urgent. But I don't say anything. And I don't grab his arm. I go read a magazine. I find this:

> "I've never found an explanation for why the human race has so many languages. When the brain became a language brain, it obviously needed to develop an intense degree of plasticity. Such plasticity allows languages to be logical, coherent systems and yet be extremely variable. The same brain that thinks in words and symbols is also a brain that has to be freed up with regard to sexual turn-on and partnering. God knows why sex attitudes have been subject to the corresponding degrees of modification and variety as language. I suspect there's a close parallel between the two. The brain doesn't seem incredibly efficient with regard to sex."

John Money said that. The same John Money who, with surgeon Howard W. Jones, performed the first sex change operation in the United States in 1965 at Johns Hopkins University and Hospital in Baltimore.

Money also tells about the *hijra* of India who disgrace their families because they are too effeminate: "The ultimate stage of the *hijra* is to get up the courage to go through the amputation of penis and testicles. They had no anesthetic." Money also answers anyone who might think that "heartless members of the medical profession are forcing these poor darlings to go and get themselves cut up and mutilated," or who think the medical profession should leave them alone. "You'd have lots of patients willing to get a gun and blow off their own genitals if you don't do it. I've had several who got knives and cut themselves trying to get rid of their sex organs. That's their obsession!"

Perhaps better than all else, I understand obsession. It is of the mind. And it is language-bound. Sex is of the body. It has no words. I am stunned to learn that someone with an obsession of the mind can have parts of the body surgically removed. This is my brother I speak of. This is not some lunatic named Carl who becomes Carlene. This is my brother.

So while we're out in that cabin on Puget Sound, I'll tell him about LuAnn. She is the sort of woman who orders the in-season fruit and a little cottage cheese. I am the sort of woman who orders a double cheeseburger and fries. LuAnn and I are sitting in her car. She has a huge orange, and she peels it so the peel falls off in one neat strip. I have a sack of oranges, the small ones. The peel of my orange comes off in hunks about the size of a baby's nail. "Oh, you bought the *juice* oranges," LuAnn says to me. Her emphasis on the word "juice" makes me want to die or something. I lack the courage to admit my ignorance, so I smile and breathe "yes," as if I know some secret, when I'm wanting to scream at her about how my mother didn't teach me about fruit and my own blood pounds in my head wanting out, out.

> There is a pattern to this thought as there is a pattern for a jumpsuit. Sew the sleeve to the leg, sew the leg to the collar. Put the garment on. Sew the mouth shut. This is how I tell about being quiet because I am bad, and because I cannot stand it when he beats me or my brother.

"The first time I got caught in your clothes was when I was four years old and you were over at Sarah what's-her-name's babysitting. Dad beat me so hard I thought I was going to die. I really thought I was going to die. That was the day I made up my mind I would *never* get caught again. And I never got caught again." My brother goes on to say he continued to go through my things until I was hospitalized. A mystery is solved.

He wore my clothes. He played in my makeup. I kept saying, back   15
then, that someone was going through my stuff. I kept saying it and saying it. I told the counselor at school. "Someone goes in my room when I'm not there, and I *know* it — goes in there and wears my clothes and goes through my stuff." I was assured by the counselor that this was not so. I was assured by my mother that this was not so. I thought my mother was doing it, snooping around for clues like mothers do. It made me a little crazy, so I started deliberately leaving things in a certain order so that I would be able to prove to myself that someone, indeed, was going through my belongings. No one, not one person, ever believed that my room was being ransacked; I was accused of just making it up. A paranoid fixation.

And all the time it was old Goldilocks.

So I tell my brother to promise me he'll see someone who counsels adult children from dysfunctional families. I tell him he needs to deal with the fact that he was physically abused on a daily basis. He tells me he doesn't remember being beaten except on three occasions. He wants me to get into a support group for families of people who are having a sex change. Support groups are people who are in the same boat. Except no one has any oars in the water.

I tell him I know how it feels to think you are in the wrong body. I tell him how I wanted my boyfriend to put a gun up inside me and blow the woman out, how I thought wearing spiked heels and low-cut dresses would somehow help my crisis, that putting on an ultrafeminine outside would mask the maleness I felt needed hiding. I tell him it's the rule, rather than the exception, that people from families like ours have very spooky sexual identity problems. He tells me that his sexuality is a birth defect. I recognize the lingo. It's support-group-for-transsexuals lingo. He tells me he sits down to pee. He told his therapist that he used to wet all over the floor. His therapist said, "You can't aim the bullets if you don't touch the gun." Lingo. My brother is hell-bent for castration, the castration that started before he had language: the castration of abuse. He will simply finish what was set in motion long ago.

I will tell my brother about the time I took ten sacks of oranges into a school so that I could teach metaphor. The school was for special students—those who were socially or intellectually impaired. I had planned to have them peel the oranges as I spoke about how much the world is like the orange. I handed out the oranges. The students refused to peel them, not because they wanted to make life difficult for me— they were enchanted with the gift. One child asked if he could have an orange to take home to his little brother. Another said he would bring me ten dollars the next day if I would give him a sack of oranges. And I knew I was at home, that these children and I shared something that *makes* the leap of mind the metaphor attempts. And something in me healed.

A neighbor of mine takes pantyhose and cuts them up and sews them up after stuffing them. Then she puts these things into Mason jars and sells them, you know, to put out on the mantel for conversation. They are little penises and little scrotums, complete with hair. She calls them "Pickled Peters."

A friend of mine had a sister who had a sex change operation. This young woman had her breasts removed and ran around the house with no shirt on before the stitches were taken out. She answered the door one evening. A young man had come to call on my friend. The sex-changed sister invited him in and offered him some black bean soup as if she were perfectly normal with her red surgical wounds and her black stitches. The young man left and never went back. A couple years later, my friend's sister/brother died when she ran a car into a concrete bridge railing. I hope for a happier ending. For my brother, for myself, for all of us.

My brother calls. He's done his toenails: Shimmering Cinnamon. And he's left his wife and children and purchased some nightgowns at a yard sale. His hair is getting longer. He wears a special bra. Most of the people he works with know about the changes in his life. His voice is not the same voice I've heard for years; he sounds happy.

My brother calls. He's always envied me, my woman's body. The same body I live in and have cursed for its softness. He asks me how I feel about myself. He says, "You know, you are really our father's first-born son." He tells me he used to want to be me because I was the only person our father almost loved.

The drama of life. After I saw that woman in the bus station eat an orange as if it were an apple, I went out into the street and smoked a joint with some guy I'd met on the bus. Then I hailed a cab and went to a tattoo parlor. The tattoo artist tried to talk me into getting a nice bird or butterfly design; I had chosen a design on his wall that appealed to me — a symbol I didn't know the meaning of. It is the Yin-Yang, and it's tattooed above my right ankle bone. I suppose my drugged, crazed consciousness knew more than I knew: that yin combines with yang to produce all that comes to be. I am drawn to androgyny.

Of course there is the nagging possibility that my brother's di-   25
lemma is genetic. Our father used to dress in drag on Halloween, and he made a beautiful woman. One year, the year my mother cut my brother's blond curls off, my father taped those curls to his own head and tied a silk scarf over the tape. Even his close friends didn't know it was him. And my youngest daughter was a body builder for a while, her lean body as muscular as a man's. And my sons are beautiful, not handsome: they look androgynous.

Then there's my grandson. I saw him when he was less than an hour old. He was naked and had hiccups. I watched as he had his first bath, and I heard him cry. He had not been named yet, but his little crib had a blue card affixed to it with tape. And on the card were the words "Baby Boy." There was no doubt in me that the words were true.

When my brother was born, my father was off flying jets in Korea. I went to the hospital with my grandfather to get my mother and this new brother. I remember how I wanted a sister, and I remember looking at him as my mother held him in the front seat of the car. I was certain he was a sister, certain that my mother was joking. She removed his diaper to show me that he was a boy. I still didn't believe her. Considering what has happened lately, I wonder if my child-skewed consciousness knew more than the anatomical proof suggested.

I try to make peace with myself. I try to understand his decision to alter himself. I try to think of him as her. I write his woman name, and I feel like I'm betraying myself. I try to be open-minded, but something in me shuts down. I think we humans are in big trouble, that many of us don't really have a clue as to what acceptable human behavior is. Something in me says no to all this, that this surgery business is the ultimate betrayal of the self. And yet, I want my brother to be happy.

It was in the city of San Antonio that my father had his surgery. I rode the bus from Kansas to Texas, and arrived at the hospital two days after the operation to find my father sitting in the solarium playing solitaire. He had a type of cancer that particularly thrived on testosterone. And so he was castrated in order to ease his pain and to stop the growth of tumors. He died six months later.

Back in the sleep of the large world of dreams, I have done surgeries   *30*
under water in which I float my father's testicles back into him, and he —
the brutal man he was — emerges from the pool a tan and smiling man,
parting the surface of the water with his perfect head. He loves all the
grief away.

I will tell my brother all I know of oranges, that if you squeeze the
orange peel into a flame, small fires happen because of the volatile oil in
the peel. Also, if you squeeze the peel and it gets into your cat's eyes, the
cat will blink and blink. I will tell him there is no perfect rhyme for the
word "orange," and that if we can just make up a good word we can be
immortal. We will become obsessed with finding the right word, and I
will be joyous at our legitimate pursuit.

I have purchased a black camisole with lace to send to my new
sister. And a card. On the outside of the card there's a drawing of a
woman sitting by a pond and a zebra is off to the left. Inside are these
words: "The past is ended. Be happy." And I have asked my companions
to hold me and I have cried. My self is wet and small. But it is not dark.
Sometimes, if no one touches me, I will die.

Sister, you are the best craziness of the family. Brother, love what
you love.

FOR DISCUSSION AND WRITING

1. Point out instances in which the author purposefully fails to provide
    enough information with which to immediately comprehend the expo-
    sition. Do you believe that the author is successful in what she is trying
    to do? Why, or why not? At several such times, the author provides the
    necessary information many paragraphs after the initial reference is
    made. Why do you think the author does this? Would you have written
    it differently? Explain.

2. Point out examples in which the author juxtaposes two disparate ideas
    or occurrences without stating what relation they have to each other.
    What relations does the author imply with each of these juxtapositions?

3. It is surprising that the author refers so frequently to her parents when
    she focuses the exposition elsewhere. Do you believe that these details
    are relevant? Why, or why not?

4. What autobiographical details can you glean from the essay? What bio-
    graphical details are provided about the brother? What do your answers
    tell you about the focus of the story?

5. Explain what significance the author's tattoo holds for her.

6. Explain what oranges mean to the author. Do they have more than one meaning for her? Cite passages from the selection to support your opinion.

7. The author writes, "Perhaps better than all else, I understand obsession. It is of the mind. And it is language-bound. Sex is of the body. It has no words" (par. 12). The author's brother, however, is proof that this is a false dichotomy. Explain. What other evidence is presented in rebuttal to this belief?

LATE NIGHT THOUGHTS ON LISTENING TO MAHLER'S NINTH SYMPHONY

Lewis Thomas

Among the very best essayists writing today are three physicians: Richard Selzer, F. Gonzalez-Crussi, and Lewis Thomas. Selzer's *Taking the World in for Repairs* and Gonzalez-Crussi's *Notes of an Anatomist* are both highly acclaimed, as are the essay collections of Lewis Thomas: *The Lives of a Cell: Notes of a Biology Watcher* (1974); *The Medusa and the Snail: More Notes of a Biology Watcher* (1979); and *Late Night Thoughts on Listening to Mahler's Ninth Symphony* (1983).

Born in 1913, Thomas completed his medical degree at Harvard in 1937, after which he served as a medical officer in the South Pacific during World War II and then assumed positions in a variety of prestigious institutions and medical schools: the Rockefeller Institute, Tulane University, the University of Minnesota, New York University and Bellevue Hospital, and the Yale University School of Medicine. He was president of the Sloan-Kettering Institute in New York, one of the world's leading centers for the study and treatment of cancer, from 1973 to 1980, and is now its chancellor.

He has published approximately two hundred scientific papers and has drafted countless reports and funding proposals. In that "practical" type of writing, however, he could not express his hopes, fears, joys, and sorrows—the other dimension of humans or, one might even say, the human dimension of humans. The following essay explains Thomas's attitude toward the future of mankind.

I cannot listen to Mahler's Ninth Symphony with anything like the old melancholy mixed with the high pleasure I used to take from this music. There was a time, not long ago, when what I heard, especially in the final movement, was an open acknowledgment of death and at the same time a quiet celebration of the tranquillity connected to the process. I took this music as a metaphor for reassurance, confirming my own strong hunch that the dying of every living creature, the most natural of all experiences, has to be a peaceful experience. I rely on nature. The long passages on all the strings at the end, as close as music can come to expressing silence itself, I used to hear as Mahler's idea of leave-taking at its best. But always, I have heard this music as a solitary, private listener, thinking about death.

Now I hear it differently. I cannot listen to the last movement of the Mahler Ninth without the door-smashing intrusion of a huge new thought: death everywhere, the dying of everything, the end of humanity. The easy sadness expressed with such gentleness and delicacy by that repeated phrase on faded strings, over and over again, no longer comes to me as old, familiar news of the cycle of living and dying. All through the last notes my mind swarms with images of a world in which the thermonuclear bombs have begun to explode, in New York and San Francisco, in Moscow and Leningrad, in Paris, in Paris, in Paris. In Oxford and Cambridge, in Edinburgh. I cannot push away the thought of a cloud of radioactivity drifting along the Engadin, from the Moloja Pass to Ftan, killing off the part of the earth I love more than any other part.

I am old enough by this time to be used to the notion of dying, saddened by the glimpse when it has occurred but only transiently knocked down, able to regain my feet quickly at the thought of continuity, any day. I have acquired and held in affection until very recently another sideline of an idea which serves me well at dark times: the life of the earth is the same as the life of an organism: the great round being possesses a mind: the mind contains an infinite number of thoughts and memories: when I reach my time I may find myself still hanging around in some sort of midair, one of those small thoughts, drawn back into the memory of the earth: in that peculiar sense I will be alive.

Now all that has changed. I cannot think that way anymore. Not while those things are still in place, aimed everywhere, ready for launching.

This is a bad enough thing for the people in my generation. We can 5
put up with it, I suppose, since we must. We are moving along anyway, like it or not. I can even set aside my private fancy about hanging around, in midair.

What I cannot imagine, what I cannot put up with, the thought that keeps grinding its way into my mind, making the Mahler into a hideous noise close to killing me, is what it would be like to be young. How do the young stand it? How can they keep their sanity? If I were very young, sixteen or seventeen years old, I think I would begin, perhaps very slowly and imperceptibly, to go crazy.

There is a short passage near the very end of the Mahler in which the almost vanishing violins, all engaged in a sustained backward glance, are edged aside for a few bars by the cellos. Those lower notes pick up fragments from the first movement, as though prepared to begin everything all over again, and then the cellos subside and disappear, like an exhalation. I used to hear this as a wonderful few seconds of encouragement: we'll be back, we're still here, keep going, keep going.

Now, with a pamphlet in front of me on a corner of my desk, published by the Congressional Office of Technology Assessment, entitled *MX Basing,* an analysis of all the alternative strategies for placement and protection of hundreds of these missiles, each capable of creating artificial suns to vaporize a hundred Hiroshimas, collectively capable of destroying the life of any continent, I cannot hear the same Mahler. Now, those cellos sound in my mind like the opening of all the hatches and the instant before ignition.

If I were sixteen or seventeen years old, I would not feel the cracking of my own brain, but I would know for sure that the whole world was coming unhinged. I can remember with some clarity what it was like to be sixteen. I had discovered the Brahms symphonies. I knew that there was something going on in the late Beethoven quartets that I would have to figure out, and I knew that there was plenty of time ahead for all the figuring I would ever have to do. I had never heard of Mahler. I was in no hurry. I was a college sophomore and had decided that Wallace Stevens and I possessed a comprehensive understanding of everything needed for a life. The years stretched away forever ahead, forever. My great-great grandfather had come from Wales, leaving his signature in the family Bible on the same page that carried, a century later, my father's signature. It never crossed my mind to wonder about the twenty-first century; it was just there, given, somewhere in the sure distance.

The man on television, Sunday midday, middle-aged and solid,   *10* nice-looking chap, all the facts at his fingertips, more dependable looking than most high-school principals, is talking about civilian defense, his responsibility in Washington. It can make an enormous difference, he is saying. Instead of the outright death of eighty million American citizens in twenty minutes, he says, we can, by careful planning and practice, get that number down to only forty million, maybe even twenty. The thing to do, he says, is to evacuate the cities quickly and have everyone get under shelter in the countryside. That way we can recover, and meanwhile we will have retaliated, incinerating all of Soviet society, he says. What about radioactive fallout? he is asked. Well, he says. Anyway, he says, if the Russians know they can only destroy forty million of us instead of eighty million, this will deter them. Of course, he adds, they have the capacity to kill all two hundred and twenty million of us if they were to try real hard, but they know we can do the same to them. If the figure is only forty million this will deter them, not worth the trouble, not worth the risk. Eighty million would be another matter, we should guard ourselves against losing that many all at once, he says.

If I were sixteen or seventeen years old and had to listen to that, or read things like that, I would want to give up listening and reading. I would begin thinking up new kinds of sounds, different from any music heard before, and I would be twisting and turning to rid myself of human language.

FOR DISCUSSION AND WRITING

1. How has the Atomic Age changed Thomas?

2. What sorts of readers is Thomas writing for? What is the evidence for your conclusion?

3. Lewis Thomas is a physician and cancer researcher who has written hundreds of scientific papers. What do you think is his purpose in writing essays such as "Late Night Thoughts"?

4. Does the essay supply enough detail for a reader unfamiliar with Mahler's Ninth Symphony to understand Thomas's point? Explain.

5. In this essay, is Lewis Thomas logical or illogical? Is the question of logic relevant? Explain your answer.

6. Thomas draws his information about nuclear bombs and atomic war from various sources. Are these sources reliable? Is reliability (or lack thereof) of sources a major concern in this essay?

7. At any point in the essay, are you confused because you lack the requisite world knowledge? At any point, do you lack knowledge of specific references but feel that your lack of knowledge does not impede your understanding of the essay? Explain.

8. "The realization that humankind can annihilate itself is depressing." Does this statement express the main point of the essay adequately? Explain.

9. The essay was written almost ten years ago. Has the situation described by Thomas changed appreciably? How so, or why not?

NATURE

Ralph Waldo Emerson

No other writer or philosopher has had a greater influence on American values and attitudes than has Ralph Waldo Emerson (1803–1882), particularly in his hymns to individuality. In the essay "Self-Reliance" he writes, "To believe your own thought, to believe that what is true for you in your private heart is true for all men — is genius." And in "The American Scholar," he advises, "The world is nothing, the man is all; in yourself is the law of all nature . . . in yourself slumbers the whole of Reason; it is for you to know all; it is for you to dare all."

Emerson is identified with a philosophical movement known as transcendentalism, which is not a systematic body of thought, but what might be called a group of related viewpoints. One aspect of transcendentalism is the belief in the oversoul, the universal soul of which all of us are a part. Another aspect of transcendentalism is the belief that whether or not there exists a reality outside the mind, we can know only what is in our own minds; hence, we construct "reality."

Emerson's life was not glamorous or mysterious. He married twice (his first wife having died after barely a year of marriage), raised a family, and served for a time as a Congregational minister. He traveled a good deal, particularly in the northeast, on lecture tours and visited Europe twice. He became a powerful figure in the intellectual and cultural life of the nation. Henry David Thoreau was massively indebted to Emerson, his friend and mentor, and without Emerson it is unlikely that Walt Whitman would have produced his masterpiece, *Leaves of Grass*.

"Nature," first published in 1836, sets forth a number of the ideas that have made Emerson so important to the American intellectual scene. First, in the world of nature one finds more truth and beauty than in the world of human artifice and culture. Second, it is the human that really creates nature; the eyes simply convey the raw data. Third, through nature one comes to know God. Fourth, great philosophers are also great poets, for, as Keats said, truth and beauty are one and the same.

As you read "Nature," think about the ways in which it expresses the spirit of America.

The rounded world is fair to see,
Nine times folded in mystery:
Though baffled seers cannot impart
The secret of its laboring heart,
Throb thine with Nature's throbbing breast,
And all is clear from east to west.
Spirit that lurks each form within
Beckons to spirit of its kin;
Self-kindled every atom glows,
And hints the future which it owes.

There are days which occur in this climate, at almost any season of the year, wherein the world reaches its perfection; when the air, the heavenly bodies and the earth, make a harmony, as if nature would indulge her offspring; when, in these bleak upper sides of the planet, nothing is to desire that we have heard of the happiest latitudes, and we bask in the shining hours of Florida and Cuba; when everything that has life gives sign of satisfaction, and the cattle that lie on the ground seem to have great and tranquil thoughts. These halcyons may be looked for with a little more assurance in that pure October weather which we distinguish by the name of the Indian summer. The day, immeasurably long, sleeps over the broad hills and warm wide fields. To have lived through all its sunny hours, seems longevity enough. The solitary places do not seem quite lonely. At the gates of the forest, the surprised man of the world is forced to leave his city estimates of great and small, wise and foolish. The knapsack of custom falls off his back with the first step he takes into these precincts. Here is sanctity which shames our religions, and reality which discredits our heroes. Here we find Nature to be the circumstance which dwarfs every other circumstance, and judges like a god all men that come to her. We have crept out of our close and crowded houses into the night and morning, and we see what majestic beauties daily wrap us in their bosom. How willingly we would escape the barriers which render them comparatively impotent, escape the sophistication and second thought, and suffer nature to intrance us. The tempered light of the woods is like a perpetual morning, and is stimulating and heroic. The anciently-reported spells of these places creep on us. The stems of pines, hemlocks and oaks almost gleam like iron on the excited eye. The incommunicable trees begin to persuade us to live with them, and quit our life of solemn trifles. Here no history, or church, or state, is interpolated on the divine sky and the immortal year. How easily we might walk onward into the opening landscape, absorbed by new pictures and by thoughts fast succeeding each other, until by degrees the recollection of home was crowded out of the mind, all memory obliterated by the tyranny of the present, and we were led in triumph by nature.

These enchantments are medicinal, they sober and heal us. These are plain pleasures, kindly and native to us. We come to our own, and make friends with matter, which the ambitious chatter of the schools would persuade us to despise. We never can part with it; the mind loves its old home: as water to our thirst, so is the rock, the ground, to our eyes and hands and feet. It is firm water; it is cold flame; what health, what affinity! Ever an old friend, ever like a dear friend and brother when we chat affectedly with strangers, comes in this honest face, and takes a grave liberty with us, and shames us out of our nonsense. Cities give not the human senses room enough. We go out daily and nightly to feed the eyes on the horizon, and require so much scope, just as we need water for our bath. There are all degrees of natural influence, from these quarantine powers of nature, up to her dearest and gravest ministrations to the imagination and the soul. There is the bucket of cold water from the spring, the wood-fire to which the chilled traveller rushes for safety — and there is the sublime moral of autumn and of noon. We nestle in nature, and draw our living as parasites from her roots and grains, and we receive glances from the heavenly bodies, which call us to solitude and foretell the remotest future. The blue zenith is the point in which romance and reality meet. I think if we should be rapt away into all that and dream of heaven, and should converse with Gabriel and Uriel, the upper sky would be all that would remain of our furniture.

It seems as if the day was not wholly profane in which we have given heed to some natural object. The fall of snowflakes in a still air, preserving to each crystal its perfect form; the blowing of sleet over a wide sheet of water, and over plains; the waving rye-field; the mimic waving of acres of houstonia, whose innumerable florets whiten and ripple before the eye; the reflections of trees and flowers in glassy lakes; the musical, steaming, odorous south wind, which converts all trees to wind-harps; the crackling and spurting of hemlock in the flames, or of pine logs, which yield glory to the walls and faces in the sitting-room — these are the music and pictures of the most ancient religion. My house stands in low land, with limited outlook, and on the skirt of the village. But I go with my friend to the shore of our little river, and with one stroke of the paddle I leave the village politics and personalities, yes, and the world of villages and personalities, behind, and pass into a delicate realm of sunset and moonlight, too bright almost for spotted man to enter without novitiate and probation. We penetrate bodily this incredible beauty; we dip our hands in this painted element; our eyes are bathed in these lights and forms. A holiday, a *villeggiatura,* a royal revel, the proudest, most heart-rejoicing festival that valor and beauty, power and taste, ever decked and enjoyed, establishes itself on the instant. These sunset clouds, these delicately emerging stars, with their private and ineffable glances, signify it and proffer it. I am taught the poorness of our invention, the ugliness of towns and palaces. Art and luxury have early learned that they must work as enhancement and sequel to this original beauty. I am over-instructed for my return. Henceforth I shall be hard to please. I cannot go back to toys. I am grown expensive and sophisticated. I can no longer live without elegance, but a countryman shall be my master of revels. He who knows the most; he who knows what sweets and virtues are in the ground, the waters, the plants, the heavens, and how to come at these enchantments, is the rich and royal man. Only as far as the masters of the world have called in nature to their aid, can they reach the height of magnificence. This is the meaning of their hanging-gardens, villas, garden-houses, islands, parks and preserves, to back their faulty personality with these strong accessories. I do not wonder that the landed interest should be invincible in the State with these dangerous auxiliaries. These bribe and invite; not kings, not palaces, not men, not women, but these tender and poetic stars, eloquent of secret promises. We heard what the rich man said, we knew of his villa, his grove, his wine and his company, but the provocation and point of the invitation came out of these beguiling stars. In their soft glances I see what men strove to realize in some Versailles, or Paphos, or Ctesiphon. Indeed, it is the magical lights of the horizon and the blue sky for the background which save all our works of art, which were otherwise bawbles. When the rich tax the poor with servility and obsequiousness, they should consider the effect of men reputed to be the possessors of nature, on imaginative minds. Ah! if the rich were rich as the poor fancy riches! A boy hears a military band play on the field at night, and he has kings and queens and famous chivalry palpably before him. He hears the echoes of a horn in a hill country, in the Notch Mountains, for example, which converts the mountains into an Aeolian harp — and this supernatural *tiralira* restores to him the Dorian mythology, Apollo, Diana, and all divine hunters and huntresses. Can a musical note be so lofty, so haughtily beautiful! To the poor young poet, thus fabulous is his picture of society; he is loyal; he respects the rich; they are rich for the sake of his imagination; how poor his fancy would be, if they were not rich! That they have some high-fenced grove which they call a park; that they live in larger and better-garnished saloons than he has visited, and go in coaches, keeping only the society of the elegant, to watering-places and to distant cities — these make the groundwork from which he has delineated estates of romance, compared with which their actual possessions are shanties and paddocks. The muse herself betrays her son, and enhances the gifts of wealth and well-born beauty by a radiation out of the air, and clouds, and forests that skirt the road — a certain haughty favor, as if from patrician genii to patricians, a kind of aristocracy in nature, a prince of the power of the air.

The moral sensibility which makes Edens and Tempes so easily, may not be always found, but the material landscape is never far off. We can find these enchantments without visiting the Como Lake, or the Madeira Islands. We exaggerate the praises of local scenery. In every landscape the point of astonishment is the meeting of the sky and the earth, and that is seen from the first hillock as well as from the top of the Alleghanies. The stars at night stoop down over the brownest, homeliest common with all the spiritual magnificence which they shed on the Campagna, or on the marble deserts of Egypt. The uprolled clouds and the colors of morning and evening will transfigure maples and alders. The difference between landscape and landscape is small, but there is great difference in the beholders. There is nothing so wonderful in any particular landscape as the necessity of being beautiful under which every landscape lies. Nature cannot be surprised in undress. Beauty breaks in everywhere.

But it is very easy to outrun the sympathy of readers on this topic,   *5*
which schoolmen called *natura naturata,* or nature passive. One can hardly
speak directly of it without excess. It is as easy to broach in mixed
companies what is called "the subject of religion." A susceptible person
does not like to indulge his tastes in this kind without the apology of
some trivial necessity: he goes to see a wood-lot, or to look at the crops,
or to fetch a plant or a mineral from a remote locality, or he carries a
fowling-piece or a fishing-rod. I suppose this shame must have a good
reason. A dilettanteism in nature is barren and unworthy. The fop of
fields is no better than his brother of Broadway. Men are naturally hunters and inquisitive of wood-craft, and I suppose that such a gazetteer as
woodcutters and Indians should furnish facts for, would take place in the
most sumptuous drawing-rooms of all the "Wreaths" and "Flora's chap-
lets" of the bookshops; yet ordinarily, whether we are too clumsy for so
subtle a topic, or from whatever cause, as soon as men begin to write on
nature, they fall into euphuism. Frivolity is a most unfit tribute to Pan,
who ought to be represented in the mythology as the most continent of
gods. I would not be frivolous before the admirable reserve and prudence
of time, yet I cannot renounce the rights of returning often to this old
topic. The multitude of false churches accredits the true religion. Literature, poetry, science are the homage of man to this unfathomed secret,
concerning which no sane man can affect an indifference or incuriosity.
Nature is loved by what is best in us. It is loved as the city of God,
although, or rather because there is no citizen. The sunset is unlike
anything that is underneath it: it wants men. And the beauty of nature
must always seem unreal and mocking, until the landscape has human
figures that are as good as itself. If there were good men, there would
never be this rapture in nature. If the king is in the palace, nobody looks
at the walls. It is when he is gone, and the house is filled with grooms
and gazers, that we turn from the people to find relief in the majestic
men that are suggested by the pictures and the architecture. The critics
who complain of the sickly separation of the beauty of nature from the
thing to be done, must consider that our hunting of the picturesque is
inseparable from our protest against false society. Man is fallen; nature is
erect, and serves as a differential thermometer, detecting the presence or
absence of the divine sentiment in man. By fault of our dulness and
selfishness we are looking up to nature, but when we are convalescent,
nature will look up to us. We see the foaming brook with compunction:
if our own life flowed with the right energy, we should shame the brook.
The stream of zeal sparkles with real fire, and not with reflex rays of sun
and moon. Nature may be as selfishly studied as trade. Astronomy to
the selfish becomes astrology; psychology, mesmerism (with intent to
show where our spoons are gone); and anatomy and physiology become
phrenology and palmistry.

But taking timely warning, and leaving many things unsaid on this
topic, let us not longer omit our homage to the Efficient Nature, *natura*

naturans, the quick cause before which all forms flee as the driven snows; itself secret, its works driven before it in flocks and multitudes (as the ancients represented nature by Proteus, a shepherd) and in undescribable variety. It publishes itself in creatures, reaching from particles and spiculae through transformation on transformation to the highest symmetries, arriving at consummate results without a shock or a leap. A little heat, that is a little motion, is all that differences the bald, dazzling white and deadly cold poles of the earth from the prolific tropical climates. All changes pass without violence, by reason of the two cardinal conditions of boundless space and boundless time. Geology has initiated us into the secularity of nature, and taught us to disuse our dame-school measures, and exchange our Mosaic and Ptolemaic schemes for her large style. We knew nothing rightly, for want of perspective. Now we learn what patient periods must round themselves before the rock is formed; then before the rock is broken, and the first lichen race has disintegrated the thinnest external plate into soil, and opened the door for the remote Flora, Fauna, Ceres, and Pomona to come in. How far off yet is the trilobite! how far the quadruped! how inconceivably remote is man! All duly arrive, and then race after race of men. It is a long way from granite to the oyster; farther yet to Plato and the preaching of the immortality of the soul. Yet all must come, as surely as the first atom has two sides.

Motion or change and identity or rest are the first and second secrets of nature: Motion and Rest. The whole code of her laws may be written on the thumbnail, or the signet of a ring. The whirling bubble on the surface of a brook admits us to the secret of the mechanics of the sky. Every shell on the beach is a key to it. A little water made to rotate in a cup explains the formation of the simpler shells; the addition of matter from year to year arrives at last at the most complex forms; and yet so poor is nature with all her craft, that from the beginning to the end of the universe she has but one stuff—but one stuff with its two ends, to serve up all her dream-like variety. Compound it how she will, star, sand, fire, water, tree, man, it is still one stuff, and betrays the same properties.

Nature is always consistent, though she feigns to contravene her own laws. She keeps her laws, and seems to transcend them. She arms and equips an animal to find its place and living in the earth, and at the same time she arms and equips another animal to destroy it. Space exists to divide creatures; but by clothing the sides of a bird with a few feathers she gives him a petty omnipresence. The direction is forever onward, but the artist still goes back for materials and begins again with the first elements on the most advanced stage: otherwise all goes to ruin. If we look at her work, we seem to catch a glance of a system in transition. Plants are the young of the world, vessels of health and vigor; but they grope ever upward towards consciousness; the trees are imperfect men, and seem to bemoan their imprisonment, rooted in the ground. The animal is the novice and probationer of a more advanced order. The men, though young, having tasted the first drop from the cup of thought, are already dissipated; the maples and ferns are still uncorrupt; yet no doubt when they come to consciousness they too will curse and swear. Flowers so strictly belong to youth that we adult men soon come to feel that their beautiful generations concern not us: we have had our day; now let the children have theirs. The flowers jilt us, and we are old bachelors with our ridiculous tenderness.

Things are so strictly related, that according to the skill of the eye, from any one object the parts and properties of any other may be predicted. If we had eyes to see it, a bit of stone from the city wall would certify us of the necessity that man must exist, as readily as the city. That identity makes us all one, and reduces to nothing great intervals on our customary scale. We talk of deviations from natural life, as if artificial life were not also natural. The smoothest curled courtier in the boudoirs of a palace has an animal nature, rude and aboriginal as a white bear, omnipotent to its own ends, and is directly related, there amid essences and billets-doux, to Himmaleh mountain-chains and the axis of the globe. If we consider how much we are nature's, we need not be superstitious about towns, as if that terrific or benefic force did not find us there also, and fashion cities. Nature, who made the mason, made the house. We may easily hear too much of rural influences. The cool disengaged air of natural objects makes them enviable to us, chafed and irritable creatures with red faces, and we think we shall be as grand as they if we camp out and eat roots; but let us be men instead of woodchucks and the oak and the elm shall gladly serve us, though we sit in chairs of ivory on carpets of silk.

This guiding identity runs through all the surprises and contrasts *10* of the piece, and characterizes every law. Man carries the world in his head, the whole astronomy and chemistry suspended in a thought. Because the history of nature is charactered in his brain, therefore is he the prophet and discoverer of her secrets. Every known fact in natural science was divined by the presentiment of somebody, before it was actually verified. A man does not tie his shoe without recognizing laws which bind the farthest regions of nature: moon, plant, gas, crystal, are concrete geometry and numbers. Common sense knows its own, and recognizes the fact at first sight in chemical experiment. The common sense of Franklin, Dalton, Davy and Black is the same common sense which made the arrangements which now it discovers.

If the identity expresses organized rest, the counter action runs also into organization. The astronomers said, 'Give us matter and a little motion and we will construct the universe. It is not enough that we should have matter, we must also have a single impulse, one shove to launch the mass and generate the harmony of the centrifugal and centripetal forces. Once heave the ball from the hand, and we can show how all

this mighty order grew.' 'A very unreasonable postulate,' said the meta-
physicians, 'and a plain begging of the question. Could you not prevail
to know the genesis of projection, as well as the continuation of it?'
Nature, meanwhile, had not waited for the discussion, but, right or
wrong, bestowed the impulse, and the balls rolled. It was no great affair,
a mere push, but the astronomers were right in making much of it, for
there is no end to the consequences of the act. That famous aboriginal
push propagates itself through all the balls of the system, and through
every atom of every ball; through all the races of creatures, and through
the history and performance of every individual. Exaggeration is in the
course of things. Nature sends no creature, no man into the world without adding a small excess of his proper quality. Given the planet, it is
still necessary to add the impulse; so to every creature nature added a
little violence of direction in its proper path, a shove to put it on its way;
in every instance a slight generosity, a drop too much. Without electricity the air would rot, and without this violence of direction which men
and women have, without a spice of bigot and fanatic, no excitement,
no efficiency. We aim above the mark to hit the mark. Every act hath
some falsehood of exaggeration in it. And when now and then comes
along some sad, sharp-eyed man, who sees how paltry a game is played,
and refuses to play but blabs the secret; how then? Is the bird flown? O
no, the wary Nature sends a new troop of fairer forms, of lordlier youths,
with a little more excess of direction to hold them fast to their several
aim; makes them a little wrong-headed in that direction in which they
are rightest, and on goes the game again with new whirl, for a generation
or two more. The child with his sweet pranks, the fool of his senses,
commanded by every sight and sound, without any power to compare
and rank his sensations, abandoned to a whistle or a painted chip, to a
lead dragoon or a gingerbread-dog, individualizing everything, general-
izing nothing, delighted with every new thing, lies down at night over-
powered by the fatigue which this day of continual pretty madness has
incurred. But Nature had answered her purpose with the curly, dimpled
lunatic. She has tasked every faculty, and has secured the symmetrical
growth of the bodily frame by all these attitudes and exertions — an end
of the first importance, which could not be trusted to any care less
perfect than her own. This glitter, this opaline lustre plays round the top
of every toy to his eye to insure his fidelity, and he is deceived to his
good. We are made alive and kept alive by the same arts. Let the stoics
say what they please, we do not eat for the good of living, but because
the meat is savory and the appetite is keen. The vegetable life does not
content itself with casting from the flower or the tree a single seed, but
it fills the air and earth with a prodigality of seeds, that, if thousands
perish, thousands may plant themselves; that hundreds may come up,
that tens may live to maturity; that at least one may replace the parent.
All things betray the same calculated profusion. The excess of fear with

which the animal frame is hedged round, shrinking from cold, starting at sight of a snake or at a sudden noise, protects us, through a multitude of groundless alarms, from some one real danger at last. The lover seeks in marriage his private felicity and perfection, with no prospective end; and nature hides in his happiness her own end, namely progeny, or the perpetuity of the race.

But the craft with which the world is made, runs also into the mind and character of men. No man is quite sane; each has a vein of folly in his composition, a slight determination of blood to the head, to make sure of holding him hard to some one point which nature had taken to heart. Great causes are never tried on their merits; but the cause is reduced to particulars to suit the size of the partisans, and the contention is ever hottest on minor matters. Not less remarkable is the overfaith of each man in the importance of what he has to do or say. The poet, the prophet, has a higher value for what he utters than any hearer, and therefore it gets spoken. The strong, self-complacent Luther declares with an emphasis not to be mistaken, that "God himself cannot do without wise men." Jacob Behmen and George Fox betray their egotism in the pertinacity of their controversial tracts, and James Naylor once suffered himself to be worshipped as the Christ. Each prophet comes presently to identify himself with his thought, and to esteem his hat and shoes sacred. However this may discredit such persons with the judicious, it helps them with the people, as it gives heat, pungency and publicity to their words. A similar experience is not infrequent in private life. Each young and ardent person writes a diary, in which, when the hours of prayer and penitence arrive, he inscribes his soul. The pages thus written are to him burning and fragrant; he reads them on his knees by midnight and by the morning star; he wets them with his tears; they are sacred; too good for the world, and hardly yet to be shown to the dearest friend. This is the man-child that is born to the soul, and her life still circulates in the babe. The umbilical cord has not yet been cut. After some time has elapsed, he begins to wish to admit his friend to this hallowed experience, and with hesitation, yet with firmness, exposes the pages to his eye. Will they not burn his eyes? The friend coldly turns them over, and passes from the writing to conversation, with easy transition, which strikes the other party with astonishment and vexation. He cannot suspect the writing itself. Days and nights of fervid like, of communion with angels of darkness and of light have engraved their shadowy characters on their tear-stained book. He suspects the intelligence or the heart of his friend. Is there then no friend? He cannot yet credit that one may have impressive experience and yet may not know how to put his private fact into literature: and perhaps the discovery that wisdom has other tongues and ministers than we, that though we should hold our peace the truth would not the less be spoken, might check injuriously the flames of our zeal. A man can only speak so long as he does not feel his speech to be partial and inadequate. It is partial, but he does not see it to be so whilst he utters it. As soon as he is released from the instinctive and particular and sees its partiality, he shuts his mouth in disgust. For no man can write anything who does not think that what he writes is for the time the history of the world; or do anything well who does not esteem his work to be of importance. My work may be of none, but I must not think it of none, or I shall not do it with impunity.

In like manner, there is throughout nature something mocking, something that leads us on and on, but arrives nowhere; keeps no faith with us. All promise outruns the performance. We live in a system of approximations. Every end is prospective of some other end, which is also temporary; a round and final success nowhere. We are encamped in nature, not domesticated. Hunger and thirst lead us on to eat and to drink; but bread and wine, mix and cook them how you will, leave us hungry and thirsty, after the stomach is full. It is the same with all our arts and performances. Our music, our poetry, our language itself are not satisfactions, but suggestions. The hunger for wealth, which reduces the planet to a garden, fools the eager pursuer. What is the end sought? Plainly to secure the ends of good sense and beauty from the intrusion of deformity or vulgarity of any kind. But what an operose method! What a train of means to secure a little conversation! This palace of brick and stone, these servants, this kitchen, these stables, horses and equipage, this bank-stock and file of mortgages; trade to all the world, country-house and cottage by the waterside, all for a little conversation, high, clear and spiritual! Could it not be had as well by beggars on the highway? No, all these things came from successive efforts of these beggars to remove friction from the wheels of life, and give opportunity. Conversation, character, were the avowed ends; wealth was good as it appeased the animal cravings, cured the smoky chimney, silenced the creaking door, brought friends together in a warm and quiet room, and kept the children and the dinner-table in a different apartment. Thought, virtue, beauty, were the ends; but it was known that men of thought and virtue sometimes had the headache, or wet feet, or could lose good time whilst the room was getting warm in winter days. Unluckily, in the exertions necessary to remove these inconveniences, the main attention has been diverted to this object; the old aims have been lost sight of, and to remove friction has come to be the end. That is the ridicule of rich men; and Boston, London, Vienna, and now the governments generally of the world, are cities and governments of the rich; and the masses are not men, but *poor* men, that is, men who would be rich; this is the ridicule of the class, that they arrive with pains and sweat and fury nowhere; when all is done, it is for nothing. They are like one who has interrupted the conversation of a company to make his speech, and now has forgotten what he went to say. The appearance strikes the eye everywhere of an aimless society, of aimless nations. Were the ends of nature so great and cogent as to exact this immense sacrifice of men?

Quite analogous to the deceits in life, there is, as might be expected, a similar effect on the eye from the face of external nature. There is in woods and waters a certain enticement and flattery, together with a failure to yield a present satisfaction. This disappointment is felt in every landscape. I have seen the softness and beauty of the summer clouds floating feathery overhead, enjoying, as it seemed, their height and privilege of motion, whilst yet they appeared not so much the drapery of this place and hour, as forelooking to some pavilions and gardens of festivity beyond. It is an odd jealousy, but the poet finds himself not near enough to his object. The pine-tree, the river, the bank of flowers before him does not seem to be nature. Nature is still elsewhere. This or this is but outskirt and a far-off reflection and echo of the triumph that has passed by and is now at its glancing splendor and heyday, perchance in the neighboring fields, or, if you stand in the field, then in the adjacent woods. The present object shall give you this sense of stillness that follows a pageant which has just gone by. What splendid distance, what recesses of ineffable pomp and loveliness in the sunset! But who can go where they are, or lay his hand or plant his foot thereon? Off they fall from the round world forever and ever. It is the same among the men and women as among the silent trees; always a referred existence, an absence, never a presence and satisfaction. Is it that beauty can never be grasped? in persons and in landscape is equally inaccessible? The accepted and betrothed lover has lost the wildest charm of his maiden in her acceptance of him. She was heaven whilst he pursued her as a star: she cannot be heaven if she stoops to such a one as he.

What shall we say of this omnipresent appearance of that first projectile impulse, of this flattery and balking of so many well-meaning creatures? Must we not suppose somewhere in the universe a slight treachery and derision? Are we not engaged to a serious resentment of this use that is made of us? Are we tickled trout, and fools of nature? One look at the face of heaven and earth lays all petulance at rest, and soothes us to wiser convictions. To the intelligent, nature converts itself into a vast promise, and will not be rashly explained. Her secret is untold. Many and many an Oedipus arrives; he has the whole mystery teeming in his brain. Alas! the same sorcery has spoiled his skill; no syllable can he shape on his lips. Her mighty orbit vaults like the fresh rainbow into the deep, but no archangel's wing was yet strong enough to follow it and report of the return of the curve. But it also appears that our actions are seconded and disposed to greater conclusions than we designed. We are escorted on every hand through life by spiritual agents, and a beneficent purpose lies in wait for us. We cannot bandy words with Nature, or deal with her as we deal with persons. If we measure our individual forces against hers we may easily feel as if we were the sport of an insuperable destiny. But if, instead of identifying ourselves with the work, we feel that the soul of the Workman streams through us, we shall find the peace of the morning dwelling first in our hearts, and the fathomless powers of gravity and chemistry, and, over them, of life, pre-existing within us in their highest form.

The uneasiness which the thought of our helplessness in the chain of causes occasions us, results from looking too much at one condition of nature, namely, Motion. But the drag is never taken from the wheel. Wherever the impulse exceeds, the Rest or Identity insinuates its compensation. All over the wide fields of earth grows the prunella or self-heal. After every foolish day we sleep off the fumes and furies of its hours; and though we are always engaged with particulars, and often enslaved to them, we bring with us to every experiment the innate universal laws. These, while they exist in the mind as ideas, stand around us in nature forever embodied, a present sanity to expose and cure the insanity of men. Our servitude to particulars betrays us into a hundred foolish expectations. We anticipate a new era from the invention of a locomotive, or a balloon; the new engine brings with it the old checks. They say that by electro-magnetism your salad shall be grown from the seed whilst your fowl is roasting for dinner; it is a symbol of our modern aims and endeavors, of our condensation and acceleration of objects; but nothing is gained; nature cannot be cheated; man's life is but seventy salads long, grow they swift or grow they slow. In these checks and impossibilities, however, we find our advantage, not less than in the impulses. Let the victory fall where it will, we are on that side. And the knowledge that we traverse the whole scale of being, from the centre to the poles of nature, and have some stake in every possibility, lends that sublime lustre to death, which philosophy and religion have too outwardly and literally striven to express in the popular doctrine of the immortality of the soul. The reality is more excellent than the report. Here is no ruin, no discontinuity, no spent ball. The divine circulations never rest nor linger. Nature is the incarnation of a thought, and turns to a thought again, as ice becomes water and gas. The world is mind precipitated, and the volatile essence is forever escaping again into the state of free thought. Hence the virtue and pungency of the influence on the mind of natural objects, whether inorganic or organized. Man imprisoned, man crystalized, man vegetative, speaks to man impersonated. That power which does not respect quantity, which makes the whole and the particle its equal channel, delegates its smile to the morning, and distils its essence into every drop of rain. Every moment instructs, and every object; for wisdom is infused into every form. It has been poured into us as blood; it convulsed us as pain; it slid into us as pleasure; it enveloped us in dull, melancholy days, or in days of cheerful labor; we did not guess its essence until after a long time.

FOR DISCUSSION AND WRITING

1. Several times in the essay, Emerson compares two scenes: nature and the civilized world. What does the author imply with this comparison? (The poem with which the essay begins might help you arrive at an answer.)

2. In regard to manner, Emerson states that most writings about nature are euphuistic. Look up the definition of *euphuistic* in a dictionary. In what ways do you think that Emerson's own essay is euphuistic? In what ways is it not? Does Emerson intend the essay to be euphuistic?

3. Given Emerson's views of the world and of reality, do you think that he would regard the reader of this essay as a miner who digs information and concepts out of the text or as a detective who constructs the meaning of text in his or her own mind?

4. Kenneth Burke, a highly influential theorist about language and literature, explains two kinds of structure for texts, *syllogistic progression* and *qualitative progression:*

> *Syllogistic progression* is the form of a perfectly conducted argument, advancing step by step. It is the form of a mystery story, where everything falls together. . . . It is the form of a demonstration in Euclid. To go from A to E through stages B, C, and D is to obtain such form. We call it syllogistic because, given certain things, certain things must follow, the premises forcing the conclusion. . . .
>
> *Qualitative progression* . . . is subtler. Instead of one incident in the plot preparing us for some other possible incident of plot (as Macbeth's murder of Duncan prepares us for the dying of Macbeth), the presence of one quality prepares us for the introduction of another (the grotesque seriousness of the murder scene preparing us for the grotesque buffoonery of the porter scene). . . . (124–25)

Explain why you think form in "Nature" is either syllogistic or qualitative. Give evidence from the text to support your opinion.

5. Emerson talks about two basic laws of nature: motion/change and identity/rest. Does the first law logically contradict the second? Why, or why not? Does one law take precedence over the other?

6. Does Emerson believe in the scientific method? Explain.

7. Does Emerson view nature as perfect or not? Explain.

8. The last paragraph of the essay pretty well summarizes Emerson's philosophy. In your own words, state that philosophy. Explain why you either agree or disagree with it.

9. Emerson attempts to give the reader a feeling for the ineffable qualities of nature. Cite examples of this from the text.

10. For a man who is obviously smitten by nature, Emerson makes many surprising statements in this essay—for example, the passage in which the author tells us to "be men instead of woodchucks" (par. 9). Cite other examples in which Emerson surprises the reader. Explain why you think these surprises strengthen or weaken the text.

11. Find three instances in which Emerson illustrates a difficult and abstract concept with concrete examples.

SOUNDING

Mark Twain

Born in Florida, Missouri, in 1835, Samuel Langhorne Clemens grew up in Hannibal, on the shores of the Mississippi. His life is an American legend: he became a Mississippi River steamboat pilot; in 1861, he and his brother Orion went to the Nevada Territory, where Sam prospected for gold and silver and became a newspaper reporter for the *Territorial Enterprise*. In the following years, he reported for the *Sacramento Union*, the *Alta Californian*, and the *New York Tribune*.

His first book was *Innocents Abroad*, an account of a journey to the Mediterranean and the Holy Land. Other books followed, among them *The Adventures of Tom Sawyer* (1876), *The Adventures of Huckleberry Finn* (1883), and *A Connecticut Yankee in King Arthur's Court* (1889). *Life on the Mississippi*, from which the following selection is taken, was published in 1883.

No other American author — with the possible exception of Ernest Hemingway — has achieved such wide readership as has Mark Twain. *The Adventures of Tom Sawyer* is a children's classic, and many rank *The Adventures of Huckleberry Finn* with Nathaniel Hawthorne's *Scarlet Letter* and Herman Melville's *Moby Dick* as our nation's greatest novels.

The year Samuel Clemens was born, Halley's Comet appeared. It returned in 1910, the year of his death.

As you read "Sounding," you will appreciate Mark Twain's ability to explain clearly and interestingly — and the wistful humor that characterizes many of his autobiographical writings.

When the river is very low, and one's steamboat is "drawing all the water" there is in the channel — or a few inches more, as was often the case in the old times — one must be painfully circumspect in his piloting. We used to have to "sound" a number of particularly bad places almost every trip when the river was at a very low stage.

Sounding is done in this way: The boat ties up at the shore, just above the shoal crossing; the pilot not on watch takes his "cub" or steersman and a picked crew of men (sometimes an officer also), and goes out in the yawl — provided the boat has not that rare and sumptuous luxury, a regularly devised "sounding-boat" — and proceeds to hunt for the best water, the pilot on duty watching his movements through a spyglass, meantime, and in some instances assisting by signals of the boat's whistle, signifying "try higher up" or "try lower down"; for the surface of the water, like an oil-painting, is more expressive and intelligible when inspected from a little distance than very close at hand. The whistle signals are seldom necessary, however; never, perhaps, except when the wind confuses the significant ripples upon the water's surface. When the yawl has reached the shoal place, the speed is slackened, the pilot begins to sound the depth with a pole ten or twelve feet long, and the steersman at the tiller obeys the order to "hold her up to starboard"; or "let her fall off to larboard";[1] or "steady — steady as you go."

When the measurements indicate that the yawl is approaching the shoalest part of the reef, the command is given to "Ease all!" Then the men stop rowing and the yawl drifts with the current. The next order is, "Stand by with the buoy!" The moment the shallowest point is reached, the pilot delivers the order, "Let go the buoy!" and over she goes. If the pilot is not satisfied, he sounds the place again; if he finds better water higher up or lower down, he removes the buoy to that place. Being finally satisfied, he gives the order, and all the men stand their oars straight up in the air, in line; a blast from the boat's whistle indicates that the signal has been seen; then the men "give way" on their oars and lay the yawl alongside the buoy; the steamer comes creeping carefully down, is pointed straight at the buoy, husbands her power for the coming struggle, and presently, at the critical moment, turns on all her steam and goes grinding and wallowing over the buoy and the sand, and gains the deep water beyond. Or maybe she doesn't; maybe she "strikes and swings." Then she has to while away several hours (or days) sparring herself off.

Sometimes a buoy is not laid at all, but the yawl goes ahead, hunting the best water, and the steamer follows along in its wake. Often there is a deal of fun and excitement about sounding, especially if it is a glorious summer day, or a blustering night. But in winter the cold and the peril take most of the fun out of it.

A buoy is nothing but a board four or five feet long, with one end   5
turned up; it is a reversed schoolhouse bench, with one of the supports left and the other removed. It is anchored on the shoalest part of the reef by a rope with a heavy stone made fast to the end of it. But for the resistance of the turned-up end of the reversed bench, the current would pull the buoy under water. At night, a paper lantern with a candle in it is fastened on top of the buoy, and this can be seen a mile or more, a little glimmering spark in the waste of blackness.

Nothing delights a cub so much as an opportunity to go out sounding. There is such an air of adventure about it; often there is danger; it is so gaudy and man-of-war-like to sit up in the stern-sheets and steer a swift yawl; there is something fine about the exultant spring of the boat when an experienced old sailor crew throw their souls into the oars; it is lovely to see the white foam stream away from the bows; there is music in the rush of the water; it is deliciously exhilarating, in summer, to go speeding over the breezy expanses of the river when the world of wavelets is dancing in the sun. It is such grandeur, too, to the cub, to get a chance to give an order; for often the pilot will simply say, "Let her go

---

[1]The term "larboard" is never used at sea, now, to signify the left hand; but was always used on the river in my time.

about!" and leave the rest to the cub, who instantly cries, in his sternest tone of command, "Ease, starboard! Strong on the larboard! Starboard, give way! With a will, men!" The cub enjoys sounding for the further reason that the eyes of the passengers are watching all the yawl's movements with absorbing interest, if the time be daylight; and if it be night, he knows that those same wondering eyes are fastened upon the yawl's lantern as it glides out into the gloom and dims away in the remote distance.

One trip a pretty girl of sixteen spent her time in our pilot-house with her uncle and aunt, every day and all day long. I fell in love with her. So did Mr. Thornburg's cub, Tom G. Tom and I had been bosom friends until this time; but now a coolness began to arise. I told the girl a good many of my river adventures, and made myself out a good deal of a hero; Tom tried to make himself appear to be a hero, too, and succeeded to some extent, but then he always had a way of embroidering. However, virtue is its own reward, so I was a barely perceptible trifle ahead in the contest. About this time something happened which promised handsomely for me: the pilots decided to sound the crossing at the head of 21. This would occur about nine or ten o'clock at night, when the passengers would be still up; it would be Mr. Thornburg's watch, therefore my chief would have to do the sounding. We had a perfect love of a sounding-boat—long, trim, graceful, and as fleet as a greyhound; her thwarts were cushioned; she carried twelve oarsmen; one of the mates was always sent in her to transmit orders to her crew, for ours was a steamer where no end of "style" was put on.

We tied up at the shore above 21, and got ready. It was a foul night, and the river was so wide, there, that a landsman's uneducated eyes could discern no opposite shore through such a gloom. The passengers were alert and interested; everything was satisfactory. As I hurried through the engine-room, picturesquely gotten up in storm toggery, I met Tom, and could not forbear delivering myself of a mean speech:

"Ain't you glad *you* don't have to go out sounding?"

Tom was passing on, but he quickly turned, and said: 10

"Now just for that, you can go and get the sounding-pole yourself. I was going after it, but I'd see you in Halifax, now, before I'd do it."

"Who wants you to get it? I don't. It's in the sounding-boat."

"It ain't, either. It's been new-painted; and it's been up on the ladies' cabin-guards two days, drying."

I flew back, and shortly arrived among the crowd of watching and wondering ladies just in time to hear the command:

"Give way, men!"   15

I looked over, and there was the gallant sounding-boat booming away, the unprincipled Tom presiding at the tiller, and my chief sitting by him with the sounding-pole which I had been sent on a fool's errand to fetch. Then that young girl said to me:

"Oh, how awful to have to go out in that little boat on such a night! Do you think there is any danger?"

I would rather have been stabbed. I went off, full of venom, to help in the pilot-house. By and by the boat's lantern disappeared, and after an interval a wee spark glimmered upon the face of the water a mile away. Mr. Thornburg blew the whistle in acknowledgment, backed the steamer out, and made for it. We flew along for a while, then slackened steam and went cautiously gliding toward the spark. Presently Mr. Thornburg exclaimed:

"Hello, the buoy lantern's out!"

He stopped the engines. A moment or two later he said: 20

"Why, there it is again!"

So he came ahead on the engines once more, and rang for the leads. Gradually the water shoaled up, and then began to deepen again! Mr. Thornburg muttered:

"Well, I don't understand this. I believe that buoy has drifted off the reef. Seems to be a little too far to the left. No matter, it is safest to run over it, anyhow."

So, in that solid world of darkness we went creeping down on the light. Just as our bows were in the act of plowing over it, Mr. Thornburg seized the bell-ropes, rang a startling peal, and exclaimed:

"My soul, it's the sounding-boat!"   25

A sudden chorus of wild alarms burst out far below—a pause—and then a sound of grinding and crashing followed. Mr. Thornburg exclaimed:

"There! the paddle-wheel has ground the sounding-boat to lucifer matches! Run! See who is killed!"

I was on the main-deck in the twinkling of an eye. My chief and the third mate and nearly all the men were safe. They had discovered their danger when it was too late to pull out of the way; then, when the great guards overshadowed them a moment later, they were prepared and knew what to do; at my chief's order they sprang at the right instant, seized the guard, and were hauled aboard. The next moment the sounding-yawl swept aft to the wheel and was struck and splintered to atoms. Two of the men and the cub Tom were missing—a fact which spread like wildfire over the boat. The passengers came flocking to the forward gangway, ladies and all, anxious-eyed, white-faced, and talked in awed voices of the dreadful thing. And often and again I heard them say, "Poor fellows! poor boy, poor boy!"

By this time the boat's yawl was manned and away, to search for the missing. Now a faint call was heard, off to the left. The yawl had disappeared in the other direction. Half the people rushed to one side to encourage the swimmer with their shouts; the other half rushed the other way to shriek to the yawl to turn about. By the callings the swimmer was approaching, but some said the sound showed failing strength. The crowd massed themselves against the boiler-deck railings, leaning over and staring into the gloom; and every faint and fainter cry wrung from them such words as "Ah, poor fellow, poor fellow! is there *no* way to save him?"

But still the cries held out, and drew nearer, and presently the voice said pluckily: 30

"I can make it! Stand by with a rope!"

What a rousing cheer they gave him! The chief mate took his stand in the glare of a torch-basket, a coil of rope in his hand, and his men grouped about him. The next moment the swimmer's face appeared in the circle of light, and in another one the owner of it was hauled aboard, limp and drenched, while cheer on cheer went up. It was that devil Tom.

The yawl crew searched everywhere, but found no sign of the two men. They probably failed to catch the guard, tumbled back, and were struck by the wheel and killed. Tom had never jumped for the guard at all, but had plunged head first into the river and dived under the wheel. It was nothing; I could have done it easy enough, and I said so; but everybody went on just the same, making a wonderful to-do over that ass, as if he had done something great. That girl couldn't seem to have enough of that pitiful "hero" the rest of the trip; but little I cared; I loathed her, anyway.

The way we came to mistake the sounding-boat's lantern for the buoy light was this: My chief said that after laying the buoy he fell away and watched it till it seemed to be secure; then he took up a position a hundred yards below it and a little to one side of the steamer's course, headed the sounding-boat up-stream, and waited. Having to wait some time, he and the officer got to talking; he looked up when he judged that the steamer was about on the reef; saw that the buoy was gone, but supposed that the steamer had already run over it; he went on with his talk; he noticed that the steamer was getting very close down to him, but that was the correct thing; it was her business to shave him closely, for convenience in taking him aboard; he was expecting her to sheer off, until the last moment; then it flashed upon him that she was trying to run him down, mistaking his lantern for the buoy light; so he sang out, "Stand by to spring for the guard, men!" and the next instant the jump was made.

FOR DISCUSSION AND WRITING

1. If "Sounding" is typical of the whole of *Life on the Mississippi,* the book from which the chapter is taken, would you say that Mark Twain idealizes the time and place, the "steamboat era" on the Mississippi? Here is another version of that scene:

These florid palaces [the steamboats], garishly painted and gilded, pine smoke belching from their stacks, seized America in the bulk and set it afloat on the rivers. It was not altogether an America of spiritual loveliness, nor were the boats wholly instruments of creative fulfillment. The trade of steamboating was carried on in a competition which was typical of the age and far worse than anything the pioneering railroads achieved. It was an American commerce, without conscience, responsibility, or control. The financial returns it offered were so great that, whatever happened to boats, crews, or passengers, owners might count on profits. The proverbial frequency of disasters rested on snags, groundings, and lack of skill to some extent, but more than all else on fraudulent jerry-building and inferior material. The soundly built boat was the exception, a product of occasional pride or responsibility; the average boat was assembled from inferior timber and machinery, thrown together with the least possible expense, and hurried out to snare her portion of the unimaginable profits before her seams opened or her boiler heads blew off. Once launched, she entered a competition ruthless and inconceivably corrupt. No device for the fraudulent capture of freight and fares was overlooked. Everything that chicanery, sabotage, bribery, and malfeasance could devise was part of the commonplace mechanism of the trade. (DeVoto 108–09)

2. From the standpoint of purpose, explain why, in your opinion, Mark Twain's view of the steamboat era differs from that of Bernard DeVoto. In your opinion, why did Mark Twain write "Sounding"? What evidence do you have for your opinion?

3. Consider "Sounding" from the standpoint of relation. Is the story about Tom G. relevant or irrelevant to Mark Twain's purpose? Explain.

4. In regard to manner, explain some of the techniques Twain uses to make his explanation clear.

5. Does Twain provide you with enough information to understand the reason for sounding and how it is carried out? Explain.

6. With regard to manner, in what part of the selection might the reader take Twain's statements with a grain of salt? Why?

7. What are the most obvious and accessible sources for information about Mississippi steamboating before the Civil War? (To answer this question, you might want to preview the discussion of using the library on pages 577–83.)

THE SLOW PACIFIC SWELL

Yvor Winters

A superb poet and perceptive critic, Yvor Winters is not much in the consciousness of the current literary world. For example, the editors of the highly influential *Norton Anthology of American Literature* include none of his works; his name does not appear in the index. Although the quantity of poetry he produced during his career is relatively small, the quality is very high indeed. His verse ranges from the lighthearted "In Praise of California Wines" to his glorious paean to love, "The Marriage."

In discussing "The Morality of Poetry," Winters sets forth this criterion: "We may say that a poem in the first place should offer us new perceptions, not only of the exterior universe, but of human experience as well; it should add, in other words, to what we have already seen."

Yvor Winters was born in 1900 and was for years professor of English at Stanford University. He died in 1960.

As "The Slow Pacific Swell" indicates, Winters, like Emerson, believes that we can learn profound lessons from nature.

Far out of sight forever stands the sea,
Bounding the land with pale tranquility.
When a small child, I watched it from a hill
At thirty miles or more. The vision still
Lies in the eye, soft blue and far away: 5
The rain has washed the dust from April day;
Paint-brush and lupine lie against the ground;
The wind above the hill-top has the sound
Of distant water in unbroken sky;
Dark and precise the little steamers ply —   10
Firm in direction they seem not to stir.
That is illusion. The artificer
Of quiet, distance holds me in a vise
And holds the ocean steady to my eyes.

Once when I rounded Flattery, the sea   15
Hove its loose weight like sand to tangle me
Upon the washing deck, to crush the hull;
Subsiding, dragged flesh at the bone. The skull
Felt the retreating wash of dreaming hair.
Half drenched in dissolution, I lay bare.   20
I scarcely pulled myself erect; I came
Back slowly, slowly knew myself the same.
That was the ocean. From the ship we saw
Gray whales for miles: the long sweep of the jaw,
The blunt head plunging clean above the wave.   25

And one rose in a tent of sea and gave
A darkening shudder; water fell away;
The whale stood shining, and then sank in spray.

A landsman, I. The sea is but a sound.
I would be near it on a sandy mound,   *30*
And hear the steady rushing of the deep
While I lay stinging in the sand with sleep.
I have lived inland long. The land is numb.
It stands beneath the feet, and one may come
Walking securely, till the sea extends   *35*
Its limber margin, and precision ends.
By night a chaos of commingling power,
The whole Pacific hovers hour by hour.
The slow Pacific swell stirs on the sand,
Sleeping to sink away, withdrawing land,   *40*
Heaving and wrinkled in the moon, and blind;
Or gathers seaward, ebbing out of mind.

FOR DISCUSSION AND WRITING

1. What was the sea like when Winters as a young child watched it from a hill? What was the sea like when Winters rounded Cape Flattery on a boat? What is the sea like in the final stanza?

2. What do these three scenes mean? What do they symbolize, or stand for?

3. Since Winters chose to write a poem, he was not free to use any words that might pop into his mind, because he needed to maintain his meter (iambic pentameter) and rhyme (for example, hill-still, ground-sound, sand-land). One might say that to a certain extent, language controlled Winters. In what ways does language always control writers, even when they are composing poetry?

4. The language available to writers sometimes limits their possibilities for expression. Explain how language also very frequently creates new possibilities and gives writers unexpected insights.

5. In regard to purpose, why do you think Winters wrote the poem?

6. State the main point of the poem.

7. Using this poem as your specific example, explain why you, as a reader, do or do not enjoy poetry.

4

Thinking Critically about Argument and Persuasion*

In this chapter, you will learn two of the most important aspects of critical reading: how to detect and analyze faulty or dishonest arguments and how to construct valid, convincing arguments.

Of course, much that you have learned in other chapters of this book applies to argument. For example, to argue successfully, you must judge what your reader needs to know and how you can establish your own credibility; thus, the discussion of the writer-reader contract in Chapter 3 will be valuable to you, as will the questioning techniques explained in that chapter.

THE MEANING OF "ARGUMENT"

We must clarify the meaning of *argument* as we use that word in this chapter. *Argument* here does not mean "fight" or even "dispute," as in "We got into a terrible argument." Rather, an argument consists of a *claim that cannot be conclusively proved* together with the *backing for that claim*. That is, there is no point in arguing about claims that can be

---

*Throughout this chapter, our debt to Stephen Toulmin is obvious. *The Uses of Argument* is the source of our analysis of argument.

proved conclusively through empirical evidence. For instance, if someone claimed that Scholastic Aptitude Test scores of high school seniors
declined in the years from 1967 to 1986, and you challenged the claim,
you could simply be referred to data easily accessible in a source such as
The World Almanac for 1988, where you would find the following statistics: verbal scores declined from 466 points to 431, and math scores fell
from 492 to 475. As long as you trust the source, there is nothing further
to be said. However, someone claiming that the Scholastic Aptitude Test
perpetuates inequality in American society, which may or may not be
true, would have a considerable job ahead to provide backing that would
convince others; the person making the claim certainly would have to do
much more than cite statistics to compose a convincing argument. This
chapter concerns the "much more" that makes up true arguments.

In summary, then, we do not argue about claims that can be proved
conclusively through empirical evidence, claims such as the following:

> The grade-point average of the typical senior at St. Olaf College is
> 2.75.

> In the campaign for mayor of _____, the Re-
> publican candidate spent \$350,000, and the Democratic spent
> \$361,000.

> In the first month after its publication, the novel *Teeth* sold 500,000
> copies.

Real arguments are based on claims about the *probable;* that is, an effective argument establishes the high probability of a claim such as the
following:

> In their conservatism and career goals, the seniors at St. Olaf Col-
> lege represent the new breed of Americans who will determine this
> nation's future.

> In the campaign for mayor of _____, the
> Democratic candidate was superior to the Republican.

> The new novel *Teeth* is a commercial success because it panders to
> the lurid interests and materialistic values of the American reading
> public.

For Discussion: Thinking about Claims

Each of the following claims involves the evaluative term good, better, *or*
best. *What sorts of backing would be needed in order to convince a reader that the
claim is valid? Which of the claims might result in an argument?*
Example:
Claim: *The weather in San Diego is usually good.*
Backing: *(1) Definition of the term* good *weather: weather with the
following characteristics: no extremes in temperature, little precipitation,*

and skies that are generally sunny. (2) Data concerning the weather in San Diego: The average temperature is 63.66°; high, 98°; low, 38°. Average precipitation: .69 inches. Clear days in 1985, 146; partly cloudy, 120; cloudy, 99.

1. *White Pine State is a good university.*
2. *The Golden Delicious is a good apple.*
3. *Amana manufactures good refrigerators.*
4. *The Amana is a better refrigerator than the General Electric.*
5. *The Ford Aerostar is a better vehicle than the Chevrolet Astro.*
6. *Truman was a better president than Eisenhower.*
7. *Picasso was a better artist than Dali.*
8. *Colgate is the best toothpaste available.*
9. *Stanford is the best university in the United States.*
10. Moby Dick *is the best American novel.*

ARGUABLE AND UNARGUABLE CLAIMS

Arguable claims have two characteristics: *definition* and *uncertainty*. A good way to appreciate these characteristics is to take a look at an unarguable claim, such as this one:

Changes in the life-styles of Americans would improve their health.

No one would challenge that claim; it is too broad and ill-defined to generate an argument. But suppose the claim were narrowed and focused, like this:

If every American stopped smoking, the general health of the nation would improve.

There is still no argument, for we are already convinced that smoking is unhealthy. In other words, the claim now lacks uncertainty; hence, there is no reason for us to want backing.

Exercise: Arguable Claims

In your opinion, which of the following claims are arguable, and which are not arguable? Using the concepts of definition *and* uncertainty, *explain your judgments. (You may disagree with a claim, yet believe that it is arguable.)*

1. *Some people oppose abortion.*
2. *Any law that limits the rights of citizens to own firearms is a step away from democracy and toward a totalitarian government.*
3. *Since it is a common practice in both commercial and scholarly publishing for editors to correct and revise the work submitted to them by authors, it should also be acceptable for college students to get editorial help with their papers before submitting them to a teacher.*
4. *Because pollution increasingly threatens life on earth, funds should be devoted to cleaning up and preserving the environment.*

5. *The language of the United States has been and is English; therefore, the information on official documents, such as ballots, should be printed only in English.*

6. *Every college student should be required either (a) to demonstrate proficiency with computers or (b) to take a course in basic computer science.*

7. *No college student should be required to take courses in a foreign language.*

8. *Government officials should have no sources of income that might create a conflict of interests.*

9. *A film is pornographic if it offends the average viewer in a community.*

THE STRUCTURE OF ARGUMENTS

Here is a simple argument that some people would question:

By playing tennis, my daughter learned the competitive skills that enabled her to succeed in business.

In order to be convincing, the arguer must provide *backing* for the *claim* that tennis was the basis for the daughter's success, as well as *evidence* that the daughter is a success.

Claim: By playing tennis, my daughter learned the competitive skills that enabled her to succeed in business.
Backing: To be a successful tennis player, you must be completely dedicated, willing to sacrifice all of your spare time for practice. You must also develop the ability to concentrate, letting nothing distract you from your goal: winning. Finally, a good tennis player has no sympathy for the opponent; the only consideration is winning.
Evidence: When my daughter went into business, she sacrificed everything for the sake of her construction company, just as she had sacrificed everything for tennis. She concentrated totally on making the business a success, letting nothing distract her; you might say that she kept her eye on the ball. And she was ruthless with competitors, cutting them out whenever possible, just as she had learned to be a coldblooded winner in tennis.

This argument (about which you should be skeptical) illustrates the difference between *backing* and *evidence*. Backing is intended to convince the reader of the validity of the claim on which the argument is based. If the claim is not valid, then there can be no argument. For example, if I claim that requiring students at Utopia University to be computer-literate would raise the overall grade-point average of the institution, I must, at the very least, give readers enough backing to convince them that the grade-point average needs to be raised and that students are not computer-literate. If I intend to argue that funding trauma centers in Salt Lake County would lower the death toll of victims of automobile accidents, shootings, and industrial accidents, I must provide backing to demonstrate that such units are not currently available. (If students at Utopia University are already computer-literate, and if their overall grade-point average is higher than those at Harvard, Princeton, and Yale, then I would have no argument. If Salt Lake County already has enough trauma centers, then I would have no argument.)

When we analyze arguments, then, we find the claim — which may be at the beginning or the end, depending on the argument's organization — and examine the *backing* for the claim and the *evidence* on which the argument is based. Are they adequate? Are they convincing? Does the claim need more backing? Is the conclusion based on sufficient evidence?

The arguer also might need to include *qualifications* that limit the scope of the claim. For example,

> By playing tennis, my daughter learned the competitive skills that enabled her to succeed in business. *Of course, I'm not claiming that tennis is the only reason for her success. After all, I gave her three million dollars with which to start her business, and her uncle the mayor made certain that she got some lucrative contracts from the city.*

The primary structural members of arguments are, then,

- the claim
- backing for the claim
- evidence for the conclusion
- qualification(s)

Exercise: Structure of Arguments

1. *Is the argument about the tennis-playing daughter — even with the backing, evidence, and qualification — convincing? Explain your answer.*

2. *The linguistic and social activist Noam Chomsky gives an example of an argument that he thinks is grotesque. Explain your reaction to the argument. Keeping in mind the elements of argument just discussed, do you agree with Chomsky that this argument is grotesque? Why, or why not? Does the argument convince you? How so? What counterarguments could you put forth?*

> *Suppose you rent a car and I buy a car. Who's going to take better care of it? Well, the answer is that I'm going to take better care of it because I have a capital investment in it. You're not going to take care of it at all. If you hear a rattle, you're just going to take it back to Hertz and let somebody else worry about it. If I hear a rattle, I'm going to take it to the garage because I don't want to get in trouble later on. In general, I'm going to take better care of the car I own than you're going to take of the car you rent. Suppose I own a person and you rent a person. Who's going to take better care of that person? Well, parity of argument, I'm going to take better care of that person than you are. Consequently, it follows that slavery is much more moral than capitalism. Slavery is a system in which you own people and therefore take care of them. Capitalism, which has a free labor market,*

is a system in which you rent people. If you own capital, you rent people and then you don't care about them at all. You use them up, throw them away, get new people. So the free market in labor is totally immoral, whereas slavery is quite moral. (Olson and Faigley 17–18)

THREE ANALYTICAL QUESTIONS ABOUT ARGUMENTS

From the structure of arguments, we can derive three important questions that help critical readers analyze arguments and determine their validity.

1. *Is the backing for the claim adequate?* Does the claim need backing?
2. *Is the evidence for the conclusion adequate?* Is it reliable? Relevant?
3. *Is the claim adequately qualified?* Does the claim need to be qualified?

If you will make those questions a part of your mental file of techniques for critical reading, you will find them extremely useful not only in your college work but throughout your personal and professional life.

Exercise: Analyzing an Argument

To study the anatomy of an argument, we need a specimen to work on; asking important questions about a hypothetical argument is like studying literature without reading actual poems and stories. Here is a classic argument. Samuel Johnson, the great eighteenth-century man of letters who compiled the first modern dictionary, wrote an argument for freeing a slave, Joseph Knight, who had been kidnapped as a child and sold to a Scottish gentleman. Knight's lawyer used Johnson's argument, and the court did indeed set Knight free. Read the argument carefully, and then apply the three questions: (1) Is the backing adequate? (2) Is the evidence adequate? (3) What are the qualifications? In your opinion, is the argument convincing or not? Explain. (The sentences are numbered for your convenience in referring to them.)

[1] It must be agreed that in most ages many countries have had part of their inhabitants in a state of slavery; yet it may be doubted whether slavery can ever be supposed the natural condition of man. [2] It is impossible not to conceive that men in their original state were equal; and very difficult to imagine how one would be subjected to another except by violent compulsion. [3] An individual may, indeed, forfeit his liberty by a crime; but he cannot by that crime forfeit the liberty of his children. [4] What is true of a criminal seems true likewise of a captive. [5] A man may accept life from a conquering enemy on condition of perpetual servitude; but it is very doubtful whether he can entail that servitude on his descendants; for no man can stipulate without commission for another. [6] The condition which he himself accepts, his son or grandson perhaps would have rejected. [7] If we

should admit, what perhaps with more reason may be denied, that there are certain relations between man and man which may make slavery necessary and just, yet it can never be proved that he who is now suing for his freedom ever stood in any of these relations. [8] He is certainly subject by no law, but that of violence, to his present master; who pretends no claim to his obedience, but that he bought him from a merchant of slaves, whose right to sell him never was examined. [9] It is said that, according to the constitutions of Jamaica, he was legally enslaved; these constitutions are merely positive; and apparently injurious to the rights of mankind, because whoever is exposed to sale is condemned to slavery without appeal; by whatever fraud or violence he might originally have been brought into the merchant's power. [10] In our own time Princes have been sold, by wretches to whose care they were entrusted, that they might have an European education; but when once they were brought to a market in the plantations, little would avail either their dignity or their wrongs. [11] The laws of Jamaica afford a Negro no redress. [12] His colour is considered as sufficient testimony against him. [13] It is to be lamented that moral right should ever give way to political convenience. [14] But if temptations of interest are sometimes too strong for human virtue, let us at least retain a virtue where there is no temptation to quit it. [15] In the present case there is apparent right on one side, and no convenience on the other. [16] Inhabitants of this island can neither gain riches nor power by taking away the liberty of any part of the human species. [17] The sum of the argument is this: — The rights of nature must be some way forfeited before they can be justly taken away: That the defendant has by any act forfeited the rights of nature we require to be proved; and if no proof of such forfeiture can be given, we doubt not but the justice of the court will declare him free.

LOGIC

Logic can, in many ways, be regarded as the formal study of argumentation. It is concerned with the basic statements in an argument, specifically, with how they relate to each other. Consider the following:

I am a mother though my child is dead. He did not die of an incurable disease, of a virus beyond the ken of medical science. He was not taken from me by a foreign enemy while defending his country. No, he was needlessly slaughtered on the highway. A drunk driver ran broadside into his motorcycle. My son was shot fifty feet through the air by the collision and hit the blacktop at forty-five miles per hour.

My son's assassin is not yet out of high school and yet that boy was able to walk into a liquor store and purchase two sixpacks of beer, most of which he drank that evening. This boy does not have the mental capability to graduate from high school in the prescribed time (he was held back in his senior year), and yet the law has given him the right to purchase alcohol and decide for himself what is appropriate behavior with regard to alcoholic consumption. I do not trust most of my adult friends to make such mature judgments. How can anyone trust the eighteen-year-old?

The law must change. Statistics have shown that states which have a minimum drinking age of twenty-one years also have significantly fewer automobile accidents caused by drunken teenagers. I lost my son, but why do any of the rest of us have to suffer as I have? Please, support legislation to increase the drinking age to twenty-one.

In a critique of this argument, we might note the mother's appeal to sympathy and how the descriptive words work in her favor. The negative connotations of such emotionally charged words as *assassin* and *slaughtered* tend to put the listener on the side of the mother in opposition to the teenager.

However, logical analysis of argument consciously ignores such factors as delivery and style and focuses only on the structure of the argument. The structure of the mother's appeal is as follows:

States with a drinking age of twenty-one have a lower rate of drunk-driving accidents among teenagers than states with a lower age.
Our state has a drinking age of less than twenty-one [implied in the mother's statements].
Therefore, to reduce the number of teenage drunk-driving accidents, we should raise the legal age for drinking.
Readers should act to support legislation on this matter.

The logician is careful to remove words that have strong connotations and background material that is not strictly pertinent. Note how the logician outlines the argument. All of the background information provided by the mother is omitted.

Logic, then, is concerned with how well the argument holds together — the internal consistency of the argument. For example, the following argument is internally consistent. As a result, the fourth statement, or *conclusion,* must follow from the first three statements, the *premises:*

The moon is made of green cheese.
All cheese has bacteria.
All bacteria are a form of life.
The moon is inhabited by life forms.

Of course, the moon is not made of green cheese, and so the argument, though internally consistent, is not sound because one of the premises is not true. The logician should be and is concerned with how an internally consistent argument relates to the outside world. That is to say, the logician is concerned not only with the structure of argument, but also its truth.

An argument, then, can be *valid* — internally consistent — without being *sound*, or true. Here is a valid argument that is obviously untrue:

> All quarterbacks are female.
> George is a quarterback.
> Therefore, George is female.

If it is true that all quarterbacks are female, then the conclusion that George is female will also be true. Nevertheless, whether the premise is true or false, the argument is nonetheless valid.

Exercise: Argument Log

During one twenty-four hour period, keep a record of the arguments that you read and hear. Note the claim and the backing and evidence. If the argument is written (in a newspaper or magazine), perhaps you can cut it out and have it available for discussion. If you hear the argument (on radio or television, for instance), write down as many details as possible. Advertisements, the newspaper's editorial page, and candidates' speeches are good sources for arguments.

Once you have compiled your log of arguments, analyze them, asking these questions about each one:

1. Who, actually, is the arguer? *(A television announcer in an ad is not the arguer; the sponsor of the ad is.) How does the nature of the arguer influence your judgment?*

2. Where did the argument appear? *(On public television? On the editorial page of the newspaper? In an advertisement for a product? In a bull session with your friends?) What influence do place and time (scene) have on the argument?*

3. What is the purpose of the argument? *What does the arguer say the purpose is? In your opinion, is that the real purpose? Explain.*

FALLACIES

Arguers sometimes stumble into illogical reasoning accidentally and sometimes use fallacious arguments purposely to bamboozle others.

An awareness of fallacies — many of which are subtle and require some thought before they can be recognized — is essential for critical thinking. To demonstrate the nature of the fallacies, we will analyze three categories in some detail: ad hominem, ambiguity, and circular reasoning; we will then briefly consider a number of the most common fallacies.

Three Logical Fallacies

AD HOMINEM The Latin term *ad hominem* means "against the man." The ad hominem fallacy is to attack the person advancing the argument rather than the argument itself.

As we saw in Chapter 3, the background of the author of a book or article is an important consideration. For instance, if the author of an article on the prevention of heart disease is the chief of cardiology at a major hospital, we have reason to trust his or her statements more than we would if the author were a health faddist with no specialized training or institutional affiliation. We might even question the veracity of an author if we discovered (in a biography or a review of the work, for example) that he or she had reason to be disingenuous or had lied in the past.

Our knowledge of the author can lead us to suspect the validity or truth of his or her argument, but we cannot dismiss the argument simply by claiming that the arguer is not an expert in the field or is a liar. History is full of examples of "nonexperts" who turned out to be right (Galileo among them), and even pathological liars can sometimes tell the truth.

The ad hominem argument ranges from extremely abusive tirades to subtle innuendoes, yet in each case the reference is not to the argument but to the person proposing it. The fallacy is committed whenever a district attorney questions the reliability of a witness in a criminal trial by citing the fact that the witness is known to have consorted with thieves and lowlifes. As an extreme example, imagine Pontius Pilate questioning the moral authority of Jesus on the basis of the people with whom Jesus associated!

Another example of the ad hominem fallacy is the maxim "Let him who is completely guiltless cast the first stone." In essence, this argument insists that the person proposing must be a role model for his or her own argument; otherwise the argument itself is rendered invalid. The counter to this proposition is expressed in another proverb: "Do as I say, not as I do."

Ad hominem arguments are generally not as blatant as these examples. Consider the situation of the most popular president in recent memory, Ronald Reagan. Mr. Reagan espoused a basic moral commitment to the family as the fabric of society and continuously reaffirmed his faith. However, political pundits noted that the president's own family was in shambles. His first marriage had ended in divorce, and children from both his first and second marriages seemed estranged from their father. This incongruity was used as an ad hominem argument against President Reagan and his philosophy. One should not attack a person's argument only on the basis of the arguer's character.

Exercise: Ad Hominem

Find examples of ad hominem fallacies and the arguments they are responding to. Determine whether the arguments have an implied assumption that the fallacy addresses or whether the fallacy has no relevance whatsoever. Almost certainly, you can find examples in your daily newspaper and in popular magazines. (Political cartoons are often ad hominem attacks.)

AMBIGUITY Often, the words we take for granted need to be scrutinized carefully when they are used in an argument, for they are sometimes ambiguous, that is, capable of more than one meaning. Ambiguity can arise either from an individual word or from the construction of a sentence. Consider the following example:

> My neighbor John is a dirty rat.
> All rats have four legs and a tail.
> Therefore, John has four legs and a tail.

Rat is used metaphorically in the first premise and literally in the second, so the argument is invalid. However, the following sentence is ambiguous because sentence structure is faulty:

> Flying jets can be dangerous.

Does the sentence mean *"To fly jets can be dangerous"* or *"Jets can be dangerous when they are flying"*?

Most arguments that contain ambiguity are, of course, much more subtle in their transgressions than are the examples above. Words that convey value judgments are often ambiguous. Think, for example, of the various interpretations people give to such common words as *patriot*, *intelligent*, and *ignorant*.

> The true patriot says, "My country, right or wrong."
> The true patriot says, "I will not fight for my country in an unjust war."

> An intelligent person is one who can live a happy life regardless of how the world views him or her.
> An intelligent person is one with an IQ of at least 110.

> Marva is so ignorant that she doesn't even know how to check the oil in her car.
> Marva is so ignorant that she hasn't ever heard of T. S. Eliot.

Exercise: Ambiguity

1. *List three words that have strong connotations, and then discuss how differences in opinion could result from using these words to characterize situations. For example, people who support the right-to-life position often call physicians who perform abortions "murderers," but those who hold the pro-choice position would not use that word in this context. You can find specific examples in such magazines as* Time *and* Newsweek *and, of course, in the newspaper.*

2. *Explain the ambiguity of terms in the following selection. In your opinion, did the author use the ambiguous terms purposely? If so, why did he use them?*

Toys 'Я Cussed

> *While many women still pay homage to Barbie at places like Evelyn Burkhalter's Barbie Hall of Fame, others have a beef with America's best-*

known doll. Many critics feel that the toy fills young women with unreal-
istic expectations, leading them to a life of vapid consumerism, endless
exercise, eating disorders and worse. In short, Barbie kills.

Listed below, some of the cultural viruses that lie dormant in other seemingly innocent toys, such as:

Mr. Potato Head *Playing with Mr. Potato Head encourages young people
to believe that parts of their bodies, especially facial features, are disposable.
The ultimate example of the dangers of prolonged exposure to Mr. Potato
Head: Michael Jackson.*

Etch a Sketch *Touted as a creative toy, the only thing this magnetic box
"etches" into a child's mind is an insatiable desire for a constant stream of
new images. There is a direct correlation between the introduction of Etch a
Sketch in the sixties and the proliferation of MTV in the eighties.*

Pickup Sticks *Teaches children to "pick up" things. And what do kids
usually pick up? Foul language. Facts of life from street corners. Annoying,
disfiguring diseases. Members of the opposite sex. Members of the same
sex. Bad morals. Crazy notions. Wild dances. And after picking up all
this, they must then pick up the pieces of their shattered lives.*

Erector Sets *Erector, erection — who do they think they're fooling? Leaves
us with men who can perform only with use of intricate machinery.*

Pop-Up Books *Same as above. Substitute magazines for machinery.*
(Rahlman 20)

3. *In the Gorgias, a Platonic dialogue, Socrates presents the following argument. Is it valid? If not, why?*

SOCRATES: *Well now, a man who has learned building is a builder, is he
not?*
GORGIAS: *Yes.*
SOCRATES: *And he who has learned music, a musician?*
GORGIAS: *Yes.*
SOCRATES: *Then he who has learned medicine is a medical man, and so
on with the rest on the same principle; anyone who has learned a certain art
has the qualification acquired by his particular knowledge?*
GORGIAS: *Certainly.*
SOCRATES: *And so, on this principle, he who has learned what is just is
just?*
GORGIAS: *Absolutely, I presume.*

CIRCULAR REASONING Circular reasoning, also known as *begging the
question,* is the error committed when the arguer uses the conclusion as a
supporting proposition. For example, I claim, "Students at Xenophobia
State University are all very intelligent." You ask me to support my claim,
and I reply, "Only intelligent students attend Xenophobia State U." This

reflexive argument does not leave the audience any more enlightened or convinced.

Here is another circular argument: "It is good to be neat and clean because everyone should be neat and clean." The argument fails to answer the essential question that it raises: *Why* should everyone be neat and clean?

Most circular arguments arise when the conclusion is stated in two or more different ways. For example, think about the following:

> The problem with divided spending jurisdiction is that it produces incentives for each committee, acting independently of all other committees, to spend more than it would if committees cooperated. Consequently the combined expenditures exceed what all committees acting in concert would spend. (Cogan 281)

The author's conclusion, marked by the word *consequently,* is really a restatement of the proposition that divided committees, acting independently of one another, are inclined to spend more. A truly valid argument, and one which the author obviously had in mind, is that there are incentives (a key word in this paragraph) for committees to spend more when they act separately than when they act in union. While most readers would understand what the author is getting at, he has argued in a circle.

A Checklist of Informal Fallacies*

The following are other common informal fallacies that a critical reader should be on the lookout for.

ACCIDENT The fallacy of accident (the opposite of hasty generalization, which is explained below) occurs when the arguer applies a general principle to an individual case without considering the circumstances. For example, wheat products are healthy foods, eaten by millions of people throughout the world. To claim that Dianne should eat wheat because it is nutritious and healthy is a fallacy, however, because Dianne is allergic to wheat.

AD IGNORANTIAM (ARGUING ON THE BASIS OF IGNORANCE) Suppose we claim, "No one has proved that the Abominable Snowman (yeti, Bigfoot) doesn't exist, so this creature must be very sly and elusive." This is an argument based on ignorance; it says, in effect, "The abominable snowman must be very clever because no one has been able to prove that he or she exists." We cannot base conclusions on what is unknown.

---

*Many of the examples in this section are adapted from S. Morris Engel, *With Good Reason.*

AD MISERICORDIAM (APPEAL TO PITY) The classic example of appealing to pity is the story of the person who murdered both of his parents by hacking them to pieces with an ax and asked the judge for mercy because he was an orphan. *Argumentum ad misericordiam* is common in the courts, where lawyers ask judges and juries to be lenient with clients who have suffered unhappy childhoods.

BANDWAGON "Everyone else is doing it, so you should too" is the gist of this fallacious argument, used, of course, as the appeal in many advertisements. The counterstatement is this: What is good for others may not be good for me.

THE BLACK–AND–WHITE FALLACY (FALLACY OF BIFURCATION) The black-and-white fallacy could just as well have been named the either-or fallacy. It is the error of assuming that there are only two choices when in fact there is at least a third. A voter who likes neither the Republican nor the Democratic candidate in a general election and who, therefore, does not vote at all is committing this fallacy, because he or she has the option of writing in an alternative candidate.

This fallacy can be used in a very persuasive but coercive manner. Consider the statement "Either you love your country unconditionally, or you are a traitor." The rhetorical stance of this statement is almost a defiant dare to disagree at the expense of being branded a traitor. It cows the intended audience into accepting the argument's premise (that you must love your country unconditionally) without allowing for a more complex mixture of feelings, both positive and negative.

COMPLEX QUESTION Some questions are a trap, regardless of whether one answers yes or no. The most famous complex question is, of course, "Have you stopped beating your wife?" A man who answers yes, is admitting that at one time he did beat her; if he answers no, he implies that he is currently a wife-beater. Another example: a detective asks a suspect, "What did you use to wipe your fingerprints from the gun?" If the suspect answers, "Nothing," the implication is that he or she did use the gun.

COMPOSITION In the fallacy of composition, the arguer assumes that what is valid for individual members of a class will also be valid for the class as whole. Consider this example: "Australians drink more beer per capita than do Americans; therefore, Australian breweries produce more beer annually than do American breweries." However, the population of the United States is about 250,000,000, whereas the population of Australia is only about 16,000,000. Salespeople purposefully commit the fallacy of composition when they tell the customer that the price of the product is very reasonable and affordable because the installment payments to be made each month are themselves fairly low. What is not stressed is the number of months that such a payment is made and the sum total.

DIVISION The fallacy of division is the opposite of the fallacy of composition. What is true of the whole is assumed to be true of the individual parts of the whole. For example, *The World Almanac* for 1990 reports that the average annual wage in Wyoming in 1988 was $19,097. It is committing the fallacy of division to conclude on the basis of this fact, that Professor John Smith of the University of Wyoming earned $19,097 in 1988.

EQUIVOCATION When the meaning of a key word in an argument shifts, the fallacy of equivocation occurs. Here are examples:

> Some dogs have fuzzy ears.
> My dog has fuzzy ears.
> Therefore, my dog is some dog!

In the first sentence, *some* is an adjective limiting the class of dogs being talked about; in the third, *some* is an adjective applied to one particular dog.

> Cabinetmakers are disappearing.
> My uncle is a cabinetmaker.
> Therefore, he is disappearing.

In the first statement, *disappearing* means "becoming scarcer"; in the third, it means "vanishing."

> No one can doubt that the miracles reported in the Bible actually took place, for miracles are still part of our lives. Just look around you, and you'll see the miracles of modern science, such as television, computers, heart transplants, and genetic engineering.

In the first instance, *miracles* refers to supernatural occurrences brought about by God; in the second instance, the word refers to products of human intelligence and ingenuity.

FALSE CAUSE (POST HOC, ERGO PROPTER HOC) The translation of the Latin *post hoc, ergo propter hoc* as "after this, therefore because of this" succinctly defines the error of this fallacy: the assumption that there is a causal link between two events simply because one precedes the other.

Obviously, false cause is most apt to occur when the correlation between the events is noted very few times, or only once. Nonetheless, the fallacy could arise even if two events were known to occur one after the other repeatedly. For example, the ancients always prayed to the sun during an eclipse so that light might once again shine on the earth; of course, each time they prayed, their wishes were seemingly granted, for the sun always came out from behind the moon.

You can take some simple precautions against falling into the trap of false cause. First, make repeated observations so that you reduce the likelihood of assuming that two random events are related. Second, try to determine whether the same event ever occurs without the antecedent. In such a case, the grounds for assuming a causal relationship are very shaky. (You might, by the way, notice that scientists often employ these same techniques in their use of statistics and control groups.)

HASTY GENERALIZATION When you reach a conclusion on the basis of insufficient evidence, you have committed the fallacy of hasty generalization. Consider this example:

> When Maria graduated from Misanthropy State College, she was offered a position as an engineer at Emeu Aviation, with a starting salary of $95,000 per year. Graduates of Misanthropy State get wonderful job offers.

> While he was jogging, James Fixx suffered a heart attack and died. Jogging causes heart attacks.

REIFICATION (FALLACY OF HYPOSTATIZATION) This fallacy occurs when a person regards an abstract concept as if it were a concrete thing. For example, the claim that a bureaucracy's reason for existence is simply to sustain itself refers to the bureaucracy as if it were a living organism with an instinct for self-preservation. A bureaucracy is not a living, breathing entity; the people who work in it are (although some pundits would argue with this point).

SWEEPING GENERALIZATION Often, a general statement applies to most of the instances under discussion, but not to all of them; when this is the case, it is a fallacy to generalize. For example, aerobic exercise is beneficial to most people, but not to those with heart conditions; therefore, it is fallacious to state that everyone should engage in aerobic exercises. Here is another example of sweeping generalization:

> The Constitution gives citizens the right to bear arms; therefore, the police were violating Jones's rights when they confiscated his automatic pistol after the judge had declared him insane.

Exercise: Fallacies

Explain the problems with the following arguments, and name the fallacies that they illustrate.

1. *I never should have loaned my car to my son. He drove it for one day, and the next day the transmission went bad.*

2. *Having received a D on a term paper, a student tries to convince the professor to raise the grade. "My father just left my mother, and my older brother*

is now in jail for drunk driving. When Mother sees this grade, it will be more than she can bear, considering her other problems."

3. *Some dogs have fleas. My dog has fleas. Therefore, my dog is some dog.*

4. *Every qualified citizen should serve two years in the United States military. We must defend the stately marble temple of democracy.*

5. *The governor has proposed that air pollution standards be tightened within the next two years. However, everyone knows that the governor is under the control of the Sierra Club and other environmental groups, so no one takes him seriously.*

6. *To learn Chinese well enough to read* The People's Daily, *one must learn about 2,500 characters. Since each of these characters is easy to learn, it is easy to learn to read Chinese.*

7. *Blacksmiths are gradually disappearing. Herb is a blacksmith. Therefore, Herb is gradually disappearing.*

8. *The printouts on my computer are garbled, so there must be something wrong with the new disks that I bought yesterday.*

9. *No one can prove conclusively that mental telepathy is impossible. Therefore, it must be the case that my friend sent me a telepathic message from Germany; otherwise, how would I have known that he drank beer and ate sausage in Munich?*

10. *A father was advising his son about the future. "If you don't go to college and prepare for a career, you'll wind up with a routine, dull job that you'll hate."*

11. *I believe in the Golden Rule, which says, "Do unto others as you would have them do unto you." Since I would want to give a classmate the correct answers during a final examination, my classmates should give me the correct answers.*

12. *Nature improves animal species by eliminating the less fit members. Therefore, we should eliminate unfit people in American society.*

13. *Only man is rational. No woman is a man. Therefore, no woman is rational.*

14. *"Who did you pass on the road," the King went on, holding his hand out to the Messenger for some hay.*

"Nobody," said the Messenger.

"Quite right," said the King, "this lady saw him too. So of course Nobody walks slower than you."

"I do my best," the Messenger said in a sullen tone. "I'm sure nobody walks much faster than I do."

"He can't do that," said the King, "or else he'd have been here first" (Lewis Carroll, Through the Looking Glass).

15. *Since Susan is a resident of Beverly Hills, she must be wealthy.*

16. *"God exists." "How do you know?" "Because the Bible says so." "How do you know the Bible is true?" "Because it's the word of God."*

17. *Was it through stupidity or calculated malice that the registrar botched up the class schedule this semester?*

REVIEW

1. What is an argument?

2. Explain *definition* and *uncertainty*.

3. Explain *backing, evidence,* and *qualification*.

4. Explain why an argument can be logically valid, but untrue.

5. Explain the fallacy of ad hominem.

6. Explain the fallacy of ambiguity.

7. Explain *circular reasoning*.

SUGGESTIONS FOR WRITING

1. Choose an important issue regarding your college or university, and write an argument supporting your claim regarding that issue.

2. After you have read and discussed the selections that follow, choose the one by either Eric Corley, Bill Brubaker, Franklin E. Zimring and Gordon Hawkins, C. S. Lewis, or Steven Zak, and use its methods to develop an argument for a claim you believe in. In a sense you will be *imitating,* but in a very special sense: you will not be mimicking your source, but using it as a model. (This kind of imitation is, finally, inevitable for writers. Consciously or not, we all use the techniques that we find in the works we read.)

ETHICS AND ANIMALS

Steven Zak

> Several magazines are geared to educated, middle-class Americans—the sort of people who might well donate money to their *alma maters,* be active in local and state politics, watch public television instead of or as well as the commercial channels, attend the theater and symphony concerts, send their children to prestige colleges, and read the book review sections of the Sunday newspaper. This group of Americans would be likely to subscribe to *The Atlantic Monthly, Harper's, The New Yorker, The New York Review of Books,* and *Sports Illustrated.* As you read "Ethics and Animals," keep in mind that these are the people for whom it was written.

In December of 1986 members of an "animal-liberation" group called True Friends broke into the Sema, Inc., laboratories in Rockville, Maryland, and took four baby chimpanzees from among the facility's 600 primates. The four animals, part of a group of thirty being used in hepatitis research, had been housed individually in "isolettes"—small stainless-steel chambers with sealed glass doors. A videotape produced by True Friends shows other primates that remained behind. Some sit behind glass on wire floors, staring blankly. One rocks endlessly, banging violently against the side of his cage. Another lies dead on his cage's floor.

The "liberation" action attracted widespread media attention to Sema, which is a contractor for the National Institutes of Health, the federal agency that funds most of the animal research in this country. Subsequently the NIH conducted an investigation into conditions at the lab and concluded that the use of isolettes is justified to prevent the spread of diseases among infected animals. For members of True Friends and other animal-rights groups, however, such a scientific justification is irrelevant to what they see as a moral wrong; these activists remain frustrated over conditions at the laboratory. This conflict between the NIH and animal-rights groups mirrors the tension between animal researchers and animal-rights advocates generally. The researchers' position is that their use of animals is necessary to advance human health care and that liberation actions waste precious resources and impede the progress of science and medicine. The animal-rights advocates' position is that animal research is an ethical travesty that justifies extraordinary, and even illegal, measures.

The Sema action is part of a series that numbers some six dozen to date and that began, in 1979, with a raid on the New York University Medical Center, in which members of a group known as the Animal Liberation Front (ALF) took a cat and two guinea pigs. The trend toward civil disobedience is growing. For example, last April members of animal-rights groups demonstrated at research institutions across the country (and in other countries, including Great Britain and Japan), sometimes blocking entrances to them by forming human chains. In the United States more than 130 activists were arrested, for offenses ranging from blocking a doorway and trespassing to burglary.

To judge by everything from talk-show programs to booming membership enrollment in animal-rights groups (U.S. membership in all groups is estimated at 10 million), the American public is increasingly receptive to the animal-rights position. Even some researchers admit that raids by groups like True Friends and the ALF have exposed egregious conditions in particular labs and have been the catalyst for needed reforms in the law. But many members of animal-rights groups feel that the recent reforms do not go nearly far enough. Through dramatic animal-liberation actions and similar tactics, they hope to force what they fear is a complacent public to confront a difficult philosophical issue: whether animals, who are known to have feelings and psychological lives, ought to be treated as mere instruments of science and other human endeavors.

The ALF is probably the most active of the world's underground animal-rights groups. It originated in England, where the animal-protection movement itself began, in 1824, with the founding of the Royal Society for the Prevention of Cruelty to Animals. The ALF evolved from a group called the Band of Mercy, whose members sabotaged the vehicles of hunters and destroyed guns used on bird shoots. It now has members across Europe, and in Australia, New Zealand, Africa, and Canada, as well as the United States. It does not, however, constitute a unified global network. The American wing of the ALF was formed in 1979. The number of its members is unknown, but their ages range from eighteen to over sixty. Some are students, some are blue-collar workers, and many belong to the suburban middle class.

Animal-rights activists feel acute frustration over a number of issues, including hunting and trapping, the destruction of animals' natural habitats, and the raising of animals for food. But for now the ALF considers animal research the most powerful symbol of human dominion over and exploitation of animals, and it devotes most of its energies to that issue. The public has been ambivalent, sometimes cheering the ALF on, at other times denouncing the group as "hooligans." However one chooses to characterize the ALF, it and other groups like it hold an uncompromising "rights view" of ethics toward animals. The rights view distinguishes the animal-protection movement of today from that of the past and is the source of the movement's radicalism.

"THEY ALL HAVE A RIGHT TO LIVE"

Early animal-protection advocates and groups, like the RSPCA, seldom talked about rights. They condemned cruelty — that is, acts that produce or reveal bad character. In early-nineteenth-century England campaigners against the popular sport of bull-baiting argued that it "fostered every bad and barbarous principle of our nature." Modern activists have abandoned the argument that cruelty is demeaning to human character ("virtue thought") in favor of the idea that the lives of animals have intrinsic value ("rights thought"). Rights thought doesn't necessarily preclude the consideration of virtue, but it mandates that the measure of virtue be the foreseeable consequences to others of one's acts.

"Michele" is thirty-five and works in a bank in the East. She has participated in many of the major ALF actions in the United States. One of the missions involved freeing rats, and she is scornful of the idea that rats aren't worth the effort. "That attitude is rather pathetic, really," she says. "These animals feel pain just like dogs, but abusing them doesn't arouse constituents' ire, so they don't get the same consideration. They all have a right to live their lives. Cuteness should not be a factor."

While most people would agree that animals should not be tortured, there is no consensus about animals' right to live (or, more precisely, their right not to be killed). Even if one can argue, as the British cleric Humphrey Primatt did in 1776, that "pain is pain, whether it be inflicted on man or on beast," it is more difficult to argue that the life of, say, a dog is qualitatively the same as that of a human being. To this, many animal-rights activists would say that every morally relevant characteristic that is lacking in all animals (rationality might be one, according to some ways of defining that term) is also lacking in some "marginal" human beings, such as infants, or the senile, or the severely retarded. Therefore, the activists argue, if marginal human beings have the right to live, it is arbitrary to hold that animals do not. Opponents of this point of view often focus on the differences between animals and "normal" human beings, asserting, for instance, that unlike most human adults, animals do not live by moral rules and therefore are not part of the human "moral community."

The credibility of the animal-rights viewpoint, however, need not   *10* stand or fall with the "marginal human beings" argument. Lives don't have to be qualitatively the same to be worthy of equal respect. One's perception that another life has value comes as much from an appreciation of its uniqueness as from the recognition that it has characteristics that are shared by one's own life. (Who would compare the life of a whale to that of a marginal human being?) One can imagine that the lives of various kinds of animals differ radically, even as a result of having dissimilar bodies and environments — that being an octopus feels different from being an orangutan or an oriole. The orangutan cannot be redescribed as the octopus minus, or plus, this or that mental characteristic; conceptually, nothing could be added to or taken from the octopus that would make it the equivalent of the oriole. Likewise, animals are not simply rudimentary human beings, God's false steps, made before He finally got it right with us.

Recognizing differences, however, puts one on tentative moral ground. It is easy to argue that likes ought to be treated alike. Differences bring problems: How do we think about things that are unlike? Against what do we measure and evaluate them? What combinations of likeness and difference lead to what sorts of moral consideration? Such problems may seem unmanageable, and yet in a human context we routinely face ones similar in kind if not quite in degree: our ethics must account for dissimilarities between men and women, citizens and aliens, the autonomous and the helpless, the fully developed and the merely potential, such as children or fetuses. We never solve these problems with finality, but we confront them.

One might be tempted to say that the problems are complicated enough without bringing animals into them. There is a certain attractiveness to the idea that animals — lacking membership in the human and moral communities, and unable to reciprocate moral concern — deserve little consideration from us. After all, doesn't one have obligations toward members of one's family and community that do not apply to outsiders? Yet this appeal to a sense of community fails to take into account certain people who likewise lack membership and yet have moral claims against us. Consider future people, particularly those who will live in the distant future. Suppose that our dumping of certain toxic wastes could be predicted to cause widespread cancer among people five hundred years in the future. Would we not have a heavy moral burden to refrain from such dumping? Probably most of us would say that we would. Yet in what meaningful sense can it be said that people we will never meet, who will never do anything for us, and whose cultures and ethical systems will likely be profoundly different from our own, are members of our community? Membership may count for something, but it is clearly not a necessary condition for moral entitlement. Also, some animals — my dog, for instance — may more sensibly be characterized as members of our community than may some human beings, such as those of the distant future.

Both advocates and opponents of animal rights also invoke utilitarianism in support of their points of view. Utilitarianism holds that an act or practice is measured by adding up the good and the bad consequences — classically, pleasure and pain — and seeing which come out ahead. There are those who would exclude animals from moral consideration on the grounds that the benefits of exploiting them outweigh the harm. Ironically, though, it was utilitarianism, first formulated by Jeremy Bentham in the eighteenth century, that brought animals squarely into the realm of moral consideration. If an act or practice has good and bad consequences for animals, then these must be entered into the moral arithmetic. And the calculation must be genuinely disinterested. One may not baldly assert that one's own interests count for more. Animal researchers may truly believe that they are impartially weighing all interests when they conclude that human interests overwhelm those of animals. But a skeptical reader will seldom be persuaded that they are in fact doing so. For instance, a spokesperson for a research institution that was raided by the ALF wrote in the *Los Angeles Times* that we should not be "more concerned with the fate of these few dogs than with the millions of people who are cancer victims." Note the apparent weighing: "few" versus "millions." But her lack of impartiality was soon revealed by this rhetorical question: "Would they [the ALF] really save an animal in exchange for the life of a child?"

Even true utilitarianism is incomplete, though, without taking account of rights. For example, suppose a small group of aboriginal tribespeople were captured and bred for experiments that would benefit millions of other people by, say, resulting in more crash-worthy cars. Would the use of such people be morally acceptable? Surely it would not, and that point illustrates an important function of rights thought: to put limits on what can be done to individuals, even for the good of the many. Rights thought dictates that we cannot kill one rights-holder to save another—or even more than one other—whether or not the life of the former is "different" from that of the latter.

Those who seek to justify the exploitation of animals often claim *15* that it comes down to a choice: kill an animal or allow a human being to die. But this claim is misleading, because a choice so posed has already been made. The very act of considering the taking of life X to save life Y reduces X to the status of a mere instrument. Consider the problem in a purely human context. Imagine that if Joe doesn't get a new kidney he will die. Sam, the only known potential donor with a properly matching kidney, himself has only one kidney and has not consented to give it—and his life—up for Joe. Is there really a choice? If the only way to save Joe is to kill Sam, then we would be unable to do so—and no one would say that we chose Sam over Joe. Such a choice would never even be contemplated.

In another kind of situation there *is* a choice. Imagine that Joe and Sam both need a kidney to survive, but we have only one in our kidney bank. It may be that we should give the kidney to Joe, a member of our community, rather than to Sam, who lives in some distant country (though this is far from clear—maybe flipping a coin would be more fair). Sam (or the loser of the coin flip) could not complain that his rights had been violated, because moral claims to some resource—positive claims—must always be dependent on the availability of that resource. But the right not to be treated as if one were a mere resource or instrument—negative, defensive claims— is most fundamentally what it means to say that one has rights. And this is what members of the ALF have in mind when they declare that animals, like human beings, have rights.

Where, one might wonder, should the line be drawn? Must we treat dragonflies the same as dolphins? Surely not. Distinctions must be made, though to judge definitively which animals must be ruled out as holders

of rights may be impossible even in principle. In legal or moral discourse we are virtually never able to draw clear lines. This does not mean
that drawing a line anywhere, arbitrarily, is as good as drawing one anywhere else.

The line-drawing metaphor, though, implies classifying entities in
a binary way: as either above the line, and so entitled to moral consideration, or not. Binary thinking misses nuances of our moral intuition.
Entities without rights may still deserve moral consideration on other
grounds: one may think that a dragonfly doesn't quite qualify for rights
yet believe that it would be wrong to crush one without good reason.
And not all entities with rights need be treated in precisely the same way.
This is apparent when one compares animals over whom we have assumed custody with wild animals. The former, I think, have rights to
our affirmative aid, while the latter have such rights only in certain
circumstances. Similar distinctions can be made among human beings,
and also between human beings and particular animals. For example, I
recently spent $1,000 on medical care on my dog, and I think he had a
right to that care, but I have never given such an amount to a needy
person on the street. Rights thought, then, implies neither that moral
consideration ought to be extended only to the holders of rights nor that
all rights-holders must be treated with a rigid equality. It implies only
that rights-holders should never be treated as if they, or their kind, didn't
matter.

ANIMALS, REFRIGERATORS, AND CAN OPENERS

The question of man's relationship with animals goes back at least
to Aristotle, who granted that animals have certain senses — hunger,
thirst, a sense of touch — but who held that they lack rationality and
therefore as "the lower sort [they] are by nature slaves, and . . . should
be under the rule of a master." Seven centuries later Saint Augustine
added the authority of the Church, arguing that "Christ himself
[teaches] that to refrain from the killing of animals . . . is the height of
superstition, for there are no common rights between us and the
beasts. . . ." Early in the seventeenth century René Descartes argued
that, lacking language, animals cannot have thoughts or souls and thus
are machines.

One may be inclined to dismiss such beliefs as archaic oddities, but   *20*
even today some people act as if animals were unfeeling things. I worked
in a research lab for several summers during college, and I remember
that it was a natural tendency to lose all empathy with one's animal
subjects. My supervisor seemed actually to delight in swinging rats
around by their tails and flinging them against a concrete wall as a way
of stunning the animals before killing them. Rats and rabbits, to those

who injected, weighed, and dissected them, were little different from cultures in a petri dish: they were just things to manipulate and observe. Feelings of what may have been moral revulsion were taken for squeamishness, and for most of my lab mates those feelings subsided with time.

The first animal-welfare law in the United States, passed in New York State in 1828, emphasized the protection of animals useful in agriculture. It also promoted human virtue with a ban on "maliciously and cruelly" beating or torturing horses, sheep, or cattle. Today courts still tend to focus on human character, ruling against human beings only for perpetrating the most shocking and senseless abuse of animals. Indeed, courts sometimes have difficulty taking animal-abuse cases seriously. For instance, in 1986 a California man who had been convicted of allowing a fifty-year-old tortoise, Rocky, in his petting zoo to suffer untreated from maladies including infected eyes, labored breathing, and dehydration appealed the lower court's order removing the animal from his custody. The state argued that the defendant's rights to Rocky should be terminated just as parental rights might be terminated for abusing a child. The court, in rejecting this analogy, quipped that while "a child preparing for homework or cleaning a bedroom may exhibit turtle-like qualities or creep toward school in turtle pace, we decline to equate title to a tortoise to the relationship between a parent and a child." Not to be outdone, another judge wrote, in a concurring opinion, that "hopefully our decision will forestall the same problem should we be faced with Rocky II."

Most states leave the regulation of medical research to Washington. In 1966 Congress passed the Laboratory Animal Welfare Act, whose stated purpose was not only to provide humane care for animals but also to protect the owners of dogs and cats from theft by proscribing the use of stolen animals. (Note the vocabulary of property law; animals have long been legally classified as property.) Congress then passed the Animal Welfare Act of 1970, which expanded the provisions of the 1966 act to include more species of animals and to regulate more people who handle animals. The AWA was further amended in 1976 and in 1985.

The current version of the AWA mandates that research institutions meet certain minimum requirements for the handling and the housing of animals, and requires the "appropriate" use of pain-killers. But the act does not regulate research or experimentation itself, and allows researchers to withhold anesthetics or tranquilizers "when scientifically necessary." Further, while the act purports to regulate dealers who buy animals at auctions and other markets to sell to laboratories, it does little to protect those animals. For instance, dealers often buy animals at "trade days," or outdoor bazaars of dogs and cats; some people bring cats by the sackful, and, according to one activist, "sometimes you see the blood coming through."

The 1985 amendments to the AWA were an attempt to improve the treatment of animals in laboratories, to improve enforcement, to encourage the consideration of alternative research methods that use fewer or no animals, and to minimize duplication in experiments. One notable change is that for the first time, research institutions using primates must keep them in environments conducive to their psychological well-being; however, some animal-rights activists have expressed skepticism, since the social and psychological needs of primates are complex, and the primary concern of researchers is not the interests of their animal subjects. Last September a symposium on the psychological well-being of captive primates was held at Harvard University. Some participants contended that we lack data on the needs of the thirty to forty species of primates now used in laboratories. Others suggested that the benefits of companionship and social life are obvious.

The U.S. Department of Agriculture is responsible for promulgating regulations under the AWA and enforcing the law. Under current USDA regulations the cages of primates need only have floor space equal to three times the area occupied by the animal "when standing on four feet" — in the words of the USDA, which has apparently forgotten that primates have hands. The 1985 amendments required the USDA to publish final revised regulations, including regulations on the well-being of primates, by December of 1986. At this writing the department has yet to comply, and some activists charge that the NIH and the Office of Management and Budget have delayed the publication of the new regulations and attempted to undermine them.

One may believe that virtue thought — which underlies current law — and rights thought should protect animals equally. After all, wouldn't a virtuous person or society respect the interests of animals? But virtue thought allows the law to disregard these interests, because virtue can be measured by at least two yardsticks: by the foreseeable effects of an act on the interests of an animal or by the social utility of the act. The latter standard was applied in a 1983 case in Maryland in which a researcher appealed his conviction for cruelty to animals after he had performed experiments that resulted in monkeys' mutilating their hands. Overturning the conviction, the Maryland Court of Appeals wrote that "there are certain normal human activities to which the infliction of pain to an animal is purely incidental" — thus the actor is not a sadist — and that the state legislature had intended for these activities to be exempt from the law protecting animals.

The law, of course, is not monolithic. Some judges have expressed great sympathy for animals. On the whole, though, the law doesn't recognize animal rights. Under the Uniform Commercial Code, for instance, animals — along with refrigerators and can openers — constitute "goods."

ALTERNATIVES TO US-VERSUS-THEM

Estimates of the number of animals used each year in laboratories in the United States range from 17 million to 100 million: 200,000 dogs, 50,000 cats, 60,000 primates, 1.5 million guinea pigs, hamsters, and rabbits, 200,000 wild animals, thousands of farm animals and birds, and millions of rats and mice. The conditions in general — lack of exercise, isolation from other animals, lengthy confinement in tiny cages — are stressful. Many experiments are painful or produce fear, anxiety, or depression. For instance, in 1987 researchers at the Armed Forces Radio-biology Research Institute reported that nine monkeys were subjected to whole-body irradiation; as a result, within two hours six of the monkeys were vomiting and hypersalivating. In a proposed experiment at the University of Washington pregnant monkeys, kept in isolation, will be infected with the simian AIDS virus; their offspring, infected or not, will be separated from the mothers at birth.

Not all animals in laboratories, of course, are subjects of medical research. In the United States each year some 10 million animals are used in testing products and for other commercial purposes. For instance, the United States Surgical Corporation, in Norwalk, Connecticut, uses hundreds of dogs each year to train salesmen in the use of the company's surgical staple gun. In 1981 and 1982 a group called Friends of Animals brought two lawsuits against United States Surgical to halt these prac-tices. The company successfully argued in court that Friends of Animals lacked "standing" to sue, since no member of the organization had been injured by the practice; after some further legal maneuvering by Friends of Animals both suits were dropped. Last November a New York City animal-rights advocate was arrested as she planted a bomb outside United States Surgical's headquarters.

In 1987, according to the USDA, 130,373 animals were subjected   30
to pain or distress unrelieved by drugs for "the purpose of research or testing." This figure, which represents nearly seven percent of the 1,969,123 animals reported to the USDA that year as having been "used in experimentation," ignores members of species not protected by the AWA (cold-blooded animals, mice, rats, birds, and farm animals). More-over, there is reason to believe that the USDA's figures are low. For example, according to the USDA, no primates were subjected to distress in the state of Maryland, the home of Sema, in any year from 1980 to 1987, the last year for which data are available.

Steps seemingly favorable to animals have been taken in recent years. In addition to the passage of the 1985 amendments to the AWA, the Public Health Service, which includes the NIH, has revised its "Pol-icy on Humane Care and Use of Laboratory Animals," and new legisla-tion has given legal force to much of this policy. Under the revised

policy, institutions receiving NIH or other PHS funds for animal research must have an "institutional animal care and use committee" consisting of at least five members, including one nonscientist and one
person not affiliated with the institution.

Many activists are pessimistic about these changes, however. They
argue that the NIH has suspended funds at noncompliant research institutions only in response to political pressure, and assert that the suspen-
sions are intended as a token gesture, to help the NIH regain lost
credibility. They note that Sema, which continues to keep primates in
isolation cages (as regulations permit), is an NIH contractor whose principal investigators are NIH employees. As to the makeup of the animal-
care committees, animal-rights advocates say that researchers control
who is appointed to them. In the words of one activist, "The brethren
get to choose."

However one interprets these changes, much remains the same. For
example, the AWA authorizes the USDA to confiscate animals from
laboratories not in compliance with regulations, but only if the animal
"is no longer required . . . to carry out the research, test or experiment";
the PHS policy mandates pain relief "unless the procedure is justified for
scientific reasons." Fundamentally, the underlying attitude that animals
may appropriately be used and discarded persists.

If the law is ever to reflect the idea that animals have rights, more-
drastic steps — such as extending the protection of the Constitution to
animals — must be taken. Constitutional protection for animals is not an
outlandish proposition. The late U.S. Supreme Court Justice William O.
Douglas wrote once, in a dissenting opinion, that the day should come
when "all of the forms of life . . . will stand before the court — the
pileated woodpecker as well as the coyote and bear, the lemmings as well
as the trout in the streams."

Suppose, just suppose, that the AWA were replaced by an animal- 35
rights act, which would prohibit the use by human beings of any animals
to their detriment. What would be the effect on medical research, education, and product testing? Microorganisms; tissue, organ, and cell cultures; physical and chemical systems that mimic biological functions;
computer programs and mathematical models that simulate biological
interactions; epidemiologic data bases; and clinical studies have all been
used to reduce the number of animals used in experiments, demonstrations, and tests. A 1988 study by the National Research Council, while
finding that researchers lack the means to replace all animals in labs, did
conclude that current and prospective alternative techniques could reduce
the number of animals — particularly mammals — used in research.

Perhaps the report would have been more optimistic if scientists
were as zealous about conducting research to find alternatives as they are
about animal research. But we should not be misled by discussions of
alternatives into thinking that the issue is merely empirical. It is broader

than just whether subject A and procedure X can be replaced by surrogate B and Y. We could undergo a shift in world view: instead of imagining that we have a divine mandate to dominate and make use of everything else in the universe, we could have a sense of belonging to the world and of kinship with the other creatures in it. The us-versus-them thinking that weighs animal suffering against human gain could give way to an appreciation that "us" includes "them." That's an alternative too.

Some researchers may insist that scientists should not be constrained in their quest for knowledge, but this is a romantic notion of scientific freedom that never was and should not be. Science is always constrained, by economic and social priorities and by ethics. Sometimes, paradoxically, it is also freed by these constraints, because a barrier in one direction forces it to cut another path, in an area that might have remained unexplored.

Barriers against the exploitation of animals ought to be erected in the law, because law not only enforces morality but defines it. Until the law protects the interests of animals, the animal-rights movement will by definition be radical. And whether or not one approves of breaking the law to remedy its shortcomings, one can expect such activities to continue. "I believe that you should do for others as you would have done for you," one member of the ALF says. "If you were being used in painful experiments, you'd want someone to come to your rescue."

FOR DISCUSSION AND WRITING

1. Two terms are important in this argument: "virtue thought" and "rights thought." (a) Define each. (b) Explain the distinctions between the two. (c) Explain why these distinctions are important to the argument.

2. Why does Zak disagree with virtue thought? What backing does he have for his position?

3. Zak states his basic claim in the last paragraph of the argument: "Barriers against the exploitation of animals ought to be erected in the law, because law not only enforces morality but defines it." How firm a position do you think Zak takes on this claim? Do you believe that one must accept this claim without qualification in order for the argument to succeed?

4. Explain why the following sentences define the argument that Zak develops in "Ethics and Animals": "The researchers' position is that their use of animals is necessary to advance human health care and that liberation actions waste precious resources and impede the progress of science and medicine. The animal-rights advocates' position is that animal research is an ethical travesty that justifies extraordinary, and even illegal, measures" (par. 2).

5. What sort of backing does Zak provide for his claim? Is the backing convincing?

6. On the basis of manner, would you say that the argument is as readable as possible? If you feel it is unclear, explain its shortcomings. If you feel it is clearly stated and developed, point out some of the ways in which Zak helps the reader.

7. From the standpoint of relation, do you think that paragraph 19, which outlines the history of human relationship with animals, is relevant? Explain why the paragraph is or is not relevant.

8. Do you have any questions about the quality of the argument? Explain. (Does the information in the argument seem reliable? Why, or why not?)

9. Explain why the argument centers on the problem of viewing animals either as agencies or agents. What are the different consequences of these views in the scene of modern medical research?

10. From the standpoint of quantity, is the evidence sufficient to support the claim? (That is, does the evidence convince you that there is a basis for argument?)

HACKERS IN JAIL

Eric Corley

> Every month, *Harper's* publishes "Readings," a collection of excerpts from various unusual or even offbeat sources (for example, five clauses from the contract that Vanessa Redgrave demands of journalists who want to interview her; one brief story from *Real Animal Heroes: True Stories of Courage, Devotion, and Sacrifice,* edited by Paul Drew Stevens; and a very short story from China). "Free the Hacker Two" appeared in the "Readings" section of *Harper's* September 1989 issue. The piece was originally published in the spring issue of *2600,* "the hacker quarterly."
>
> Corley's claim is that hacking is not wrong. His conclusion is that hackers should not be punished. Is his backing for the claim adequate? Does he have sufficient evidence for his conclusion? Does he qualify his claim appropriately? In short, is Corley's argument strong or weak, valid or invalid?

By now you've probably all heard about Kevin Mitnick. Mitnick, twenty-five, is an overweight, bespectacled computer junkie known as a "dark-side" hacker for his willingness to use a computer as a weapon. He allegedly used a computer to break into Defense Department computer systems, sabotage business computers, and electronically harass anyone — including a probation officer and FBI agents — who got in his way. He was arrested late last year, after being turned in by a friend who said Mitnick was "a menace to society."

Mitnick has an amazing history, to say the least. He and a friend logged into a North American Air Defense Command computer in Colorado Springs in 1979. The friend said they did not interfere with any defense operation. They just "got in, looked around, and got out."

Investigators believe that Mitnick also may have disseminated a false report, carried by a news service in April 1988, that Security Pacific National Bank lost $400 million. The report appeared four days after Mitnick had been turned down for a job at Security Pacific. He also learned how to disrupt telephone-company operations and disconnected the phones of celebrities such as Kristy McNichol.

Last February, Herbert Zinn Jr., an eighteen-year-old hacker who broke into U.S. military and AT&T computers, was sentenced to nine months in federal prison. A dropout from Mather High School in Chicago, Zinn (a.k.a. "Shadow Hawk") was sixteen at the time he committed the intrusions, using his home computer and a modem. Zinn penetrated a Bell Labs computer in Naperville, Illinois, an AT&T computer in Burlington, North Carolina, and another AT&T computer at Robbins Air Force base in Georgia. He copied fifty-five programs, including complex software relating to computer design and artificial intelligence. Although no classified material was involved, the government claims that the programs he copied from a NATO computer linked with the U.S. missile command are "highly sensitive."

During his trial in January, Zinn spoke in his own defense, saying   5
that he copied the programs to educate himself and not to sell them or share them. Zinn is still in jail.

When people actually start going to jail for playing with computers, it's time to ask some very serious questions.

Let's start with Mitnick. Here we have what appears to be a nasty, vindictive human being. But is this reason enough to lock him up without bail? In normal times in almost any democratic society, the answer would be a resounding *no*. But there are special circumstances here: computers. Doing nasty things with computers is considered infinitely worse than doing nasty things without computers. As a result, Mitnick had less success seeking bail than he would if he had been charged with murder. Prison authorities wouldn't even let him use the phone for fear of what he might do.

Pretend for a moment that computers don't exist. Mitnick disconnects Kristy McNichol's phone using wire clippers. That's vandalism, maybe trespassing, good for a fine of maybe $100. He and a friend walk into the North American Air Defense Command Center one day. They don't break anything and they soon leave. Had they been caught, they would have been thrown off the grounds or, at worst, arrested for trespassing and held overnight. (The person who left the door unlocked would be fired.)

In our society such a person would be classified as a mischief-maker. Such people exist everywhere. But because Mitnick used computers to perform his mischief, he's treated as though he's another John Hinckley.

Society is indeed endangered by what's happening here, but that's   10
not Mitnick's fault. He simply demonstrated how vulnerable our information — and our way of life — has become. If one person can cause such chaos, then clearly the system is falling apart at the seams.

The Zinn case is equally deplorable. A bright kid is languishing in prison because he didn't know when to curb his intellectual curiosity. The newspapers accused Zinn of stealing software, but all he did was *copy* some programs. If these programs were so valuable, why in hell was he able to download them over the phone lines?

The message here is that some of our nation's brightest kids are being imprisoned for being a little too inquisitive, and that's frightening. Much can be learned from what hackers uncover. Hackers may not be knights in shining armor, but the notion that they are dangerous criminals could not be further from the truth. These are kids doing what kids have always done. The only difference is that they've learned how to use a tool that most people have ignored. And until more of us know how to use that tool, there will be many more abuses — not just abuses *of* the tool but abuses *by* the tool. That's where the real danger lies.

Hacking is not wrong. Hacking is healthy. Hacking is *not* the same as stealing. Hacking uncovers design flaws and security deficiencies. Above all, hacking proves that the ingenuity of a single mind is still the most powerful tool of all.

We are hackers. We always will be. Our spirits will not be crushed by these horrible events. Call us co-conspirators, fellow anarchists, whatever you want. We intend to keep learning. To suppress this desire is contrary to everything that is human.

Like the authors who rose to defend Salman Rushdie from the long   *15*
arm of hysteria, we must rise to defend those endangered by the hacker witch-hunts. After all, they can't lock us *all* up. And unless they do, hacking is here to stay.

FOR DISCUSSION AND WRITING

1. Is the argument logical? Does it contain fallacies? Explain.

2. Is the following an accurate structural analysis of Corley's argument?

   > *Claim:* Hackers should not be punished. (Hacking should be decriminalized.)
   > *Evidence:* Both Kevin Mitnick and Herbert Zinn, Jr., have been prosecuted for hacking.
   > *Backing:* Similar crimes that do not involve computers either go unpunished or incur light penalties.
   > *Qualification:* None.

   Explain why you think that the structural analysis is or is not accurate.

3. Is the evidence for the claim adequate and appropriate?

4. Is the backing adequate and appropriate?

5. State the gist of Corley's argument.

6. The argument first appeared in *2600,* the "hacker quarterly," and was reprinted in the September 1989 issue of *Harper's.* Does your knowledge of these sources affect your judgment of the argument?

7. Is the argument adequate from the standpoint of quality? Explain.

8. Do you agree with Corley's views on intellectual property (such as computer programs)? Do you think he would consider unauthorized appropriation of a personal computer (hardware) more or less serious than the appropriation of a computer program (software)?

9. Explain why you agree or disagree with Corley's argument that the punishments meted out to the two hackers were unduly severe because computers were involved.

PROFITS VS. INJURY: DOES THE HUMAN TOLL OF BOXING OUTWEIGH ITS MERITS AS A SPORT?

Bill Brubaker

> *The Washington Post National Weekly Edition* does not attempt to be up-to-the-minute on the latest-breaking news; its purpose is to provide background for and discussion of the news and issues of the day. A recent issue contains such diverse articles as these: "The White House Tough Guy," a profile of John Sununu, President Bush's chief of staff; "Open for Business," a look into the future of the world's economy; "The Price of Oil Riches," a report on Valdez, Alaska, one year after the great oil spill; "Disappearing Dakota," an article about the decline of population in North Dakota; and "Israel's New Tactic," an analysis of the expulsion of West Bank Palestinians who do not meet stringent residency requirements.
>
> The issues that Brubaker deals with in "Profits vs. Injury" are not headline news, but the moral and legal ramifications of professional boxing — like those of capital punishment, euthanasia, and abortion — make the subject one that informed citizens should consider.

When Larry Holmes, the former world heavyweight boxing champion, wants to get dressed, he must ask his wife, Diane, for help. "The thumb on my right hand can no longer bend," Holmes explains. "Without my thumb, I can't put on my tie or fasten the top button of my shirt. The thumb is just froze, you know? Guess it'll be like that forever."

Holmes says his thumb won't bend because he defended too many titles with a broken right hand. "I fought Mike Tyson with a broke right hand," he says. "I fought 'Bonecrusher' Smith with a broke hand. I fought David Bey with a broke hand. Man, I've had so many problems with this thumb, I've asked the doctors to cut it off. But they won't."

If Holmes had only risked injury to his right hand, his story wouldn't be so troubling. But during a career that lasted 15 years, Holmes says he routinely put his health on the line.

"I fought Michael Spinks with a slipped disc in my neck," he says. "I fought Kenny Norton with my left biceps pulled off my arm. I fought Muhammad Ali with eight stitches in my eye. I fought Leroy Jones with a twisted ankle. Man, I've fought with fevers, stomachaches, everything. But, you know, you've got to do it. The opportunity to pick yourself up a few million dollars doesn't come often. It's like a once-in-a-lifetime dream."

Holmes always was considered one of the more sensible boxing champions. A seventh-grade dropout, he managed to save most of the $16 million he earned in the ring. But when it came to his health, Holmes acknowledges, "I really didn't care about the dangers that were involved. You know, that's how fighters are."

Boxing is as safe as it ever has been. Prefight medical exams have become more rigid. The maximum number of rounds for world-title fights has been reduced from 15 to 12. The World Boxing Council (WBC) has teamed up with the University of California at Los Angeles to study ring injuries. Johns Hopkins University is in the midst of a four-year study on health risks to amateur fighters.

But, as Larry Holmes will attest, boxing remains a brutal activity, often undertaken by men more concerned with escaping poverty than injury and overseen by state and foreign-government commissions that do not share the same rules or medical standards.

Jose Sulaiman, president of the WBC, which sanctions world-title fights, has long been one of the sport's staunchest supporters. But Sulaiman acknowledges: "If we do not give a priority to safety, boxing could die in 25 years. There are not too many societies that will be ready to accept legalized assassination."

By some accounts, more than 500 boxers have died of ring-related injuries over the last 80 years. The American Medical Association and British Medical Association have called for an outright ban on boxing. But there is a prevailing view that if boxing were banned, the show would go on—in barns, warehouses and back alleys, with no medical supervision. Accepting that, some doctors say it is better to join the boxing establishment than to fight it.

"We say to doctors in both the AMA and BMA: Instead of contin- 10 uing your negative criticism, come up with positive thoughts. Let's sit down and try to make the sport safe," says Adrian Whiteson, a London physician who is cochairman of the WBC medical committee. "Because kids are always going to box. Put two infants in a playpen, put one toy between them, and before long they're going to be scratching each other and throwing punches. It's natural. We're aggressive people. I wish we weren't."

But aggressiveness is not the overriding problem in boxing: It's the determination of many fighters to compete when they are medically impaired and the inability of some trainers, managers, promoters and regulating organizations to stop them. Some snapshots:

On Sept. 17, 1986, Wilfred Benitez, a financially troubled former WBC welterweight champion, appeared in Baltimore for a 10-round fight. Benitez won the fight but was suspended indefinitely when a medical examination after the fight found evidence of chronic traumatic encephalopathy—or punch-drunk syndrome. "Benitez had looked terrible in the fight," recalls Lawrence Charnas, neurologist for the Maryland State Athletic Commission. "He'd throw a punch and miss, and he actually lost his balance in the ropes. In the postfight exam, he clearly demonstrated motor impairment."

How did Benitez get licensed in Maryland to begin with? Until July 1987, the state commission did not require boxers to undergo pre-fight neurological exams. "Benitez never appealed his suspension," Charnas says, "and I don't believe he fought again." Wrong. Ten weeks later, Benitez appeared in a fight in Argentina, where he lost on a seventh-round technical knockout.

On Dec. 12, 1987, Cuba's undefeated super-heavyweight, Leonardo Martinez Fizz, dislocated his right shoulder during the first round of an amateur fight in Santa Clara, Cuba, against Tevin George of the United States. With his right arm hurting, Martinez used his left hand in the second round and battered George so badly the fight had to be stopped. For all his heroics, Martinez Fizz had to spend two weeks in a rehabilitative hospital in Havana.

Why was Martinez Fizz allowed to continue the fight with a dislo-   15
cated shoulder? "There wasn't efficient communication between the athlete and the trainer," says Cuba's top sports medicine specialist, Dr. Armando Pancorbo. "He should not have continued to fight because he risked having serious problems with his shoulder for his entire life."

The Cuban team doctor, Oscar Ramirez, says Martinez Fizz did not complain of an injury between rounds. "This is characteristic of boxers," he says. "You go to a corner to see a boxer who has an injury, and he says, 'Doctor, I can continue. I have nothing. Give me a chance.'"

On Oct. 31, 1986, the New Jersey State Athletic Control Board suspended Brian Baronet, a junior welterweight from South Africa, after a knockout in Atlantic City. Baronet was told he would remain on suspension until he had a complete medical exam, including a brain scan. Baronet went home to South Africa, apparently to retire. But last year he attempted a comeback, and on June 17 he died of a brain injury after being knocked out in a fight in Durban, South Africa.

Why had the local South African boxing commission allowed Baronet to fight while under suspension in New Jersey? The commission had not been notified of the New Jersey suspension. "At the time we weren't exchanging information and results with overseas commissions," New Jersey boxing commission chairman Larry Hazzard says. "Now, we are. But getting information from overseas is still a problem. Sometimes there are inaccuracies in the records."

Medical standards in boxing are as disparate as the hundreds of commissions — from Paraguay to Pennsylvania — that govern the sport. Some commissions, such as the one in New York, require a boxer to have an annual electroencephalogram (EEG). Others, such as in Maryland, do not. "An EEG is an expensive, insensitive and inappropriate test to screen individuals," says Charnas, the Maryland neurologist. "It's stupid. You can quote me."

Some commissions, such as in New Jersey, do not allow a boxer   20
who has competed in a four-round bout to fight again for 14 days.

Others, such as in California, allow the same boxer to fight every two days. Most commissions will license a boxer who has undergone surgery for a detached retina. The boxing commissions in California and Britain will not. The WBC voted in 1984 to ban boxers with detached retinas. The organization reversed itself when Maurice Hope, a British boxer who had undergone surgery for a detached retina, submitted medical evidence that he was fit to fight. The reversal cleared the way for Sugar Ray Leonard, who had also had surgery for a detached retina, to make a comeback.

Whiteson says he does not agree with his organization's policy, which allows a boxer to compete after retina surgery if he is cleared by two ophthalmologists. "A boxer with a detached retina shouldn't go into the ring, whether they're Sugar Ray Leonard or anyone else," Whiteson says. "Your eyes, you need them. At the end of the day, I hope Sugar Ray Leonard gets away with it."

Sulaiman has formed a committee to study whether the rule should again be reversed. "I favor stopping boxers with a detached retina," he says. "But the way it is now, some doctors say yes, some doctors say no. There is no consensus."

There is a consensus on minimum standards for prefight examinations, although these guidelines are not always followed. In May 1987, for example, a Baltimore middleweight, James (Morris) Jones, was licensed by the Maryland commission and allowed to fight even though he had not undergone the required ophthalmological exam. "A decision was made by the commission to make an exception in that area," says Dennis Gring, the commission's executive secretary.

At the world-title level, prefight exams usually are rigorous. But the world organizations cannot impose their standards on member commissions. At a WBC convention last year, for example, the WBC medical committee discussed AIDS testing—an important issue in a sport where blood often is in evidence. Whiteson concluded that no legislation could be passed "due to the different rules and regulations in force [in member commissions] . . . concerning the confidentiality of handling the results."

In the United States, some commission officials believe there is only one solution to this medical discordance: the formation of a national regulatory agency. In 1987, Democratic Rep. Bill Richardson of New Mexico introduced a bill to establish a nonprofit corporation that would set minimum standards for state commissions. The bill died in a subcommittee but probably will be resubmitted this year.

Of course, it is doubtful anyone could stop a medically impaired boxer from at least attempting to fight. As Holmes says, that's how boxers are.

Holmes says he skipped the official weigh-in before his successful 1980 bout with Muhammad Ali because "I didn't want anybody to notice the eight stitches in my right eye." Now 39, Holmes says he would make a comeback if the price was right. "And if I was 50 years old, I'd probably do the same."

New York commission chairman Randy Gordon was not surprised last summer when junior lightweight Harold (The Shadow) Knight insisted on fighting after a CAT scan found an abnormality in his brain.

"He said, 'It's nothing,'" Gordon explains. "I said, 'How do you know that it's nothing?' He said, 'I don't get dizzy. I don't have any problems with it.' I understand why Harold wanted to fight. He's an outstanding fighter. He stands to make a lot of money in his career."

Rejected by New York, Knight applied for a license in New Jersey.   30
"Of course, we told him he couldn't fight here, either," Hazzard says. "But he wanted to fight bad, even with his problem. I guess that's the athlete's mentality. Somehow, maybe he has this idea that he's skillful enough to keep from getting hurt."

The WBC has been the most progressive organization in boxing safety. In 1976, it instituted a requirement that boxers undergo prefight medical exams that include an EEG, chest X-ray, blood and eye tests and a CAT scan (if he has not had one within the past year). The WBC also urged managers to "report immediately to their boxing commissions and doctors every accident that may have occurred during training." But neither the recommendation nor prefight exam stopped lightweight champion Julio Cesar Chavez from fighting fellow Mexican Jose Luis Ramirez in Las Vegas last October with injured ribs.

On Sept. 10, Chavez was treated in the emergency room of St. Joseph Riverside Hospital in Warren, Ohio, for what his promoter, Don King, describes as a hairline rib fracture. Chavez says that when he resumed training 10 days later he wore a protective jacket and received injections to prevent inflammation. According to the Nevada State Athletic Commission, Chavez did not disclose the injury during the mandatory prefight exam. King says Chavez's doctor examined the boxer and found his ribs had healed sufficiently for him to fight. Chavez says he might have been doing something "dangerous" because his ribs still "hurt."

Flip Homansky, a Nevada commission doctor, says Chavez may have escaped detection of his injury by masking pain during the prefight physical. Advised early last month that Chavez had fought with a fractured rib, Sulaiman said: "We're opposed to boxers competing when they are not in top condition. Chavez never told us of this injury."

Whiteson says he was troubled that Chavez did not report the injury. "He was putting his health and his sport on the line," Whiteson says. "If we want the sport to survive, then everybody's got to be honest." Chavez says he did not postpone the fight because "there was too much money involved."

This is, after all, a business. As 19-year-old lightweight David Gon- 35
zales told a Washington Post reporter last October, two months after his
opponent in a California state title fight died of a cerebral hemorrhage:
"No, I never had no thoughts [of retiring] 'cause this is the way I make
my money. You know, this is my living. You know, this was just like
somebody got hurt at the job. So I just keep on going."

Sulaiman echoes others in his business when he offers this justification for the sport: "A certain percentage of the world is born with a
drive or desire to be violent. They are violent in their own areas, in their
ghettos. These are the candidates to become boxers. Boxing is the reason
to take them out of that area and bring them into one that will give them
the opportunity to live a decent life."

Such was the case with James Jones, who, inspired by a sparring
exhibition by Sugar Ray Leonard near his home in Baltimore, began
fighting as an amateur in 1980. Jones set up a training room in the
basement of his family's rowhouse and painted the word CHAMP in
large red letters on the floor. "His dream was to become like Sugar Ray,"
says his sister, Bertha Wright.

Jones graduated from high school in 1981 and continued fighting as
an amateur while working as a movie-theater usher. He stopped boxing
in 1985 after becoming a father.

Aressie Jones was delighted when the second youngest of her eight
children quit boxing. "Morris' father had died of tuberculosis and a
brother had drowned during a seizure," Wright says. "My mother always said she wouldn't be able to make it if something happened to
Morris." Early in 1987, Morris Jones decided to resume boxing as a
professional. "He told my mom, 'Ma, when I make the big money I'm
going to do a lot of things for you,'" Wright says. On May 2, 1987,
Jones prepared to make his debut as a fill-in at a boxing show at Prince
George's Community College in Maryland. He would receive $350 to
fight Charles Ingram of Washington, D.C., who was appearing in his
second professional bout. "James was very excited," Wright says. "But
he told his family, 'I don't want any of you to go to the fight. You'll all
worry too much.'"

At 9 that evening, Jones stepped into the ring for a scheduled six- 40
rounder. The fighters seemed evenly matched and Ingram was awarded
the first three rounds. Twenty-three seconds into the fourth round, Ingram hit Jones on his chin with an overhand right. Jones fell straight
back, hit his head on the floor of the ring and lost consciousness.
Jones was taken to a nearby hospital, comatose and paralyzed on his left
side, the result of a blood clot on the right side of his brain. Jones un-
derwent brain surgery, after which he remained comatose and partially
paralyzed.

Dr. Saied Jamshidi, the neurosurgeon who operated on Jones,
says the injury was caused by a blow to the head. Jamshidi says it was

impossible to determine if Jones had neurological abnormalities before the fight. Charnas, the state boxing commission neurologist, says Jones' injury was unavoidable. "The only way to avoid that is to not have people get into boxing."

Jones awoke from the coma on May 10, 1987 — Mothers Day — and soon regained some movement in his left side. A subsequent medical report stated that he suffers from memory deficits so severe that he forgets to wear a coat when he goes outside in cold weather.

Jones, 26, now lives with his mother. He has recovered some memory and much of the movement on his left side. "Simple things he can understand," Wright says. "More complicated things he can't. He speaks very well, but sometimes he'll repeat something four or five times, not realizing he'd already said it."

So far, Jones' medical bills have totaled about $500,000, according to members of his family. He receives a monthly Social Security disability check for $269 but has no personal insurance, and he was covered for only $1,000 through the Maryland boxing commission.

On a recent afternoon, Morris Jones sat in his living room reflecting   45 upon the knockout that altered the course of his life. "I wanted to become a pro boxer so I'd be a positive image for my son," he says. "Now, I don't know what I'll do. I still love boxing, even though it messed my whole life up. When I watch it on TV I don't get angry or sad. I just think: Well, I guess I wasn't meant to be a boxer."

FOR DISCUSSION AND WRITING

1. Could Brubaker be accused of the fallacy of hasty generalization? Explain your judgment.

2. Does Brubaker make effective use of statistics in his argument? Explain.

3. Is either of the following an adequate statement of Brubaker's claim?
   a. Boxing should be outlawed.
   b. Boxing should be more closely regulated.
   If neither is adequate, give an adequate statement of the claim.

4. Is the following an accurate and adequate analysis of the argument?

   Claim: (a) Boxing should be outlawed, or (b) boxing should be more closely regulated.
   Evidence: The many cases of boxing mayhem cited in the argument.
   Backing: The cases of bad regulation cited in the argument.
   Qualification: None.

5. From the standpoint of quantity, is the evidence sufficient to be convincing?

6. From the standpoint of quality, is the evidence reliable?

7. From the standpoint of quantity, is the backing sufficient?

8. From the standpoint of quality, is the backing sufficient?

9. In your opinion, is Brubaker biased or unbiased? Explain.

10. What is your own opinion about boxing? Explain why this argument did or did not alter your opinion in any way.

ON BOXING

Joyce Carol Oates

Joyce Carol Oates is one of the most prolific authors in the history of literature. Her first book, a collection of short stories, was published in 1963. By 1989, she had published eighteen novels, fourteen volumes of stories, several books of poems, and various collections of essays. Counting just novels and collections of short stories, Oates averaged more than a book a year between 1963 and 1989. Interestingly, when they visited the United States in 1987, Soviet Premier Mikhail Gorbachev and his wife, Raisa, both professed their admiration for Oates's work.

Among Oates's more significant works are the novels *A Garden of Earthly Delights* (1967); *Expensive People* (1968); *them* (1969), which won the National Book Award; *Wonderland* (1971); *Do with Me What You Will* (1974); and *You Must Remember This* (1987). Two collections of short stories have also received much critical attention: *Wheel of Love* (1970) and *A Sentimental Education* (1981).

In her novels and short stories, as in the selection below, violence has consistently fascinated Oates, and none of her works is more violent than *them,* a nonfiction novel set in Detroit. It is the story of "Maureen Wendell," the pseudonym of a young woman who had been Oates's student at the University of Detroit. "My initial feeling about her life was, 'This must be fiction, this can't all be real!' My more permanent feeling was, 'This is the only kind of fiction that is real.'" And in the following essay, she says, "Nor can I think of boxing in writerly terms as a metaphor for something else. . . . Life *is* like boxing in many unsettling respects. But boxing is only like boxing."

Oates was born in Lockport, New York, in 1938. Her family were working class, Catholic, and rural. She attended Syracuse University and graduated Phi Beta Kappa; according to one of her professors, she was the most brilliant student he had ever known. She took an M.A. at Wisconsin and married Raymond Joseph Smith. She has taught at Rice University, the University of Detroit, and the University of Windsor in Ontario. Currently, she teaches at Princeton, where she and her husband edit the literary magazine *The Ontario Review.*

"Profits vs. Injury," by Bill Brubaker, is a straightforward argument against boxing. "On Boxing" can be read as a defense of boxing and as a counterstatement to Brubaker. As you read, notice the arguments that Oates develops. In what ways do her methods of argument differ from Brubaker's?

How can you enjoy so brutal a sport, people sometimes ask me. Or pointedly don't ask.

And it's too complex to answer. In any case I don't "enjoy" boxing in the usual sense of the word, and never have; boxing isn't invariably "brutal"; and I don't think of it as a "sport."

Nor can I think of boxing in writerly terms as a metaphor for something else. No one whose interest began as mine did in childhood—as an offshoot of my father's interest—is likely to think of boxing as a symbol of something beyond itself, as if its uniqueness were merely an abbreviation, or iconographic; though I can entertain the proposition that life is a metaphor for boxing—for one of those bouts that go on and on, round following round, jabs, missed punches, clinches, nothing determined, again the bell and again and you and your opponent so evenly matched it's impossible not to see that your opponent *is* you: and why this struggle on an elevated platform enclosed by ropes as in a pen beneath hot crude pitiless lights in the presence of an impatient crowd?—that sort of hellish-writerly metaphor. Life *is* like boxing in many unsettling respects. But boxing is only like boxing.

For if you have seen five hundred boxing matches you have seen   5
five hundred boxing matches and their common denominator, which certainly exists, is not of primary interest to you. "If the Host is only a symbol," as the Catholic writer Flannery O'Connor once remarked. "I'd say the hell with it." . . .

> *Why are you a boxer, Irish featherweight champion Barry McGuigan was asked. He said: "I can't be a poet. I can't tell stories . . ."*

Each boxing match is a story—a unique and highly condensed drama without words. Even when nothing sensational happens: then the drama is "merely" psychological. Boxers are there to establish an absolute experience, a public accounting of the outermost limits of their beings; they will know, as few of us can know of ourselves, what physical and psychic power they possess—of how much, or how little, they are capable. To enter the ring near-naked and to risk one's life is to make of one's audience voyeurs of a kind: boxing is so intimate. It is to ease out of sanity's consciousness and into another, difficult to name. It is to risk, and sometimes to realize, the agony of which *agon* (Greek, "contest") is the root.

In the boxing ring there are two principal players, overseen by a shadowy third. The ceremonial ringing of the bell is a summoning to full wakefulness for both boxers and spectators. It sets into motion, too, the authority of Time.

The boxers will bring to the fight everything that is themselves, and everything will be exposed—including secrets about themselves they cannot fully realize. The physical self, the maleness, one might say, underlying the "self." There are boxers possessed of such remarkable intuition, such uncanny prescience, one would think they were somehow recalling their fights, not fighting them as we watch. There are boxers who perform skillfully, but mechanically, who cannot improvise in response to another's alteration of strategy; there are boxers performing at the peak of their talent who come to realize, mid-fight, that it will not be enough; there are boxers — including great champions — whose careers end abruptly, and irrevocably, as we watch. There has been at least one boxer possessed of an extraordinary and disquieting awareness not only of his opponent's every move and anticipated move but of the audience's keenest shifts in mood as well, for which he seems to have felt personally responsible — Cassius Clay/Muhammad Ali, of course. "The Sweet Science of Bruising" celebrates the physicality of men even as it dramatizes the limitations, sometimes tragic, more often poignant, of the physical. Though male spectators identify with boxers no boxer behaves like a "normal" man when he is in the ring and no combination of blows is "natural." All is style.

Every talent must unfold itself in fighting. So Nietzsche speaks of the Hellenic past, the history of the "contest" — athletic, and otherwise — by which Greek youths were educated into Greek citizenry. Without the ferocity of competition, without, even, "envy, jealousy, and ambition" in the contest, the Hellenic city, like the Hellenic man, degenerated. If death is a risk, death is also the prize — for the winning athlete.

In the boxing ring, even in our greatly humanized times, death   10
is always a possibility — which is why some of us prefer to watch films or tapes of fights already past, already defined as history. Or, in some instances, art. (Though to prepare for writing this mosaic-like essay I saw tapes of two infamous "death" fights of recent times: the Lupe Pintor–Johnny Owen bantamweight match of 1982, and the Ray Mancini–Duk Koo-Kim lightweight match of the same year. In both instances the boxers died as a consequence of their astonishing resilience and apparent indefatigability — their "heart," as it's known in boxing circles.) Most of the time, however, death in the ring is extremely unlikely; a statistically rare possibility like your possible death tomorrow morning in an automobile accident or in next month's headlined airline disaster or in a freak accident involving a fall on the stairs or in the bathtub, a skull fracture, subarachnoid hemorrhage. Spectators at "death" fights often claim afterward that what happened simply seemed to happen — unpredictably, in a sense accidentally. Only in retrospect does death appear to have been inevitable.

If a boxing match is a story it is an always wayward story, one in which anything can happen. And in a matter of seconds. Split seconds! (Muhammad Ali boasted that he could throw a punch faster than the eye could follow, and he may have been right.) In no other sport can so much take place in so brief a period of time, and so irrevocably.

Because a boxing match is a story without words, this doesn't mean that it has no text or no language, that it is somehow "brute," "primitive," "inarticulate," only that the text is improvised in action; the language a dialogue between the boxers of the most refined sort (one might say, as much neurological as psychological: a dialogue of split-second reflexes) in a joint response to the mysterious will of the audience which is always that the fight be a worthy one so that the crude paraphernalia of the setting — ring, lights, ropes, stained canvas, the staring onlookers themselves — be erased, forgotten. (As in the theater or the church, settings are erased by way, ideally, of transcendent action.) Ringside announcers give to the wordless spectacle a narrative unity, yet boxing as performance is more clearly akin to dance or music than narrative.

To turn from an ordinary preliminary match to a "Fight of the Century" like those between Joe Louis and Billy Conn, Joe Frazier and Muhammad Ali, Marvin Hagler and Thomas Hearns is to turn from listening or half-listening to a guitar being idly plucked to hearing Bach's *Well-Tempered Clavier* perfectly executed, and that too is part of the story's mystery: so much happens so swiftly and with such heart-stopping subtlety you cannot absorb it except to know that something profound is happening and it is happening in a place beyond words.

I try to catch my opponent on the tip of his nose because I try to punch the bone into his brain.
— MIKE TYSON,
heavyweight contender

Boxing's claim is that it is superior to life in that it is, ideally, superior to all accident. It contains nothing that is not fully willed.

The boxer meets an opponent who is a dream–distortion of himself in the sense that his weaknesses, his capacity to fail and to be seriously hurt, his intellectual miscalculations — all can be interpreted as strengths belonging to the Other; the parameters of his private being are nothing less than boundless assertions of the Other's self. This is dream, or nightmare: my strengths are not fully my own, but my opponent's weaknesses; my failure is not fully my own, but my opponent's triumph. He is my shadow-self, not my (mere) shadow. The boxing match as "serious, complete, and of a certain magnitude" — to refer to Aristotle's

15

definition of tragedy — is an event that necessarily subsumes both boxers, as any ceremony subsumes its participants. (Which is why one can say, for instance, that the greatest fight of Muhammad Ali's career was one of the few fights Ali lost — the first heroic match with Frazier.)

The old boxing adage — a truism surely untrue — that you cannot be knocked out if you see the blow coming, and if you *will* yourself not to be knocked out, has its subtler, more daunting significance: nothing that happens to the boxer in the ring, including death — "his" death — is not of his own will or failure of will. The suggestion is of a world-model in which we are humanly responsible not only for our own acts but for those performed against us.

Which is why, though springing from life, boxing is not a metaphor for life but a unique, closed, self-referential world, obliquely akin to those severe religions in which the individual is both "free" and "determined" — in one sense possessed of a will tantamount to God's, in another totally helpless. The Puritan sensibility would have understood a mouth filling with blood, an eye popped out of its socket — fit punishment for an instant's negligence.

A boxing trainer's most difficult task is said to be to persuade a young boxer to get up and continue fighting after he has been knocked down. And if the boxer has been knocked down by a blow he hadn't seen coming — which is usually the case — how can he hope to protect himself from being knocked down again? and again? The invisible blow is after all — invisible.

"Normal" behavior in the ring would be unbearable to watch, deeply shameful: for "normal" beings share with all living creatures the instinct to persevere, as Spinoza said, in their own being. The boxer must somehow learn, by what effort of will non-boxers surely cannot guess, to inhibit his own instinct for survival; he must learn to exert his "will" over his merely human and animal impulses, not only to flee pain but to flee the unknown. In psychic terms this sounds like magic. Levitation. Sanity turned inside out, "madness" revealed as a higher and more pragmatic form of sanity.

The fighters in the ring are time-bound — surely nothing is so excruciatingly long as a fiercely contested three-minute round — but the fight itself is timeless. In a sense it becomes all fights, as the boxers are all boxers. By way of films, tapes, and photographs it quickly becomes history for us, even, at times, art. Time, like the possibility of death, is the invisible adversary of which the boxers — and the referee, the seconds, the spectators — are keenly aware. When a boxer is "knocked out" it does not mean, as it's commonly thought, that he has been knocked unconscious, or even incapacitated; it means rather more poetically that he has been knocked out of Time. (The referee's dramatic count of ten constitutes a metaphysical parenthesis of a kind through which the fallen boxer must penetrate if he hopes to continue in Time.) There are in a

20

sense two dimensions of Time abruptly operant: while the standing boxer is *in time* the fallen boxer is *out of time*. Counted out, he is counted "dead" — in symbolic mimicry of the sport's ancient tradition in which he would very likely be dead. (Though, as we may recall, the canny Romans reserved for themselves as spectators the death blow itself: the triumphant gladiator was obliged to wait for a directive from outside the arena before he finished off his opponent.)

If boxing is a sport it is the most tragic of all sports because more than any human activity it consumes the very excellence it displays — its drama is this very consumption. To expend oneself in fighting the greatest fight of one's life is to begin by necessity the downward turn that next time may be a plunge, an abrupt fall into the abyss. *I am the greatest* says Muhammad Ali. *I am the greatest* says Marvelous Marvin Hagler. You always think you're going to win, Jack Dempsey wryly observed in his old age, otherwise you couldn't fight at all. The punishment — to the body, the brain, the spirit — a man must endure to become even a moderately good boxer is inconceivable to most of us whose idea of personal risk is largely ego-related or emotional. But the punishment as it begins to show in even a young and vigorous boxer is closely gauged by his rivals, who are waiting for him to slip. (After junior-welterweight champion Aaron Pryor won a lackluster fight last year a younger boxer in his weight division, interviewed at ringside, said with a smile: "My mouth is watering." And there was twenty-nine-year-old Billy Costello's bold statement — "If I can't beat an old man [of thirty-three] then I should retire" — shortly before his bout with Alexis Arguello, in which he was knocked out in an early round.)

In the ring, boxers inhabit a curious sort of "slow" time — amateurs never box beyond three rounds, and for most amateurs those nine minutes are exhausting — while outside the ring they inhabit an alarmingly accelerated time. A twenty-three-year-old boxer is no longer young in the sense in which a twenty-three-year-old man is young; a thirty-five-year-old is frankly old. (Which is why Muhammad Ali made a tragic mistake in continuing his career after he had lost his title for the second time — to come out of retirement, aged thirty-eight, to fight Larry Holmes, and why Holmes made a similar mistake, years later, in needlessly exposing himself to injury, as well as professional embarrassment, by meeting with the light-heavyweight champion Michael Spinks. The victory of the thirty-seven-year-old Jersey Joe Walcott over the thirty-year-old Ezzard Charles, for the heavyweight title in 1951, is *sui generis*. And Archie Moore is *sui generis*.) All athletes age rapidly but none so rapidly and so visibly as the boxer.

So it is, the experience of watching great fighters of the past is radically different from having seen them perform when they were reigning champions. Jack Johnson, Jack Dempsey, Joe Louis, Sugar Ray Robinson, Rocky Marciano, Muhammad Ali, Joe Frazier — as spectators we know not only how a fight but how a career ends. The trajectory not merely of ten or fifteen rounds but that of an entire life . . .

Everything that man esteems
Endures a moment or a day.
Love's pleasure drives his love away,
The painter's brush consumes his dreams;
The herald's cry, the soldier's tread
Exhaust his glory and his might:
Whatever flames upon the night
Man's own resinous heart has fed.

—WILLIAM BUTLER YEATS, *from "The Resurrection"*

When I see blood, I become a bull.

— MARVIN HAGLER

I have no difficulty justifying boxing as a sport because I have never thought of it as a sport.

There is nothing fundamentally playful about it; nothing that seems   25
to belong to daylight, to pleasure. At its moments of greatest intensity it seems to contain so complete and so powerful an image of life—life's beauty, vulnerability, despair, incalculable and often self-destructive courage—that boxing *is* life, and hardly a mere game. During a superior boxing match (Ali-Frazier I, for instance) we are deeply moved by the body's communion with itself by way of another's intransigent flesh. The body's dialogue with its shadow-self—or Death. Baseball, football, basketball—these quintessentially American pastimes are recognizably sports because they involve play: they are games. One *plays* football, one doesn't *play* boxing.

Observing team sports, teams of adult men, one sees how men are children in the most felicitous sense of the word. But boxing in its elemental ferocity cannot be assimilated into childhood. (Though very young men box, even professionally, and many world champions began boxing in their early or mid-teens. By the time he was sixteen Jack Dempsey, rootless and adrift in the West, was fighting for small sums of money in unrefereed saloon fights in which—in the natural course of things—he might have been killed.) Spectators at public games derive much of their pleasure from reliving the communal emotions of childhood but spectators at boxing matches relive the murderous infancy of the race. Hence the occasional savagery of boxing crowds—the crowd, largely Hispanic, that cheered as the Welshman Johnny Owen was pounded into insensibility by the Mexican bantamweight champion

Lupe Pintor, for instance — and the excitement when a man begins to seriously bleed.

Marvelous Marvin Hagler, speaking of blood, is speaking, of course, of his own.

Considered in the abstract the boxing ring is an altar of sorts, one of those legendary spaces where the laws of a nation are suspended: inside the ropes, during an officially regulated three-minute round, a man may be killed at his opponent's hands but he cannot be legally murdered. Boxing inhabits a sacred space predating civilization; or, to use D. H. Lawrence's phrase, before God was love. If it suggests a savage ceremony or a rite of atonement it also suggests the futility of such gestures. For what possible atonement is the fight waged if it must shortly be waged again . . . and again? The boxing match is the very image, the more terrifying for being so stylized, of mankind's collective aggression; its ongoing historical madness.

FOR DISCUSSION AND WRITING

1. In some ways, Oates refuses to make an argument on boxing's behalf. At the beginning of this essay she writes,

   > How can you enjoy so brutal a sport, people sometimes ask me. Or pointedly don't ask.
   > And it's too complex to answer. In any case I don't "enjoy" boxing in the usual sense of the word, and never have; boxing isn't invariably "brutal"; and I don't think of it as a "sport."

   Later, she repeats herself by stating, "I have no difficulty justifying boxing as a sport because I have never thought of it as a sport" (par. 24). In a strictly logical sense, does Oates's refusal to consider boxing a sport obviate the requirement to justify its existence?

2. Do you believe that Oates really *is* trying to justify boxing even though she attempts to define away the argument? Why, or why not?

3. In another part of the essay not included in this selection, Oates notes,

   > In December 1984 the American Medical Association passed a resolution calling for the abolition of boxing on the principle that while other sports involved as much, or even more, risk to life and health — the most dangerous sports being football, auto racing, hang gliding, mountain climbing, and ice hockey, with boxing in about seventh place — boxing is the only sport in which the objective is to cause injury. . . . To say that the rate of death and injury in the ring is not extraordinary set beside the rates of other sports is to misread the nature of the criticism brought to bear against

boxing (and not against other sports). Clearly, boxing's very image is repulsive to many people because it cannot be assimilated into what we wish to know about civilized man.

Do you think that this argument is more persuasive than that of the selection in calling for the maintenance of boxing as a "sport" or profession? Why, or why not?

4. At least one implication of this passage is that boxing should not be banned because other, more dangerous sports are not banned. What would the logician have to say about the validity of this argument?

5. Do you think that the purpose of this essay is to present an argument? To persuade? Why, or why not?

6. Do you think Oates would be willing to attend boxing matches in which the opponents wore protective head gear like that which is worn during sparring? Would Brubaker? Explain.

7. What did Flannery O'Connor mean when she wrote, "If the Host is only a symbol, I'd say the hell with it" (par. 5)? What is Oates's point in quoting O'Connor? Do you see boxing as metaphorical?

8. Oates makes a surprising claim for a writer when she states that boxing is not a metaphor for anything else. Do you agree with her? Is she herself consistent in this assertion? Why, or why not?

9. It would be difficult to state that the essay has one particular gist, for it develops several ideas. Do you feel that the writing is disjointed as a result? What are some of the points developed in the essay?

10. The essay violates the writer–reader contract concerning relation in that the subsections do not relate to each other except in the broadest terms. Does this make the entire piece more difficult to understand? Does each subsection violate or uphold the contract regarding relation?

11. Oates is a respected author and essayist, but she is not generally known as an expert on boxing. (She implies that she saw films of two infamous fights for the first time only in preparation for writing this essay.) Does this undermine her authority in writing about boxing? Explain why or why not, and cite passages from the text to support your view.

PILTDOWN REVISITED

Stephen Jay Gould

Stephen Jay Gould, a professor at Harvard University, is a noted paleontologist who has been very successful in promoting public interest in evolutionary theory. His monthly columns are a popular feature in the magazine *Natural History,* and his widely respected books include *Ever Since Darwin, The Mismeasure of Man, Hen's Teeth and Horse's Toes,* and *The Panda's Thumb,* from which "Piltdown Revisited" is excerpted.

The following selection is of interest for several reasons. First, as Gould points out himself, mysteries are fascinating, especially those that spring from actual occurrences. In this article, Gould tries to determine who perpetrated one of science's greatest hoaxes. In addition, he considers why the scientific community was, in general, so completely fooled. Gould uses logic in attempting to solve a mystery while also analyzing why the members of the scientific community deserted their own allegiance to well-reasoned thought and careful weighing of the evidence. The Piltdown hoax is a humbling example of people's inability to be truly objective.

In "Piltdown Revisited," Gould discusses Pierre Teilhard de Chardin in detail, so the following information might enhance your appreciation of the article. Teilhard, a Jesuit priest, achieved great prominence posthumously when his book *The Phenomenon of Man* was published shortly after his death. In it, Teilhard proposed that the evolution of the universe was directed towards a certain goal, known as the Omega Point, with which individual consciousness would ultimately become completely integrated. Less widely known is the fact that Teilhard was also a noted paleontologist involved with the discovery of Peking man, *Homo erectus.* Because Peking man's development was intermediate between *Australopithecus,* an African hominid, and *Homo sapiens,* it provided science with important clues about the evolutionary history of our species.

Nothing is quite so fascinating as a well-aged mystery. Many connoisseurs regard Josephine Tey's *The Daughter of Time* as the greatest detective story ever written because its protagonist is Richard III, not the modern and insignificant murderer of Roger Ackroyd. The old chestnuts are perennial sources for impassioned and fruitless debate. Who was Jack the Ripper? Was Shakespeare Shakespeare?

My profession of paleontology offered its entry to the first rank of historical conundrums a quarter-century ago: In 1953, Piltdown man was exposed as a certain fraud perpetrated by a very uncertain hoaxer. Since then, interest has never flagged. People who cannot tell *Tyrannosaurus* from *Allosaurus* have firm opinions about the identity of Piltdown's forger. Rather than simply ask "whodunit?" this column treats what I regard as an intellectually more interesting issue: why did anyone ever accept Piltdown man in the first place? I was led to address the subject by recent and prominent news reports adding — with abysmally poor evidence, in my opinion — yet another prominent suspect to the list. Also, as an old mystery reader, I cannot refrain from expressing my own prejudice, all in due time.

In 1912, Charles Dawson, a lawyer and amateur archaeologist from Sussex, brought several cranial fragments to Arthur Smith Woodward, Keeper of Geology at the British Museum (Natural History). The first, he said, had been unearthed by workmen from a gravel pit in 1908. Since then, he had searched the spoil heaps and found a few more fragments. The bones, worn and deeply stained, seemed indigenous to the ancient gravel; they were not the remains of a more recent interment. Yet the skull appeared remarkably modern in form, although the bones were unusually thick.

Smith Woodward, excited as such a measured man could be, accompanied Dawson to Piltdown and there, with Father Teilhard de Chardin, looked for further evidence in the spoil heaps. (Yes, believe it or not, the same Teilhard who, as a mature scientist and theologian, became such a cult figure some fifteen years ago with his attempt to reconcile evolution, nature, and God in *The Phenomenon of Man*. Teilhard had come to England in 1908 to study at the Jesuit College in Hastings, near Piltdown. He met Dawson in a quarry on May 31, 1909; the mature solicitor and the young French Jesuit became warm friends, colleagues, and coexplorers.)

On one of their joint expeditions, Dawson found the famous man- 5 dible, or lower jaw. Like the skull fragments, the jaw was deeply stained, but it seemed to be as apish in form as the cranium was human. Nonetheless, it contained two molar teeth, worn flat in a manner commonly encountered in humans, but never in apes. Unfortunately, the jaw was broken in just the two places that might have settled its relationship with the skull: the chin region, with all its marks of distinction between ape and human, and the area of articulation with the cranium.

Armed with skull fragments, the lower jaw, and an associated collection of worked flints and bone, plus a number of mammalian fossils to fix the age as ancient, Smith Woodward and Dawson made their splash before the Geological Society of London on December 18, 1912. Their reception was mixed, although on the whole favorable. No one smelled fraud, but the association of such a human cranium with such an apish jaw indicated to some critics that remains of two separate animals might have been mixed together in the quarry.

During the next three years, Dawson and Smith Woodward countered with a series of further discoveries that, in retrospect, could not have been better programmed to dispel doubt. In 1913, Father Teilhard found the all-important lower canine tooth. It, too, was apish in form but strongly worn in a human manner. Then, in 1915, Dawson convinced most of his detractors by finding the same association of two thick-skulled human cranial fragments with an apish tooth worn in a human manner at a second site two miles from the original finds.

Henry Fairfield Osborn, leading American paleontologist and converted critic, wrote:

> If there is a Providence hanging over the affairs of prehistoric men, it certainly manifested itself in this case, because the three fragments of the second Piltdown man found by Dawson are exactly those which we would have selected to confirm the comparison with the original type. . . . Placed side by side with the corresponding fossils of the first Piltdown man they agree precisely; there is not a shadow of a difference.

Providence, unbeknown to Osborn, walked in human form at Piltdown.

For the next thirty years, Piltdown occupied an uncomfortable but acknowledged place in human prehistory. Then, in 1949, Kenneth P. Oakley applied his fluorine test to the Piltdown remains. Bones pick up fluorine as a function of their time of residence in a deposit and the fluorine content of surrounding rocks and soil. Both the skull and jaw of Piltdown contained barely detectable amounts of fluorine; they could not have lain long in the gravels. Oakley still did not suspect fakery. He proposed that Piltdown, after all, had been a relatively recent interment into ancient gravels.

But a few years later, in collaboration with J. S. Weiner and W. E. le   *10*
Gros Clark, Oakley finally considered the obvious alternative — that the "interment" had been made in this century with intent to defraud. He found that the skull and jaw had been artifically stained, the flints and bone worked with modern blades, and the associated mammals, although genuine fossils, imported from elsewhere. Moreover, the teeth had been filed down to simulate human wear. The old anomaly — an apish jaw with a human cranium — was resolved in the most parsimonious way of all. The skull *did* belong to a modern human; the jaw was an orangutan's.

But who had foisted such a monstrous hoax upon scientists so anxious for such a find that they remained blind to an obvious resolution of its anomalies? Of the original trio, Teilhard was dismissed as a young and unwitting dupe. No one has ever (and rightly, in my opinion) suspected Smith Woodward, the superstraight arrow who devoted his life to the reality of Piltdown and who, past eighty and blind, dictated in retirement his last book with its chauvinistic title, *The Earliest Englishman* (1948).

Suspicion instead has focused on Dawson. Opportunity he certainly had, although no one has ever established a satisfactory motive. Dawson was a highly respected amateur with several important finds to his credit. He was overenthusiastic and uncritical, perhaps even a bit unscrupulous in his dealings with other amateurs, but no direct evidence of his complicity has ever come to light. Nevertheless, the circumstantial case is strong and well summarized by J.S. Weiner in the *The Piltdown Forgery* (Oxford University Press, 1955).

Supporters of Dawson have maintained that a more professional scientist must have been involved, at least as a coconspirator, because the finds were so cleverly faked. I have always regarded this as a poor argument, advanced by scientists largely to assuage their embarrassment that such an indifferently designed hoax was not detected sooner. The staining, to be sure, had been done consummately. But the "tools" had been poorly carved and the teeth crudely filed — scratch marks were noted as soon as scientists looked with the right hypothesis in mind. Le Gros Clark wrote: "The evidences of artificial abrasion immediately sprang to the eye. Indeed so obvious did they seem it may well be asked — how was it that they had escaped notice before." The forger's main skill consisted in knowing what to leave out — discarding the chin and articulation.

In November 1978, Piltdown reappeared prominently in the news because yet another scientist had been implicated as a possible coconspirator. Shortly before he died at age ninety-three, J.A. Douglas, emeritus professor of geology at Oxford, made a tape recording suggesting that his predecessor in the chair, W.J. Sollas, was the culprit. In support of this assertion, Douglas offered only three items scarcely ranking as evidence in my book: (1) Sollas and Smith Woodward were bitter enemies. (So what, Academia is a den of vipers, but verbal sparring and elaborate hoaxing are responses of differing magnitude.) (2) In 1910, Douglas gave Sollas some mastodon bones that could have been used as part of the imported fauna. (But such bones and teeth are not rare.) (3) Sollas once received a package of potassium bichromate and neither Douglas nor Sollas's photographer could figure out why he had wanted it. Potassium bichromate was used in staining the Piltdown bones. (It was also an important chemical in photography, and I do not regard the alleged confusion of Sollas's photographer as a strong sign that the professor had some nefarious usages in mind.) In short, I find the evidence against Sollas so weak that I wonder why the leading scientific journals of England and the United States gave it so much space. I would exclude Sollas completely, were it not for the paradox that his famous book, *Ancient Hunters,* supports Smith Woodward's views about Piltdown in terms so obsequiously glowing that it could be read as subtle sarcasm.

Only three hypotheses make much sense to me. First, Dawson was   15 widely suspected and disliked by some amateur archeologists (and equally acclaimed by others). Some compatriots regarded him as a fraud. Others were bitterly jealous of his standing among professionals. Perhaps one of his colleagues devised this complex and peculiar form of revenge. The second hypothesis, and the most probable in my view, holds that

Dawson acted alone, whether for fame or to show up the world of professionals we do not know.

The third hypothesis is much more interesting. It would render Piltdown as a joke that went too far, rather than a malicious forgery. It represents the "pet theory" of many prominent vertebrate paleontologists who knew the man well. I have sifted all the evidence, trying hard to knock it down. Instead, I find it consistent and plausible, although not the leading contender. A.S. Romer, late head of the museum I inhabit at Harvard and America's finest vertebrate paleontologist, often stated his suspicions to me. Louis Leakey also believed it. His autobiography refers anonymously to a "second man," but internal evidence clearly implicates a certain individual to anyone in the know.

It is often hard to remember a man in his youth after old age imposes a different persona. Teilhard de Chardin became an austere and almost Godlike figure to many in his later years; he was widely hailed as a leading prophet of our age. But he was once a fun-loving young student. He knew Dawson for three years before Smith Woodward entered the story. He may have had access, from a previous assignment in Egypt, to mammalian bones (probably from Tunisia and Malta) that formed part of the "imported" fauna at Piltdown. I can easily imagine Dawson and Teilhard, over long hours in field and pub, hatching a plot for different reasons: Dawson to expose the gullibility of pompous professionals; Teilhard to rub English noses once again with the taunt that their nation had no legitimate human fossils, while France reveled in a superabundance that made her the queen of anthropology. Perhaps they worked together, never expecting that the leading lights of English science would fasten upon Piltdown with such gusto. Perhaps they expected to come clean but could not.

Teilhard left England to become a stretcher bearer during World War I. Dawson, on this view, persevered and completed the plot with a second Piltdown find in 1915. But then the joke ran away and became a nightmare. Dawson sickened unexpectedly and died in 1916. Teilhard could not return before the war's end. By that time, the three leading lights of British anthropology and paleontology — Arthur Smith Woodward, Grafton Elliot Smith, and Arthur Keith — had staked their careers on the reality of Piltdown. (Indeed they ended up as two Sir Arthurs and one Sir Grafton, largely for their part in putting England on the anthropological map.) Had Teilhard confessed in 1918, his promising career (which later included a major role in describing the legitimate Peking man) would have ended abruptly. So he followed the Psalmist and the motto of Sussex University, later established just a few miles from Piltdown — "Be still, and know. . . ." — to his dying day. Possible. Just possible.

All this speculation provides endless fun and controversy, but what about the prior and more interesting question: why had anyone believed

Piltdown in the first place? It was an improbable creature from the start. Why had anyone admitted to our lineage an ancestor with a fully modern cranium and the unmodified jaw of an ape?

Indeed, Piltdown never lacked detractors. Its temporary reign was born in conflict and nurtured throughout by controversy. Many scientists continued to believe that Piltdown was an artifact composed of two animals accidentally commingled in the same deposit. In the early 1940s, for example, Franz Weidenreich, perhaps the world's greatest human anatomist, wrote (with devastating accuracy in hindsight): "*Eoanthropus* ['dawn man,' the official designation of Piltdown] should be erased from the list of human fossils. It is the artificial combination of fragments of a modern human braincase with orang-utanglike mandible and teeth." To this apostasy, Sir Arthur Keith responded with bitter irony: "This is one way of getting rid of facts which do not fit into a preconceived theory; the usual way pursued by men of science is, not to get rid of facts, but frame theory to fit them."

Moreover, had anyone been inclined to pursue the matter, there were published grounds for suspecting fraud from the start. A dental anatomist, C.W. Lyne, stated that the canine found by Teilhard was a young tooth, just erupted before Piltdown's death, and that its intensity of wear could not be reconciled with its age. Others voiced strong doubts about the ancient manufacture of Piltdown's tools. In amateur circles of Sussex, some of Dawson's colleagues concluded that Piltdown must be a fake, but they did not publish their beliefs.

If we are to learn anything about the nature of scientific inquiry from Piltdown—rather than just reveling in the joys of gossip—we will have to resolve the paradox of its easy acceptance. I think that I can identify at least four categories of reasons for the ready welcome accorded to such a misfit by all the greatest English paleontologists. All four contravene the usual mythology about scientific practice—that facts are "hard" and primary and that scientific understanding increases by patient collection and sifting of these objective bits of pure information. Instead, they display science as a human activity, motivated by hope, cultural prejudice, and the pursuit of glory, yet stumbling in its erratic path toward a better understanding of nature.

The imposition of strong hope upon dubious evidence. Before Piltdown, English paleoanthropology was mired in a limbo now occupied by students of extraterrestrial life: endless fields for speculation and no direct evidence. Beyond some flint "cultures" of doubtful human workmanship and some bones strongly suspected as products of recent interments into ancient gravels, England knew nothing of its most ancient ancestors. France, on the other hand, had been blessed with a superabundance of Neanderthals, Cro-Magnons and their associated art and tools. French anthropologists delighted in rubbing English noses with this marked disparity of evidence. Piltdown could not have been better designed to turn the tables. It seemed to predate Neanderthal by a considerable stretch of time. If human fossils had a fully modern cranium hundreds of thousands of years before beetle-browed Neanderthal appeared, then Piltdown must be our ancestor and the French Neanderthals a side branch. Smith Woodward proclaimed: "The Neanderthal race was a degenerate offshoot of early man while surviving modern man may have arisen directly from the primitive source of which the Piltdown skull provides the first discovered evidence." This international rivalry has often been mentioned by Piltdown's commentators, but a variety of equally important factors have usually escaped notice.

Reduction of anomaly by fit with cultural biases. A human cranium with an ape's jaw strikes us today as sufficiently incongruous to merit strong suspicion. Not so in 1913. At that time, many leading paleontologists maintained an a priori preference largely cultural in origin, for "brain primacy" in human evolution. The argument rested on a false inference from contemporary importance to historical priority: we rule today by virtue of our intelligence. Therefore, in our evolution, an enlarged brain must have preceded and inspired all other alterations of our body. We should expect to find human ancestors with enlarged, perhaps nearly modern, brains and a distinctly simian body. (Ironically, nature followed an opposite path. Our earliest ancestors, the australopithecines, were fully erect but still small brained.) Thus, Piltdown neatly matched a widely anticipated result. Grafton Elliot Smith wrote in 1924:

> The outstanding interest of the Piltdown skull is in the confirmation it affords of the view that in the evolution of Man the brain led the way. It is the veriest truism that Man has emerged from the simian state in virtue of the enrichment of the structure of his mind. . . . The brain attained what may be termed the human rank at a time when the jaws and face, and no doubt the body also, still retained much of the uncouthness of Man's simian ancestors. In other words, Man at first . . . was merely an Ape with an overgrown brain. The importance of the Piltdown skull lies in the fact that it affords tangible confirmation of these inferences.

Piltdown also buttressed some all too familiar racial views among white Europeans. In the 1930s and 1940s, following the discovery of Peking man in strata approximately equal in age with the Piltdown gravels, phyletic trees based on Piltdown and affirming the antiquity of white supremacy began to appear in the literature (although they were never adopted by Piltdown's chief champions, Smith Woodward, Smith, and Keith). Peking man (originally called *Sinanthropus,* but now placed in *Homo erectus*) lived in China with a brain two-thirds modern size, while Piltdown man, with its fully developed brain, inhabited England. If Piltdown, as the earliest Englishman, was the progenitor of white races, while other hues must trace their ancestry to *Homo erectus,* then whites crossed the threshold to full humanity long before other people. As longer residents in this exalted state, whites must excel in the arts of civilization.

Reduction of anomaly by matching fact to expectation. We know, in ret-rospect, that Piltdown had a human cranium and an ape's jaw. As such, it provides an ideal opportunity for testing what scientists do when faced with uncomfortable anomaly. G.E. Smith and others may have advo-cated an evolutionary head start for the brain, but no one dreamed of an independence so complete that brains might become fully human before jaws changed at all! Piltdown was distressingly too good to be true.

If Keith was right in his taunt to Weidenreich, then Piltdown's champions should have modeled their theories to the uncomfortable fact of a human cranium and an ape's jaw. Instead, they modeled the "facts" — another illustration that information always reaches us through the strong filters of culture, hope, and expectation. As a persistent theme in "pure" description of the Piltdown remains, we learn from all its major supporters that the skull, although remarkably modern, contains a suite of definitely simian characters! Smith Woodward, in fact, origi-nally estimated the cranial capacity at a mere 1,070 cc (compared with a modern average of 1,400 to 1,500), although Keith later convinced him to raise the figure nearer to the low end of our modern spectrum. Graf-ton Elliot Smith, describing the brain cast in the original paper of 1913, found unmistakable signs of incipient expansion in areas that mark the higher mental faculties in modern brains. He concluded: "We must re-gard this as being the most primitive and most simian human brain so far recorded; one, moreover, such as might reasonably have been ex-pected to be associated in one and the same individual with the mandible which so definitely indicates the zoological rank of its original posses-sor." Just a year before Oakley's revelation, Sir Arthur Keith wrote in his last major work (1948): "His forehead was like that of the orang, devoid of a supraorbital torus; in its modeling his frontal bone presented many points of resemblance to that of the orang of Borneo and Sumatra." Modern *Homo sapiens,* I hasten to add, also lacks a supraorbital torus, or brow ridge.

Careful examination of the jaw also revealed a set of remarkably human features for such an apish jaw (beyond the forged wear of the teeth). Sir Arthur Keith repeatedly emphasized, for example, that the teeth were inserted into the jaw in a human, rather than a simian, fashion.

Prevention of discovery by practice. In former years, the British Mu-seum did not occupy the vanguard in maintaining open and accessible collections — a happy trend of recent years, and one that has helped to lift the odor of mustiness (literally and figuratively) from major research museums. Like the stereotype of a librarian who protects books by guarding them from use, Piltdown's keepers severely restricted access to the original bones. Researchers were often permitted to look but not touch; only the set of plaster casts could be handled. Everyone praised the casts for their accuracy of proportion and detail, but the detection of fraud required access to the originals — artificial staining and wear of teeth cannot be discovered in plaster. Louis Leakey writes in his autobiography:

> As I write this book in 1972 and ask myself how it was that the forgery remained unmasked for so many years, I have turned my mind back to 1933, when I first went to see Dr. Bather, Smith Woodward's successor. . . . I told him that I wished to make a careful examination of the Piltdown fossils, since I was preparing a textbook on early man. I was taken into the basement to be shown the specimens, which were lifted out of a safe and laid on a table. Next to each fossil was an excellent cast. I was not allowed to handle the originals in any way, but merely to look at them and satisfy myself that the casts were really good replicas. Then, abruptly, the originals were removed and locked up again, and I was left for the rest of the morning with only the casts to study.
>
> It is my belief now that it was under these conditions that all visiting scientists were permitted to examine the Piltdown specimens, and that the situation changed only when they came under the care of my friend and contemporary Kenneth Oakley. He did not see the necessity of treating the fragments as if they were the crown jewels but, rather, considered them simply as important fossils — to be looked after carefully, but from which the maximum scientific evidence should be obtained.

Henry Fairfield Osborn, although not known as a generous man, paid almost obsequious homage to Smith Woodward in his treatise on the historical path of human progress, *Man Rises to Parnassus* (1927). He had been a skeptic before his visit to the British Museum in 1921. Then, on Sunday morning, July 24, "after attending a most memorable service in Westminster Abbey," Osborn "repaired to the British Museum to see the fossil remains of the now thoroughly vindicated Dawn Man of Great Britain." (He, at least, as head of the American Museum of Natural History, got to see the originals.) Osborn swiftly converted and proclaimed Piltdown "a discovery of transcendent importance to the prehistory of man." He then added: "We have to be reminded over and over again that Nature is full of paradoxes and that the order of the universe is not the human order." Yet Osborn had seen little but the human order on two levels — the comedy of fraud and the subtler, yet ineluctable, imposition of theory upon nature. Somehow, I am not distressed that the human order must veil all our interactions with the universe, for the veil is translucent, however strong its texture.

POSTSCRIPT

Our fascination with Piltdown never seems to abate. This article, published originally in March, 1979, elicited a flurry of correspondence, some acerbic, some congratulatory. It centered, of course, upon Teilhard. I was not trying to be cute by writing at length about Teilhard while stating briefly that Dawson acting alone accounts best for the facts. The case against Dawson had been made admirably by Weiner, and I had nothing to add to it. I continued to regard Weiner's as the most probable hypothesis. But I also believed that the only reasonable alternative (since the second Piltdown site established Dawson's complicity in my view) was a coconspiracy — an accomplice for Dawson. The other current proposals, involving Sollas or even G.E. Smith himself, seemed to me so improbable or off-the-wall that I wondered why so little attention had focussed upon the only recognized scientist who had been with Dawson from the start — especially since several of Teilhard's prominent colleagues in vertebrate paleontology harbored private thoughts (or had made cryptically worded public statements) about his possible role.

Ashley Montagu wrote on December 3, 1979, and told me that he had broken the news to Teilhard himself after Oakley's revelation of the fraud — and that Teilhard's astonishment seemed too genuine to represent dissembling: "I feel sure you're wrong about Teilhard. I knew him well, and, in fact, was the first to tell him, the day after it was announced in *The New York Times,* of the hoax. His reaction could hardly have been faked. I have not the slightest doubt that the faker was Dawson." In Paris last September, I spoke with several of Teilhard's contemporaries and scientific colleagues, including Pierre P. Grassé and Jean Piveteau; all regarded any thought of his complicity as monstrous. Père Francois Russo, S.J., later sent me a copy of the letter that Teilhard wrote to Kenneth P. Oakley after Oakley had exposed the fraud. He hoped that this document would assuage my doubts about his coreligionist. Instead my doubts intensified; for, in this letter, Teilhard made a fatal slip. Intrigued by my new role as sleuth, I visited Kenneth Oakley in England on April 16, 1980. He showed me additional documents of Teilhard, and shared other doubts with me. I now believe that the balance of evidence clearly implicates Teilhard as a coconspirator with Dawson in the Piltdown plot. I will present the entire case in *Natural History Magazine* in the summer or fall of 1980; but for now, let me mention the internal evidence from Teilhard's first letter to Oakley alone.

Teilhard begins the letter by expressing satisfaction. "I congratulate you most sincerely on your solution of the Piltdown problem . . . I am fundamentally pleased by your conclusions, in spite of the fact that, sentimentally speaking, it spoils one of my brightest and earliest paleontological memories." He continues with his thoughts on "the psychological riddle," or whodunit. He agrees with all others in dismissing Smith

Woodward, but he also refuses to implicate Dawson, citing his thorough knowledge of Dawson's character and abilities: "He was a methodical and enthusiastic character . . . In addition, his deep friendship for Sir Arthur makes it almost unthinkable that he should have systematically deceived his associate several years. When we were in the field, I never noticed anything suspicious in his behavior." Teilhard ends by proposing, halfheartedly by his own admission, that the whole affair might have been an accident engendered when an amateur collector threw out some ape bones onto a spoil heap that also contained some human skull fragments (although Teilhard does not tell us how such a hypothesis could possibly account for the same association two miles away at the second Piltdown site).

Teilhard's slip occurs in his description of the second Piltdown find. Teilhard writes: "He just brought me to the site of Locality 2 and explained me (sic) that he had found the isolated molar and the small pieces of skull in the heaps of rubble and pebbles raked at the surface of the field." Now we know (see Weiner, p. 142) that Dawson did take Teilhard to the second site for a prospecting trip in 1913. He also took Smith Woodward there in 1914. But neither visit led to any discovery; no fossils were found at the second site until 1915. Dawson wrote to Smith Woodward on January 20, 1915 to announce the discovery of two cranial fragments. In July 1915, he wrote again with good news about the discovery of a molar tooth. Smith Woodward assumed (and stated in print) that Dawson had unearthed the specimens in 1915 (see Weiner, p. 144). Dawson became seriously ill later in 1915 and died the next year. Smith Woodward never obtained more precise information from him about the second find. Now, the damning point: Teilhard states explicitly, in the letter quoted above, that Dawson told him about both the tooth and the skull fragments of the second site. But Claude Cuénot, Teilhard's biographer, states that Teilhard was called up for service in December, 1914; and we know that he was at the front on January 22, 1915 (pp. 22–23). But if Dawson did not "officially" discover the molar until July, 1915, how could Teilhard have known about it *unless he was involved in the hoax*. I regard it as unlikely that Dawson would show the material to an innocent Teilhard in 1913 and then withhold it from Smith Woodward for two years (especially after taking Smith Woodward to the second site for two days of prospecting in 1914). Teilhard and Smith Woodward were friends and might have compared notes at any time; such an inconsistency on Dawson's part could have blown his cover entirely.

Second, Teilhard states in his letter to Oakley that he did not meet Dawson until 1911: "I knew Dawson very well, since I worked with him and Sir Arthur three or four times at Piltdown (after a chance meeting in a quarry near Hastings in 1911)." Yet it is certain that Teilhard met Dawson during the spring or summer of 1909 (see Weiner, p. 90). Dawson introduced Teilhard to Smith Woodward, and Teilhard submitted some fossils he had found, including a rare tooth of an early mammal, to Smith Woodward late in 1909. When Smith Woodward described this material before the Geological Society of London in 1911, Dawson, in the discussion following Smith Woodward's talk, paid tribute to the "patient and skilled assistance" given to him by Teilhard and another priest since 1909. I don't regard this as a damning point. A first meeting in 1911 would still be early enough for complicity (Dawson "found" his first piece of the Piltdown skull in the autumn of 1911, although he states that a workman had given him a fragment "some years" earlier), and I would never hold a mistake of two years against a man who tried to remember the event forty years later. Still, a later (and incorrect) date, right upon the heels of Dawson's find, certainly averts suspicion.

Moving away from the fascination of whodunit to the theme of my original essay (why did anyone ever believe it in the first place), another colleague sent me an interesting article from *Nature* (the leading scientific periodical in England), November 13, 1913, from the midst of the initial discussions. In it, David Waterston of King's College, University of London, correctly (and definitely) stated that the skull was human, the jaw an ape's. He concludes: "It seems to me to be as inconsequent to refer the mandible and the cranium to the same individual as it would be to articulate a chimpanzee foot with the bones of an essentially human thigh and leg." The correct explanation had been available from the start, but hope, desire, and prejudice prevented its acceptance.

FOR DISCUSSION AND WRITING

1. Briefly explain the four reasons that Gould advances for the success of the Piltdown hoax.

2. Summarize the data that supported the authenticity of the Piltdown remains. What was the first incontrovertible evidence that Piltdown man was a fraud? Once it was known that Piltdown was inauthentic, what other evidence that the fossils were not real became readily apparent?

3. Summarize the structure of Dawson's argument in favor of the authenticity of Piltdown man. (Claim? Evidence? Backing? Qualification?)

4. Summarize the structure of Gould's argument.

5. In your opinion, was Teilhard de Chardin aware of the hoax? Give the backing for your claim.

6. What level of world knowledge outside the field of paleontology does Gould presume that his readers possess? Does a reader require at least some knowledge of paleontology in order to appreciate the essay? Explain.

7. The essay seems to have two main points. What are they? Do you think that multiple gists necessarily make a piece of writing more confusing? Explain.

8. Why does Gould believe Dawson and Teilhard perpetrated the hoax? Were you interested in the reasons that Gould advances for their actions? Why, or why not? Were the purposes credible?

9. What cultural and intellectual ideas of the time led the experts to believe in Piltdown man?

10. According to Gould, what should be the relationship between facts and theory?

11. Gould gives one example in which the scientists actually changed a "fact" in their rush to believe in the Piltdown man. What fact was changed?

12. Although several scientists were very close to discovering the full truth of the case, it appears from the information supplied by Gould that not one of the authorities who suspected the hoax ever attempted to duplicate it himself. Why do you think that is so?

THE CREATION OF PATRIARCHY

Gerda Lerner

> This essay interprets history from the feminist point of view. Until
> recently, history in the West was almost always a story told by men:
> *Charles Austin* Beard, *James Anthony* Froude, *Edward* Gibbon, *Thomas
> Babington* Macaulay, *Arnold* Toynbee, and *George Macaulay* Trevelyan come
> to mind when one thinks about the "standard" historians. Studies such as
> "The Creation of Patriarchy" give us an important new way of looking at
> our past.
>
> Gerda Lerner is a distinguished academic, Robinson-Edwards Professor
> of History and Senior Distinguished Professor at the University of Wiscon-
> sin in Madison. She is a former president of the Organization of American
> Historians and the author of six books on the place of women in history,
> including *Black Women in White America, The Female Experience: An Ameri-
> can Documentary,* and *The Majority Finds Its Past: Placing Women in History*.
>
> In the selection that follows—from her 1986 study, *The Creation of Pa-
> triarchy*—Gerda Lerner argues that "even where women appear to be mar-
> ginal, this is the result of patriarchal intervention" and that "the system of
> patriarchy is a historic construct; it has a beginning; it will have an end."
> As you read, pay attention to the nature of Lerner's argument. What meth-
> ods does she use to convince you, the reader, of her point? Are there
> weaknesses in the argument? Are there particular strengths?

Patriarchy is a historic creation formed by men and women in a
process which took nearly 2500 years to its completion. In its earliest
form patriarchy appeared as the archaic state. The basic unit of its organization was the patriarchal family, which both expressed and constantly
generated its rules and values. We have seen how integrally definitions of
gender affected the formation of the state. Let us briefly review the way
in which gender became created, defined, and established.

The roles and behavior deemed appropriate to the sexes were expressed in values, customs, laws, and social roles. They also, and very
importantly, were expressed in leading metaphors, which became part of
the cultural construct and explanatory system.

The sexuality of women, consisting of their sexual and their reproductive capacities and services, was commodified even prior to the creation of Western civilization. The development of agriculture in the
Neolithic period fostered the inter-tribal "exchange of women," not only
as a means of avoiding incessant warfare by the cementing of marriage
alliances but also because societies with more women could produce
more children. In contrast to the economic needs of hunting/gathering
societies, agriculturists could use the labor of children to increase production and accumulate surpluses. Men-as-a-group had rights in women
which women-as-a-group did not have in men. Women themselves be-

came a resource, acquired by men much as the land was acquired by men. Women were exchanged or bought in marriages for the benefit of their families; later, they were conquered or bought in slavery, where their sexual services were part of their labor and where their children were the property of their masters. In every known society it was women of conquered tribes who were first enslaved, whereas men were killed. It was only after men had learned how to enslave the women of groups who could be defined as strangers, that they learned how to enslave men of those groups and, later, subordinates from within their own societies.

Thus, the enslavement of women, combining both racism and sexism, preceded the formation of classes and class oppression. Class differences were, at their very beginnings, expressed and constituted in terms of patriarchal relations. Class is not a separate construct from gender; rather, class is expressed in generic terms.

By the second millennium B.C. in Mesopotamian societies, the daughters of the poor were sold into marriage or prostitution in order to advance the economic interests of their families. The daughters of men of property could command a bride price, paid by the family of the groom to the family of the bride, which frequently enabled the bride's family to secure more financially advantageous marriages for their sons, thus improving the family's economic position. If a husband or father could not pay his debt, his wife and children could be used as pawns, becoming debt slaves to the creditor. These conditions were so firmly established by 1750 B.C. that Hammurabic law made a decisive improvement in the lot of debt pawns by limiting their terms of service to three years, where earlier it had been for life.

The product of this commodification of women — bride price, sale price, and children — was appropriated by men. It may very well represent the first accumulation of private property. The enslavement of women of conquered tribes became not only a status symbol for nobles and warriors, but it actually enabled the conquerors to acquire tangible wealth through selling or trading the product of the slaves' labor and their reproductive product, slave children.

Claude Lévi-Strauss, to whom we owe the concept of "the exchange of women," speaks of the reification of women, which occurred as its consequence. But it is not women who are reified and commodified, it is women's sexuality and reproductive capacity which is so treated. The distinction is important. Women never became "things," nor were they so perceived. Women, no matter how exploited and abused, retained their power to act and to choose to the same, often very limited extent, as men of their group. But women *always and to this day* lived in a relatively greater state of un-freedom than did men. Since their sexuality, an aspect of their body, was controlled by others, women were not only actually disadvantaged but psychologically restrained in a very special way. For women, as for men of subordinate and oppressed groups, history consisted of their struggle for emancipation and freedom from necessity. But women struggled against different forms of oppression and dominance than did men, and their struggle, up to this time, has lagged behind that of men.

The first gender-defined social role for women was to be those who were exchanged in marriage transactions. The obverse gender role for men was to be those who did the exchanging or who defined the terms of the exchanges.

Another gender-defined role for women was that of the "stand-in" wife, which became established and institutionalized for women of elite groups. This role gave such women considerable power and privileges, but it depended on their attachment to elite men and was based, minimally, on their satisfactory performance in rendering these men sexual and reproductive services. If a woman failed to meet these demands, she was quickly replaced and thereby lost all her privileges and standing.

The gender-defined role of warrior led men to acquire power over   10
men and women of conquered tribes. Such war-induced conquest usually occurred over people already differentiated from the victors by race, ethnicity, or simple tribal difference. In its ultimate origin, "difference" as a distinguishing mark between the conquered and the conquerors was based on the first clearly observable difference, that between the sexes. Men had learned how to assert and exercise power over people slightly different from themselves in the primary exchange of women. In so doing, men acquired the knowledge necessary to elevate "difference" of whatever kind into a criterion for dominance.

From its inception in slavery, class dominance took different forms for enslaved men and women: men were primarily exploited as workers; women were always exploited as workers, as providers of sexual services, and as reproducers. The historical record of every slave society offers evidence for this generalization. The sexual exploitation of lower-class women by upper-class men can be shown in antiquity, under feudalism, in the bourgeois households of nineteenth- and twentieth-century Europe, in the complex sex/race relations between women of the colonized countries and their male colonizers — it is ubiquitous and pervasive. For women, sexual exploitation is the very mark of class exploitation.

At any given moment in history, each "class" is constituted of two distinct classes — men and women.

The class position of women became consolidated and actualized through their sexual relationships. It always was expressed within degrees of unfreedom on a spectrum ranging from the slave woman, whose sexual and reproductive capacity was commodified as she herself was; to the slave-concubine, whose sexual performance might elevate her own status or that of her children; then to the "free" wife, whose sexual and reproductive services to one man of the upper classes entitled her to property and legal rights. While each of these groups had vastly different obligations and privileges in regard to property, law, and economic resources, they shared the unfreedom of being sexually and reproductively controlled by men. We can best express the complexity of women's various levels of dependency and freedom by comparing each woman with her brother and considering how the sister's and brother's lives and opportunities would differ.

Class for men was and is based on their relationship to the means of production: those who owned the means of production could dominate those who did not. The owners of the means of production also acquired the commodity of female sexual services, both from women of their own class and from women of the subordinate classes. In Ancient Mesopotamia, in classical antiquity, and in slave societies, dominant males also acquired, as property, the product of the reproductive capacity of subordinate women—children, to be worked, traded, married off, or sold as slaves, as the case might be. For women, class is mediated through their sexual ties to a man. It is through the man that women have access to or are denied access to the means of production and to resources. It is through their sexual behavior that they gain access to class. "Respectable women" gain access to class through their fathers and husbands, but breaking the sexual rules can at once declass them. The gender definition of sexual "deviance" marks a woman as "not respectable," which in fact consigns her to the lowest class status possible. Women who withhold heterosexual services (such as single women, nuns, lesbians) are connected to the dominant man in their family of origin and through him gain access to resources. Or, alternatively, they are declassed. In some historical periods, convents and other enclaves for single women created some sheltered space, in which such women could function and retain their respectability. But the vast majority of single women are, by definition, marginal and dependent on the protection of male kin. This is true throughout historical time up to the middle of the twentieth century in the Western world and still is true in most of the underdeveloped countries today. The group of independent, self-supporting women which exists in every society is small and usually highly vulnerable to economic disaster.

Economic oppression and exploitation are based as much on the commodification of female sexuality and the appropriation by men of women's labor power and her reproductive power as on the direct economic acquisition of resources and persons.

The archaic state in the Ancient Near East emerged in the second millennium B.C. from the twin roots of men's sexual dominance over women and the exploitation by some men of others. From its inception,

15

the archaic state was organized in such a way that the dependence of male family heads on the king or the state bureaucracy was compensated for by their dominance over their families. Male family heads allocated the resources of society to their families the way the state allocated the resources of society to them. The control of male family heads over their female kin and minor sons was as important to the existence of the state as was the control of the king over his soldiers. This is reflected in the various compilations of Mesopotamian laws, especially in the large number of laws dealing with the regulation of female sexuality.

From the second millennium B.C. forward control over the sexual behavior of citizens has been a major means of social control in every state society. Conversely, class hierarchy is constantly reconstituted in the family through sexual dominance. Regardless of the political or economic system, the kind of personality which can function in a hierarchical system is created and nurtured within the patriarchal family.

The patriarchal family has been amazingly resilient and varied in different times and places. Oriental patriarchy encompassed polygamy and female enclosure in harems. Patriarchy in classical antiquity and in its European development was based upon monogamy, but in all its forms a double sexual standard, which disadvantages women, was part of the system. In modern industrial states, such as in the United States, property relations within the family develop along more egalitarian lines than those in which the father holds absolute power, yet the economic and sexual power relations within the family do not necessarily change. In some cases, sexual relations are more egalitarian, while economic relations remain patriarchal; in other cases the pattern is reversed. In all cases, however, such changes within the family do not alter the basic male dominance in the public realm, in institutions and in government.

The family not merely mirrors the order in the state and educates its children to follow it, it also creates and constantly reinforces that order.

It should be noted that when we speak of relative improvements in   20
the status of women in a given society, this frequently means only that we are seeing improvements in the degree in which their situation affords them opportunities to exert some leverage within the system of patriarchy. Where women have relatively more economic power, they are able to have somewhat more control over their lives than in societies where they have no economic power. Similarly, the existence of women's groups, associations, or economic networks serves to increase the ability of women to counteract the dictates of their particular patriarchal system. Some anthropologists and historians have called this relative improvement women's "freedom." Such a designation is illusory and unwarranted. Reforms and legal changes, while ameliorating the condition of women and an essential part of the process of emancipating them,

will not basically change patriarchy. Such reforms need to be integrated within a vast cultural revolution in order to transform patriarchy and thus abolish it.

The system of patriarchy can function only with the cooperation of women. This cooperation is secured by a variety of means: gender indoctrination; educational deprivation; the denial to women of knowledge of their history; the dividing of women, one from the other, by defining "respectability" and "deviance" according to women's sexual activities; by restraints and outright coercion; by discrimination in access to economic resources and political power; and by awarding class privileges to conforming women.

For nearly four thousand years women have shaped their lives and acted under the umbrella of patriarchy, specifically a form of patriarchy best described as paternalistic dominance. The term describes the relationship of a dominant group, considered superior, to a subordinate group, considered inferior, in which the dominance is mitigated by mutual obligations and reciprocal rights. The dominated exchange submission for protection, unpaid labor for maintenance. In the patriarchal family, responsibilities and obligations are not equally distributed among those to be protected: the male children's subordination to the father's dominance is temporary; it lasts until they themselves become heads of households. The subordination of female children and of wives is lifelong. Daughters can escape it only if they place themselves as wives under the dominance/protection of another man. The basis of paternalism is an unwritten contract for exchange: economic support and protection given by the male for subordination in all matters, sexual service, and unpaid domestic service given by the female. Yet the relationship frequently continues in fact and in law, even when the male partner has defaulted on his obligation.

It was a rational choice for women, under conditions of public powerlessness and economic dependency, to choose strong protectors for themselves and their children. Women always shared the class privileges of men of their class *as long as they were under "the protection" of a man.* For women, other than those of the lower classes, the "reciprocal agreement" went like this: in exchange for your sexual, economic, political, and intellectual subordination to men you may share the power of men of your class to exploit men and women of the lower class. In class society it is difficult for people who themselves have some power, however limited and circumscribed, to see themselves also as deprived and subordinated. Class and racial privileges serve to undercut the ability of women to see themselves as part of a coherent group, which, in fact, they are not, since women uniquely of all oppressed groups occur in all strata of the society. The formation of a group consciousness of women must proceed along different lines. That is the reason why theoretical formulations, which have been appropriate to other oppressed groups, are so inadequate in explaining and conceptualizing the subordination of women.

Women have for millennia participated in the process of their own subordination because they have been psychologically shaped so as to internalize the idea of their own inferiority. The unawareness of their own history of struggle and achievement has been one of the major means of keeping women subordinate.

The connectedness of women to familial structures made any de-   25 velopment of female solidarity and group cohesiveness extremely problematic. Each individual woman was linked to her male kin in her family of origin through ties which implied specific obligations. Her indoctrination, from early childhood on, emphasized her obligation not only to make an economic contribution to the kin and household but also to accept a marriage partner in line with family interests. Another way of saying this is to say that sexual control of women was linked to paternalistic protection and that, in the various stages of her life, she exchanged male protectors, but she never outgrew the childlike state of being subordinate and under protection.

Other oppressed classes and groups were impelled toward group consciousness by the very conditions of their subordinate status. The slave could clearly mark a line between the interests and bonds to his/ her own family and the ties of subservience/protection linking him/her with the master. In fact, protection by slave parents of their own family against the master was one of the most important causes of slave resistance. "Free" women, on the other hand, learned early that their kin would cast them out, should they ever rebel against their dominance. In traditional and peasant societies there are many recorded instances of female family members tolerating and even participating in the chastisement, torture, even death of a girl who had transgressed against the family "honor." In Biblical times, the entire community gathered to stone the adulteress to death. Similar practices prevailed in Sicily, Greece, and Albania into the twentieth century. Bangladesh fathers and husbands cast out their daughters and wives who had been raped by invading soldiers, consigning them to prostitution. Thus, women were often forced to flee from one "protector" to the other, their "freedom" frequently defined only by their ability to manipulate between these protectors.

Most significant of all the impediments toward developing group consciousness for women was the absence of a tradition which would reaffirm the independence and autonomy of women at any period in the past. There had never been any woman or group of women who had lived without male protection, as far as most women knew. There had never been any group of persons like them who had done anything significant for themselves. Women had no history—so they were told;

so they believed. Thus, ultimately, it was men's hegemony over the symbol system which most decisively disadvantaged women.

Male hegemony over the symbol system took two forms: educational deprivation of women and male monopoly on definition. The former happened inadvertently, more the consequence of class dominance and the accession of military elites to power. Throughout historical times, there have always been large loopholes for women of the elite classes, whose access to education was one of the major aspects of their class privilege. But male dominance over definition has been deliberate and pervasive, and the existence of individual highly educated and creative women has, for nearly four thousand years, left barely an imprint on it.

We have seen how men appropriated and then transformed the major symbols of female power: the power of the Mother-Goddess and the fertility-goddesses. We have seen how men constructed theologies based on the counterfactual metaphor of male procreativity and redefined female existence in a narrow and sexually dependent way. We have seen, finally, how the very metaphors for gender have expressed the male as norm and the female as deviant; the male as whole and powerful, the female as unfinished, mutilated, and lacking in autonomy. On the basis of such symbolic constructs, embedded in Greek philosophy, the Judeo-Christian theologies, and the legal tradition on which Western civilization is built, men have explained the world in their own terms and defined the important questions so as to make themselves the center of discourse.

By making the term "man" subsume "woman" and arrogate to 30 itself the representation of all of humanity, men have built a conceptual error of vast proportion into all of their thought. By taking the half for the whole, they have not only missed the essence of whatever they are describing, but they have distorted it in such a fashion that they cannot see it correctly. As long as men believed the earth to be flat, they could not understand its reality, its function, and its actual relationship to other bodies in the universe. As long as men believe their experiences, their viewpoint, and their ideas represent all of human experience and all of human thought, they are not only unable to define correctly in the abstract, but they are unable to describe reality accurately.

The androcentric fallacy, which is built into all the mental constructs of Western civilization, cannot be rectified simply by "adding women." What it demands for rectification is a radical restructuring of thought and analysis which once and for all accepts the fact that humanity consists in equal parts of men and women and that the experiences, thoughts, and insights of both sexes must be represented in every generalization that is made about human beings.

Today, historical development has for the first time created the necessary conditions by which large groups of women—finally, all women—can emancipate themselves from subordination. Since women's thought has been imprisoned in a confining and erroneous patriarchal framework, the transforming of the consciousness of women about ourselves and our thought is a precondition for change.

We have opened this book with a discussion of the significance of history for human consciousness and psychic well-being. History gives meaning to human life and connects each life to immortality, but history has yet another function. In preserving the collective past and reinterpreting it to the present, human beings define their potential and explore the limits of their possibilities. We learn from the past not only what people before us did and thought and intended, but we also learn how they failed and erred. From the days of the Babylonian king-lists forward, the record of the past has been written and interpreted by men and has primarily focused on the deeds, actions, and intentions of males. With the advent of writing, human knowledge moved forward by tremendous leaps and at a much faster rate than ever before. While, as we have seen, women had participated in maintaining the oral tradition and religious and cultic functions in the preliterate period and for almost a millennium thereafter, their educational disadvantaging and their symbolic dethroning had a profound impact on their future development. The gap between the experience of those who could or might (in the case of lower-class males) participate in the creating of the symbol system and those who merely acted but did not interpret became increasingly greater.

In her brilliant work *The Second Sex*,[1] Simone de Beauvoir focused on the historical end product of this development. She described man as autonomous and transcendent, woman as immanent. But her analysis ignored history. Explaining "why women lack concrete means for organizing themselves into a unit" in defense of their own interests, she stated flatly: "They [women] have no past, no history, no religion of their own." De Beauvoir is right in her observation that woman has not "transcended," if by transcendence one means the definition and interpretation of human knowledge. But she was wrong in thinking that therefore woman has had no history. Two decades of Women's History scholarship have disproven this fallacy by unearthing an unending list of sources and uncovering and interpreting the hidden history of women. This process of creating a history of women is still ongoing and will

[1]Simone de Beauvoir, *The Second Sex* (New York, 1953), introduction, xxii, both quotes. De Beauvoir based this erroneous generalization on the androcentric historical scholarship available to her at the time of the writing of her book, but has to date not corrected it.

need to continue for a long time. We are only beginning to understand its implications.

The myth that women are marginal to the creation of history and   *35* civilization has profoundly affected the psychology of women and men. It has given men a skewed and essentially erroneous view of their place in human society and in the universe. For women, as shown in the case of Simone de Beauvoir, who surely is one of the best-educated women of her generation, history seemed for millennia to offer only negative lessons and no precedent for significant action, heroism, or liberating example. Most difficult of all was the seeming absence of a tradition which would reaffirm the independence and autonomy of women. It seemed that there had never been any woman or group of women who had lived without male protection. It is significant that all the important examples to the contrary were expressed in myth and fable: amazons, dragon-slayers, women with magic powers. But in real life, women had no history — so they were told and so they believed. And because they had no history they had no future alternatives.

In one sense, class struggle can be described as a struggle for the control of the symbol systems of a given society. The oppressed group, while it shares in and partakes of the leading symbols controlled by the dominant, also develops its own symbols. These become in time of revolutionary change, important forces in the creation of alternatives. Another way of saying this is that revolutionary ideas can be generated only when the oppressed have an alternative to the symbol and meaning system of those who dominate them. Thus, slaves living in an environment controlled by their masters and physically subject to the masters' total control, could maintain their humanity and at times set limits to the masters' power by holding on to their own "culture." Such a culture consisted of collective memories, carefully kept alive, of a prior state of freedom and of alternatives to the masters' ritual, symbols, and beliefs. What was decisive for the individual was the ability to identify him/ herself with a state different from that of enslavement or subordination. Thus, all males, whether enslaved or economically or racially oppressed, could still identify with those like them — other males — who showed transcendent qualities in the symbol systems of the master. No matter how degraded, each male slave or peasant was like to the master in his relationship to God. This was not the case for women. Quite the contrary — in Western civilization up to the time of the Protestant Reformation no woman, no matter how elevated or privileged, could feel her humanity reinforced and confirmed by imagining persons like her — female persons — in positions of intellectual authority and in direct relationship to God.

Where there is no precedent, one cannot imagine alternatives to existing conditions. It is this feature of male hegemony which has been most damaging to women and has ensured their subordinate status for millennia. The denial to women of their history has reinforced their acceptance of the ideology of patriarchy and has undermined the individual woman's sense of self-worth. Men's version of history, legitimized as the "universal truth," has presented women as marginal to civilization and as the victim of historical process. To be so presented and to believe it is almost worse than being entirely forgotten. The picture is false, on both counts, as we now know, but women's progress through history has been marked by their struggle against this disabling distortion.

Moreover, for more than 2500 years women have been educationally disadvantaged and deprived of the conditions under which to develop abstract thought. Obviously thought is not based on sex; the capacity for thought is inherent in humanity; it can be fostered or discouraged, but it cannot ultimately be restrained. This is certainly true for thought generated by and concerned with daily living, the level of thought on which most men and women operate all their lives. But the generating of abstract thought and of new conceptual models — theory formation — is another matter. This activity depends on the individual thinker's education in the best of existing traditions and on the thinker's acceptance by a group of educated persons who, by criticism and interaction, provide "cultural prodding." It depends on having private time. Finally, it depends on the individual thinker being capable of absorbing such knowledge and then making a creative leap into a new ordering. Women, historically, have been unable to avail themselves of all of these necessary preconditions. Educational discrimination has disadvantaged them in access to knowledge; "cultural prodding," which is institutionalized in the upper reaches of the religious and academic establishments, has been unavailable to them. Universally, women of all classes had less leisure time than men, and, due to their child-rearing and family service function, what free time they had was generally not their own. The time of thinking men, their work and study time, has since the inception of Greek philosophy been respected as private. Like Aristotle's slaves, women "who with their bodies minister to the needs of life" have for more than 2500 years suffered the disadvantages of fragmented, constantly interrupted time. Finally, the kind of character development which makes for a mind capable of seeing new connections and fashioning a new order of abstractions has been exactly the opposite of that required of women, trained to accept their subordinate and service-oriented position in society.

Yet there have always existed a tiny minority of privileged women, usually from the ruling elite, who had some access to the same kind of education as did their brothers. From the ranks of such women have come the intellectuals, the thinkers, the writers, the artists. It is such women, throughout history, who have been able to give us a female perspective, an alternative to androcentric thought. They have done so at a tremendous cost and with great difficulty.

Those women, who have been admitted to the center of intellectual   *40* activity of their day and especially in the past hundred years, academically trained women, have first had to learn "how to think like a man." In the process, many of them have so internalized that learning that they have lost the ability to conceive of alternatives. The way to think abstractly is to define precisely, to create models in the mind and generalize from them. Such thought, men have taught us, must be based on the exclusion of feelings. Women, like the poor, the subordinate, the marginals, have close knowledge of ambiguity, of feelings mixed with thought, of value judgments coloring abstractions. Women have always experienced the reality of self and community, known it, and shared it with each other. Yet, living in a world in which they are devalued, their experience bears the stigma of insignificance. Thus they have learned to mistrust their own experience and devalue it. What wisdom can there be in menses? What source of knowledge in the milk-filled breast? What food for abstraction in the daily routine of feeding and cleaning? Patriarchal thought has relegated such gender-defined experiences to the realm of the "natural," the non-transcendent. Women's knowledge becomes mere "intuition," women's talk becomes "gossip." Women deal with the irredeemably particular: they experience reality daily, hourly, in their service function (taking care of food and dirt); in their constantly interruptable time; their splintered attention. Can one generalize while the particular tugs at one's sleeve? He who makes symbols and explains the world and she who takes care of his bodily and psychic needs and of his children—the gulf between them is enormous.

Historically, thinking women have had to choose between living a woman's life, with its joys, dailiness, and immediacy, and living a man's life in order to think. The choice for generations of educated women has been cruel and costly. Others have deliberately chosen an existence outside of the sex-gender system, by living alone or with other women. Some of the most significant advances in women's thought were given us by such women, whose personal struggle for an alternative mode of living infused their thinking. But such women, for most of historical time, have been forced to live on the margins of society; they were considered "deviant" and as such found it difficult to generalize from their experience to others and to win influence and approval. Why no female system-builders? Because one cannot think universals when one's self is excluded from the generic.

The social cost of having excluded women from the human enterprise of constructing abstract thought has never been reckoned. We can begin to understand the cost of it to thinking women when we accurately name what was done to us and describe, no matter how painful it may be, the ways in which we have participated in the enterprise. We have long known that rape has been a way of terrorizing us and keeping us in subjection. Now we also know that we have participated, although unwittingly, in the rape of our minds.

Creative women, writers and artists, have similarly struggled against a distorting reality. A literary canon, which defined itself by the Bible, the Greek classics, and Milton, would necessarily bury the significance and the meaning of women's literary work, as historians buried the activities of women. The effort to resurrect this meaning and to re-evaluate women's literary and artistic work is recent. Feminist literary criticism and poetics have introduced us to a reading of women's literature, which finds a hidden, deliberately "slant," yet powerful worldview. Through the reinterpretations of feminist literary critics we are uncovering among women writers of the eighteenth and nineteenth centuries a female language of metaphors, symbols, and myths. Their themes often are profoundly subversive of the male tradition. They feature criticism of the Biblical interpretation of Adam's fall; rejection of the goddess/witch dichotomy; projection or fear of the split self. The powerful aspect of woman's creativity becomes symbolized in heroines endowed with magical powers of goodness or in strong women who are banished to cellars or to live as "the madwoman in the attic." Others write in metaphors upgrading the confined domestic space, making it serve, symbolically as the world.[1]

For centuries, we find in the works of literary women a pathetic, almost desperate search for Women's History, long before historical studies as such exist. Nineteenth-century female writers avidly read the work of eighteenth-century female novelists; over and over again they read the "lives" of queens, abbesses, poets, learned women. Early "compilers" searched the Bible and all historical sources to which they had access to create weighty tomes with female heroines.

Women's literary voices, successfully marginalized and trivialized   45
by the dominant male establishment, nevertheless survived. The voices of anonymous women were present as a steady undercurrent in the oral tradition, in folksong and nursery rhymes, tales of powerful witches and good fairies. In stitchery, embroidery, and quilting women's artistic creativity expressed an alternate vision. In letters, diaries, prayers, and song the symbol-making force of women's creativity pulsed and persisted.

All of this work will be the subject of our inquiry in the next volume. How did women manage to survive under male cultural hegemony; what was their influence and impact on the patriarchal symbol system; how and under what conditions did they come to create an

[1]Sandra N. Gilbert and Susan Gubar, *The Madwoman in the Attic: The Woman Writer and the Nineteenth Century Literacy Imagination* (New Haven, 1984).

alternate, feminist world-view? These are the questions we will examine in order to chart the rise of feminist consciousness as a historical phenomenon.

Women and men have entered historical process under different conditions and have passed through it at different rates of speed. If recording, defining, and interpreting the past marks man's entry into history, this occurred for males in the third millennium B.C. It occurred for women (and only some of them) with a few notable exceptions in the nineteenth century. Until then, all History was for women pre-History.

Women's lack of knowledge of our own history of struggle and achievement has been one of the major means of keeping us subordinate. But even those of us already defining ourselves as feminist thinkers and engaged in the process of critiquing traditional systems of ideas are still held back by unacknowledged restraints embedded deeply within our psyches. Emergent woman faces a challenge to her very definition of self. How can her daring thought — naming the hitherto unnamed, asking the questions defined by all authorities as "non-existent" — how can such thought coexist with her life as woman? In stepping out of the constructs of patriarchal thought, she faces, as Mary Daly put it, "existential nothingness." And more immediately, she fears the threat of loss of communication with, approval by, and love from the man (or the men) in her life. Withdrawal of love and the designation of thinking women as "deviant" have historically been the means of discouraging women's intellectual work. In the past, and now, many emergent women have turned to other women as love objects and reinforcers of self. Heterosexual feminists, too, have throughout the ages drawn strength from their friendships with women, from chosen celibacy, or from the separation of sex from love. No thinking man has ever been threatened in his self-definition and his love life as the price for his thinking. We should not underestimate the significance of that aspect of gender control as a force restraining women from full participation in the process of creating thought systems. Fortunately, for this generation of educated women, liberation has meant the breaking of this emotional hold and the conscious reinforcement of our selves through the support of other women.

Nor is this the end of our difficulties. In line with our historic gender-conditioning, women have aimed to please and have sought to avoid disapproval. This is poor preparation for making the leap into the unknown required of those who fashion new systems. Moreover, each emergent woman has been schooled in patriarchal thought. We each hold at least one great man in our heads. The lack of knowledge of the female past has deprived us of female heroines, a fact which is only recently being corrected through the development of Women's History. So, for a long time, thinking women have refurbished the idea systems created by men, engaging in a dialogue with the great male minds in their heads. Elizabeth Cady Stanton took on the Bible, the Church fathers, the founders of the American republic. Kate Millet argued with Freud, Norman Mailer, and the liberal literary establishment; Simone de Beauvoir with Sartre, Marx, and Camus; all Marxist-Feminists are in a dialogue with Marx and Engels and some also with Freud. In this dialogue woman intends merely to accept whatever she finds useful to her in the great man's system. But in these systems woman—as a concept, a collective entity, an individual—is marginal or subsumed.

In accepting such dialogue, thinking woman stays far longer than   *50* is useful within the boundaries or the question-setting defined by the "great men." And just as long as she does, the source of new insight is closed to her.

Revolutionary thought has always been based on upgrading the experience of the oppressed. The peasant had to learn to trust in the significance of his life experience before he could dare to challenge the feudal lords. The industrial worker had to become "class-conscious," the Black "race-conscious" before liberating thought could develop into revolutionary theory. The oppressed have acted and learned simultaneously—the process of becoming the newly conscious person or group is in itself liberating. So with women.

The shift in consciousness we must make occurs in two steps: we must, at least for a time, be woman-centered. We must, as far as possible, leave patriarchal thought behind.

To be woman-centered means: asking if women were central to this argument, how would it be defined? It means ignoring all evidence of women's marginality, because, even where women appear to be marginal, this is the result of patriarchal intervention; frequently also it is merely an appearance. The basic assumption should be that it is inconceivable for anything ever to have taken place in the world in which women were not involved, except if they were prevented from participation through coercion and repression.

When using methods and concepts from traditional systems of thought, it means using them from the vantage point of the centrality of women. Women cannot be put into the empty spaces of patriarchal thought and systems—in moving to the center, they transform the system.

To step outside of patriarchal thought means: Being skeptical to-   *55* ward every known system of thought; being critical of all assumptions, ordering values and definitions.

Testing one's statement by trusting our own, the female experience. Since such experience has usually been trivialized or ignored, it means overcoming the deep-seated resistance within ourselves toward accepting ourselves and our knowledge as valid. It means getting rid of the great men in our heads and substituting for them ourselves, our sisters, our anonymous foremothers.

Being critical toward our own thought, which is, after all, thought trained in the patriarchal tradition. Finally, it means developing intellectual courage, the courage to stand alone, the courage to reach farther than our grasp, the courage to risk failure. Perhaps the greatest challenge to thinking women is the challenge to move from the desire for safety and approval to the most "unfeminine" quality of all — that of intellectual arrogance, the supreme hubris which asserts to itself the right to reorder the world. The hubris of the godmakers, the hubris of the male system-builders.

The system of patriarchy is a historic construct; it has a beginning; it will have an end. Its time seems to have nearly run its course — it no longer serves the needs of men or women and in its inextricable linkage to militarism, hierarchy, and racism it threatens the very existence of life on earth.

What will come after, what kind of structure will be the foundation for alternate forms of social organization we cannot yet know. We are living in an age of unprecedented transformation. We are in the process of becoming. But we already know that woman's mind, at last unfettered after so many millennia, will have its share in providing vision, ordering, solutions. Women at long last are demanding, as men did in the Renaissance, the right to explain, the right to define. Women, in thinking themselves out of patriarchy add transforming insights to the process of redefinition.

As long as both men and women regard the subordination of half   *60* the human race to the other as "natural," it is impossible to envision a society in which differences do not connote either dominance or subordination. The feminist critique of the patriarchal edifice of knowledge is laying the groundwork for a correct analysis of reality, one which at the very least can distinguish the whole from a part. Women's History, the essential tool in creating feminist consciousness in women, is providing the body of experience against which new theory can be tested and the ground on which women of vision can stand.

A feminist world-view will enable women and men to free their minds from patriarchal thought and practice and at last to build a world free of dominance and hierarchy, a world that is truly human.

FOR DISCUSSION AND WRITING

1. Lerner writes,

> It was only after men had learned how to enslave the women of groups who could be defined as strangers, that they learned how to enslave men of those groups and, later, subordinates from within their own societies.

> Thus, the enslavement of women, combining both racism and sexism, preceded the formation of classes and class oppression. (pars. 3–4)

Does this argument have any backing or reservations? (You will want to reread quite a few of the succeeding paragraphs to answer this question fully.)

2. The following pairs of sentences seem to be contradictory. Do you believe that they are, indeed, contradictory? (You might benefit from rereading the text in which these sentences appear.) How would you rewrite these sentences so that they would be clearer?

> Thus, the enslavement of women, combining both racism and sexism, preceded the formation of classes and class oppression. . . . Class is not a separate construct from gender; rather class is expressed in generic terms. (par. 4)

> The product of this commodification of women — bride price, sale price, and children — was appropriated by men. . . . But it is not women who are reified and commodified, it is women's sexuality and reproductive capacity which is so treated. (par. 6, 7)

> Women, no matter how exploited and abused, retained their power to act and to choose to the same, often very limited extent, as men of their group. But women *always and to this day* lived in a relatively greater state of un-freedom than did men. (par. 7)

3. What qualifications does Lerner make to her claim that "the vast majority of single women are, by definition, marginal and dependent on the protection of male kin"? (par. 14)

4. According to Lerner, how is the cooperation of women within the patriarchal system ensured?

5. Do you believe that Lerner would agree with the statement that women are an oppressed class? Explain.

6. The title of this essay could just as easily be "The Liberation from Patriarchy." Explain.

7. Lerner makes a startling pronouncement when she writes that women entered history in the nineteenth century. How does Lerner define history? Is this definition different from that which you normally use? If women's history is such a recent phenomenon, how can women ever have the rich history that Lerner's essay calls for?

8. In terms of manner, this essay is written almost in terms of a manifesto, such as the Declaration of Independence, rather than as a carefully constructed argument. Explain.

A GAME OF CHICKEN
Franklin E. Zimring and Gordon Hawkins

In the foreword to *Capital Punishment and the American Agenda,* from which the following selection is taken, the respected journalist Tom Wicker says,

> In a radical departure from other books on the death penalty in America, [Zimring and Hawkins] even argue that its abolition would not be so much a profound advance as "society . . . catching up with itself." In their view, Americans "have in fact already outgrown the social and political conditions in which capital punishment can continue to be practiced." (ix)

In his essay about boxing, Bill Brubaker raises ethical questions. Whether one is in favor or against that sport, those questions must be addressed. Regardless of one's stand on capital punishment—pro or con—one must face the issues raised by Zimring and Hawkins.

Franklin E. Zimring is professor of law and director of the Earl Warren Legal Institute at the University of California, Berkeley. Gordon Hawkins is a senior fellow of the Earl Warren Institute. He was formerly director of the Sydney University Institute of Criminology.

On August 12, 1984, these paragraphs appeared in the *New York Times:*

> With 221 condemned prisoners, Florida has the most crowded death row in the country, and the crowd is growing by 25 a year. The Department of Corrections estimates the number of condemned prisoners could grow to 300 by July 1986.
>
> The agency plans to ask the Legislature for authority to build a separate facility to house the estimated 800 condemned prisoners expected—assuming the pace of executions does not accelerate sharply—by the year 2000.[1]

These projections are remarkable. Even more remarkable is the matter-of-fact manner in which such extraordinary numbers were reported: eight hundred prisoners on death row in one of fifty states, and this in a state where the current governor is "widely known for the speed with which he signs death warrants."[2] How many will be executed? How will they be selected? What will happen next?

The circumstances of capital punishment in the United States of the 1980s are unprecedented. At the midpoint of the decade some 1,700 prisoners were held by state authorities under "active sentences of death,"

[1]Rangel, "Florida's Death Row Population Booms," *N.Y. Times,* Aug. 12, 1984, at D4, col. 3.
[2]*Id.*

cases where no outstanding court order or executive decision has reversed a death sentence following a murder conviction. The American
megaprison now has, increasingly, a mega–death row as its seventh circle. Either we are on the verge of a momentous change in American
execution policy, or we are engaged in a gruesome charade.

The enormity of the death row backlog in contemporary America
can be demonstrated in a variety of statistical comparisons. This is by far
the largest collection of the condemned in American history. It exceeds
by a factor of five the total number of executions in the United States
and Western Europe in the previous twenty-five years.[3] In many American states, if present trends in both death sentences and executions continue for a very few years, the number of those awaiting execution will
equal the number executed in the past half-century.[4]

ONE EXECUTION A DAY?

For the country as a whole, the supply of condemned prisoners
vastly exceeds any objective measure of demands for executions. Eleven
persons were executed in the United States between 1977 and the end of
1983.[5] During 1984, partially in response to a Supreme Court mandate
to curtail and expedite federal court review,[6] the annual rate of execution
in the United States reached twenty-one.[7]

Although the increase demonstrates the role that constitutional   5
courts can have on the pace of executions, even twenty-one executions a
year leaves an American prison population stocked with seventy times as
many condemned as can be executed. And this is not merely a seventy-
year supply; it is an endlessly growing stockpile. To keep pace with the
number of death sentences issued annually under state penal schemes
approved by the U.S. Supreme Court is to live in a nation that executes
about 300 per year, and perhaps one for each day of the year.

---

[3]The number executed under civil authority in the United States from January 1960
to June 20, 1984, was 211. *See* Bureau of Justice Statistics, U.S. Department of Justice,
Capital Punishment 1982, at 14, Table 1 (1984); Bureau of Justice Statistics, U.S. Department of Justice, *Bulletin: Capital Punishment 1983,* at 1 (1984). The Western world
figure was obtained from Amnesty International, *Report: The Death Penalty* (1979).
[4]Florida is the first major state to have a death row population (212 in 1984) well in
excess of prisoners executed during 1935–85 (178). The total number of legal executions under civil authority in America from January 1900 to August 1, 1985, is 7,312.
See W. Bowers, *Legal Homicide: Death as Punishment in America 1864–1982,* at 54, Table
2–3 (1984) (hereafter W. Bowers, *Legal Homicide*): Bureau of Justice Statistics. U.S.
Department of Justice, *Bulletin: Capital Punishment 1983,* at 1 (1984); NAACP Legal
Defense and Educational Fund, Inc., *Death Row, U.S.A.* 3 (Aug. 1, 1985) (hereafter
Death Row, U.S.A.).
[5]*Death Row, U.S.A.,* at 3.
[6]*Barefoot v. Estelle,* 103 S. Ct. 3383 (1983); *see also* Weisberg, "Deregulating Death,"
1983 Sup. Ct. Rev. 305.
[7]*Death Row, U.S.A.,* at 3.

That number represents almost twice as many as the peak year of executions in the United States in this century[8] and more than three times as many as the annual total reported by South Africa,[9] now the leading executioner among those nations with accurate reporting. Furthermore, this rate would only be a break-even point. More than one a day would be necessary to reduce the large death row population, many more to achieve a swift and certain execution policy. Anything less (and we will not see one execution a day) creates an endlessly rising backlog and a subsidiary selection process to accompany the procedures that have already produced the fraternity of the condemned.

Executive clemency and intentional delay will restrict the number of executions. State appellate courts and state executive branch maneuvers will serve as the major control on death row populations (with death from suicide and natural causes also of significance). Such methods will prove troublesome but necessary for keeping the number of executions within tolerable limits, to the extent that federal courts withdraw as the primary execution management instrument in the American governmental organization. But none of these measures can reduce the ever-growing death row population.

Moreover, these control mechanisms move the question of who shall live and who shall die away from legal guidelines and the judicial process into an area with neither laws nor principles for guidance.[10] This fundamental inequity led the U.S. Supreme Court to strike down the previously administered death penalty laws in *Furman* v. *Georgia*.[11] Yet it is the inevitable result of implementing the penalty in ways that the courts have since approved.

The situation is not temporary. Unless there are tremendous increases in executions or remarkable decreases in death sentences, then backlog, delay, and occasional executions striking "like lightning"[12] must be seen as integral to the American system.

The whole of Part II is about the implications of and possible solutions to the capital punishment impasse, but in this chapter our ambitions are more modest: to convey a sense of the special problems that

10

---

[8] *See* W. Bowers, *Legal Homicide,* at 25, Table 1–4; *see also* note 4. The peak year was 1935 with 199 executions.

[9] According to South African government figures, 100 executions were carried out in 1982 for criminal offenses. Amnesty International, *Amnesty International Report 1983,* at 81 (1983).

[10] *See, e.g.,* Dix, "Appellate Review of the Decision to Impose Death," 68 *Geo. L.J.* 97 (1980).

[11] In *Furman* v. *Georgia,* 408 U.S. 239, 310 (1972), Justice Stewart concluded "that the Eighth and Fourteenth Amendments cannot tolerate the infliction of a sentence of death under legal systems that permit this unique penalty to be so wantonly and so freakishly imposed."

[12] *Id.* at 39 ("These death sentences are cruel and unusual in the same way that being struck by lightning is cruel and unusual").

current conditions generate for American political and judicial institutions, and the general society. Seventeen hundred death row prisoners and a few dozen executions a year—apparently the choice is between a permanent Reign of Terror or an execution policy that makes mockery of the legal standards governing the use of the death penalty. These are circumstances that almost no one would wish as American public policy. How did this situation come to be?

One simple explanation deserves preliminary attention before we examine the complex causes of present conditions. In this view, capital punishment would be no problem but for the meddlesome intervention of the federal courts. The "pileup" or "logjam" on death row was created by judicial interference with the will of elected state legislators, juries, and judges. Thus, the vast disparity between the condemned and the executed resulted from the judicially imposed moratorium that existed from 1967 through 1977, and the country could live at equilibrium with a modest number of executions (whatever that might mean).

Several indications in recent history dispute the accuracy of this view. The backlog of death sentences produced by the first five years of the moratorium was in fact drastically reduced by the Supreme Court's decision in *Furman* v. *Georgia*.[13] Furthermore, the most dramatic growth in death row populations occurred after 1976, when the U.S. Supreme Court gave its constitutional approval to state capital sentencing statutes in *Gregg* v. *Georgia*.[14] The seven years following that landmark decision produced eleven executions and about 100 times that number of death row inhabitants. In this whole period only twelve states, less than a third of those with capital punishment statutes, performed any executions.[15]

Blaming the courts may be a popular indoor sport, but it misinterprets the extent and breadth of ambivalence over capital punishment in the United States and the crisis of political accountability represented by the current contrast between the many who are condemned and the few who are executed. The game of "blame it on the courts" also ignores a fundamental aspect of American public opinion: Those who support the concept of capital punishment do not necessarily want any executions, and most would be horrified by the kind of perpetual bloodbath that would ensue were the criminal law to keep its promises literally. From the standpoint of public opinion, perhaps the best of all possible worlds is one with the death penalty on the statute books, but no executions.

---

[13]The implication of the judgment in *Furman* striking down sentences of capital punishment in the cases before the Court was that most extant statutes in American jurisdictions were unconstitutional and as a result 633 prisoners were removed from death row. *See* M. Meltsner, *Cruel and Unusual: The Supreme Court and Capital Punishment* 292–3 (1974).

[14]428 U.S. 153 (1976).

[15]*Death Row, U.S.A.*, at 3.

PASSING THE BUCK

Current conditions represent a "crisis of statesmanship" in American political life. Insofar as it produces a situation that nobody wants, it may be compared to the game of "chicken" that provides the title of this chapter.

That game was lucidly described by Bertrand Russell: *15*

> This sport is called "Chicken!" It is played by choosing a long straight road with a white line down the middle and starting two very fast cars towards each other from opposite ends. Each car is expected to keep the wheels of one side on the white line. As they approach each other mutual destruction becomes more and more imminent. If one of them swerves from the white line before the other, the other, as he passes, shouts "Chicken!," and the one who has swerved becomes an object of contempt.[16]

In the game of chicken, the one who swerves to avoid a crash loses. The problem is that if neither participant is willing to become that loser, a catastrophe that nobody wants will occur; but if the potentially fatal crash is truly not desired, why does it so frequently happen? Because each participant is also unwilling to pay the price of "chickening out" and will take great risk to pass that cost to his or her opponent.

The comparison between the absurd mathematics of capital punishment policy and the classic game of chicken is both powerful and incomplete. With respect to the disparity between death sentences and executions, and the continuation of executions themselves, many, if not most, key actors in the American government — in our constitutional courts, in the higher reaches of state government, and in state supreme courts — would rather function in circumstances greatly different from those described in preceding pages. The simplest, and for many the best, solution for these key actors would be the end of executions. Further, many of these agents of state and federal government have the power individually or collectively to stop executions, just as both drivers in a chicken game can avert disaster by swerving or stopping.

At all levels of government, however, to halt executions is perceived as an unpopular act, inviting accusations of autocratic and elitist policy, and negative consequences either in electoral politics or with respect to the legitimacy of judicial institutions. Each authoritative actor would prefer that someone else stop executions — the archetypical situation in chicken. The difference is this: The price of action in the capital punishment game is not one of facing the accusation of cowardice, but rather of accepting the consequences of bravery.

[16]B. Russell, *Common Sense and Nuclear Warfare* (1959).

This situation is exacerbated by the multiplicity of elements in the distribution of power over criminal justice policy generally and capital punishment in particular. Many government actors are available to halt executions in a particular jurisdiction. In the 1980s no death sentences can be enforced without decisions by local prosecutors; the local judiciary, with or without a jury; state appellate courts; federal courts; the U.S. Supreme Court; and executive clemency review processes, frequently including the governor of the executing jurisdiction.

The result can be two kinds of buck passing. First, all these avenues of decision make it possible for the individual hoping to shift responsibility onto another to envisage a number of potential candidates for that honor. Second, in the later stages of review, those who hold the power to reverse executions face the apparent seal of approval on the decision to execute that has been conferred by all of the preceding review processes. Proponents of execution can remind the governor that six other decision makers have already affirmed the legitimacy of the procedure. This momentum generates an unwillingness to upset a decision so resolutely endorsed by a series of other presumably responsible actors — a form of passing the buck backward.

In Chapter 7 we tell the story of Velma Barfield, a North Carolina   20
grandmother executed in 1984. One aspect of that event will serve here, however, as a classic case of buck passing. Then-Governor Hunt, in rejecting Mrs. Barfield's clemency petition, said: "I cannot in good conscience justify making an exception to the law as enacted by our State Legislature, or overruling those 12 jurors who, after hearing the evidence, concluded that Mrs. Barfield should pay the maximum penalty for her brutal actions."[17]

Students of rhetoric can benefit by studying this pronouncement, a vintage example of passing the buck backward. It is also a notable instance of endorsing "the maximum penalty" without actually naming it.

Ironically, the same theory that leads to passing the buck backward also encourages passing it forward. Prosecutors can tell themselves to leave it to the jury, juries to the judge, the judge to the appellate court, and so on. This avoidance of responsibility recently led the U.S. Supreme Court to invalidate a death sentence after the prosecutor had encouraged the jury to impose the penalty, claiming that any error would be corrected by future review.[18] The prosecutor, in his closing arguments, had said to the jury: "Now [the defense attorneys insinuate] that your decision is the final decision and that they're gonna take Bobby Caldwell out in front of the Courthouse in moments and string him up and that is terribly, terribly unfair. For they know, as I know, and as [the]

[17]"Carolina Slayer Fails in Her Bid for a Reprieve," *N.Y. Times,* Sept. 28, 1984, at Al, col. 2.
[18]*Caldwell* v. *Mississippi,* 105 S. Ct. 2633 (1985).

Judge . . . has told you, that the decision you render is automatically reviewed by the Supreme Court."[19] The Court did hold that Caldwell's sentence was unconstitutional, but the prosecutor in the case was only verbalizing what every decision maker involved in a death penalty case realizes.

Even though successive participants in the process may be looking to future reviews to take the responsibility away from them — and thus pay the cost of being brave — the result may be the opposite, because of the apparent constraint imposed by the unanimity of prior reviews. Those who look to others in the system to be brave unwittingly raise the perceived price of bravery for those who must act after them.

Buck passing has been a crucial problem in the context of capital punishment in the United States since the 1960s. The federal courts were for so long the single agency preventing executions that many other responsible actors began to depend on the courts' assumption of that role and evaded the practice of individualized decision making. Even the state legislatures that enthusiastically enacted capital punishment statutes after *Furman* v. *Georgia* could do so in comfortable anticipation of subsequent federal judicial disapproval.

As Chapter 2 demonstrated, state legislatures could act knowing courts were hostile, thereby daring the courts to rescue the system from the consequences of the new laws. They were free to pass both symbolic legislation — and the buck. By the time U.S. Supreme Court became impatient with this role for the federal courts, and with the institutional criticism it had absorbed, traditional mechanisms of restraint had been literally abandoned. Other processes and practices that might have been developed around a declining trend in executions were probably aborted.

One illustration of the displacement of other control processes, probably caused by federal court intervention, is the pattern of executive commutation of sentences. Official statistics report the number of such commutations in 1960 at twenty-two, a figure equal to more than ten percent of the 210 persons on death row at the end of that year. By the end of 1967, when the death row population had more than doubled to 435, the number of commutations reported dropped to thirteen, and the more significant percentage of commutations to the death row population had dropped from ten percent to three percent.[20] Executive clemency, seldom popular with executives, was believed less necessary in an era when federal court intervention had brought executions to a virtual halt.

Although federalizing of capital punishment disabled local pressures to decrease the use of the penalty, there is nothing wrong with

---

[19]*Id.* at 2640.
[20]Statistics for 1960 were derived from U.S. Department of Justice, *National Prisoner Statistics* 2, Figure A (March 1961). Statistics for 1967 were derived from U.S. Department of Justice, *National Prisoner Statistics* 12, Table 4 (June 1968).

centralizing the control of executions in a branch of the federal government. Federal control is both more efficient and, given the national scope of the issue, more appropriate than a patchwork of state and local controls. After all, during the base year of 1960, when twenty-two sentences were commuted and federal oversight was not prominent, two-and-one-half times as many prisoners were executed as were spared.[21] The point is that the "stop-and-go" character of Supreme Court judgments about the validity of state death penalty provisions probably increased the number of persons sentenced to death over the past ten years and contributed to the high ratio of death sentences to executions.

One illustration of this phenomenon concerns recent trends in executive clemency. Once the governors became accustomed to forgoing responsibility for commutation, they were disinclined to accept political responsibility for death row population control even when the Supreme Court changed course. With the exception of 1976, the year the signals were shifted, government statistics report no post-*Gregg* year in which commutation of sentence reached even four percent of the nation's death row population.[22] Some of the numbers are gallows humor. In 1979, with 588 prisoners on death row, a national total of four sentence commutations was reported, less than one percent of the condemned population. In 1980, when the number on death row at the end of the year jumped 100 to 688, the number of commutations decreased from four to two.[23]

Executive clemency measures behavior at only one point in the complex series of decisions that determines the death row population. A broader gauge of stop-and-go effects on the complex political process that has led to death row inflation is the number of death sentences produced by the constellation of prosecutorial, judicial, jury, and state appellate court decision making referred to earlier. Figure 5.1, taken from federally collected statistics, shows trends in death sentences by year for the South, always the nation's capital punishment capital.

The striking element in these data is the difference between pre- and post-*Furman* v. *Georgia* death sentences. Before 1972, when that decision was announced, the number of new death sentences each year in the Southern states averaged about fifty, with the trend, if any, downward. After a year of rapid legislative adjustment in 1973, the number of new death sentences each year more than doubled, and there is no year after 1973 in which the number of new death sentences in the South did not substantially exceed the number of such sentences issued in any year prior to *Furman*.

30

[21]U.S. Department of Justice, *National Prisoner Statistics* 1 (March 1961).
[22]Bureau of Justice Statistics, U.S. Department of Justice, *Capital Punishment* (yearly issues 1976–83).
[23]Bureau of Justice Statistics, U.S. Department of Justice, *Capital Punishment 1979*, at Table 17 (1980); Bureau of Justice Statistics, U.S. Department of Justice, *Capital Punishment 1980*, Table 17 (1981).

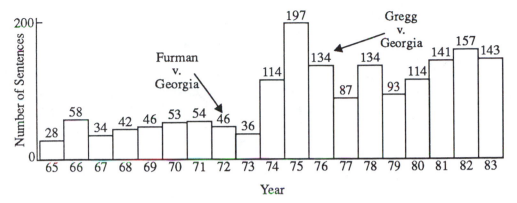

FIGURE 5.1. New death sentences by year in the South.

BLAME IT ON THE COURT?

While there might be other explanations for this pattern, certainly one element in the equation is that the institutional controls operating before the Supreme Court's apparent preemption of the issue ceased to operate after *Furman*. As with executive clemency, these controls were not reasserted when the court staged its strategic withdrawal from prohibiting capital punishment in 1976. From 1977 through 1983, the annual average of new death sentences in the South was well above double the average in the decade preceding *Furman*.

The matter extends beyond the behavior of prosecutors and judges to that of state legislatures. Relieving the legislative process of ultimate responsibility and then restoring legislative power is an almost certain prescription for a high volume of death sentences. More troublesome is the possibility that a hands-off attitude concerning executions in the future might produce a greater number than would have occurred with a more consistent judicial role.

Although one may only speculate as to what might have happened with a different course of events, one thing seems clear: There is no way for federal courts to play a truly neutral role in execution policy in the United States. The prior role of the courts, and the legislative and popular reactions to it, have set forces in motion that have had significant effect on death sentencing and may have some effect on executions. Whether the Supreme Court contends with this legacy actively or passively in the future, much of what will happen will be attributable to that institution's work. Either way, there is a case for a more sophisticated version of "blame it on the Court."

All of this is complicated by the allocations of responsibility for criminal justice policy in the United States when constitutional values are not implicated. Unlike much of the Western world, the locus of penal policy in the United States is state government, not the national government. State government is both more parochial and traditionally less associated with statesmanship, in the sense of resisting the perceived popular will, than is national government in general and the federal Supreme Court in particular. An illustration of a divergence between federal and state practices with respect to capital punishment emerges from official statistics on executions and death row populations. In the twelve years preceding the Supreme Court's pronouncement in *Furman* v. *Georgia*, despite a multitude of federal crimes for which the death penalty was available, only one prisoner was executed under federal jurisdiction.[24] Less than one-half of one percent of executions during the period occurred under federal jurisdiction.

More important, the federal government has successfully avoided the pileup of death sentences that has produced the disparity between death row populations and any imaginable level of executions in so many American states. During 1960–83, while the death row population in the nation as a whole grew sixfold, the number of prisoners under federal jurisdiction facing death sentences has varied between zero and two and has remained at zero since 1977.[25] The United States is experiencing a de facto moratorium on capital punishment at the federal level, but the allocation of responsibility in criminal justice matters to the states has rendered this fact almost invisible and possibly irrelevant.

35

AN INAPT ANALOGY?

Is it inaccurate to characterize executions in the mid-1980s as a game of chicken? The car crash in chicken is a circumstance that neither player wishes, but are there not political actors in the United States who really favor current circumstances? Is this not what opinion polls and the pronouncements of candidates for public office are telling us? Not quite.

The behavior of public officials in the period before and after executions is in marked contrast to their discussions of capital punishment during political campaigns. While there is talk about the need for the law to keep its promises, political figures are not usually enthusiastic about specific executions. Indeed, the odd lot of late adolescents who gather around prison boundaries to cheer on the eve of scheduled executions is usually regarded as deviant by the same public that supports capital punishment. James Reston described the hideous performance of the crowd that gathered to witness the execution of Velma Barfield:

[24]The last federally authorized execution occurred in Iowa in 1963. Bureau of Justice Statistics, U.S. Department of Justice, *Capital Punishment 1982,* at Table 5 (1984).
[25]Bureau of Justice Statistics, U.S. Department of Justice, *Capital Punishment* (yearly issues 1960–83).

[A] clutch of death-penalty boosters egged on the state. "Hip, hip hurrah . . . K-I-L-L." "Burn, bitch, burn." Their delirious, high-pitched cackles floated over the scene like a bad odor. . . . At 2 a.m. the cheerleaders, inspired by the collective sadism induced by the spectacle, began to chant "Kill her! Kill her! Kill her!" and at 2:15 it was as if the home team had just scored the winning touchdown.[26]

No holder of statewide office has been known to join the cheers anywhere in the United States.

The most that can be said for the opinion of policy makers toward executions is that they are willing to permit executions; there are indeed many responsible government officials willing to allow execution as the costs of maintaining capital punishment statutes. But does this defeat the analogy between teenaged games of chicken and executions? Remember that there are drivers willing to risk catastrophic crashes to avoid the label of cowardice. If there were not, there would be no participants in chicken and no crashes to explain.

Current execution policy and games of chicken are similar in two further respects—the avoidance of personal responsibility for fateful outcomes and the sharp differences between public and private attitudes of key actors. When the cars collide in a chicken game, those involved in the crash tend to avoid ascriptions of personal responsibility for the outcome. The crash is viewed more as the product of fate or an act of God than as anyone's fault. Similarly, executions are regarded as the demand of "the law" as an abstraction or an expression of "the will of the people." The multiplicity of individual decisions necessary for an execution merge into a single depersonalized act of the state. The phenomenon of passing the buck facilitates this imagery, which may be one reason why passing the buck is so common in capital punishment cases. The people who make decisions in these matters frequently talk and think as if no individual is in charge. That this image gives comfort, that this state of diffuse responsibility is felt necessary, seems powerful evidence of ambivalence about legal execution in the United States.

A final parallel between highway bravado and execution policy concerns the distinction between private views and public behavior that may be of critical importance in predicting outcome. The price of chickening out on the highway is public knowledge that the accident avoider lacks the bravado to carry through. If risk-taking behavior of this sort could be decided by truly secret ballot, we doubt that any collisions would occur.

We cannot say that those who hold power on such matters would abolish the death penalty. We *can* say that the public reaction to decisions about capital punishment is regarded as vitally important by decision

40

[26]Reston, "Invitation to a Poisoning," *Vanity Fair,* Feb. 1985, at 82, 101.

makers at all levels of government, and that the perceived public reaction has decisive impact on how decisions are made and explained.

The factors we have discussed here provide a context in which the future of capital punishment will be worked out. We shall return to many of the concepts and examples in this chapter as we discuss, successively, each of these aspects of present policy—lethal injection (Chapter 6); the short-term future of executions (Chapter 7); and prospects for the longer term (Chapter 8).

FOR DISCUSSION AND WRITING

1. Is the following argument logical or illogical? Explain.
   If capital punishment deters potential murderers, then painful forms of execution should be more effective than those that are relatively painless. Thus, advocates of capital punishment should also advocate methods of execution such as death by fire at the stake.

2. In the final three paragraphs, the authors briefly allude to possible qualifications to their claim. What are these?

3. Which of the following two statements is a truncated argument? Explain.
   a. There is a steady increase in the death row population.
   b. There is an untenable increase in the death row population.

4. The argument for the death penalty appears simple enough: an eye for an eye, a tooth for a tooth. What backing can you give for this proposition? Is the basis for the backing primarily moral or pragmatic?

5. How do the following data influence your judgment of the quality of this argument? (a) Franklin E. Zimring is professor of law and director of the Earl Warren Legal Institute at the University of California, Berkeley. Gordon Hawkins is a senior fellow of the Earl Warren Legal Institute. He was formerly director of the Sydney University Institute of Criminology. (b) The book from which the selection is taken was published by Cambridge University Press.

6. What elements of scene are important in this argument?

7. In regard to manner, did you find this selection easy to understand or difficult? Explain. Did the authors' failure to relate their "game of chicken" metaphor to actual cases make the argument more difficult to understand?

8. Does this selection advance an argument against capital punishment? If not, what is the claim?

9. Who are the two drivers in the game of chicken?

10. What are the reasons for the pileup of convicts on death row?

THE NATURALIST AND
THE SUPERNATURALIST

C. S. Lewis

C. S. Lewis has enjoyed several special niches in the literary field. He has written successful fantasies, many of which assume the trappings of science fiction but are really allegories dealing with the moral and theological issues of the human race. The fabulous nature of these stories, which take place on other planets inhabited by alien cultures, overwhelms any scientific or factual elements of the plots. Other books are not science fiction but are just as phantasmagorical. *The Screwtape Letters,* for example, is a novel in which the Devil lends his nephew advice on how best to corrupt the souls of humans, thus leading them to eternal damnation.

Lewis has also written some very important theological analyses of Christianity of which the following selection is one example. Another is *The Problem of Pain,* which considers suffering from the Christian perspective. In addition, Lewis has won acclaim for scholarly works dealing with the notion of romantic love throughout history *(Allegory of Love)* and Milton's epic poem *Paradise Lost (Preface to* Paradise Lost).

Lewis's scholarly work is a direct result of the position he held as Fellow and Tutor of Magdalen College, Oxford, from 1925 until 1954. Prior to that time, Lewis had studied at University College, Oxford, after serving as a second lieutenant in the Somerset Light Infantry during World War I. During the Second World War, Lewis was heard over the British Broadcasting Corporation and gave talks on religion to the Royal Air Force. He died in 1963.

The following essay is an example of logical argumentation in its purest form. If you accept Lewis's premises, it is very hard to deny his conclusions.

"Gracious!" exclaimed Mrs. Snip, "and is there a
place where people venture to live above ground?"
"I never heard of people living *under* ground," replied
Tim, "before I came to Giant-Land." "Came to
Giant-Land!" cried Mrs. Snip, "why, isn't
everywhere Giant-Land?"
ROLAND QUIZZ, *Giant-Land,* chap. xxxii.

I use the word *Miracle* to mean an interference with Nature by supernatural power.[1] Unless there exists, in addition to Nature, something else which we may call the supernatural, there can be no miracles.

[1]This definition is not that which would be given by many theologians. I am adopting it not because I think it an improvement upon theirs but precisely because, being crude and "popular," it enables me most easily to treat those questions which "the common reader" probably has in mind when he takes up a book on Miracles.

Some people believe that nothing exists except Nature; I call these people *Naturalists*. Others think that, besides Nature, there exists something else: I call them *Supernaturalists*. Our first question, therefore, is whether the Naturalists or the Supernaturalists are right. And here comes our first difficulty.

Before the Naturalist and the Supernaturalist can begin to discuss their difference of opinion, they must surely have an agreed definition both of Nature and of Supernature. But unfortunately it is almost impossible to get such a definition. Just because the Naturalist thinks that nothing but Nature exists, the word *Nature* means to him merely "everything" or "the whole show" or "whatever there is." And if that is what we mean by Nature, then of course nothing else exists. The real question between him and the Supernaturalist has evaded us. Some philosophers have defined Nature as "What we perceive with our five senses." But this also is unsatisfactory; for we do not perceive our own emotions in that way, and yet they are presumably "natural" events. In order to avoid this deadlock and to discover what the Naturalist and the Supernaturalist are really differing about, we must approach our problem in a more roundabout way.

I begin by considering the following sentences. (1) Are those his natural teeth or a set? (2) The dog in his natural state is covered with fleas. (3) I love to get away from tilled lands and metalled roads and be alone with Nature. (4) Do be natural. Why are you so affected? (5) It may have been wrong to kiss her but it was very natural.

A common thread of meaning in all these usages can easily be discovered. The natural teeth are those which grow in the mouth; we do not have to design them, make them, or fit them. The dog's natural state is the one he will be in if no one takes soap and water and prevents it. The countryside where Nature reigns supreme is the one where soil, weather and vegetation produce their results unhelped and unimpeded by man. Natural behaviour is the behaviour which people would exhibit if they were not at the pains to alter it. The natural kiss is the kiss which will be given if moral or prudential considerations do not intervene. In all the examples Nature means what happens "of itself" or "of its own accord": what you do not need to labour for; what you will get if you take no measures to stop it. The Greek word for Nature (Physis) is connected with the Greek verb for "to grow"; Latin *Natura*, with the verb "to be born." The Natural is what springs up, or comes forth, or arrives, or goes on, *of its own accord:* the given, what is there already: the spontaneous, the unintended, the unsolicited.

What the Naturalist believes is that the ultimate Fact, the thing you can't go behind, is a vast process in space and time which is *going on of its own accord*. Inside that total system every particular event (such as your sitting reading this book) happens because some other event has hap- 5 pened; in the long run, because the Total Event is happening. Each particular thing (such as this page) is what it is because other things are what they are; and so, eventually, because the whole system is what it is. All the things and events are so completely interlocked that no one of them can claim the slightest independence from "the whole show." None of them exists "on its own" or "goes on of its own accord" except in the sense that it exhibits, at some particular place and time, that general "existence on its own" or "behaviour of its own accord" which belongs to "Nature" (the great total interlocked event) as a whole. Thus no thoroughgoing Naturalist believes in free will: for free will would mean that human beings have the power of independent action, the power of doing something more or other than what was involved by the total series of events. And any such separate power of originating events is what the Naturalist denies. Spontaneity, originality, action "on its own," is a privilege reserved for "the whole show," which he calls *Nature*.

The Supernaturalist agrees with the Naturalist that there must be something which exists in its own right; some basic Fact whose existence it would be nonsensical to try to explain because this Fact is itself the ground or starting-point of all explanations. But he does not identify this Fact with "the whole show." He thinks that things fall into two classes. In the first class we find either things or (more probably) One Thing which is basic and original, which exists on its own. In the second we find things which are merely derivative from that One Thing. The one basic Thing has caused all the other things to be. It exists on its own; they exist because it exists. They will cease to exist if it ever ceases to maintain them in existence; they will be altered if it ever alters them.

The difference between the two views might be expressed by saying that Naturalism gives us a democratic, Supernaturalism a monarchical, picture of reality. The Naturalist thinks that the privilege of "being on its own" resides in the total mass of things, just as in a democracy sovereignty resides in the whole mass of the people. The Supernaturalist thinks that this privilege belongs to some things or (more probably) One Thing and not to others—just as, in a real monarchy, the king has sovereignty and the people have not. And just as, in a democracy, all citizens are equal, so for the Naturalist one thing or event is as good as another, in the sense that they are all equally dependent on the total system of things. Indeed each of them is only the way in which the character of that total system exhibits itself at a particular point in space and time. The Supernaturalist, on the other hand, believes that the one original or self-existent thing is on a different level from, and more important than, all other things.

At this point a suspicion may occur that Supernaturalism first arose from reading into the universe the structure of monarchical societies.

But then of course it may with equal reason be suspected that Naturalism has arisen from reading into it the structure of modern democracies. The two suspicions thus cancel out and give us no help in deciding which theory is more likely to be true. They do indeed remind us that Supernaturalism is the characteristic philosophy of a monarchical age and Naturalism of a democratic, in the sense that Supernaturalism, even if false, would have been believed by the great mass of unthinking people four hundred years ago, just as Naturalism, even if false, will be believed by the great mass of unthinking people to-day.

Everyone will have seen that the One Self-existent Thing — or the small class of self-existent things — in which Supernaturalists believe, is what we call God or the gods. I propose for the rest of this book to treat only that form of Supernaturalism which believes in one God; partly because polytheism is not likely to be a live issue for most of my readers, and partly because those who believed in many gods very seldom, in fact, regarded their gods as creators of the universe and as self-existent. The gods of Greece were not really supernatural in the strict sense which I am giving to the word. They were products of the total system of things and included within it. This introduces an important distinction.

The difference between Naturalism and Supernaturalism is not exactly the same as the difference between belief in a God and disbelief. Naturalism, without ceasing to be itself, could admit a certain kind of God. The great interlocking event called Nature might be such as to produce at some stage a great cosmic consciousness, an indwelling "God" arising from the whole process as human mind arises (according to the Naturalists) from human organisms. A Naturalist would not object to that sort of God. The reason is this. Such a God would not stand outside Nature or the total system, would not be existing "on his own." It would still be "the whole show" which was the basic Fact, and such a God would merely be one of the things (even if he were the most interesting) which the basic Fact contained. What Naturalism cannot accept is the idea of a God who stands outside Nature and made it. 10

We are now in a position to state the difference between the Naturalist and the Supernaturalist despite the fact that they do not mean the same by the word Nature. The Naturalist believes that a great process, or "becoming," exists "on its own" in space and time, and that nothing else exists — what we call particular things and events being only the parts into which we analyse the great process or the shapes which that process takes at given moments and given points in space. This single, total reality he calls Nature. The Supernaturalist believes that one Thing exists on its own and has produced the framework of space and time and the procession of systematically connected events which fill them. This framework, and this filling, he calls Nature. It may, or may not, be the only reality which the one Primary Thing has produced. There might be other systems in addition to the one we call Nature.

In that sense there might be several "Natures." This conception must be kept quite distinct from what is commonly called "plurality of worlds" — i.e. different solar systems or different galaxies, "island universes" existing in widely separated parts of a single space and time. These, however remote, would be parts of the same Nature as our own sun: it and they would be interlocked by being in relations to one another, spatial and temporal relations and causal relations as well. And it is just this reciprocal interlocking within a system which makes it what we call a Nature. Other Natures might not be spatio-temporal at all: or, if any of them were, their space and time would have no spatial or temporal relation to ours. It is just this discontinuity, this failure of interlocking, which would justify us in calling them different Natures. This does not mean that there would be absolutely no relation between them; they would be related by their common derivation from a single Supernatural source. They would, in this respect, be like different novels by a single author; the events in one story have no relation to the events in another *except* that they are invented by the same author. To find the relation between them you must go right back to the author's mind: there is no cutting across from anything Mr. Pickwick says in *Pickwick Papers* to anything Mrs. Gamp hears in *Martin Chuzzlewit*. Similarly there would be no normal cutting across from an event in one Nature to an event in any other. By a "normal" relation I mean one which occurs in virtue of the character of the two systems. We have to put in the qualification "normal" because we do not know in advance that God might not bring two Natures into partial contact at some particular point: that is, He might allow *selected* events in the one to produce results in the other. There would thus be, at certain points, a partial interlocking; but this would not turn the two Natures into one, for the total reciprocity which makes a Nature would still be lacking, and the anomalous interlockings would arise not from what either system was in itself but from the Divine act which was bringing them together. If this occurred each of the two Natures would be "supernatural" in relation to the other: but the fact of their contact would be supernatural in a more absolute sense — not as being beyond this or that Nature but beyond any and every Nature. It would be one kind of Miracle. The other kind would be Divine "interference" not by the bringing together of two Natures, but simply.

All this is, at present, purely speculative. It by no means follows from Supernaturalism that Miracles of any sort do in fact occur. God (the primary thing) may never in fact interfere with the natural system He has created. If He has created more natural systems than one, He may never cause them to impinge on one another.

But that is a question for further consideration. If we decide that Nature is not the only thing there is, then we cannot say in advance whether she is safe from miracles or not. There are things outside her: we do not yet know whether they can get in. The gates may be barred, or they may not. But if Naturalism is true, then we do know in advance that miracles are impossible: nothing can come into Nature from the outside because there is nothing outside to come in, Nature being everything. No doubt, events which we in our ignorance should mistake for miracles might occur: but they would in reality be (just like the commonest events) an inevitable result of the character of the whole system.

Our first choice, therefore, must be between Naturalism and Supernaturalism.   15

FOR DISCUSSION AND WRITING

1. What is Lewis's claim?

2. He gives no evidence for the claim. Does he need evidence? Explain why or why not.

3. What is his backing for the claim?

4. Point out instances in which Lewis uses analogy to support or clarify his point. Are these analogies successful?

5. Are you a naturalist or a supernaturalist? Present some backing for your position. (Does any empirical evidence — facts and figures — relate to your claim?)

6. Lewis starts by defining *miracle, naturalist,* and *supernaturalist*. Why are these definitions crucial for the argument? (What happens to the argument if the reader does not accept the definitions?)

7. In regard to manner, most readers would say that C. S. Lewis is a remarkably clear writer, making complex ideas relatively easy to understand. What are some of the ways in which Lewis makes his argument easy to follow?

8. What conclusions can you draw about Lewis (the agent) on the basis of the work (his act).

9. What influence do you think scene has had on Lewis's thinking? Recall that for more than a quarter of a century he was a tutor at Oxford and that he was an infantry officer in World War I. What would be a reliable source to consult for more information about the scenes of Lewis's life (i.e., his biography)?

10. How was Lewis's novel *The Screwtape Letters* reccived when it first came out? What source would you consult to learn what critics thought of the book?

11. Why is the definition of *miracle* with which Lewis begins his argument important to the argument?

A MODEST PROPOSAL

For Preventing the Children of Poor People in Ireland from Being a Burden to Their Parents or Country, and for Making Them Beneficial to the Public

Jonathan Swift

Swift is best known for *Gulliver's Travels,* published in 1726. Often viewed as a children's book, this work is actually a devastating satire on the manners and morals of the author's contemporaries in the British Isles. "A Modest Proposal" (1729) is one of the greatest works of irony in the English language, and it is widely reprinted in essay collections because it is such a perfect model of its genre.

Swift was born in Dublin in 1667. He took his B.A. at Trinity College in Dublin and then became secretary to Sir William Temple, an influential nobleman. In 1700, Swift became a vicar in the Anglican Church and in 1701 took his doctor of divinity degree at Trinity College. Among his literary works are *A Tale of a Tub* (1704), *The Battle of the Books,* and "Verses on the Death of Dr. Swift" (1731).

In 1713, Swift was made Dean of St. Patrick's Cathedral in Dublin. In 1742, Swift was committed to the care of guardians, his health and his memory having deteriorated. He died in 1745 and was buried in St. Patrick's Cathedral.

Before you read this essay, you might want to review the discussion of the writer-reader contract in Chapter 3 and refresh your memory about purposeful "violations" of the terms of that contract.

It is a melancholy object to those who walk through this great town or travel in the country, when they see the streets, the roads, and cabin doors, crowded with beggars of the female-sex, followed by three, four, or six children, all in rags and importuning every passenger for an alms. These mothers, instead of being able to work for their honest livelihood, are forced to employ all their time in strolling to beg sustenance for their helpless infants, who, as they grow up, either turn thieves for want of work, or leave their dear native country to fight for the Pretender in Spain, or sell themselves to the Barbadoes.

I think it is agreed by all parties that this prodigious number of children in the arms, or on the backs, or at the heels of their mothers, and frequently of their fathers, is in the present deplorable state of the kingdom a very great additional grievance; and therefore whoever could find out a fair, cheap, and easy method of making these children sound, useful members of the commonwealth would deserve so well of the public as to have his statue set up for a preserver of the nation.

But my intention is very far from being confined to provide only for the children of professed beggars; it is of a much greater extent, and shall take in the whole number of infants at a certain age who are born of parents in effect as little able to support them as those who demand our charity in the streets.

As to my own part, having turned my thoughts for many years upon this important subject, and maturely weighed the several schemes of other projectors, I have always found them grossly mistaken in their computation. It is true, a child just dropped from its dam may be supported by her milk for a solar year, with little other nourishment; at most not above the value of two shillings, which the mother may certainly get, or the value in scraps, by her lawful occupation of begging; and it is exactly at one year old that I propose to provide for them in such a manner as instead of being a charge upon their parents or the parish, or wanting food and raiment for the rest of their lives, they shall on the contrary contribute to the feeding, and partly to the clothing, of many thousands.

There is likewise another great advantage in my scheme, that it will prevent those voluntary abortions, and that horrid practice of women murdering their bastard children, alas, too frequent among us, sacrificing the poor innocent babes, I doubt, more to avoid the expense than the shame, which would move tears and pity in the most savage and inhuman breast.

The number of souls in this kingdom being usually reckoned one million and a half, of these I calculate there may be about two hundred thousand couple whose wives are breeders; from which number I subtract thirty thousand couples who are able to maintain their own children, although I apprehend there cannot be so many under the present distresses of the kingdom; but this being granted, there will remain an hundred and seventy thousand breeders. I again subtract fifty thousand for those women who miscarry, or whose children die by accident or disease within the year. There only remain an hundred and twenty thousand children of poor parents annually born. The question therefore is, how this number shall be reared and provided for, which, as I have already said, under the present situation of affairs, is utterly impossible by all the methods hitherto proposed. For we can neither employ them in handicraft or agriculture; we neither build houses (I mean in the country) nor cultivate land. They can very seldom pick up a livelihood by stealing till they arrive at six years old, except where they are of towardly parts; although I confess they learn the rudiments much earlier, during which time they can however be looked upon only as probationers, as I have been informed by a principal gentleman in the county of Cavan, who protested to me that he never knew above one or two instances under the age of six, even in a part of the kingdom so renowned for the quickest proficiency in that art.

I am assured by our merchants that a boy or a girl before twelve years old is no salable commodity; and even when they come to this age they will not yield above three pounds, or three pounds and half a crown

5

at most on the Exchange; which cannot turn to account either to the parents or the kingdom, the charge of nutriment and rags having been at least four times that value.

I shall now therefore humbly propose my own thoughts, which I hope will not be liable to the least objection.

I have been assured by a very knowing American of my acquaintance in London, that a young healthy child well nursed is at a year old a most delicious, nourishing, and wholesome food, whether stewed, roasted, baked, or boiled; and I make no doubt that it will equally serve in a fricassee or a ragout.

I do therefore humbly offer it to public consideration that of the hundred and twenty thousand children, already computed, twenty thousand may be reserved for breed, whereof only one fourth part to be males, which is more than we allow to sheep, black cattle, or swine; and my reason is that these children are seldom the fruits of marriage, a circumstance not much regarded by our savages, therefore one male will be sufficient to serve four females. That the remaining hundred thousand may at a year old be offered in sale to the persons of quality and fortune through the kingdom, always advising the mother to let them suck plentifully in the last month, so as to render them plump and fat for a good table. A child will make two dishes at an entertainment for friends; and when the family dines alone, the fore or hind quarter will make a reasonable dish, and seasoned with a little pepper or salt will be very good boiled on the fourth day, especially in winter.

I have reckoned upon a medium that a child just born will weigh twelve pounds, and in a solar year if tolerably nursed increaseth to twenty-eight pounds.

I grant this food will be somewhat dear, and therefore very proper for landlords, who, as they have already devoured most of the parents, seem to have the best title to the children.

Infant's flesh will be in season throughout the year, but more plentiful in March, and a little before and after. For we are told by a grave author, an eminent French physician, that fish being a prolific diet, there are more children born in Roman Catholic countries about nine months after Lent than at any other season; therefore, reckoning a year after Lent, the markets will be more glutted than usual, because the number of popish infants is at least three to one in this kingdom; and therefore it will have one other collateral advantage, by lessening the number of Papists among us.

I have already computed the charge of nursing a beggar's child (in which list I reckon all cottagers, laborers, and four fifths of the farmers) to be about two shillings per annum, rags included; and I believe no gentleman would repine to give ten shillings for the carcass of a good fat child, which, as I have said, will make four dishes of excellent nutritive meat, when he hath only some particular friend or his own family to

10

dine with him. Thus the squire will learn to be a good landlord, and grow popular among the tenants; the mother will have eight shillings net profit, and be fit for work till she produces another child.

Those who are more thrifty (as I must confess the times require) 15 may flay the carcass; the skin of which artificially dressed will make admirable gloves for ladies, and summer boots for fine gentlemen.

As to our city of Dublin, shambles may be appointed for this purpose in the most convenient parts of it, and butchers we may be assured will not be wanting; although I rather recommend buying the children alive, and dressing them hot from the knife as we do roasting pigs.

A very worthy person, a true lover of his country, and whose virtues I highly esteem, was lately pleased in discoursing on this matter to offer a refinement upon my scheme. He said that many gentlemen of this kingdom, having of late destroyed their deer, he conceived that the want of venison might be well supplied by the bodies of young lads and maidens, not exceeding fourteen years of age nor under twelve, so great a number of both sexes in every county being now ready to starve for want of work and service; and these to be disposed of by their parents, if alive, or otherwise by their nearest relations. But with due deference to so excellent a friend and so deserving a patriot, I cannot be altogether in his sentiments; for as to the males, my American acquaintance assured me from frequent experience that their flesh was generally tough and lean, like that of our schoolboys, by continual exercise, and their taste disagreeable; and to fatten them would not answer the charge. Then as to the females, it would, I think with humble submission, be a loss to the public, because they soon would become breeders themselves: and besides, it is not improbable that some scrupulous people might be apt to censure such a practice (although indeed very unjustly) as a little bordering upon cruelty; which, I confess, hath always been with me the strongest objection against any project, how well soever intended.

But in order to justify my friend, he confessed that this expedient was put into his head by the famous Psalmanazar, a native of the island Formosa, who came from thence to London above twenty years ago, and in conversation told my friend that in his country when any young person happened to be put to death, the executioner sold the carcass to persons of quality as a prime dainty; and that in his time the body of a plump girl of fifteen, who was crucified for an attempt to poison the emperor, was sold to his Imperial Majesty's prime minister of state, and other great mandarins of the court, in joints from the gibbet, at four hundred crowns. Neither indeed can I deny that if the same use were made of several plump young girls in this town, who without one single groat to their fortunes cannot stir abroad without a chair, and appear at the playhouse and assemblies in foreign fineries which they never will pay for, the kingdom would not be the worse.

Some persons of a desponding spirit are in great concern about that vast number of poor people who are aged, diseased, or maimed, and I have been desired to employ my thoughts what course may be taken to ease the nation of so grievous an encumbrance. But I am not in the least pain upon that matter, because it is very well known that they are every day dying and rotting by cold and famine, and filth and vermin, as fast as can be reasonably expected. And as to the younger laborers, they are now in almost as hopeful a condition. They cannot get work, and consequently pine away for want of nourishment to a degree that if at any time they are accidentially hired to common labor, they have not strength to perform it; and thus the country and themselves are happily delivered from the evils to come.

I have too long digressed, and therefore shall return to my subject.   20
I think the advantages by the proposal which I have made are obvious and many, as well as of the highest importance.

For first, as I have already observed, it would greatly lessen the number of Papists, with whom we are yearly overrun, being the principal breeders of the nation as well as our most dangerous enemies: and who stay at home on purpose to deliver the kingdom to the Pretender, hoping to take their advantage by the absence of so many good Protestants, who have chosen rather to leave their country than to stay at home and pay tithes against their conscience to an Episcopal curate.

Secondly, the poorer tenants will have something valuable of their own, which by law may be made liable to distress, and help to pay their landlord's rent, their corn and cattle being already seized and money a thing unknown.

Thirdly, whereas the maintenance of an hundred thousand children, from two years old and upwards, cannot be computed at less than ten shillings a piece per annum, the nation's stock will be thereby increased fifty thousand pounds per annum, besides the profit of a new dish introduced to the tables of all gentlemen of fortune in the kingdom who have any refinement in taste. And the money will circulate among ourselves, the goods being entirely of our own growth and manufacture.

Fourthly, the constant breeders, besides the gain of eight shillings sterling per annum by the sale of their children, will be rid of the charge of maintaining them after the first year.

Fifthly, this food would likewise bring great custom to taverns,   25
where the vintners will certainly be so prudent as to procure the best receipts for dressing it to perfection, and consequently have their houses frequented by all the fine gentlemen, who justly value themselves upon their knowledge in good eating; and a skillful cook, who understands how to oblige his guests, will contrive to make it as expensive as they please.

Sixthly, this would be a great inducement to marriage, which all wise nations have either encouraged by rewards or enforced by laws and penalties. It would increase the care and tenderness of mothers toward their children, when they were sure of a settlement for life to the poor babes, provided in some sort by the public, to their annual profit instead of expense. We should see an honest emulation among the married women, which of them could bring the fattest child to the market. Men would become as fond of their wives during the time of their pregnancy as they are now of their mares in foal, their cows in calf, or sows when they are ready to farrow; nor offer to beat or kick them (as is too frequent a practice) for fear of a miscarriage.

Many other advantages might be enumerated. For instance, the addition of some thousand carcasses in our exportation of barreled beef, the propagation of swine's flesh, and improvement in the art of making good bacon, so much wanted among us by the great destruction of pigs, too frequent at our tables, which are no way comparable in taste or magnificence to a well-grown, fat, yearling child, which roasted whole will make a considerable figure at a lord mayor's feast or any other public entertainment. But this and many others I omit, being studious of brevity.

Supposing that one thousand families in this city would be constant customers for infants' flesh, besides others who might have it at merry meetings, particularly weddings and christenings, I compute that Dublin would take off annually about twenty thousand carcasses, and the rest of the kingdom (where probably they will be sold somewhat cheaper) the remaining eighty thousand.

I can think of no one objection that will possibly be raised against this proposal, unless it should be urged that the number of people will be thereby much lessened in the kingdom. This I freely own, and it was indeed one principal design in offering it to the world. I desire the reader will observe, that I calculate my remedy for this one individual kingdom of Ireland and for no other that ever was, is, or I think ever can be upon earth. Therefore let no man talk to me of other expedients: of taxing our absentees at five shillings a pound: of using neither clothes nor household furniture except what is of our own growth and manufacture: of utterly rejecting the materials and instruments that promote foreign luxury: of curing the expensiveness of pride, vanity, idleness, and gaming in our women: of introducing a vein of parsimony, prudence, and temperance: of learning to love our country, in the want of which we differ even from Laplanders and the inhabitants of Topinamboo: of quitting our animosities and factions, nor acting any longer like the Jews, who were murdering one another at the very moment their city was taken: of being a little cautious not to sell our country and conscience for nothing: of teaching landlords to have at least one degree of mercy toward their tenants: lastly, of putting a spirit of honesty, industry, and skill into our shopkeepers; who, if a resolution could now be taken to buy only our native goods, would immediately unite to cheat and exact upon us in the price, the measure, and the goodness, nor could ever yet be brought to make one fair proposal of just dealing, though often and earnestly invited to it.

Therefore I repeat, let no man talk to me of these and the like   30
expedients, till he hath at least some glimpse of hope that there will ever be some hearty and sincere attempt to put them in practice.

But as to myself, having been wearied out for many years with offering vain, idle, visionary thoughts, and at length utterly despairing of success, I fortunately fell upon this proposal, which, as it is wholly new, so it hath something solid and real, of no expense and little trouble, full in our own power, and whereby we can incur no danger in disobliging England. For this kind of commodity will not bear exportation, the flesh being of too tender a consistence to admit a long continuance in salt, although perhaps I could name a country which would be glad to eat up our whole nation without it.

After all, I am not so violently bent upon my own opinion as to reject any offer proposed by wise men, which shall be found equally innocent, cheap, easy, and effectual. But before something of that kind shall be advanced in contradiction to my scheme, and offering a better, I desire the author or authors will be pleased maturely to consider two points. First, as things now stand, how they will be able to find food and raiment for an hundred thousand useless mouths and backs. And secondly, there being a round million of creatures in human figure throughout this kingdom, whose sole subsistence put into a common stock would leave them in debt two millions of pounds sterling, adding those who are beggars by profession to the bulk of farmers, cottagers, and laborers, with their wives and children who are beggars in effect; I desire those politicians who dislike my overture, and may perhaps be so bold to attempt an answer, that they will first ask the parents of these mortals whether they would not at this day think it a great happiness to have been sold for food at a year old in the manner I prescribe, and thereby have avoided such a perpetual scene of misfortunes as they have since gone through by the oppression of landlords, the impossibility of paying rent without money or trade, the want of common sustenance, with neither house nor clothes to cover them from the inclemencies of the weather, and the most inevitable prospect of entailing the like or greater miseries upon their breed forever.

I profess, in the sincerity of my heart, that I have not the least personal interest in endeavoring to promote this necessary work, having no other motive than the public good of my country, by advancing our trade, providing for infants, relieving the poor, and giving some pleasure to the rich. I have no children by which I can propose to get a single penny; the youngest being nine years old, and my wife past childbearing.

FOR DISCUSSION AND WRITING

1. Briefly outline Swift's argument: claim, backing, evidence, qualification.

2. Swift ends his ironic tour de force by assuring the reader,

   > I profess, in the sincerity of my heart, that I have not the least personal interest in endeavoring to promote this necessary work, having no other motive than the public good of my country, by advancing our trade, providing for infants, relieving the poor, and giving some pleasure to the rich. I have no children by which I can propose to get a single penny; the youngest being nine years old, and my wife past childbearing.

   What would be the purpose and effect of such a testimonial in an argument that was *not* ironic? What is its ironic effect?

3. Why would a skillful arguer start with premises on which everyone could agree before introducing the controversial claim? Explain how Swift captures his readers' sympathy and agreement before he jolts them with his claim.

4. What means does Swift use to satirize scientific thought? What else is the subject of his attacks?

5. In regard to manner, Swift uses irony to advance his argument. What are the advantages and the disadvantages of this device? Might some readers fail to perceive the irony and thus conclude that Swift was a monster?

6. How would the concept of world knowledge help explain why some readers might fail to perceive Swift's irony and read the essay as a literal argument for butchering and consuming children?

7. State the ironic gist of the essay. State the literal gist.

8. Why does Swift talk of "a child just dropped from its dam" (par. 4) rather than of "a newborn child" and of "breeders" (par. 6) rather than "mothers"? Check the meanings of *drop* and *dam*. (What source would you use to find what those terms meant in the eighteenth century?)

9. Swift uses statistics to back his argument. Do you think that his statistics were accurate? Does their accuracy matter? Explain.

CIVIL DISOBEDIENCE

Henry David Thoreau

From the standpoint of adventure — exploring new territory, crossing oceans in sailing ships, fighting battles — Thoreau's biography is fairly uneventful. He was born in Concord, Massachusetts, in 1817 and lived in that city all of his life, except for a few years during childhood, his college days at nearby Harvard, and a few months on Staten Island in 1843. Thoreau did not marry. His most complex and lasting relationship was with his neighbor, Ralph Waldo Emerson, the venerated American apostle of nature and self-reliance.

In 1849, Thoreau published his journal *A Week on the Concord and Merrimack Rivers*. Thoreau's major work — and one of the most important in the canon of American literature — is *Walden* (1854), a detailed account of a year that he spent in a cabin at Walden Pond, near Cambridge. Thoreau died in 1862.

For reasons that will become obvious as you read "Civil Disobedience," this essay profoundly influenced both Mahatma Gandhi and Martin Luther King, Jr.

I heartily accept the motto, — "That government is best which governs least;" and I should like to see it acted up to more rapidly and systematically. Carried out, it finally amounts to this, which also I believe, — "That government is best which governs not at all;" and when men are prepared for it, that will be the kind of government which they will have. Government is at best but an expedient; but most governments are usually, and all governments are sometimes, inexpedient. The objections which have been brought against a standing army, and they are many and weighty, and deserve to prevail, may also at last be brought against a standing government. The standing army is only an arm of the standing government. The government itself, which is only the mode which the people have chosen to execute their will, is equally liable to be abused and perverted before the people can act through it. Witness the present Mexican war, the work of comparatively a few individuals using the standing government as their tool; for, in the outset, the people would not have consented to this measure.

This American government, — what is it but a tradition, though a recent one, endeavoring to transmit itself unimpaired to posterity, but each instant losing some of its integrity? It has not the vitality and force of a single living man; for a single man can bend it to his will. It is a sort of wooden gun to the people themselves; and, if ever they should use it in earnest as a real one against each other, it will surely split. But it is not the less necessary for this; for the people must have some complicated machinery or other, and hear its din, to satisfy that idea of government which they have. Governments show thus how successfully men can be imposed on, even impose on themselves, for their own advantage. It is excellent, we must all allow; yet this government never of itself furthered any enterprise, but by the alacrity with which it got out of its way. *It* does not keep the country free. *It* does not settle the West. *It* does not educate. The character inherent in the American people has done all that has been accomplished; and it would have done somewhat more, if the government had not sometimes got in its way. For government is an expedient by which men would fain succeed in letting one another alone; and, as has been said, when it is most expedient, the governed are most let alone by it. Trade and commerce, if they were not made of India rubber, would never manage to bounce over the obstacles which legislators are continually putting in their way; and, if one were to judge these men wholly by the effects of their actions, and not partly by their intentions, they would deserve to be classed and punished with those mischievous persons who put obstructions on the railroads.

But, to speak practically and as a citizen, unlike those who call themselves no-government men, I ask for, not at once no government, but *at once* a better government. Let every man make known what kind of government would command his respect, and that will be one step toward obtaining it.

After all, the practical reason why, when the power is once in the hands of the people, a majority are permitted, and for a long period continue, to rule, is not because they are most likely to be in the right, nor because this seems fairest to the minority, but because they are physically the strongest. But a government in which the majority rule in all cases cannot be based on justice, even as far as men understand it. Can there not be a government in which majorities do not virtually decide right and wrong, but conscience? — in which majorities decide only those questions to which the rule of expediency is applicable? Must the citizen ever for a moment, or in the least degree, resign his conscience to the legislator? Why has every man a conscience, then? I think that we should be men first, and subjects afterward. It is not desirable to cultivate a respect for the law, so much as for the right. The only obligation which I have a right to assume, is to do at any time what I think right. It is truly enough said, that a corporation has no conscience; but a corporation of conscientious men is a corporation with a conscience. Law never made men a whit more just; and, by means of their respect for it, even the well-disposed are daily made the agents of injustice. A common and natural result of an undue respect for law is, that you may see a file of soldiers, colonel, captain, corporal, privates, powder-monkeys and all, marching in admirable order over hill and dale to the wars, against their wills, aye, against their common sense and consciences, which makes it very steep marching indeed, and produces a palpitation of the heart. They have no doubt that it is a damnable business in which they are concerned; they are all peaceably inclined. Now, what are they? Men at

all? or small moveable forts and magazines, at the service of some unscrupulous man in power? Visit the Navy Yard, and behold a marine,
such a man as an American government can make, or such as it can make
a man with its black arts, a mere shadow and reminiscence of humanity,
a man laid out alive and standing, and already, as one may say, buried
under arms with funeral accompaniments, though it may be

> "Not a drum was heard, nor a funeral note,
>   As his corse to the ramparts we hurried;
> Not a soldier discharged his farewell shot
>   O'er the grave where our hero we buried."

The mass of men serve the State thus, not as men mainly, but as   5
machines, with their bodies. They are the standing army, and the militia,
jailers, constables, *posse comitatus,* &c. In most cases there is no free
exercise whatever of the judgment or of the moral sense; but they put
themselves on a level with wood and earth and stones; and wooden men
can perhaps be manufactured that will serve the purpose as well. Such
command no more respect than men of straw, or a lump of dirt. They
have the same sort of worth only as horses and dogs. Yet such as these
even are commonly esteemed good citizens. Others, as most legislators,
politicians, lawyers, ministers, and office-holders, serve the State chiefly
with their heads; and, as they rarely make any moral distinctions, they
are as likely to serve the devil, without intending it, as God. A very few,
as heroes, patriots, martyrs, reformers in the great sense, and *men,* serve
the State with their consciences also, and so necessarily resist it for the
most part; and they are commonly treated by it as enemies. A wise man
will only be useful as a man, and will not submit to be "clay," and "stop
a hole to keep the wind away," but leave that office to his dust at least: —

> "I am too high-born to be propertied,
>   To be a secondary at control,
>   Or useful serving-man and instrument
>   To any sovereign state throughout the world."

He who gives himself entirely to his fellow-men appears to them
useless and selfish; but he who gives himself partially to them is pronounced a benefactor and philanthropist.

How does it become a man to behave toward this American government to-day? I answer that he cannot without disgrace be associated
with it. I cannot for an instant recognize that political organization as *my*
government which is the *slave's* government also.

All men recognize the right of revolution; that is, the right to refuse
allegiance to and to resist the government, when its tyranny or its inef-
ficiency are great and unendurable. But almost all say that such is not the
case now. But such was the case, they think, in the Revolution of '75. If
one were to tell me that this was a bad government because it taxed

certain foreign commodities brought to its ports, it is most probable that I should not make an ado about it, for I can do without them: all machines have their friction; and possibly this does enough good to counterbalance the evil. At any rate, it is a great evil to make a stir about it. But when the friction comes to have its machine, and oppression and robbery are organized, I say, let us not have such a machine any longer. In other words, when a sixth of the population of a nation which has undertaken to be the refuge of liberty are slaves, and a whole country is unjustly overrun and conquered by a foreign army, and subjected to military law, I think that it is not too soon for honest men to rebel and revolutionize. What makes this duty the more urgent is the fact, that the country so overrun is not our own, but ours is the invading army.

Paley, a common authority with many on moral questions, in his chapter on the "Duty of Submission to Civil Government," resolves all civil obligation into expedience; and he proceeds to say, "that so long as the interest of the whole society requires it, that is, so long as the established government cannot be resisted or changed without public inconveniency, it is the will of God that the established government be obeyed, and no longer." — "This principle being admitted, the justice of every particular case of resistance is reduced to a computation of the quantity of the danger and grievance on the one side, and of the probability and expense of redressing it on the other." Of this, he says, every man shall judge for himself. But Paley appears never to have contemplated those cases to which the rule of expediency does not apply, in which a people, as well as an individual, must do justice, cost what it may. If I have unjustly wrested a plank from a drowning man, I must restore it to him though I drown myself. This, according to Paley, would be inconvenient. But he that would save his life, in such a case, shall lose it. This people must cease to hold slaves, and to make war on Mexico, though it cost them their existence as a people.

In their practice, nations agree with Paley; but does any one think   10
that Massachusetts does exactly what is right at the present crisis?

> "A drab of state, a cloth-o'-silver slut,
> To have her train borne up, and her soul trail in the dirt."

Practically speaking, the opponents to a reform in Massachusetts are not a hundred thousand politicians at the South, but a hundred thousand merchants and farmers here, who are more interested in commerce and agriculture than they are in humanity, and are not prepared to do justice to the slave and to Mexico, *cost what it may*. I quarrel not with far-off foes, but with those who, near at home, co-operate with, and do the bidding of those far away, and without whom the latter would be harmless. We are accustomed to say, that the mass of men are unprepared; but improvement is slow, because the few are not materially wiser or better than the many. It is not so important that many should be as good as you, as that there be some absolute goodness somewhere; for that will leaven the whole lump. There are thousands who are *in opinion* opposed to slavery and to the war, who yet in effect do nothing to put an end to them; who, esteeming themselves children of Washington and Franklin, sit down with their hands in their pockets, and say that they know not what to do, and do nothing; who even postpone the question of freedom to the question of free-trade, and quietly read the prices-current along with the latest advices from Mexico, after dinner, and, it may be, fall asleep over them both. What is the price-current of an honest man and patriot to-day? They hesitate, and they regret, and sometimes they petition; but they do nothing in earnest and with effect. They will wait, well disposed, for others to remedy the evil, that they may no longer have it to regret. At most, they give only a cheap vote, and a feeble countenance and God-speed, to the right, as it goes by them. There are nine hundred and ninety-nine patrons of virtue to one virtuous man; but it is easier to deal with the real possessor of a thing than with the temporary guardian of it.

All voting is a sort of gaming, like chequers or backgammon, with a slight moral tinge to it, a playing with right and wrong, with moral questions; and betting naturally accompanies it. The character of the voters is not staked. I cast my vote, perchance, as I think right; but I am not vitally concerned that that right should prevail. I am willing to leave it to the majority. Its obligation, therefore, never exceeds that of expedience. Even voting *for the right* is *doing* nothing for it. It is only expressing to men feebly your desire that it should prevail. A wise man will not leave the right to the mercy of chance, nor wish it to prevail through the power of the majority. There is but little virtue in the action of masses of men. When the majority shall at length vote for the abolition of slavery, it will be because they are indifferent to slavery, or because there is but little slavery left to be abolished by their vote. *They* will then be the only slaves. Only *his* vote can hasten the abolition of slavery who asserts his own freedom by his vote.

I hear of a convention to be held at Baltimore, or elsewhere, for the selection of a candidate for the Presidency, made up chiefly of editors, and men who are politicians by profession; but I think, what is it to any independent, intelligent, and respectable man what decision they may come to, shall we not have the advantage of his wisdom and honesty, nevertheless? Can we not count upon some independent votes? Are there not many individuals in the country who do not attend conventions? But no: I find that the respectable man, so called, has immediately drifted from his position, and despairs of his country, when his country has more reason to despair of him. He forthwith adopts one of the candidates thus selected as the only *available* one, thus proving that he is himself *available* for any purposes of the demagogue. His vote is of no more worth than that of any unprincipled foreigner or hireling native, who may have been bought. Oh for a man who is a *man,* and, as my neighbor says, has a bone in his back which you cannot pass your hand through! Our statistics are at fault: the population has been returned too large. How many *men* are there to a square thousand miles in this country? Hardly one. Does not America offer any inducement for men to settle here? The American has dwindled into an Odd Fellow, — one who may be known by the development of his organ of gregariousness, and a manifest lack of intellect and cheerful self-reliance; whose first and chief concern, on coming into the world, is to see that the alms-houses are in good repair; and, before yet he has lawfully donned the virile garb, to collect a fund for the support of the widows and orphans that may be; who, in short, ventures to live only by the aid of the mutual insurance company, which has promised to bury him decently.

It is not a man's duty, as a matter of course, to devote himself to the eradication of any, even the most enormous wrong; he may still properly have other concerns to engage him; but it is his duty, at least, to wash his hands of it, and, if he gives it no thought longer, not to give it practically his support. If I devote myself to other pursuits and contemplations, I must first see, at least, that I do not pursue them sitting upon another man's shoulders. I must get off him first, that he may pursue his contemplations too. See what gross inconsistency is tolerated. I have heard some of my townsmen say, "I should like to have them order me out to help put down an insurrection of the slaves, or to march to Mexico, — see if I would go;" and yet these very men have each, directly by their allegiance, and so indirectly, at least, by their money, furnished a substitute. The soldier is applauded who refuses to serve in an unjust war by those who do not refuse to sustain the unjust government which makes the war; is applauded by those whose own act and authority he disregards and sets at nought; as if the State were penitent to that degree that it hired one to scourge it while it sinned, but not to that degree that it left off sinning for a moment. Thus, under the name of order and civil government, we are all made at last to pay homage to and support our own meanness. After the first blush of sin, comes its indifference; and from immoral it becomes, as it were, *un*moral, and not quite unnecessary to that life which we have made.

The broadest and most prevalent error requires the most disinterested virtue to sustain it. The slight reproach to which the virtue of patriotism is commonly liable, the noble are most likely to incur. Those who, while they disapprove of the character and measures of a government, yield to it their allegiance and support, are undoubtedly its most conscientious supporters, and so frequently the most serious obstacles to reform. Some are petitioning the State to dissolve the Union, to disregard the requisitions of the President. Why do they not dissolve it themselves, — the union between themselves and the State, — and refuse to pay their quota into its treasury? Do not they stand in the same relation to the State, that the State does to the Union? And have not the same reasons prevented the State from resisting the Union, which have prevented them from resisting the State?

How can a man be satisfied to entertain an opinion merely, and   15 enjoy *it*? Is there any enjoyment in it, if his opinion is that he is aggrieved? If you are cheated out of a single dollar by your neighbor, you do not rest satisfied with knowing that you are cheated, or with saying that you are cheated, or even with petitioning him to pay you your due; but you take effectual steps at once to obtain the full amount, and see that you are never cheated again. Action from principle, — the perception and the performance of right, — changes things and relations; it is essentially revolutionary, and does not consist wholly with any thing which was. It not only divides states and churches, it divides families; aye, it divides the *individual,* separating the diabolical in him from the divine.

Unjust laws exist: shall we be content to obey them, or shall we endeavor to amend them, and obey them until we have succeeded, or shall we transgress them at once? Men generally, under such a government as this, think that they ought to wait until they have persuaded the majority to alter them. They think that, if they should resist, the remedy would be worse than the evil. But it is the fault of the government itself that the remedy *is* worse than the evil. *It* makes it worse. Why is it not more apt to anticipate and provide for reform? Why does it not cherish its wise minority? Why does it cry and resist before it is hurt? Why does it not encourage its citizens to be on the alert to point out its faults, and *do* better than it would have them? Why does it always crucify Christ, and excommunicate Copernicus and Luther, and pronounce Washington and Franklin rebels?

One would think, that a deliberate and practical denial of its authority was the only offence never contemplated by government; else, why has it not assigned its definite, its suitable and proportionate penalty? If a man who has no property refuses but once to earn nine shillings for the State, he is put in prison for a period unlimited by any law that I know, and determined only by the discretion of those who placed him there; but if he should steal ninety times nine shillings from the State, he is soon permitted to go at large again.

If the injustice is part of the necessary friction of the machine of government, let it go, let it go: perchance it will wear smooth, — certainly the machine will wear out. If the injustice has a spring, or a pulley, or a rope, or a crank, exclusively for itself, then perhaps you may consider whether the remedy will not be worse than the evil; but if it is of such a nature that it requires you to be the agent of injustice to another, then, I say, break the law. Let your life be a counter friction to stop the machine. What I have to do is to see, at any rate, that I do not lend myself to the wrong which I condemn.

As for adopting the ways which the State has provided for remedying the evil, I know not of such ways. They take too much time, and a man's life will be gone. I have other affairs to attend to. I came into this world, not chiefly to make this a good place to live in, but to live in it, be it good or bad. A man has not every thing to do, but something; and because he cannot do *every thing,* it is not necessary that he should do *something* wrong. It is not my business to be petitioning the governor or the legislature any more than it is theirs to petition me; and, if they should not hear my petition, what should I do then? But in this case the State has provided no way: its very Constitution is the evil. This may seem to be harsh and stubborn and unconciliatory; but it is to treat with the utmost kindness and consideration the only spirit that can appreciate or deserves it. So is all change for the better, like birth and death which convulse the body.

I do not hesitate to say, that those who call themselves abolitionists   *20* should at once effectually withdraw their support, both in person and property, from the government of Massachusetts, and not wait till they constitute a majority of one, before they suffer the right to prevail through them. I think that it is enough if they have God on their side, without waiting for that other one. Moreover, any man more right than his neighbors, constitutes a majority of one already.

I meet this American government, or its representative the State government, directly, and face to face, once a year, no more, in the person of its tax-gatherer; this is the only mode in which a man situated as I am necessarily meets it; and it then says distinctly, Recognize me; and the simplest, the most effectual, and, in the present posture of affairs, the indispensablest mode of treating with it on this head, of expressing your little satisfaction with and love for it, is to deny it then. My civil neighbor, the tax-gatherer, is the very man I have to deal with, — for it is, after all, with men and not with parchment that I quarrel, — and he has voluntarily chosen to be an agent of the government. How shall he ever know well what he is and does as an officer of the government, or as a man, until he is obliged to consider whether he shall treat me, his neighbor, for whom he has respect, as a neighbor and well-disposed man, or as a maniac and disturber of the peace, and see if he can get over this obstruction to his neighborliness without a ruder and more impetuous thought or speech corresponding with his action? I know this well, that if one thousand, if one hundred, if ten men whom I could name, — if ten *honest* men only, — aye, if *one* HONEST man, in this State of Massachusetts, *ceasing to hold slaves,* were actually to withdraw from this co-partnership, and be locked up in the county jail therefor, it would be the abolition of slavery in America. For it matters not how small the beginning may seem to be: what is once well done is done for ever. But we love better to talk about it: that we say is our mission. Reform keeps many scores of newspapers in its service, but not one man. If my esteemed neighbor, the State's ambassador, who will devote his days to the settlement of the question of human rights in the Council Chamber, instead of being threatened with the prisons of Carolina, were to sit down the prisoner of Massachusetts, that State which is so anxious to foist the sin of slavery upon her sister, — though at present she can discover only an act of inhospitality to be the ground of a quarrel with her, — the Legislature would not wholly waive the subject the following winter.

Under a government which imprisons any unjustly, the true place for a just man is also a prison. The proper place to-day, the only place which Massachusetts has provided for her freer and less desponding spirits, is in her prisons, to be put out and locked out of the State by her own act, as they have already put themselves out by their principles. It is there that the fugitive slave, and the Mexican prisoner on parole, and the Indian come to plead the wrongs of his race, should find them; on that separate, but more free and honorable ground, where the State places those who are not *with* her but *against* her, — the only house in a slave-state in which a free man can abide with honor. If any think that their influence would be lost there, and their voices no longer afflict the ear of the State, that they would not be as an enemy within its walls, they do not know by how much truth is stronger than error, nor how much more eloquently and effectively he can combat injustice who has experienced a little in his own person. Cast your whole vote, not a strip of paper merely, but your whole influence. A minority is powerless while it conforms to the majority; it is not even a minority then; but it is irresistible when it clogs by its whole weight. If the alternative is to keep all just men in prison, or give up war and slavery, the State will not hesitate which to choose. If a thousand men were not to pay their tax-bills this year, that would not be a violent and bloody measure, as it would be to pay them, and enable the State to commit violence and shed innocent blood. This is, in fact, the definition of a peaceable revolution, if any such is possible. If the tax-gatherer, or any other public officer, asks me, as one has done, "But what shall I do?" my answer is, "If you really wish to do any thing, resign your office." When the subject has refused allegiance, and the officer has resigned his office, then the revolution is accomplished. But even suppose blood should flow. Is there not a sort of blood shed when the conscience is wounded? Through this wound a man's real manhood and immortality flow out, and he bleeds to an everlasting death. I see this blood flowing now.

I have contemplated the imprisonment of the offender, rather than the seizure of his goods, — though both will serve the same purpose, — because they who assert the purest right, and consequently are most dangerous to a corrupt State, commonly have not spent much time in accumulating property. To such the State renders comparatively small service, and a slight tax is wont to appear exorbitant, particularly if they are obliged to earn it by special labor with their hands. If there were one who lived wholly without the use of money, the State itself would hesitate to demand it of him. But the rich man — not to make any invidious comparison — is always sold to the institution which makes him rich. Absolutely speaking, the more money, the less virtue; for money comes between a man and his objects, and obtains them for him; and it was certainly no great virtue to obtain it. It puts to rest many questions which he would otherwise be taxed to answer; while the only new question which it puts is the hard but superfluous one, how to spend it. Thus his moral ground is taken from under his feet. The opportunities of living are diminished in proportion as what are called the "means" are increased. The best thing a man can do for his culture when he is rich is to endeavour to carry out those schemes which he entertained when he was poor. Christ answered the Herodians according to their condition. "Show me the tribute-money," said he; — and one took a penny out of his pocket; — If you use money which has the image of Caesar on it, and which he has made current and valuable, that is, *if you are men of the State,* and gladly enjoy the advantages of Caesar's government, then pay him back some of his own when he demands it; "Render therefore to Caesar that which is Caesar's, and to God those things which are God's," — leaving them no wiser than before as to which was which; for they did not wish to know.

When I converse with the freest of my neighbors, I perceive that, whatever they may say about the magnitude and seriousness of the question, and their regard for the public tranquillity, the long and the short of the matter is, that they cannot spare the protection of the existing government, and they dread the consequences of disobedience to it to their property and families. For my own part, I should not like to think that I ever rely on the protection of the State. But, if I deny the authority of the State when it presents its tax-bill, it will soon take and waste all my property, and so harass me and my children without end. This is hard. This makes it impossible for a man to live honestly and at the same time comfortably in outward respects. It will not be worth the while to accumulate property; that would be sure to go again. You must hire or squat somewhere, and raise but a small crop, and eat that soon. You must live within yourself, and depend upon yourself, always tucked up and ready for a start, and not have many affairs. A man may grow rich in Turkey even, if he will be in all respects a good subject of the Turkish government. Confucius said, — "If a State is governed by the principles of reason, poverty and misery are subjects of shame; if a State is not governed by the principles of reason, riches and honors are the subjects of shame." No: until I want the protection of Massachusetts to be extended to me in some distant southern port, where my liberty is endangered, or until I am bent solely on building up an estate at home by peaceful enterprise, I can afford to refuse allegiance to Massachusetts, and her right to my property and life. It costs me less in every sense to incur the penalty of disobedience to the State, than it would to obey. I should feel as if I were worth less in that case.

Some years ago, the State met me in behalf of the church, and   25
commanded me to pay a certain sum toward the support of a clergyman whose preaching my father attended, but never I myself. "Pay it," it said, "or be locked up in the jail." I declined to pay. But, unfortunately, another man saw fit to pay it. I did not see why the schoolmaster should be taxed to support the priest, and not the priest the schoolmaster; for I was not the State's schoolmaster, but I supported myself by voluntary subscription. I did not see why the lyceum should not present its tax-bill, and have the State to back its demand, as well as the church. However, at the request of the selectmen, I condescended to make some such statement as this in writing: — "Know all men by these presents, that I, Henry Thoreau, do not wish to be regarded as a member of any incorporated society which I have not joined." This I gave to the town-clerk; and he has it. The State, having thus learned that I did not wish to be regarded as a member of that church, has never made a like demand on me since; though it said that it must adhere to its original presumption that time. If I had known how to name them, I should then have signed off in detail from all the societies which I never signed on to; but I did not know where to find a complete list.

I have paid no poll-tax for six years. I was put into a jail once on this account, for one night; and, as I stood considering the walls of solid stone, two or three feet thick, the door of wood and iron, a foot thick, and the iron grating which strained the light, I could not help being struck with the foolishness of that institution which treated me as if I were mere flesh and blood and bones, to be locked up. I wondered that it should have concluded at length that this was the best use it could put me to, and had never thought to avail itself of my services in some way. I saw that, if there was a wall of stone between me and my townsmen, there was a still more difficult one to climb or break through, before they could get to be as free as I was. I did not for a moment feel confined, and the walls seemed a great waste of stone and mortar. I felt as if I alone of all my townsmen had paid my tax. They plainly did not know how to treat me, but behaved like persons who are underbred. In every threat and in every compliment there was a blunder; for they thought that my chief desire was to stand the other side of that stone wall. I could not but smile to see how industriously they locked the door on my meditations, which followed them out again without let or hinderance, and *they* were really all that was dangerous. As they could not reach me, they had resolved to punish my body; just as boys, if they cannot come at some person against whom they have a spite, will abuse his dog. I saw that the State was half-witted, that it was timid as a lone woman with her silver spoons, and that it did not know its friends from its foes, and I lost all my remaining respect for it, and pitied it.

Thus the State never intentionally confronts a man's sense, intellectual or moral, but only his body, his senses. It is not armed with superior wit or honesty, but with superior physical strength. I was not born to be forced. I will breathe after my own fashion. Let us see who is the strongest. What force has a multitude? They only can force me who obey a higher law than I. They force me to become like themselves. I do not hear of *men* being *forced* to live this way or that by masses of men. What sort of life were that to live? When I meet a government which says to me, "Your money or your life," why should I be in haste to give it my money? It may be in a great strait, and not know what to do: I cannot help that. It must help itself; do as I do. It is not worth the while to snivel about it. I am not responsible for the successful working of the machinery of society. I am not the son of the engineer. I perceive that, when an acorn and a chestnut fall side by side, the one does not remain inert to make way for the other, but both obey their own laws, and spring and grow and flourish as best they can, till one, perchance, overshadows and destroys the other. If a plant cannot live according to its nature, it dies; and so a man.

The night in prison was novel and interesting enough. The prisoners in their shirt-sleeves were enjoying a chat and the evening air in the door-way, when I entered. But the jailer said, "Come, boys, it is time to lock up;" and so they dispersed, and I heard the sound of their steps returning into the hollow apartments. My room-mate was introduced to me by the jailer, as "a first-rate fellow and a clever man." When the door was locked, he showed me where to hang my hat, and how he managed matters there. The rooms were whitewashed once a month; and this one, at least, was the whitest, most simply furnished, and probably the neatest apartment in the town. He naturally wanted to know where I came from, and what brought me there; and, when I had told him, I asked him in my turn how he came there, presuming him to be an honest man, of course; and, as the world goes, I believe he was. "Why," said he, "they accuse me of burning a barn; but I never did it." As near as I could discover, he had probably gone to bed in a barn when drunk, and smoked his pipe there; and so a barn was burnt. He had the reputation of being a clever man, had been there some three months waiting for his trial to come on, and would have to wait as much longer; but he was quite domesticated and contented, since he got his board for nothing, and thought that he was well treated.

He occupied one window, and I the other; and I saw, that if one stayed there long, his principal business would be to look out the window. I had soon read all the tracts that were left there, and examined where former prisoners had broken out, and where a grate had been sawed off, and heard the history of the various occupants of that room; for I found that even here there was a history and a gossip which never circulated beyond the walls of the jail. Probably this is the only house in the town where verses are composed, which are afterward printed in a circular form, but not published. I was shown quite a long list of verses which were composed by some young men who had been detected in an attempt to escape, who avenged themselves by singing them.

I pumped my fellow-prisoner as dry as I could, for fear I should never see him again; but at length he showed me which was my bed, and left me to blow out the lamp.

It was like travelling into a far country, such as I had never expected to behold, to lie there for one night. It seemed to me that I never had heard the town-clock strike before, nor the evening sounds of the village; for we slept with the windows open, which were inside the grating. It was to see my native village in the light of the middle ages, and our Concord was turned into a Rhine stream, and visions of knights and castles passed before me. They were the voices of old burghers that I heard in the streets. I was an involuntary spectator and auditor of whatever was done and said in the kitchen of the adjacent village-inn, — a wholly new and rare experience to me. It was a closer view of my native town. I was fairly inside of it. I never had seen its institutions before. This is one of its peculiar institutions; for it is a shire town. I began to comprehend what its inhabitants were about.

In the morning, our breakfasts were put through the hole in the door, in small oblong-square tin pans, made to fit, and holding a pint of chocolate, with brown bread, and an iron spoon. When they called for the vessels again, I was green enough to return what bread I had left; but my comrade seized it, and said that I should lay that up for lunch or dinner. Soon after, he was let out to work at haying in a neighboring field, whither he went every day, and would not be back till noon; so he bade me good-day, saying that he doubted if he should see me again.

When I came out of prison, — for some one interfered, and paid the tax, — I did not perceive that great changes had taken place on the common, such as he observed who went in a youth, and emerged a tottering and gray-headed man; and yet a change had to my eyes come over the scene, — the town, and State, and country, — greater than any that mere time could effect. I saw yet more distinctly the State in which I lived. I saw to what extent the people among whom I lived could be trusted as good neighbors and friends; that their friendship was for summer weather only; that they did not greatly purpose to do right; that they were a distinct race from me by their prejudices and superstitions, as the Chinamen and Malays are; that, in their sacrifices to humanity, they ran no risks, not even to their property; that, after all, they were not so noble but they treated the thief as he had treated them, and hoped, by a certain outward observance and a few prayers, and by walking in a particular straight though useless path from time to time, to save their souls. This may be to judge my neighbors harshly; for I believe that most of them are not aware that they have such an institution as the jail in their village.

It was formerly the custom in our village, when a poor debtor came out of jail, for his acquaintances to salute him, looking through their fingers, which were crossed to represent the grating of a jail window, "How do ye do?" My neighbors did not thus salute me, but first looked at me, and then at one another, as if I had returned from a long journey. I was put into jail as I was going to the shoemaker's to get a shoe which was mended. When I was let out the next morning, I proceeded to finish my errand, and, having put on my mended shoe, joined a huckleberry party, who were impatient to put themselves under my conduct; and in half an hour, — for the horse was soon tackled, — was in the midst of a huckleberry field, on one of our highest hills, two miles off; and then the State was nowhere to be seen.

This is the whole history of "My Prisons."

I have never declined paying the highway tax, because I am as desirous of being a good neighbor as I am of being a bad subject; and, as for supporting schools, I am doing my part to educate my fellow-countrymen now. It is for no particular item in the tax-bill that I refuse to pay it. I simply wish to refuse allegiance to the State, to withdraw and stand aloof from it effectually. I do not care to trace the course of my dollar, if I could, till it buys a man, or a musket to shoot one with, — the dollar is innocent, — but I am concerned to trace the effects of my allegiance. In fact, I quietly declare war with the State, after my fashion, though I will still make what use and get what advantage of her I can, as is usual in such cases.

If others pay the tax which is demanded of me, from a sympathy with the State, they do but what they have already done in their own case, or rather they abet injustice to a greater extent than the State requires. If they pay the tax from a mistaken interest in the individual taxed, to save his property or prevent his going to jail, it is because they have not considered wisely how far they let their private feelings interfere with the public good.

This, then, is my position at present. But one cannot be too much 30 on his guard in such a case, lest his action be biassed by obstinacy, or an undue regard for the opinions of men. Let him see that he does only what belongs to himself and to the hour.

I think sometimes, Why, this people mean well; they are only ignorant; they would do better if they knew how: why give your neighbors this pain to treat you as they are not inclined to? But I think, again, this is no reason why I should do as they do, or permit others to suffer much greater pain of a different kind. Again, I sometimes say to myself, When many millions of men, without heat, without ill-will, without personal feeling of any kind, demand of you a few shillings only, without the possibility, such is their constitution, of retracting or altering their present demand, and without the possibility, on your side, of appeal to any other millions, why expose yourself to this overwhelming brute force? You do not resist cold and hunger, the winds and the waves, thus obstinately; you quietly submit to a thousand similar necessities. You do not put your head into the fire. But just in proportion as I regard this as not wholly a brute force, but partly a human force, and consider that I have relations to those millions as to so many millions of men, and not of mere brute or inanimate things, I see that appeal is possible, first and instantaneously, from them to the Maker of them, and secondly, from them to themselves. But, if I put my head deliberately into the fire, there is no appeal to fire or to the Maker of fire, and I have only myself to blame. If I could convince myself that I have any right to be satisfied with men as they are, and to treat them accordingly, and not according, in some respects, to my requisitions and expectations of what they and I ought to be, then, like a good Mussulman and fatalist, I should endeavor to be satisfied with things as they are, and say it is the will of God. And, above all, there is this difference between resisting this and a purely brute or natural force, that I can resist this with some effect; but I cannot expect, like Orpheus, to change the nature of the rocks and trees and beasts.

I do not wish to quarrel with any man or nation. I do not wish to split hairs, to make fine distinctions, or set myself up as better than my neighbors. I seek rather, I may say, even an excuse for conforming to the laws of the land. I am but too ready to conform to them. Indeed I have reason to suspect myself on this head; and each year, as the tax-gatherer comes round, I find myself disposed to review the acts and position of the general and state governments, and the spirit of the people, to discover a pretext for conformity. I believe that the State will soon be able to take all my work of this sort out of my hands, and then I shall be no better a patriot than my fellow-countrymen. Seen from a lower point of view, the Constitution, with all its faults, is very good; the law and the courts are very respectable; even this State and this American government are, in many respects, very admirable and rare things, to be thankful for, such as a great many have described them; but seen from a point of view a little higher, they are what I have described them; seen from a higher still, and the highest, who shall say what they are, or that they are worth looking at or thinking of at all?

However, the government does not concern me much, and I shall bestow the fewest possible thoughts on it. It is not many moments that I live under a government, even in this world. If a man is thought-free, fancy-free, imagination-free, that which *is not* never for a long time appearing *to be* to him, unwise rulers or reformers cannot fatally interrupt him.

I know that most men think differently from myself; but those whose lives are by profession devoted to the study of these or kindred subjects, content me as little as any. Statesmen and legislators, standing so completely within the institution, never distinctly and nakedly behold it. They speak of moving society, but have no resting-place without it. They may be men of a certain experience and discrimination, and have no doubt invented ingenious and even useful systems, for which we sincerely thank them; but all their wit and usefulness lie within certain not very wide limits. They are wont to forget that the world is not governed by policy and expediency. Webster never goes behind government, and so cannot speak with authority about it. His words are wisdom to those legislators who contemplate no essential reform in the existing government; but for thinkers, and those who legislate for all time, he never once glances at the subject. I know of those whose serene and wise speculations on this theme would soon reveal the limits of his mind's range and hospitality. Yet, compared with the cheap professions of most reformers, and the still cheaper wisdom and eloquence of politicians in general, his are almost the only sensible and valuable words, and we thank Heaven for him. Comparatively, he is always strong, original, and, above all, practical. Still his quality is not wisdom, but prudence. The lawyer's truth is not Truth, but consistency, or a consistent expediency. Truth is always in harmony with herself, and is not concerned chiefly to reveal the justice that may consist with wrong-doing. He well deserves to be called as he has been called, the Defender of the Constitution. There are really no blows to be given by him but defensive ones. He is not a leader, but a follower. His leaders are the men of '87. "I have never made an effort," he says, "and never propose to make an effort; I have never countenanced an effort, and never mean to countenance an effort, to disturb the arrangement as originally made, by which the various States came into the Union." Still thinking of the sanction which the Constitution gives to slavery, he says, "Because it was a part of the original compact, — let it stand." Notwithstanding his special acuteness and ability, he is unable to take a fact out of its merely political relations, and behold it as it lies absolutely to be disposed of by the intellect, — what, for instance, it behoves a man to do here in America to-day with regard to slavery, but ventures, or is driven, to make some such desperate answer as the following, while professing to speak absolutely, and as a private man, — from which what new and singular code of social duties might be inferred? — "The manner," says he, "in which the government of those States where slavery exists are to regulate it, is for their own consideration, under their responsibility to their constituents, to the general laws of propriety, humanity, and justice, and to God. Associations formed elsewhere, springing from a feeling of humanity, or any other cause, have nothing whatever to do with it. They have never received any encouragement from me, and they never will."

They who know of no purer sources of truth, who have traced up 35 its stream no higher, stand, and wisely stand, by the Bible and the Constitution, and drink at it there with reverence and humility; but they who behold where it comes trickling into this lake or that pool, gird up their loins once more, and continue their pilgrimage toward its fountain-head.

No man with a genius for legislation has appeared in America. They are rare in the history of the world. There are orators, politicians, and eloquent men, by the thousand; but the speaker has not yet opened his mouth to speak, who is capable of settling the much-vexed questions of the day. We love eloquence for its own sake, and not for any truth which it may utter, or any heroism it may inspire. Our legislators have not yet learned the comparative value of free-trade and of freedom, of union, and of rectitude, to a nation. They have no genius or talent for comparatively humble questions of taxation and finance, commerce and manufactures and agriculture. If we were left solely to the wordy wit of legislators in Congress for our guidance, uncorrected by the seasonable experience and the effectual complaints of the people, America would not long retain her rank among the nations. For eighteen hundred years, though perchance I have no right to say it, the New Testament has been written; yet where is the legislator who has wisdom and practical talent enough to avail himself of the light which it sheds on the science of legislation?

The authority of government, even such as I am willing to submit to, — for I will cheerfully obey those who know and can do better than I, and in many things even those who neither know nor can do so well, — is still an impure one: to be strictly just, it must have the sanction and consent of the governed. It can have no pure right over my person and property but what I concede to it. The progress from an absolute to a limited monarchy, from a limited monarchy to a democracy, is a progress toward a true respect for the individual. Is a democracy, such as we know it, the last improvement possible in government? Is it not possible to take a step further towards recognizing and organizing the rights of man? There will never be a really free and enlightened State, until the State comes to recognize the individual as a higher and independent power, from which all its own power and authority are derived, and treats him accordingly. I please myself with imagining a State at last which can afford to be just to all men, and to treat the individual with respect as a neighbor; which even would not think it inconsistent with its own repose, if a few were to live aloof from it, not meddling with it, nor embraced by it, who fulfilled all the duties of neighbors and fellow-men. A State which bore this kind of fruit, and suffered it to drop off as fast as it ripened, would prepare the way for a still more perfect and glorious State, which also I have imagined, but not yet anywhere seen.

FOR DISCUSSION AND WRITING

1. Explain why the following statement is either logical or illogical: "The authority of government, even such as I am willing to submit to, — for I will cheerfully obey those who know and can do better than I, and in many things even those who neither know nor can do so well, — is still an impure one: to be strictly just, it must have the sanction and the consent of the governed. It can have no right over my person and my property but what I concede to it." (par. 37)

2. What is Thoreau's claim?

3. In many ways, Thoreau argues for radical self-centeredness. What backing does he provide for such a position? Explain why you agree or disagree with him.

4. Thoreau uses metaphors to characterize obedience to and action by the government. How do these metaphors add to the persuasiveness of the argument?

5. Near the beginning of his essay, Thoreau says, "That government is best which governs not at all" (par. 1). Then he mounts a withering assault on the United States federal government, accusing it of becoming a standing government against Mexico, asserting that the government has never furthered any enterprise, does not keep the nation free, does not educate, and so on. Finally, however, he states, "I ask for, not at once no government, but *at once* a better government" (par. 3). Most people would agree with the final statement. Do you think that most would also agree that the government which governs not at all is best? Explain.

6. Characterize Thoreau's tone. Is he calm and reasonable, or strident and impatient? Which of the following are most like "Civil Disobedience" in tone: "Hackers in Jail," "Profits Vs. Injury," "A Game of Chicken," "The Natural and the Supernatural," or "Ethics and Animals"? If you were to write your own version of "Civil Disobedience," would you change the tone? In what way or ways?

7. "Civil Disobedience" influenced Mahatma Gandhi and Martin Luther King, Jr., as well as other international figures. Explain why, in your opinion, it has had such an impact. (It will be useful to think in terms of agent, scene, and purpose.)

8. Would Thoreau agree with the adage that "if you are not a part of the solution, then you must be part of the problem"? Explain.

9. In Thoreau's view, what is the moral authority by which a democracy exists? What moral authority should a state abide by?

10. Evaluate the essay from the standpoint of quantity. Could Thoreau have deleted parts? If so, which ones?

11. What circumstances of scene generated the purpose for the argument?

12. State the gist of the argument. Explain why you think it either does or does not concern civil disobedience.

13. In regard to relation, evaluate Thoreau's account of his night in prison. Is the narrative relevant to his argument?

14. According to Thoreau, two specific problems undercut the authority of the government. What are these problems? Do you agree with Thoreau's conclusions about these problems? (What source would you consult to find background on the problems?)

THE LONELINESS OF
THE MILITARY HISTORIAN

Margaret Atwood

Margaret Eleanor Atwood, born in 1939, is one of Canada's (and North America's) most highly admired writers. Her book of poetry, *The Circle Game* (1964), won the Governor General's Award; her second novel, *Surfacing* (1972), deals with the archetypal theme of the search for a father. Other works include two volumes of selected poems (1976, 1988) and the novel *The Cat's Eye* (1989). Atwood's best-known work is *The Handmaid's Tale* (1986), a science fiction story about an America in the near future, when the world has been virtually destroyed by pollution and religious fundamentalists have seized control of the government. (The movie version of *The Handmaid's Tale* starred Robert Duvall and Faye Dunaway.)

As you read "The Loneliness of the Military Historian," think about the ways in which Margaret Atwood might agree or disagree with what John Keegan, one very prominent military historian, says in the introduction to his book on great generals in history: "The leader of men in warfare can show himself to his followers only through a mask, a mask that he must make for himself, but a mask made in such a form as will mark him to men of his time and place as the leader they want and need." Is each war different, or are all wars fundamentally the same?

If we take this poem to be an argument, what is the claim? Is the poem successful or unsuccessful as an argument?

Confess: it's my profession
that alarms you.
This is why few people ask me to dinner,
though Lord knows I don't go out of my way to
   be scary.   5
I wear dresses of sensible cut
and unalarming shades of beige,
I smell of lavender and go to the hairdresser's:
no prophetess mane of mine
complete with snakes, will frighten the   10
   youngsters.
If my eyes roll and I mutter,
if my arms are gloved in blood right up to the
   elbow,
if I clutch at my heart and scream in horror   15
like a third-rate actress chewing up a mad scene,
I do it in private and nobody sees
but the bathroom mirror.

In general I might agree with you:
women should not contemplate war,   20
should not weigh tactics impartially,
or evade the word *enemy*,
or view both sides and denounce nothing.
Women should march for peace,
or hand out white feathers to inspire bravery,   25
spit themselves on bayonets
to protect their babies,
whose skulls will be split anyway,
or, having been raped repeatedly,
hang themselves with their own hair.   30
These are the functions that inspire general
    comfort.
That, and the knitting of socks for the troops
and a sort of moral cheerleading.
Also: mourning the dead.   35
Sons, lovers, and so forth.
All the killed children.

Instead of this, I tell
what I hope will pass as truth.
A blunt thing, not lovely.   40
The truth is seldom welcome,
especially at dinner,
though I am good at what I do.
My trade is in courage and atrocities.
I look at them and do not condemn.   45
I write things down the way they happened,
as near as can be remembered.
I don't ask *why* because it is mostly the same.
Wars happen because the ones who start them
think they can win.   50

In my dreams there is glamour.
The Vikings leave their fields
each year for a few months of killing and
    plunder,
much as the boys go hunting.   55
In real life they were farmers.
They come back loaded with splendor.
The Arabs ride against Crusaders
with scimitars that could sever
silk in the air.   60
A swift cut to the horse's neck

and a hunk of armor crashes down
like a tower. Fire against metal.
A poet might say: romance against banality.
When awake, I know better. 65

Despite the propaganda, there are no monsters,
or none that can be finally buried.
Finish one off and circumstances
and the radio create another.
Believe me: whole armies have prayed fervently 70
to God all night and meant it,
and been slaughtered anyway.
Brutality wins frequently,
and large outcomes have turned on the
    invention 75
of a mechanical device, viz. radar.

True, sometimes valor counts for something,
as at Thermopylae. Sometimes being right,
though ultimate virtue by agreed tradition
is decided by the winner. 80
Sometimes men throw themselves on grenades
and burst like paper bags of guts
to save their comrades.
I can admire that.
But rats and cholera have won many wars. 85
Those, and potatoes
or the absence of them.
It's no use pinning all those medals
across the chests of the dead.
Impressive, but I know too much. 90
Grand exploits merely depress me.

In the interests of research
I have walked on many battlefields
that once were liquid with pulped
men's bodies and spangled with burst 95
shells and splayed bone.
All of them have been green again
by the time I got there.
Each has inspired a few good quotes in its day.
Sad marble angels brood like hens 100
over the grassy nests where nothing hatches.
(The angels could just as well be described as
    vulgar,
or pitiless, depending on camera angle.)

The word *glory* figures a lot on gateways.   105
Of course I pick a flower or two
from each, and press it in the hotel
Bible, for a souvenir.
I'm as human as you.

But it's no use asking me for a final statement.   110
As I say, I deal in tactics.
Also statistics:
for every year of peace there have been four
    hundred
years of war.   115

FOR DISCUSSION AND WRITING

1. The narrator states that "it's no use asking me for a final statement" (line 110). Why does she write this? Do you believe that the poem itself has a final statement — that is, a claim — to make? If so, what is it? If not, explain why not.

2. Atwood cites a statistic: "for every year of peace there have been four hundred years of war" (line 113). Do you believe this statistic to be true or false? Does the author intend it to be taken literally? Why, or why not? What backing or qualification do you think Atwood would present to reinforce her argument?

3. What do you think that the poem is meant to persuade the reader to believe in or take action with? Do you think that it is effective in its purpose? Why, or why not?

4. The narrator states that "women should not contemplate war" (line 20), yet that is her very profession. Does the narrator see this as a contradiction? Why, or why not? (Remember, the "speaker" in the poem is a fictional character, not Margaret Atwood.)

5. This poem has many examples of wild, graphic scenes of horror counterbalanced by a dispassionate analysis or staid imagery. Give several examples of this. Why do you think the author uses this technique?

6. Do you think that the military historian is avoided because of the subject of her profession or her attitude toward it? Explain.

7. The tone of the poem is dispassionate. Does this tone contradict or agree with the intention of the piece?

8. Do you feel that it would be more productive to view the poem as a narrative or as exposition? Do you base your answer on the fact that the text is a poem, on the subject matter, or on some other factor? Explain.

THE DECLARATION
OF INDEPENDENCE

Of the Declaration of Independence, the *Concise Columbia Encyclopedia* says:

Adopted July 4, 1776, by delegates of the Thirteen Colonies, announcing their separation from Great Britain and creation of the United States. It was written almost totally by Thomas Jefferson. The opening paragraphs state the American ideal of government, based on the theory of natural rights. The Declaration of Independence is the most important of all American historical documents; its combination of general principles and abstract theory of government with a detailed enumeration of specific grievances and injustices makes it one of the great political documents of the West.

Nonetheless, we wonder how many Americans have carefully and critically read the Declaration and given it the thought it deserves.

When in the Course of human events, it becomes necessary for one people to dissolve the political bands which have connected them with another, and to assume among the powers of the earth, the separate and equal station to which the Laws of Nature and of Nature's God entitle them, a decent respect to the opinions of mankind requires that they should declare the causes which impel them to the separation.

We hold these truths to be self-evident, that all men are created equal, that they are endowed by their Creator with certain unalienable Rights, that among these are Life, Liberty and the pursuit of Happiness. — That to secure these rights, Governments are instituted among Men, deriving their just powers from the consent of the governed. — That whenever any Form of Government becomes destructive of these ends, it is the Right of the People to alter or to abolish it, and to institute new Government, laying its foundation on such principles and organizing its powers in such form, as to them shall seem most likely to effect their Safety and Happiness. Prudence, indeed, will dictate that Governments long established should not be changed for light and transient causes; and accordingly all experience hath shewn, that mankind are more disposed to suffer, while evils are sufferable, than to right themselves by abolishing the forms to which they are accustomed. But when a long train of abuses and usurpations, pursuing invariably the same Object evinces a design to reduce them under absolute Despotism, it is their right, it is their duty, to throw off such Government, and to provide new Guards for their future security. — Such has been the patient sufferance of these Colonies; and such is now the necessity which constrains them to alter their former Systems of Government. The history of the

present King of Great Britain is a history of repeated injuries and usurpations, all having in direct object the establishment of an absolute Tyranny over these States. To prove this, let Facts be submitted to a candid
world.

He has refused his Assent to Laws, the most wholesome and necessary for the public good.

He has forbidden his Governors to pass Laws of immediate and
pressing importance, unless suspended in their operation till his Assent
should be obtained; and when so suspended, he has utterly neglected to
attend to them.

He has refused to pass other Laws for the accommodation of large   5
districts of people, unless those people would relinquish the right of
Representation in the Legislature, a right inestimable to them and formidable to tyrants only.

He has called together legislative bodies at places unusual, uncomfortable, and distant from the depository of their public Records, for the
sole purpose of fatiguing them into compliance with his measures.

He has dissolved Representative Houses repeatedly, for opposing
with manly firmness his invasions on the rights of the people.

He has refused for a long time, after such dissolutions, to cause
others to be elected; whereby the Legislative powers, incapable of Anni-
hilation, have returned to the People at large for their exercise; the State
remaining in the meantime exposed to all the dangers of invasion from
without, and convulsions within.

He has endeavoured to prevent the population of these States; for
that purpose obstructing the Laws for Naturalization of Foreigners; refusing to pass others to encourage their migrations hither, and raising
the conditions of new Appropriations of Lands.

He has obstructed the Administration of Justice, by refusing his   10
Assent to Laws for establishing Judiciary powers.

He has made Judges dependent on his Will alone, for the tenure of
their offices, and the amount and payment of their salaries.

He has erected a multitude of New Offices, and sent hither swarms
of Officers to harass our people, and eat out their substance.

He has kept among us, in times of peace, Standing Armies without
the Consent of our legislatures.

He has affected to render the Military independent of and superior
to the Civil power.

He has combined with others to subject us to a jurisdiction foreign   15
to our constitution, and unacknowledged by our laws; giving his Assent
to their Acts of pretended Legislation:

For Quartering large bodies of armed troops among us:

For protecting them, by a mock Trial, from punishment for any
Murders which they should commit on the Inhabitants of these States:

For cutting off our Trade with all parts of the world:

For imposing Taxes on us without our Consent:

For depriving us in many cases, of the benefits of Trial by Jury: *20*

For transporting us beyond Seas to be tried for pretended offences:

For abolishing the free System of English Laws in a neighbouring Province, establishing therein an Arbitrary government, and enlarging its Boundaries so as to render it at once an example and fit instrument for introducing the same absolute rule into these Colonies:

For taking away our Charters, abolishing our most valuable Laws, and altering fundamentally the Forms of our Governments:

For suspending our own Legislatures and declaring themselves invested with power to legislate for us in all cases whatsoever.

He has abdicated Government here, by declaring us out of his *25* Protection and waging War against us.

He has plundered our seas, ravaged our Coasts, burnt our towns, and destroyed the lives of our people.

He is at this time transporting large Armies of foreign Mercenaries to compleat the works of death, desolation and tyranny, already begun with circumstances of Cruelty & perfidy scarcely paralleled in the most barbarous ages, and totally unworthy the Head of a civilized nation.

He has constrained our fellow Citizens taken Captive on the high Seas to bear Arms against their Country, to become the executioners of their friends and Brethren, or to fall themselves by their Hands.

He has excited domestic insurrections amongst us, and has endeavoured to bring on the inhabitants of our frontiers, the merciless Indian Savages, whose known rule of warfare, is an undistinguished destruction of all ages, sexes and conditions.

In every stage of these Oppressions we have Petitioned for Redress *30* in the most humble terms: our repeated Petitions have been answered only by repeated injury. A Prince, whose character is thus marked by every act which may define a Tyrant, is unfit to be the ruler of a free people.

Nor have we been wanting in attention to our British brethren. We have warned them from time to time of attempts by their legislature to extend an unwarrantable jurisdiction over us. We have reminded them of the circumstances of our emigration and settlement here. We have appealed to their native justice and magnanimity, and we have conjured them by the ties of our common kindred to disavow these usurpations, which, would inevitably interrupt our connections and correspondence. They too have been deaf to the voice of justice and of consanguinity. We must, therefore, acquiesce in the necessity, which denounces our Separation, and hold them, as we hold the rest of mankind, Enemies in War, in Peace Friends.

We, therefore, the Representatives of the United States of America, in General Congress, Assembled, appealing to the Supreme Judge of the world for the rectitude of our intentions, do, in the Name, and by Authority of the good People of these Colonies, solemnly publish and declare, That these United Colonies are, and of Right ought to be Free and Independent States; that they are Absolved from all Allegiance to the British Crown, and that all political connection between them and the State of Great Britain, is and ought to be totally dissolved; and that as Free and Independent States, they have full Power to levy War, conclude Peace, contract Alliances, establish Commerce, and to do all other Acts and Things which Independent States may of right do.

And for the support of this Declaration, with a firm reliance on the protection of divine Providence, we mutually pledge to each other our Lives, our Fortunes and our sacred Honor.

FOR DISCUSSION AND WRITING

1. The following is a list of some of the background knowledge that a reader needs for a full understanding of the Declaration of Independence:
   a. the philosophy of John Locke
   b. the concept of Laws of Nature, as it was held in the eighteenth century
   c. the Divine Right of Kings
   d. the Continental Congress
   e. the biography and philosophy of Thomas Jefferson
   In how many of these areas of knowledge are you proficient? What sources would you consult to learn about those with which you are insufficiently familiar?

2. Can the Declaration of Independence mean exactly the same to you as it did to a contemporary of Jefferson attending the Continental Congress? Explain.

3. In what sense might it be said that the Declaration of Independence is a holy document, like the Bible and the Koran?

4. What are the consequences for the argument in the Declaration if we deny the self-evident truths? Is it, for instance, a self-evident truth that all men are created equal? Explain.

5. What is a declaration? How does a declaration differ from a statement and an appeal? (What source would you consult for information regarding this question?)

6. In regard to the previous question, which of the following statements seems strange to you?
   a. I hereby declare that I am free.
   b. I hereby hope that I am free.
   c. I hereby vow that I am free.
   d. I hereby guess that I am free.
   Explain this strangeness.

TO HIS COY MISTRESS

Andrew Marvell

"To His Coy Mistress" is almost as widely known as Joyce Kilmer's "Trees" ("Poems are made by fools like me, / But only God can make a tree"); however, most readers would judge "To His Coy Mistress" superior to "Trees" in almost every respect: in the subtlety of its "message"; in the vividness and appropriateness of its images; in the nuances of its language. After one or two readings, "Trees" is exhausted; "To His Coy Mistress" seems almost limitless in what it can give readers.

Born in 1621, Andrew Marvell was the son of a Puritan clergyman. Educated at Cambridge, he became the colleague of John Milton, author of *Paradise Lost,* and served in Parliament during the last twenty years of life, until his death in 1678. He is remembered for a small body of lyric poems that were published after his death. "The Garden" and "To His Coy Mistress" are widely admired for their wit and their balance of levity and seriousness.

Your first purpose in reading this poem should be pleasure, for it is a wonderful, subtle, slightly off-color, joyous piece of writing. You might also "use" the poem in two other ways: first, as a document in the history of sexism and, second, as an example of faulty, unfair, but persuasive argument.

Had we but world enough, and time,
This coyness, lady, were no crime.
We could sit down and think which way
To walk, and pass our long love's day;
Thou by the Indian Ganges' side   *5*
Should'st rubies find; I by the tide
Of Humber would complain. I would
Love you ten years before the Flood;
And you should, if you please, refuse
Till the conversion of the Jews.   *10*

My vegetable love should grow
Vaster than empires, and more slow.
An hundred years should go to praise
Thine eyes, and on thy forehead gaze;
Two hundred to adore each breast,   *15*
But thirty thousand to the rest;
An age at least to every part,
And the last age should show your heart.
For, lady, you deserve this state,
Nor would I love at lower rate.   *20*

But at my back I always hear
Time's winged chariot hurrying near;
And yonder all before us lie

Deserts of vast eternity.
Thy beauty shall no more be found,   25
Nor in thy marble vault shall sound
My echoing song; then worms shall try
That long preserved virginity,
And your quaint honor turn to dust,
And into ashes all my lust.   30
The grave's a fine and private place,
But none, I think, do there embrace.

Now therefore, while the youthful hue
Sits on thy skin like morning dew,
And while thy willing soul transpires   35
At every pore with instant fires,
Now let us sport us while we may;
And now, like am'rous birds of prey,
Rather at once our time devour,
Than languish in his slow-chapped power.   40
Let us roll all our strength, and all
Our sweetness, up into one ball;
And tear our pleasure with rough strife
Through the iron gates of life.
Thus, though we cannot make our sun   45
Stand still, yet we will make him run.

FOR DISCUSSION AND WRITING

1. Point out the gaps in the logic of this argument.

2. In what way or ways is the argument unfair?

3. If the arguer expects his coy mistress to "fall for" the argument, what must his opinion of her be?

4. Is the argument comic or serious? Or in tone is it a mixture of the comic and the serious? Explain.

5. Would it be valid to say that this is a bad poem because it is based on fallacious logic and unfair argument? Explain.

6. Is the poem, like "A Modest Proposal," ironic? Explain.

7. Assess the poem on the basis of the writer–reader contract (quality, quantity, manner, relation).

8. Interpret the poem from the standpoint of the *agent* (the speaker in the poem). What do we learn about the agent when we consider the *act* itself (the argument), the *purpose* of the act, the *agency* (the poem in which the argument is embodied)?

5

Researched Writing

In this chapter, you will learn how to use the library to find facts, opinions, and discussions regarding the subjects that you write about. You will also learn how to incorporate the facts, opinions, and discussions that you find into your own writing.

It is essential to distinguish between opinion and *prejudice:* a prejudice has no credible backing, that is, no basis or an inadequate basis in fact or logic. On the other hand, an opinion should be supported by known facts and certainly should not contradict them. This test of an opinion is crucial in persuading those that do not share your belief that the opinion is nonetheless valid.

As Chapter 4 pointed out, the basis for an argument is a claim: the Buick LeSabre is (or is not) a better value than the Ford Taurus; Jones will (or will not) make a better member of the city council than Smith; the income tax should (or should not) be abolished since it is (or is not) unconstitutional; the government should (or should not) provide financial aid to all needy college students; every college graduate should (or should not) be required to demonstrate proficiency in a foreign language.

A claim that is backed up is no longer just prejudice; it becomes an opinion. The quality of the argument, therefore, depends on the quality of the backing; adequate, credible backing is necessary to convince a reader. Finding this backing is the first step in preparing a research paper.

USING THE LIBRARY TO FIND SOURCES FOR BACKING AN OPINION

There are many sources for backing: interviews with experts, laboratory experiments, personal experience. However, the most common sources, as you probably already know, are published materials.

Understanding how to use the library to find these sources is, obviously, essential. The following discussion will help you.

Two Types of References

There are two basic types of reference books in a library. Some books are themselves sources of information on the subject at hand; that is, they provide the researcher with facts, opinions, analyses, and so forth. Other reference books do not themselves contain information on a given subject but provide citations to sources that do.

A general encyclopedia, such as *Collier's Encyclopedia,* the *World Book Encyclopedia,* or the *Encyclopaedia Britannica,* is a familiar example of the first type. General encyclopedias contain articles that provide succinct overviews of the topics. By their very nature, they cannot be comprehensive. Nonetheless, they are very useful guides to a subject with which you are not familiar, since all of the entries have been reviewed by experts in the various fields. In fact, many of the articles have been written by such experts. Bear in mind, however, that although general encyclopedias are a good place to begin your research, most of the sources you will need may not be located in the reference section of the library at all but, rather, in the "stacks" — the main book collection, discussed later in this chapter.

In contrast to encyclopedias and other works that are themselves sources of information about topics, indexes and bibliographies (which usually *are* located in the reference room) are works whose whole purpose is simply to lead researchers to appropriate sources. An index is an inventory of the various topics covered by magazines and journals; indexes do not generally list any books, however. A bibliography is an inventory of both books *and* articles; unlike indexes, though, bibliographies usually cover only one specific subject.

Bibliographies and indexes are useful when an encyclopedia is insufficient for your purpose and you need in-depth information. Because serials — magazines, journals, quarterlies, and other such publications that are produced on a regular basis and consecutively numbered — are constantly being published, indexes themselves are continuously updated with new volumes that cover the most recent period. Many indexes are published on a frequent basis (for instance, each month) in softcover, with cumulative hardcover editions published less often (perhaps each year or each quarter). Indexes, then, are an obvious choice when you want the most current information on a topic.

The most widely known index is the *Reader's Guide to Periodical Literature.* You yourself have probably made some use of it in doing research for a class paper. The *Reader's Guide,* in general, catalogs the articles of popular magazines, some 180 in all. It is organized alphabetically by topic heading, with each relevant article from the surveyed periodicals listed below the heading. The title of the article, the name of the periodical, its volume and page numbers, and the date of publication are listed for each citation.

Be aware, however, that the distinctions made here among types of reference books are not exact. For example, at the end of an encyclopedia article you will find short bibliographies that can be used for additional sources of information. In fact, bibliographies are quite common features of information sources such as review articles and digests (discussed in greater detail below) as well as of encyclopedia entries. Nonetheless, the main reason for looking through an encyclopedia, review article, or digest is not for its references but for the information about the subject matter within that text. Additional references are generally only a secondary consideration when one uses these sources.

Criteria for Evaluating a Text's Authority

The answers to these three questions will give you, the critical reader, insight into the authority of the text:

1. What are the author's credentials in writing about the topic at hand?
2. What do others think about the author's work?
3. What is the consensus on the subject matter being dealt with?

These questions can help you organize your use of the library when you are doing research.

WHAT ARE THE AUTHOR'S CREDENTIALS? Information about the author, if not available within the book itself (where some of it may be questionable), can probably be found at any library with a typical reference section. To begin with, an author who is well known might be listed as an entry in an encyclopedia. Remember, though, that the fame or even importance of an author, as indicated by an encyclopedia listing, is not in itself proof of the author's authority on the subject matter you are interested in. For example, a scientist who is an expert on nuclear fission might step outside of his or her field of study to write an article on the influence of nuclear weapons in foreign relations, but the scientist has now moved into the realm of politics.

Another source of biographical information on the author is a series of books whose titles all begin with *Who's Who.* The original series, simply called *Who's Who,* is an alphabetic listing of important British personages that is published in England. Included for each entry is a thumbnail biographical sketch. Additional *Who's Who* series include *Who's Who in America* and *Who's Who in Medicine,* as well as other volumes. Although a *Who's Who* offers only very brief articles, it can provide quick, useful information on the background of an author. These valid reference books, by the way, are not to be confused with other, so-called vanity series such as *Who's Who in American High Schools,* in which the listings are included primarily to sell copies of the books to those listed.

Current Biography and the *New York Times Biographical Service* offer articles on current newsmakers, and *Contemporary Authors* contains biographies of current authors. It is important to be aware that *Contemporary Authors* does not limit itself to writers of fiction, and can be extremely useful if you're looking for information on the author of a factual piece of writing. The *Dictionary of American Biography* and the *National Cyclopedia of American Biography* are also excellent sources of biographical information. (The terms *dictionary, encyclopedia,* and *cyclopedia* are often used interchangeably. All contain articles rather than the one-sentence descriptions most commonly found in everyday desktop dictionaries.)

The *Reader's Guide to Periodical Literature* can be used to find articles on and by a particular author. However, the *Reader's Guide,* for the most part, covers only the more popular and general magazines published. If you are interested in obtaining in-depth information on an author, it is often advisable also to consult specialized indexes for a particular field of study. There are indexes for the social sciences, the humanities, business, general science, applied science and technology, biology and agriculture, law, education, and art, among others. They will refer you to hundreds of professional journals you would otherwise miss if you consulted only the *Reader's Guide.* Such indexes are so numerous that your best approach may be to consult a reference librarian, whom you should never hesitate to ask so long as you have looked in the obvious places first.

WHAT DO OTHERS THINK ABOUT THE AUTHOR'S WORK? Certain reference books collect book reviews so that you can determine what critics thought of a particular work itself (and perhaps, incidentally, of its author). *Book Review Digest* collects reviews from over seventy magazines and journals and provides a brief summary of each review. *Book Review Digest* also cites the source of the review article so that anyone interested in reading the original can go to that source.

Contemporary Authors not only offers summary biographies, as noted above, but also contains discussions of each author's major works, his or her thematic concerns, and brief critical quotes drawn from a multitude of sources.

General and specialized indexes and encyclopedias are also useful aids in researching the opinions that others hold of the author in question. Here is a sampling of specialized indexes: *Index to International Statistics, Index to Legal Periodicals, Index to Scientific and Technical Proceedings, Index to Scientific Reviews, Index to Social Sciences and Humanities Proceedings,* and *Index to U.S. Government Periodicals.*

WHAT IS THE CONSENSUS ON THE SUBJECT MATTER? Encyclopedia articles are excellent overviews of the accepted body of thought about a given subject because they do not emphasize matters that are in dispute by the authorities in the field. Therefore, if reasonably current, they are handy aids to evaluation of a work you are researching. Is the work speculative? Controversial? Are there large gaps in the facts that it covers, or does it by and large cover the relevant material? You can often use the encyclopedia as the basis for determining the answers to these questions.

While you might want to consult a general reference encyclopedia, such as the *Encylopaedia Britannica, World Book Encyclopedia,* or *Collier's Encyclopedia,* you should also be aware that there are many specialized encyclopedias that might be of greater benefit. Among the topics covered by specialized encyclopedias are American history, the Middle Ages, philosophy, the Bible, world literature, jazz, chemistry, psychology, prehistoric life, Judaism, urban planning, and statistics. A few of the specialized encyclopedias are *Encyclopedia of Associations, Encyclopedia of Business Information Sources, Encyclopedia of Information Systems and Services, Encyclopedia of the Social Sciences,* and *Encyclopedia of World Art.* There is even an *Encyclopedia of Food.*

Like encyclopedia articles, *review articles* attempt to present an overview of a subject, but they are generally more comprehensive and technical. A review article is not simply a critique of one book or essay but is instead an encapsulation of the most current knowledge in particular fields, including a listing of all or much of the relevant literature and commentaries on it.

There are several ways to locate review articles. First, there are series of review articles for the natural, applied, and behavioral sciences, the titles of which all start with *Annual Review of . . .* and conclude with the subject that is covered. For example, there is an *Annual Review of Anthropology,* an *Annual Review of Microbiology,* an *Annual Review of Fluid Mechanics,* and so on. In addition, there is the *Index to Scientific Reviews,* which cites review articles not only for the same subjects covered by the *Annual Review* series but also for other fields of study related to the sciences.

To find review articles on topics outside the sciences, you can also use indexes, but such indexes will also contain references to other kinds of written material. You can try to determine whether the reference is a review article by noting the number of footnotes in the text and the number of bibliographic entries cited. An article that contains a large number of either might be a review. Certain indexes supply this information in advance.

The older the text, the greater the possibility that the information it contains is outdated or has been disproved. It is a good idea, therefore, to find out when the text was written. In almost all cases a book is copyrighted within a year after it is written; thus, the original copyright date, which in most books can be found on the back of the title page, is a useful indicator.

If you are stumped in your effort to find an appropriate reference book for your topic, or if you want to make sure that you have exhausted the possibilities within the reference section of the library, you should consult the ultimate reference book: the *Guide to Reference Books,* edited by Eugene Sheehy. It is a comprehensive listing of the reference materials available on a given subject. There you will find an amazing array of sources, many if not most of which you probably have never heard of but which could be very helpful in your research.

The Stacks

So far, we have discussed using encyclopedias, reviews of the work, and indexes and bibliographies. Let us also note the obvious. Although the reference section of the library can be invaluable — not only in supplying important information directly but also in guiding the researcher to additional sources such as magazines and journals — it is hardly the largest part of the library. The main stacks constitute most of a typical library. They contain complete books, not just articles, on various subjects, and often it is to these books that you will be led if you require a great deal of research on a topic.

The first step in finding the books you need is to go to the library's catalog. A book that is listed in the catalog is among the library's holdings, and the call number indicates exactly where that book is to be found. Most catalogs, as you are probably aware, refer to the library's possessions in three ways: by author, by title, and by subject matter. All three types of references may be interfiled (in the case of hard copy), or there might be separate card catalogs for subject and for author/title.

Even though the catalog is fairly straightforward, you need to be aware of several points. First, a catalog will note the journals in the collection, but it will not list the individual articles. Various indexes found within the reference section of the library serve that function. Second, the system that libraries use in arranging their catalogs by subject matter is often not readily apparent to the researcher.

Two books are invaluable sources of information on how the catalog is arranged by subject. The first is actually a two-volume work entitled *Library of Congress Subject Headings*. It is the standard used by libraries across the nation to organize their catalogs by subject. It lists in alphabetical order the appropriate term to be used for a subject and cross-references synonyms that are not used in cataloging with the terms that are. In addition, the *Library of Congress Subject Headings* lists under each subject heading other subject headings that are related but are either narrower or broader in scope. This cross-referencing system is extremely useful if you wish to expand your search to related topics. Even more important, the cross-referencing is necessary when you have found a subject heading that is only related to your concern but is not specifically what you are looking for. The cross-referencing system enables you to follow a trail of interrelated terms until you find the most appropriate subject heading, at which point you can consult the card catalog for the volumes that are listed under that same heading.

The second reference book is the *Libary of Congress Subject Headings: A Guide to Subdivision Practice*. It explains the standard means by which a broad topic is divided into subheadings. Because a topic could have hundreds of books listed under it, a knowledge of the subheadings used can be crucial. For example, you can determine whether your library contains a bibliographic reference book about a given topic by consulting the catalog under the listed subheading and then under the sub-subheading of "bibliography."

Librarians can be invaluable to the experienced as well as to the novice researcher. Although the classification system will be a standard one used by many other libraries, each library has its own method of placing its materials within the building. Moreover, each library will have only some of the available reference materials. While it is a good idea to search the library yourself for appropriate materials, the librarian can often save you hours of frustrating effort in your search for information.

A final note: No such overview as this can detail all the resources that are available to, or the methods to be employed by, the library researcher. We strongly recommend that you familiarize yourself with your college or university library or libraries. Learn where to locate the various reference books discussed in this chapter; look through the catalog, and try searching for particular books in the stacks; acquaint yourself with any special collections that the library houses. While supremely organized, a library is also supremely complex, and only practice will make you a competent researcher.

Library research enables one to answer questions: What bearing does the concept of "natural law" have on our understanding of the United States Constitution? Would it be possible for me to install a new sewer main, and if so, how do I do it? What are the most important arguments for and against making automatic weapons illegal? How do critics evaluate the latest biography of Samuel Taylor Coleridge? Where did the Reverend Robert Schuller take his doctoral degree? What famous clients has F. Lee Bailey defended?

And, of course, the library is the main resource for backing and evidence in many arguments — such as "The Death Penalty: For Whom the Bell Tolls," which follows. We have annotated this argument to show you how we have used and documented sources. You should also be a critical reader, asking questions about quality, quantity, manner, and relation; judging the reliability of sources; and determining whether the argument is coherent or fragmented.

RESEARCH FOR AN ARGUMENT

In our opinion, capital punishment should be abolished. We developed an argument that we believed would stand a good chance of convincing readers — that is, our purpose was to convince those who favor capital punishment to change their minds. Although we knew a good deal about our subject, we needed to find (1) expert opinions that favor capital punishment, (2) expert opinions that oppose capital punishment, (3) the primary arguments for and against capital punishment, and (4) the backing for those arguments. We knew that the literature on capital punishment is massive — more than we could to cover in months of research. For this reason, we resolved to limit our sources to (a) the opinions of experts after 1977 (when Gary Gilmore was executed in Utah after a ten-year moratorium on the death penalty in the United States), although for specific purposes we did include two earlier sources (by Koestler and Kant); and (b) the details of only one capital case (that of Joseph Giarratano).

It is very important to realize that our research might well have resulted in our changing our own opinion. It is always possible that gaining more extensive knowledge on a subject will change the research-er's viewpoint. *We were not looking exclusively for sources that would verify our opinion.*

The following step-by-step account of how we did our research can serve as a rough guide when you do library research on a topic.

1. First we read articles in encyclopedias: the *Americana,* the *Britannica,* and the computerized *Academic American Encyclopedia* by Grolier. The *Americana* article was particularly useful, because it contained a short bibliography:

> Hugo Adam Bedau, *Death Is Different* (1987)
> Eugene B. Block, *When Men Play God: The Fallacy of Capital Punishment* (1984)
> John Lawrence, *The History of Capital Punishment* (1983)
> Bonnie Szumski, Lynn Hall, and Susan Bursell, eds., *The Death Penalty: Opposing Viewpoints* (1986)
> Franklin E. Zimring and Gordon Hawkins, *Capital Punishment and the American Agenda* (1986)

Since these sources were listed in the *Americana,* we had some assurance that they would be authoritative and reliable, and, as you will see, we relied extensively on *Death Is Different, The Death Penalty: Opposing Viewpoints,* and *Capital Punishment and the American Agenda.*

2. Next we surveyed the library catalog, which at the University of California at Irvine (where we do most of our research) is computerized. The library contained ninety-six volumes cataloged under "capital punishment," and we went to the stacks to scan only those that were related to our subject. (For instance, we did not look for volumes about capital punishment in foreign countries.) In the several hours that we spent in the stacks examining books, we found several that we might have used but one that was clearly essential: Roger Hood, *The Death*

Penalty: A World-Wide Perspective (1989), which is a report to the United Nations Committee on Crime Prevention and Control. Another book that interested us, but that we did not use in our argument, is *Rites of Execution: Capital Punishment and the Transformation of American Culture, 1776–1865* (1989).

3. For more careful scrutiny at our leisure, we checked out Bedau, *Death Is Different: Studies in the Morality, Law, and Politics of Capital Punishment;* Hood, *The Death Penalty: A World-Wide Perspective: A Report to the United Nations Committee on Crime Prevention;* Koestler, *Reflections on Hanging; The Death Penalty: Opposing Viewpoints,* eds. Szumski, Hall, and Bursell; and Zimring and Hawkins, *Capital Punishment and the American Agenda.*

4. We then surveyed periodical indexes — *Reader's Guide* and *Info-Trac* — and found more than two hundred articles on the death penalty. (*InfoTrac* is a computerized index of magazines published since 1988.) We scanned a number of the articles and found one that is particularly significant and useful: Horgan's "The Death Penalty."

5. Since we wanted to discuss one troublesome case in some detail, we looked at articles that dealt with individual convicted murderers and chose Joseph Giarratano as the most interesting and instructive case study. Articles on the Giarratano case appeared in *The Nation, Newsweek,* and *U.S. News and World Report,* among other magazines. We also checked the *New York Times Index* to find newspaper accounts of the Giarratano case.

6. We had now assembled our materials. We had taken notes on some of the sources; we had photocopied three articles from the *New York Times;* we checked out six significant books so that we could read them carefully.

AN ARGUMENT AGAINST THE DEATH PENALTY

The following is the argument that resulted from our research and planning. As you read this essay, pay close attention to the annotations, which explain how and why we used our sources.

The form that we use to indicate our sources is the one preferred by the *Modern Language Association of America.* The form that you use in your own writing will depend on the field in which you were writing (social sciences, natural sciences) and the publication for which you are writing (newspaper, magazine, scholarly journal). The general rule is this: If you use a fact, an opinion, or an idea from a source, be sure to let your readers know exactly where you got the material and where they can go to check your accuracy and to learn more about what the source has to say.

1"

1/2"

Firstname Surname

Professor _____

English _____

26 March 1992

Doublespace

The Death Penalty: For Whom the Bell Tolls

Some legal issues gain depth and importance because they con
cern basic religious, ethical, and social values. Abortion, ho-

1"

mosexual marriage, euthanasia (or the right to death with dignity), the allocation and financing of medical care--these involve both legal intricacies and the most fundamental beliefs of

1"

the citizenry. Capital punishment is another such issue. (In
1977 (<u>Coker v. Georgia</u>), the Supreme Court in effect limited
capital punishment to crimes that result in a victim's death,
even though some state laws provide the death penalty for such
crimes as kidnapping and rape of a child (Hood 31).)

The solemnity and social importance of the death penalty is
made vividly clear when a public official speaks of capital punishment in a jocular or cynical way. Orange County Superior
Court Judge Robert R. Fitzgerald has sentenced six men to death;
he calls them his "basketball team." "I keep waiting for one of
them to score some points," he is quoted as saying (Hicks A36).

Most people who hold a valid opinion, pro or con, regarding
the death penalty would find such an attitude repellent in the
extreme. For our society, unlike some others, holds life to be
of great value, even the supreme value.

<u>Arguments in Favor of the Death Penalty</u>

Two arguments in favor of capital punishment are incontro-

1"

Using parentheses to indicate sources for facts and ideas **(paragraph 1)**
The parenthetical notation—(Hood 31)—indicates that we found the information about the supreme court in the book by Hood on page 31. To find out all necessary information about Hood's book, turn to the alphabetical "Works Cited" section at the end of this essay (beginning on page 624), where you will find the author's full name, the full title of the book, the place of publication, the publisher, and the date of publication.

Using parentheses to indicate sources for facts and ideas **(paragraph 2)**
The information about Judge Fitzgerald came from page A36 of a newspaper article by Hicks. For full information on the source, see the Hicks entry in the "Works Cited" section.

Stating your own opinions and conclusions **(paragraph 3)**
No documentation is necessary for the commentary on Judge Fitzgerald because that is our opinion and does not come from a research source.

vertible. The first is this: executing a criminal prevents him or her from committing another crime. If the other reasons for supporting the death penalty were as ironclad as this one, it would be irrational to argue against capital punishment. The second irrefutable argument for capital punishment is that it provides the loved ones of the murder victim with revenge. In fact, under Islamic law, the relatives of the victim have the choice of reprieving the murderer, with or without compensation; indeed, in Saudi Arabia and Iran, the guardian of the victim has the right to perform the execution himself (presumably not her-self) or to hire someone to do it (Hood 77-80). However, arguing in favor of the death penalty on the basis of revenge counters the widely held Judeo-Christian ethic of forgiveness and the equally prevalent sense that human life is sacred and to be sac-rificed only for the larger good.

5   Arguments favoring the death penalty hold that it (1) is moral, (2) deters potential murderers, (3) saves the state money, (4) fulfills the concept of justice, and (5) is more humane than life imprisonment.

Is the death penalty moral? Expert opinion is divided. For example, Ernest van den Haag, respected professor of juris-prudence and public policy at Fordham University, argues, "His crime morally sets the murderer apart from his victim. The vic-tim did, and therefore the murderer does not, deserve to live. His life cannot be sacred if that of his victim was" (61). How-ever, Michael E. Endres, professor of criminal justice at Xavier University in Cincinnati, says that capital punishment is immoral

Paraphrasing, or stating information from a source in your
own words **(paragraph 4)**
The source of the information about Islamic law is pages 77–78 in Hood. We are
using information from Hood but not quoting him directly; thus, quotation marks
would be improper.

Stating your own opinions and conclusions **(paragraph 5)**
We do not need documentation for our list of arguments in favor of the death
penalty because the list comes from our general knowledge of the subject; it is our
list, not someone else's. However, if we had drawn the list from a source,
documentation would have been necessary.

Identifying the author of a source **(paragraph 6)**
Notice that in the text we have mentioned Ernest van den Haag, the author of the
quoted opinion; therefore, we do not need to repeat his name in the parenthetical
documentation. The citation—(61)—means that the quotation comes from page 61
of the source listed under van den Haag in the "Works Cited." Since this is an
exact quotation of *less than five lines,* it is run right into our text with quotation
marks to set it apart.

because

> the death penalty serves no rehabilitative purpose; it
> exceeds the requirements of justice and social unity;
> alternatives to it may serve the same purpose as well;
> finally, the incapacitation or special deterrence of a
> given offender is insured by execution, but there are
> other effective ways to inhibit reoffending. (67)

If it is moral to execute convicted, responsible adults, is
it also moral to execute children or adults who are mentally retarded or insane? Arthur Koestler tells of a horrifyingly interesting case that bears on our question:

> In 1748, William York, a boy of ten, was sentenced to
> death for murder. Chief Justice Willis postponed the
> execution to find out whether it was proper to hang the
> child. All the judges concurred that it was. Their
> ruling deserves to be quoted because it epitomizes the
> judges' blind belief, throughout the centuries, in the
> unique and irreplaceable deterrent effect of the death-
> penalty. The judges ruled that the child--"is cer-
> tainly a proper subject for capital punishment, and
> ought to suffer; for it would be a very dangerous con-
> sequence to have it thought that children may commit
> such atrocious crimes with impunity. There are many
> crimes of the most heinous nature . . . which children
> are very capable of committing; and which they may in
> some circumstances be under strong temptation to com-
> mit; and therefore, though the taking away the life of

Identifying the author of a source;
using indentation to show that you are quoting **(paragraph 6)**
The author of the quotation, Michael E. Endres, is identified in the introduction
to the quotation; thus his name need not appear in the parentheses. The exact
source of the quotation is found in the "Works Cited" under Endres. Note also
that quotations more than five lines long are usually indented ten spaces and
appear without quotation marks. We cite and quote van den Haag and Endres as
backing for our point that opinion about the morality of the death penalty is
divided. Without this backing, our contention would have been considerably
weakened, since critical readers would have suspected that we could not find even
one example of such disagreement.

a boy of ten years old may savour of cruelty, yet as

the example of this boy's punishment may be a means of

deterring other children from the like offenses; and as

the sparing of this boy, merely on account of his age,

will probably have a quite contrary tendency, in jus-

tice to the publick, the law ought to take its course."

(13-14)

Undoubtedly, public morality has changed since 1748, but only in

1990 did Missouri raise its age limit for capital punishment from

fourteen to sixteen ("Juveniles" 1). Is a sixteen-year-old a

responsible adult? If not, should an offender this young be ex-

ecuted as "a means of deterring other children from the like of-

fenses"? Currently, more than seventy-five death-row inmates

committed their crimes before they were eighteen years old, and

in the last decade, at least four such offenders have been ex-

ecuted (Horgan 19). It is most interesting to note that the

United States of America joins only four other nations in execut-

ing juvenile offenders: Bangladesh, Barbados, Iran, and Iraq

(Horgan 19).

Diminished mental capacity is a mitigating factor in capital

offenses, and psychiatric evidence must be considered in all such

cases (Hood 63-64). However, psychiatrists who assess the

defendant's mental state from the standpoint of both mitigation

and potential for further violence are often in a double bind,

for the very condition that mitigates the crime may, from another

point of view, be the factor that makes the defendant a bad risk

(Hood 64). Furthermore, psychiatry is more an art than a science

Identifying the author of a source;
using indentation to show that you are quoting (paragraph 7)
The source is quoted exactly and is more than five lines; thus the material is indented. The quoted passage will be found on pages 13–14 of the Koestler source listed in "Works Cited."

Anonymous articles as sources **(paragraph 7)**
The material on age limits for juveniles is an anonymous newspaper article. Full information appears under "Juveniles" in the "Works Cited" section.

Showing the sources of fact **(paragraph 7)**
Both of the facts about the execution of minors come from page 19 of Horgan.

Giving credit for both facts and opinions **(paragraph 8)**
The two citations from Hood are quite different. The first one (concerning psychiatric evidence) is a *fact* that we gained from Hood's book. The second one is Hood's *opinion,* not a fact. Since the opinion is Hood's, not ours, we must give Hood credit as our source.

and thus does not provide conclusive evidence for a decision regarding life or death.

The moral and ethical questions regarding capital punishment
are open to so much controversy that it would be difficult for an
informed person to take a definitive stand one way or another on
whether the death penalty is or is not moral and ethical.

Does the death penalty deter potential murderers? On the
basis of masses of evidence, we can only conclude, with Hood,
that this is an unanswered question: "The evidence as a whole
gives no positive support to the deterrent hypothesis" (167).
One might argue, of course, that the mere existence of the death
penalty is not a deterrent unless executions are actually carried
out. Thus, as the number of executions increases, the frequency
of murder should decline. According to Hood (117-148), no evidence indicates that more frequent executions lead to lower homicide rates. For example, the last executions in Australia took
place in the mid-1960s, but "the reported homicide rate per
100,000 of population has fallen, and the murder rate has remained constant" (Hood 124-25); in the United States, when the
first execution took place after a decade-long moratorium, the
homicide rate almost doubled, from 4.8 per 100,000 to 8.8 (Hood
126). Some admittedly inconclusive evidence suggests that executions may actually bring about more murders. One study, reported
by Horgan, indicates that in New York State between 1907 and
1963, the number of murders rose by an average of a bit more than
two in the month following an execution (17).

Dividing murders into two categories is useful when one con-

The authors' own conclusions (paragraph 9)
The paragraph states our conclusion, not that of a source.

Identifying the author of a source (paragraph 10)
The exact quotation is from Hood, page 167. Since we mention Hood in the lead-in to the quotation, we do not need his name in the parentheses giving the page number.

Using summaries and examples (paragraph 10)
Documentation in the paragraph indicates that we are (1) giving our summary of pages 117–148 of Hood, (2) using a specific fact from pages 124–25 of Hood, (3) using another specific fact from page 126 of Hood, and using one specific fact from page 17 of Horgan. On pages 117–148, Hood sets forth the results of numerous studies of the death penalty, but within the limits of our argument, we cannot deal with all of them. Thus, we show the readers where to turn for more detailed information, and we give two specific examples (pages 124–25 and 126) so that readers will have some idea of the kind of evidence that Hood sets forth.

siders the deterrence argument: what Bedau terms "'carefully contemplated murders,' such as 'murder for hire'" (172) and so-
called crimes of passion. As Bedau points out, those who carefully plan murders do so with a view of avoiding detection and
punishment; hence, the threat of the death penalty plays little
or no role in the decision to commit the crime. No threat would
deter the killer who is carried away by uncontrollable rage or
hatred.

If capital punishment is a deterrent, then painful methods
of execution surely would have more effect than painless ones,
yet Texas, Utah, and other states have adopted lethal injection
as the method of execution--ameliorating the severity of the
death penalty, supposedly for "humanitarian" reasons. On the
other hand, California and other states that use lethal gas as a
means of execution do not make the agony of death by asphyxiation
a matter of public knowledge. If the death penalty is a deterrent, the agonies of execution should not be ameliorated, as in
Texas, or kept hidden from the public, as in California.

Since we cannot responsibly claim that the threat of the
death penalty reduces the number of murders, the argument for
capital punishment on the basis of its deterrent effect crumbles.

From a strictly utilitarian point of view, is capital punishment cost-effective? According to Robert L. Spangenberg, an
attorney who directs the Boston Legal Assistance Project, "states
spend anywhere from $1.6 million to $3.2 million to obtain and
carry out a capital sentence; states could incarcerate someone
for 100 years or more for less money" (Horgan 18).

Using another's ideas to support one's own concepts **(paragraph 11)**
The idea of positing two categories of murder is our own, but we draw on Bedau for concepts regarding one type of murder. As the citation indicates, Bedau's discussion of "carefully contemplated murders" is found on page 172.

15

     Even if executing convicted murderers turns out to be more expensive than incarcerating them, a cost/benefit analysis might reveal that the death penalty is economically sound, providing such social benefits as protection from potential murderers. However, as Bedau says,

> Since no adequate cost/benefit analysis of the death penalty exists, there is no way to resolve these questions from that standpoint at this time. Moreover, it can be argued that we cannot have such an analysis without already establishing in some way or other the relative value of innocent lives versus guilty lives. (38)

     It appears, then, that economic, utilitarian arguments in favor of capital punishment have no solid basis.

     What about the concept of justice in regard to the death penalty?

     Immanuel Kant argued that justice demands--consists in--complete equality; thus, if one murders, the commensurate punishment is death. Bedau (17) quotes from <u>The Metaphysical Elements of Justice</u>:

> What kind and what degree of punishment does public legal justice adopt as its principle? None other than the principle of equality . . . , that is, the principle of not treating one side more favorably than the other. Accordingly, any undeserved evil that you inflict on someone else among the people is one that you do to yourself. . . . Only the law of retribution . . .

***Documentation when you use one source that you find in
another source* (paragraph 18)**
The problem with documentation here is a bit complicated. We found the
quotation from Kant on page 17 of Bedau, as we indicate: "Bedau (17) quotes
from *The Metaphysical Elements of Justice*." The quotation, however, is from page
101 of Kant's book, and we indicate that fact in the parentheses at the end of the
quotation. Thus our documentation informs readers where the quotation appears
in Bedau's book and the exact page it comes from in Kant's book. We know
Bedau's source because *he* documented adequately; that is, he provided a citation
and a list of references (sources). Notice that the "Works Cited" list at the end of
this paper includes exact information about the book by Kant from which Bedau
took the quotation.

> can determine exactly the kind and degree of punish-
> ment. . . . All other standards fluctuate back and
> forth and, because extraneous considerations are mixed
> with them, they cannot be compatible with the principle
> of pure and strict legal justice. (Kant 101)

As Bedau points out, the principle of equality applies to murderers who are intrinsically vicious and have rationally willed to
kill another. "If modern criminologists and psychologists are
correct, however," says Bedau, "most murders are not committed by
persons whose state of mind can be described as Kant implies"
(17). Even if we accept Kant's principle of justice, we find
that it is inapplicable in the real world.

Is it more humane to execute a convicted murderer than to
require him or her to spend years, or life, in prison? It is, of
course, impossible to make such a judgment <u>for</u> the condemned.
Lifers in prison do commit suicide, and convicted murderers do
ask for death rather than life imprisonment. As Bedau says, however, it is impossible to determine which is more severe, life in
prison or death, for there is no way to compare the two alternatives (27). We do know, however, that death makes it impossible
to correct errors in judgment. In any case, society does not
base its penalties on the preferences of the convicted.

Anecdotal evidence does cast doubt on the humaneness of the
death penalty. In 1990, Jesse Joseph Tafero was electrocuted for
the murder of two policemen in Florida.

> When a prison official threw the switch, a sponge de-
> livering electricity to Tafero's skull burst into

Using quotation marks **(paragraph 18)**
Quotation marks indicate that we have used an exact quotation from page 17 of Bedau's book.

Paraphrasing **(paragraph 19)**
From Bedau, page 27 we gained the idea that it is impossible to determine whether life in prison or death is the more severe punishment, but we paraphrased Bedau's idea (stated it in our own words); thus, we did not use quotation marks.

> flames. The executioner cut the current for six sec-
> onds--during which Tafero, smoke pouring from his
> hooded head, moved and breathed, according to eyewit-
> nesses--and then shocked him again. After a total of
> six minutes and three jolts, Tafero was pronounced
> dead. The electric chair was introduced in the U.S.
> 100 years ago as a humane alternative to hanging.
> (Horgan 19)

And in regard to the humaneness of capital punishment, it is well
to ponder the fact that hydrogen cyanide in the gas chamber
brings about death by asphyxiation as the gas combines with the
enzymes necessary for cellular oxidation.

The Death Penalty: A Case History

The logical, hypothetical, and abstract nature of argument
gains body and soul when the pros and cons are applied to an actual case--when a human drama illustrates the theories, the opinions, and the statistics.

In February of 1991, Joe Giarratano was just eighty-two
hours away from the electric chair; his only chance for life was
commutation of his sentence by Virginia Governor L. Douglas
Wilder. Giarratano's story is worth considering.

In 1979, he confessed to murder. The Nation gives this account of the crime:

> One morning in February 1979 in Norfolk, Virginia, Jo-
> seph Giarratano awoke in a drugged haze to discover the
> bodies of two women with whom he shared an apartment.
> Michelle Kline, 15, had been strangled in her bed. Her

Indentation to indicate exact quotation **(paragraph 20)**
Indentation indicates a direct quotation. The parenthetical citation indicates that the quotation is from Horgan, page 19.

Common knowledge, or facts that do not need to be documented **(paragraph 20)**
The fact about hydrogen cyanide does not need documentation. It can be considered common knowledge and can be verified through common reference sources such as encyclopedias.

mother, Toni Kline, lay in the blood-drenched bathroom, her carotid artery severed.

> Unable to remember what had happened the night before, Giarratano panicked and fled to his home state of Florida. "By the time I got off the bus in Jackson-ville," he says, "I decided I must have murdered Toni and Michelle." As soon as he arrived he turned himself in to the first policeman he saw and confessed.
>
> (Hooker 485)

In a one-day trial that was over before noon, Giarratano was found guilty of murder in the first degree and was in due course sentenced to death in Virginia's electric chair. He now says that he was so high on drugs and so utterly convinced of his own evil that he admitted to the crimes even though he could not re-member having committed them. "'I was convinced that I was evil, and had to be punished for what I did. . . . All I wanted to do was die,' Giarratano said" (Hooker 486).

When he was convicted, Giarratano was a drug addict and al-coholic "who suffered frequent delusions, hallucinations, and blackouts" (Hooker 485). During the first part of his confine-ment prior to the scheduled execution, authorities administered antipsychotic medication to Giarratano for four years. In 1981, he was on the verge of being executed when a judge found him men-tally incompetent (Kaplan and Cohn 56). Wanting to die, however, he withdrew from all medication so that he would appear rational enough to be executed. Free of drugs for the first time in years, Giarratano found a new will to live and began to study law

***Quotations within quotations* (paragraph 24)**

As we indicate, we have directly quoted Giarratano, but we found that quotation in Hooker's article on page 486. In cases like this, one must be certain that readers know who is being quoted and where the quote comes from. The use of both types of quotation marks (" '. . .' ") indicates that we are quoting Hooker, who is quoting Giarratano. In other words, we have a direct quotation within a direct quotation. In the paragraph that follows, we quote only Hooker and thus use only the double quotation marks (". . .").

in an effort to save himself from the electric chair. So successful was his self-education that "[I]n the tightly knit community of lawyers, scholars and opponents of capital punishment, he
is considered more a colleague than a convict" (Margolick A1).
Working in behalf of another convict, Giarratano collaborated in
developing a novel legal argument whereby both the fair trial
clauses of the Sixth Amendment to the Constitution and the due
process clause of the Fourteenth guarantee counsel, not simply
through the process of normal appeals, but through the very last
legal remedies (Margolick B6).

By the fall of 1990, Giarratano had two final hopes of
avoiding execution: a decision by the Supreme Court and clemency
or commutation by the governor of Virginia. Here is how
Giarratano assessed his chances with the Supreme Court:

> "I've got Brennan and Marshall for sure, just because
> it's a death case. I think we've got a shot at
> Blackmun and a good shot at Stevens. That fifth vote's
> going to be tough. O'Connor seems to have a streak of
> fairness in her at times, and White could go either
> way. I don't know enough about Kennedy to know where
> he fits in. Scalia and Rehnquist seem to be walking
> together hand in hand on all this; their attitude in
> death cases is 'kill 'em.' So forget them."
> (Margolick B6)

In its issue of October 2, 1990, the New York Times reported
that Thurgood Marshall was the only dissenter in an opinion that
denied Giarratano v. Procunier, No. 89-7661, in which Giarratano

Quotations within quotations **(paragraph 26)**
The indentation shows that we are quoting Margolick (page B6), and the quotation marks show that Margolick is quoting Giarratano. This is another example of how researchers indicate that they are using quotes within quotes.

argued that "the lower courts had improperly put 'the state's interest in finality' above questions of fundamental fairness" ("Death Penalty" A18). Would Governor Wilder commute the death sentence?

Wilder had opposed the death penalty, but reversed himself on the issue in his gubernatorial campaign (Margolick B6). Newsweek for March 4, 1991, reports that Giarratano, tensely waiting for the governor's decision, joked with Marie Deans, a friend and supporter,

> "If I win," he said, "I'm going to kiss the biggest, ugliest guard I can find."
>
> Twenty minutes later the phone down the hallway rang. Deans picked it up. Wilder had just commuted the death sentence to life with the possibility of parole in 2004. Deans beamed. Giarratano was stunned. "Did I hear you right?" he asked. "You did it!" The short, pudgy 33-year-old inmate leaped and almost hit the roof of his cage. He beckoned to one of his jailers, whom he indeed tried to kiss. Then he sat down to enjoy the "first meal" of his new life: reheated lake trout and some coffee. (Kaplan and Cohn 56)

Politics, Reasonable Doubt, and the Death Sentence

The governor's commutation of the death sentence raises two questions: Was Wilder's motive at least in part political? Was Giarratano guilty beyond reasonable doubt?

The Giarratano case had aracted national and international interest (Kaplan and Cohn 56). Through the efforts of Marie

Quotations within quotations **(paragraph 28)**

Here is another example of quotes within a quotation. The article by Kaplan and Cohn reports what Giarratano said when he received news of the commutation.

Deans, Columnist James J. Kilpatrick became interested in the
case and wrote four articles supporting Giarratano. Mike
Farrell, of M*A*S*H fame, became an advocate. The European Parliament passed a resolution supporting Giarratano. The
governor's office received more than seven thousand letters and
phone calls supporting Giarratano, with only 120 opposed to clemency. The Giarratano case was featured on the television programs 20-20 and Nightwatch. Governor Wilder was, then, under
considerable public and political pressure to grant clemency to
Giarratano. As Newsweek puts it,

> In announcing his decision, Wilder denied he was
> swayed. In a six-page statement that granted clemency
> but not a new trial, he insisted that his powers "can-
> not be implemented based upon popular appeal." His
> policy chief, Walter MacFarlane, says the decision was
> "strictly on the merits"--although the statement never
> does explain the reasons for clemency. Some Wilder
> observers accuse him of political gamesmanship in a
> case where mercy meant lile risk. Larry Sabato, who
> teaches political science at the University of Vir-
> ginia, says he needed to solidify support in the Holly-
> wood community, which is a source of financing for
> prominent Democrats. Wilder also had to be wary of
> seeming soft on the death penalty. Here, Giarratano's
> timing proved politically fortuitous for both of them.
> Because two other, less controversial, death sentences
> were carried out in late 1990, Wilder is insulated from

charges that he is lenient on crime. (Kaplan and Cohn 56)

Whether or not Governor Wilder acted on the basis of political motives, politics is a factor in capital punishment. Zimring and Hawkins state flatly, "It is no coincidence that the list of actively executing countries matches that of politically oppressive countries" (6). In other words, in the view of some reputable authorities, there is a correlation between political repression and the death penalty.

If Governor Wilder was not swayed by political concerns, was there enough evidence to give him the basis for reasonable doubt of Giarratano's guilt? Here are facts to which the governor had access:

(1) Giarratano's various confessions did not add up; they were conflicting (Margolick B6).

It soon became clear that without his confessions, Giarratano could not have been convicted. He made five in all, but only the fifth bore a passing resemblance to the physical evidence at the scene of the crime, and only that one was presented at the trial. But police officers testified that they had coached their suspect, spoon-feeding their version of the facts to him. (Hooker 486)

(2) During the trial, State Psychiatrist Miller Ryans warned that Giarratano's confessions might well have been the product of mental disorder (Hooker 486).

(3) Giarratano confessed to strangling Michelle Kline with

his hands, but, as a pathologist testified in 1990, "The hall-marks of manual strangulation are not present" (Hooker 486).

35

(4) Giarratano is left-handed, and his right hand is neuro-logically impaired, yet a forensic expert testified that Toni Kline had been stabbed from behind by a right-handed person (Hooker 486).

(5) "Numerous unidentified fingerprints and nine hair samples that did not belong to Giarratano or either of his al-leged victims were discovered in the apartment, along with a driver's license belonging to another man" (Hooker 486).

(6) Footprints at the crime scene could not have been made by Giarratano's boots (Margolick B6).

(7) "[T]he blood found on his boots did not match that of Toni Kline, and . . . hair found on Michelle Kline did not match his" (Margolick B6).

On the basis of this evidence, it is reasonable to conclude that Governor Wilder's decision to commute the sentence may well not have been politically motivated, yet the taint remains: the possibility that Giarratano is alive today because a politician was considering his own future--which raises the possibility that others have been executed because of political ambitions. In Charlottesville, the Daily Progress said of Virginia Attorney General Mary Sue Terry, who opposed clemency for Giarratano, "She is not afraid, it seems, to risk the death of a possibly innocent man, sacrificed for her own ego and political ambitions" (Margolick B6).

40

If capital punishment could be made nonpolitical, and if it

were possible infallibly to establish guilt beyond reasonable
doubt, proponents of the death penalty would be on much more
solid ground. However, to isolate the death penalty from political concerns would be to alter the processes of American democracy and, indeed, to change basic human nature. And it hardly
needs saying that no human enterprise will ever be infallible.

Capital Punishment: Cruel and Unusual

    There is, then, no agreement about the morality, the deter-
rent value, the utilitarian effectiveness, the justice, or the
humaneness of the death penalty. The Giarratano case demonstrates (a) that capital punishment is a political issue, and
that political considerations will always make administration of
the death penalty unequal and capricious; (b) that establishing
guilt beyond a reasonable doubt is, at least in some cases, difficult. In other words, there is always a possibility that an
innocent person will be put to death.

> In the past 18 years, at least 27 people condemned to
> death have later been found innocent by a higher court.
> Some of these reversals came about through sheer seren-
> dipity. The innocence of Randall Dale Adams, released
> [in 1989] after spending 12 years on death row in Texas
> for murdering a police officer, came to light only be-
> cause a filmmaker happened to take an interest in the
> case. Others have not been so lucky. From 1900 to
> 1985, at least 23 Americans were executed for crimes
> they did not commit, according to a 1987 report in the
> Stanford Law Review. (Horgan 18)

The Eighth Amendment of the U. S. Constitution states, "Excessive bail shall not be required, nor excessive fines imposed, nor cruel and unusual punishments inflicted." Obviously, the Supreme Court does not hold that the death penalty, per se, is cruel and unusual, since executions occur regularly. Yet from a variety of standpoints, imposition of the death penalty is, indeed, unusual.

A murderer who is black, kills a white person, and has no money to pay for legal defense has a lesser chance of escaping the death penalty than does an affluent white who kills a black person. As Bedau says, "All the sociological evidence points to the conclusion that the death penalty is the poor man's justice; hence the epigram, 'Those without the capital get the punishment'" (43). Since 1976, 84 percent of murderers who have been executed killed a white person, even though half of the murder victims in the United States are black. During that same period, no white has been executed for killing a black person (Horgan 18). Hood (106) assembled telling data on the death sentences given to intraracial and interracial murderers:

	Texas	Florida	Georgia
White kills black	1.4%	0	3%
White kills white	9.5%	24%	0
Black kills white	13.2%	47%	22%
Black kills black	2.5%	1%	1%

Though the statistics do not differentiate types of murders (for instance, murders for profit, crimes of passion), it is abundantly clear that in Texas, Florida, and Georgia it is a good

deal more perilous for a black person to kill a white than for a
white person to kill a black. It is more <u>unusual</u> for a black
person to escape the death penalty. If it is not cruel, the
death penalty is at least unusual in many cases.

Whether a punishment is cruel depends to a certain extent on
the pain that it brings to the victim; thus, it would be easy to
gain consensus about boiling in oil or stoning as a method of
execution. In the eighteenth century, hanging meant death by
strangulation, for the victim was hoisted upon the gallows, not
suddenly dropped a sufficient distance to bring instantaneous
unconsciousness; the old method of hanging would probably be
judged cruel. As Bedau says, "The sense of 'cruel and unusual
punishment' has to be taken from the properties of those punitive
acts and practices that have been judged to be morally unacceptable in a particular historic time and place" (105). It would
seem that Americans currently do not judge capital punishment to
be cruel, for about 75 percent of the public supports it (Horgan
17), yet in the view of developing world standards, American
death penalty laws and those who support them appear little less
than barbaric. Nation after nation has abolished capital punishment: Portugal, 1976; Denmark, 1978; Nicaragua and Norway, 1979;
France, 1981; the Netherlands, 1982; Australia, 1985; The Philip-
pines and East Germany, 1987; Cambodia, New Zealand, and Romania,
1989; Namibia, 1990 (Horgan 17). Alone among the Western democracies, the United States is going counter to the trend toward
abolition and to the main objective of the United Nations in the
field of capital punishment, which is "to progressively restrict

.

the number of offenses for which the death penalty might be imposed with a view to its eventual abolition" (Hood v).

45

One can argue reasonably and convincingly that the death penalty is cruel and unusual.

I believe that capital punishment dehumanizes my society and
hence robs me of part of my humanity. The Declaration of Independence sets the standard: "We hold these Truths to be self-evident,
that all Men are created equal, that they are endowed by their
Creator with certain unalienable rights, that among these are
Life, Liberty, and the Pursuit of Happiness." Individuals or the
state can take life only when no alternative exists, and quite
obviously alternatives to capital punishment do exist.

John Donne said it, and Ernest Hemingway echoed it: "any man's
<u>death</u> diminishes <u>me</u>, because I am involved in <u>Mankinde</u>; And
therefore never send to know for whom the <u>bell</u> tolls; It tolls
for <u>thee</u>"--and me.

Making certain the readers know what sources your documentation refers to
(paragraph 44)
The dates of abolition are all from Horgan, page 17. The fact that among
Western democracies only the United States is going counter to the trend toward
abolition is from Hood, page v, as is the direct quotation.

Works Cited

Bedau, Adam Hugo. <u>Death Is Different: Studies in the Morality,</u>
     <u>Law, and Politics of Capital Punishment</u>. Boston: North-
     eastern UP, 1987.

"Death Penalty." <u>New York Times</u> 2 Oct. 1990, natl. ed.: A18.

Endres, Michael E. "The Morality of Capital Punishment."
     [excerpt]. <u>The Death Penalty: Opposing Viewpoints</u>. Ed.
     Bonnie Szumski, Lynn Hall, and Susan Bursell. St. Paul:
     Greenhaven Press, 1986. 62-67.

Hicks, Jerry. "O. C. Judge Decries Delay in Executing the
     'Deserving.'" <u>Los Angeles Times</u> 9 June 1991, Orange County
     ed.: A1+.

Hood, Roger. <u>The Death Penalty: A World-Wide Perspective; A</u>
     <u>Report to the United Nations Committee on Crime Prevention</u>
     <u>and Control</u>. Oxford: Oxford UP, 1989.

Hooker, Stephen. "The Killing of Joe Giarratano." <u>The Nation</u> 29
     Oct. 1990: 485-86.

Horgan, John. "The Death Penalty." <u>Scientific American</u> July
     1990: 17-19.

Kant, Immanuel. <u>The Metaphysical Elements of Justice</u>. 1797.
     Trans. John Ladd. Indianapolis: Bobbs, 1965.

Kaplan, David A., and Bob Cohn. "Pardon Me, Governor Wilder."
     <u>Newsweek</u> 4 Mar. 1991: 56.

"Juveniles." <u>Lifelines</u> [National Coalition to Abolish the Death
     Penalty] April/May/June 1991: 1.

Koestler, Arthur. <u>Reflections on Hanging</u>. New York: Macmillan,
     1957.

Book (Bedau)

Name of author (last name first). Title of book (underlined or in italics). Place of publication. Publisher (UP means "University Press"). Date of publication.

Anonymous newspaper article ("Death Penalty")

Title of article (in quotation marks). Name of newspaper (underlined, or in italics). Date of newspaper. Edition of newspaper (e.g., "National Edition"). Page on which the article is found, including the section. (The article is found in section A on page 18.)

Anthology or Collection (Endres)

An anthology or collection is a book made up of selections from other sources: books, magazines, newspapers, and so on. Author of the original book or article (last name first). Title of the original book or article (underlined or in italics). Note indicating that only one excerpt from the book appears. The title of the collection in which the excerpt appears (underlined or in italics). The names of the editors of the collection. ("Ed." means "editor" or "editors.") Place of publication of the collection. Publisher of the collection. Date of publication of the collection. Pages in the collection on which the selection appears.

Signed article in a newspaper (Hicks)

Name of author (last name first). Title of article (in quotation marks). Name of newspaper (underlined or in italics). Date of issue in which the article appeared. Edition of the newspaper. Page(s) on which the article appears and the section in which it begins. (Article begins on page 1 of section A. The plus sign, +, indicates that the article goes on to other pages.)

Book (Hood)

See Bedau (above).

Magazine article (Hooker)

Name of author (last name first). Title of article (in quotation marks). Name of magazine or journal (underlined or in italics). Date of magazine or journal. Pages on which the article appears.

Magazine article (Horgan)

See Hooker (above).

Translation (Kant)

Trans. ("translator") indicates that the book was translated.

Magazine article (Kaplan)

See Hooker (above).

Anonymous article in a newsletter (Juveniles)

Title of article (in quotation marks). Title of newsletter (underlined or in italics). Identity of organization that publishes the newsletter. (Since the newsletter is not well known, the name of the publishing organization is supplied, in brackets, for the reader.) Date of publication. Page number.

Book (Koestler)

See Bedau (above).

Surname 21

Margolick, David. "Legal Scholar on Death Row Fights to Halt Own
    Execution." <u>New York Times</u> 5 Mar. 1990, natl. ed.: A1+.
van den Haag, Ernest. <u>The Death Penalty: A Debate</u>. <u>The Death</u>
    <u>Penalty: Opposing Viewpoints</u>. Ed. Bonnie Szumski, Lynn Hall,
    and Susan Bursell. St. Paul: Greenhaven Press, 1986. 58-61.
Zimring, Franklin E., and Gordon Hawkins. <u>Capital Punishment and</u>
    <u>the American Agenda</u>. Cambridge: Cambridge UP, 1986.

Magazine article **(Margolick)**
See Hooker (above).

Anthology or collection **(van den Haag)**
See Endres (above).

Book **(Zimring)**
See Bedau (above).

Exercise: Research Paper

1. *At any point, did you lack the specific world knowledge to enable you to understand a part of the argument? Be specific in your answer.*

2. *Were the authors of the sources used in the paper reliable? Explain why you think they were or were not.*

3. *Do you think that the authors of the paper let their own purpose unduly influence their presentation of sources and evidence? In other words, do you think that the authors of the argument stacked the deck in their own favor? Explain.*

4. *What influence do the current place and time (the United States in the 1990s) have on your understanding of the argument? In what ways do time and place influence the argument?*

5. *What about medium? The argument has been published in a college textbook. In what ways might that fact have influenced the authors of the argument?*

6. *What do you think was the purpose of the authors? Give evidence (logical arguments, facts) for your opinion.*

7. *Did the argument or the sources used for the argument always provide enough information for you to grasp the point? At any time, was information superfluous? (Judge the* quantity *of information in the argument.)*

8. *Did you feel that the authors of the argument knew what they were talking about and that they were being honest with their readers? Were the sources used in the argument reliable? (Judge the* quality *of the argument.)*

9. *Was the argument developed as clearly as possible? Was it obscure at times? Explain. (Judge the* manner *of the argument.)*

10. *Was anything in the argument irrelevant? Should some parts of the argument have been deleted? (Judge the* relation *of the parts of the argument to the whole.)*

11. *In your own words, state the claim of the argument.*

12. *Explain why you think the claim is either arguable or unarguable.*

13. *Do the authors provide adequate backing for the claim? Explain.*

14. *Do the authors provide adequate evidence for the conclusion? Explain.*

15. *Do the authors qualify the argument adequately? Explain.*

16. *At any point, does the logic in the argument break down? Be specific in your answer.*

REVIEW

1. What is the difference between *opinion* and *prejudice?*

2. What are primary and secondary reference sources? Give an example of each.

3. What is a bibliography?

4. What is a periodical index? Name one that is often used.

5. Explain how you would go about checking an author's credibility. Be specific. What sources would you consult?

6. Does your library publish a guide to its use? Where can a student obtain a copy?

7. What cataloging system does your library use, Dewey decimal or Library of Congress? How does each work?

8. If you use a quotation of more than five lines, how do you indicate where the quotation begins and ends?

9. If you use a quotation of more than five lines and it contains a quotation from another source, how do you indicate where the internal quotation begins and ends?

10. What is a paraphrase? How do readers know that you are paraphrasing a source?

11. Give an example of common knowledge that would not need documentation in a paper.

12. In the system of documentation used in "The Death Penalty: For Whom the Bell Tolls," there are two methods of showing the author of a source such as a book. Explain those methods.

SUGGESTIONS FOR WRITING

1. Do an analysis of "The Death Penalty: For Whom the Bell Tolls." Whether you agree or disagree with the claim that the death penalty should be abolished, you can judge the strengths and weaknesses of the argument. In your analysis, be specific. If you find gaps in logic, explain in detail. If you think that the data are erroneous, give the accurate data (and the sources where you obtained them).

2. Write an autobiographical account of a significant moment in your life (e.g., your decision to go to college, the loss of someone important to you, a serious failure, a great triumph). Use library resources to develop your narrative. For example, if you write about your decision to attend college, you will probably want to know about the advantages (and disadvantages) of a college education, and you will find such information in the library. If you were to write about the death of a loved one, you would find many discussions of grief and its effects. In other words, no matter how "personal" your subject might be, you can find resources that will add to your understanding — and your reader's.

3. What unanswered questions have bothered you? Should the United States rely on nuclear energy to replace fossil fuel in the generation of electricity? Are determinate prison sentences more effective in preventing crime than indeterminate sentences? What was the critical reception of *Moby Dick* when it was first published? What are the reading habits of Americans today? Who determines what programs will appear on

television, and what is the process whereby the decision is made? In what ways does commerce influence art in the film industry? What are the current trends in higher education (e.g., kinds of students entering college, preferred majors, government funding)? Write a research paper that answers one of your questions.

4. Write an argument for or against a proposition. For example: (1) American medicine should/should not be socialized, after the model of Canada. (2) The draft—universal military service—should/should not be restored. (3) Senators and members of Congress should/should not be limited to two terms. (4) Alcoholic beverages should/should not be regulated substances, as are narcotics. (5) Fraternities and sororities should/should not be banned at your college or university.

(continued)

Bill Brubaker, "Profits vs. Injury: Does the Human Toll of Boxing Outweigh Its Merits as a Sport?" from *The Washington Post National Weekly Edition*, March 6–12, 1989. Reprinted by permission of the publisher. Copyright 1989.

Paddy Calistro, "Surf Citified" from *Los Angeles Times Magazine*, 4:28 (July 17, 1988), 37. Reprinted by permission of the author.

Truman Capote, *In Cold Blood* by Truman Capote. Copyright © 1965 by Truman Capote. Reprinted by permission of Random House, Inc.

Frank Conroy, "White Days and Red Nights" from *Stop-Time* by Frank Conroy. Copyright © 1965, 1966, 1967 by Frank Conroy. Used by permission of Viking Penguin, a division of Penguin Books USA Inc.

Eric Corley, "Hackers in Jail" from *Harper's*. September 1989. 22, 24, 26. Reprinted by permission of Eric Corley.

Annie Dillard, "The Interior Life" from *An American Childhood* by Annie Dillard. Copyright © 1987 by Annie Dillard. Reprinted by permission of Harper-Collins Publishers, Inc.

"Donner Party" from *The New Columbia Encyclopedia*, 4th edition. Copyright © 1975 by Columbia University Press.

Loren Eiseley, "The Angry Winter" from *The Unexpected Universe*. Copyright © 1968 by Loren Eiseley, reprinted by permission of Harcourt Brace Jovanovich, Inc.

Douglas B. Feaver, "All the Excuses Can't Hide the Outrage of the Iran Air Tragedy." Copyright © 1988, The Washington Post. Reprinted with permission.

Edward Finegan, "Popular And Scholarly Views of 'Good English'". Reprinted by permission of the publisher from Finegan, Edward, *Attitudes Toward English Usage*. (New York: Teachers College Press, © 1980 by Teachers College, Columbia University. All rights reserved.), pages 5–17.

Robert Frost, "Desert Places" from *The Poetry of Robert Frost*. Edited by Edward Connery Lathem. Copyright 1936 by Robert Frost. Copyright © 1964 by Lesley Frost Ballantine. Copyright © 1969 by Holt, Rinehart and Winston. Reprinted by permission of Henry Holt and Company, Inc.

Stephen Jay Gould, "Piltdown Revisited" is reprinted from *The Panda's Thumb, More Reflections in Natural History* by Stephen Jay Gould, by permission of W. W. Norton & Company, Inc. Copyright © 1980 by Stephen Jay Gould.

Earle Hackett, "The Bleeders" from *Blood* by Earle Hackett. Reprinted by permission of Omni International from a *Saturday Review* book.

Stephen W. Hawking, "Our Picture of the Universe" from *A Brief History of Time* by Stepen W. Hawking. Copyright © 1988 by Stephen W. Hawking. Used by permission of Bantam Books, a division of Bantam Doubleday Dell Publishing Group, Inc.

John Hersey, "The Fire" from *Hiroshima* by John Hersey. Copyright 1946, © 1985 and renewed 1973 by John Hersey. Reprinted by permission of Alfred A. Knopf, Inc.

Bruce Horovitz, "Giveaway Assures that Aspen Smells of Aspen." Copyright © 1989 *Los Angeles Times*. Reprinted by permission.

Zora Neale Hurston, "How It Feels to Be Colored Me" from *I Love Myself When I Am Laughing*. Reprinted by permission of the Estate of Zora Neale Hurston.

Gerda Lerner, "The Creation of Patriarchy" from *The Creation of Patriarchy* by Gerda Lerner. Copyright © 1986 by Oxford University Press, Inc. Reprinted by permission.

C. S. Lewis, *Miracles: How God Intervenes in Human Affairs*, by C. S. Lewis, copyright 1947, 1960 by C. S. Lewis. Reprinted by permission of HarperCollins Publishers ltd.

Barry Lopez, "Arctic Dreams" from *Arctic Dreams* by Barry Lopez. Copyright © 1986 by Barry Holstun Lopez. Reprinted with permission of Charles Scribner's Sons, an imprint of Macmillan Publishing Company.

Peter Matthiessen, "November 6" from *The Snow Leopard* by Peter Matthiessen. Copyright © 1978 by Peter Matthiessen. Used by permission of Viking Penguin, a division of Pensuin Books USA Inc.

Mary McCarthy, "The Vassar Girl" from *On the Contrary: Articles of Belief, 1946-1961* by Mary McCarthy. Reprinted by permission of the McCarthy Trust.

John McPhee, "Ice Pond" from *Table of Contents* by John McPhee. Copyright © 1980, 1981, 1982, 1983, 1984, 1985 by John McPhee. Reprinted by permission of Farrar, Straus & Giroux, Inc. Excerpt from *The Pine Barrens*, by John McPhee. Copyright © 1967, 1968 by John McPhee. Reprinted by permission of Farrar, Straus & Giroux, Inc.

Barbara Mellix, "From Outside, In" originally appeared in *The Georgia Review*, volume XLI, No. 2 (Summer 1987), © 1987 by the University of Georgia, © 1987 by Barbara Mellix. Reprinted by permission of Barbara Mellix and *The Georgia Review*.

Alan Moorehead, "The Long Egyptian Night" from *The Blue Nile*, Vintage Edition. Copyright © 1962, 1972 by Alan Moorehead. Reprinted by permission of HarperCollins.

Eleanor Munro, "On the Pilgrim's Path to Lourdes" from *Best American Essays, 1988*. Reprinted by permission of Georges Borchardt, Inc. for the author. Copyright © 1987 by Eleanor Munro.

John G. Neihardt, "The First Cure" from *Black Elk Speaks* by John G. Neihardt by permission of University of Nebraska Press. Copyright 1932, 1959, 1972 by John G. Neihardt. Copyright © 1961 by the John G. Neihardt Trust.

Joyce Carol Oates, from *On Boxing* by Joyce Carol Oates. Copyright © 1987 by Ontario Review, Inc. Reprinted by permission of Doubleday, a division of Bantam Doubleday Dell Publishing Group, Inc.

George Orwell, "Politics and the English Language." Copyright © 1946 by Sonia Brownell Orwell and renewed 1974 by Sonia Orwell, reprinted from *Shooting an Elephant and Other Essays*, by permission of Harcourt Brace Jovanovich, Inc.

Katherine Ann Porter, "St. Augustine and the Bullfight" from *The Collected Essays and Occasional Writings of Katherine Anne Porter*. Copyright © 1970 by Katherine Anne Porter. Reprinted by permission of Houghton Mifflin Company/Seymour Lawrence. All rights reserved.

Reed Kirk Rahlman, "Toys R Cussed" from *California* Magazine, May 1989. Reprinted by permission of the publisher.

Janice C. Redish, "The Language of the Bureaucracy" from *Literacy for Life*, edited by Richard W. Bailey and Robin Melanie Fosheim. Reprinted by permission of the Modern Language Association of America.

Richard Rodriguez, "The Achievement of Desire" from *Hunger of Memory* by Richard Rodriguez. Copyright © 1982 by Richard Rodriguez. Reprinted by permission of David R. Godine, Publisher.

Mike Rose, "Lives on The Boundary" from *Lives on the Boundary* by Mike Rose. Reprinted by permission of The Free Press, a Division of Macmillan, Inc. Copyright © 1989 by Mike Rose.

Judy Ruiz, "Oranges and Sweet Sister Boy" from *The Best American Essays*, 1989, editor Geoffrey Wolff. Ticknor & Fields, 1989. First published in *Iowa Woman*. Copyright © 1988 by Iowa Woman Endeavors.

Elizabeth Salter, "A Tent at Maamba" from *Daisy Bates*, published by Coward, McCann and Geoghegan. Reprinted by permission of Putnam Publishing Group.

John Simon, "U, Non-U, and You" from *Paradigms Lost: Reflections on Literacy and Its Decline* by John Simon. Copyright © 1976, 1977, 1978, 1979, 1980 by John Simon. Reprinted by permission of Clarkson N. Potter, Inc., a division of Crown Publishers, Inc.

"Tim Falls in Love" is reproduced as it appeared in the August 1988 issue of *Harper's Magazine*. Reprinted by permission of Lands' End.

Lewis Thomas, "Late Night Thoughts on Listening to Mahler's Ninth" from *Late Night Thoughts on Listening to Mahler's Ninth* by Lewis Thomas. Copyright © 1982 by Lewis Thomas. Used by permission of Viking Penguin, a division of Penguin Books USA, Inc.

James Boyd White, "The Invisible Discourse of the Law: Reflections on Legal Literacy and General Education" from *Literacy for Life*, edited by Richard W. Bailey and Robin Melanie Fosheim. Reprinted by permission of The Modern Language Association of America.

Yvor Winters, "The Slow Pacific Swell" from *Collected Poems* by Yvor Winters. Reprinted by permission of The Ohio University Press/Swallow Press, Athens.

Steven Zak, "Ethics and Animals" *The Atlantic*, March 1989. Reprinted by permission of *The Atlantic*. Copyright © 1989 by the Atlantic Monthly Company.

Franklin E. Zimring and Gordon Hawkins, "A Game of Chicken" from *Capital Punishment and the American Agenda* by Franklin E. Zimring and Gordon Hawkins. Copyright © 1986 by Cambridge University Press. Reprinted by permission of Cambridge University Press.